PRESS

SAP PRESS is a joint initiative of SAP and Galileo Press. The know-how offered by SAP specialists combined with the expertise of the publishing house Galileo Press offers the reader expert books in the field. SAP PRESS features first-hand information and expert advice, and provides useful skills for professional decision-making.

SAP PRESS offers a variety of books on technical and business related topics for the SAP user. For further information, please visit our website: *www.sap-press.com*.

Jörg Thomas Dickersbach, Gerhard Keller, Klaus Weihrauch
Production Planning and Control with SAP
2006, approx. 400 pp., ISBN 1-59229-106-6

Martin Murray
SAP MM — Functionality and Technical Configuration
2006, 504 pp., ISBN 1-59229-072-8

Gerd Hartmann, Ulrich Schmidt
Product Lifecycle Management with SAP
2005, 620 pp., ISBN 1-59229-036-1

Michael Hölzer, Michael Schramm
Quality Management with SAP
2005, 538 pp., ISBN 1-59229-051-5

Optimize Your SAP ERP Financials Implementation

Shivesh Sharma

Optimize Your SAP ERP
Financials Implementation

Bonn • Boston

ISBN 978-1-59229-160-1

1st Edition 2008

Editors Jawahara Saidullah, Jutta VanStean
Copy Editor Julie McNamee
Cover Design Silke Braun
Layout Design Vera Brauner
Production Todd Brown, Steffi Ehrentraut
Typesetting Publishers' Design and Production Services, Inc.
Printed and bound in Germany

© 2008 by Galileo Press
SAP PRESS is an imprint of Galileo Press,
Boston (MA), USA
Bonn, Germany

Contents

Contents at a Glance

5   Optimizing Financial Business Processes: Accounts Payable and Accounts Receivable 215

9 Improving General Ledger Management 469

10   Achieving Faster Closes 547

11   Special Purpose Ledger 579

"Finance is the art of passing currency from hand to hand until it finally disappears."
                                                            —*Robert W. Sarnoff*

Preface

Finance is the fulcrum around which most of the functions of an organization revolve. SAP Enterprise Resource Planning (SAP ERP) provides one of the most comprehensive enterprise-wide business software solutions. In this book, you'll learn about how you can implement some of the most common functions of finance using SAP ERP.

SAP ERP Financials help an organization achieve efficiencies by leveraging the integrated perspective of an organization. It helps focus the efforts of financial management into value-adding activities by supporting a process-driven approach, streamlining consolidation, and achieving faster closes.

With the introduction of Strategic Enterprise Management (SEM) and Financial Supply Chain Management (FSCM), financial management can focus more time on the strategic aspects of planning and monitoring and less on burdensome reconciliation activities.

Let's get into the nitty-gritty of what this book is trying to accomplish by looking at the SAP ERP versions on which this book is based.

SAP ERP 2005 and ECC 6.0

With the extreme pace of innovation, it becomes evident that whatever was amazing five years ago is now mundane and basic functionality. This book is based on SAP ERP 2005, ECC version 6.0, which is the latest version that SAP AG is proposing for fresh implementations and upgrades. However, you will also be introduced to the differences between it and the previous versions (SAP R/3 4.7/4.6C) wherever applicable. Please note that to ensure you understand the latest functionality, the differences prior to 4.6C have *not* been detailed because they are practically prehistoric.

Let's look at the core themes of this book next.

SAP ERP Financials: Process Orientation

At a very high level, the key challenges and business drivers you face while implementing Financials IT systems is the *quality of reporting*. One of the important contributors to the challenges you'll face is the lack of understanding of the business process and how it is mapped in the system. Understanding how the business process affects reporting is one of the key aspects of a successful Financials implementation.

Determining who needs the information, which also determines where the information source should reside, is another important aspect of reporting requirements. This understanding simplifies the reporting structure and helps in designing simpler financial and business processes.

So one of the core themes of this book is to help you understand the various business processes, such as procurement to payment, order to cash, and so on, and to explain the finance system as a wraparound of these business processes.

> **Note**
>
> Finance is not an island but is tightly integrated with other business activities. The focus of this book is to explain the flora and fauna and the entire ecosystem of finance and how it all comes together from a process perspective.

Understanding finance as a part of business processes will help improve and optimize your financial business processes. You will be able to construct the framework in which you are operating and then visualize how you can make this process better in terms of reduced timelines or reduced operating costs. This leads to the next theme, which is the primary focus of this book: optimization.

SAP ERP Financials Optimization

This book provides an opportunity for you to think through the various tools and methodologies that are considered the best practices and then choose those that best meet your requirements from a financial perspective. This practical approach enables you to deal with situations based on the tools available from SAP ERP. The most important thing to understand in ERP implementations is the need to constantly improve the business processes as per the changing market conditions.

> **Note**
>
> An ERP implementation is not a one-time activity that is done when you implement SAP ERP for the first time. The first implementation extracts the maximum business benefits. However, if you have the basic structure set up, you are ready to launch your organization into a growth trajectory via incremental improvements, which can reap you significantly large business benefits.

Markets change, customers change, competitor landscapes change, and the business processes also change. So what was perfectly in sync with the market realities suddenly becomes outdated.

> **Enterprise Mashups**
>
> The latest buzzword—which is not really a word yet—is the creation of enterprise *mashups*, in which systems can be created using service-oriented architecture (SOA) that allows you to operate in a seamless fashion with your business partners.

To keep pace with the new realities of your organization, you should establish your core processes and then build your ecosystem around it. So the first step is to understand your unique base scenario and then to come up with a solution that meets your requirements within the budgetary and timeline constraints. Good consultants do this all the time. They optimize the solution that can be implemented to give you the maximum business benefit.

This book arms you with the basics of SAP ERP Financials, which allows you to navigate through a complex set of choices to meet your unique financial requirements.

How This Book Is Organized

Consider this book organized into three broad parts:

▶ Part I Structure of SAP ERP Financials and SAP ERP Enterprise (Chapters 1, 2, and 3)

▶ Part II Business Process View of Financial Accounting (Chapters 4, 5, 6, and 7)

▶ Part III Financial General Ledger, Closing, and Consolidations (Chapters 8, 9, 10, 11, and 12)

Chapter 13 wraps up and summarizes what is learned in this book.

Let's take a brief look at these parts before we proceed further.

Part I: Structure of SAP ERP Financials and SAP ERP Enterprise

Chapters 1, 2, and 3, the first part of this book, explore the SAP ERP architecture, implementation methodologies, structure, value proposition, and business case outline. Then you move on to a detailed look of SAP ERP Financials and the various application components within Financials.

After you understand the depth and breadth of the solution landscape, you are introduced to the SAP ERP enterprise structure and how it fits together across logistics, human resources (HR) management, Financials, and controlling. You also learn various pros and cons of selecting organizational entities and mapping them per SAP suggested best practices.

Part II: Business Process View of Financial Accounting

The second part consists of Chapters 4 to 7 where you will learn about optimizing financial accounting subledgers.

After you understand the overall structure of SAP ERP from a financial perspective, Chapter 4 introduces you to the overall business processes of procurement, sales, quality management, and plant maintenance, and how these are mapped in SAP ERP. You also learn the integration points and hand-offs to finance for each of these processes.

After you understand the organization as a whole, Chapter 5 delves into the details of accounts payable and accounts receivable configuration, followed by bank accounting in Chapter 6, and assets accounting in Chapter 7. This covers all the subledgers of financial accounting.

Part III: Financial General Ledger, Closing, and Consolidations

The third part focuses primarily on getting your financial statements right.

After you understand the overall structure of SAP ERP from a subledger perspective, you are ready to learn more about the main General Ledger (GL). Chapter 8 discusses the global settings that need to be made in financial accounting.

After you've learned the key global settings, you are ready to understand the new General Ledger (GL) in Chapter 9. Chapter 10 discusses the key month end close accelerators. Chapter 11 delves into a detailed understanding of the special purpose ledger, and Chapter 12 details the consolidation functions using ECCS.

This covers all the Financial Accounting components.

The book concludes with Chapter 13, which summarizes the major concepts and take aways, while also giving you some direction for the future.

> **Tip**
>
> Each of these five parts covers different aspects of finance and builds on each preceding part, so it makes sense to read the book in sequence. However, if you need details about a particular topic and are already aware of the basics, feel free to start from the beginning of each part.

Summary

ERP implementation is not a magic bullet that can help you change your organization in one go. You need to constantly change the way you operate by building a core enterprise structure and then enhancing it by using an extension of the existing business process mappings. That is why you need to continuously strive to optimize your information technology landscape by looking for ways to improve your business processes.

SAP ERP consulting relies on learning from the experiences of others and adopting best practices from multiple implementations. You will find a lot of hidden functionality and important insights in this book that you can implement in your organization to improve your financial processes. You will also learn how SAP ERP Financials has evolved, and you will become familiar with the new functionalities that are available for you in SAP ERP ECC 6.0.

In Chapter 1, you will be introduced to the SAP ERP solution and the direction in which SAP AG is moving to support the new realities of the marketplace. It also allows you to take a look at identifying the business benefits for your SAP ERP implementation by following the value engineering roadmap offering. Let's begin our journey of learning for SAP ERP Financials with Chapter 1.

Let's review SAP ERP projects, the philosophy behind them, and the typical methodologies used in industry for an SAP ERP implementation.

1   Implementing SAP ERP

SAP provides one of the most comprehensive enterprise-wide business software solutions. In this chapter, you'll explore the SAP ERP solution by focusing on the key aspects of the implementation rationale, approach, and some of the key issues. This chapter is the building block for the next chapter, in which you learn more about the SAP ERP Financials solution.

The process of implementing SAP has been well defined and documented in various publications. You can read the SAP PRESS book *Managing Organizational Change during SAP Implementations* for additional and more detailed information. The implementation approach has different nuances depending on whom you talk to, but the overall theme is conceptually the same. So let's begin by highlighting the reasons for implementing SAP ERP.

1.1   Reasons for Implementing SAP ERP

At a very high level, SAP ERP, or any IT system for that matter, is implemented to achieve a business goal that is important to the sponsor or executive management. To start with, executive management (CEOs, CIOs, CFOs, etc.) outlines the issues critical to the organization and to its shareholders. During that process, executive management also comes to the realization that the current IT system does not support that vision of the organization, or that the IT system needs to be improved to support changing market conditions and to better align with current business realities.

For instance, a CFO might realize that the financial reporting is extremely complex, and it takes a significant amount of manual effort to close the books. So instead of working on financial analysis and decision making, the financial organization is trying to get the financial books closed. The final numbers always cause confusion as well because there are too many systems of record (SORs) with conflicting numbers.

The problem identified by the CFO trickles down to the IT department in terms of business requirements. IT in turn identifies the roadmap to achieve that business goal. This is how the journey of an ERP implementation project typically begins, with a simple abstract goal. The goal helps structure and formalize the overall value proposition of the IT ERP project.

Usually a detailed analysis of the options available for an SAP ERP implementation is done. At this point, the organization looks at the various tools available that meet the desired objective. So a CFO might look at, for instance, SAP Financials and Oracle Financials as the solution for the organization. Based on a detailed analysis of organizational needs and goal assessment, the organization chooses a particular software product and signs a contract with the software provider.

> **Note**
>
> Founded in 1972, SAP AG is the industry leader in providing collaborative business solutions for all major industry sectors and markets.

After the organization chooses SAP, a more detailed level analysis is done to evaluate the components of the SAP architecture that should be implemented and when. This leads to the SAP ERP roadmap.

1.2   SAP ERP Implementation Roadmap

Your organization now must determine which components need to be implemented first. You have to define how to transition from legacy systems to the SAP ERP. In addition, you might already be on SAP but want to implement additional components or simplify your architectural landscape. This is called defining your SAP ERP implementation roadmap.

To define the roadmap, you must first understand the current offering of SAP, which is discussed next, followed by the factors that influence the roadmap, and the SAP ERP value engineering roadmap offering that allows you to structure your implementation roadmap for maximum benefit. The next section details the evolution of SAP ERP 2005 to its current avatar.

1.2.1   Evolution of SAP ERP 2005

SAP ERP has evolved continuously each year from its initial release in 1972 to a broader offering as shown in Figure 1.1. The current release shown in the figure is SAP ERP 2005 with add-on components. SAP plans to release the next level of ERP every five years to align with the customer's upgrade cycles, which means the next release would be in 2010.

Figure 1.1 and Figure 1.2 illustrate the system architecture and the SAP ERP solution landscape respectively.

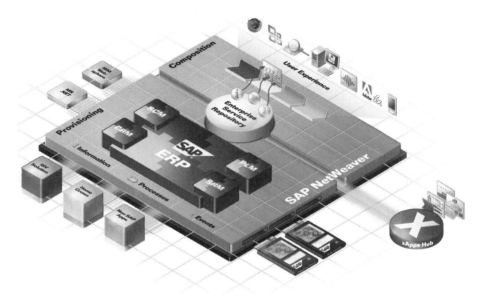

Figure 1.1 SAP ERP Landscape

Figure 1.1 illustrates the SAP ERP landscape along with the other components that integrate with SAP ERP. As shown in the figure, **SAP ERP** is the core enterprise business application, which can be hooked up to SAP Supply Chain Management (**SCM**), Customer Relationship Management (**CRM**), Supplier Relationship Management (**SRM**), and Product Lifecycle Management (**PLM**).

All these components sit on the **SAP NetWeaver** platform, which allows you to integrate disparate homegrown and non-SAP systems into one unified system. You can also hook up additional platforms seamlessly, such as IBM WebSphere, Microsoft .NET, SAP Executive Search, and the SAP BI accelerator.

All these can also be used to feed the Enterprise Services Repository (ES Repository), which allows you to tailor the user experience into multiple content delivery models. You can also integrate cross-application tools that allow you to further enrich the user experience.

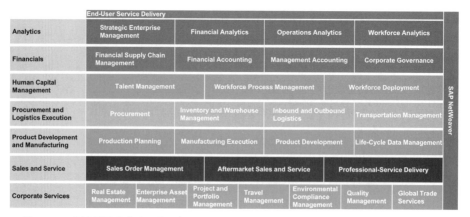

Figure 1.2 SAP ERP Solution Stack

Figure 1.2 shows you the SAP ERP solution stack in more detail with component-level stacks, such as Analytics, Financials, Human Capital Management, Procurement and Logistics Execution, Product Development and Manufacturing, Sales and Service, and Corporate Services. These can then be further subdivided into individual components. Let's take a detailed look at Financials. The Financials stack can be segregated into Financial Supply Chain Management, Financial Accounting, Management Accounting, and Corporate Governance.

Figure 1.1 and Figure 1.2 highlight the multitude of options that are available to an organization as well as the multiple ways to architect your SAP ERP solution. Multiple options create confusion and the need to prioritize the implementation of select modules for a select architecture to derive the maximum business benefits.

> **Note**
>
> With SAP ERP Financials, you can choose to implement SAP ERP Financial Accounting, SAP ERP Management Accounting, SAP ERP Corporate Governance, or SAP ERP Financial Supply Chain Management components.
>
> Within these components, there are multiple options in SAP ERP Financial Accounting, such as Accounts Receivable, Accounts Payable, Asset Accounting, New General Ledger, and so on. In addition to the SAP R/3 reporting stack for SAP ERP Financials, you can also implement SAP SEM and use SAP financial analytics.

Arriving at the preferred roadmap for the organization is very important and requires a clear understanding of IT strategy and the business value derived from each of the evaluated options.

1.2.2   SAP ERP Roadmap Analysis Factors

Broadly speaking, the SAP ERP implementation roadmap can vary depending on the following factors:

▶ Money available to implement an SAP ERP system

▶ Current system landscape and alignment with current business objectives

▶ Business benefit of the project

▶ Timelines of the project

▶ Resource availability: Business versus IT versus consulting

▶ Involvement of the sponsor in the project

▶ Consulting partner

▶ Client or customer IT team structure

▶ Business team structure: Super users

▶ Business team availability

▶ Culture of the client

Additional variables can also affect the way you implement and manage an SAP ERP project, and the implementation methodology depends on the unique project situation. On a very broad level, the business goal of the project or the value proposition of the project drives the implementation methodology. So the business goal can be one of these:

▶ Integrating the processes

▶ Automating the processes

▶ Making the system more efficient

▶ Making the system more flexible

▶ Improving reporting capabilities

▶ Improving business intelligence capabilities

However, not all of these are equally important. Some are more important than others, some are must haves, and some have conflicting goals such as making the system more flexible to business requirements and making the system more efficient. Although both of these are important, the question is which one is more important.

Assigning the correct importance helps determine what you implement and how you implement it. How do you resolve the deadlock between conflicting business goals? You need to understand the impact of each business goal on the return on investment (ROI) or net present value (NPV) of the IT investment. Whichever contributes more to the ROI wins. Therefore, to design an effective roadmap, you should focus on the following aspects:

▶ Aligning business priorities with the system implementation timeline

▶ Reducing the total cost of ownership by retiring legacy systems

▶ Reducing the infrastructure and maintenance burden by rationalizing the application portfolio

▶ Creating a timeline for benefit realization

1.2.3   SAP Value Engineering Roadmap Offering

SAP AG provides a detailed value engineering roadmap offering that can be used to map the implementation schedule for an SAP ERP project. Let's take a look at the process of coming up with a roadmap solution for a SAP ERP implementation as shown in Figure 1.3.

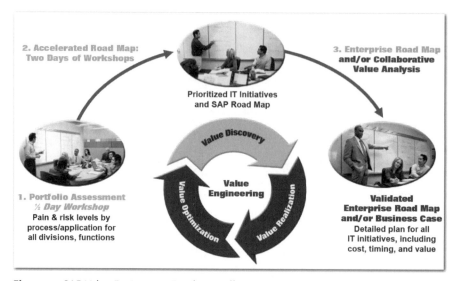

Figure 1.3 SAP Value Engineering Roadmap Offering

As shown in Figure 1.3, the SAP ERP implementation roadmap analysis can be segregated into three stages:

▶ **Value Discovery**

▶ **Value Realization**

▶ **Value Optimization**

The process of finalizing the SAP ERP implementation roadmap begins by understanding the current portfolio assessment in which a detailed analysis of pain/risk levels by process/application for all divisions and functions is performed. Portfolio Assessment can be preceded by an ASUG *benchmarking survey,* which can be used to analyze the current SAP ERP landscape of existing customers.

Note

To read more about the benchmarking survey, visit *www.benchmarking.sap.com/ cgi-bin/qwebcorporate.dll?idx=VAD5GH.*

A typical high-level finding of a benchmarking survey for Finance and Procurement is shown in Figure 1.4.

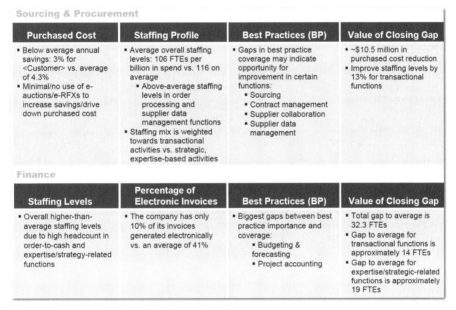

Figure 1.4 Typical Benchmarking Survey Results

Example

For the Finance area, you can grasp the staffing levels, percentage of electronic invoices, and the gaps between the current organization processes across industries. This also gives you the value of closing gap in terms of manpower allocation, transactional efficiency, and strategic reporting analysis capabilities, which then translates to business benefits and business case build up for the SAP ERP module level implementation.

Portfolio Assessment involves understanding the detailed IT landscape currently implemented and analyzing whether it supports the current vision of the organization. This forms the basis of the next detailed level roadmap workshop, which then feeds the prioritized IT initiatives and the SAP ERP roadmap. At the end of the workshop, it is important to come up with a deliverable that explains which processes should be implemented in SAP ERP first and the rationale for the same.

Figure 1.5 illustrates the high-level financial business processes mapped for the sample organization and highlights the avenues for achieving cost savings and strategic benefit along with technical resources, organizational readiness, and transition costs. This tool can then be used for mapping the project scope and the timelines for the implementation of these subprocesses by understanding the feasibility of implementation and the business value that can be realized from the implementation.

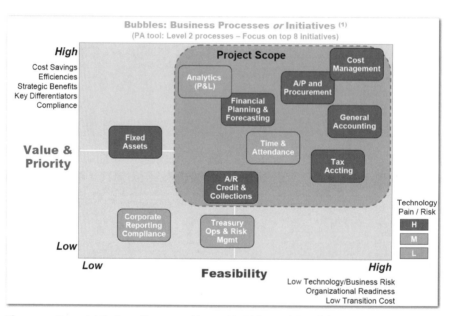

Figure 1.5 Financial Business Processes Mapped in Value and Feasibility

It is very important to then follow this up with the enterprise roadmap and value analysis. The SAP value engineering group provides the Value Lifecycle Manager (see Figure 1.6), which helps integrate all of the steps for outlining your SAP ERP implementation roadmap along with the finalized business case:

▶ **Align with executive objectives**

This contains the executive interview guide.

▶ **Facilitate discovery workshops**

This helps you detail the interview structure, identify the pain points, and showcase the best practices and solution enablers.

▶ **Develop the business case**

In this step, you identify the value drivers and key performance indicators (KPIs) and perform a detailed benefits analysis.

▶ **Quantify the business case**

In this step, you identify project costs, understand the timing of the benefits, and outline the financial assumptions.

▶ **Review and validate the business case summary**

This involves detailing the financial impact, costs and benefits analysis, detailed value tree analysis, and graphical representation of the value tree.

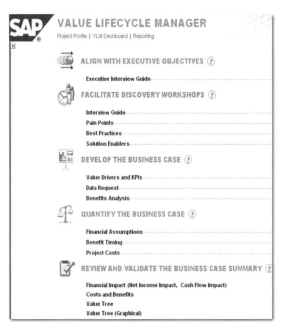

Figure 1.6 SAP Value Lifecycle Manager

Note

Treating an SAP ERP implementation as a capital project ensures that the business case of the SAP ERP implementation is finalized before embarking on it.

All these process components will help you validate the business case and the enterprise roadmap, which contains the detailed plan for all IT initiatives along with the cost timing and value.

Tips

▶ Finance personnel must apply financial modeling to SAP ERP project implementations because the implementation can make or break a company.

▶ The Finance department can help in developing models (based on ROI, NPV, and Discount Cash Flow [DCF]) to quantify the business benefits achieved by implementing SAP ERP.

▶ Equally important is the process of monitoring the value realized as you implement SAP ERP. After you quantify the business benefit realization metrics, it is important that you track them and ensure that the business goals are achieved. The Finance department should play a crucial role in monitoring the business benefits when they are realized and keeping a tab on missed benefits.

Next, you'll learn more about the various options available to implement the SAP ERP roadmap and how you can tailor your SAP ERP solution to meet specific business requirements.

1.3   Types of SAP Implementations

The SAP landscape and evolving business requirements necessitate that you tailor your implementation to meet the requirements that make the most sense. In this section, you will learn about the different flavors of SAP implementations and the approach needed in each of the scenarios. Depending on the roadmap identified by your organization, you might be implementing the following *types* of SAP ERP implementations as described in the next sections.

1.3.1   Production Support

A production support implementation supports the current SAP ERP functionality, which requires minor tweaks to the existing components. This is the most common form of SAP ERP project. Typically, the company matures as an SAP user after two to three years when most of the basic functionality has been implemented. This aspect of the business is managed mostly by the company's internal IT staff. Typical production support activities include completing a series of checklists at month end and year end as part of the closing process. In addition, you might also be asked to create a new financial report that includes additional levels of detail for analysis.

1.3.2   Enhancing an Existing SAP ERP Implementation

This applies to more than the ongoing production support and requires you to tweak your existing system to meet changing needs. This can involve implementing new components or reconfiguring existing components to meet the needs. This typically requires the involvement of external SAP ERP consultants who have done it before and are more familiar with the process. Carefully mapping your desired SAP ERP landscape versus the existing SAP ERP landscape is an important step before starting mini enhancements because this keeps things in perspective. Figure 1.7 illustrates the process of mapping the new Financials functionality needed to support the new business requirements.

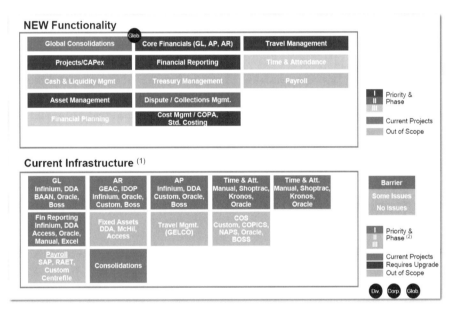

Figure 1.7 Financials Analysis of System Landscape for Improvements by Phase

1.3.3   Upgrading SAP ERP to a New Version

As you learned earlier, SAP will be releasing a new version of SAP ERP core functionality every five years. The SAP ERP release strategy is shown in Figure 1.8. So every five years, your organization will need to make an upgrade decision. The key aspects to consider while doing so include your support agreement with SAP, the licensing agreement, and a host of other organizational factors.

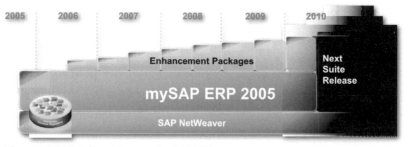

Figure 1.8 SAP Release Strategy for SAP ERP

As shown in Figure 1.8, SAP will provide additional enhancement packages that can be implemented during that time frame if those packages drive business benefit realization. Some of the proposed enhancement packages are shown in Figure 1.9. From a financial perspective, the new enhancement packages that will further simplify the business processes are: Credit and Collections, Fast Closing, and Treasury in the Functionality track. The new features that will become available in the Enterprise SOA (service-oriented architecture) track are: Financial Shared Services and Procure to Pay. From the Simplification track, Accounting to Reporting will become available, which will integrate your accounting reporting.

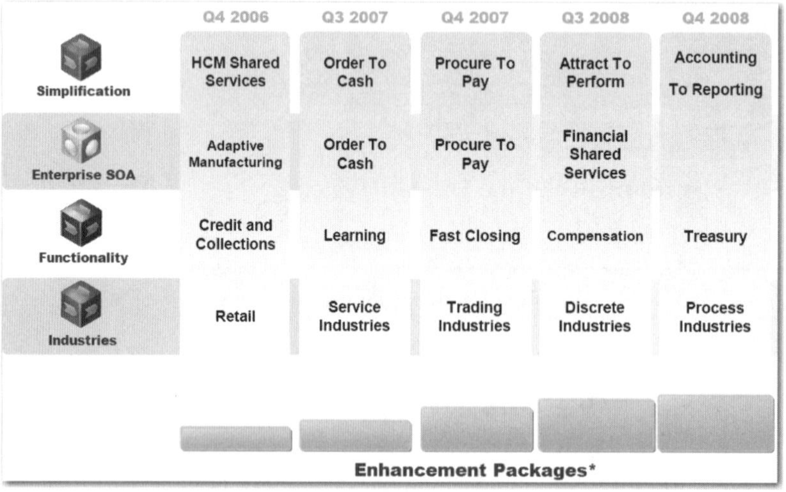

	Q4 2006	Q3 2007	Q4 2007	Q3 2008	Q4 2008
Simplification	HCM Shared Services	Order To Cash	Procure To Pay	Attract To Perform	Accounting To Reporting
Enterprise SOA	Adaptive Manufacturing	Order To Cash	Procure To Pay	Financial Shared Services	
Functionality	Credit and Collections	Learning	Fast Closing	Compensation	Treasury
Industries	Retail	Service Industries	Trading Industries	Discrete Industries	Process Industries

Enhancement Packages*

Figure 1.9 Enhancement Packages from 2006 to 2008

While upgrading SAP ERP, an organization also must choose to perform a technical upgrade, a technical *and* functional upgrade, or a strategic upgrade to SAP ERP. This is decided after carefully considering the benefits of the functional upgrade. A strategic upgrade focuses on increasing revenue, whereas a technical upgrade focuses more on reducing costs. A functional upgrade is somewhat in the middle with a mixture of increasing revenues and reducing costs. Some of the approaches taken and the benefits achieved are shown in Figure 1.10.

Strategic Upgrade to SAP ERP
- Adopted SAP to deploy Enterprise SOA infastructure
- Deployed composites to deploy operational dashboards
- Intergrated xMII for manufacturing shop floor analytics
- Lowered post-merger costs of intergration with Maytag

Functional Upgrade to SAP ERP
- Modernized financial accounting capabilities
- Lower technical infrastructure costs
- Reduced customizations to manage
- One project to upgrade ERP and retire instances

Technical Upgrade to SAP ERP
- Access to new funtionality
- Reduction in maintenance and testing costs
- Reduce number of customizations to maintain
- One project to upgrade ERP and implement support Packs

Figure 1.10 Methods of Upgrading with Business Benefits

The following are some other goals that a company might have for opting for a technical upgrade:

▶ To cleanse master data

▶ To remove redundant and unwanted configurations

▶ To harmonize business processes

▶ To enhance performance of the SAP ERP system

Typically, risk-averse organizations perform a technical upgrade followed by a functional enhancement and then a strategic upgrade. This helps reduce the risk and disruption to the business processes. However, most of the upgrade projects will fall in the category of functional upgrades.

1.3.4 New Implementations

This involves implementing SAP ERP from scratch in a new SAP ERP landscape. New implementations allow you to discard previous practices and incorporate best practices by modifying and reengineering the business processes. This can be due to the new functionality, which is available in the system, as well as due to an increased understanding of the new business realities. Some of the existing clients might also decide to implement SAP ERP from scratch when the previous implementation does not reflect the current realities.

A completely new ERP implementation is a rare event in the current business environment with 41,500 installations already done by SAP. Currently, most of the new SAP ERP implementations are happening in the mid-size segment where companies have disparate systems (which do not talk to each other or require complex maintenance) because the company has grown from a small company to a mid-size company.

As you move from the top to the bottom (production support to new implementation) in the implementation types list, the implementation becomes more complex and demanding from the business perspective. Each of the preceding implementations can have *subtypes* of the SAP ERP implementation:

▶ Implementing new functionality using standard SAP ERP

▶ Customizing SAP ERP using ABAP (Advanced Business Application Programming) or new user interface tools to meet business requirements

Keep the following in mind when you are planning a new implementation:

▶ **The KISS principle (Keep It Simple Stupid)**
It is strongly advised that you follow the first approach of implementing using standard SAP ERP functionality. Otherwise, you'll need an army of developers to maintain the system.

▶ **Minimize development objects**
Keep your development objects to the minimum, and take the maximum benefit out of the standard SAP ERP functionality available. Use Smart Forms and configurable objects.

▶ **Hire business savvy SAP ERP business analysts and configurators**
Hire more SAP ERP business analysts who have implemented the functionality before. This ensures that you do not end up with too many development objects, which are tougher to maintain and support in the future.

All of these implementation types have very different timelines and very different requirements in terms of methodology. In the next section, you'll learn about the SAP ERP implementation methodologies.

1.4 SAP Implementation Methodologies

As you already know, SAP ERP projects are performed for a multitude of business reasons and require varying levels of skills. However, it is important to follow the same set of rules—called the implementation methodology—while implementing any SAP ERP project. So let's delineate the typical implementation methodologies being used globally to implement SAP ERP.

Implementation methodologies help structure the implementation in a way that helps you achieve business objectives. It involves taking on a more method-oriented perspective and translates to a toolkit or a roadmap that helps us get there.

1.4.1 Evolution from ASAP to ValueSAP to Solution Manager

SAP has continuously evolved the approach to implementing the SAP suite of applications due to the following significant changes:

▶ An ever-evolving system landscape with more integration opportunities across other software vendors

▶ An increasingly complex suite of applications

▶ Portalization or webization of SAP ERP

▶ Need to implement SAP ERP solutions in an ever-shortening time frame

SAP has kept pace with all of this by evolving from the Accelerated SAP Implementation (ASAP) methodology- and toolkit-based solution approach to the ValueSAP benefits realization approach and then, in the current avatar, to the Solution Manager integrated project management and benefits tracking approach. Figure 1.11 shows the evolution from ASAP to ValueSAP to SAP Solution Manager.

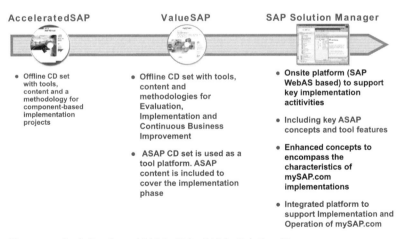

Figure 1.11 Evolution from ASAP to ValueSAP to Solution Manager

The following subsections dive deeper into each of these implementation methodologies to show you the various ways of implementing SAP.

1.4.2 ASAP Methodology

ASAP consists of identifying a toolkit of SAP ERP accelerators (based on the best practices of SAP ERP implementations for customers from around the world) that consists of a number of templates, questions, and scenarios. Most of the companies use SAP AG's ASAP methodology, which has now been replaced by Solution Manager.

Different consulting companies add and subtract templates depending on their previous experiences, however, so think of ASAP as a general toolkit with the modification and enhancements coming from different consulting companies depending on their experience and learning.

> **Example: Tailored Methodologies**
>
> Fujitsu Consulting uses Macroscope™ integrated with ASAP to integrate its overall service offering to the market in one umbrella. For example, if Fujitsu Consulting has developed proprietary tools to manage upgrades, then the ASAP methodology would include the various tools for reverse business engineering and custom utilities that help in understanding the upgrade and accelerating the implementation even further. In addition, companies add their industry-specific experience, which helps in further refining the toolkit to implement SAP ERP.

Primarily, however, most of the consulting companies start with ASAP/Solution Manager and then add their own nuances depending on the organizational environment and industry solution.

1.4.3 ASAP Phases of an SAP Implementation

The following sequential phases are part of ASAP methodology, which are also illustrated in Figure 1.12:

Figure 1.12 ASAP Project Lifecycle Phases (Source SAP AG)

1. Project preparation

   The project framework is defined, and team members are mobilized.

2. Business blueprint

The business processes are defined, and the Business Blueprint document is signed off.

3. Realization

The system is configured along with the unit testing. Data mappings and data requirements are finalized for migration.

4. Final preparation

Integration testing, conversion testing, and end user training are completed.

5. Go-Live & support

The legacy data is migrated to SAP, and the new system is activated with post go-live support.

You should follow this methodology and perform gate checks at each stage so that the project scope is finalized and detailed at a more granular level as you go along. Sometimes, organizations skip a stage and proceed ahead. These mistakes are extremely costly and harder to correct because you are much deeper into the implementation. Even though this is a fairly old approach, it still holds water. Next, you'll learn about the variations of this approach and how the SAP ERP implementation approach has progressed over time.

1.4.4 ValueSAP Implementation Approach

As SAP evolved into one of the premier choices for ERP, many organizations started implementing SAP on an organization-wide basis. This led to longer project implementation times, which in turn led to higher costs. This led to concerns among the corporate world about how beneficial it was to implement the system in their organizations. SAP answered by coming up with the ValueSAP-based approach, in which the business drivers became the focus of the implementation. The toolkit available to implement SAP expanded to include the evaluation of the SAP implementation and the business benefits realization aspect.

In addition, the focus was more on continuously improving the business benefits of using SAP as the tool to enable change management within the organization. SAP also tried to help track how organizations were evolving per the market conditions. This tool also started giving more insights into benchmarking business processes of the organization against the best in business, which were also going through a similar ordeal of adapting to the continuously changing business environment and increasing globalization of the economy.

1.4.5 Solution Manager: Managing SAP Implementations

Solution Manager is an overall approach to managing SAP implementations that provides the integrated platform to manage the project. So the key question is how Solution Manager is different from ASAP/ValueSAP methodologies. Solution Manager provides these added features:

▶ Multiple procedures for functional and technical implementations are now available. Previously, there was just one way of doing things (ASAP), but as SAP ERP evolved, variations needed to be accommodated to ensure the optimal implementation solution.

▶ More product-related information is an inherent part of Solution Manager.

▶ An integrated approach is used for managing the go-live analysis and platform for supporting the SAP ERP landscape.

▶ The business process repository contains the business process scenarios and business process definitions.

▶ Earlier business blueprinting was based on a Q&A database that was not tied to the implementation. But Solution Manager provides additional tools for scoping and blueprinting, which can then be tied together to the testing process as well.

▶ The focus of Solution Manager shifted to a process-oriented perspective. ASAP and ValueSAP were focused on implementing SAP ERP modules such as Materials Management (MM), Sales and Distribution (SD), and so on. Now the focus is on Procure to Pay.

The SAP Solution Manager is an integrated platform that runs centrally in a customer's solution landscape and ensures the technical capability of the supporting distributed system. Solution Manager helps implement SAP, then operates it, and optimizes it over a longer time horizon so that the processes can be continuously improved and the business benefits realized. The components of Solution Manager (review Figure 1.13) are described as follows:

▶ **Project Management**
This component can be used to enable the metrics from Solution Manager that are related to configuration objects, training documentation, and other details.

▶ **Knowledge Management**
This component can be used to manage the documentation pertaining to training user manuals, business process documentation related to blueprint, and so on.

▶ **Knowledge Transfer**
This component can be used to manage the knowledge transfer from the consulting partner to the customer's IT personnel.

▶ **Change Management**
This can be used to monitor the change controls to the project scope. In addition, it can be used to enable change management activities by acting as one central repository for all of the organization's documentation.

▶ **Test Management**
Solution Manager can be used to manage test cases and execute them automatically as per the business scenario. In addition, Solution Manager can be integrated with the best of breed testing solutions (Mercury Quality Center, and so on) to support testing requirements.

▶ **Solution Monitoring**
This component can be used to monitor the system across landscapes and is especially useful to the SAP ERP basis team.

Figure 1.13 Solution Manager Components

▶ **Support Desk**
Solution Manager can also be used to manage the help desk ticketing process and assign it to relevant personnel according to predefined rules.

▸ **Service Delivery**
Service delivery can be used by SAP AG to provide support for OSS messages and can be used by SAP to log in to the various customer systems.

Now that you understand the various implementation approaches and toolkits, let's take a look at the team structure that is used to implement an SAP ERP project.

1.5   SAP Implementation Team Structure

An SAP implementation is an ongoing process improvement initiative to realign the business needs in the changing environment. Thus the implementation team structure is highly fluid depending on the purpose of the implementation. The financial implementation team must be strong and composed of the same set of members throughout the implementation of the project.

1.5.1   Typical SAP Implementation Structure

Each SAP implementation has its own level of complexity, and the staffing structure is defined in the Project Preparation phase of the project per the ASAP methodology. The key theme is to define a mechanism of communication that allows everyone to talk to each other and move forward. Also the business must be involved in the implementation from a methodology perspective as well as from a key decision perspective. Defining a suitable project structure is crucial to achieving the business goals and involving the business owners/stakeholders of the project throughout the project. The two streams of activities must be the following:

▸ **Business change and operational readiness**
This stream ensures that the business is ready for change. This team initially includes the business personnel who are part of the core implementation team. This team later gets extended to power users who then help ensure that the organization wide change is accepted.

▸ **Technology integration**
This team supports the technical process implementation, testing of the configured business processes, and their delivery. This team is comprised of IT personnel who are more involved in the business process design and testing activities and are responsible for the delivery of an error-free product to the business.

Both these streams have to constantly talk to each other and support each other to realize the business objectives. Some of the SAP ERP implementations struggle because of a lack of clarity regarding business change and site readiness, so it is important to keep these two streams integrated as a cohesive whole to support an effective SAP ERP implementation. Clearly delineating the individual roles and responsibilities to support the project is also important.

A sample project organization structure is shown in Figure 1.14. As you can see, process teams (Sales & Distribution, Purchasing, Financials, BW, Inventory Mgmt) interact with other technical teams (technical team, interface team, and data team). The process teams are the link between the project and the business; however, the technical teams have little interaction with the business.

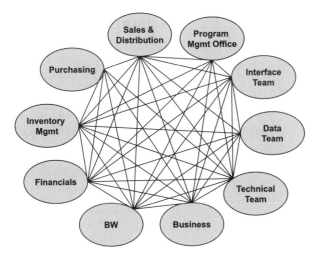

Figure 1.14 Typical SAP Project Organization Structure

The project needs this web of interactions, managed and coordinated by the *Program Management Office*, so you need to set up guidelines and rules by which the project team should work together. You'll learn more about these guidelines in the next section.

1.5.2 Project Operating Rhythm

To execute an SAP ERP implementation project, it is imperative that you define the guidelines by which the project should be run. The project operating rhythm connotes the guidelines by which the project is run and managed, including how you will be managing the project over the project lifecycle, the status reporting mechanism and communication mechanism within the team and across the business, and the key milestones that are crucial to the overall success of the project.

The operating rhythm helps define the rules and framework that will be used to implement the project. It also contributes to the cohesion within the team and helps the team move forward in the right direction.

> **Tip**
>
> Define the operating rhythm of the project early in the lifecycle of the project. It can get more refined as the project moves along.

Now that you understand the typical SAP ERP implementation structure, let's consider the role of the SAP Financials consultant.

1.6 Role of SAP ERP Financials Consultants in an SAP ERP Implementation

SAP ERP Financials consultants help define and structure the SAP ERP implementation. They are necessary because a lot of legacy and go-forward reporting resides in financial systems. In addition to outlining financial and controlling processes, these consultants also provide the following perspective to other integrated processes:

▶ Integration perspective

▶ Accounting perspective

▶ Management reporting perspective

These perspectives are detailed next.

1.6.1 Integration Perspective

Financials consultants help analyze the integration touch-points from across the modules and help fill in the gaps in many situations. They also act as a common conduit of information transfer across the teams to help keep the team together and focused on the right issues. For example, MM account determination and SD account determination help drive integration of finance with the purchasing and sales teams. While defining the account determination, a lot of cross-team interaction happens, and the finance consultant acts as an integrator across the teams.

Because SAP ERP is an integrated business solution, often there is confusion regarding who owns a particular piece. A typical example is Logistics Invoice Verification, which SAP ERP houses in Logistics, even though this is an accounts payable function and must be defined in conjunction with the

Financials consultant. It is important that these integration touch-points are owned and managed by the financial team.

1.6.2   Accounting and Audit Perspective

When defining a business process mapped to an SAP solution, often the tie breaker of how the process is configured depends on how the accounting should work. For example, when receiving goods, whether the material stock needs to be maintained in the system or whether it can be expensed is decided per accounting guidelines. Depending on which way you go, the configuration would be different for the material purchasing and inventory management. Financials consultants help analyze the pros and cons of each process from an accounting perspective. This exercise is especially important in account determination for MM and SD. This, in turn, helps define the Month End process, which cuts down on the number of days to close the books.

In addition, sometimes the process needs to be redesigned to accommodate the accounting and audit perspective, which most of the other teams forget. So the Financials consultant helps ensure that the delegation of authority and segregation of duties are adhered to according to corporate guidelines. A classic example involves the release strategies that need to be defined for purchase order approval. These are typically owned by the controlling department but need to be configured by the logistics consultant, so the finance team acts as a keeper of accounting and audit perspective in the implementation.

1.6.3   Management Reporting Perspective

In a non-ERP legacy system, the management reports typically come from the Financials system. In SAP, management reporting is distributed across individual applications; however, these applications require a unique perspective from the Financials consultant to communicate the same to other teams.

SAP ERP Financials teams help analyze the management reporting requirements and then finalize the individual reporting requirements across all modules. For example, one of the most important after effects of an SAP ERP implementation is the integration of the stock ledger to the GL accounting ledger. In a legacy environment, these were two ledgers; the stock ledger was managed by MM, and the valuation ledger was maintained by Financials. With the implementation of SAP ERP, the valuation and stock value are

integrated and housed in MM, which means MM owns inventory management reporting in post-SAP ERP.

The most important factor in implementing SAP ERP is the labor and time
involved in the implementation effort, so it's very important that you understand the role of financial consultants along with the SAP ERP implementation team structure. These important criteria influence how you roll out the
implementation.

The next section describes these choices and what parameters affect these
choices.

1.7 Big Bang Versus Phased Implementation Approach

Making the decision of selecting the big bang or the phase approach is of
crucial importance because it affects the overall cost and timelines of an SAP
implementation. When companies roll out SAP ERP projects for the first
time, the crucial decision is whether to do a Big Bang (one-time replacement
of legacy systems) approach or to take a Phased Implementation approach
(interface-driven approach). The key to the choice is the amount of risk and
the change readiness barometer within an organization.

Some of the significant factors that determine which implementation approach to use are shown in Figure 1.15. As shown in the figure, Corporate
Strategy, Value/ROI, Business Risk, Technology Risk, and Technical Prerequisites help define which implementation approach you should use when rol-
ling out SAP ERP.

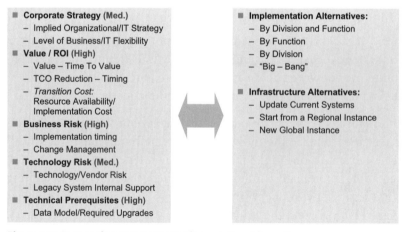

Figure 1.15 Factors that Determine Implementation Alternatives

1.7.1 Big Bang Approach

The Big Bang approach is required when the legacy systems have aged a lot and the organization has become sluggish and unresponsive to the current market needs and environment. The following are the key benefits of the Big Bang approach:

▸ **Holistic perspective**
It provides a more thorough look at the organization by looking at all the systems in place.

▸ **More re-enginneering products**
More business process engineering opportunities are available when you go live with a lot of functionality.

▸ **Entire SAP ERP suite**
 SAP's entire suite of applications can be used to fulfill the business requirements.

▸ **Legacy maintenance savings**
Significant savings can be achieved by replacing many systems because you don't have to worry about designing interfaces in the interim.

▸ **Incorporating Best Practices**
An organization can quickly ramp up its processes in line with the best in the business.

▸ **Less change fatigue**
Because the implementation occurs all at one time, users don't have to adjust continuously. The change is rapid and final, which enables the business to focus on more strategic activities than the timelines of IT implementation.

The Big Bang approach is more costly, however, and sometimes is a marathon that strains the organization in terms of business commitment to the project and the impact of the changing economic and competitive environment.

1.7.2 Phased Implementation

In a phased implementation, on the other hand, the project is divided into multiple releases as shown in Figure 1.16. Primarily, you need to define your implementation in phases. In Figure 1.16, Phase I and Phase II make up the foundation of the organization. Later phases are also planned, but it is important to identify the business processes that will cover most of the business organization.

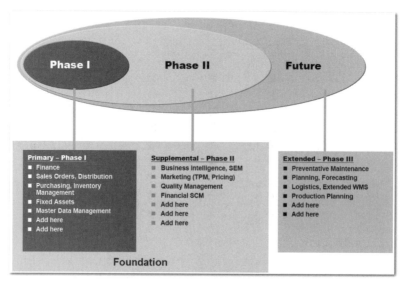

Figure 1.16 Phased Approach

The following list and Figure 1.17 show you the factors used for analyzing when various processes should be implemented:

▶ **Solution Fit to Requirements**
This maps the overall fit of SAP ERP with the current business processes of the organization.

▶ **Critical Business/IT Need**
This identifies the priority due to the lack of functionality in existing systems.

▶ **Potential Business Value**
This maps the business benefit of implementing SAP ERP for the identified business process.

▶ **Organizational Risk Readiness**
This identifies the acceptance of the solution from a change management perspective as well as the level of implementation effort.

After you have analyzed the preceding factors, you can map the functionality to the phases as shown in Figure 1.18. You can map the implementation of business processes in phases. For example, Value Management Office is mapped to Phase 1 and partially to Phase 2.

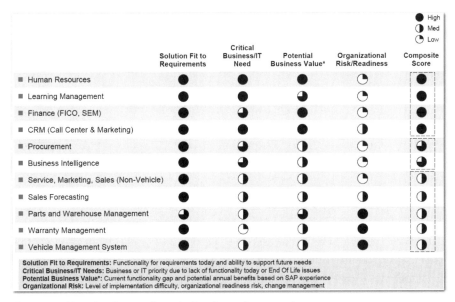

	Solution Fit to Requirements	Critical Business/IT Need	Potential Business Value*	Organizational Risk/Readiness	Composite Score
■ Human Resources	●	●	●	◑	●
■ Learning Management	●	●	◕	◔	●
■ Finance (FICO, SEM)	●	◕	●	◔	●
■ CRM (Call Center & Marketing)	●	●	●	○	●
■ Procurement	●	◕	◐	◔	◕
■ Business Intelligence	●	◕	◐	◔	◕
■ Service, Marketing, Sales (Non-Vehicle)	●	○	○	◔	◐
■ Sales Forecasting	●	○	○	○	○
■ Parts and Warehouse Management	◕	○	◕	●	○
■ Warranty Management	●	◔	◐	●	○
■ Vehicle Management System	●	○	○	●	○

High ● Med ◑ Low ◔

Solution Fit to Requirements: Functionality for requirements today and ability to support future needs
Critical Business/IT Needs: Business or IT priority due to lack of functionality today or End Of Life issues
Potential Business Value*: Current functionality gap and potential annual benefits based on SAP experience
Organizational Risk: Level of implementation difficulty, organizational readiness risk, change management

Figure 1.17 Mapping Process Areas to Readiness Assessment

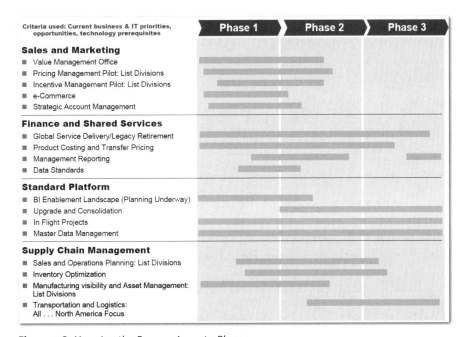

Criteria used: Current business & IT priorities, opportunities, technology prerequisites

Phase 1 ▷ Phase 2 ▷ Phase 3

Sales and Marketing
- ■ Value Management Office
- ■ Pricing Management Pilot: List Divisions
- ■ Incentive Management Pilot: List Divisions
- ■ e-Commerce
- ■ Strategic Account Management

Finance and Shared Services
- ■ Global Service Delivery/Legacy Retirement
- ■ Product Costing and Transfer Pricing
- ■ Management Reporting
- ■ Data Standards

Standard Platform
- ■ BI Enablement Landscape (Planning Underway)
- ■ Upgrade and Consolidation
- ■ In Flight Projects
- ■ Master Data Management

Supply Chain Management
- ■ Sales and Operations Planning: List Divisions
- ■ Inventory Optimization
- ■ Manufacturing visibility and Asset Management: List Divisions
- ■ Transportation and Logistics: All . . . North America Focus

Figure 1.18 Mapping the Process Areas to Phases

Phased implementation helps focus on the following:

- **Low hanging fruits**
  Some areas can benefit by immediate transition to SAP.

- **Change management readiness is more from business**
  The business gradually transitions from legacy systems to an SAP environment that is more integrated and requires more rigor from business. This reduces the extent of shock experienced when users first experience SAP.

- **Small but significant victories**
  Typically, SAP implementations are organization-wide efforts that impact a huge population. This means that the projects tend to linger for some time. Having multiple releases helps the project team savor the go-live and renews their vigor and confidence to go on to the next leg of the journey. These small but significant victories go a long way to contribute to the overall success of the project.

- **Reduce the risk**
  The risk of failure is reduced because you can test the waters and then keep adding new functionality.

- **Users of pilot implementations become system champions**
  If the system is implemented well, then the users of the pilot sites can be groomed to be the system champions. This helps speed system acceptance and usage.

Now that you understand the broad types of implementation approaches, let's move on to discuss how these need to be coordinated and managed across geographies.

1.8 Managing Global Rollouts and Local Requirements

Global rollouts, characterized by a dispersed geographic footprint, are extremely critical to the overall success of the organization. When designing a global rollout, segregating the global requirements that unify an organization becomes imperative. This is called *global design*. However, to meet statutory and other local requirements, you must also carefully outline the local design issues and incorporate that as part of the local design.

1.8.1 Managing the Global Footprint

To manage the global footprint, you must establish the guidelines for identifying a unified global design. Figure 1.19 highlights the challenges of the local requirements while implementing a global template. Local requirements need to be identified early in the project to ensure that they can be met by local developments and country versions. At the same time, however, you must ensure that the local customizations do not diverge too much from the global design.

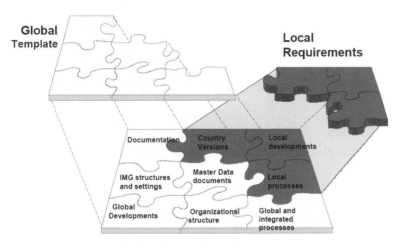

Figure 1.19 Managing Global Rollouts with Local Requirements

Financial Perspective: Global Versus Local Design

From a Financials perspective, statutory requirements differ across countries and economic regions. So the local statutory requirements might be mapped in the country chart of accounts. The best practice is to define one common global chart of accounts. So it's very important to cater to not only local requirements but also to the global financial requirements where the company is listed on the stock exchange.

In SAP implementations, global design consistency achieves the following:

▶ Standardizing business processes across divisions

▶ Improving process opportunities

▶ Evolving as one company by using numerous initiatives that aim at cutting the overheads and streamlining the reporting structure

Having a common strategy when you start implementing an SAP ERP solution is very important. Global rollouts are also difficult to manage and implement due to the following reasons:

▶ Cultural differences across countries

▶ Time-zone management issues

▶ Evolving consensus on the best practices across countries

▶ Different financial requirements across countries

Best Practice

It makes sense to consolidate all the different instances of SAP in one global instance because it helps reduce the infrastructure maintenance efforts. This also drives out inefficient local processes and allows you to pick and choose the best practices across locations.

1.8.2 Key Challenges for Global Rollouts

Here are the key challenges for global rollouts:

▶ Establish one global operating rhythm that also accommodates the local way of working.

▶ Change management in different geographic regions needs to be managed differently.

▶ Adopt common master data global standards and establish a data governance model going forward.

▶ Ensure that the scope is tightly managed.

1.8.3 Key Lessons from Global Rollouts

Now let's review some lessons to be learned from previous global rollouts:

▶ Ensure that project sponsorship has been bought into, and keep the communication lines open with project sponsors throughout the duration of the project.

▶ Follow established methodologies for implementation.

▶ Review the deliverable of each phase, and follow a strict change control and scope management process.

▶ Standardize documentation templates, communication plans, the ABAP development lifecycle, and the deliverable sign-off process.

▶ Focus on program management, which is extremely critical in managing the global rollouts.

▶ Be flexible to adjust to changes during the course of the project.

- ▶ Involve business representations across the divisions and countries early in the project.
- ▶ Test and test some more before deploying.
- ▶ Manage deployment and cutover synchronously with business divisions.

Now let's discuss how projects can be best managed across time zones and countries, which is always a challenge for global rollouts.

1.8.4 Managing Projects Across Time Zones and Countries

In an ever-changing project team structure and focus on lowering the costs of SAP implementations, more and more development work is moving offshore to countries such as India, which have built a huge knowledge base of SAP ERP consultants and implementation experience. In addition, many SAP ERP projects occur concurrently across continents. With multiple teams designing an SAP ERP system across time zones, focusing on the overall global design is very important.

This means there are new challenges for managing the project and organizing the team structure across time zones. This also affects the operating rhythm of the project because the meeting time (overlapping time) is limited to the common time zones across the teams. The development process can use the "follow the sun approach (SAP's help desk approach) to maintain seamless around-the-clock project operations, which might alleviate some of the pain regarding ever-tighter timelines. But this means more resource redundancy and more cost overall and more project management effort to coordinate the offshore resources.

1.9 Summary

In this chapter, you learned about the rationale of SAP ERP implementation and the roadmap of SAP ERP implementation focusing on Financials. The SAP ERP value engineering approach to roadmap finalization was also detailed to map the ERP portfolio along with timelines and business benefits. You also learned the various implementation methodologies, ASAP, ValueSAP, and Solution Manager, to manage your SAP implementations. In addition, we discussed the team structure of a typical SAP ERP implementation and the role of the SAP ERP Financials consultant. We also highlighted the challenges and approaches for global rollouts while meeting local requirements.

In Chapter 2, you'll learn more about the SAP ERP from the Financials perspective.

This chapter provides an overview of SAP ERP Financials and delves into the evolution of the solution from a Transactional Orientation to Financial Analytics and Strategy perspective.

2 The SAP ERP Financials Solution

In Chapter 1, you learned about the SAP ERP solution in general, as well as details about the suggested roadmap and implementation methodologies. This chapter outlines the overall structure of the SAP ERP Financials solution to help you understand how the solution works.

SAP ERP provides a broad range of financial solutions that can meet even the most complex financial requirements. However, it is very important that you understand what is best for you. Implementing a complex solution for a simple business process will add more complexity without achieving the requisite business benefit. So you need to weigh your choices and optimize your financial solution to your requirements.

Besides learning why you should implement SAP ERP Financials, this chapter provides you with the various options you can choose from for that implementation. Choosing is always tough in SAP ERP because you can implement the same requirement in multiple ways, so read this chapter keeping your own requirements and limitations in mind.

Let's start with understanding the key requirements for implementing an integrated financial business solution.

2.1 Key Requirements for the Financials ERP Solution

One of the most direct ways of judging an SAP ERP implementation is to find out how closely the system meets the current and future business requirements. Before evaluating the SAP ERP solution, you should understand the market realities, such as faster design to market and nontraditional competitors with the advent of Internet, globalization, and disruptive technologies that change the way things work overnight. In addition, you need to carefully consider whether the current system supports the vision of your organization and the current and future business requirements.

So if you are introducing a new product line, you must consider what that will do to your existing customer base. Will you gain new customers? How will you support your new customer base? The objective of this section is to understand what business users really want from an integrated financial solution. Let's first understand who the key users of a financial system in an organization are.

2.1.1   Finance System Stakeholders

Finance has multiple stakeholders that need to be satisfied and managed. Here are some of the key stakeholders who are customers of financial information or need inputs from Finance:

▶ **Senior management**
Executives need to know whether they are making the right strategic and tactical decisions to support value creation. Finance needs to warn them well in advance so that they can initiate corrective action. Senior management includes CEO, CIO, CFO, and so on.

▶ **Auditors and regulators**
With Enron and other accounting scandals, organizations are finding that auditors and regulators demand more transparency and the establishment of better controls and checks. Finance needs to ensure that appropriate security, internal controls, and compliance measures are established to meet their requirements. Internal auditors and external auditors include PriceWaterhouseCoopers, Ernst and Young, and so on.

▶ **Business managers**
Business managers need financial information to manage the costs and revenues of their business units. With the advent of the credit crunch, capital has become scarce and business managers need to justify the investment and capital they seek from the board. Also business managers need to make sure that only optimal business initiatives are financed. Key business users are cost center managers and division managers.

▶ **Shareholders**
Shareholders demand more visibility in company processes, and management is always under siege from activist investors if their expectations are not being met. Also shareholders have increased expectations about earnings per share, and their time horizon is extremely short, so they need to see results quarter after quarter. Examples of shareholders include pri-

vate equity groups such as Blackstone, hedge fund activists, and financial institutional investors, as well as small investors who own the share of the listed or unlisted companies.

▶ **Financial operations**

There is increasingly a move toward shared services and streamlining financial operations to reduce the costs and increase the overall revenue per finance employee. The aim is to accelerate the turnaround time to get the cash. This involves the traditional users of financial information such as finance managers and accountants.

Now that you understand the enlarged users of the financial information, it is important to understand how the role of chief financial officer (CFO) has changed. Previously, the CFO was just responsible for financial and statutory reporting, and the key role was to act as a controller who was basically responsible for publishing balance sheets and liaising with auditors and setting up internal controls in the organization. In the next subsection, you'll see the myriad hats that a CFO has to put on now.

2.1.2 Chief Financial Officer: A New Role

Being part of senior management, a CFO needs to be one of the most important sponsors of an SAP ERP Financials implementation. To understand what will get the attention of the CFO, you must understand the role of the CFO in this modern era. Because finance is evolving to meet multiple needs across these diverse stakeholders, the role of the CFO is changing to be a trusted adviser to the business. So instead of the CFO being just an accountant, more and more organizations are now blending the role of strategic planner with the CFO role. This further broadens the perspective of the financial organization to be more integrated with business.

With the new impetus on providing robust, timely and accurate information to business units, the financial organization is becoming a partner to business to search new business ideas, assess their ROI opportunity, and fund them as required. The focus of finance is thus shifting from a transaction-oriented system to that of a decision enabler.

As shown in Figure 2.1, the role is changing to move toward **Business Insight** and less toward financial transactions, which until now comprised approximately half of the finance time and effort. So how do you reduce the share of financial transactions from **46%** to **32%**? That can only be achieved by the following:

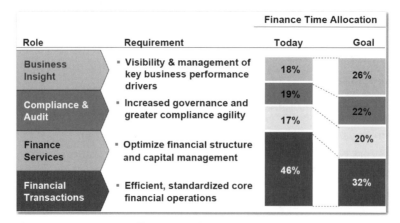

Figure 2.1 Finance Time Allocation: Today and Future (Source: CFO Magazine)

▶ Implementing integrated enterprise-wide systems to accelerate the closing cycle and doing away with a fragmented IT structure.

▶ Standardizing ERP systems.

▶ Automating the labor-intensive processes to reduce manual errors that require lengthy reconciliation efforts.

▶ Integrating the compliance and governance efforts in the system design.

▶ Reducing the dependency on Microsoft Excel because this creates multiple flavors of the same sheet that become dependent on individuals rather than being driven by a process-oriented perspective. Excel creates multiple islands of information that then need to be combined together manually.

▶ Standardizing processes globally so that everybody follows the same closing timeline and month-end closing processes.

▶ Using data warehousing capabilities to generate strategic reporting and analysis.

▶ Standardizing planning, forecasting, and analysis templates so that everybody uses the same set of tools.

You should be able to quantify the benefits that you gain by streamlining your financial operations as shown in Figure 2.2

Typical drivers for an SAP ERP Financials implementation are outlined in Figure 2.2, which highlights the savings that can be achieved by implementing integrated Financials. Again you need to choose the business drivers that make sense from your organization's perspective.

Now that you understand the current business requirements, let's explore some history of the SAP ERP Financials solution to appreciate how the current SAP ERP Financials solution has evolved over time.

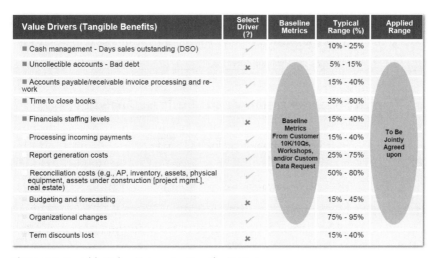

Value Drivers (Tangible Benefits)	Select Driver (?)	Baseline Metrics	Typical Range (%)	Applied Range
■ Cash management - Days sales outstanding (DSO)	✓		10% - 25%	
■ Uncollectible accounts - Bad debt	✗		5% - 15%	
■ Accounts payable/receivable invoice processing and re-work	✓		15% - 40%	
■ Time to close books	✓		35% - 80%	
■ Financials staffing levels	✗	Baseline Metrics From Customer 10K/10Qs, Workshops, and/or Custom Data Request	15% - 40%	To Be Jointly Agreed upon
Processing incoming payments	✓		15% - 40%	
Report generation costs	✓		25% - 75%	
Reconciliation costs (e.g., AP, inventory, assets, physical equipment, assets under construction [project mgmt.], real estate)	✓		50% - 80%	
Budgeting and forecasting	✗		15% - 45%	
Organizational changes	✓		75% - 95%	
Term discounts lost	✗		15% - 40%	

Figure 2.2 Tangible Value Drivers to Map the Savings

2.2 SAP ERP Financials Direction: A Historical Perspective

With the continuous evolution of the Web as a strategic tool to enhance competition and bolster the relationship with customers, SAP ERP has evolved from a client/server transaction-based system to a Web-powered enterprise planning system, as well as a tool to manage the ecosystem of IT for the organization. So let's start this history discussion with SAP R/3.

2.2.1 Financials Versus Controlling

The SAP R/3 Financials system was designed to manage both financial accounting and management accounting. The financial accounting tool was known as FI (Financial Accounting), and Management Accounting was termed CO (Controlling). The overall solution was historically known as FI-CO, and there was a clear-cut distinction between the two sub-processes. However, as time went by, the distinction became less and less evident as organizations started doing more disclosures and as Sarbanes-Oxley came into being. So conceptually, the SAP solution became SAP Financials, whereby both the solutions (FI and CO) became more integrated and harder to distinguish. This book focuses on the Financials aspect of SAP ERP Financials and a detailed look into controlling is outside its scope. However, you will gain a general understanding of controlling in this chapter.

SAP also added other tools such as Financial Supply Chain Management (FSCM), which took a process-oriented view of managing the Financials, and linked it to the supply chain of Accounts Receivable (A/R) and Accounts Payable (A/P). Overall, the solution became broader, more process focused, and more attuned to the business realities of more transparent disclosure requirements following the Enron debacle.

2.2.2 Transaction Orientation Versus Business Analytics

The SAP R/3 platform was based on capturing the nuances of the business from a transaction-orientation perspective. However as organizations adopted SAP ERP by replacing disparate legacy systems, SAP ERP became one system of record (SOR).

Organizations continued having different best-of-breed solutions for Business Intelligence (BI) reporting. The best-of-breed solutions provided more flexibility and were more customizable. However, over time, it became very difficult to manage this reporting because there were multiple best-of-breed solutions for each piece.

This led SAP to come up with a comprehensive suite of BI products, including the core Business Information Warehouse (BW) and Strategic Enterprise Management (SEM), Customer Relationship Management (CRM), and Advanced Planning and Optimization (APO) product suites. It became easier to collate data across these product suites and the SAP R/3 core, which also helped organizations simplify the system landscape. Organizations could now get rid of multiple interfaces connecting the best-of-breed solutions with SAP. Management of IT systems became much easier because SAP ERP now became both *one system of record (SOR)* and *one system of intelligence (SOI)*.

2.2.3 Business Warehouse and Strategic Enterprise Management

As SAP developed its BI application, known as the SAP Business Information Warehouse (SAP BW), it saw an opportunity to move beyond the normal planning processes and incorporate *strategic perspective* into its BI tools. This is how SAP *Strategic Enterprise Management* (SEM) came into being. SEM was a mechanism for organizations to *operationalize* strategy. This meant taking the strategic planning process down to the individual key performance indicators (KPIs) and providing a common measurable framework to understand the effectiveness of a strategy. The two broad components of SEM are:

▶ **Corporate Performance Measurement**
   This component is based on the Balanced Scorecard concept of Robert Kaplan and David Norton. For additional information it is recommended that you read the SAP PRESS book, *CPM Balanced Score Card with SAP* to learn more about this.

▶ **Business Planning and Simulation**
The Business Planning and Simulation component extended the planning tools of cost center accounting, profit center accounting, and other controlling tools to a broader set and provided a mechanism to track the overall goal of the organization against the transaction matrices.

Now that you understand the history and evolution of SAP ERP Financials, let's move on to the future vision of SAP from the financial perspective.

2.2.4 SAP ERP Financials Goals

The current direction of SAP ERP Financials, based on information and updates gleaned from recent SAPPHIRE conferences, is to become:

▶ More user friendly

▶ More interoperable across disparate systems

▶ More focused on harnessing the data captured in transactional systems

▶ More about BI-based solutions

▶ One system for the organization

▶ A more nimble and Web-based software design

Regarding the last item in the list, the key change has been changing the reporting platform from the one based out of individual SAP R/3 modules to a common BW where data can be collated, sliced, and diced as per the requirement of the organization.

The New SAP Model: Think Smaller

As you might be aware, SAP AG is trying to revamp its market offering by providing a robust solution that taps into the faster-growing small- and medium business market. This has driven SAP to focus its efforts more on Web-based applications with the implementation being more hands-on to support the customers every inch of the way. The new mid-market offering, formerly code-named A1S, is now called SAP Business ByDesign, and was launched in the U.S. in September of 2007.

Next you'll learn more about the SAP ERP solution set available for financial business processes.

2.3 SAP ERP Financials: A Snapshot View

SAP ERP Financials is a complete solution to handle the myriad and continuously evolving financial needs as discussed in the previous section. This section describes the current SAP ERP offering and how it is evolving to meet these business needs.

2.3.1 SAP ERP Financials Solution Stack

The SAP ERP Financials solution helps you overcome these multiple goals by providing an integrated enterprise-wide financial-management platform. Let's take a look at the overall SAP ERP solution discussed in the previous chapter and shown in Figure 2.3.

End-User Service Delivery				
Analytics	Strategic Enterprise Management	Financial Analytics	Operations Analytics	Workforce Analytics
Financials	Financial Supply Chain Management	Financial Accounting	Management Accounting	Corporate Governance
Human Capital Management	Talent Management	Workforce Process Management		Workforce Deployment
Procurement and Logistics Execution	Procurement	Inventory and Warehouse Management	Inbound and Outbound Logistics	Transportation Management
Product Development and Manufacturing	Production Planning	Manufacturing Execution	Product Development	Life-Cycle Data Management
Sales and Service	Sales Order Management	Aftermarket Sales and Service		Professional-Service Delivery
Corporate Services	Real Estate Management / Enterprise Asset Management	Project and Portfolio Management / Travel Management	Environmental Compliance Management	Quality Management / Global Trade Services

Figure 2.3 SAP ERP Stack

As you see in Figure 2.3, the Financials component broadly comprises *Financials* (Financial Supply Chain Management, Financial Accounting, Management Accounting, and Corporate Governance) and *Analytics* (Strategic Enterprise Management and Financial Analytics). These can then be further delineated into the detailed level footprint as shown in Figure 2.4. Some of these components also touch other SAP ERP components as well. Review the figure to become familiar with the delineated components.

Strategic Enterprise Management	Shareholder Relationship Management	Strategy Management	Performance Measurement	Strategic Planning & Simulation	Business Consolidation
Business Analyliltics	Financial Analytics	Customer Relationship Analytics	Supply Chain Analylitics	Human Resource Analytics	Product Life-cycle Analytics
Accounting	Financial Statements	General Ledger & Sub Ledgers	Revenue and Cost Accounting	Order and Project Accounting	Product and Service Cost Calculation
Finanacial Supply Chain Management	Cost Management	Electronic Bill Presentment and Payment	Dispute Management / In-House Cash	Cash and Liquidity Management	Treasury & Risk Management
Corporate Services	Real Estate Management		Travel Management	Incentive and Commision Management	
Financial Portal Solutions	Manager Self-Service		Corporate Finance Portal		

Figure 2.4 SAP Financials Solution Components

These can also be represented in detail as shown in Figures 2.5, 2.6, 2.7, and 2.8. Figure 2.5 shows you the Financial Accounting and Managerial Accounting components in detail, and Figure 2.6 shows you the details of Strategic Enterprise Management and Financial Analytics.

Figure 2.5 Financial Accounting and Management Accounting

We will cover Financial Accounting and Management Accounting in detail in subsequent chapters.

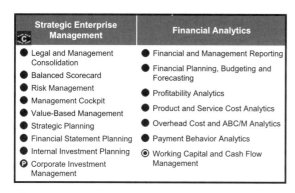

Figure 2.6 Strategic Enterprise Management and Financial Analytics

Figure 2.7 shows you the detail level components of Financial Supply Chain Management, and Figure 2.8 shows you the Corporate Governance components.

Figure 2.7 Financial Supply Chain Management

Figure 2.8 Corporate Governance Solution

We'll cover Financial Supply Chain Management and Corporate Governance in brief later in this chapter.

2.3.2 SAP ERP Financial Solution Release Strategy

As you learned in Chapter 1, going forward, SAP will be releasing a new version of SAP ERP core functionality every five years. The SAP ERP release strategy is shown in Figure 2.9.

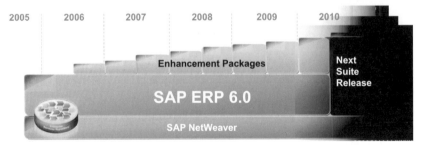

Figure 2.9 SAP Release Strategy

The enhancement packages pertaining to SAP ERP Financials are shown in Figure 2.10.

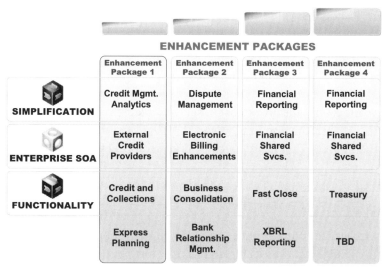

Figure 2.10 Enhancement Packages for SAP ERP Financials

As you can see, the focus is on credit management in **Enhancement Package 1**, FSCM and consolidation in **Enhancement Package 2**, and financial reporting, shared services, and fast close from Enterprise Package 3 onwards.

Enhancement Package 1

This comprises simplifying **Credit Management Analytics**, linking to **External Credit Providers** using SOA, and key changes in the functionality of **Credit and Collections**. Credit management has now been made part of FSCM, where you get extended credit management functionality. The other component of Enhancement Package 1 is **Express Planning**.

Enhancement Package 2

This comprises additional features in **Dispute Management** and **Electronic Billing Enhancements,** which allow you to optimize and streamline your financial supply chain management. Both of these deliver significant savings in cash collections and receivable management by accelerating cash cycle and reducing working capital requirements. In addition, Business Consolidation allows you to define more business focused parameters of consolidation. The package also contains enhancements for Bank Relationship Management which allow you to navigate through the complex inter-relationships with banks in the international SWIFT format.

Enhancement Package 3

The focus of enhancement package 3 is on beefing the financial reporting by adding more analytical capabilities using **Financial Reporting and Extensible Business Reporting Language (XBRL) Reporting** for consolidation. In addition, with the increased trend towards a common shared services center, SAP plans to provide an extension set to implement Financial Shared Services. With the introduction of the new GL, SAP plans to further enhance its offerings to support Fast Close across a diverse and heterogeneous ERP environment.

Enhancement Package 4

Enhancement package four continues to build on the reporting capabilities available in SAP ERP Financials using Financial Reporting. In addition, it will attempt to smooth the wrinkles of the previous enhancement on Financial Shared Services and make it more robust. You will also see more Treasury components which allow you to manage your financial supply chain lifecycle in a more improved fashion.

> **Note**
>
> The first two packages are already available, while the other two are due by 2008 and 2009 respectively. For additional detail about SAP's release strategy go to *http://www.sap.com/services/pdf/BWP_WP_Release_Strategy.pdf*. For detailed information about the support pack release strategy of SAP go to *http://service.sap.com/sp-stacks*.

Next you'll learn about the SAP ERP Easy Access for SAP ERP Financials.

2.3.3 SAP Easy Access for SAP Financials

Figure 2.11 shows the SAP Easy Access interface and the subcomponents that can be accessed from the SAP menu. SAP Easy Access for SAP ERP Financials is structured according to groups, modules, and sub modules. These groups are further divided into modules. Following are the broad groups in SAP Easy Access:

- ▶ Financial Accounting
- ▶ Financial Supply Chain Management
- ▶ Controlling
- ▶ Enterprise Controlling
- ▶ Strategic Enterprise Management

- ► Investment Management
- ► Project Systems
- ► Real Estate Management
- ► Flexible Real Estate Management
- ► Bank Applications

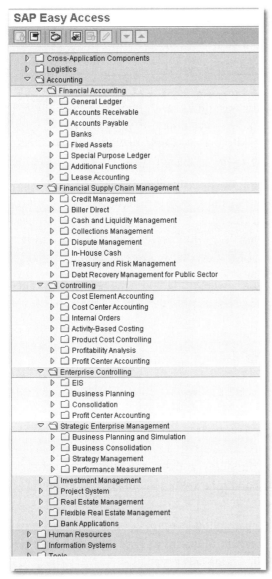

Figure 2.11 Financials End User Menu Path: Components

Financial Accounting is divided into:

- General Ledger
- Accounts Receivable
- Accounts Payable
- Banks
- Fixed Assets
- Special Purpose Ledger
- Lease Accounting
- Additional Functions

> **Note**
>
> Additional Functions is a part of accounts receivable and accounts payable modules.

Figure 2.11 also shows the components for Financial Supply Chain Management, Controlling, Enterprise Controlling, and Strategic Enterprise Management. Now that you understand the spectrum of the SAP ERP Financials solution, let's look at FSCM in more detail in the next section to provide a holistic understanding of the SAP ERP Financials business suite.

You'll learn about the core Financial Accounting and Management Accounting SAP ERP tools in much more detail in later chapters (Chapters 4 to 17).

2.4 Financial Supply Chain Management

SAP FSCM is an integrated approach to managing all cash-related processes and helping design better controls and more visibility. The following list represents the overall goals:

- Reduce the working capital
- Reduce the operating expenses
- Better understand and predict cash flow

Implementing a financial supply chain allows you to control the various parameters of your financial processes. FSCM instills a supply chain perspective into managing your Financials collections and payables.

2.4.1 FSCM Process Areas

FSCM covers the process areas shown in Figure 2.12. These processes range from **Credit Management** to **Treasury and Risk Management**. Following are the key SAP solutions to handle these processes:

▶ **SAP Credit Management**
This is used to integrate the credit limit assessment across multiple systems and then act as a common place where credit is managed.

▶ **SAP Biller Direct**
This covers electronic bill presentment and payment, which includes issuing invoices and settling invoices with the payment from vendor.

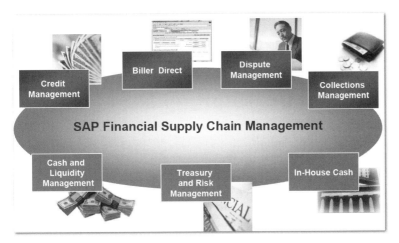

Figure 2.12 SAP FSCM Components

▶ **SAP Bill Consolidator**
This covers the electronic bill consolidation by issuing the invoice and then receiving the settlement and payment from the customer.

▶ **SAP Dispute Management**
This is primarily used for resolving disputes for invoices that are underpaid.

▶ **SAP In-House Cash Management**
This component is used to manage the finance working capital.

▶ **Treasury and Risk Management**
This component is used to forecast cash and finance working capital.

▶ **Cash and Liquidity Management**
This is used to forecast cash and liquidity management and reconcile the same as you progress.

Previously, most of these components were part of accounts payable, accounts receivable, and banking, but SAP ERP is trying to map these processes so that the financial supply chain can be managed from paying the cash to vendors to receiving the cash from customers. Typically, these processes are used to provide one uniform view of the overall cash requirements for the company.

2.4.2 Business Benefits of SAP Financial Supply Chain Management

The following *business benefits* can be realized by implementing SAP FSCM:

▶ Shorter settlement cycles

▶ Faster dispute resolution

▶ Lower costs of payment and billing

▶ Less bad or doubtful debt

▶ Improved cash flow management

▶ Reduced working capital

▶ Decreased nonproductive float

SAP FSCM helps manage the cash flow activity across all business processes from suppliers to products to customers. It streamlines financial business processes and supplements traditional methods of communication with partners. In the next section, you'll learn about the corporate governance tools that are available from the SAP ERP Financials suite of applications.

2.5 Corporate Governance

Corporate governance is the system of rules and regulations under which a corporation is directed and controlled by the corporate board members. It lays down the ethics and compliance standards that an organization should follow. The importance of corporate governance was highlighted because of the stricter controls enforced by Sarbanes-Oxley in the wake of the Enron scandal. SAP provides the tools and techniques discussed next to support the corporate governance model stipulated by the board of directors.

2.5.1 Audit Information System

The Audit Information System (AIS) is aimed at improving the quality of system, business, and tax audits and consists of preconfigured SAP standard programs and reports disclosing audit-relevant information from multiple SAP applications. AIS also provides an export interface for totals and documents that can be used with leading external auditing tools.

2.5.2 Management of Internal Controls

This is used to support management in assessing and reporting on the effectiveness of the company's internal control system as required by the Sarbanes-Oxley Act and similar regulations. This has been designed to help organizations comply with section 404 of the Sarbanes-Oxley Act.

2.5.3 Risk Management

Risk management is used to catalog risks such as economic indicators, competitive landscape, and other external and internal factors that can derail an organization. SAP SEM provides you with an integrated view of risks across the organization. In addition, the risks identified can also be integrated with the strategic planning of the organization to understand new dimensions, demystify future scenarios, and help you perform business planning and simulation.

2.5.4 Whistleblower Complaints

Whistleblower Complaints is an HTML-based service offered as part of SAP ERP. This functionality is used to send anonymous complaints to comply with section 301 of the Sarbanes-Oxley Act, which requires companies to establish a process for collecting anonymous information.

2.5.5 Segregation of Duties

You can use the Virsa compliance calculator for SAP to determine whether the segregation of duties is adhered to within the organization. SAP bought Virsa to further enhance its system offering from the security and audit perspective. The following variations of Virsa are available: Role Expert, Firefighter, and Access Enforcer. These help in defining appropriate roles and ensure that your SAP system meets the compliance standards. Figure 2.13 displays the stack of Virsa mapped across the stages for end-to-end compliance with corporate standards. It allows you to generate audit reports, which can prove to the external auditors that the SAP ERP system complies with the segregation of duties.

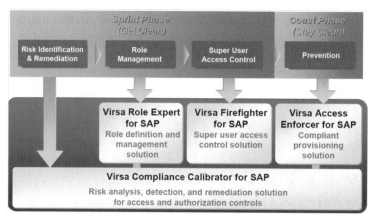

Figure 2.13 Virsa Enables End-to-End Compliance

2.6 Summary

In this chapter, we discussed the SAP ERP Financials solution itself. You learned about the requirements of implementing SAP ERP Financials, its historical perspective, the current SAP ERP Financials solution, and the future
enhancements that will be available in Enterprise Packages 1, 2, 3 and 4. In
addition you learned about the Financial Supply Chain Management (FSCM)
and Corporate Governance and Risk Control (GRC) solutions available in SAP
ERP.

Overall SAP ERP Financials can enable financial business process transformation by providing an integrated platform to manage all your financial business
processes. The new integrated General Ledger allows you to map your most
complex business process in financial statement terms while FSCM provides
you with an integrated toolkit to smooth out the wrinkles in your financial
value chain. Instead of doing a post mortem analysis, SAP Financials allows
you to perform analytical reporting to anticipate and control your future by
providing you increased reporting capabilities, instilling better financial audit
and control checkpoints and better control of your financial processes.

It is clear, therefore, that you can use SAP ERP Financials to enable financial
transformation by automating critical and labor intensive financial processes
and reducing the time for month-end closing processes, freeing up crucial
time for strategic financial analytics.

In Chapter 3, we'll discuss the process of configuring an optimal enterprise
structure in SAP ERP.

What are the key organizational entities? How are they mapped in SAP? Defining organizational entities correctly can simplify the reporting requirement and can significantly affect the timelines of an SAP ERP implementation.

3 Choosing the Optimal Enterprise Structure

From this chapter forward, we will discuss the details of implementing and optimizing SAP ERP Financials. The first step in implementing the SAP ERP solution is to understand the organizational structure and how it needs to be mapped in SAP ERP.

The SAP ERP enterprise structure is the fundamental data framework within the SAP ERP system. It sits above the master data and transaction data. Typically, master data is created with reference to the SAP enterprise structure. Let's say you want to create a material master. The material master should be created with reference to a plant. In this example, material is the master data, and plant is the logistics enterprise entity. Now an inventory transaction (goods receipt, goods issue, etc.) is done for a particular material and plant.

A common mistake organizations make is to map their current organizational structure into SAP ERP. That is not the best thing because the current structure might not be meeting your current reporting and process requirements. So think about how your organization will look five years from now and then design your structure.

> **Tip**
>
> Changing the core organization structure is not easy in SAP ERP, so listen to the consultants who have done it before. This will help you design a flexible organizational structure that will hold true even when you overhaul your organization.

If you define your organizational entities correctly the first time, you will be able to fully use the breadth and depth of the SAP ERP functionality. Otherwise, you'll end up with costly workarounds. Understanding the SAP organizational entities available and how other companies have used them will help you design your optimal organizational structure.

This chapter outlines the available organizational entities and how best to design a structure that suits your organization. Next, you'll learn about organization entities and how best to approach the process of defining your own.

3.1 Introduction to Organizational Entities

The decisions concerning organization entities set the tone for the overall project implementation, so it's very important to finalize these after carefully considering all the pros and cons of each option. This section covers the basic objectives and some caveats for defining an organization's enterprise structure.

3.1.1 Organizational Structure Mapping Approach

To map organizational entities, the best approach is to conduct a workshop early in the blueprinting phase, which is conducted typically by a consulting partner. The agenda of the workshop is to first present an overview of the SAP enterprise structure and then discuss all available options by detailing the advantages and disadvantages of choosing the possible options. At the end of the workshop, the goal is to have a documented enterprise structure that will be the basis of the ongoing implementation.

The agenda of an enterprise-mapping workshop should be to finalize an optimal enterprise structure that meets business requirements. The SAP ERP enterprise structure is initially outlined during the project preparation phase and then further detailed as part of the business blueprint.

> **Note**
>
> Review the project phases outlined in Chapter 1 as part of ASAP projects phases from Project Preparation, Business Blueprint, Realization, and Final Cutover, to Go Live and Support. It is very important to define your structure early and stick to it as this decides the overall complexity of the implementation.

As you learned earlier, the SAP ERP enterprise structure sits above the master data and transaction data. So let's take a look at the purpose of defining the SAP ERP enterprise structure.

3.1.2 Purpose of Defining the SAP ERP Enterprise Structure

The basic objectives of defining the enterprise structure are:

▶ To fulfill your business needs.

▶ To define and outline the internal and external reporting requirements. So at the time of defining your enterprise structure, think of all the ways you might need reporting to be extracted out of the system.

▶ To map the physical organizational entities to the SAP organization entities so that you can visualize how your organization will look and feel in SAP ERP.

Now that you understand the purpose of defining enterprise structure, let's discuss the overall impact of the enterprise structure.

3.1.3 Impact of the SAP Enterprise Structure

The SAP ERP enterprise structure design affects *everything*, including the following:

▶ Reporting

▶ Master data design

▶ Inter-company processing

▶ Ability to use standard reporting

▶ Data complexity

Keep in mind that, once defined, it's very difficult to change the core SAP ERP enterprise structure. So consider carefully before you implement an enterprise structure because it is very difficult to change configuration midway in the project. Take your time and think of all the possibilities and considerations that can have an impact on your SAP ERP enterprise structure.

3.1.4 Evaluation Criteria for Mapping Your Organization to SAP ERP Enterprise Structure

SAP ERP provides you with many options that you can interpret in multiple ways, so it's very important that you follow some golden rules while mapping your organization to SAP. Consider the following aspects when designing your own organization structure:

▶ Do not try to map your existing legacy system structure to the SAP enterprise structure. Think fresh. Think new.

▶ List what you liked about your legacy structure.

▶ List what you hate about your organization structure.

▶ Think of *what if* scenarios. The real organizational structure is sometimes hidden. You might have a formal organizational structure and an informal organization structure that nobody wants to talk about. These imaginary scenarios help you come up with the real enterprise-wide structure that makes sense rather quickly. Some scenarios might include:

- **What happens if your organization gets taken over by a new company?**
  Think of a scenario where your organization gets taken over by a new company and then analyze how the new merged entity would look. This will help you identify the core organization structure.

- **What happens if your company takes over a related business?**
  This scenario lets you identify your growth opportunities and the areas you think need more granular reporting than is currently needed.

- **What if you acquire a new plant in a different state?**
  This scenario lets you think about your logistics organizational entities and how they relates to accounting in terms of fixed assets, banking, general ledger (GL), and accounts payable setup.

- **What if you decide to decommission or sell a plant?**
  This scenario helps you simplify some of your complex reporting requirements.

- Think from an outsider's perspective first and then from an insider's perspective.

- Use the best practices applicable to your industry and provided by SAP or a SAP consulting partner.

- Traditionally the reporting structure was fragmented and there were no standardized processes across organizations. It is very important that you start thinking about driving your organization toward common processes and best practices. You can achieve this by treating your company as *one company*, since that drives your reporting understanding and rationalization of organizational structure.

- Some companies have multiple instances of SAP ERP and other legacy systems, which complicates the enterprise structure. Ask simple questions such as what will be the enterprise structure if you had one global instance of SAP ERP. Will your enterprise structure change?

These simple questions and considerations help you solve the complex puzzle of identifying the business requirements of SAP ERP enterprise structure. In addition, these need to be married against the following technical considerations:

- Technical design complexity
- Master data upkeep and maintenance

► Consolidation structure and inter-company processing-related activities

► Statutory versus management reporting requirements

► Ability to use standard out-of-the-box reporting

First you should learn the meaning of individual organizational entities, and then the assignment options available. Finally you can map your organization to the SAP ERP enterprise structure.

3.1.5   Configuring the SAP ERP Enterprise Structure

In this subsection, you'll learn how to configure the SAP enterprise structure via the SAP Implementation Guide (IMG). The transaction code for the IMG is SPRO. After you execute SPRO, choose SAP Reference IMG to see the SAP Customizing Implementation Guide.

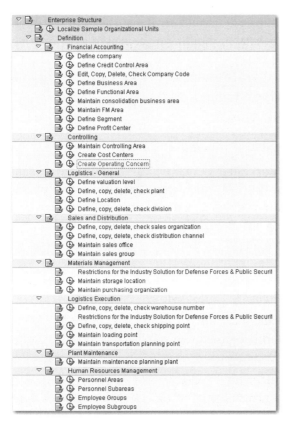

Figure 3.1 SAP Enterprise Structure Definition, Assignment, and Consistency Check

The SAP Customizing Implementation Guide for defining enterprise structure is shown in Figure 3.1 for key organizational elements. You can use the

Localize Sample Organizational Units to import the sample organization units by country. **Release Notes** identify specific information pertaining to new nodes that were added.

Tip

For each implementation, you can define your own IMG by identifying the components you need to implement.

As you can see in Figure 3.1, the configuration guide for enterprise structure is organized by SAP ERP components such as **Financial Accounting, Controlling, Logistics-General, Sales and Distribution, Materials Management, Logistics Execution, Plant Maintenance, and Human Resources Management**. In addition, you can also perform **Consistency Check** for checking sales and distribution settings.

You will learn about all these organizational elements in detail in this chapter. First, you'll learn about the Financial Accounting organization structure.

3.2 Financial Enterprise Structure Organizational Entities

Let's first take a deeper look at financial organizational entities. Each organizational entity needs to be defined after carefully understanding the overall enterprise-wide requirements. However, the Finance department owns the Financial Accounting organizational units. Financial organization entities primarily define at what level you are defining your balance sheet and profit and loss (P&L) statements along with other statutory reporting requirements such as segment reporting, cost of sales reporting, and so on. In addition, you can also specify the structure of your consolidation requirements using financial enterprise structure entities. Figure 3.2 breaks down the previous figure in more detail to show the menu path.

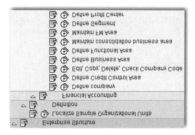

Figure 3.2 SAP Financial Entities Configuration

In Figure 3.2, you can see the key Financial Accounting entities. Next, you'll learn about one of the most important enterprise entities for financials: the company code.

3.2.1 Company Code

Company code is an independent accounting entity for which a complete self-contained set of accounts can be drawn up. It represents a legal entity and a balanced legal set of books. The salient points of a company code are as follows:

▶ All the financial transactions are posted in a company code. This includes the entry of all transactions that must be posted and the creation of all items for legal individual financial statements, such as the balance sheet and the P&L statement.

▶ When posting any financial transaction, the company code assignment is required. This can be either a manual assignment or be derived automatically from other data elements.

▶ A company code has a unique alphanumeric four-character key.

▶ Assignments required at this level include country, fiscal year, chart of accounts, accounting currency, and base language.

▶ Periods and currencies are driven by a company code.

▶ Legal balance sheet and P&L statements are created at company code level.

▶ This is the minimum mandatory structure required to use Financial Accounting.

In SAP ERP, you can either configure using the menu path or by using the transaction code. Sometimes configuration objects do not have a transaction code available. In that case, you have to use the menu path. Also, at the start, we suggest that you use the menu path **IMG • Enterprise structure • Definition • Financial Accounting • Edit, Copy, Delete, Check Company Code • Copy. Delete, Check Company Code** because it allows you to become familiar with the system. However, using the Transaction OX02 or EC01 will get you to the screen shown in Figure 3.3.

After you click on the option **Copy, delete, check company code,** you reach the screen shown in Figure 3.4.

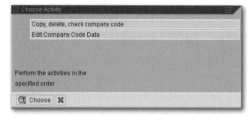

Figure 3.3 SAP Company Code Definition

Here you can click on the Copy icon (the second icon from left that looks like two sheets of paper). This gives you a pop-up window where you can enter the source company code (in this case, **US01**) and your new company code (in this case, **US00**) as shown in Figure 3.4.

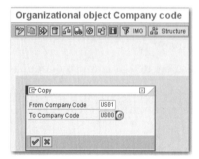

Figure 3.4 Copying a Company Code from an Existing One (Transaction Code EC01)

You can then copy all the settings from **US01** to **US00**. While this is being copied, the system asks for the currency needed for target company code. You can choose to change it at this point. As shown in Figure 3.5, you can change the company code currency to other than the source company code currency. In this case, you decided to keep the same currency. In addition, you might also get a message about copying the GL accounts where you can choose to either copy or not copy the GL accounts already created in the source company code.

Figure 3.5 Option to Change the Company Code Currency

This action leads to the next screen as shown in Figure 3.6 where you can enter the name and address of the new company code created.

Figure 3.6 Entering Company Code Name, City, Country, Currency, and Language

You can maintain the address and other communication details by clicking on the Address icon (envelope with address details) in Figure 3.6. After you click on the Address icon, a pop-up window opens where you can maintain the address details as shown in Figure 3.7.

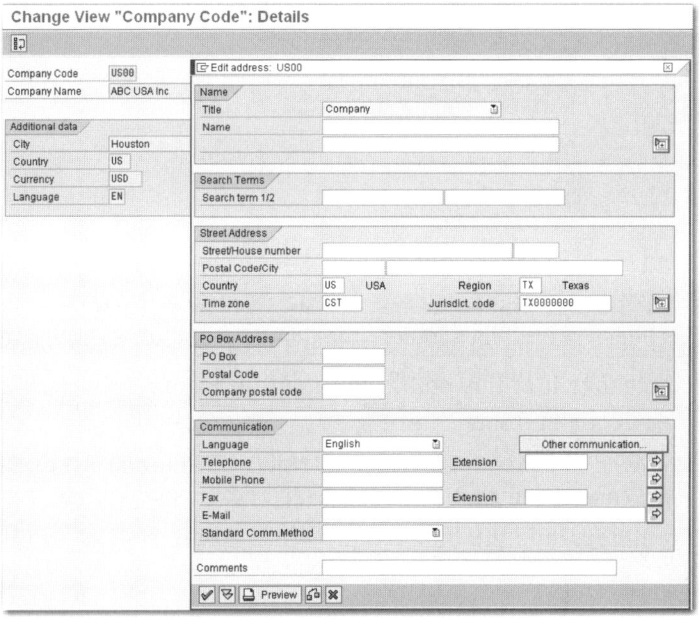

Figure 3.7 Address Details of Company Code

The result is the copying of all other relevant configuration information that needs to happen for a company code. You will get a message that the company code US00 was successfully copied from US01 as shown in Figure 3.8.

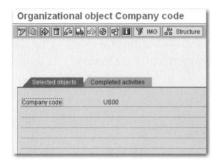

Figure 3.8 New Company Code Is Created

If you want to see what this new company looks like, you have to go back and choose the other option: **Edit Company Code Data** as shown in Figure 3.9.

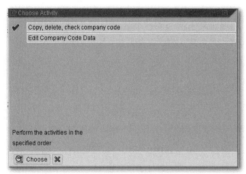

Figure 3.9 Edit an Existing Company Code

This allows you to return to this company code later as you saw in Figures 3.6 and 3.7, where you can make changes to the address details. Now that the company code has been created, let's look at the details of the company code that has been created. The Company Code Global data definition is outlined in Figure 3.10.

The menu path is **IMG • Financial Accounting (New) • Financial Accounting Global Settings (New) • Global Parameters for Company Code • Enter Global Parameters**, and the transaction code is OBY6.

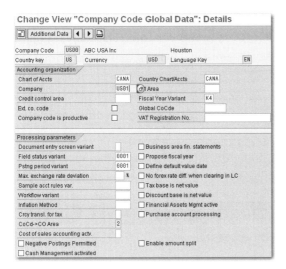

Figure 3.10 Company Code Global Data Definition

The key parameters that are populated for a company code are as follows (these were populated in the previous step using Transaction EC01):

▶ **Country Key**
This identifies the country where the company code is based.

▶ **Currency**
This identifies the company code currency.

▶ **Language Key**
This denotes the language in which the company code would be managed.

In addition, various accounting organization assignments are also made for a company code as follows, based on the following source company code settings:

▶ **Chart of Accounts (Chart of Accts)**
This is the operative chart of accounts in which all the company code transactions are posted.

▶ **Country Chart of Accounts (Country Chart/Accts)**
These are the country-specific chart of accounts that need to be maintained only if required.

▶ **Company**
This is the legal consolidation unit that is tied to the company code.

▶ **Credit Control Area**
This is the organization entity that controls how credit is managed for customers.

▶ **FM Area**

This is the financial management area that needs to be maintained only if you have implemented funds management.

▶ **Fiscal Year Variant**

This identifies the fiscal year applicable for the company code. For example, K4 symbolizes the calendar year as the fiscal year with four special periods.

We'll cover the various organization entities and their assignment to the company code later in this chapter.

Notes

Remember this about the company code relationship:

▶ Each client can have multiple company codes.

▶ A company code can be assigned to only one chart of accounts, one chart of depreciation, one Controlling area, and one company.

These settings can be changed if desired in the screen shown in Figure 3.10. We will discuss these objects in detail as well. Additional data related to taxes and other ID numbers can be maintained in the next screen (see Figure 3.11), which appears when you click on the **Additional Data** tab shown in Figure 3.10.

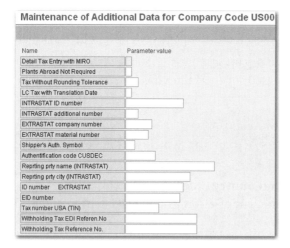

Figure 3.11 Company Code Additional Information

From SAP ERP 6.0 onwards, new settings related to **Detail Tax Entry with MIRO, Plants Abroad Not Required, Tax Without Rounding Tolerance**, and so on have also been added.

3.2.2   Company

Company is the organization entity that is defined for the *consolidation module*. Company is the smallest organizational unit for which individual financial statements are created according to the relevant legal requirements. It represents a legal entity, which could be a subsidiary, joint venture, affiliate, or branch. A company does not require the legal books to exist in SAP ERP. Salient points regarding a company organizational unit are as follows:

▶ Company can represent a legal entity or a group of legal entities.

▶ Company can also be used to take into account non-SAP financial data through import.

▶ Company is used as an internal trading partner as well in intercompany transactions.

▶ Each intercompany transaction is tagged and automatically eliminated during the consolidation process.

▶ Only a single-level roll up is possible in legal consolidation.

▶ Multiple company codes can be assigned to one company for consolidation.

▶ A company can include one or more company codes.

The menu path you will need to use is **IMG • Enterprise Structure • Definition • Financial Accounting • Define Company**.

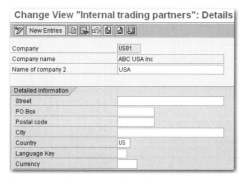

Figure 3.12 Defining a New Company

As you see in Figure 3.12, the only things that you enter here are the **Company name**, address, and **Currency**-related information.

Note
In Figure 3.10, company US01 has been assigned the company code US00. You will learn more about assignments in Section 3.11.

3.2.3   Business Area

The business segment or division in which a group/conglomerate operates can be set up as a *business area.* This is typically used for SEC segment-level reporting. Financial statements can be created for business areas for internal purposes. The definition of the business area is optional, however.

You can use the menu path **IMG • Enterprise structure • Definition • Financial Accounting • Define Business Area** or the transaction code OX03. In the example shown in Figure 3.13, you have created business areas for each of your consulting divisions, assuming you work for a consulting company.

Figure 3.13 Defining a New Business Area

3.2.4   Consolidation Business Area

This is the business area that is defined for consolidation purposes across company codes for segment-level reporting. This accounting unit represents a central business area for which you can generate a balance sheet that can be included in the business area consolidation. You can use the menu path **IMG • Enterprise structure • Definition • Financial Accounting • Maintain Consolidation Business Area**. Figure 3.14 displays the screen where you can maintain consolidation business areas.

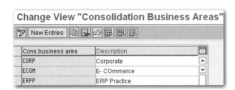

Figure 3.14 Defining a New Consolidation Business Area

3.2.5   Financial Management Area

Financial Management or the **FM area** (see Figure 3.15) is used for financial budgeting and is used in SAP Funds Management. Each company code is assigned a financial management area, if you are using funds management functionality. The menu path is **IMG • Enterprise structure • Definition • Financial Accounting • Maintain FM Area**.

Figure 3.15 Defining a New Financial Management Area

3.2.6 Functional Area

The functional area categorizes an organization into groups so that you can map the cost of goods sold to each of these groupings. This is used for *cost of sales* reporting. These historically represented different departments within an organization, such as Marketing, Production, Sales, Administration, and Research & Development. The menu path is **IMG • Enterprise Structure • Definition • Financial Accounting • Define Functional Area**.

> **Note**
>
> The menu path is not valid from ERP 5.0 onwards so you can use the transaction code **FM_FUNCTION** to create, change, or display a functional area.

Figure 3.16 shows you the screen for changing the parameters of a functional area. You can maintain the **Description**, the **Validity Period** (to and from dates), and the **Authorization Group**. **Authorization Group** helps you control who can access the functional area.

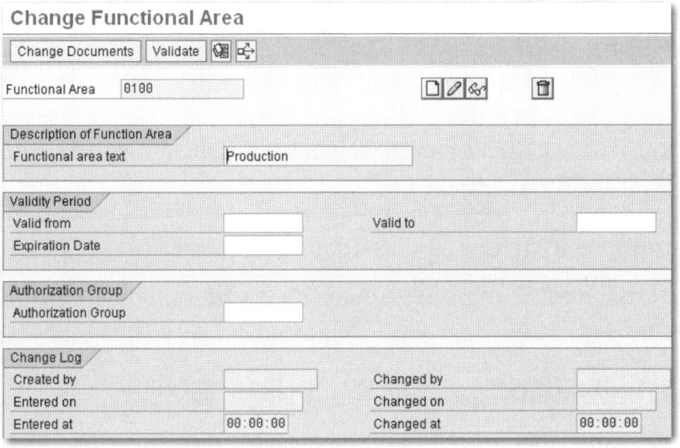

Figure 3.16 Defining a New Functional Area

> **Note**
>
> Typically, substitution rules were used for determining the functional area automatically when posting, but in the latest SAP ERP release, you can use a derivation strategy to determine the functional area.

3.2.7 Segment

This new enterprise object was introduced with the new GL. Segment is used for segmental reporting as per the SEC and International Financial Reporting Standards (IFRS) guidelines of increased disclosure. The menu path is **IMG • Enterprise Structure • Definition • Financial Accounting • Define Segment**.

Figure 3.17 shows you the screen where you have defined segments from a retail company's perspective. The categorization for a retailer can be cash and carry customers, department stores, food retail, nonfood specialty stores, and others.

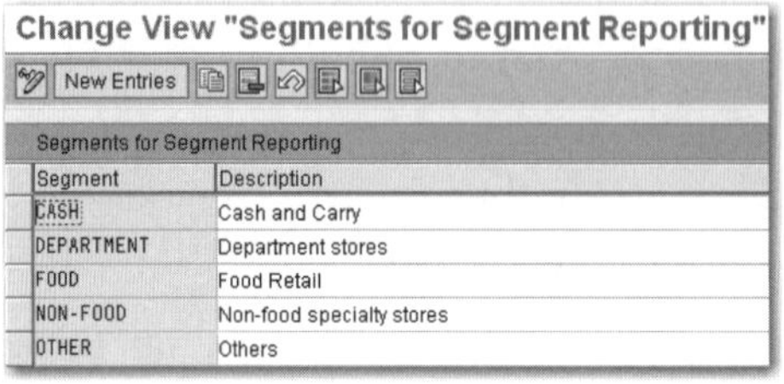

Figure 3.17 Defining Segments

3.2.8 Profit Center

A profit center is an entity that resides in Controlling and represents an area of responsibility within your company; that is, it provides an internal view of your organization. Profit center is typically a unit that manages both *costs and revenues* and behaves as an independent operating unit for which a separate operating statement and balance sheet can be calculated. Following are some of the salient points concerning profit centers:

► Each profit center must be assigned to a standard hierarchy.

► Profit centers can be created as regions, functions, products, or a combination of these attributes.

► Some of the organizations create a one-to-one assignment with cost center.

► Each profit center can be assigned to one Controlling area.

▸ Profit centers are statistical cost objects and must be derived from a real cost object.

You can use the menu path **IMG • Enterprise structure • Definition • Financial Accounting • Define Profit Center • EC-PCA: Create Profit Center** or the transaction code KE51. Profit centers were part of Enterprise Controlling but with the advent of the new GL, these have also been included in Financial Accounting.

3.2.9 Chart of Accounts

This is a listing of all GL accounts that are required to record Financial Accounting transactions. Some things to remember about chart of accounts are that:

▸ Multiple charts of account can be defined in a client.

▸ Chart of accounts can be used in multiple company codes.

▸ Chart of accounts controls account classification and classifies all accounting entries.

▸ An operating chart of accounts, a country chart of accounts, and a group chart of accounts can be used in parallel.

▸ A country chart of accounts is used to satisfy specific account numbering requirements, particularly in some European and South American countries.

▸ A group chart of accounts is used for legal consolidation.

▸ An operative chart of accounts is defined at a company-code level and determines the structure of the balance sheet within a company code.

Tip

A company code can be assigned to only one operative chart of accounts.

Some caveats related to the structuring of chart of accounts are:

▸ Typically, one of the operative chart of accounts is also made the group chart of accounts.

▸ If group and operative chart of accounts are different, then these need to be mapped account by account.

▸ It's always best to have one common chart of accounts.

▸ Multiple charts of account increase the amount of maintenance.

3.2.10 Chart of Depreciation

This is a main organizational unit for fixed assets, and it houses the possible methods of depreciation for the company code. Typically one chart of depreciation is usually set by country. Each depreciation area is used to calculate a type of depreciation (book, income tax, federal, etc.). The depreciation calculation keys determine the formula used for depreciation.

The chart of depreciation relationship to other financial enterprise entities is enumerated as follows:

▶ A chart of depreciation can only be assigned to one chart of accounts.

▶ A chart of depreciation may cover one or multiple company codes.

▶ A company code can only be assigned to one chart of depreciation.

3.2.11 Credit Control Area

Credit processing in SAP ERP Financials is governed via the credit control area. The credit control area controls the way credit is managed in accounting and sales and distribution. You can use this menu path: **IMG • Enterprise structure • Definition • Financial Accounting • Define Credit Control Area**.

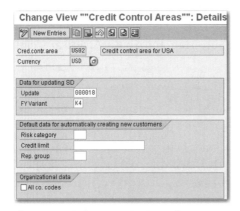

Figure 3.18 Defining Credit Control Area

Figure 3.18 shows you the screen for defining the credit control area and some of the important settings for the same. The credit control area requires the definition of the following fields:

▶ **Currency**
This is the currency in which the credit limits are monitored.

▶ **Update**
Update is the most important field from the credit control area perspective

because it lays the rules for managing the customer credit. The following update rules can be defined as applicable for a credit control area:

- ▶ **Blank**: No update from sales and distribution documents. This means that credit control limits will not be affected from sales and distribution and is only used when sales and distribution is not implemented.

- ▶ **000012:** Open order value on time axis, delivery and billing document value. This means that the system will include the open order value along with the delivery and billing document value to determine the credit used by the customer.

- ▶ **000015**: Open delivery and billing document value. This means that the system will only consider the delivery documents and the billing document value.

- ▶ **000018:** Open delivery value for sales order, open billing document value. This means that the system will consider only the open delivery value and open billing document value.

- ▶ **F Y Variant**
  This is the applicable fiscal year variant. K4 stands for the calendar year as fiscal year with 4 special periods.

- ▶ **Risk Category, Credit Limit, and Rep. Group**
  These fields can be used to enter the default value for creating customers.

- ▶ **All co. codes**
  If you set this indicator, then your credit control area can be entered for all the company codes.

This completes our discussion of the Financial Accounting entities. Let's now take a brief look at the Controlling entities.

3.3   Controlling Organizational Entities

Controlling entities are used to manage the management reporting structure of an organization. The owner of Controlling organizational entities is typically the cost controller who manages the entities in consultation with operational department heads. Unlike financial organization entities that can be solely defined by the Finance department, Controlling organization entities (especially cost center) need to be defined in conjunction with operational process teams. In addition, you need to involve your HR department to incorporate the organizational structure when defining your Controlling entities. Overall, the guiding principles should be the strategy and vision of the organization going forward.

With that said, let's take a look at the Controlling organization entities (operating concern, Controlling area, and cost centers) in detail.

3.3.1 Operating Concern

This is the organizational entity that tracks the profitability of an organization and structures the enterprise from a profitability perspective. Operating concern is the highest organizational unit in Controlling, and is activated for Controlling-Profitability Analysis (CO-PA). When you create an operating concern, then only the operating concern object is created. All the other details get created when you create the master data and characteristic for operating concern. The menu path is: **IMG • Enterprise structure • Definition • Controlling • Create Operating Concern**.

3.3.2 Controlling Area

This is the umbrella organizational entity for Controlling that is used for managerial reporting and cost accounting purposes. All the cost activities can happen in only one Controlling area, not across Controlling areas. All the costing activities require a Controlling area.

The Controlling area represents a common unit of cost structure for which costs and revenue are managed, allocated, and distributed. For example, if you want to transfer primary costs, allocate them or perform any costing planning, all these activities happen within a Controlling area.

After following the menu path **IMG • Enterprise structure • Definition • Controlling • Maintain Controlling Area • Copy, Delete, Check Controlling Area** or using the transaction code EC16 you click on **Maintain Controlling area**, and then choose **Copy, Delete, Check Controlling Area** to get to the screen shown in Figure 3.19.

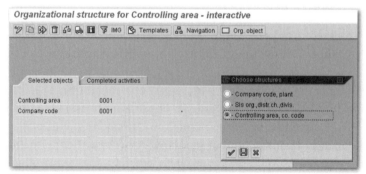

Figure 3.19 Copying an Existing Controlling Area

To copy a Controlling area, select the template **Controlling area, co. code** after clicking on **Templates**.

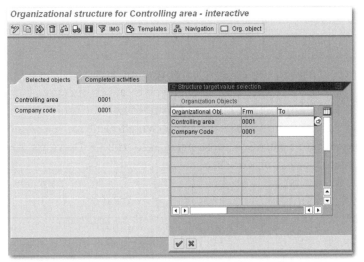

Figure 3.20 Entering a Target Company Code and Controlling Area

In Figure 3.20, you have to enter the target company code and Controlling area. The system asks you whether you want to copy all the GL accounts and which currency you want for your Controlling area. In this case, assume that the currency was specified as USD. This creates a new Controlling area and company code, along with the assignments. In the preceding example, you created US00 as the Controlling area that tied to company code US00 as well.

3.3.3   Cost Center

The cost center is the smallest entity in Controlling that represents an area of responsibility at which the costs are managed in your company. You can also implement budgeting at a cost center level in your company. The salient points for a cost center are listed here:

▸ Cost centers typically represent departments within an organization.

▸ Each cost center can be assigned to only one Controlling area, one profit center, and one company code.

▸ Each cost center must be assigned to a standard hierarchy structure.

▸ Cost centers are used to analyze planned and actual costs at the cost center level.

The menu path is **IMG • Enterprise Structure • Definition • Financial Accounting • Define Profit Center • EC-PCA: Create Profit Center,** and the Transaction is KS01.

Next you'll learn more about the logistics organizational entities.

3.4 Logistics Organizational Entities

In this section, you'll learn more about the logistics organizational entities. They support the logistics modules of SAP ERP, which need to be created so that you can map your business processes to the SAP ERP system. For example, you manufacture and process your goods in a physical location. That physical location is typically created in SAP ERP as a plant. This helps you understand that your plant in St Louis is number 1000 versus the plant in Chicago, which is 2000. So all your material masters and other transaction data is then recorded in these two plants as they occur.

3.4.1 Valuation Level

The valuation level defines level at which you will valuate your inventory or stockable materials. The valuation level can be either plant or company code. Plant is the recommended valuation level in most situations. This is mandatory if you plan to implement production planning, costing, or the SAP Retail Information System solution. Figure 3.21 shows the two toggle boxes available for you. In this example, you have chosen **Valuation area is a plant**.

Use the menu path **IMG • Enterprise Structure • Definition • Logistics— General • Define Valuation Level** or the transaction code OX14.

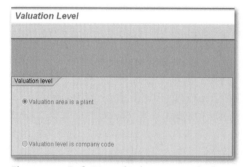

Figure 3.21 Definition of Valuation Level: Plant or Company Code

The choice of valuation level affects the following:

▶ Maintenance of material master records

▶ GL accounts in which the material stocks are managed

▶ GL accounts to which material transactions are posted

Valuation area is most commonly set at the plant level to allow for the material valuation at a plant level. If you set the valuation area at the company code level, then the material data will be valuated at the company code level.

Note

It is very difficult to switch between valuation levels after you have production data. Making a clear choice early is important because any change requires a data conversion effort and consulting help.

3.4.2 Plant

A plant is an organizational logistics unit relevant for production, procurement, plant maintenance, and materials planning. This corresponds to a physical location where materials are managed and is an operational unit within a company code. Examples of a plant include a production facility, branch office, distribution center, warehouse, or anywhere where stock is kept. Some salient features of plant are as follows:

▶ A plant is not a financial entity even though the valuation happens at a plant level.

▶ A plant has bigger implications in other logistics modules such as Materials Management (MM), Sales and Distribution (SD), Production Planning (PP), and Logistics Execution (LE), which includes shipping and transportation.

▶ Materials Requirement Planning (MRP) is run at the plant level and available to promise functionality resides at the plant level.

▶ Valuation prices (standard price and moving average price) is defined by the plant.

You can use this menu path: **IMG • Enterprise Structure • Definition • Logistics—General • Define, Copy, Delete, Check Plant • Copy, Delete, Check Plant** and this transaction code: **EC02 (Copying)**.

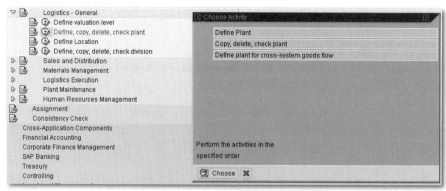

Figure 3.22 Logistics Enterprise Structure: Defining Plant

As shown in Figure 3.22, to create a plant, you choose **Define Plant**. You can also copy an existing plant by choosing **Copy, delete, check plant**. This opens up an interface that is similar to what you saw earlier when copying a company code or Controlling area. If you clicked on **Define Plant**, then the next screen would appear as shown in Figure 3.23, where you can enter the name and address details of the plant that you want to create.

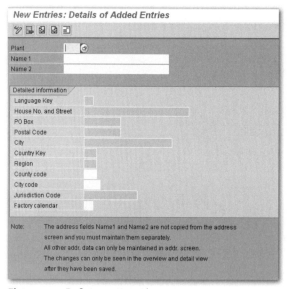

Figure 3.23 Defining a New Plant: Basics

After entering the details and saving the data, your plant has been created. Now you need to make sure that it is properly assigned to the right hierarchy elements.

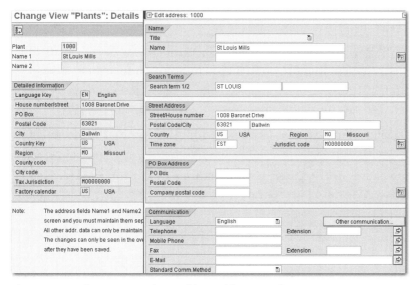

Figure 3.24 Defining a New Plant: Adding Address Details

3.4.3 Location

A location allows a plant to be classified according to spatial or situation criteria. You can assign an asset, functional location, equipment, or work center to a location. This is primarily used for reporting and is for informative assignment only. The menu path is **IMG • Enterprise Structure • Definition • Logistics—General • Define Location**. Note that location is inherently defined in conjunction with a plant.

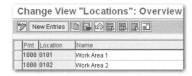

Figure 3.25 Figure 3.25 Defining a New Location

Figure 3.25 shows the two locations that have been defined **0101** and **0102** for **Work Area 1** and **Work Area 2**, respectively.

3.4.4 Storage Location

The storage location is where materials are physically stored in a plant. It allows the distinction of materials stocks within a plant. Some of the salient points of a storage location are as follows:

▸ Stock is managed only on a quantity basis at a storage location. As we discussed, the value is maintained only at a plant level, if the valuation level is plant.

▸ Physical inventory can be carried out at the storage location level.

▸ A separate material master view needs to be created for each storage location.

▸ Each goods movement (issue or receipt) needs a storage location.

▸ Movements across storage locations within the same plant do not have any financial impact.

The menu path is **IMG • Enterprise Structure • Definition • Materials Management • Maintain Storage Location** and the transaction code: OX09.

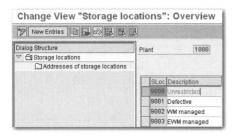

Figure 3.26 Define Storage Location

As shown in Figure 3.26, storage location is also inherently tied to a plant. After you define the storage location **9000** as **Unrestricted**, you can also maintain the address of the storage location by clicking on **Addresses of storage locations** in the left pane.

3.4.5 Storage Bin

This is the bin within a storage location where materials are stored. To implement inventory tracking at the storage bin level, you should implement SAP Warehouse Management (WM). SAP WM is implemented typically in manufacturing and engineering companies (such as automobile manufacturers) where you have too many materials masters that need to be tracked and managed separately by bin.

3.5 Relationship Between Financial and Logistics Entities

In earlier sections, you learned the definitions of financial and logistics organization entities. However, SAP ERP is an integrated system in which both of these come together (in addition to a host of other organization entities) to allow you to map your processes end-to-end. So let's consider the broad relationship between general logistics units and their link to accounting at this point. This is illustrated in Figures 3.27 and 3.28.

> **Note**
>
> I wanted to come up with a universally applicable entity-relationship diagram (ERD) across the SAP ERP landscape. But as with any system, there are too many ifs and buts that are unique to each organization and that make it really difficult to come up with a universal ERD. However, it's very important for you to understand what is technically possible. Then you need to apply your business common sense to come up with your own custom ERD.

As shown in Figure 3.27, the storage bin **(Bin 1)** is tied to the storage location **(Storage Location 1)**, which is assigned to a plant **(Plant 1)** that is assigned to a company code **(Company Code 1).** Hopefully, this gives you an understanding of how you can map your organizational entities to SAP ERP and understand the bigger picture.

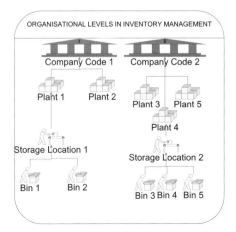

Figure 3.27 Schematic for Organizational Levels in Inventory Management

Figure 3.28 further details additional financial components and the interlinkage with logistics components. The figure also details the various types of financial statements that can be created at different levels, such as business area statements, company code statements, and the consolidation group level statements for the company and the consolidation business area.

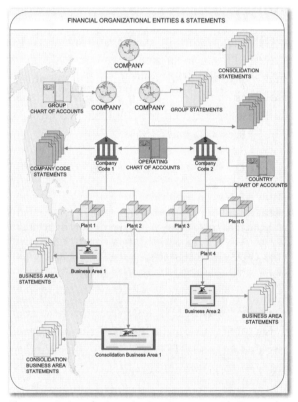

Figure 3.28 Sample Organization Structure with Financials and Logistics

As you can see from Figure 3.28, plants (**Plant 1 and Plant 2**) are assigned to a company code (**Company Code 1**), which can then be assigned to a **COMPANY,** which can then be assigned to another **COMPANY**. In addition, you can assign plants (Plant 1) to business areas (**Business Area 1**), which can then be assigned to a consolidation business area **(Consolidation Business Area 1)**. Also, the country chart of accounts and operating chart of accounts need to be assigned at a company code level.

After you understand the mish mash of these assignments and distinguish the subtle differences between each of these entities (such as company code versus company), which can be very confusing, you are ready to understand much more complex inter-relationships. You'll learn about the detailed analysis of the assignments later in Chapter 3. For now make a mental note of each of these entities and how they fit into the overall schema of SAP ERP.

Next, you'll learn about the purchasing organizational entities.

3.6 Purchasing Organizational Entities

Now that you understand the general logistics and financial organizational unit, let's take a look at the purchasing organizational entities. Purchasing organizational entities are organizational units that need to be created if you are using purchasing in materials management. These identify the overall structure of purchasing, and the assignment of purchasing to accounting determines whether you are organizing purchasing in a centralized or decentralized fashion. Purchasing has two main organization entities: purchasing organization and purchasing group.

3.6.1 Purchasing Organization

This is the organization entity responsible for procuring materials or services for one or more plants and for negotiating general conditions of purchase with vendors. This also assumes legal responsibility for all external purchase transactions. The menu path is **IMG • Enterprise structure • Definition • Materials Management • Maintain Purchasing Organization**.

You can also define a *reference purchasing organization* that allows you to maintain the central terms and conditions that can be used by other purchasing organizations. This is especially useful if you can pool your buying together and get quantity discounts and favorable payment terms as a result of the pooling.

Typically, organizations have one central purchasing group that coordinates the purchase of high-value and high-volume items, and then you have local-level purchasing organizations that can be set up to tailor to local purchasing requirements. However, organizations are moving away from multiple purchasing departments and are making purchasing part of shared services to maximize pooling benefits.

3.6.2 Purchasing Group

The purchasing organization is further subdivided into purchasing groups (buyer groups), which are responsible for day-to-day buying activities. These can represent a single buyer or a group of buyers depending on your organization.

Let's now discuss how the purchasing group can be defined in the SAP materials management module. Take note of the menu path: **IMG • Materials Management • Purchasing • Create Purchasing Groups**.

Remember, a purchasing group is one of the primary purchasing objects by which you define the release strategies that define the level of approvals required to approve a certain purchase order limit. In the next section, you'll learn about the sales organizational entities.

3.7   Sales and Distribution Organizational Entities

Sales and distribution organizational entities form a framework in which all the sales business transactions, such as sales order, sales inquiry, and so on, are processed. To learn about the organizational entities in sales and distribution, first take a look at sales organization.

3.7.1   Sales Organization

This is the organizational entity responsible for selling materials and services, for negotiating sales conditions, and for product liability and rights of recourse. This is the highest level of summarization for sales statistics. The customer master is created for a sales organization in sales and distribution. The menu path you can use is **IMG • Enterprise Structure • Definition • Sales and Distribution • Define, Copy, Delete, Check Sales organization • Define Sales Organization**.

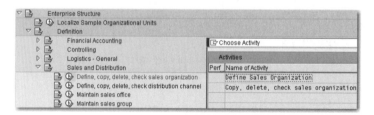

Figure 3.29 Menu Path for Sales and Distribution Organization Entities

Figure 3.29 shows the menu path along with the activity that needs to be selected for creating a new sales organization.

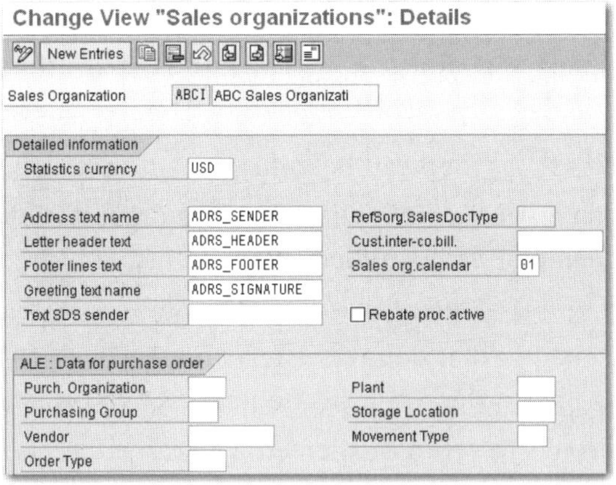

Figure 3.30 Defining a Sales Organization

To create a new sales organization, you can copy it from a predefined sales organization provided in the system and then modify the appropriate fields (see Figure 3.30). The sales organization needs the following key fields defined:

▶ **Statistics currency**
This defines the currency applicable for the sales organization as a default.

▶ **Text names**
Address/Letter header/Footer Lines/Greeting/SDS Sender: These are all the form types defined for the sales organization for communication.

▶ **Ref Sales Org Doc Type**
This is the reference sales organization used for the definition of allowed document types. If all the document types need to be allowed, you have to leave this blank.

▶ **Customer Inter Company Billing**
This defines the customer number that is used for intercompany billing and for defining the sales organization in opportunity management.

▶ **Rebate Processing Active**
This needs to be checked if you need to activate rebate processing for a sales organization.

▶ **ALE Data for Purchase Order**
This denotes the ALE-related data for external systems from a purchasing perspective: **Purch. Organization, Purchasing Group, Vendor, Order**

Type, Plant, Storage Location, Movement Type. These are typically used to pre-populate external data.

Next, you'll learn how to check whether the sales organization has been successfully created and whether there are any missing entries. The menu path is **IMG • Enterprise Structure • Definition • Sales and Distribution • Define, Copy, Delete, Check Sales Organization • Copy, Delete, Check Sales Organization** and the transaction code is EC04.

You can also create a sales organization by copying the sales organization from another one using the same method as you used for the Controlling area and company code. The transaction code for copying, checking and deleting a sales organization is EC04.

Figure 3.31 shows the sales organization entry screen where you can check whether the configuration is correct. To get to this screen, you can either use the F8 function key or click on **Organization Object • Check org.object**. This shows you the pop-up window as shown in Figure 3.31 where you can enter the **Sales Org.** as **ABCI**.

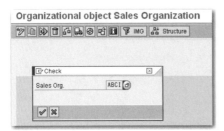

Figure 3.31 Checking the Sales Organization Configuration

After you click on the green check box or press Enter, you see the message displayed in Figure 3.32, **All foreign key dependencies are correct**, only if all the settings have been performed correctly.

Figure 3.32 Checking Sales Organization Configuration: Results

If you press Enter or click on the green check box, you go to the screen shown in Figure 3.33 where you will get the message that the sales org. ABCI was checked for errors in the **Completed activities** tab.

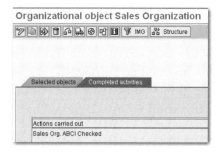

Figure 3.33 Sales Organization Configuration Checked

3.7.2 Division

Division is the organizational unit that pertains to the internal organizational responsibility for sales and revenues of goods and services. This is typically related to the product groups or product lines that the company is engaged in selling. The menu path (illustrated in Figure 3.34) is **IMG • Enterprise structure • Definition • Logistics - General • Define, Copy, Delete, Check Division**. The transaction code is EC06.

> **Note**
>
> Division resides in logistics-general rather than in sales and distribution.

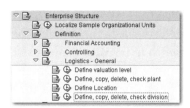

Figure 3.34 Defining a New Division: Menu Path

Figure 3.35 shows sample divisions created based on the range of products or product family. The figure shows the hypothetical division for Apple, Inc., and these are categorized as per the logical product family.

Figure 3.35 Defining a New Division

For the purpose of illustration, let's continue defining the sales and distribution aspects of Apple Inc.

3.7.3 Distribution Channel

This entity represents the channel by which materials and services reach their customers. The distribution channel also denotes the strategies by which an organization distributes the goods and services to customers. Examples of these are wholesale, retail, direct sales, and so on. Distribution channels can be used to differentiate sales statistics, achieve flexible pricing, and define responsibilities within an organization.

You can use the menu path **IMG • Enterprise Structure • Definition • Sales and Distribution • Define, Copy, Delete, Check Distribution Channel** or the transaction code EC05. Figure 3.36 shows the various channels by which products reach the consumers.

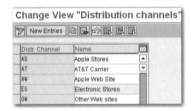

Figure 3.36 Defining the Distribution Channel

Similar to the sales organization check, you can also check the distribution channel for configuration errors. The transaction code is **IMG • Enterprise Structure • Definition • Sales and Distribution • Define, Copy, Delete, Check Distribution Channel • Copy, Delete, Check Distribution Channel**, and the Transaction is EC05.

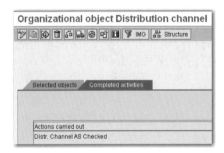

Figure 3.37 Figure 3.37 Checking the Distribution Channel Configuration

Figure 3.37 shows the end results of checking the distribution channel **AS** which you would have entered in the pop-up box that appears after you choose **Organization Unit • Check org.object**.

3.7.4 Sales Area

A sales area determines the distribution channel used by a sales organization to sell a division's products. It is important to clearly identify how you are selling a particular product.

> **Note**
>
> Sales area equals sales organization plus division plus distribution channel. It identifies the overall strategy of sales for an organization by delineating the unique combinations of selling a particular product in different regions.

Theoretically, sales areas can be mapped by combining all the sales organizations with all the divisions and all the distribution channels. However, not all the combinations are logical examples. For example, Apple Inc. currently sells iPhones only via AT&T. Other Apple products, however, are not available from AT&T.

A sales document can only be assigned one sales area, and during sales order processing, you can define the validity checks for pricing and business processing such as delivery and confirmation by sales area.

The sales area is the organizational unit that ties everything together and outlines the possibilities from sales. The entities in the sales area are tied to Financial Accounting. All the other organization entities are for sales reporting and categorization purposes only.

3.7.5 Sales Office

This is a physical location, typically a branch office, which is responsible for the sales of certain products and services within a particular geographical area. A customer can be assigned a sales office in the customer master. This represents the geographical perspective of a sales organization. Some of the salient points of a sales office include the following:

▶ The sales office can be assigned to one or more sales areas.

▶ The sales office needs to have a physical address.

▶ Sales personnel can be assigned to a sales office.

- ▶ Each sales document is tied to a sales office.
- ▶ This can be used to select the list of sales document.

The menu path is **IMG • Enterprise Structure • Definition • Sales and Distribution • Maintain Sales Office**.

Figure 3.38 Defining a New Sales Office

Figure 3.38 shows you the possible sales offices that can be maintained by geography. This is how you have organized your sales offices physically. So if you have an office in the U.S. Midwest that controls all the sales-related activities in the Midwest, then you need to maintain it as a sales office.

3.7.6 Sales Group

This is one level below the sales office. It can be used to group personnel working for a common product family or to segregate the industry focus within the Sales department. Some of the salient points of a sales office are as follows:

- ▶ The sales group can be assigned to one or more sales offices.
- ▶ Sales personnel can be assigned to a sales group.
- ▶ The sales group is a selection criterion for lists of sales documents.

You can use the menu path: **IMG • Enterprise Structure • Definition • Sales and Distribution • Maintain Sales Group**.

Figure 3.39 shows you the categorization of sales into logical groups such as **Hardware** and **Software**. This is primarily based on how you have categorized your sales personnel.

Figure 3.39 Defining a New Sales Group

3.7.7 Credit Control Area

The Credit Control Area (FI-AR) is used in credit management for customers to group similar types of customers in one credit control area and set credit limits for customers. One credit control area can be assigned to multiple company codes, and one company code can have multiple credit control areas.

This completes all the sales and distribution organization entities. In the next section, you'll learn about the logistics execution organization entities.

3.8 Logistics Execution Organizational Entities

Logistics execution organization entities pertain primarily to shipping, transportation, and warehousing processes. Here you need to define the entities that control the business transactions related to inbound and outbound delivery, along with the shipment processes. Figure 3.40 shows you how to get to the enterprise structure menu for configuring organizational entities for logistics execution.

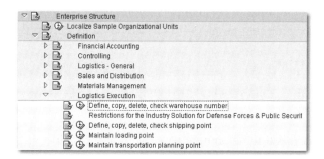

Figure 3.40 Menu Path for Configuring Logistics Execution Entities

3.8.1 Warehouse Number/Warehouse Complex

This identifies a complex physical warehouse structure within a warehouse management system. The physical location is usually decisive for assigning the definition of the warehouse number. A warehouse number groups together storage types and storage bins that are organized and maintained as a complete unit.

All the activities within a warehouse, such as stock placements and stock removals of materials, are executed within a warehouse number. You can use the menu path **IMG • Enterprise Structure • Definition • Logistics Execution • Define, Copy, Delete, Check Warehouse Number • Copy, Delete, Check Distribution Channel** or the transaction code EC09.

Figure 3.41 Defining a New Warehouse Number

Figure 3.41 shows how a new warehouse number is defined. Typical categorization for warehouse management can be central warehousing with the complete warehouse management implemented, or lean warehouse management, which can be implemented without stocks valuation and linkage of the same to accounting.

3.8.2 Shipping Point

The shipping point is the physical location from which you ship the goods, for example, the warehouse's loading ramp number. The shipping point is defined on the basis of a combination of plants, shipping conditions, and loading groups. You need a shipping point to ship a delivery and to receive it as well.

You can use the menu path **IMG • Enterprise Structure • Definition • Logistics Execution • Define, Copy, Delete, Check Shipping Point • Copy, Delete, Check Shipping Point** or the transaction code EC07.

Here are the key fields that need to be entered when you define a **Shipping Point**, as shown in Figure 3.42:

▶ **Departure Zone**
This typically corresponds to the ZIP code of the country and denotes the region where the shipping point is located.

▶ **Loading Time (Determine Load. Time)**
This is the difference between the loading time and the goods issue time. It can be configured as route dependent, independent, not applicable with no loading time, or default from the shipping point.

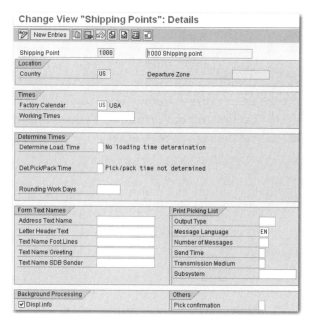

Figure 3.42 Defining a New Shipping Point

▶ **Pick/Pack Time (Det. Pick/Pack Time)**
This is the difference between material availability time and loading time. It can also be configured as not applicable, route dependent, route independent, or default from the shipping point.

▶ **Pick Confirmation**
This is set as **A** if you want picking confirmation to be a mandatory step before you can do post goods issue.

3.8.3   Loading Point

This is the subdivision of shipping point and is typically optional. It denotes the exact physical location where the loading of a delivery item takes place, for instance, bay 13 of warehouse number 5. The menu path is **IMG • Enterprise Structure • Definition • Logistics Execution • Maintain Loading Point** and the transaction code EC07.

Figure 3.43 illustrates the menu path along with the pop-up screen that allows you to enter the **Shipping Point/Receiving Pt** for which you want to define the **Loading Point**.

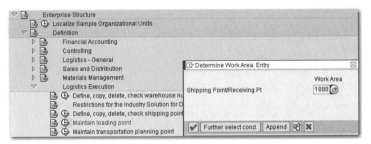

Figure 3.43 Entering the Loading Point Within the Shipping Point

After you select a shipping point, you can maintain the loading point as shown in Figure 3.44.

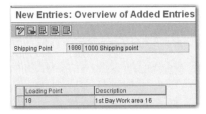

Figure 3.44 Defining a New Loading Point

3.8.4 Transportation Planning Point

This outlines the responsibility area for planning a particular type of transportation, for example, rail versus truck. A shipment is assigned to one transportation planning point. A transportation planning point is also the link to the company code for transportation processing. The menu path is **IMG • Enterprise Structure • Definition • Logistics Execution • Maintain Transportation Planning Point**. Figure 3.45 shows how you can maintain **ABCD** as a **New Transport Pl Pt** with appropriate address details along with any communication details.

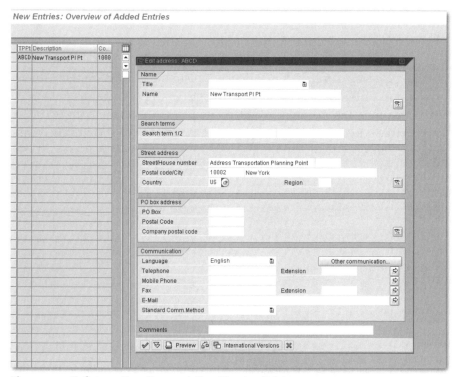

Figure 3.45 Defining a New Transportation Planning Point

Let's now take a look at the plant maintenance organizational entities.

3.9   Plant Maintenance Organizational Entities

Plant Maintenance organizational entities control how the business transactions are processed in plant maintenance and customer service. Plant maintenance primarily inherits all the logistics general entities. In this section, you'll learn about any additional entities that need to be defined specifically for plant maintenance. These organizational units are most significant to the maintenance planner so that they can chart out the planning structure of the organization from the maintenance perspective. For example, the maintenance planner might decide that for five logistics plants, the maintenance planning should be organized and managed by one maintenance planning plant.

3.9.1 Maintenance Planning Plant

This is created in addition to the normal logistics plant if you need to do maintenance planning for a particular plant. This allows you to map maintenance planning correctly if maintenance planning is done centrally for several plants in one plant. Figure 3.46 shows you how to get to the screen for maintaining the maintenance planning plant. The menu path is **IMG • Enterprise Structure • Definition • Plant Maintenance • Maintain Maintenance Planning Plant.**

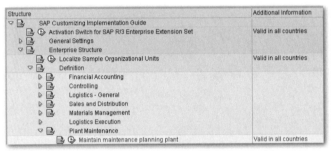

Figure 3.46 Menu Path for Maintenance Plant Org Entities

Figure 3.47 displays the screen for maintaining the maintenance planning plant.

Figure 3.47 Defining a New Maintenance Planning Plant

All the maintenance tasks for the technical objects in plant maintenance, such as equipment and task lists, are planned and prepared at the maintenance planning plant. The following activities can be performed at the maintenance planning plant:

▸ Defining task lists

▸ Material planning based on bills of material in task lists and orders

▸ Managing and scheduling maintenance plans

▸ Creating maintenance notifications

▸ Executing maintenance orders

Let's now move on to learning about HR related organizational entities.

3.10   Human Resources Organizational Entities

Human Resources (HR) organizational entities help you structure your HR transactions from personnel administrative, time management, and payroll perspectives. These are controlled by your HR manager; however, the Finance department also influences some of the organizational entities from the cost management and allocation perspective.

3.10.1   Personnel Area

This is the organizational unit at which all the HR processes are managed. This is organized according to the aspects of personnel, time management, and payroll. These should be created with a four-character key. The best practice is to copy from an SAP template personnel area and then modify to update the additional attributes. The menu path is **IMG • Enterprise Structure • Definition • Human Resources Management • Personnel Areas • Personnel Areas** or you can use the transaction code EC10.

Using Transaction EC10, you can maintain the personnel area identifier along with the address details as shown in Figure 3.48. It's best to copy this personnel area from another personnel area because it will copy other dependent configuration objects as well.

Figure 3.48 Defining a New Personnel Area

Figure 3.48 shows how you have maintained **NAUS** as the personnel area applicable for **North America US**. You can also maintain the address of the personnel area by using the Envelope icon shown in Figure 3.48. The address should be the address of the head office for that particular personnel area. After you save the personnel area, you will get the message shown in Figure 3.49.

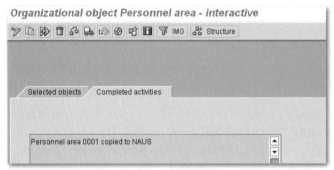

Figure 3.49 Copying the Personnel Area from the Standard SAP Personnel Area

3.10.2 Personnel Subarea

A personnel area can be subdivided into several subareas according to some logical grouping. For example, you might choose to group your personnel area by geography. Personnel subareas contain business characteristics such as geography. Groupings for personnel subareas can be used for validating master data and time data. In addition, you can use personnel subareas to check the plausibility of data that you enter. You can use the menu path **IMG • Enterprise Structure • Definition • Human Resources Management • Personnel Subareas** or the transaction code EC11. The personnel subarea along with its menu path is shown in Figure 3.50.

Figure 3.50 Defining a New Personnel Subarea: Menu Path

First enter the personnel area and then enter the subareas within the personnel area as shown in Figure 3.51.

In the example shown in Figure 3.51, you choose to maintain your personnel subareas as per geography. **SOUT** represents the **Southern US**, and **NORT** represents the **Northern US**.

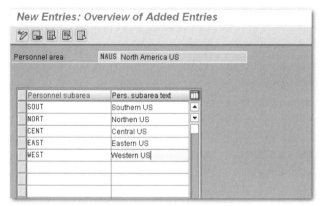

Figure 3.51 Defining a New Personnel Subarea

3.10.3 Employee Groups

This allows you to divide employees into groups and then define their relationship within an enterprise. The relationship identifies whether the employee is salaried or hourly, and the parameters differentiate the various activities in HR. SAP ERP has most of the standard employee groups available by country, and you should use those as your starting point and then add the ones specific to your organization's way of structuring your employees. The functions of employee groups are as follows:

▶ Employee groups allow you to generate default data entry values, for example, for the payroll accounting area or an employee's basic pay.

▶ Employee groups serve as selection criteria for reporting.

▶ Employee groups constitute an authorization check unit.

The menu path is **IMG • Enterprise Structure • Definition • Human Resources Management • Employee Groups**. The typical employee groups within an enterprise are shown in Figure 3.52. Some of these are **Salaried employee**, **Inactive employee**, and **Temp/Seasonal**.

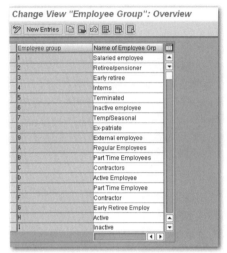

Figure 3.52 Defining a New Employee Group

3.10.4 Employee Subgroup

Employee subgroups can be defined to further segregate employee groups. Features are allocated to these in the later steps. This helps to outline the personnel structure of an organization as well as provides opportunities to segregate HR data for reporting and control purposes as listed here:

▶ The employee subgroup grouping enables you to differentiate how an employee is dealt with in payroll.

▶ The employee subgroup grouping enables you to determine the permissible wage types, appraisal criteria, leave quota, and work schedules.

▶ The employee subgroup enables you to define data entry default values, for example, for the payroll accounting area or an employee's basic pay.

▶ The employee subgroup is a selection criterion for evaluations.

▶ Employee subgroups are authorization check units.

The menu path is **IMG • Enterprise Structure • Definition • Human Resources Management • Employee Groups**. Some sample employee subgroups are shown in Figure 3.53, such as **Salaried Employees** and **Student Employee**.

After getting this introduction to all the organizational units across financial, Controlling, logistics, purchasing, logistics execution, plant maintenance, and HR management, we can proceed to the assignment possibilities of each of these organizational units.

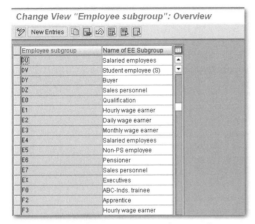

Figure 3.53 Defining a New Employee Subgroup

3.11 Assignment of Organizational Entities

SAP ERP is an integrated system, which requires that all its enterprise entities need to talk to each other. The only way to do this is by assigning these organizational units to each other across module components. In this section, you will learn the various assignments that build the organizational hierarchy in the system.

However, understanding the rules of assignment clearly is important. Sometimes organizational structures do not meet the technical requirements of assignments. In that case, you have to find a feasible workaround or add organizational objects in other modules to ensure that you get your optimal organizational structure. Figure 3.54 shows you the assignments possible for building your enterprise structure.

3.11.1 Company Code(s) to Company (N:1 or 1:1)

Remember, that company is used for consolidation, whereas company code is the accounting entity for which you can generate individual balance sheets and where all the financial transactions are recorded. Multiple company codes can be assigned to one company. Take note of the menu path: **IMG • Enterprise Structure • Assignment • Financial Accounting • Assign Company Code to Company**.

We'll cover all the assignments, including Logistics, Purchasing, Sales and Distribution, Plant Maintenance, Logistics Execution, and HR management, to give you a thorough perspective of other organizational areas. To give you a capsule view of the assignments, you'll learn how an assignment is actually performed along with the rules for assignment, caveats, and relationships (many to one, many to many, one to many, etc.) in each of the assignments. Let's begin with the Financial Accounting assignments.

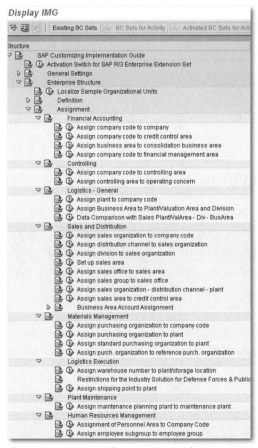

Figure 3.54 Menu Path: Organizational Entities Assignments

Figure 3.55 shows how **Company US01** has been assigned to **Co...** (company code) **US01**. The list gets populated for all the company codes, and you just enter the correct company.

Figure 3.55 Assigning Company Code to Company

You can assign multiple companies to a company, however. The assignment of multiple companies to a company helps in outlining the consolidation structure of your organization. There are certain rules to keep in mind for assignments:

▶ A company code can be assigned to only one company.

▶ Multiple company codes can be assigned to one company; in other words, a company can consist of multiple company codes.

Now let's take a look at the relationships:

▶ Company to company code: One to many

▶ Company code to company: One to one

Keep this caveat in mind when dealing with company codes: Only company codes with the same *chart of accounts* and *fiscal year variant* can be assigned to the same company. Figure 3.56 shows you a schematic relationship of company code and company.

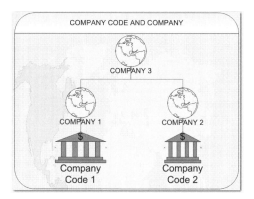

Figure 3.56 Hierarchical Relationship of Company Code to Company

3.11.2 Company Code(s) to Credit Control Area (N:1 or 1:1)

In this step, the credit control area is assigned to a company code. This is the link between SAP ERP Financials Accounts Receivable and Sales and Distribution modules as well. The credit control area is tied to sales and distribution by update rules. By this assignment, you are linking SAP ERP Financials with sales and distribution in terms of credit control. The menu path is **IMG • Enterprise Structure • Assignment • Financial Accounting • Assign Company Code to Credit Control Area**.

Figure 3.57 shows the assignment of company code (**Co.** as shown in Figure 3.57) **US00** to credit control area (**CCAr** as shown in Figure 3.5) **US02**.

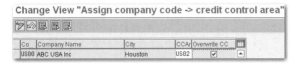

Figure 3.57 Assigning the Credit Control Area to the Company Code

Here are the rules for assignment:

▶ A company code can be assigned to only one credit control area.

▶ Multiple company codes can be assigned to one credit control area; in other words, a credit control area can span multiple company codes.

Keep the following in mind about relationships:

▶ Credit control area to company code: One to many

▶ Company code to credit control area: One to one

There are a couple of caveats to keep in mind:

▶ If you set the **Overwrite CC** area (the last indicator shown in Figure 3.57), then during document posting, you can override the credit control area.

▶ After the document is posted, the credit control area cannot be changed.

3.11.3 Business Area to Consolidation Business Area (N:1 or 1:1)

Business areas need to be assigned to consolidation business areas for group reporting purposes. The menu path is **IMG • Enterprise Structure • Assignment • Financial Accounting • Assign Business Area to Consolidation Business Area**.

Figure 3.58 shows the assignment of **Business Area 9001** to the **Cons. bus. area** (consolidation business area) **0001**.

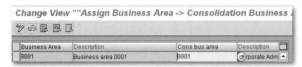

Figure 3.58 Assigning Business Area to Consolidation Business Area

Remember this about the relationship:

▶ Business area to consolidation business area: Many to one

▶ Consolidation business area to business area: One to many

3.11.4 Company Code to Financial Management Area (N:1 or 1:1)

Company codes need to be assigned to Financial Management areas if you need to activate funds management for the particular company code so that budgeting can be done using funds management. If you do not use this setting, then Funds Management is not active for a particular company code. The menu path is **IMG • Enterprise Structure • Assignment • Financial Accounting • Assign Company Code to Financial Management Area**. Figure 3.59 shows the assignment of company code to the financial management area.

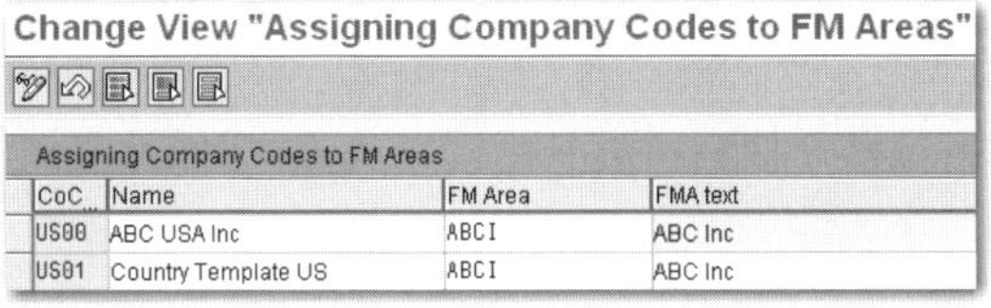

Figure 3.59 Assigning Company Code to Financial Management Area

Keep this in mind about the relationship:

▶ Company code to financial management area: Many to one

▶ Financial management area to company code: One to many

3.11.5 Profit Center to Company Code (N:1 or N:N)

Multiple profit centers can be assigned to one company code. This is a new node because of the introduction of the new GL. The menu path is **IMG • Enterprise Structure • Assignment • Financial Accounting • Assign Profit Center to Company Code,** and the transaction code is KE56. Here are the rules for assignment:

▶ A profit center can be assigned to a specific company code.

▶ If you do not make this assignment, then the profit center is assigned to all the company codes.

▶ Multiple profit centers can be assigned to one company code. Rephrasing, a company code can consist of multiple profit centers.

> **Note**
>
> If you do not make this assignment, then the profit center is assigned to all the company codes.

3.11.6   Company Code to Controlling Area (N:1 or 1:1)

The company code and Controlling areas do not have to exist in a one-to-one relationship. Multiple company codes assigned to a Controlling area activate the cross-company code Controlling. Overall, you have the following options for this assignment:

▸ The company code can correspond to exactly one Controlling area.

▸ Several company codes can correspond to one Controlling area.

Remember the setting in the company code definition (Transaction OBY6), which automatically gets populated as **2** if you set up cross-company code accounting. If you have assigned only one company code to a Controlling area, then you will see **1** in the company code definition. The menu path is **IMG • Enterprise Structure • Assignment • Controlling Area • Assign Company Code to Controlling Area** or the transaction code OKKP.

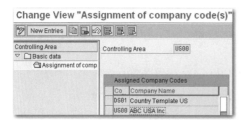

Figure 3.60 Assigning Company Codes to the Controlling Area

Figure 3.60 shows the assignment of multiple company codes to the Controlling area. Here are the rules of assignment:

▸ A company code is assigned to only one Controlling area.

▸ A Controlling area can contain multiple company codes.

> **Note**
>
> Multiple company codes can only be assigned to the same Controlling area if they have the same fiscal year variant and operating chart of accounts, as shown in Figure 3.61.

> **Best Practice**
>
> Define one Controlling area for your entire organization.

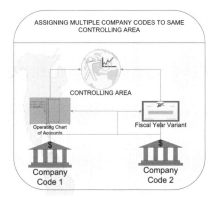

Figure 3.61 Relationship of Company Code and Controlling Area

As always, keep this in mind about relationships:

▶ Company code to Controlling area: One to one
▶ Controlling area to company code: One to many

Keep these points in mind regarding the assignments of cost center and profit center hierarchies along with the cost objects:

▶ There can only be one cost center and profit center standard hierarchy per Controlling area.
▶ The cost center and profit center standard hierarchy are assigned to a Controlling area.
▶ Cost objects are also assigned to a Controlling area.

3.11.7 Controlling Area to Operating Concern (N:1 or 1:1)

The operating concern is the highest level of Controlling entity at which profitability and contribution margins need to be analyzed within a client. The operating concern gets information from sales and distribution, cost accounting, finance, and non-SAP sources. It can be compared to a holistic report card of sales and distribution seen from a financial perspective. The menu path is **IMG • Enterprise Structure • Assignment • Controlling Area • Assign Controlling Area to Operating Concern**. Figure 3.62 shows the assignment of Controlling area **US00** and **US01** to operating concern **US00**.

Change View "Assignment Operating concern -> CO Area"

COAr	Name	OpCo	Name
US00	ABC Controlling Area	US00	Operating Concern ABC Inc
US01	Kostenrechnungskreis US01	US00	Operating Concern ABC Inc

Figure 3.62 Assign Controlling Area to Operating Concern

Here are the rules for assignment, as illustrated in Figure 3.63:

▸ A Controlling area is assigned to only one operating concern.

▸ An operating concern can have multiple Controlling areas assigned to it.

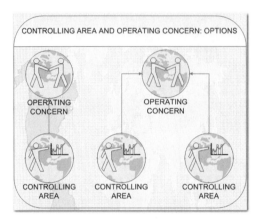

Figure 3.63 Controlling Area and Operating Concern (1:1/N:1)

Keep this in mind about relationships:

▸ Controlling area to operating concern: One to one

▸ Operating concern to Controlling area: One to many

Best Practice

Remember, typically one operating concern is defined per organization.

3.11.8 Assign Plant(s) to Company Code (N:1 or 1:1)

Multiple plants can be assigned to one company code. One plant can be assigned to only one company code. The menu path is **IMG • Enterprise Structure • Assignment • Logistics—General • Assign Plant to Company Code**. Figure 3.64 shows the assignment of plant (s) to the company code. As you can see, plants **1000** and **US01** have been assigned to the company code **US00**.

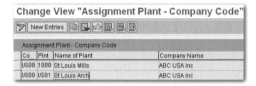

Figure 3.64 Assign Plants to the Company Code

These are the rules for assignment:

- A plant is assigned to only company code.
- A company code can have multiple plants assigned to it.

Remember this about relationships:

- Plant to company code: One to one
- Company code to plant: One to many

3.11.9 Assigning the Business Area to the Plant/ Valuation Area and Division (N:N)

Business areas are assigned for a combination of plant/valuation area and division. This helps integrate the business area (Financials component) with the plant (Logistics component). Generally, the plant and valuation area are the same, as you saw in Section 3.4.1: The menu path is **IMG • Enterprise Structure • Assignment • Logistics—General • Assign Business Area to Plant/Valuation Area and Division** and the transaction code is OMJ7. Figure 3.65 shows the submenu that comes up when you execute Transaction OMJ7.

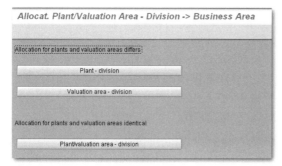

Figure 3.65 Assigning the Business Area for the Plant/Valuation Area and Division

First you can make the plant, division, and business area assignment as shown in Figure 3.66 by clicking on **Plant-division.**

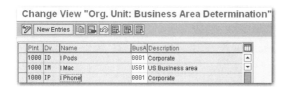

Figure 3.66 Assigning the Business Area to the Plant and Division

The same plant can be assigned to multiple business areas (seen as **BusA** in Figure 3.66) as well by choosing a different division, shown as **Dv** in Figure 3.66. After completing this entry, you can make the valuation area, division, and business area as shown in Figure 3.67 by clicking on **Valuation area–division**, as seen in Figure 3.65.

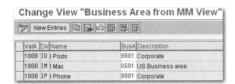

Figure 3.67 Assigning the Valuation Area and Division to the Business Area

You can also check whether the configuration pertaining to the business area has been done as shown in Figure 3.68. If all the entries exist in the table, then you will get a message that **All entries already exist**. **No update**. Otherwise, the system will have updated the missing business areas.

Figure 3.68 Checking for Missing Business Area for Valuation Areas

The menu path is **IMG • Enterprise Structure • Assignment • Logistics— General • Data Comparison with Sales Plant/ValArea–Div—BusArea** and the transaction code is OMJM. Here are the rules for assignment:

▸ A plant/valuation area can be assigned to multiple business areas.

▸ The same business area can be assigned to multiple plants.

▸ A plant/valuation area and division can be assigned to only one business area.

Remember this about relationships:

▸ Plant to business area: Many to many

▸ Plant and division to business area: One to one

▸ Business area to plant: One to many

▸ Business area to plant and division: One to many

In the next subsections, we'll cover the sales and distribution assignments. These assignments are typically done by the sales and distribution team in consultation with the finance team.

3.11.10 Assigning Sales Organization(s) to the Company Code

Here you will learn to assign sales organizations to the company code. This helps in linking Sales and Distribution components to Financials components. Let's take a look at the menu path for assigning sales organizations to the company code. Figure 3.69 shows how you can get to the screen for assigning sales organizations to the company code.

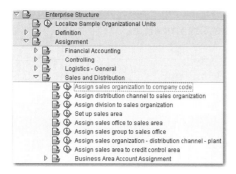

Figure 3.69 Menu path for Assigning Sales Organization Entities

The menu path is **IMG • Enterprise Structure • Assignment • Sales and Distribution • Assign Sales Organization to Company Code**. Figure 3.70 shows you the assignment of the sales organization (**SOrg.in** Figure 3.70) **ABCI** to company code (**Co...** in Figure 3.70) **US00**.

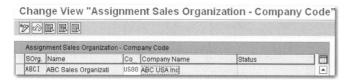

Figure 3.70 Assigning the Sales Organization to the Company Code

Here are the rules for assignment:

▶ The sales organization can only be assigned to one company code.

▶ One company code can have multiple sales organizations assigned to it.

- Assigning the sales organization to the company code establishes the link between SAP Sales and Distribution and SAP ERP Financials.

Keep this in mind about relationships:

- Sales organization to company code: One to one
- Company code to sales organization: One to many

3.11.11 Assigning the Distribution Channel to the Sales Organization

Now you can assign the distribution channel to the sales organization, which helps in setting up internal sales and the distribution structure. The menu path is **IMG • Enterprise Structure • Assignment • Sales and Distribution • Assign Distribution Channel to Sales Organization**.

Figure 3.71 shows you the assignment of the distribution channels (**DChl** with values of **AS**, **AT**, **AW**, **ES**, and **OW** in Figure 3.71) defined previously to the sales organization (**SOrg**. in Figure 3.70 with values of **ABCI**).

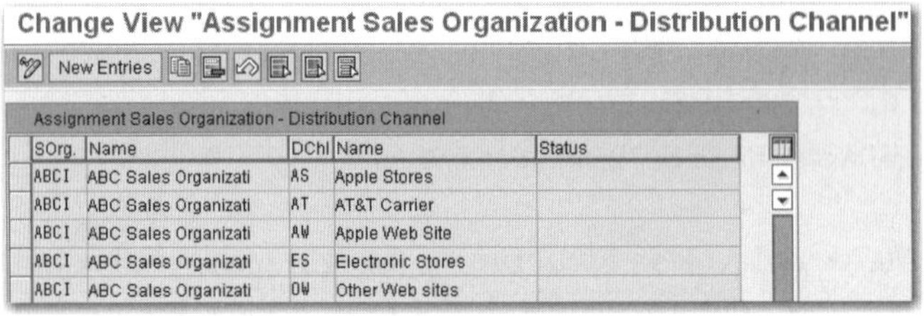
Change View "Assignment Sales Organization - Distribution Channel"

New Entries

Assignment Sales Organization - Distribution Channel

SOrg.	Name	DChl	Name	Status
ABCI	ABC Sales Organizati	AS	Apple Stores	
ABCI	ABC Sales Organizati	AT	AT&T Carrier	
ABCI	ABC Sales Organizati	AW	Apple Web Site	
ABCI	ABC Sales Organizati	ES	Electronic Stores	
ABCI	ABC Sales Organizati	OW	Other Web sites	

Figure 3.71 Assigning the Distribution Channel to the Sales Organization

Rules for assignment:

- Multiple distribution channels can be assigned to multiple sales organizations.
- The relationship of the sales organization to the distribution channel is many to many.

3.11.12 Assigning the Division to the Sales Organization

In this step, you assign the division to the sales organization, which helps define your sales enterprise structure. These assignments are then used to structure your sales area in subsequent steps. The menu path is **IMG • Enterprise Structure • Assignment • Sales and Distribution • Assign Division to Sales Organization**. Figure 3.72 shows how to assign the sales organization (**SOrg.**) **ABCI** to the divisions (**Dv**) **ID, IM, IP, and IT**. These can be seen in Figure 3.72.

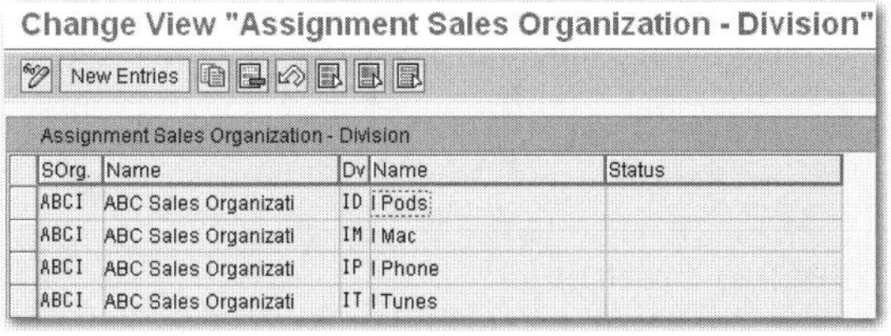

Figure 3.72 Assigning the Division to the Sales Organization

The assignment rule is that multiple divisions can be assigned to multiple sales organizations. The definition of relationships is sales organization to division: many to many

3.11.13 Setting Up the Sales Area

Now that you've made the assignments of the sales organization to the division and distribution channels, let's look at the definition of the sales area by examining the sales area for Apple Inc., which sells iPods, iMacs, iPhones, and iTunes through different distribution channels. The menu path is **IMG • Enterprise Structure • Assignment • Sales and Distribution • Set Up Sales Area**.

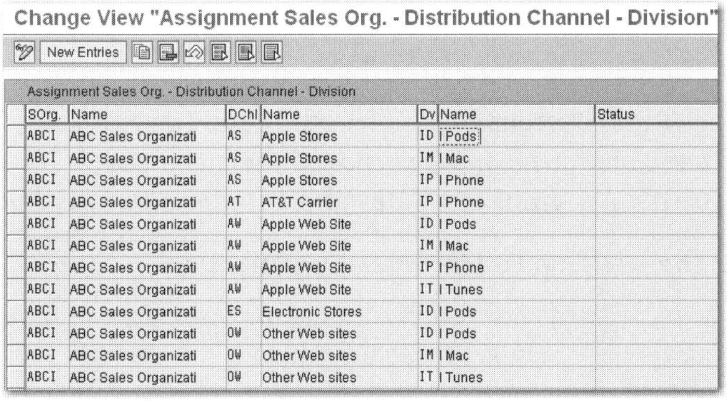

Figure 3.73 shows you how to assign the sales organization (**SOrg.**) **ABCI** to the distribution channel (**DChl**) **AS**, **AT**, **AW**, **ES**, and **OW** and divisions (**Dv**) **ID**, **IM**, **IP**, and **IT**.

Figure 3.73 Setting Up Sales Area

> **Note**
>
> For illustrative purposes, assume that the Apple product group is considered a division. So the only way iPhone is being distributed right now is via Apple stores, the Apple website, and AT&T, which does not sell any other Apple products. Note this distinction in the sales areas that have been set up.

3.11.14 Assigning the Sales Office to the Sales Area

Now you assign the sales office to the sales area, which we defined in the previous step. This is important for setting up the sales structure for reporting purposes. The menu path is **IMG • Enterprise Structure • Assignment • Sales and Distribution • Assign Sales Office to Sales Area**.

Figure 3.74 shows how you can assign the sales organization (**SOrg.** in Figure 3.73) **ABCI,** distribution channel (**DChl** in Figure 3.74) **AS,** and divisions (**Dv** in Figure 3.74) **ID** and **IP** to sales office **(SOff.** in Figure 3.74) **EURO** and **MWUS.**

Change View "Assignment Sales Office - Sales Area": Overview

SOrg.	Name	DChl	Name	Dv	Name	SOff.	Description
ABCI	ABC Sales Organizati	AS	Apple Stores	ID	I Pods	EURO	Europe
ABCI	ABC Sales Organizati	AS	Apple Stores	ID	I Pods	MWUS	Midwest USA
ABCI	ABC Sales Organizati	AS	Apple Stores	IP	I Phone	EURO	Europe
ABCI	ABC Sales Organizati	AS	Apple Stores	IP	I Phone	MWUS	Midwest USA

Figure 3.74 Assigning the Sales Office to the Sales Area

The rule for assignment is that multiple sales offices can be assigned to multiple sales areas. Sales areas have a many to many relationship with sales offices.

3.11.15 Assigning the Sales Group to the Sales Office

In this step, you assign the sales group to the sales office. This is important for setting up the sales structure for reporting purposes. The menu path is **IMG • Enterprise Structure • Assignment • Sales and Distribution • Assign Sales Office to Sales Area**.

Change View "Assignment Sales Organization/Distribution Channel - Plan

SOrg.	Name	DChCust/Mt	Name	Plnt	Name 1	Status
ABCI	ABC Sales Organizati	AS	Apple Stores	1000	St Louis Mills	
ABCI	ABC Sales Organizati	AS	Apple Stores	US01	St Louis Arch	

Figure 3.75 Assigning the Sales Group to the Sales Office

Figure 3.75 shows how you can assign the sales offices **(SOff.** in Figure 3.75) **EURO and MWUS** to the sales groups **(SGrp** in Figure 3.75) **HRW** and **SW**. The rule for assignment is that multiple sales offices can be assigned to multiple sales groups The sales groups have a many to many relationship with the sales offices.

3.11.16 Assigning the Sales Organization and Distribution Channel to the Plant

In this step, you assign the sales organization and distribution channel to the plant. Ideally, you should restrict these to the ones from which you will be shipping the goods via that distribution channel. The menu path is **IMG • Enterprise Structure • Assignment • Sales and Distribution • Assign Sales Organization-Distribution Channel-Plant**.

SOrg.	Name	DChCust/Mt	Name	Plnt	Name 1	Status
ABCI	ABC Sales Organizati	AS	Apple Stores	1000	St Louis Mills	
ABCI	ABC Sales Organizati	AS	Apple Stores	US01	St Louis Arch	

Figure 3.76 Assigning Plants to the Sales Organization and Distribution Channel

Figure 3.76 shows how you can assign the sales organization **(SOrg.** in Figure 3.76) **ABCI** and distribution channel **(DChl** in Figure 3.76) **AS** to plants **(Plnt** in Figure 3.76**) 1000** and **US01**. The sales organization and distribution channel has a many to many relationship with the plant.

3.11.17 Assigning the Sales Area to the Credit Control Area

In this step, you assign the sales area to the credit control area. This establishes the link between Sales and Distribution and Financials. In our example, you assigned all the sales area to the same credit control area US02. The menu path is **IMG • Enterprise Structure • Assignment • Sales and Distribution • Assign Sales Area to Credit Control Area**.

Figure 3.77 shows how you can assign the sales organization **(SOrg.** in Figure 3.77) **ABCI** and distribution channel **(DChl** in Figure 3.77) **AS, AT, AW, ES, OW,** and divisions **(Dv** in Figure 3.77) **ID, IM, IT, and IP** to the credit control area **(CCAr** in Figure 3.77) **US02**.

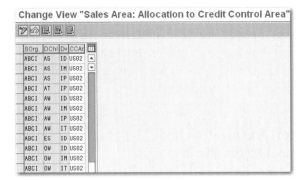

Figure 3.77 Assigning the Sales Area to the Credit Control Area

Remember these rules for assignment:

▸ One sales area can be assigned one credit control area only.

▸ One credit control area can be tied to multiple sales areas.

These are the relationships:

▸ Sales area to credit control area: One to one

▸ Credit control area to sales area: One to many

3.11.18 Business Area Account Assignment: Define Rules by Sales Area

Now you can assign the rules of how the business area will be determined by the sales area. The following rules can be maintained by the sales area:

▸ Business area determination from plant/division.

▸ Business area determination from sales area.

▸ Business area determination from the sales organization/distribution channel item division.

The menu path is **IMG • Enterprise Structure • Assignment • Sales and Distribution • Business Area Account Assignment • Define Rules By Sales Area**. Figure 3.78 shows how you can assign the sales organization (**SOrg.** in Figure 3.78) **ABCI** and distribution channel (**DChl** in Figure 3.78) **AS, AT, AW, ES, OW,** and divisions (**Dv** in Figure 3.78) **ID, IM, IT,** and **IP** to the business area determination rule (**Rule** in Figure 3.78) **2**.

In the example, you have chosen the option **2**. Here the business area is determined from the sales area. Only when you choose option **2** do you need to maintain the entries in the next step.

Change View "Org.Unit: Sales Area - Business Area Determination Rule"

SOrg.	DChl	Dv	Name	Rule
ABCI		ID	I Pods	2
ABCI	AS	IM	I Mac	2
ABCI	AS	IP	I Phone	2
ABCI	AT	IP	I Phone	2
ABCI	AW	ID	I Pods	2
ABCI	AW	IM	I Mac	2
ABCI	AW	IP	I Phone	2
ABCI	AW	IT	I Tunes	2
ABCI	ES	ID	I Pods	2
ABCI	OW	ID	I Pods	2
ABCI	OW	IM	I Mac	2
ABCI	OW	IT	I Tunes	2
Z001	01	01	Product Division 01	1

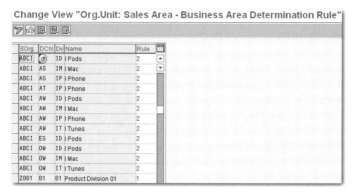

Figure 3.78 Business Area Determination Rule

3.11.19 Assigning the Business Area to the Sales Area

This is only applicable if you have defined that rule 2 is applicable in the previous step. The menu path is **IMG • Enterprise Structure • Assignment • Sales and Distribution • Business Area Account Assignment • Define Rules By Sales Area**.

Figure 3.79 shows how you can assign the sales organization (**SOrg.** in Figure 3.79) **ABCI** and distribution channel (**DChl** in Figure 3.79) **AS**, **AT**, **AW**, **ES**, **OW**, and divisions (**Dv** in Figure 3.79) **ID**, **IM**, **IT**, and **IP** to the business area (**BusA** in Figure 3.79) **0001**.

Change View "Sales Area - Business Area Determination SlsOrg/DstCh"

SOrg.	DChl	Dv	Name	BusA	Description
ABCI	AS	ID	I Pods	0001	Corporate
ABCI	AS	IM	I Mac	0001	Corporate
ABCI	AS	IP	I Phone	0001	Corporate
ABCI	AT	IP	I Phone	0001	Corporate
ABCI	AW	ID	I Pods	0001	Corporate
ABCI	AW	IM	I Mac	0001	Corporate
ABCI	AW	IP	I Phone	0001	Corporate
ABCI	AW	IT	I Tunes	0001	Corporate
ABCI	ES	ID	I Pods	0001	Corporate
ABCI	OW	ID	I Pods	0001	Corporate
ABCI	OW	IM	I Mac	0001	Corporate
ABCI	OW	IT	I Tunes	0001	rporate

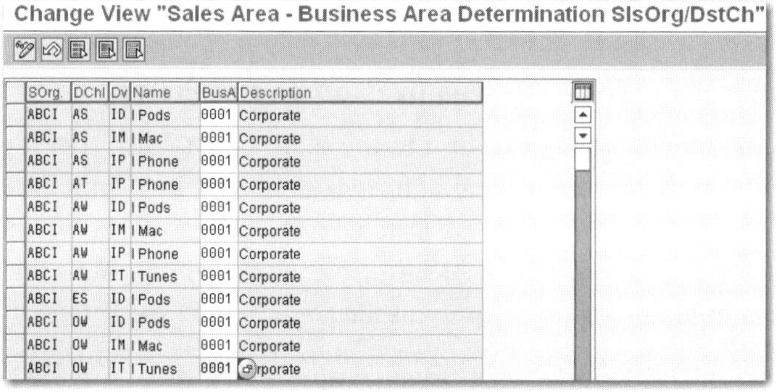

Figure 3.79 Assigning the Business Area to the Sales Area

> **Note**
>
> You can only maintain the entries if you have maintained the business rule as **2** in the previous step.

Next we will start covering the purchasing assignments, which are done by the purchasing team in consultation with the finance team.

3.11.20 Assigning the Purchasing Organization to the Company Code

Here you will learn to assign the purchasing organization to the company code. Assigning the purchasing organization to the company code establishes the link between materials management purchasing and financials. The menu path is **IMG • Enterprise Structure • Assignment • Materials Management • Assign Purchasing Organization to Company Code**.

In this step, you assign **US00** company code (**CoCd** in Figure 3.80) to the purchasing organization (**POrg** in Figure 3.80) **US01** as shown in Figure 3.80.

POrg	Description	CoCd	Company Name	Status	
US01	US Purchasing org.	US00	ABC USA Inc		

Figure 3.80 Assigning the Purchasing Organization to the Company Code

The rule for assignment is that one purchasing organization can only be assigned to one company code, which defaults at the time of the purchasing document creation. At the time of document entry, however, you can change the company code.

3.11.21 Assigning the Purchasing Organization to the Plant

Here you assign the purchasing organization to the plant to establish the link between purchasing and logistics. This assignment defines which purchase organizations are responsible for making a purchase to the plant. The menu path is **IMG • Enterprise Structure • Assignment • Materials Management • Assign Purchasing Organization to Plant**.

In this step, you assign **US01** purchasing organization (**POrg** in Figure 3.81) to plants (**Plnt** in Figure 3.81) **1000** and **US01** as shown in Figure 3.81.

Change View "Assign Purchasing Organization to Plant"

POrg	Description	Plnt	Name 1	Status
US01	US Purchasing org.	1000	St Louis Mills	
US01	US Purchasing org.	US01	St Louis Arch	

Figure 3.81 Assigning the Purchasing Organization to the Plant

The rule for assignment is that many purchasing organizations can be assigned to many plants and vice versa. However, the company code of these purchasing organizations should be same. The relationship is many to many.

In addition, you can assign the plant to a default purchasing organization. This is especially useful if one plant has multiple purchasing organizations assigned. Also, remember that a purchasing organization can be assigned to a reference purchasing organization. This allows the contracts and purchase orders to be accessible to other purchasing organizations.

Next we'll start covering the logistics-execution assignments, which are the responsibility of your inventory management team in consultation with your logistics team.

3.11.22   Assigning a Warehouse Number to the Plant and Storage Location

In this step, you assign the warehouse number to the plant and storage location. This establishes the link between warehouse management and general logistics. You also can represent the warehouse management system correctly by identifying the storage locations and plants that make up the warehouse complex. These assignments are typically made by your inventory management team. The menu path is **IMG • Enterprise Structure • Assignment • Logistics Execution • Assign Warehouse Number to Plant/Storage Location**.

In this step, you assign the plant (**Plnt** in Figure 3.82) **1000** and storage location (**Sloc** in Figure 3.82) **9000** and **9001** to warehouse number (**WhN** in Figure 3.82) **100** as shown in Figure 3.82.

Figure 3.82 Assigning the Warehouse Number to the Plant and Storage Location

3.11.23   Assigning Shipping Points to the Plant

In this step, you assign the shipping points to the plant to establish the link between the logistics execution from the shipping perspective and the general logistics team. This assignment is typically done by your transportation planning team, which comes under the umbrella of logistics execution as well. The menu path is **IMG • Enterprise Structure • Assignment • Logistics Execution • Assign Shipping Points to Plants**.

Figure 3.83 Assign Shipping Points to Plants

In this step, you assign the shipping point **1000** to plant **1000**. The first step is to place the cursor on the plant as shown in Figure 3.83, and then click the **Assign** button. This will give you the small pop up window shown in Figure 3.83 (**Shipping Points • Plants: Choose Shipping Point**) at the bottom right, where you need to select the shipping point **1000**. Press Enter, and then the shipping point will be assigned to the plant.

The rule for assignment is that many shipping points can be assigned to many plants and vice versa. The relationship is many to many.

3.11.24 Assigning the Maintenance Planning Plant to the Maintenance Plant

Now you assign the maintenance planning plant, which is needed for planning purposes, to the logistics maintenance plant. This establishes the link between plant maintenance and general logistics. This assignment is typically done by the maintenance planner. The menu path is **IMG • Enterprise Structure • Assignment • Plant Maintenance • Assign Maintenance Planning Plant to Maintenance Plant**.

The assignment is shown in Figure 3.84 where plant (Plnt in Figure 3.84) **1000** is assigned to maintenance planning plant (**PlPl** in Figure 3.84) **1000**.

The rule for assignment is that one maintenance plant is assigned to one maintenance planning plant. The maintenance plant to maintenance planning plant relationship is one to one.

Change View "Allocation of PlanPlants to MaintPlants"			
Plnt	Name 1	PlPl	Name 1
0001	Werk 0001		
1000	St Louis Mills	1000	St Louis Mills

Figure 3.84 Assign Maintenance Planning Plant to Maintenance Plant

In the next subsections, we cover the HR management assignment.

3.11.25 Assigning the Personnel Area to the Company Code

In this step, you'll assign the personnel area to the company code. This assignment establishes the link between HR personnel administration and SAP ERP Financials and is typically done by the HR department in consultation with the finance department. The menu path is **IMG • Enterprise Structure • Assignment • Human Resources Management • Assignment of Personnel Area to Company Code**.

The assignment is shown in Figure 3.85 where personnel area (**Pers. area**) is assigned to **Company Code US00**.

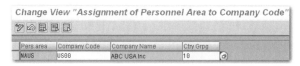

Figure 3.85 Assign the Personnel Area to the Company Code

Rules for assignment:

▸ Multiple personnel areas can be assigned to the same company code.

▸ One personnel area can be assigned to one company code

Relationships:

▸ Company code to personnel area: One to many

▸ Personnel area to company code: One to one

> **Note**
>
> The personnel area to company code assignment is one of the links between financial and HR management.

3.11.26 Assigning the Employee Subgroup to the Employee Group

In this step, you assign the employee subgroup to the employee group. In addition, you determine whether the employee group/employee subgroup combinations are allowed for the country groupings. For example, the employee subgroup for trainees should be assigned to the employee group active and not to the employee group pensioners. The menu path is **IMG • Enterprise Structure • Assignment • Human Resources Management • Assign Employee Subgroup to Employee Group**.

The assignment is shown in Figure 3.86 for **Employee Group (EEG)** of **Salaried employee** and the corresponding employee subgroups (**Esgrp**) allowed for the employee group.

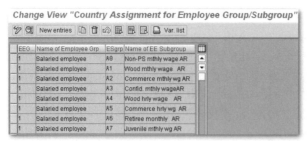

Figure 3.86 Assignment of the Employee Subgroup to the Employee Group

The rule for assignment is that multiple employee subgroups can be assigned to an employee.

This completes all the assignments that can be done in SAP ERP enterprise structure. Now that you understand the broad definition of each of the organizational entities, let's look at some sample decision points in mapping your organization. We will be primarily focusing on financial entities, but we'll touch on some of the logistics components as well.

3.12 Key Financial Organizational Mapping Decisions and Best Practices

Now that you have outlined the organization entities and how they are assigned to each other, you need to take a look at the key decisions to be made, during the beginning of the *business blueprinting* of the project. We'll also highlight the *best practices* for mapping the organizational elements, but it is important that you consider the various local organizational level perspectives before finalizing your organization structure.

3.12.1 Company Codes per Country, per Legal Entity, or per Organizational Business Unit

Company codes are typically set up to represent the financial structure of the company from the eyes of the regulatory agencies. That perspective primarily dictates at what level company codes are created.

However, you can choose to create a company code by organizational business unit if the businesses are extremely diverse and need to be audited separately. Typically, it is one company code per country. However, when the organization is set up to have multiple holding companies within a country, then the same are also created in the system. The advantages of having company codes by country include the following:

▶ Legal consolidation is most efficient because you can immediately have independent sets of books by country. This avoids the need to run consolidation to get the books by country.

▶ Management reporting is more efficient because the management is typically by countries.

▶ Master data maintenance is less burdensome.

There are also advantages of using the company code as a legal entity:

▶ Legal consolidation is more efficient.

▶ Master data maintenance is less burdensome and more clearly understood.

▶ Intercompany transactional activity is more streamlined and understandable.

▶ Best suited for auditors because you can easily prepare an auditable set of books.

The advantages of using the company code as an organizational unit include the following:

▶ Can maintain the credit limits, chart of accounts, and customer payment analysis and reporting at the organization unit level.

▶ More localized reporting is available.

Best Practices

▶ Create company code by legal entity, and, if possible, make sure that you have one primary legal entity by country.

▶ You can choose to create multiple company codes for holding companies within the same country.

▶ Use segment-level reporting capability in the new GL to supplement the legal reporting capability by company code.

▶ When classifying company codes, do not consider interdivisional transactions as intercompany transactions.

▶ Do not try to solve all your reporting problems by company code definition.

There is one caveat you should keep in mind. If you implement the new GL, then it makes sense to only use the company code as a legal entity because all the other division-level reporting can be managed in sub ledgers.

3.12.2 Currency Decisions in the Company Code

The currency decision is one of the most important decisions for a company code because it deeply affects the currency translation issue, which is one of the thorniest issues that Finance departments deal with at month end. Typically, the country of the company code decides the currency. For holding companies that are primarily for listing on the security exchanges only, it makes sense to define the currency as the currency of the global headquarters. This helps in consolidation and quick understanding of the currency translation exchange gains and losses. The currency of a company code has huge implications in terms of currency translation gains and losses.

> **Best Practices**
>
> ▸ Company code currency should be the one in which the maximum number of transactions happen in that company code.
> ▸ Company code currency is also influenced by the currency where the holding company is listed.

3.12.3 Chart of Accounts: Global Versus By Country

Chart of accounts is one of the most time-consuming exercises in the GL. Organizations have the option to have one *global chart of accounts* or *one chart of account per country* to make sure that local accounting requirements are met. To make a better decision, map out your global GL transactions by country. If you have too many transactions occurring in diverse countries with diverse businesses, then it makes sense to have separate charts of account for those countries.

Here are the advantages of having one global chart of accounts:

▸ Increases global control to adopt one common accounting standard across the organization
▸ Helps in standardizing and rationalizing the GL structure
▸ Helps drive consistency in accounting rules and guidelines
▸ Simplifies the global consolidation process and reduces the variables during month-end close
▸ Minimizes master data maintenance

These are the advantages of using country-specific charts of account:

▸ Flexibility to meet country-specific local requirements
▸ More suitable if you have diverse businesses across countries

> **Best Practice**
>
> Keep a common global chart of accounts.

3.12.4 One Controlling Area Versus Multiple Controlling Areas by Region

Most organizations implement one Controlling area across all company codes. This allows one view of the costing across the organization because you don't need to run multiple reports to get an overall perspective. Also organizations implementing multiple Controlling areas have multiple currencies, which makes the comparison of costs much more difficult.

However, if you need to differentiate the costing across diverse business divisions within a conglomerate, then you can choose to implement multiple Controlling areas by division or by region. Another reason to implement multiple Controlling areas is if you have multiple global headquarters, based on different divisions, in different countries, and you need to track costs and revenue in different currencies. These are the advantages of one global Controlling area:

▶ Increased reporting capability for global reporting using standard out-of-the-box reports

▶ Global allocations

▶ Helps standardize the Controlling processes across the organization

These are the advantages of a regional Controlling area:

▶ Flexibility to meet local managerial reporting requirements

▶ Minimizes system performance issues

▶ Allows you to define multiple standard and cost center hierarchies to support local reporting

---

Best Practice

Use one Controlling area per organization.

3.12.5 Currency of Controlling Area

As we discussed earlier, the company code currency drives the legal reporting. You can choose to define the Controlling area currency as per the management currency. So even if you have the holding company in the United Kingdom, if your market and the majority of management sits in the United States, it's best to define the Controlling area currency as USD, while the group currency (currency for consolidation and legal reporting) can be GBP.

Best Practice

Management currency should be Controlling area currency.

3.12.6 One Operating Concern Versus Multiple Operating Concerns by Region

Most of the organizations implement one operating concern across all Controlling areas. This allows one view of the profitability of the organization. However, if you need to differentiate the profitability view across diverse business divisions within a conglomerate, then you can choose to implement multiple Controlling areas by division. You can also choose to differentiate operating concerns by region. These are the advantages of one global operating concern:

▶ Global profitability reporting capability using standard out-of-the-box reports

▶ One common yardstick for judging performance of the organization units across the enterprise

Here are the advantages of regional operating concern:

▶ Provides specific regional subdivision of profitability analysis reporting

▶ Minimizes performance issues

▶ Meets local reporting requirements

Best Practice

Use one operating concern per organization.

3.12.7 Cost Centers Standard Hierarchy Definition: By Department or By Division

When defining a cost center standard hierarchy, it's important to understand the middle-level management reporting requirements as well as executive management reporting requirements. If it is a decentralized organization where middle-level management makes most of the decisions regarding cost management and control, it makes sense to implement a standard hierarchy by departments. On the other hand, if it is a top-driven centrally managed corporation, then the cost center hierarchy needs to mirror the business unit structure.

Best Practices

▶ Implement cost center standard hierarchy at the lowest level capturing both the nuances, and then create one as standard hierarchy and the other as an alternative hierarchy.

▶ Cost center structure is very flexible and can be customized in multiple ways to meet business requirements.

3.12.8 Profit Center Hierarchy Definition

The profit center hierarchy definition should be created only when the managing person of the profit center is responsible for the revenue and costs combined together.

Best Practices

- Keep the profit center structure extremely simple.
- Keep the number acutely low, and you'll get a structure that is strikingly effective and supremely simple.

Also remember the following:

- Typically, organizations map cost center and profit center similarly, which is not the correct approach.
- A politically correct profit center structure is not the best organization structure for any of the organization entities.

3.12.9 Business Area Versus Profit Center

The business area was typically implemented in the earlier days of SAP R/3 when profit center accounting was not offered as a solution. The business area is in Financials (external reporting), whereas the profit center is in Controlling (internal reporting). The business area is typically derived from an assignment of the plant and division. However, the profit center is maintained in a Controlling area. The default setting is that the created profit center is applicable across all company codes, but you can choose to assign it to a company code.

Over time, this distinction has blurred as internal reporting within Profit Center Accounting (PCA) can also be tailored toward external reporting, especially with the new GL. So, theoretically, you can implement both the business area and the profit center if you want to distinguish the external reporting from the internal reporting.

Note

The distinction between a business area and profit center can be obtained from the SAP Service Marketplace (*http://service.sap.com*) by accessing SAP Note 321190.

SAP is focusing more on profit center accounting and less on the business area for future developments. For fresh implementations, it makes sense for organizations to only implement profit center accounting and use its reporting capabilities to generate the segment-level reporting required by the SEC and other regulatory agencies. In addition, you can choose to use segment (if you are implementing the new GL) for your segmental reporting.

For already existing implementations using the business area, organizations can continue using the business area for external reporting and choose to implement profit center accounting for additional features related to internal reporting.

3.12.10 Functional Area and Cost of Sales Accounting

Cost of sales accounting is used to generate P&L statements by comparing the revenue to the expenses incurred to obtain these revenues. Cost of sales accounting can be implemented by using the functional area and substitution rules via cost objects. Cost of sales accounting should first be activated for the company code in global data.

Note

After the company code settings have been defined, you need to configure the functional areas, such as manufacturing, marketing, administration, R&D, and so on. From SAP Release 4.7 onwards, it has become very easy to implement cost of sales because the functional area can be assigned now at the GL account level in addition to the cost object assignments. The functional area is assigned to P&L accounts at a GL level, and the same can be done by a mass change for all the GL accounts.

The functional area can also be entered directly in a cost element or in a cost center category. Now that you understand some of the key decision points when defining your organizational structure, let's look at some of the key nonfinancial decisions that impact financials

3.13 Key Nonfinancial Entity Decisions that Impact Financials

SAP ERP is an integrated business solution that meets your overall business requirements. Any change in other organization entities is bound to have ripple effects across financials. So it makes sense to take a look at some of the important aspects of nonfinancial entities that impact finance.

Let's say that the materials management team did not get their enterprise structure right. It might so happen that finance now needs to create extra cost centers to capture the costs being incurred at a more granular level. Or if the plant maintenance module was not implemented, then somebody might decide to use cost centers or some type of cost object to fulfill their reporting needs. Now if you buckle, then you might end up with an enterprise structure that does not make sense from a financial perspective. At this point, you should have constructive discussion and explain the correct utility of each of your financial enterprise entities. That is why having extra knowledge about nonfinancial entities helps in these situations, so that you can suggest the optimal structure rather than a workaround.

With that said, let's understand some of the key decision points in nonfinancial enterprise entities.

3.13.1 Plant: Physical Location Versus Logical Location

If you have locations that are physically very close to each other, then the key decision that needs to be made is whether you should create them as one plant or multiple plants. The defining factors in this case are the following:

▶ Number of transactions between the plants (high: one SAP plant; low: multiple SAP plants)

▶ Whether you need to run MRP separately (yes: multiple SAP plants; no: one SAP plant)

You should also consider whether the increased number of plants means that you now have to extend all your materials to new plants. So it's important to understand the data maintenance level effort needed when you increase the number of plants.

3.13.2 Purchasing Organization and Sales Organization Structure

The purchasing organization and sales organization are assigned to the company code. Depending on whether purchasing and sales is centralized or decentralized, you can choose to have one or multiple purchasing organizations and sales organizations respectively assigned to the same company code.

> **Note**
>
> Purchasing and sales organizations are the direct link between Materials Management and Financials (MM-FI) and Sales and Distribution and Financials (SD-FI), respectively. All the other organizational entities do not have a direct link with financials, and they need to be designed per your sales and distribution and purchasing setup. You need to make sure that these are set up correctly from a financials perspective.

3.13.3 Distinguishing the Plant and Storage Location

The plant and storage locations are organization entities of logistics. Storage location is one level below the plant, but the valuation happens only at the plant level. If you need the valuation to be at a lower level than the current plant structure, you need to create that as a plant. The valuation level decides what the enterprise structure of logistics looks like, so it's very important for you to clearly distinguish the plant and storage location.

3.13.4 How Reporting Requirements Drive
the Structure of the Design

Experience tells us that it is very important to understand the reporting requirements of the organization before designing the enterprise structure. It is also important to consider not only the current legacy reporting requirements but also future reporting requirements. After the enterprise structure has been put in place, it's very difficult to change it later. So be sure to outline the to-be state of the organization and then design the enterprise structure.

SAP ERP has so many objects that with a little bit of creativity, you can use these for almost any purpose. However, it's important to identify the correct optimal use of the objects and then stick to it. In this instance, shortcuts really do cut you short in the long run. So when you want to upgrade, find the consultant who implemented it, question the motives, and go through the process of remapping your business processes drastically.

It is very important for you to decide what is best for your organization in the long run and then implement that enterprise structure. It may mean a lot of pain in the short term, which happens whenever you deviate from the normal course, but it will definitely be worth it. While this chapter gave you some insight into Controlling, the focus of this book is FI, and we will delve deeper into it now.

3.14 Summary

In this chapter, you learned the key enterprise structure elements of Financials, Controlling, Logistics, Purchasing, Sales and Distribution, and human resources management. You also learned how these elements can be assigned to each other along with their rules of assignment, which help you define your structure. In addition, we touched on the best practices of structuring an organization to meet current and future reporting needs. This chapter gave you some insight into controlling but the focus of this book is FI, which we will cover now. Chapter 4 introduces the typical financial business processes and how these are integrated together in SAP ERP. You'll also learn the various processes and how these can be mapped to end user roles.

This chapter gives you an integrated perspective of the SAP ERP Financials solution, focusing on some of the key business processes of an organization. You will learn some interesting nuggets of integration wisdom of Financials (FI) with Materials Management (MM), Sales and Distribution (SD), Project Systems (PS), Plant Maintenance (PM), Human Resources Management (HR), Transportation, and Shipment Costs.

4 Integrated Business Process View of SAP ERP Financials

In this chapter, you will learn more about the key business processes and how these are integrated with SAP ERP Financials (FI). After learning these business processes and their touch-points with finance you will be able to appreciate the integration of SAP ERP Financials with other process teams. The integration perspective allows you to think about the end-to-end processes and helps you design an optimal solution that makes sense to your organization.

After reading this chapter and thinking about some of its insights, you might decide to automate some stream of processes thereby eliminates inefficiencies and choose to start off with some manual processes and automate them later as you build on your solution landscape. So understanding the end-to-end processes allows you to prioritize the implementation of specific modules and adopt advanced features as you go along. It is also important to understand the change readiness of your organization by the process areas, which also requires that you understand other process areas that integrate with SAP ERP Financials.

You will not only learn about the processes from an SAP ERP perspective, but you will also become familiar with typical departmental structures and how you can tailor your organizational departments to the process streams. After you understand the overall structure of SAP ERP Financials and other process areas, you might even choose to organize the Finance department by process areas rather than by the traditional departmental modular approach.

The most important takeaway from this chapter is to think of your Finance department as part of the process chain and how you add value for your organization. You will consider what extra benefits you bring to the table in terms of control, audit points, and corporate governance. Overall, the trend is to bundle the traditional financial roles as part of a shared services structure to extract maximum efficiencies. However, you need to understand what part of the finance brings strategic benefit to an organization and how you can be a partner to other process teams.

So let's first take a look at the procurement to payment process, which involves a handshake between the finance team and the purchasing and receiving process teams.

4.1 Purchase Requisition to Check Writing: Procurement to Payment

This section introduces a simple procurement cycle that starts with the creation of a purchase requisition and ends with the payment processing. It deals with SAP MM and SAP ERP Financials integration issues.

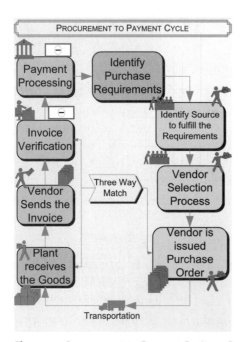

Figure 4.1 Procurement to Payment Business Process

4.1.1 Process Flow

A general procurement to payment cycle can be described from a business process perspective as shown in Figure 4.1 and as listed in the steps here:

1. Purchasing requirements are identified.

2. Source to fulfill the requirements is identified.

3. The vendor selection process occurs.

4. The purchase order or contract to vendor is issued.

5. The plant receives the goods.

6. The vendor sends the invoice physically or electronically.

7. The invoice is verified for accuracy.

8. The payment is processed.

Now that you understand the typical procurement to payment business process, let's consider the SAP ERP point of view. Because SAP ERP is a transactional-based system that requires the generation of documents at each stage, let's take a look at the documents generated in SAP ERP. The process flow of purchase requisition to check writing is illustrated in Figure 4.2, which highlights the SAP ERP documents created at each stage.

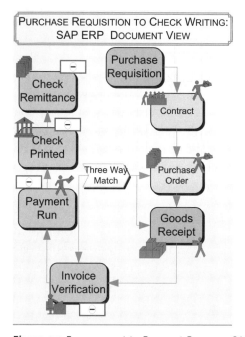

Figure 4.2 Procurement to Payment Process—SAP ERP Document View

4.1.2 Standard Operating Processes for Purchasing Processes

Figure 4.3 shows the procurement to pay process in department format. Now this may not be the structure that you adopt, but it is a good starting point for you to map your business processes to your organization. It is very important that you map these business processes to your organizational departments to ensure that you understand the hand-offs that occur between various departments. In this section, therefore, you will learn the hand-offs from different departments during the procurement cycle.

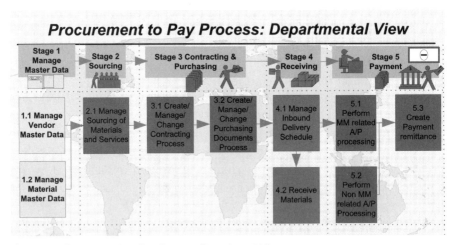

Figure 4.3 Procurement to Pay Process: Department View

A separate department is typically responsible for each stage; however, one stage can have multiple departments, or a single department can have multiple stages. So your organization has to carefully consider all the implications of the various hand-offs. This is especially important with the changing landscape globally, where it is possible that some of these steps might be outsourced to different companies or might be managed in a shared services environment.

Understanding the impact of all these factors is very important. These hand-offs with the delineation of roles and responsibilities become the standard operating procedures (SOPs). Also, it is very important to define the cycle times and metrics or service level agreements (SLA) between the various handshakes that occur across departments. The complexity of the SOPs depends on the following factors:

▸ **Number of departments**
   The larger the number of departments, the more stakeholders there are

who need to have the overall process as well as their roles and responsibilities explained. So you are looking at multiple RACIs (Responsible, Accountable, Communicated, Informed), which becomes really confusing and difficult to deal with.

- **Geographic location of departments**
  Most organizations have centralized their Accounts Payable departments, which requires establishing an efficient method to send the invoices to the central department.

- **Delegation of authority structure of the organization**
  Another key aspect that complicates this even further is the authority levels identified within an organization.

- **Number of approval levels**
  This is required for creating an invoice for a particular amount. If there are more levels, then there must be more rigid procedures in the approval process.

- **Outsourcing**
  If you have outsourced some of your routine payment processing tasks then you have to include the SLAs in the definition of hand-offs across departments.

Best Practices

- Document the hand-offs in as much detail as you can. This eliminates unnecessary confusion.
- Eliminate as many hand-offs as possible by automating them and using simplified processes.

Imagine an ideal process mapping scenario where you had process teams instead of departments. In this scenario you would just have one department that handles the procurement to payment cycle. The accountant part of the purchasing team would together drive the procurement to payment process.

Now you can go on to learn the variations of this process and understand how these are mapped in SAP ERP.

4.1.3 Multiple Scenarios for Purchasing and Representation in SAP

The various subscenarios of procurement are shown in Figure 4.4. You will learn in detail each of the following scenarios in this section:

▸ **Procurement of stock material**
This pertains to the purchase of materials, which is recorded in inventory and then consumed from inventory.

▸ **Procurement of consumable material**
This is the material that is procured and directly expensed to a cost object.

▸ **Procurement of external services**
This scenario examines the process of procuring services instead of materials.

▸ **Automated procurement**
This is the process of automating some of the procurement activities.

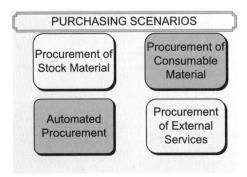

Figure 4.4 Procurement Scenarios

Let's go through each of these scenarios, including the detailed steps in each and the key differences between them. You will also learn the accounting entries at each step.

4.1.4 Procurement of Stock Material

The process of procuring a stock material is shown in Figure 4.5 and is detailed here from an accounting perspective. The requester receives the goods and performs the goods receipt in the system. If the material is valuated on a moving average price, then we update the inventory with **110 USD** and credit the **GR/IR** clearing account for the same amount.

However, if the material is valued using standard cost, then the GR/IR clearing account still gets credited by 110, but inventory is debited only with 100 USD, and the rest (10 USD) hits a price difference account. Table 4.1 highlights moving average price material.

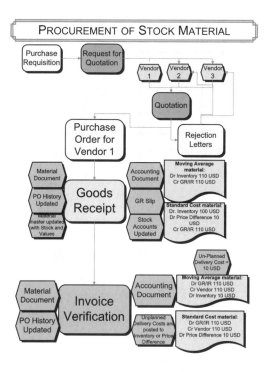

Figure 4.5 Procurement of Stock Material with Accounting Details

Credit GR/IR Clearing	110 USD
Debit Inventory	110 US

Table 4.1 Moving Average Price Material

Table 4.2 highlights the standard price.

Credit GR/IR Clearning	110 USD
Debit Inventory	100 USD
Debit Price Difference	10 USD

Table 4.2 Standard Price

When you receive the goods, you receive an *invoice* of 120 USD, due to the increased fuel price, and you agree to pay 120 USD.

Debit Gr/IR	110 USD
Credit Vendor	120 USD
Debit Inventory	10 USD

Table 4.3 Moving Average Price Material

The accounting entries appear as they do in Tables 4.3 (moving average price material) and 4.4 (standard price).

Debit GR/IR Clearing	110 USD
Credit Vendor	120 USD
Debit Price Difference	10 USD

Table 4.4 Standard Price

At the time of the *payment*, debit the vendor with 120 USD and credit the bank with 120 USD. The accounting entry is seen in Table 4.5.

Credit Bank	120 USD
Debit Vendor	120 USD

Table 4.5 Accounting Entry

Now that you understand the process of procuring a stockable material, let's turn to the process of procuring a consumable material.

4.1.5 Procurement of Consumable Materials

Consumables are not valuated in inventory and hence do not go into stock. They are not managed on a value basis (e.g., office supplies tied to a cost center, equipments bought against an asset). The system, however, does update the quantity of consumption materials that have a material master record. Consumable materials are materials purchased directly for an account assignment object. These can be purchased against the following:

- **Asset**: A
- **Cost center**: K
- **Project**: P
- **Order**: F
- **Sales order**: S

The difference between consumables and stock materials is illustrated in Figure 4.6.

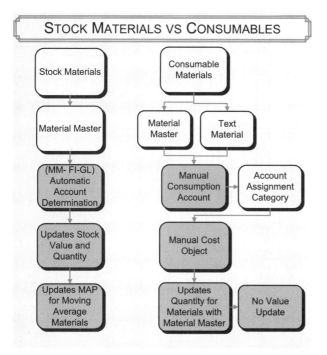

Figure 4.6 Key Differences Between Stock Materials and Consumables

The procurement process of consumable materials is shown in Figure 4.7.

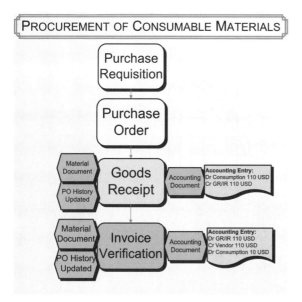

Figure 4.7 Procurement of Consumables

Let's look at the accounting entries for the scenario discussed in Section 4.1.4. Goods receipt entries are seen in Table 4.6 and those for invoice receipt in Figure 4.7.

Credit GR/IR Clearning	110 USD
Debit Consumables	110 USD

Table 4.6 Goods Receipt

Debit GR/IR Clearing	110 USD
Credit Vendor	120 USD
Debit Consumables	10 USD

Table 4.7 Invoice Receipt

For purchasing consumable materials, you can create blanket purchase orders. These are usually valid for a longer period of time. You can directly post invoices for the materials and services procured via blanked purchase order. The typical document type is **FO**, which allows you to enter purchase order validity at the header level and use the item type for blanket purchase order items. Invoice verification checks that the validity and total dollar value is within the limits. The account assignment does not need to be defined for a blanket purchase order. No material number is needed either. The significant advantage of a blanket PO is *lowered transaction costs*, which are typically used for low-value consumables. The procurement process using a blanket purchase order is shown in Figure 4.8.

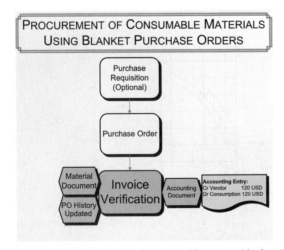

Figure 4.8 Procurement of Consumables Using Blanket Purchase Orders

As you see in Figure 4.8, you can skip the goods receipt step and still do invoicing. So it is just a *two-way match* between the purchase order and the invoice submitted by the vendor. However, this should only be used in low-value items that have large quantities. Using a blanket purchase order without recording the goods receipt lowers the transaction costs of recording multiple goods receipt for low-value transactions such as purchasing consumables. Using the previous example, the accounting entry that happens when we perform the invoice receipt is shown in Table 4.8.

Credit Vendor	120 USD
Debit Consumables	120 USD

Table 4.8 Invoice Receipt

4.1.6 Procurement of External Services

Procuring external services is different from normal procurement from the perspective of managing the services. Figure 4.9 shows the process of procuring external services.

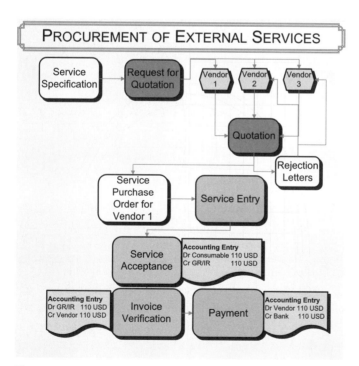

Figure 4.9 Procurement of External Services

As you can see, instead of a purchase requisition, you have to create a service specification that then gets pulled into a service purchase order for the successful vendor. After the service is performed, you have to perform the service entry sheet. Until now, no accounting entry has happened. However, when you accept the service using the service acceptance, the service is recorded in FI as shown in Figure 4.9. After that, the process is exactly the same in invoice verification where you clear the GR/IR clearing account and credit vendor. The next step is the disbursement of payment, which credits the vendor and debits your bank account.

Now that you have learned all the basic variations of the procurement processes, let's look at some of the ways to automate the procurement activities.

4.1.7 Automated Procurement

This section focuses on describing the *automated procurement process* that occurs per a set of business rules that need to be defined in preceding processes. So let's look at some of the ways you can automate the procurement activities. SAP ERP can trigger automatic creation of purchase requisitions and purchase orders if the same is set up in materials planning per these business rules:

▸ Purchase orders can be automatically created if the business rules have been defined in the material master and vendor master. There is a special indicator that sets up the same. Purchase orders are created automatically if there is an *info-record* that matches the parameters laid out in *contracts* (quantity or value based). This can also be refined by using *source lists* that filter to whom the order needs to be released.

▸ Purchase orders and purchase requisitions can also be created as an input from Materials Requirement Planning (MRP) runs. If the safety stock is reached for stock items, then the system triggers the creation of purchase requisitions and purchase orders based on business rules regarding safety stock, prior consumption, and future requirements.

We can also automate subsequent steps such as automatic goods receipt based on shipping notification. These are triggered based on order acknowledgments, loading acknowledgment, or shipping notification sent by the vendor in advance for purchase order delivery scheduling. Shipping notification sent by the vendor can be configured in the system to do an automatic goods receipt.

We can also pay based on business rules defined in the evaluated receipt settlement (ERS) process. In ERS, the vendor does not send an invoice, so the invoice receipt process does not happen. We pay based on the automatic invoice generated per the goods receipt and purchase order terms. This ensures that the onus of reconciliation is on the vendor. A typical example is payment to consulting companies based on the timesheets submitted by consultants on site. All these can be combined to generate a multitude of scenarios where you have automated procurement.

4.1.8 SAP ERP Transactions for Procurement

The key transaction codes for executing the procurement cycle are seen in Table 4.9.

Action to be Executed	Transaction Code
Purchase Requisition Create/Change/Display	ME51N/ME52N/ME53N
Release Purchase Requisition	ME54N/ME55
Purchase Order Create/Change/Display	ME21N/ME22N/ME23N
Release Purchase Order	ME29N/ME28
Outline Agreement Create/Change/Display	ME31K/ME32K/ME33K
Release Outline Agreement	ME35K
Scheduling Agreement Create/Change/Display	ME31L/ME32L/ME33L
Goods Receipt	MIGO
Service Entry Sheet	ML81N
Release Service Entry Sheet	ML85
Logistics Invoice Verification	MIRO
ERS Settlement	MRRL

Table 4.9 Procurement Cycle Transaction Codes

Now that you have learned the various business processes, let's look at the types of purchasing that can be implemented.

4.1.9 SAP Organizational Entities Part of Procurement Process

You can organize your purchasing function in multiple ways, such as:

▶ **Corporate group-wide purchasing**
One purchasing organization is responsible for all the company codes and all the plants.

▶ **Distributed purchasing**
Many purchasing organizations are responsible for different plants.

▶ **Company-specific purchasing**
In this case, the purchasing organization is tied to the company code. So each company code has its own purchasing organization.

The various options are also illustrated in Figure 4.10.

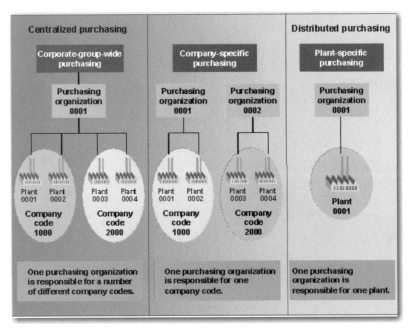

Figure 4.10 Centralized Purchasing Versus Distributed Purchasing (Source SAP AG)

In this section, you learned about the various options of organizing your purchasing organization entities depending on your organizational needs.

Best Practices

▶ Have one purchasing organization if you have centralized purchasing as this helps in driving efficiencies and cost savings.

▶ Make sure that your corporate structure is aligned to your reporting requirements.

4.1.10 Integrating Supplier Relationship Management in the Procurement Process

Until now, you just learned the traditional way of performing the procurement. However, with the introduction of Supplier Relationship Management

(SRM), it becomes imperative to understand the ecosystem in which you are operating. Now you operate in an ecosystem with your vendors, so the processes are driven by catalog searches and buying over the Internet. These processes are supported in SRM. In this section, you will learn about the self-service procurement process.

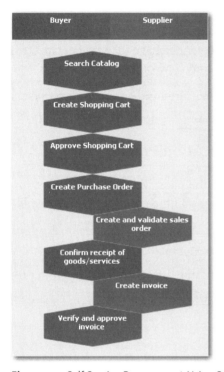

Figure 4.11 Self Service Procurement Using SAP SRM (Source SAP AG)

The process is shown in Figure 4.11. Let's consider the individual steps in the process assuming that you are looking from a buyer's perspective:

1. Search the catalog for a particular item.

2. If you find the item, you create a shopping cart.

3. This shopping cart is then approved by your manager based on a work-flow that is driven by the organization chart.

4. After the shopping cart is created, the system creates a purchase order. (If you are a seller, the system creates a sales order in your system.)

5. The goods are shipped from the seller to your warehouse.

6. When you receive the goods, you perform a confirmation that creates a confirmation number in SAP SRM; if you have an SAP ERP system, the system creates a goods receipt against the purchase order.

7. At this point, the seller can automatically create an invoice and electronically send the same to you.

8. After receiving the invoice, you can easily reconcile it against the goods receipt.

9. After receipt is verified, approve the invoice, which can then be used to create an automatic payment run.

The process is extremely seamless and supports an integrated view beyond your enterprise. Both the supplier and the vendor have the same perspective of the invoice processing, and both have one view of the entire process.

Now that you understand the processes that drive procurement, let's take a detailed look at the Sales and Distribution (SD) function of SAP ERP.

4.2   Sales Order to Cash Application Process

In this section, you will learn more about the sales cycle from order creation to order fulfillment, along with the payment by the customer. This is the SD and SAP ERP Financials integration.

4.2.1   Process Flow of Order to Cash Cycle

The order to cash cycle is clearly illustrated in Figure 4.12, starting from pre-sales activities and culminating with payment.

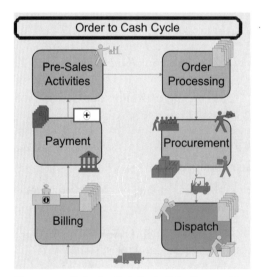

Figure 4.12 Order to Cash Cycle Sales Process View

Now that you understand the broad sales order cycle, let's take a look at the SAP view of the sales cycle, which is shown in Figure 4.13.

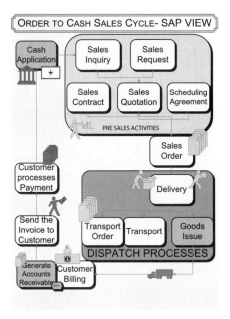

Figure 4.13 Sales Cycle: SAP View

As you see in the Figure 4.13, SAP ERP SD provides the various document types that you need to generate the record information at various stages. Let's take a more detailed look at each of these documents from the accounting perspective:

▶ **Goods issue in dispatch process**
After the material is physically shipped from your location, the system does a goods issue that reduces the inventory from the plant where the inventory was kept.

▶ **Customer billing**
In this step, you generate an invoice that automatically updates the accounts receivable. In addition, the invoice is mailed to the customer either physically or electronically.

▶ **Applying cash**
After you receive the payment, you apply the cash against your invoice, which clears the corresponding accounts receivable.

Now that you understand the mapping of the typical sales process in SAP ERP, let's take a look at how these processes are mapped to the SOPs from a sales perspective.

4.2.2 Standard Operating Procedures for Sales Processes

This section covers the hand-offs from different departments during the order to cash sales cycle. The order to cash process has been mapped in six stages as shown in Figure 4.14.

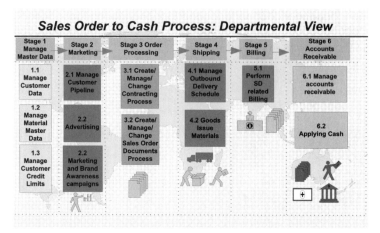

Figure 4.14 Sales Order to Cash Cycle- Departmental View

4.2.3 Multiple Scenarios for Sales and Distribution in SAP ERP

Multiple scenarios can be configured in SD by defining new sales order types to represent the scenarios. Let's look at a new scenario for SD. A rush order can be distinguished from a standard order by defining a new sales order document type for rush order.

Let's first understand the key configuration points regarding SD. These will help you identify the various objects that you need to be familiar with to understand the integration of SD with FI.

Sales Document Type

This is what you need to keep in mind about sales document types:

▶ Sales document type controls the behavior of sales order at header level.

▶ Sales document type can be restricted by sales area.

▶ Item category controls the behavior of sales order at item level by defining:

  ▶ Pricing

  ▶ Business data at item level

- ▶ Billing relevance
- ▶ Delivery relevance

Item Category and Item Usage

Remember these points:

- ▶ Item category is assigned to a sales document type to control the behavior of the document type at item level.
- ▶ Item category checks against the item category group maintained in the material master.
- ▶ Item usage can be set up using ABAP (Advanced Business Application Programming), and it is set internally to control some parameters.

Schedule Line Category

Keep the following points in mind:

- ▶ Schedule line category controls the behavior of the schedule line.
- ▶ Schedule line category is a two-digit key. The first denotes the area (Inquiry, quotation, sales order, returns, etc.), and the second identifies what happens with the schedule line within logistics. The standard second digits are enumerated here:
  - ▶ **T:** No inventory management.
  - ▶ **X:** No inventory management with goods issue.
  - ▶ **N:** No materials planning.
  - ▶ **P:** MRP relevant.
  - ▶ **V:** Consumption-based planning.

Pricing Procedure

Keep the following in mind about pricing procedure:

- ▶ Pricing procedure is the building block of configuring the pricing in SD. Pricing procedure is configured separately to mirror the business requirement and is then assigned to the sales document type.
- ▶ For a bill of material (BOM) to be relevant for Sales, BOM usage should be defined for the sales document type.
- ▶ Subitems in BOM are typically used for free goods, such as reference manuals with a software, and so on.

▸ It is also important for you to understand some of the standard delivered sales order document types drive most of the configuration.

Here are some of the SAP ERP delivered sales document types and item categories along with their phases:

▸ **Pre-Sales**

   ▸ **Inquiry**: IN: Doc Type and AFN: Standard Item

   ▸ **Quotation**: QT: Document Type and AGTX: Item Category

▸ **Sales Phase**

   ▸ **Standard Order**:

   ▸ **OR:** Doc Type and TAD: Service Item Category

   ▸ **RO:** Rush Order

   ▸ **CD:** Delivery-Free of Charge

   ▸ **CF:** Consignment

   ▸ **Cash Sales**: CS: Doc Type and BVNN: Free of Charge Item

▸ **Complaints:** Returns: RE: Doc Type and REN: Item category

These can be modified and customized to suit the unique requirements of the organization that is implementing SD.

4.2.4 Transactions Codes for Sales and Distribution

The following are the key transaction codes for sales processing:

▸ **Sales Inquiry**: Create/Change/Display: VA11/VA12/VA13.

▸ **Sales Quotation**: Create/Change/Display: VA21/VA22/VA23.

▸ **Sales Order**: Create/Change/Display: VA01/VA02/VA03.

▸ **Scheduling Agreement**: Create/Change/Display: VA31/VA32/VA33.

▸ **Contract**: Create/Change/Display: VA41/VA42/VA43.

Other key transaction codes for billing and accounts-receivable cash application are listed here:

▸ **Billing Document**: Create/Change/Display: VF01/VF02/VA03.

▸ **Billing due List**: Maintain: VF04.

▸ **Accounts Receivable**: Cash application: F-28.

Now that you understand the key transaction codes in SD, let's recap the SAP ERP organization entities for SD.

4.2.5   SAP Organizational Entities and Master Data

The sales organization entities are shown in Figure 4.15. As you learned earlier, entities that make up the sales area (division, distribution channel, sales organization) are the real organizational entities that are assigned to Financials. Sales office, sales group, and sales person are used primarily to define the reporting for SD.

Best Practice

Reporting organization entities (sales group, sales office, and sales person) are configured so that sales statistics can be obtained at a more granular level than achieved by the sales area. The sales area is needed more from an organizational assignment perspective. This keeps the overall sales structure simple and manageable and still allows an organization to have specific reporting.

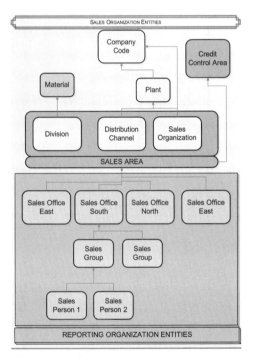

Figure 4.15 Sales Organization Entities

Customer Master and Its Roles

Managing the customer master data entity is a little bit different in SD. A customer is created as a business partner with the roles as shown in Figure 4.16. The customer can be created as a bill to, as a payer, as a ship to, or as a sold to. This allows you to enter different customer partners according to the requirement.

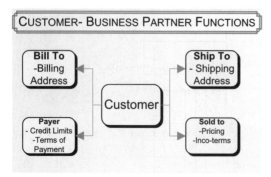

Figure 4.16 Customer Partner Functions

Next, you will learn about the accounting implications of the various business processes in SD.

4.2.6 Accounting Impact from SD Transactions

No accounts are hit during the creation of the sales order/inquiry or quotation. Let's look at the SD transactions that impact SAP ERP Financials:

▸ **Post goods issue**
It is only at the time of post goods issue that inventory (finished goods) is credited, and cost of goods sold is debited.

▸ **Billing**
During the billing process (creation of accounts receivable) revenue less sales deducts is credited, and customer is debited.

▸ **Payment receipt**
When we receive the payment from the customer, then customer is credited, and bank is debited.

Let's now go on to discover the integration touch-points between PS and FI.

4.3   Project Systems (PS-FI Integration)

In this section you will learn about project systems and how these are integrated with FI to support extensive reporting and accounting requirements. Project Systems (PS) in SAP ERP can be used to manage both large-scale and small-scale projects. It allows you to structure a project so that you can plan costs and track the actual expenditure against each of the master data elements of the project systems. Let's begin by analyzing a typical process flow for managing projects.

4.3.1 Process Flow for Project Systems

The process flow of PS can be represented from a project lifecycle perspective as shown in Figure 4.17.

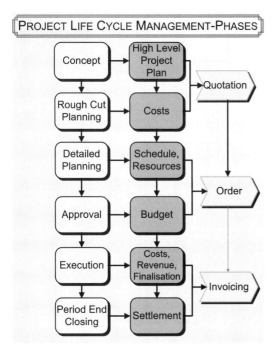

Figure 4.17 Project Lifecycle: Process View

Let's now review the different phases you must go through to execute a large project:

1. **Concept**
   Each project starts with the concept of the project that highlights the value proposition of it. At this stage, you have a high-level project plan that details the broad timelines and business benefits that need to be achieved by implementing the project. At this stage, you try to determine which vendors and partners are needed to support your organization.

2. **Rough-cut planning**
   After the high-level planning has been reviewed and approved by the re-

levant stakeholders, you need to perform a rough-cut planning where you analyze the costs on a very high level based on slightly detailed planning.

3. **Detailed planning**
After your costs and business benefits have been approved per internal organizational requirements, you need to perform detailed planning where you outline the detailed schedule and assign resources to each of the scheduled milestones. This reality check helps you analyze the reasonableness of the project objectives.

4. **Approval**
At this point, the detailed schedule and resource allocation needs to be approved by your organization for the exact budgetary allocation. You need to issue purchase orders to vendors for their involvement in the project.

5. **Execution**
After the budget is approved on the basis of the detailed plan, you start executing according to the detailed plans. The execution plan becomes more refined as you know more about the project at a task level. You actually record the costs and revenues and finalize the myriad details of the execution process.

6. **Period end closing**
After the project has been completed, you need to settle it to either an asset or against a cost object, whichever is appropriate per the accounting rules. At this stage, you invoice your customer and settle the invoices of your vendors.

4.3.2   Key Integration Points for SAP ERP Finacials and PS

Let's review the points where SAP ERP Financials and Project System integrate:

▶ **Execution and period end closing**
The key integration between FI and PS happens at the time of recording of actual costs and revenue during execution time. These costs then need to be settled at period end either to an expense or an asset.

▶ **Approval**
The budgeting process is also another key integration between FI and PS. To achieve maximum benefits, it makes sense to implement investment management in conjunction with PS. This helps you in identifying the projects and linking to your overall budgeting process.

The real benefits can only be realized if you activate availability control because this instills more fiscal prudence and discipline than any other communication from finance.

Now that you understand the various phases of a project implementation, let's map these to PS from a departmental standpoint.

4.3.3 Standard Operating Processes for Project Systems

Typically, managing a project is segregated into the six functions or stages—ranging from managing master data to period end closing—as shown in Figure 4.18.

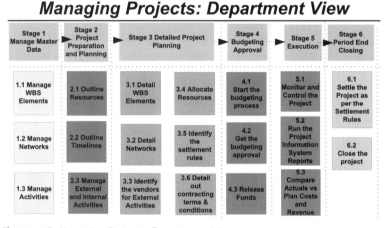

Figure 4.18 Managing Projects: Department View

Now that you understand the process flow of projects systems as well as the departmental view, you will learn about the variations that can be mapped in PS.

4.3.4 Multiple Scenarios for Projects Implementation

Let's first discuss how you can implement various planning processes in PS. Planning processes with PS are detailed here:

▶ **Date planning**
The system determines the earliest dates of activities by forward scheduling and the latest dates by backward scheduling. The difference between the earliest and the latest start dates for an activity called *float*.

▶ **Resource planning**

During resource planning, the differentiation needs to be made between externally processed and internally processed activities. For internally managed work, it is important to define the capacity requirements, do capacity analysis and leveling, and then distribute the work among internal resources, which leads to confirming and recording actual dates and costs as they happen. For externally managed work, we have to track the SLAs and manage per the contract. We can create an externally processed activity to create a purchase requisition and subsequent purchasing steps. The steps can follow the entire purchasing cycle or be limited to a specific path depending on the requirement.

▶ **Material planning**

This is used to plan the material requirements within the project systems. It can be used for transferring BOMs. PS is also integrated to Production Planning (PP) and Materials Management (MM), from the material planning perspective.

▶ **Cost planning**

The costs can be planned using two different methods:

▶ Manual cost planning in the WBS element: This can also have the sub-flavors like:

▶ Manual entry of all the costs in WBS elements.

▶ Detailed planning
This relates to primary cost and activity inputs, and is based on cost elements by period.

▶ Unit costing
This is based on cost elements and is based on how we arrived at that cost by looking up material data, activities, and variables.

▶ **Cost planning using activities**

This relates to network costing when you go one level below WBS element.

▶ **Revenue planning**

This can be done in multiple ways:

▶ Manual planning

▶ Billing plans typically for milestone billing-based projects

▶ SD documents

Budgeting Process

Salient points of budgeting processes are outlined here:

- Budgeting process sets the framework for the project and is allocated to the project during the planning process.
- Budgeting is *more binding* than cost planning. Cost planning is bottom up, whereas budgeting is typically top down.
- Budgeting can be set up to have an *availability check,* which tracks against the assigned funds set up against the budget bearing WBS elements (also referred to as controlling elements).
- Budgeting in PS can also be integrated via investment measures in controlling investment management, or it can be done only in PS.
- For managing multiple internal orders, you can use investment management to organize a group of internal orders together.
- Budgeting process is an ongoing process to track and manage the progress of the project. It is not a one-time activity
- Current Budget = Original Budget + Supplements – Returns +/- Transfers.
- Sometimes there is an additional step Release Budget, which makes the funds available for use. The release of the budget is done per the current budget.
- For multiple-year projects, the system allows you to carry forward the budgets to the next year by using the Carry-Forward functionality.
- Availability control is the functionality that can be used to stop actual postings from occurring in the first place if it is set as active. It can also be set up as passive. Passive availability control indicates that the budgeting process is being used primarily for reporting. On the other hand, active setting prevents the assignment of too many funds.
- Availability control checks the assigned value (costs incurred) against the distributable budget (budget not yet distributed to the other lower-level WBS elements).

4.3.5 Transactions for Project Systems

Master data is the most important element in managing PS. So let's take a look at some of the key master data transaction codes for PS in Table 4.10. These allow you to create a WBS element, network, and milestone.

Action	Transaction Code
WBS Create/Change/Display	CJ91/CJ92/CJ93
Network Create/Change/Display	CN01/CN02/CN03
Milestone Create/Change/Display	CN11/CN12/CN13

Table 4.10 Project Systems Transaction Codes

Now that you are familiar with the transaction codes for PS, let's take a detailed look at the organization elements in PS.

4.3.6 Organizational Entities for Project Systems

PS has no organizational structure of its own. It builds on the existing structure by making assignments to the organizational units in FI and logistics. In this section, you will learn to structure PS to meet your requirements. The building blocks of structuring PS are WBS elements, networks, and activities. The structure of these entities is shown in Figure 4.19.

As you learned earlier, the structure of PS need to be built by assigning the PS master data. The master data can be assigned to various financial and logistics organization data. Figure 4.20 illustrates the following typical assignments that are possible from PS to FI:

▶ **Project Definition**
A project can be assigned to a controlling area, company code, business area, profit center, or plant.

▶ **WBS Element**
This can be assigned to a company code, business area, cost center, equipment, or investment program.

▶ **Networks**
This can be assigned to a plant, business area, or profit center.

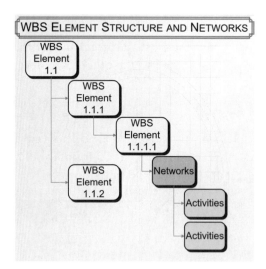

Figure 4.19 Project System: Building Blocks

▶ **Activities**

Four types of activities can be assigned to networks, and each of these activities can be assigned to different objects as follows:

▶ **Internal**

These are activities performed by internal resources within an organization. This can be assigned to a plant, work center, business area, or profit center.

▶ **External**

External activities are typically performed by external vendors and business partners. These can be assigned to a plant, purchasing organization, purchasing group, business area, or profit center.

▶ **General**

General activities can be assigned to a plant, business area, or a profit center.

▶ **Material**

Activities that consume material need an assignment to the purchasing group, purchasing organization, or plant.

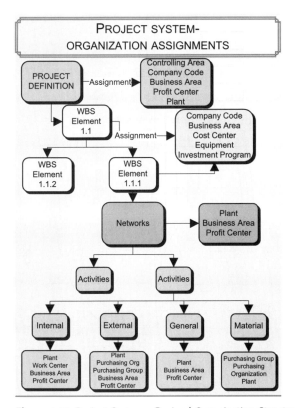

Figure 4.20 Project Systems: Derived Organization Structure

PS organization elements are used to build up the necessary level of detail to manage the budgeting process that occurs at the WBS level. Network is the lowest level and is settled to the WBS elements to which the network is assigned.

Here are the task-level assignments for WBS element:

▶ **Budgeting**
Original budgeting, availability check, updates, releases.

▶ **Managing schedule**
Dates: actual, scheduled, updates.

▶ **Managing costs and revenues**
Planned versus actual.

▶ **Commitment management**
WBS element can also be used to track the commitments.

▶ **Period end processes**
Settlement at period end, results analysis, and so on.

The functions of networks are as follows:

▶ Map the flow of the project.

▶ Define the various tasks that make up the network of activities.

▶ Understand the dependencies of various tasks within a network.

▶ Plan the labor, materials, capacities, and tools to manage the project at a more granular level.

▶ Define the milestones.

4.3.7 Integration of Project Systems with other ERP Modules

PS is integrated with FI, Controlling, PP and MM. Salient capsule points of integration are mentioned next.

Currencies in Project Systems

The following currencies are maintained in parallel for managing projects:

▶ Controlling area currency

▶ Object (WBS element/network/activities) currency

▶ Transaction currency

Cost Planning Tools

These are the tools available for Cost Planning:

▶ Easy cost planning for internal orders, WBS elements, internal service requests, appropriation requests, and ad hoc estimates

▶ Manual cost planning in WBS elements; both bottom up cost planning and top down distribution is possible in manual cost planning

▶ Cost planning in networks done in multiple versions and used for detailed costing

▶ Copy planning used to create multiple plans versus actual versions

The orders that can be assigned to a project are the following:

▶ Internal orders

▶ Plant maintenance orders

▶ Sales orders

▶ Production orders

The orders can be settled to the following objects at period end:

▶ An assigned WBS element

▶ A different WBS element or to a different order

▶ A different cost object (cost center, asset, or profitability segment)

You might ask, who owns the cost after settlement. For that, review this list:

▶ After the costs are settled to a receiver, then the responsibility of costs is also transferred to the receiver.

▶ Project cash management can be used to track the payments in and out of a project.

▶ The key organizations in project cash management are the *financial management area* and *commitment items*.

In the next section, you will learn about the Plant Maintenance (PM) process and how it is integrated with FI.

4.4 Managing Plant Maintenance

Plant maintenance is especially important in the manufacturing industry where you need to maintain the plant and equipment so that they can be continuously used with minimum downtime for manufacturing. In this section, you will learn more about the process of implementing PM and how it is integrated with other components. You will also learn the key financial integration points. First let's explore the typical plant maintenance processes.

4.4.1 Process Flow

Figure 4.21 illustrates the process flow of PM.

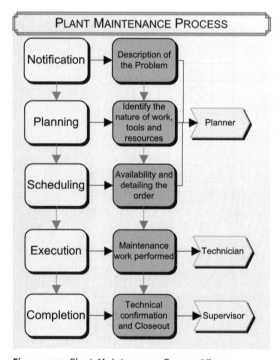

Figure 4.21 Plant Maintenance: Process View

The process flow shown in Figure 4.21 shows the SAP view of the PM along with the business perspective. Let's detail each of these steps to understand their significance and implications to SAP ERP Financials:

1. Notification

PM notification is the initiator of the PM activities. At this stage, you will have a brief description of the problem that needs to be entered in the notification.

2. Planning

After the maintenance planner receives the request, the planner needs to identify the nature of the work and the tools and resources for taking care of the maintenance notification.

3. Scheduling

Now that you have identified the details, you need to assign the resources and schedule the appropriate time to fix the problem. This involves creating a maintenance order that references the previous maintenance notification.

4. Execution

The maintenance work is performed by a technician. During this time, the actual quantity of the materials used and the labor used are recorded against the production order.

5. Completion

This is the technical confirmation and closeout of the maintenance process, which is done by the supervisor of the technician.

Now that you understand the basics of the PM let's take a look at the departmental view of PM.

4.4.2 Standard Operating Procedures for Plant Maintenance Processes

Now you will learn the various processes and structure of the plant maintenance department. Figure 4.22 shows the mapping of various SAP ERP PM business processes into a departmental view of the same.

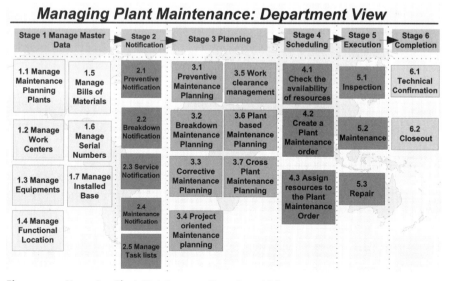

Figure 4.22 Managing Plant Maintenance: Department View

Based on these different processes and how your organization has divided these tasks, you can segregate these into different hand-offs across your organization. Now that you understand there are different types of plant maintenance, let's take a look at the different scenarios for plant maintenance that can be used to understand the multitude of ways in which you can map PM processes to meet your requirements.

4.4.3 Multiple Scenarios for Plant Maintenance

Various scenarios for PM are shown in Figure 4.23. In addition you will also learn about the links between the procurement and PM processes.

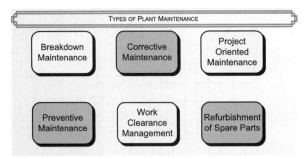

Figure 4.23 Types of Plant Maintenance

Let's take a look at each of these PM processes in detail.

Breakdown Maintenance

The breakdown maintenance process does not have the planning component. The maintenance order is immediately released upon creation, and the order can be created with or without a notification. Because the order is created when there is an emergency, these orders start with a status of TECO (technically complete), which means that all of the maintenance planning required for this order has been completed (see Figure 4.24).

Corrective Maintenance

This has all the phases of PM shown in Figure 4.22, including the planning phase.

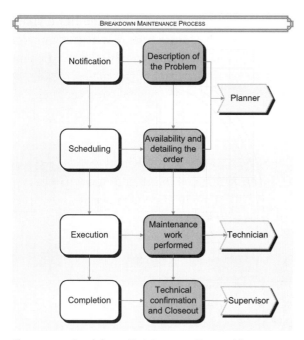

Figure 4.24 Breakdown Maintenance: Process View

Preventive Maintenance

This is done by the maintenance planner to prevent the system from breaking down. It can be based on time, performance, or conditions. In a single-cycle plan, the same activity can be performed at regular intervals. However in a strategy plan, maintenance work and inspections are performed in different cycles. These are more in line with how the wear and tear of machinery actually happens per the specifications from the manufacturer.

After these activities have been defined in the maintenance plan, they can be scheduled so that the system automatically generates a PM order with appropriate task lists defined to help define the periodicity of the tasks. Also, useful historical information is generated as you go through the series of steps. The process for executing preventive maintenance is shown in Figure 4.25.

Project-Based Maintenance

This is typically used for shutdown maintenance when the PM activities have to be orchestrated in a specific timeframe with the allocated resources. Inspections and repair work that require a shutdown of an asset are routinely performed in plants. These help in lengthening the useful life of an asset. Shutdown maintenance also improves the future operational efficiency of maintaining the asset. It helps if the tasks are managed in the form of a project and monitored and planned accordingly.

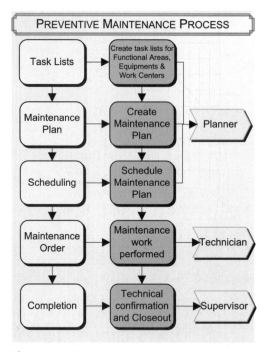

Figure 4.25 Preventive Maintenance Process

Work Clearance Management

Work clearance management (WCM) is the process for creating a safe environment for operating in the plant. It helps in ensuring that we can carry out the tasks in PM safely and without putting anybody's life in danger. The focus of this is to meet the environmental guidelines as well as guarantee the technical system is available to do PM work. There are some rules for work WCM:

▶ Maintenance orders are linked to WCM at the header level.

▶ For WCM-relevant orders, the status should be EXEC (released for execution) before any PM activity can be performed on the order.

▶ Setting the task to released depends on the WCM architecture and whether the valuation has been activated.

The process flow for WCM is shown in Figure 4.26, highlighting how the status of the order changes from one stage to the other.

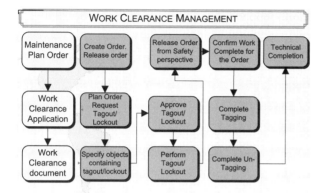

Figure 4.26 Work Clearance Management Process

Let's now take a detailed look at the WCM steps:

1. Create a plant maintenance order and release it.

2. Create a lockout of the plant equipment so that work equipment processes can be performed on the PM equipment.

3. The next step is to specify objects that contain tagout and lockouts.

4. The tagout and lockout of objects is approved.

5. The actual tagout or lockout is performed.

6. The PM order is released from the safety perspective.

7. Now the actual work is performed on the equipment, the status of the maintenance order is changed to *Certified from a safety perspective.* This completes the tagging process.

8. After the tagging process is complete, you can untag the equipment and then mark the maintenance order for technical completion.

Procuring External Services and Materials within Plant Maintenance

Sometimes, it becomes imperative to procure external materials and services to perform maintenance activities. This requires PM to be integrated with the procurement process of materials and services. The integrated process flow is shown in Figure 4.27.

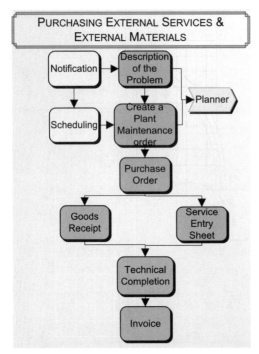

Figure 4.27 Purchasing External Services and Materials

You can create a material purchase order or a service purchase order referencing a PM order. From there, the routine procurement processes follow, including goods receipt or service entry sheet approval. After you have used the goods and performed the technical completion of the maintenance, you can pay the vendor invoice with reference to the purchase order.

Refurbishment of Spare Parts

The refurbishment of spare parts is an important PM process that is much cheaper than buying a new part. The refurbishment process is triggered when a predefined number of defective parts reaches stores. At this time, the maintenance planner creates a PM order that details the tasks, time, and other necessary information for refurbishment. Employees responsible for refurbishment withdraw the materials and then carry out the tasks as outlined in the order. When they are done, they return the refurbished material to the store (see Figure 4.28). This completes the order.

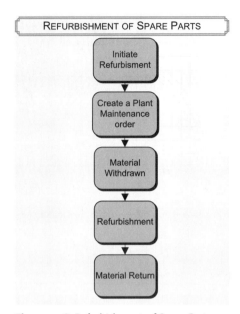

Figure 4.28 Refurbishment of Spare Parts

Now that you understand the various processes that can be undertaken in PM, let's take a look at the organization entities involved in PM processes.

4.4.4 Plant Maintenance Organizational Entities

In this section, you will learn about the PM organization entities and how these are linked to other FI entities.

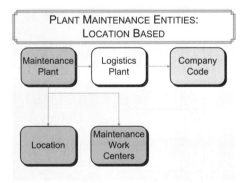

Figure 4.29 Location-Based Plant Maintenance Entities

Figure 4.29 shows the PM entities based on the location. This also shows the assignment of maintenance plant to logistics plant, which is then assigned to the company code. Figure 4.30 shows the PM entities based on planning. There are two entities from the planning perspective. The maintenance planning plant is the plant at which operational planning is done, whereas the maintenance planner group is the subdivision of planning activities within a maintenance planning plant.

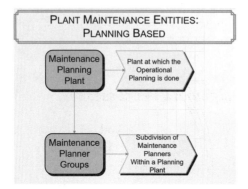

Figure 4.30 Planning-Based Plant Maintenance Entities

This section provided you with an understanding of the organization entities of PM by location and from a planning perspective. You also learned the link between PM's plant and the company code of FI.

4.4.5 Integration of Plant Maintenance with Financials

Let's also take a look at some of the configuration level settings that link FI with PM

Planning Phase

The costs in PM can be analyzed from these broad perspectives:

- **Controlling View**
  Cost element level (spare parts, labor, etc.)
- **Plant Maintenance View**
  Value category level (internal, external, and others)

In customizing, cost elements are assigned to a value category.

Completion Phase

This phase starts off with a technical understanding such as damage, cause of damage, and recording actual time required. These are recorded in technical confirmation. This indicates that the order is technically finished for PM. However, business confirmation is done by settling the costs assigned to the purchase order to appropriate cost elements. Condition-based material valuation is used to categorize refurbished materials.

You can valuate materials separately within the same valuation area by using the valuation category in the material master's accounting view. The movement type can then be tied to a condition to differentiate a refurbished, new, or defective material.

4.5   Managing Quality Management Processes

Quality is very important to deliver customer satisfaction and ensure product consistency over a long period of time. Various philosophies abound regarding quality and how it can be ingrained and improved in an organization. Some of the key philosophies of quality management (QM) are listed here:

▶ **Total Quality Management (TQM)**
This is evolving quality as a management strategy for competitive advantage. The premise is to ensure that every activity in an organization is embedded with quality. As defined by ISO (International Standards Organization): "TQM is a management approach for an organization, centered on quality, based on participation of all its members and aiming at long term success through customer satisfaction and benefits to all members of the organization and the society."

▶ **Six Sigma**
Six Sigma is a disciplined, data-driven approach to eliminating defects in any process from manufacturing to transactional, from products to services. The idea is to eliminate any variation in the process or the product. Every process should have a consistent quality. To achieve Six Sigma, a product should not have more than 3.4 defects per million opportunities.

Now that you understand some of the key philosophies of QM, let's take a look at quality processes and how you can implement these processes using the SAP ERP system solution.

4.5.1   Quality Management Process Flow

SAP ERP supports the QM processes as per the DIN EN ISO 9000 standards. QM processes are an integral part of the following SAP ERP solutions:

- ▶ **SCM Planning**
  Integration of QM with work planning and procurement planning.

- ▶ **SCM Procurement**
  Covers release of vendors, goods receipt inspections, and complaints against the vendor.

- ▶ **SCM Production**
  Inspections during production and end of production checks.

- ▶ **SCM SD**
  Customer inspections, goods issue inspections, and customer complaints

Figure 4.31 shows the processes in various stages of logistics Supply Chain Management (SCM), which have quality checks identified at various stages.

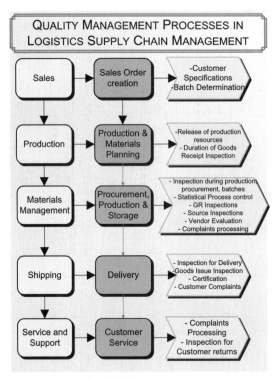

Figure 4.31 Quality Checks in SCM

Overall QM processes (seen in Figure 4.32) can be classified as one of the following:

- ▶ **Planned processes**
  These are checks that happen at various stages of logistics SCM according to the quality plan. These are detailed later in this section.

▶ **Triggered processes**
These are triggered by defects that are discovered at any stage. These are recorded in quality notification.

4.5.2 Standard Operating Procedures for Quality Management Processes

QM is typically segregated into the following functions:

▶ Master data management

▶ Quality procedures and certification affiliation

▶ Quality planning

▶ Quality inspections

▶ Quality control

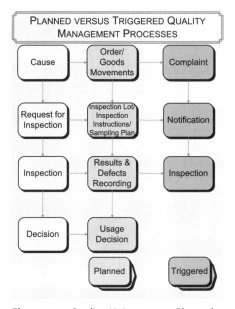

Figure 4.32 Quality Maintenance: Planned versus Triggered

These functions, along with their details from a departmental perspective, are shown in Figure 4.33.

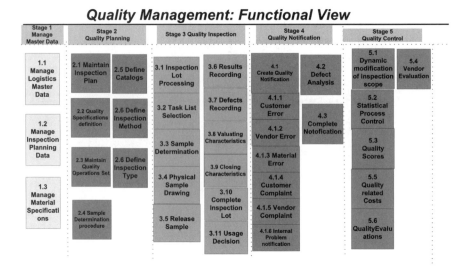

Figure 4.33 QM: Functional View

As a finance process owner, you should know about the typical process flow in quality because sometimes payment terms are contingent on the Finance department receiving the quality certification and subject to quality checks being completed and approved. In the next section, you will learn about the organization entities of QM.

4.5.3 Quality Management Organizational Entities

You have already learned that QM is an integral part of the logistics supply chain and is performed at each of the individual steps. The only way to understand the organization entities of QM is to learn how an inspection plan is created. Figure 4.34 describes the components of the inspection plan and relevant master data elements tied to it.

As you can see, an inspection plan is tied to a material and can be performed for a vendor or customer. Also the header of the inspection plan is tied to a work center and a reference operation set that identifies how many operations need to be performed for recording the inspection lot with reference to the inspection plan.

When you actually perform the inspection operation, you can tie it to material and equipment. Also various inspection characteristics, inspection methods, sampling procedures, and catalogs can be maintained when creating the inspection lot with reference to the inspection plan. In the next section, you will learn how the QM module integrates with FI and controlling.

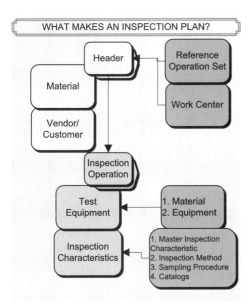

Figure 4.34 Components of an Inspection Plan

4.5.4   Integration with Financials and Controlling

Even though QM is not heavily integrated with FI, it can be used to support various checks and controls with reference to FI. Let's take a look at some of the key integration points of QM with FI:

▶ Quality costs incurred for various quality-related activities are posted to controlling by assigning appropriate cost centers or cost objects.

▶ Quality costs can also be passed to controlling by assigning a maintenance order for quality-related work and subsequent settlement to controlling and accounting. Quality costs get passed on to FI when the maintenance order is settled as per the settlement rules.

▶ QM is integrated with MM to segregate stock types such as stock available for issue versus stock not available for issue.

In this section, you learned the various QM processes and their integration with other logistics modules and FI. In the next section, you will learn about the payroll process and its integration with FI.

4.6   Managing Payroll Human Resources-Financials (HR-FI) Integration

In this section, you will learn about the integration of payroll with accounting. Before detailing the integration, let's discuss the payroll process.

4.6.1 Payroll Process Flow

Broadly, payroll is used to calculate remuneration of work performed by individual employees. Payroll is typically used to denote the following sequence of activities:

1. Calculate pay and create payroll results and remuneration statements. This consists of two elements: calculation of remuneration elements and statutory or voluntary deductions.

2. Make bank transfers or payments by checks.

3. Post results to accounting.

4. Perform other evaluations, such as taxes.

Remuneration structure can have two types of components: fixed, which is basic compensation, or variable, which is time-based compensation. This process flow is also shown in Figure 4.35.

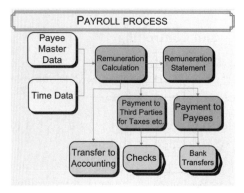

Figure 4.35 Payroll Process

Figure 4.36 shows the calculation schema for payroll processes.

You calculate the payroll using basic data and time data. After this, the additional payments and deductions as chosen by employees are also considered. All these are factored along with the statutory payments and deduction to determine the net payment amount, which is then disbursed to the employee.

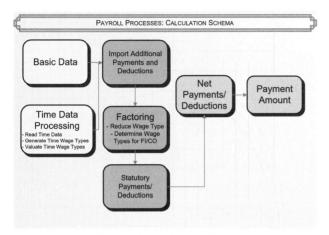

Figure 4.36 Calculation Schema for Payroll Processes

4.6.2 Standard Operating Procedures for Human Resources

The payroll process is a sub-process in the HR area. The other key sub-processes in HR are shown in Figure 4.37.

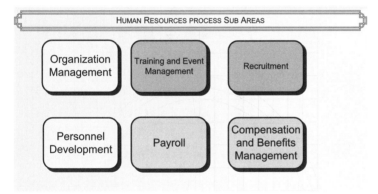

Figure 4.37 HR Process Subareas

All these components are tightly integrated with each other to support organization-wide HR functions. Figure 4.38 highlights the key HR functions. Most of these functions are HR-only processes. HR processes with a financial impact are listed here:

▶ **Time Management**
This involves defining the work schedule (number of hours per day), entering the time sheet at the end of the week, and recording absence and illness and other details regarding time entry. This can be integrated with

the procurement process for performing service entry sheets based on hours worked by employees and contractors. Then you can pay the contracting company via ERS runs, and pay employees via payroll.

▶ **Payroll**

This is covered in more detail in this section. The first step in a payroll execution is the payroll run, which involves the calculation of various payroll components by employee. Another component is the remuneration statement, which identifies the details of the payment and the deductions made. The component that matters the most is the payment to payees (employees, contractors) and third parties, which involves federal and state governments. The last step is recording the payroll transactions in accounting.

▶ **Compensation Management**

In this step, you plan your compensation strategy. This is managed by performing job pricing, which benchmarks the job role against the industry practices. It also involves budgeting for the job role and is integrated with the FI budgeting and planning process. Also you can plan long-term incentives such as bonuses, 401k plans, and so on in compensation management. You can also perform compensation administration in this module.

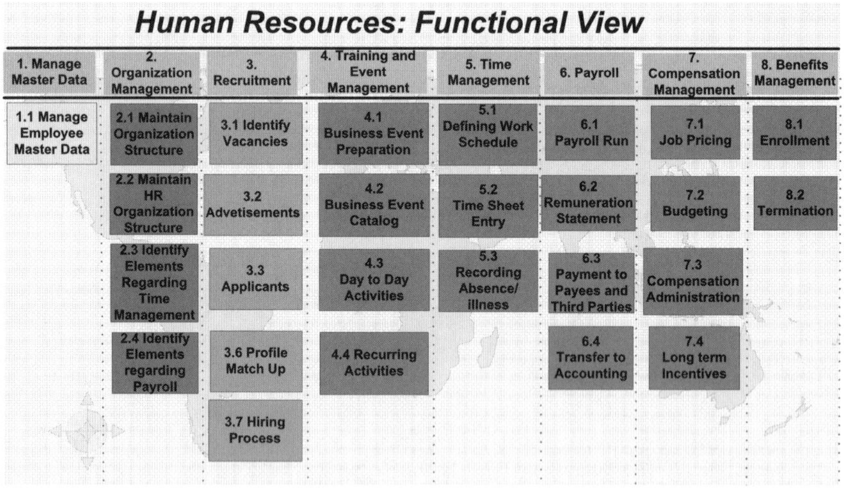

Human Resources: Functional View

1. Manage Master Data	2. Organization Management	3. Recruitment	4. Training and Event Management	5. Time Management	6. Payroll	7. Compensation Management	8. Benefits Management
1.1 Manage Employee Master Data	2.1 Maintain Organization Structure	3.1 Identify Vacancies	4.1 Business Event Preparation	5.1 Defining Work Schedule	6.1 Payroll Run	7.1 Job Pricing	8.1 Enrollment
	2.2 Maintain HR Organization Structure	3.2 Advetisements	4.2 Business Event Catalog	5.2 Time Sheet Entry	6.2 Remuneration Statement	7.2 Budgeting	8.2 Termination
	2.3 Identify Elements Regarding Time Management	3.3 Applicants	4.3 Day to Day Activities	5.3 Recording Absence/ illness	6.3 Payment to Payees and Third Parties	7.3 Compensation Administration	
	2.4 Identify Elements regarding Payroll	3.6 Profile Match Up	4.4 Recurring Activities		6.4 Transfer to Accounting	7.4 Long term Incentives	
		3.7 Hiring Process					

Figure 4.38 Human Resources: Functional View

Next, you will learn about the organizational entities relevant for HR management.

4.6.3 Organizational Entities for Human Resources Management

HR structure can be divided into three broad headings as shown in Figure 4.39.

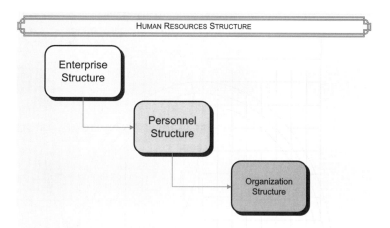

Figure 4.39 Human Resources Structure

Let's also get an idea of what is involved in each:

▶ **Enterprise Structure**
This shows the relationship of HR with other enterprise organizational entities such as company code (see Figure 4.40). The key HR organization entity is the personnel area, which represents the location. The personnel area is subdivided into the personnel subarea, which represents the departments.

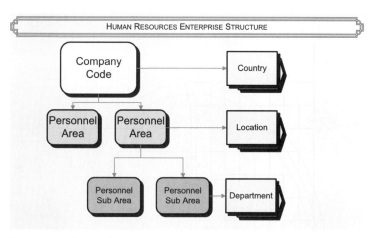

Figure 4.40 Human Resources Enterprise Structure

▶ **Personnel Structure**

This is one level below the enterprise structure and is unique to HR for internal reporting and classification purposes. The goal of the personnel structure is to segregate the employees by using employee groups. For example, you can have an employee group named **Active**, which can be further classified into employee subgroups called Trainee, Hourly, Salaried. A sample personnel structure is shown in Figure 4.41.

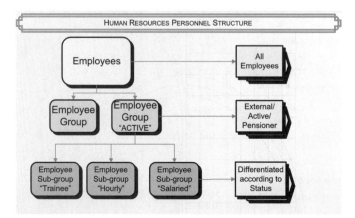

Figure 4.41 Human Resources Personnel Structure

▶ **Payroll Accounting Area and Organization Structure**

In addition to the personnel structure, you can also design your organization structure by dividing your employees into payroll accounting areas. These are exclusively used by the payroll module to define when the payroll is run and to identify the employees who are part of the payroll run (see Figure 4.42).

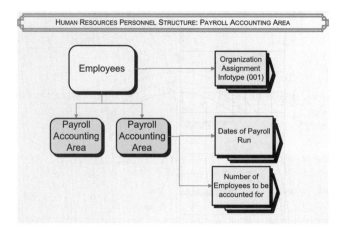

Figure 4.42 Human Resources: Payroll Accounting Area

You learned the basic structure of HR and some of the key organization elements. Now you will discover how the basic HR structure and some of the key organizational elements come together. Figure 4.43 shows the integration of personnel administration with the HR organization structure.

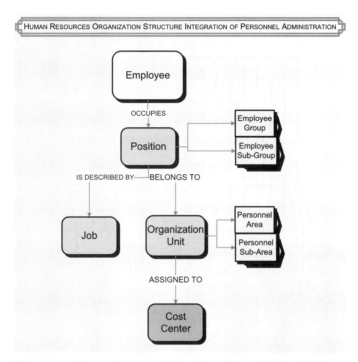

HUMAN RESOURCES ORGANIZATION STRUCTURE INTEGRATION OF PERSONNEL ADMINISTRATION

Figure 4.43 Human Resources: Integration of Organization Structure and Personnel Administration

An employee master data occupies a position in HR organizational management. The position is tied to an employee group or an employee subgroup. In addition, a position is described by a job and belongs to an organization unit, which can be assigned to a cost center. The organization unit is tied to a personnel area or personnel subarea, and the personnel area is tied to a company code. This completes the broad picture of integrating the organization entities of HR and FI. In the next section, you will learn more about the integration of HR with FI.

4.6.4 Integration of Human Resources with Financials

As you saw earlier, HR is integrated to Controlling via the cost center assignment of the organization unit. You can also assign the cost center directly in the employee master. Also for the payroll process, the payroll accounting area helps in the integration with FI when the accounting entries are posted to FI after the payroll run has been completed. The menu path is **IMG • Financial Accounting (New) • General Ledger Accounting (New) • Periodic Processing • Integration • Payroll • Define Income Statement Accounts/ Define Balance Sheet Accounts • Automatic Postings - Account Determination**.

You will learn more about integrating HR with General Ledger (GL) in Chapter 9, when we discuss GL Accounting. In the next section, you will learn how transportation and shipment costs can be managed.

4.7 Managing Transportation and Shipment Costs

Transportation costs (LE-FI integration) play a crucial role in the calculation of the price of a product. It is important to keep transportation costs low so that the product can be supplied on time and in a price-competitive manner. In this section, you will learn the flow of transportation processes and how they can be mapped to SAP ERP Financials.

4.7.1 Process Flow for Transportation

The transportation process is used for movements from vendors to plants *(inbound)*, plants to plants *(interplant movement)*, and plants to customers *(outbound)*. This is shown in Figure 4.44.

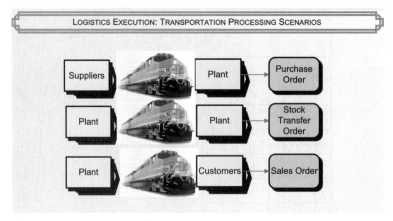

Figure 4.44 Transportation Planning Scenarios

Each of these scenarios is linked to a corresponding main document: purchase order for inbound, stock transfer order for interplant, and sales order for outbound. Transportation processing refers to the shipment of goods and is heavily dependent on the previously defined processes in logistics. Transportation processes can be segregated into the following distinct components:

▶ Transportation planning and shipment completion

▶ Shipment costs calculation (customers and vendors)

▶ Shipment costs settlement

▶ Service agent selection

▶ Management of means of transport and utilities

▶ Follow-up and supervision of shipments

▶ Management of shipment costs

The schematic describing the shipment process for inbound and outbound scenarios is outlined in Figure 4.45.

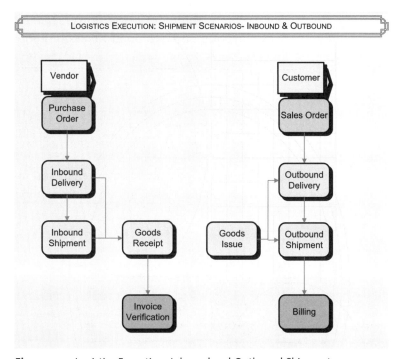

Figure 4.45 Logistics Execution: Inbound and Outbound Shipments

Transportation components in the schematic (see Figure 4.45) are the creation of the delivery and shipment documents. In addition, the goods receipt and goods issue also are linked to the transportation process.

Now that you understand the transportation components, let's take a look at the departmental or functional view of the transportation. This is detailed in the next section.

4.7.2   Standard Operating Procedures for Transportation

In this section, you will learn about the transportation process from a departmental and functional point of view. Transportation processes can be segregated into four functional areas as shown in Figure 4.46. They are discussed here:

▸ **Manage master data**
This is maintaining the master data for transportation, which includes the transportation planning point, carrier master data, and the transportation rates for various condition types.

▸ **Shipment planning**
This involves identifying the freight movement requirements, creating the shipment schedule, and creating the mode of movement from a strategic perspective. In addition, it also involves the operational identification of the routes of movement along with the creation of deliveries and creation of shipments to manage the individual deliveries.

▸ **Shipment execution**
This process area involves monitoring the shipment, confirming freight movements, and confirming routes and forwarding agents.

▸ **Freight payment**
This is an area that typically involves the payment of the freight and involves accounts payable working in conjunction with the transportation department to pay the freight carrier.

Transportation: Functional View

1. Manage Master Data	2. Shipment Planning	3. Shipment Execution	4. Freight Payment
1.1 Manage Transportation Planning Point	2.1 Identify Freight Movements Required	3.1 Confirm Freight movements	4.1 Approve Freight Service
1.2 Manage Carrier (Vendor) Master	2.2 Create Shipment Schedule	3.2 Confirm Routes and Forwarding Agents	4.2 Settle Freight Cost
1.3 Manage Transportation Rates	2.3 Identify Mode of Movement	3.3 Monitor Shipment	4.3 Invoice Verification
	2.4 Identify Routes of Movementl		4.4 Billing
	2.5 Create Deliveries		
	2.6 Create Shipment		

Figure 4.46 Transportation: Functional View

4.7.3 Multiple Scenarios for Transportation

As you saw earlier, transportation processes can be broadly segregated in three categories. Now we will detail each of these scenarios and how these can be represented in SAP ERP.

Inbound Shipments

Let's first take a look at the inbound shipments from a vendor to one of your plants using the process flow shown in Figure 4.47. The following describes the components of the inbound shipment process from shipment creation to shipment cost settlement:

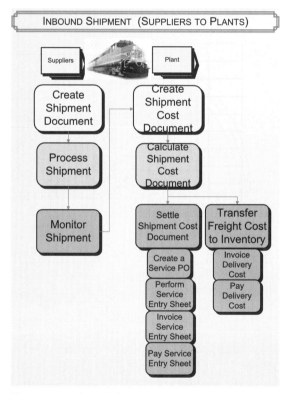

Figure 4.47 Inbound Shipment Processing

1. **Create a shipment**

   You need to create a shipment referencing a particular purchase order against which the supplier is delivering the goods. In this case, an inbound delivery is created and attached to the shipment document.

2. Process shipment

Now process the shipment going through various stages of shipment, such as planning, check in, loading start, loading end, shipment completion, and shipment end. In this step, you process the shipment by maintaining the forwarding agent, identifying any external identification parameters, and updating them as and when you receive them from your freight carrier.

3. Monitor shipment

The shipment is updated with external parameters as it goes from the origin location to the receiving location, so you can monitor the shipment lifecycle as it goes from shipment start to shipment end. In addition, you can update any tracking or bill of lading numbers from the external carrier, which helps in identifying the shipment.

4. Create shipment cost document

After you receive the material at your plant or as per your requirements, you can create a shipment cost document that is tied to the shipment.

5. Calculate shipment cost document

The shipment cost document is updated with the pricing conditions to represent the total cost of shipment. The total shipment cost is calculated and stored in the shipment cost document.

You have two options to settle the payment costs. Either you can pass on the freight cost to inventory at the destination plant, or you can expense the freight cost and pay the same to the carrier.

6. Settle shipment cost document

To pay the shipment costs as an expense item, the system allows you to create an automatic service purchase order and then performs a service entry sheet per the shipment cost calculated. This service entry sheet can then be invoiced using the normal invoice verification process and paid to the vendor.

7. Transfer shipment cost to inventory

You can also choose to transfer the shipment cost to inventory of the destination plant. In that case, the goods receipt at the destination plant with reference to the shipment cost will also create a delivery cost with reference to the receiving purchase order. The delivery costs can then be invoiced with reference to the receiving purchase order.

Outbound Shipments

Outbound shipments involve arranging a shipment to go to a customer. The process flow is shown in Figure 4.48, and the detailed process components are described here:

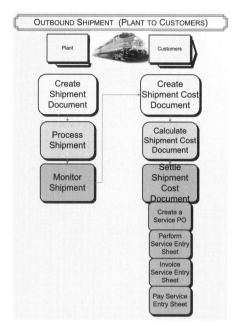

Figure 4.48 Outbound Shipment Process

1. Create a shipment

The first step is to create a shipment referencing a particular sales order against which you are delivering the goods to your customer. In this case, an outbound delivery is created and attached to the shipment document.

2. Process shipment to calculate shipment cost document

The shipment processing, monitoring, cost document, and calculating document are the same as discussed for inbound shipments.

3. Settle shipment cost document

To pay the shipment costs referencing a sales order, you have to use the automatic service purchase order created by the system and then perform a service entry sheet as per the shipment cost calculated. This service entry sheet can then be invoiced using the normal invoice verification process and paid to the vendor.

Interplant Shipment

Interplant shipments are a special case of inbound shipment where you do not have a reference purchase order. Instead, you have a stock transfer order against which you can settle the shipment delivery costs. The process flow is shown in Figure 4.49, which is similar to Figure 4.47.

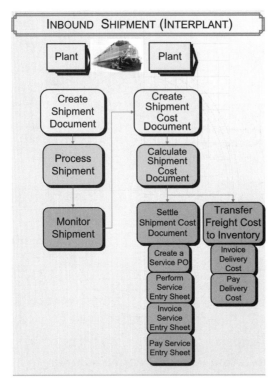

Figure 4.49 Interplant Transfer

4.7.4 Logistics Execution Organizational Entities

Now let's see how logistics execution entities are interrelated. Figure 4.50 shows the organization entities for logistics execution.

As shown in Figure 4.50, the warehouse number is the lowest entity that is tied to the storage location tied to the plant. For transportation, the loading point is the lowest entity that is tied to the shipping point tied to the plant. In addition, you have the option of defining a transportation planning point that is tied to a company code directly. The transportation planning point is also used to assign the purchasing data during the settlement process. You can assign the transportation planning point and the shipment cost type to a purchasing group, purchasing organization, and plant for creating a purchase order automatically during the settlement process discussed earlier.

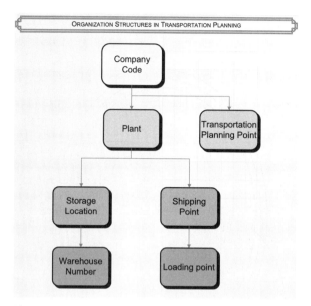

ORGANIZATION STRUCTURES IN TRANSPORTATION PLANNING

Company Code

Plant

Transportation Planning Point

Storage Location

Shipping Point

Warehouse Number

Loading point

Figure 4.50 Logistics Execution: Organization Entities for Transportation

4.7.5 Integration of Transportation Planning with Financials

Transportation planning is integrated with FI from the perspective of freight invoicing and pricing. The pricing for transportation can be defined separately from the MM pricing. The key integration point is the shipment cost calculation and the shipment cost settlement process. If you are a FI consultant, then you need to configure the shipment cost calculation and settlement functionality. The configuration of the pricing schema is done by the transportation expert.

4.8 Summary

In this chapter, you learned about the broad business processes in FI, which include purchase requisition to check writing, sales order to cash, managing project lifecycle, managing payroll, plant maintenance equipments, QM, and transportation and shipment costs. You learned the end-to-end business process flows, along with their distinction by departments and functions. You also learned about some of the variations of these business processes and how they can be mapped in SAP ERP Financials.

Overall, this chapter lays the process framework of SAP ERP FI and introduced the other process areas to help you understand their integration with

FI. It provides you with the broad understanding of the other process areas. You will need to keep referring back to Chapters 3 and 4 for your general understanding and for building your baseline knowledge about SAP ERP Financials.

In Chapter 5, you will learn how to configure and optimize accounts payable and accounts receivable.

In this chapter you will learn the key functionalities available in SAP ERP Financials to support accounts payable and accounts receivable, the two most important subledgers of accounting that are heavily oriented toward daily transaction recording and analysis.

5 Optimizing Financial Business Processes: Accounts Payable and Accounts Receivable

In this chapter you can build on the knowledge gained in Chapter 4, which focused on the integrated business process perspective of SAP ERP Financials, by delving into the details of the payment portion of the procure to pay cycle and the cash part of the order to cash cycle. Accounts payable (AP) and accounts receivable (AR) handle interactions with vendors and customers, respectively, by maintaining their subledgers per the statutory and internal reporting requirements.

We will map out the tools and techniques to implement and optimize AP and AR. Optimization is tough, especially when there are so many choices available in the mapping process in SAP ERP. So it becomes very important that you understand which functionality will give you the maximum benefit and what is the standard process available in SAP ERP. In this chapter, you will be presented with the various choices available to you in SAP ERP for implementing your AP and AR processes.

This chapter emphasizes the outlining of activities that simplify your life or help you establish a seamless process so you can derive the maximum benefit from your SAP ERP Financials implementation. Figure 5.1 illustrates how we will proceed with learning the processes covered in this chapter. Let's begin by discussing how a vendor master looks in SAP ERP.

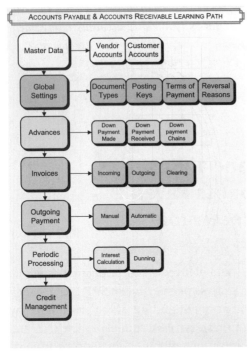

Figure 5.1 Accounts Payable and Accounts Receivable Learning Path

5.1 Vendor Master

The vendor master is the key to understanding how AP functions. In SAP ERP, master data is broken up by views. You can create master data across multiple organization entities by extending these views. A vendor master can be created for a company code (accounting view), for a purchasing organization (logistics view), or for both, depending on the nature of the vendor. Figure 5.2 shows the vendor master display screen for centrally maintained data (both company code and purchasing).

For purchasing vendor master data, the menu path is **SAP Menu • Logistics • Materials management • Purchasing • Master data • Vendor • Purchasing • Create/Change/Display/Changes/Block/Flag for deletion**, and the Transactions are MK01/MK02/MK03/MK04/MK05/MK06.

For company code vendor master data, the menu path is **SAP Menu • Accounting • Financial Accounting • Accounts Payable • Master records • Create/Change/Display/Changes/Block/Flag for deletion**, and the Transactions are FK01/FK02/FK03/FK04/FK05/FK06. Several tabs can be maintained for a vendor: Let's look at each of the individual tabs and what they contain:

Figure 5.2 Vendor Master: View (Transaction XK03)

▶ **General data—Address**
   In this tab, you can enter your vendor name and address details.

▶ **General data—Control**
   In this tab, you can enter your control parameters: **Account Control—Customer.** If a customer is also a vendor then you can establish a link between them using this field. This can then be used for clearing vendor and customer balances together. You can enter the trading partner as well in this tab. In addition, tax information can be entered here along with the reference data, which has some industry-related fields and other transportation-specific fields. Also you can maintain the withholding tax details as well.

▶ **General data: Payment transactions**
   In this tab, you can enter the bank details along with payment transaction details of the **Alternative Indicator**, **DME Indicator**, **Instruction Key**, and **Permitted Payees**.

▶ **Company code data: Accounting information**
   The most important field in this is **Reconciliation Account**, which houses the GL account that is hit when AP transactions are made against the vendor master. Also you can maintain the **Head Office** of the vendor. Head office is the remit to vendor location where the payment for any transaction with this vendor should be routed to. Other important fields that can be maintained on this screen are **Interest Indicator** for interest calculation and other **Withholding Tax Details**.

▶ **Company code data: Payment data**
   This tab outlines how the vendor is paid: **Payment Methods** (check, wire

transfer, etc.), **House Bank Details**, and the **Payment Terms** corresponding to the vendor. It also defines the **Tolerance Group** in invoice verification, which allows you to define the tolerances around the difference between what the system calculated and the actual invoice amount.

▸ **Company code data: Dunning Data**
This tab outlines the parameters for dunning data: **Dunning Procedure**, **Dunning Recipient**, **Last Dunned Date**, **Dunning Block**, and so on, and correspondence data: **Accounting Clerk**, **Clerk at Vendor**, and so on. Dunning details show up only if the vendor is also a customer.

▸ **Company code data: Withholding tax**
Withholding tax shows up only if it has been activated for the company code in the configuration.

▸ **Purchasing Organization data: Purchasing data**
This view has the **Schema Group**, which is used in pricing, and various control parameters such as **GR-Based Invoice Verification Indicator**, **Service Based Invoice Verification**, and other purchasing controls, which if selected, default to any purchasing document created for the vendor. It also has **Order Currency, Terms of Payment** and **Incoterms (Freight on board, Delivered**, etc.).

▸ **Purchasing organization data: Partner functions**
This tab helps in establishing partner functions for the vendor, such as invoice presented by, and so on.

Now let's move on to the customer master data.

5.2   Customer Master Data

Customer master is the key to understanding AR . The structure and organization of customer master data follows the same set of guidelines as the vendor master but is integrated with SAP SD rather than MM. Remember that in SAP ERP, the master data structure is broken up by views. You can create master data across multiple organization entities by extending these views.

5.2.1   Customer Master Views

Customer master can be created for a company code (accounting view) or for a sales area (sales organization plus distribution channel plus division (logistics view), or for both, depending on the nature of the customer. For example, sundry debtors/customers do not need a sales view and can be created purely as accounting vendors (created for the relevant company code) so that you can perform accounting functions with them. But for customers that have sales documents created, you need to extend them to the appropriate sales area. If a customer is also a vendor, you can establish a link between them using the Account Control—Customer. This can then be used for clearing vendor and customer balances together.

5.2.2   Creating a New Customer

Figure 5.3 shows how you can create customer master data in both SD and the sales area. You need to enter the account group, company code, distribution channel, and division to maintain a customer. The menu path for the SD customer master is **SAP Menu • Logistics • Sales and Distribution • Master Data • Business partner • Customer • Create • Sales and Distribution/Complete,** and the Transactions are VD01/XD01.

For the company code customer master data, follow the path **Company Code Customer Master Data SAP Menu • Accounting • Financial Accounting • Accounts Receivable• Master records • Create/Change/Display/Changes/ Block/Set deletion indicator**. The Transactions are FD01/FD02/FD03/FD04/ FD05/FD06.

Figure 5.3 Creating a New Customer

General Data Tabs

When you press Enter, you should be able to maintain the following in the **General data**: address, control data, payment transactions, marketing, unloading points, export data, and contact persons for the customer. Let's take a look at each of these tabs within the **General data** group:

- ▶ **General Data: Address**

  You can maintain the customer address along with the communication details in this tab. Also take a look at the international versions that house the structure for maintaining the address for different countries.

- ▶ **General Data: Control data**

  If you have a customer that also has a vendor relationship, you need to maintain the vendor master in this tab. This tab is very similar to the vendor master account control.

- ▶ **General Data: Payment transactions:**

  Bank details can be entered here. This tab is very similar to the **Vendor Payment Transactions** tab in **General data**.

- ▶ **General Data: Marketing**

  This tab is completely new. The classification section is used to classify the master data per Nielson ID, customer class, and other industry details. You can maintain the regional market classification and also assign your defined customer hierarchy. In the key figures area, you can maintain the annual sales and number of employees by year. You can also maintain the fiscal year variant and the legal status of your customer (incorporated, limited, etc.). Most of these features are useful from a sales and marketing perspective.

- ▶ **General Data: Unloading points**

  This tab is used for maintaining the unloading points along with receiving points, departments, goods receiving hours, and other information about the customer receiving process. These details are useful to your shipping department.

- ▶ **General Data: Export data**

  If your customer is involved in confidential military research and applications that are important to national security, you can maintain the usage of customer. This is important for maintaining records of your transactions with defense departments. You can maintain the usage for civilian or for military and further classify the usage to different types. These details are useful only if your customer is involved in military equipment sales and service.

- ▶ **General Data: Contact persons**

  In this section, you can maintain the contact persons with their contact details.

Now that you have taken a look at the customer master general data tabs, let's examine the Company Code tab's company code data (accounting view), whose tabs relate to account management, payment transactions, correspondence, and insurance.

Company Code Data Tabs

The customer company code data is very similar to vendor master company code data:

▶ **Company code data: Account management tab**
The most important field from the accounting perspective is the Reconciliation account, which houses the GL account that is hit when AR transactions occur against the customer master. Other fields that you can maintain here include Head Office, Cash Management Group, Interest Indicator, Previous Account Number, and Buying Group. Most of these perform the same function as in the vendor master data. However, the function is from a customer's perspective.

▶ **Company code data: Payment transactions**
This tab outlines how the customer pays: payment methods (check, wire transfer, etc.), terms of payment, tolerance groups, and house bank details. These fields are also maintained in the vendor master. Additional fields include AR Pledging Indicator and Payment Advice.

▶ **Company code data: Correspondence**
The most important section is the dunning-related information, which captures the Level of Dunning, Dunning Recipient, Last Dunned Date, Dunning Clerk, and other details. This tab also outlines how you will be corresponding with the customer accounting clerk. You can also maintain the departments to which you want to send the correspondence. Your options are sales, accounting, and legal departments. You can also choose to print your payment notices with or without cleared items.

▶ **Company code data: Insurance**
Here you can maintain the insurance policy details (policy number, amount insured, deductible, etc.) if applicable against the receivables of this customer.

Sales Area Tabs

Let's now take a look at the sales area-related tabs for a customer master:

▶ **Sales area data: Sales**
Here you can maintain the sales order-related attributes that default when you create a sales order. Some of the key attributes are Sales District, Sales

Office, Sales Group, Customer Group, and Currency. Pricing/Statistics house the attributes related to pricing procedure, including Customer Pricing Procedure, Price List, and Price Group.

▸ **Sales area data: Shipping**
In this tab, you can maintain the parameters pertaining to shipping, including the Delivering Plant, Delivery Priority, and Shipping Conditions associated with the customer. You can also define whether partial delivery is allowed for this particular customer.

Best Practice

Identify the reasons for defining the customer master. This helps significantly during the data conversion of legacy customers by cleaning up the old records.

▸ **Sales area data: Billing**
You can capture the invoicing dates relevant for this customer along with rebate and price determination settings. You can also maintain the incoterms (FOB or DEL), terms of payment, account assignment group, and taxes applicable by country and tax category.

▸ **Sales area data: Partner functions**
You can capture the various partner functions applicable for the particular customer. Some of your options are Sold to Party, Bill to Party, Payer, and Ship to Party. In addition, you can enhance the customer data to include additional tabs.

Note

The customer master is a combination of configuration and master data maintenance. Configuration can be used to define the overall strategy for master data maintenance and ongoing support.

5.3 Configuring the Vendor Master and Customer Master

In this section, you will learn how to configure and optimize a vendor master in SAP ERP Financials. You will also be introduced to best practices for configuring a vendor master. Even though most of the functionality related to a vendor master comes with a standard out of the box solution, it is important for you to understand what can be changed in the vendor master to customize it to your needs. The configuration elements for the vendor master and customer master configurations are shown in Figure 5.4. Most of these objects come preconfigured. To create a new variant, you can copy an existing object.

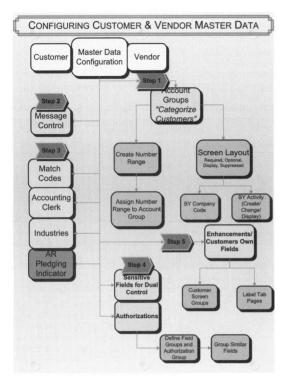

Figure 5.4 Configuring Vendor and Customer Master Data

The menu path for configuring the vendor master data is **IMG • Financial Accounting • Accounts Receivable and Accounts Payable • Vendor Accounts • Master Data**. For configuring customer master data, you can follow **IMG • Financial Accounting • Accounts Receivable and Accounts Payable • Customer Accounts• Master Data**.

Define Account Groups

The first step in configuring vendor or customer master data is to create your vendor or customer account groups. Account groups allow you to classify your vendor or customer in different groups. The menu path is **IMG • Financial Accounting • Accounts Receivable and Accounts Payable • Vendor Accounts • Master Data • Preparation for Creating Vendor Master Data • Define account groups with Screen Layouts (Vendors)**. Or, you can use Transaction OBD3. Figure 5.5 displays the screen that allows you to create vendor account groups.

Figure 5.5 Define New Account Groups

If you double click account **Group 001**, you get the screen shown in Figure 5.6.

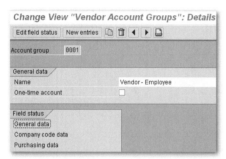

Figure 5.6 Figure 5.6 Details of a Vendor Account Group

This shows you the name of the account group. In addition, you will see the **Field status** group and the associated options: **General data**, **Company code data**, and **Purchasing data**. At this stage, a vendor account group can be defined as a **One-time account** that results in the system asking for an address at the time of recording the transaction for the vendor. To go to the next screen where the field adjustments can be done, click on one of the options in **Field status**: **General data**, **Company code data,** or **Purchasing data**, and the system takes you to the configuration setting that has already been defined for the account group.

For the customer account group, follow this path: **IMG • Financial Accounting • Accounts Receivable and Accounts Payable • Customer Accounts • Master Data • Preparations for Creating Customer Master Data • Define Account Groups with Screen Layout (Customers)**, or use Transaction OBD2. Figure 5.7 displays the basic settings pertaining to the customer account group: sold to party. You can choose to copy this and create your customer account group to customize some of these settings. Let's understand the settings:

▸ **Name**
Maintain the name of the customer account group.

▸ **One time account**

You can specify whether this account pertains to a one-time account. If you so choose, you need to enter the customer address details every time you do a transaction with this vendor.

▸ **Output determination procedure (Output determ. proc.)**

This defines the output categories and the sequence in which they appear in the document.

Remember that companies *strongly discourage* the creation of one-time customer or vendor accounts, and it is one of the most common things that auditors come hunting for. Often one-time vendors become a back-door entry to the AR ledger. Other terms for the one-time customer are dummy customer or mysterious customer. Guard yourself against the use of the one-time customer. Even if you create a one-time customer, make sure that you monitor the activity in the account carefully and religiously.

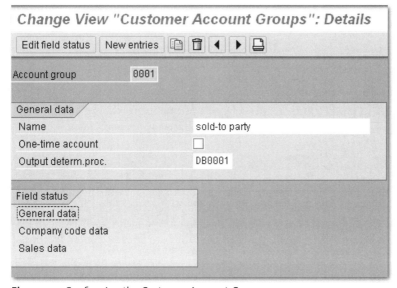

Figure 5.7 Configuring the Customer Account Group

Note
Field status settings get copied from the reference account group that was used to create the new account group.

Figure 5.8 shows the details of the **Acct group 001** along with the account management details of the company code data. You can make the following settings by each field, which is available in the vendor master:

▶ **Suppress**
Field is not visible when you go to the vendor master.

▶ **Req. Entry**
Field is a required entry when entering the vendor master.

▶ **Opt. Entry**
The field is optional and may or may-not be entered in a vendor master.

▶ **Display**
The field can only be displayed.

Figure 5.8 Defining the Screen Layout of the Vendor Master by Account Group

Best Practice
For the field status group definition (seen in Figure 5.8), leave the fields as optional unless there is a business need otherwise. Do not change a field to suppressed or display. The change typically made on this screen is to make some of the fields required for a particular account group so that users are forced to enter appropriate data in those fields.

This configuration setting allows you to tailor your account groups per your business requirements. Note that it is always a good idea to make sure that the reconciliation account is marked as a required entry. This forces the user to enter the reconciliation account every time a vendor for this account group needs to be created. Also if you have an account group for employees, make sure that you mark the **Personnel number** as **Req. entry.**

5.3.1 Define Field Status Group by Company Code and by Activity

You can also define the field status group by company code and by different transactions that can be performed on a vendor master, such as change, display, or create a vendor. The menu path for the field status group by company code is **IMG • Financial Accounting • Accounts Receivable and Accounts Payable • Vendor Accounts • Master Data • Preparation for Creating Vendor Master Data • Define Screen Layout per Company Code**.

The menu path for the field status group by activity is **IMG • Financial Accounting • Accounts Receivable and Accounts Payable • Vendor Accounts • Master Data • Preparation for Creating Vendor Master Data • Define Screen Layout per Activity (vendors)**.

Now, let's take a look at how you can create number ranges for vendor master data.

5.3.2 Define Number Ranges

Number ranges are used to assign a sequential number when you actually create a vendor master. This is to allow you to distinguish between various vendor master groups just by looking at the master record number. Figure 5.9 shows the screen for creating vendor number ranges. The menu path is **IMG • Financial Accounting • Accounts Receivable and Accounts Payable • Vendor Accounts • Master Data • Preparation for creating Vendor Master Records • Create Number Ranges for Vendor Accounts**, and the Transaction is XKN1.

Figure 5.9 Figure 5.9: Define Vendor Number ranges (Transaction XKN1)

When you click on change **Intervals** (the pencil icon), you need to add an interval to define a new number range. This will take you to the next screen as shown in Figure 5.10. If you click on the *add Interval* icon (with the plus sign) you will get a popup **Insert Interval** where you can maintain the new interval number ranges. When you click on the plus sign icon at the bottom, the number range is added. After creating the number range, you need to assign it to the account group. Customer number ranges can be similarly configured. The menu path is **IMG • Financial Accounting • Accounts Receivable and Accounts Payable • Customer Accounts • Master Data • Preparations for Creating Customer Master Data • Create Number Ranges for Customer Accounts,** and the Transaction is XDNI.

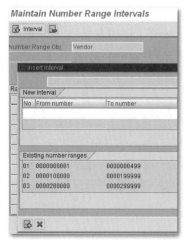

Figure 5.10 Defining a New Number Range for Vendors

5.3.3   Assign Number Ranges

Number ranges for vendor master data need to be assigned to the account group. In this step, you will learn how to assign a number range to an account group. The menu path is **IMG • Financial Accounting • Accounts Receivable and Accounts Payable • Vendor Accounts • Master Data • Preparation for creating Vendor Master Records • Assign Number Ranges to Vendor Accounts,** and the Transaction is OBAS. Figure 5.11 shows how you can assign the number range to vendor account groups. You can assign the **Number range** 01 defined in the previous step to the Account **Group 001: Vendor-Employee**.

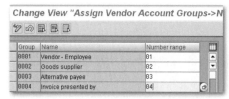

Figure 5.11 Assigning the Number Range to Vendor Account Group

5.3.4   Define Message Control

In this step, you define whether a particular message pertaining to the vendor master is a warning or an error. The system also shows the standard suggested message. The message area is F2 for customer- and vendor-related messages. The menu path is **IMG • Financial Accounting • Accounts Receivable and Accounts Payable • Vendor Accounts • Master Data • Preparation for** creating Vendor Master Records • **Change Message Control for Vendor Master Data**. This allows you to configure an error message if you need any additional controls to be implemented for the vendor master.

5.3.5 Define Match Codes

Match codes are used for searching a particular object. These help in zeroing on the correct vendor quickly with the information provided. The first step in defining a match code is to maintain search fields. After you have defined the search fields, you can maintain the match codes. For example, you can define a search field for a vendor as Name1, Name2, or City. The menu path to define search fields for match codes is **IMG • Financial Accounting • Accounts Receivable and Accounts Payable • Vendor Accounts • Master Data • Match Code • Check Search fields for Matchcodes**, and the Transaction is OBB3.

For maintaining match codes for vendors, the menu path is **IMG • Financial Accounting • Accounts Receivable and Accounts Payable • Vendor Accounts • Master Data • Match Code • Maintain Matchcodes for Vendors**, and the Transaction is OB50. The collective search help for vendors is Transaction KRED. Within that, you can define search helps that have the search fields included within them. The same logic can be used for setting up customer match codes.

5.3.6 Define Accounting Clerk

Accounting clerk is primarily put as an identifier in the vendor master to distinguish who manages the particular vendor in the AP department. These are optional definitions and are dependent on how the AP department is being managed. These can then be used later for evaluations or for correspondence. The menu path is **IMG • Financial Accounting • Accounts Receivable and Accounts Payable • Vendor Accounts • Master Data • Preparation for creating Vendor Master records • Define Accounting Clerks**.

5.3.7 Define Industries

Industry is primarily put as an identifier in the vendor master to distinguish vendors by industry and can also be used in vendor evaluations. The menu path is **IMG • Financial Accounting • Accounts Receivable and Accounts Payable • Vendor Accounts • Master Data • Preparation for creating Vendor Master records • Define Industries**.

5.3.8 Authorizations for Changing Vendor/Customer Master

The first step in the authorization definition is to define the field groups for the master records. Subsequently, you need to define group fields for vendor/customer master records as described here:

1. **Define Field Groups for Vendor Master Records**
   Define field groups for vendor master records to segregate various vendor master fields. This can be used to later control what can be changed and by whom. Use the path **IMG • Financial Accounting • Accounts Receivable and Accounts Payable • Vendor Accounts • Master Data • Preparations for Changing Vendor Master • Define Field groups for Vendor Master Records.**

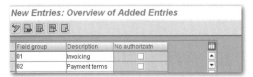

Figure 5.12 Define Field Groups for Master Records

Figure 5.12 shows the field groups that are required for categorizing vendor master records.

2. **Group Fields for Vendor Master Records**
   This is used to group together fields that have a similar level of sensitivity around them. These help in defining appropriate level of authorizations. The menu path is **IMG • Financial Accounting • Accounts Receivable and Accounts Payable • Vendor Accounts • Master Data • Preparations for Changing Vendor Master • Group Fields for Vendor Master Records.**

Figure 5.13 shows the group field definition for vendor master records. These are also assigned to the field group defined earlier.

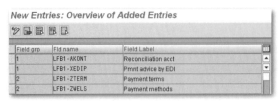

Figure 5.13 Group Fields for Vendor Master Records

3. **Sensitive Fields for Dual Control**
   This is used to have a dual control over changing specific fields of vendor master. If a field is defined as sensitive, then the vendor is blocked until

another person checks the change and confirms or rejects the change. For example, if payment terms is marked as sensitive, and somebody changes the payment terms, then the vendor is blocked until another person confirms that the change is valid. The menu path is **IMG • Financial Accounting • Accounts Receivable and Accounts Payable • Vendor Accounts • Master Data • Preparations for Creating Vendor Master • Define Sensitive Fields for Dual Control (Vendors)**. Figure 5.14 shows that you have marked payment terms as applicable for sensitive field dual control.

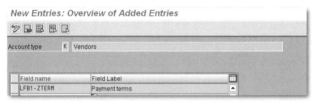

Figure 5.14 Defining Fields as Sensitive for Dual Control (Vendors)

> **Best Practice**
>
> Define payment terms, reconciliation accounts, and banking information as relevant for sensitive fields for dual control.

Most often, these settings are sufficient for you to manage your vendor master data. However, in specific instances, you can modify the vendor master data to include specific fields. This is described later in this chapter.

5.3.9 Define Customer-Specific Enhancements

This is only used if the standard settings available in the vendor master do not meet your needs. Figure 5.15 shows the vendor screen groups that have been created for some of the various industry applications. Use the menu path **IMG • Financial Accounting • Accounts Receivable and Accounts Payable • Vendor Accounts • Master Data • Preparations for Creating Vendor Master • Adoption of Customer's Own Master Data Fields • Prepare Modification Free Enhancement in Vendor Master Record**.

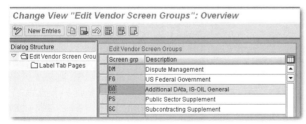

Figure 5.15 Edit Vendor Screen Groups

Here you can define your own screen groups, which then start populating in the vendor master. If you select one of the screen groups, then you need to select **Label Tab Pages** on the left side (see Figure 5.16) to see the fields and the function group that you can add to the vendor master data screen.

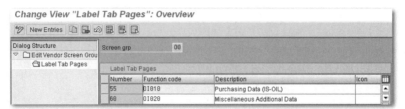

Figure 5.16 Label Tab Pages

Best Practice

Avoid extra fields in the vendor master. If it is an absolute necessity, use the functionality just described to define completely new screens. This is the suggested mechanism to enhance the vendor master. Do not develop a custom ABAP program to add a new transaction to enhance the vendor master.

5.3.10 Define Pledging Indicator

This is defined to allow customer records and their line items within a particular company code to participate in a factoring procedure. To display the factoring procedure, the same should have been activated in customer master. The menu path is **IMG • Financial Accounting • Accounts Receivable and Accounts Payable • Customer Accounts • Master Data • Preparations for Creating Customer Master Data • Define Accounts Receivable Pledging Indicator**. Figure 5.17 shows the settings that you need to make for the pledging indicator.

Figure 5.17 Defining Pledge Indicator

Note

The AR pledging status can be classified as open or still.

Next you will learn more about the global settings applicable for both AP and AR and some key concepts.

5.4 Accounts Payable and Accounts Receivable Business Transactions: Key Concepts and Global Settings

This section covers all the business transactions applicable for AP. It also describes the features and functionality available in SAP ERP to perform these business transactions.

5.4.1 Key Concepts

In this section, you will be introduced to some of the key concepts that are applicable for all the business transactions posting in SAP ERP.

Document Principle

The document principle is crucial from an audit and system sanctity perspective. Each transaction creates a unique document number. For finance, the unique number is identified by combining the document number with the company code and fiscal year. The same document number might repeat across years and company codes. Also every document number posted has a time stamp with the posting date, time, and person who posted it. Debits and credits should match for each financial transaction in GL. Financial document numbers can be displayed in finance by using Transaction FB03.

Define Document Types

Document type needs to be specified for each financial posting, or it is automatically derived based on the configuration settings. In this subsection, you will learn to define the financial document types.

Posting Keys

In SAP ERP Financials, posting keys represent debit and credit. For most transactions, posting keys get determined automatically, based on the configuration. However, it is always a good idea to understand the rules behind posting keys because they can be confusing. Some general rules for posting keys include the following:

▸ Posting keys have two digits.

▸ If the first digit is even, the posting key is a debit.

▸ If the first digit is odd, the posting key is a credit.

▸ The only exception to the preceding statements is for assets, which have 70 as debit and 75 as credit.

▸ The posting key range for vendors is 2X and 3X.

▸ The posting key range for customers is 0X and 1X

▸ The posting key for debiting a GL account is 40 and crediting a GL account is 50.

Note

With the new SAP Enjoy transactions, you do not need to know the posting keys. You just have to specify debit and credit. However, these rules are important when you are trying to post transactions using old transaction codes such as F-43 or for a data conversion program when you are combining vendors and GL accounts being loaded in the same file.

5.4.2 Global Settings

This section covers the configuration for global settings for business transactions applicable for AP. First let's look at common document settings.

Configuring Document Settings

Document settings are common across many transactions, and the configuration node is attached across most of the business transactions in the AP and AR IMG. The menu path is **IMG • Financial Accounting • Accounts Receivable and Accounts Payable • Incoming Invoices/Credit Memos • Carry Out and Check Document Settings**. You can also use **IMG • Financial Accounting • Accounts Receivable and Accounts Payable • Internal Transfer Posting • Carry Out and Check Document Settings**. So what exactly do you configure in document settings? Keep these three things in mind:

▸ Rules of posting for the document

▸ Screen design for the document

▸ Rules for changing a posted document

The document settings are based on the definition of document type. Document type and posting key configuration drives the other settings. Most of the configuration pertaining to document type and posting key is standard in AP. However, it is important to understand the details that can be changed and the impact of those changes.

> **Best Practice**
>
> To create your own document type or posting key, copy from an existing document type or posting key.

▶ **Define Document Types**

The document type needs to be specified for each financial posting, or it is automatically derived based on configuration settings. In this subsection, you will learn to define the financial document types. After you execute the transaction, you will be taken to the screen as shown in Figure 5.18. The menu path is **IMG • Financial Accounting • Accounts Receivable and Accounts Payable • Incoming Invoices/Credit Memos • Carry Out and Check Document Settings • Define Document Types**, and the Transaction is OBA7. The naming conventions for financial document types are provided here:

- ▶ **K**: Vendors
- ▶ **A**: Assets
- ▶ **D**: Customers
- ▶ **S**: Accounting Documents

Figure 5.18 Define Document Type

After you double-click, you can look at all the possible settings that are made at the document type level. Let's take a look at one of the vendor document types: KR-Vendor FI invoice shown in Figure 5.19.

Document type identifies the following parameters:

▶ **Number range associated**

The number range 19 is typically assigned to vendor invoices. So all the FI vendor invoices will begin with the numbers assigned to number range 19. Most of the companies use a 10-digit number. So your first FI invoice would be 1900000001 for a company code for a fiscal year. These numbers restart every year and for each company code.

▶ **Reversal Document Type**

This is the document type that would reverse this document type if we used reversal process (Transaction FB08).

▶ **Account Types**

The document type can be restricted by account types. Account types are assets, customers, vendor, material, or GL accounts. So you can choose that document types for assets only post to assets and GL accounts.

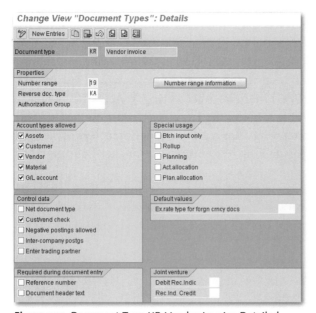

Figure 5.19 Document Type KR-Vendor Invoice Detailed

Note

You need to consider the offsetting entry that is posted in the document type. For example, in an FI AP journal entry, you should always have GL account as an allowed account type. Otherwise, you are just restricted to vendors on both debit and credit sides.

▶ **Required Fields for Entry**

You can specify **Document header text** or **Reference** as required fields by document types.

▶ **Special Usage**

The various options available here are batch input, rollup, account allocation, or plan allocation. These features are more relevant for assets and controlling functions. You can specify whether a particular document type has any of these as relevant.

▶ **Define Posting Keys**

Posting keys are used to identify whether the transaction is a debit or a credit. In the posting key (details of posting 31 are shown in Figure 5.20) configuration, you need to identify the following:

▶ Credit or debit

▶ Type of account applicable for the posting key

▶ Whether the posting key allows special GL transactions

▶ Whether the posting key allows sales-related transactions

▶ Whether the posting key is used in payment transactions

▶ The reversal posting key that should be used for reversal transactions

> **Note**
>
> It is *not* a best practice to define a new posting key. All posting keys come pre-defined in SAP ERP, and they should be sufficient. However, it is important to understand what goes on behind the posting key configuration.

The menu path is **IMG • Financial Accounting • Accounts Receivable and Accounts Payable • Incoming Invoices/Credit Memos • Carry Out and Check Document Settings • Define Posting Keys**, and the Transaction is OB41.

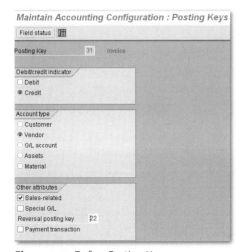

Figure 5.20 Define Posting Key

It is important to understand the field status group associated with the posting key. You can go to the **Field Status** screen (see Figure 5.21) by clicking on the **Field status** button on the upper-left side.

Figure 5.21 Field Status Group for Posting Key

Field status group controls which fields are optional, suppressed, or required for a particular posting key. This is shown in more detail in Figure 5.22.

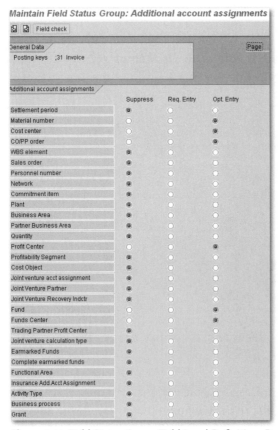

Figure 5.22 Field Status Group Field Level Definition: Required, Optional, Suppressed

It is very important that the field status groups are consistent across posting keys, movement types, and GL account master data. Sometimes you might get an error that the field status groups are inconsistent, and the message might be pointing toward the posting key. You will not get this error if you do not define your own posting key. However, you should ensure that the movement types and GL account are also synchronous as far as field status group is concerned.

Document Change Rules

Under the document change rules, you define which particular fields of a posted document can be changed and under what circumstances. So per the definition shown in Figure 5.23, document header text can be changed only if the posting period is not closed. The menu path is **IMG • Financial Accounting • Accounts Receivable and Accounts Payable • Incoming Invoices/Credit Memos • Carry Out and Check Document Settings • Document Change Rules, Document Header**.

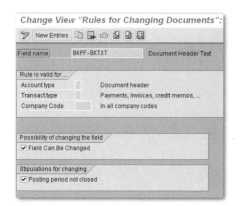

Figure 5.23 Document Change Rules Definition

Maintain Terms of Payment

These identify the terms of payment that are maintained in the vendor master. Terms of payment define the due date for payment of the vendor invoice. Most payment terms are preconfigured in AP, but it is important to understand how you can create a new one based on the settings. The menu path is **IMG • Financial Accounting • Accounts Receivable and Accounts Payable • Incoming Invoices/Credit Memos • Maintain terms of Payment**.

> **Best Practice**
>
> It is imperative to standardize the list of payment terms when you first go-live on SAP ERP. Rationalization and standardization of payment terms help simplify the configuration activities and minimize clean up efforts later.

Figure 5.24 shows the screen where you can maintain the terms of payment.

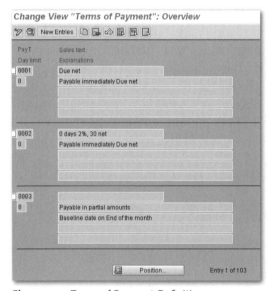

Figure 5.24 Terms of Payment Definition

> **Best Practice**
>
> To start creating a new payment terms copy a standard preconfigured payment term and start from there.

Let's take a look at the various fields that can be changed to define a new payment terms. Figure 5.25 shows the details of the payment term 112.

The key configuration fields are shown here:

▶ **Default for baseline date**
  Identifies the date used to calculate the baseline date. The payment terms shown in Figure 5.25 use the document date, which is typically the day the vendor created its invoice. So it is important to ensure that the same is captured in the document date when you are entering the vendor invoice.

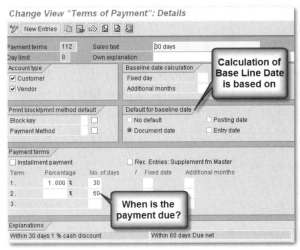

Figure 5.25 Payment terms: Definition

▶ **Number of days**

Identifies the date when the payment becomes due. For the payment terms shown in Figure 5.25, the payment is due on the 60th, and we get a 1% discount if we pay within 30 days.

▶ **Define terms of payment for installment payments**

Used to define terms of payment when the payment is split into installments/partial amounts that are paid at regular intervals. This is akin to defining group payment terms with details about individual payment terms identified for each installment. The menu path is **IMG • Financial Accounting • Accounts Receivable and Accounts Payable • Incoming Invoices/Credit Memos • Define Terms of Payment for Installment Amounts, and the Transaction is OBB9**. Figure 5.26 shows the payment terms with the installments identified

Payment terms	Inst	Percent	Pmnt term	
0009	1	30.000	0001	▲
0009	2	40.000	0001	▼
0009	3	30.000	0001	

Change View "Terms of Payment for Holdback/Retainage"

Figure 5.26 Define Terms of Payment for Installment

Figure 5.26 defines the payment terms 0009 as having three installments (1st: 30%, 2nd: 40%, 3rd: 30%) each with the payment terms of 0001.

Incoming Invoices/Credit Memo: Enjoy Transactions

From SAP R/3 4.6C onward, you can use SAP Enjoy transactions for data entry, which are much more user friendly for entering data and posting documents. Let's review steps for configuring Enjoy transactions for invoices and credit memos. First define the default document types. The menu path is **IMG • Financial Accounting • Accounts Receivable and Accounts Payable • Incoming Invoices/Credit Memos • Define Document Types for Enjoy Transactions**. Figure 5.27 shows how you can maintain the default document types by company code.

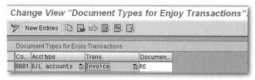

Figure 5.27 Maintain Document Type for Enjoy Transactions

You can also default tax codes for all the transactions. The menu path is **IMG • Financial Accounting • Accounts Receivable and Accounts Payable • Incoming Invoices/Credit Memos • Define Tax Codes per transaction**.

Figure 5.28 shows you the screen where you can default the tax codes by country. In the first popup, you select the country for which you are maintaining the tax codes. After you select your country, you can maintain different tax codes as relevant for invoice verification, financial accounting invoice receipt, financial accounting outgoing invoice, or relevant for all the transactions.

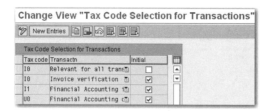

Figure 5.28 Define Tax Codes per Enjoy Transaction

If multiple tax codes are defined, then the one that is the most suitable is chosen as the default. You can also mark them as the default tax codes by clicking on the **Initial** check box. The menu path is **IMG • Financial Accounting • Accounts Receivable and Accounts Payable • Incoming Invoices/Credit Memos • Define Posting keys for Incoming Invoices/Credit Memos**.

These settings come predefined in AP and should not be changed. Let's take a look at some of the important settings relevant for incoming invoices and credit memos. Three transaction types are used for incoming invoices: **EGK (Vendor item in incoming invoice)**, **EGS (GL item in incoming invoice)**, and **EGX (Vendor item with special GL indicator)**. Figure 5.29 shows the options **EGK**, **EGS**, and **EGX** as well.

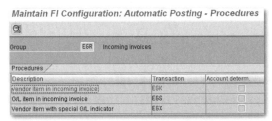

Figure 5.29 Define Posting Key for Incoming Invoices

The posting keys for EGK are 21 and 31, for EGS are 40 and 50, and for EGX, are 29 (Debit) and 39 (Credit). In the next section, you will learn how to define the configuration settings for fast entry.

Fast Entry Configuration

Fast entry screens are used if you want to enter lots of transactional data at one time. This is especially important for journal entries at month end or for a series of entries that arrive in batches and need to be performed together. The configuration is the same as defining posting keys, and the configuration pertaining to the screen layout for fast entry requires that you specify the list of fields that you want to enter when using the fast entry screen. The menu path is **IMG • Financial Accounting • Accounts Receivable and Accounts Payable • Incoming Invoices/ Credit Memo • Invoice/Credit Memo Fast Entry • Define Posting keys for Fast Entry • Define Screen Layout for GL account Items**.

Allow Negative Posting

These settings are defined to allow negative postings. The implication of permitting negative postings is that when a document is reversed, both the debit balance and the credit balance are removed from the overall balances for the particular GL account. Use the menu path **IMG • Financial Accounting • Accounts Receivable and Accounts Payable • Business transactions • Adjustment Posting/Reversal • Permit Negative Posting**.

For example, if the initial balance in GL 100000 was 0 USD, then we posted +$100 to GL 100000. If we reverse the document that posted +$100, the total debit balance reduces to zero, and the credit balance also reduces to zero, if the **Negative Posting** checkbox is selected. Otherwise, you will have $100 debit and $100 credit netting out to zero.

Define Reasons for Reversal

In this setting, you can define the reason you want to reverse a document. It is mandatory to define the reason for reversal before the system allows you to reverse the document. This is configured at client level and is shown in Figure 5.30. Follow the menu path **IMG • Financial Accounting • Accounts Receivable and Accounts Payable • Business transactions • Adjustment Posting/Reversal • Define Reason for Reversal**.

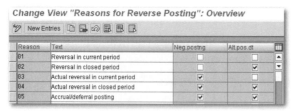

Figure 5.30 Define Reasons for Reversal

You can perform a couple of settings to be triggered by reversal reasons:

▶ **Negative Posting**
If checked, the reversal reason if chosen reduces the transaction figures, as if the transaction never happened.

▶ **Alternative posting date**
If checked, this allows you to specify an alternative posting date, which is a different date from the current fiscal period.

This completes the global settings for AP and AR. Next, you will learn settings for configuring downpayments.

5.5 Downpayments

Downpayments are used in SAP ERP to record the payment of advance or receipt of advance. Advance should be treated as an asset. However, in the vendor master or customer master, you can define only one reconciliation account. Using the downpayment functionality of SAP ERP, you can define an alternative reconciliation account, which can be mapped to assets or liabilities depending on whether you made the advance or received the advance. Downpayment functionality is mapped in SAP using the special GL indicator. This should not be confused with the special purpose ledger, which will be covered in Chapter 11. In this section, you will learn how you can maintain a subledger for advances for both vendors and customers using special GL indicators.

5.5.1 Downpayments Made—Accounts Payable

These are used to record advance payments that are given to vendors prior to your receiving the goods or services. The process of giving an advance can be done in two steps or in a single step. In the two-step process, the admin or AP clerk requests the downpayment or advance (Transaction: F-47), and the manager approves the downpayment or advance (Transaction: F-48).

Downpayment requests (F-47) create a noted item without any accounting. It is possible to route the advance request via workflow to the manager. Downpayment approvals (F-48) create a posting document that hits the appropriate reconciliation account defined in the configuration for alternative reconciliation account. In the one-step process, only F-48 is used to post the advance directly to accounting.

Downpayments are recorded in AP as a special GL indicator. Different types of advances can be configured as different special GL Indicators. The accounting entry that happens at the time of posting a downpayment made are the following:

▶ Dr Vendor with Special GL Indicator: Alternative reconciliation account.

▶ Cr Bank: GL account.

Guarantees

Guarantees made are shown in the notes to the balance sheet and are off-balance sheet items. Guarantees received, however, are not displayed on the balance sheet. The AP module allows you to track guarantees made and received. The system automatically posts the guarantee to the vendor account and the offset to a clearing account that has already been configured. This posting is made using statistical posting (Transaction F-55).

Bills of Exchange

Bills of exchange are used to record off-balance sheet items that are recorded in the balance sheet as noted items. These are cleared when the actual payment is made to clear off these liabilities. Bills of exchange are also recorded as special GL indicators in AP. Transaction F-40 is used for bill of exchange payment.

5.5.2 Downpayment Received: Accounts Receivable

These are used to record advance payments that are received from customers prior to you shipping the goods or performing the services. These are typically required in cases where the credit rating for the customer is not good. Downpayments are typically received for a partial invoice amount. The customer will pay the difference between the invoice and the advance when the customer receives the goods followed by your invoice.

The process of giving an advance can be either a two-step or single-step process. In the two-step process, the admin/AP clerk requests the recording of the advance (Transaction F-37), and the manager approves the advance (Transaction F-29). The downpayment request (F-37) creates a noted item without any accounting. It is possible to route the advance via workflow to the manager. The downpayment approval (F-29) creates a posting document that hits the appropriate reconciliation account defined in the configuration for the alternative reconciliation account. In the one-step process, only F-29 is used to post the advance. Downpayments are recorded in AR as special GL Indicators. Different types of advances can be configured as different special GL Indicators. The accounting entry to record a downpayment received is the following:

▶ Dr Bank/Cash

▶ Cr Customer with Special GL Indicator

5.5.3 Configuring Downpayments

This subsection covers the configuration pertaining to advances. A diagram illustrating the configuration process for downpayments made is shown in Figure 5.31.

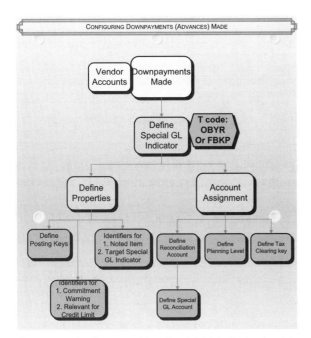

Figure 5.31 Configuring a New Special GL Indicator for Advances

The configuration process for downpayments is similar for customers. The only change you need to make is choosing the account type D instead of K. The menu path is **IMG • Financial Accounting • Accounts Receivable and Accounts Payable • Business Transactions • Define Alternative Reconciliation account for Downpayments**. You can also use the Transactions OBYR or FBKP. On executing Transaction OBYR, the screen in Figure 5.32 appears.

Maintain Accounting Configuration : Special G/L - List

Acct type	Sp.G/L	Sp.G/L ind	Description
K	A	Dwn pmt	Down payment on current assets
K	B	Financi	Financial assets down payment
K	F	Pmt req	Down payment request
K	H	Securit	Security deposit
K	I	Dwn pmt	Intangible asset down payment
K	M	Dwn pmt	Tangible asset down payment
K	O	Amortiz	Amortization down payment
K	V	Dwn pmt	Stocks down payment

Figure 5.32 Defining a new Special GL Indicator

AP has many predefined downpayments in the system. You can use those to create your own special GL indicators. Click on *New* to create a new special GL indicator. The screen shown in Figure 5.33 appears.

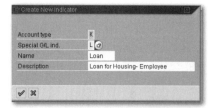

Figure 5.33 Defining a New Special GL Indicator

You need to make sure that the account type is **K** for vendor downpayments. Enter the special GL indicator that you want to define along with the description of the special GL indicator. When you are done, press the Enter key, which will take you to the screen shown in Figure 5.34. Here you need to maintain the properties of the special GL indicators as described here:

▸ **Noted items**
Check this box, if you are defining a special GL indicator as a noted item.

▸ **Relevant to credit limit**
Check this box if the downpayments recorded in this special GL indicator need to be considered for determining the overall credit limit of the customer. This is primarily relevant for customers.

▸ **Commitments warning**
This is checked if you need to get a warning when the budget for the downpayment is exceeded.

▸ **Target special GL indicator**
Here you need to maintain the downpayment request indicator (F) along with the special GL indicator so that downpayment request can be converted to a downpayment.

▸ **Posting key**
Enter the text for the downpayment postings (29 for debit and 39 for credit).

▸ **Special GL transaction types**
When you define the special GL transaction type as **Downpayment/ downpayment request**, the postings made to the special GL appear in the purchase order history. **Bill of exchange/Bill request** is used to capture the special GL indicators that capture bills of exchanges. If you have any other type of special GL indicators that do not fall in this category, you need to choose **Others**.

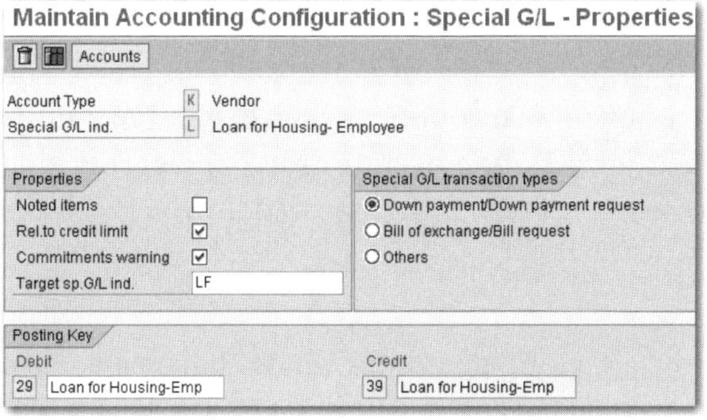

Figure 5.34 Maintaining Special GL Properties

Clicking on **Accounts** takes you to the account assignment configuration as shown in Figure 5.35.

Figure 5.35 Defining Reconciliation Account, Special GL Account, Planning Level, and Input Tax Clearing Key

Here you need to maintain the GL accounts for special GL indicators as described here:

▸ **Reconciliation account**
This is the GL account that is maintained in the vendor master for AP.

▸ **Special GL account**
This is the GL account to which you want the postings to go if you use this special GL indicator.

▸ **Planning level**
This is the planning level key that is used to map the special GL indicator to cash management. Typically, FF or FK is used in here.

▸ **Input tax clearing**
This is the account determination key that is used to map the clearing of the tax on downpayments. The key entered here can be used to automatically determine the tax clearing account. You can also use this to map multiple tax clearing accounts for multiple downpayment accounts.

You will learn more about the tax clearing in the next step.

5.5.4 Defining Tax Clearing Account for Downpayments

Here you will configure tax clearing accounts for downpayments. The menu path is **IMG • Financial Accounting • Accounts Receivable and Accounts Payable • Business Transactions • Define Account for Tax Clearing**, and the Transaction is OBXB. When you execute the transaction, you reach the screen shown in Figure 5.36.

Maintain FI Configuration: Automatic Posting - Procedures

Group   ANZ   Down payments

Procedures

Description	Transaction	Account determ.
Down payment bank posting	ANB	☐
Down Payment Requests	ANF	☐
Down payments	ANZ	☐
Customer down payment transfer posting	AUD	☐
Vendor down payment transfer posting	AUK	☐
Output tax clearing on down payments	MVA	☑
Input tax clearing on down payments	VVA	☑

Figure 5.36 Defining Tax Clearing on Downpayments

For vendor downpayments, select Transaction VVA, which represents input tax clearing. You will reach the next screen as shown in Figure 5.37 where you need to maintain the input tax clearing identifier (this was shown in Figure 5.35 as well) and the GL account.

Maintain FI Configuration: Automatic Posting - Accounts

◀ ▶ ☐ ☐ ☐   Posting Key   👤 Procedures   Rules

Chart of Accounts   CANA   Chart of accounts - North America
Transaction   VVA   Input tax clearing on down payments

Account assignment

Input tax cl...	Account

Figure 5.37 Defining Input Tax Clearing Account on Downpayments

The posting keys for input tax clearing are 40 (debit) and 50 (credit).

5.5.5 Integration of Downpayments with Logistics

The downpayment made can appear in the purchase order history via the following steps:

1. Ensure that the field status group of the alternative reconciliation account has purchase order and purchase order item as mandatory. This ensures that you have the purchase order to be available for input when you are giving the advance.

▸ This needs to be done in GL master data.

▸ You can also make the purchase order optional to achieve the desired result if there are situations where the purchase order is not available.

2. After you post the downpayment, it appears in the purchase order history as transaction type DPyt. This simple step is very useful because it allows you to generate various reports, look at the purchase order, and find out the net value that you need to pay before making your payment.

5.5.6 Downpayment Chains

This is a new feature from SAP R/3 4.7 onward. The downpayment chain is designed for long-term contracts particularly in the construction industry and groups together invoice and payment transactions carried out by two business partners. The credit side downpayment chain is used for subcontractors or vendors, whereas the debit side downpayment chain is used for customers. Because this is a new functionality from release 4.7 onward, the menu path is not in AP. The menu path is **SAP Menu • Accounting • Financial Accounting • Additional Functions • Down Payment Chains — Debit-Side Down Payment Chains • Credit-Side Down Payment Chains**, and the Transactions are SAPPCE/DPCD01/SAPPCE/DPCK01.

5.5.7 Configuring Downpayment Chains

Figure 5.38 shows you the process of configuring downpayment chains. You can use the menu path **IMG • Accounting • Financial Accounting (new) • Accounts Receivable and Accounts Payable • Business Transactions • Debit-Side and Credit-Side Down Payment Chains**.

Number Range

The first step in configuring a downpayment chain is to create a number range. The number range needs to be created by company code. Follow the menu path **IMG • Accounting • Financial Accounting (new) • Accounts Receivable and Accounts Payable • Business Transactions • Debit-Side and Credit-Side Down Payment Chains • Define Number Range Intervals**, or execute the Transaction SAPPPCE/DPCNKR.

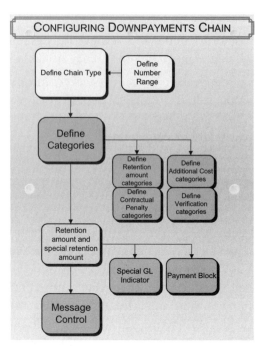

Figure 5.38 Configuring Downpayment Chain Process Flow

Chain Type

The chain type identifies the various settings related to the downpayment chains (see Figure 5.39):

▶ **Account Type**
Whether it is a debit (vendor) or credit (customer) downpayment chain.

▶ **Number Range**
This is assigned to the chain type.

▶ **Active Chain Type**
If you set this indicator, then you can use the chain type to create new downpayment chains.

▶ **Initial Status Released**
Initial status that the system should set when you create a downpayment chain.

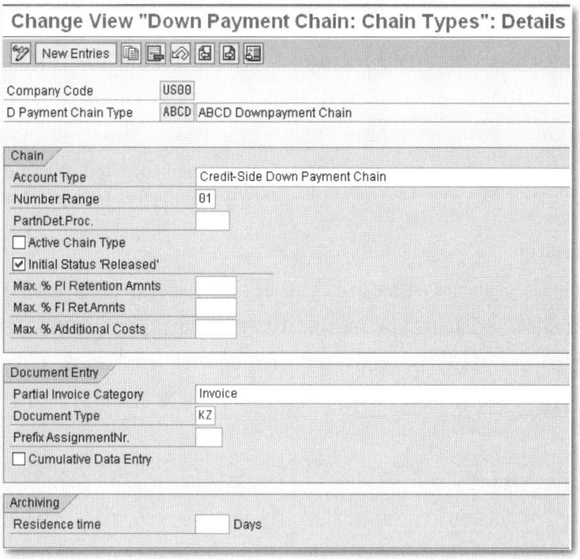

Figure 5.39 Configuring a New Downpayment Chain Type

Following are the maximum percentage for which security retention amounts, guarantee retention amounts, and additional costs can be created:

▸ **Partial Invoice Category**
Whether the partial invoices need to be posted as downpayment requests or invoices.

▸ **Cumulative Data Entry**
Where data entry is cumulative or the difference from the previous accounting document is added on.

▸ **PartnDet.Proc.**
Partner determination procedure used for the downpayment chain.

▸ **Document Type**
This is valid for the accounting documents to control document entry.

▸ **Prefix AssignmentNr.**
This is for reservation of the assignment number used.

▸ **Residence time**
After what residence time downpayment chains can be archived at the earliest.

In addition you need to define the various categories:

▶ **Retention Amount Categories**

This is required if you need to withhold money for security according to the contract terms and conditions. Retention amount categories allow you to categorize the percentage reduction that you will be making. However, you need to specify whether the retention category is applicable for partial invoice or final invoices.

▶ **Additional Cost Categories**

This allows you to define the GL account and the account type (vendor or customer), which would be used for capturing any additional costs pertaining to utilities in the project. This is created uniquely for one company code, and you need to identify the account type whether it is for vendor or for customer.

▶ **Contractual Penalty Categories**

This allows you to configure the contractual penalty category for a particular company code, which can then be maintained in the contract written with the vendor or customer.

▶ **Verification Categories**

This allows you to capture the different documentation requirements that must be met by a particular date. For example, a subcontractor must submit a quality certificate, a registration paper, and a bonded copy of a specific regulatory requirement by a certain date. These can then be a prerequisite to initiate any payment to the contractor by maintaining these conditions in the contract.

You can also specify the following additional settings:

▶ **Payment Block**

You can set up by company code and account type (vendor or customer) which payment block should be set up for the partial invoice and for the final invoice and corrections.

▶ **Special GL definition for retention amount and special retention amount**:

You can identify by company code and account type (vendor or customer), which special GL accounts need to be used for retention amounts and special retention amounts. This allows you to hit the correct special GL transaction.

▶ **Message Control**

You can use the message area /SAPPCE/DPCM1 to configure warning, error, or information messages for the downpayment chain's standard messages.

5.6 Processing Invoices in Accounts Payable and Accounts Receivable

In this section, you will learn about the business processing of invoices in AP and AR.

5.6.1 Invoicing Transactions and Clearing in Accounts Payable

Let's first look at how to invoice transactions and clear them in AP. Then we will look at the same in AR. Let's start with incoming invoices in AP.

Incoming Invoices

Incoming AP invoices can be created only in AP or created with reference to a MM document. For SAP ERP Financials invoices, follow the menu path **SAP menu • Accounting • Financial accounting • Accounts payable • Document entry • Invoice/Invoice-general**. You can also use Transactions FB60/F-43. For MM invoices, follow the path **SAP menu • Materials Management • Logistics Invoice Verification • Document entry • Enter Invoice/Park Invoice,** or use Transactions MIRO/MIR7.

As in the case of downpayment, invoice creation, posting can be a two-step process. We can park (noted item) an invoice and then post it. Parking a document does not create any accounting document. Posting updates the account balances.

> **Note**
>
> The old transaction code for invoice verification prior to release 4.6C was MRHR.

Optimizing Incoming invoices Using Logistics Invoice Verification

You can process an incoming invoice using logistics invoice verification in multiple ways. The most common being online validation of invoices by looking at the goods receipt, purchase order, and the physical invoice sent by the vendor. However, multiple automatic settlement processes are available in SAP ERP that allow you to reduce the overall reconciliation effort and shorten your processing time:

1. **Evaluated receipt settlement (ERS)**
   In this process, you do not receive the physical invoice but pay based on the goods receipt done in your system per the terms and conditions of the purchase order. The onus of reconciliation is on vendor.

2. **Consignment and pipeline settlement**
   This is typically applicable for utilities such as electricity, when you pay based on the withdrawals made in the system. The vendor receives a copy of the settlement. Again, the onus of reconciliation is on the vendor.

3. **Invoicing plan**
   Based on the dates scheduled in the purchase order, the system automatically creates the invoice and then subsequent payment is made without the vendor sending an invoice.

4. **Revaluation**
   Sometimes, some of the price changes are effective retrospectively. You can use the revaluation process to determine the difference between the old paid invoices and the effect of the new price and then pay the same to the vendor.

Open Item Clearing

Open item clearing can be done by either displaying the list of open items for the vendor or by using Transaction F-44. This helps in identifying open vendor line items that need to be either paid (credit balances) or adjusted (debit balances) against future payments. Follow **SAP Menu • Accounting • Financial Accounting • Accounts Payable • Account • Clear**, or use Transaction F-44.

Internal Transfer Posting

Internal transfer posting is used to correct errors or to transfer an amount from one vendor to another or to a GL account. It has two transactions: internal transfer posting with clearing (Transaction F-51) or internal transfer posting without clearing (Transaction F-42). In F-51, the open item is cleared against the new item created by this transaction. However, in F-42, the new item is created that exactly offsets the previous transaction but still appears in the list of open items. Use the menu path **SAP Menu • Accounting • Financial Accounting • Accounts Payable • Document Entry • Other • Transfer with clearing/ Transfer Without Clearing**, or use Transactions F-51/F-42.

5.6.2 Accounts Receivable Outgoing Invoices and Clearing

This section covers all of the business transactions applicable for AR and describes the features and functionality available in these business transactions.

Outgoing Invoices

Outgoing AR invoices can be created in AR either solely in FI or with reference to a SD logistics document. For FI, you can follow the path **SAP Menu • Accounting • Financial accounting • Accounts Receivable • Document Entry • Invoice,** or use the Transactions FB70/F-22. For SD, follow the path Sales and Distribution Document **SAP Menu • Logistics • Sales and Distribution • Billing • Billing Document • Create, or use Transaction VF01**.

Open Item Clearing

Open item clearing can be done by either displaying the list of open items for the customer or by using Transaction F-32. This helps in identifying open customer line items that need to be either paid (credit balances) or adjusted (debit balances) against future payments. Follow **SAP Menu • Accounting • Financial accounting • Accounts Receivable • Account • Clear,** or use Transaction F-32.

Internal Transfer Posting

Internal transfer posting is used to correct errors or to transfer an amount from one customer to another or to a GL account (for recognizing bad debt and transferring to a loss account). It has two variants: internal transfer posting with clearing (Transaction F-30) or internal transfer posting without clearing (Transaction F-21). In F-30, the open item is cleared against the new item created by this transaction. However, in F-21, the new item is created that exactly offsets the previous transaction but still appears in the list of open items. The menu path is **SAP Menu • Accounting • Financial accounting • Accounts Receivable • Document Entry • Other • Transfer without clearing/ Transfer with clearing**, and the Transactions are F-21/F-30.

Incoming Payments

This is the process of receiving a payment and applying it against a group of invoices submitted to the customer. You can use the menu path **SAP Menu •**

Accounting • Financial Accounting • Accounts Receivable • Document Entry • Incoming Payment or Transaction F-28.

5.7 Processing Outgoing Payments

Outgoing payments can be managed in SAP ERP to get you the maximum discounts from your vendors. Outgoing payments denotes the process of making a payment by combining a group of invoices for the same vendor. You have many choices in making your payment by due date in SAP ERP. You can make payments manually or via a payment run.

Manual Payment

In manual outgoing payments, the SAP ERP Financials system allows you to select the vendor open items (invoices and credit memos) that have not yet been paid. Depending on the payment method, either an immediate need check can be printed, or you can do a direct deposit to the bank. The menu path is **Accounting • Financial Accounting • Accounts Payable • Document Entry • Outgoing payment • Post/Post + print forms**. The Transactions are F-53/F-58.

Payment Run

The menu path for payment runs is **Accounting • Financial Accounting • Accounts Payable • Periodic processing • Payments/ Schedule Payment Program Periodically**, and the Transactions are F110/F110S. Payment runs allow you to manage the process of making payments via three simple steps:

1. **Create a payment proposal**
   This identifies the list of vendors, the payment methods, and the date when the payment run will be executed.

2. **Execute the payment run**
   Based on the proposal list, the system clears the open items, creating payment clearing documents in the process.

3. **Generation of payment transfer method**
   This step generates the check/bank transfer and also prints the remittance.

The prerequisite for defining the outgoing payment is the setup of the house bank.

Define House Banks

House banks need to be configured prior to defining settings for outgoing payments. House banks are essentially master data that must be created in the banking module. You will learn more about bank accounting in Chapter 6. The menu path for defining house banks is **IMG • Financial Accounting • Bank Accounting • Bank Accounts • Define House Banks**, and the Transaction is FI12.

Figure 5.40 shows the details required to create a house bank. You need to enter the address and other details related to the bank as well. In addition, you can define the account ID and the general account tied to the account.

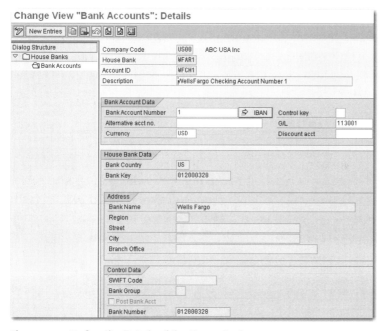

Figure 5.40 Define the Details of the House Bank:

You can customize your outgoing payments according to the following broad structure:

▶ **Global Settings**

The key settings here pertain to the definition of GL accounts, posting keys for clearing, and payment block reasons.

▶ **Manual Outgoing Payments**

These include tolerance definition, reason codes, cross-company code manual payments, and line layout related settings.

▶ **Automatic Outgoing Payments**

Automatic outgoing payments settings pertain to payment programs and their configurations.

5.7.1 Configuring Outgoing Payments: Global Settings

Various GL accounts need to be set up for discounts, differences, and clearing transactions. The menu path is **IMG • Financial Accounting • Accounts Receivable and Accounts Payable • Business transactions • Outgoing payments • Outgoing Payments Global Settings**.

The configuration pertaining to defining GL accounts for outgoing payments is shown in Figure 5.41. The figure shows the menu path, the transaction code, and the parameters by which you can maintain the GL accounts for the particular activity.

Outgoing Payments: Outgoing Payments Global Settings					
Menu path	T Code	Transaction Key	Parameters		
Define Accounts for Cash Discount Taken (actually received cash discount)	OBXU	SKE	Chart of Accounts	Tax Code	
Define Accounts for Lost Cash Discount (Difference between Cash Discount Calculated and the Discount actually claimed)	OBXV	VSK	Chart of Accounts	Tax Code	
Define Accounts for Overpayments/ Underpayments (Payment Difference by Reason Code)	OBXL	ZDI	Chart of Accounts	Tax Code	Reason Codes
Define Accounts for Exchange Rate Differences	OB09	None	Chart of Accounts	General Ledger Account	Currency and Currency Type
Define accounts for Rounding Difference	OB00	RDF	Chart of Accounts		
Define accounts for Payment differences with alternative currency	OBXO	KDW	Chart of Accounts	Tax Code	
Define Clearing accounts for Payment difference with Alternative Currency	OBXQ	KDZ	Chart of Accounts	General Modification	

Figure 5.41 Outgoing Payments GL Account Determination

Automatic Postings for Payment Program and Payment Request

In this section, you can define the posting keys for the payment program per the four scenarios: Bank posting, bill of exchange posting, bank bill liability, and payment request. These settings are shown in Figure 5.42.

Automatic postings for Payment Program and Payment Request				
Description	Transaction Code	Transaction Key	Posting key-Debit	Posting key-Credit
Payment program: Bank posting	OBXC	ZBA	40	50
Payt program: Bill of exchange/bill of payment request	OBXC	ZWE	29	39
Payt program: Bank Bill Liability	OBXC	ZWO	40	50
Payment Request	OBXP	ZAF	29	39

Figure 5.42 Automatic Posting Key Determination

The next important configuration step in global settings is the definition of payment block reasons.

Defining Payment Block Reasons

Payment block reasons are used to identify the reasons for blocking an invoice for payment. It is important for your organization to know the reasons that a particular payment might be blocked. Each organization might block payments for various reasons, such as nondelivery of items, noncompliance with certain conditions, and so on. In this step, you can configure your own payment block reasons. The menu path to follow is **IMG • Financial Accounting • Accounts Receivable and Accounts Payable • Business transactions • Outgoing Payments • Outgoing Payments Global Settings • Payment Block Reasons • Define Payment Block Reasons.** Figure 5.43 shows the payment block reasons that can be defined.

Change View "Payment Block Reasons": Overview

New Entries

Block ind.	Description	Change in pmnt prop.	Manual payments block	Not changeable
	Free for payment	☐	☐	☐
*	Skip account	☐	☐	☐
A	Blocked- manual paym	☐	☐	☐
B	Blocked for payment	☐	☐	☐
N	Postprocess inc.pmnt	☐	☐	☐
P	Payment request	☐	☐	☐
R	Invoice verification	☐	☐	☐
V	Payment clearing	☐	☐	☐
X	Goods Missing	☐	☐	☐
Z	Missing Goods	☐	☐	☐

Figure 5.43 Defining Payment Block Reasons

The following settings can be made in payment block reasons:

▶ **Change in payment proposal**
If you set this flag, then you are allowed to change or set this payment block reason during payment proposal.

▶ **Manual payments block**
This ensures that the vendor line items blocked with this payment block cannot be paid by manual entry of outgoing payments.

▶ **Not changeable**
Setting this flag disallows changing the payment block flag within a dialog transaction. This setting is especially relevant when you implement work-flow and do not want the block to be manually deleted by the users by going to document change.

These three settings are not applicable for contract AR and AP.

5.7.2 Configuring Outgoing Payments: Manual Payment

In this section, you will learn the three key configurations for manual out-going payments:

▶ Defining tolerance for vendors

▶ Defining reason codes

▶ Preparing cross company code manual payments

Define Tolerances for Vendors

These are only defined if you want to allow any variation between what you pay and what you receive on the invoice from the vendor. Some companies do not set these up because it allows you to take a look at why there are differences. The menu path is **IMG • Financial Accounting • Accounts Receivable and Accounts Payable • Business transactions • Outgoing payments • Manual Outgoing Payments • Define Tolerances (Vendors)**. However, you can choose to define these by company code if required as shown in Figure 5.44. You need to define the tolerance group name, the per-mitted percentage differences, and the absolute currency amount.

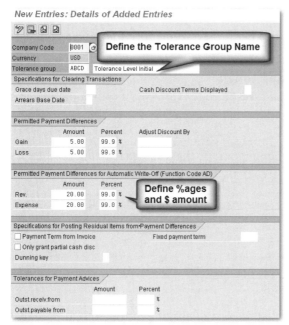

New Entries: Details of Added Entries

Company Code 0001
Currency USD
Tolerance group ABCD   Tolerance Level Initial

Define the Tolerance Group Name

Specifications for Clearing Transactions
Grace days due date   Cash Discount Terms Displayed
Arrears Base Date

Permitted Payment Differences
                Amount   Percent   Adjust Discount By
Gain   5.00   99.9 %
Loss   5.00   99.9 %

Permitted Payment Differences for Automatic Write-Off (Function Code AD)
                Amount   Percent
Rev.   20.00   99.0 %   **Define %ages and $ amount**
Expense   20.00   99.0 %

Specifications for Posting Residual Items from Payment Differences
☐ Payment Term from Invoice   Fixed payment term
☐ Only grant partial cash disc
Dunning key

Tolerances for Payment Advices
                Amount   Percent
Outst.receiv.from   %
Outst.payable from   %

Figure 5.44 Define Tolerance Groups for Vendors

Define Reason Codes:

Reason codes are used to define the reason you are overpaying or underpaying an invoice. Follow the path **IMG • Financial Accounting • Accounts Receivable and Accounts Payable • Business transactions • Outgoing payments • Manual Outgoing Payments • Overpayment/Underpayment • Define Reason Codes (Manual Outgoing Payments)**. Figure 5.45 shows the process of creating a reason code and making the necessary settings.

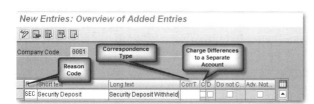

New Entries: Overview of Added Entries

Company Code 0001   Correspondence Type   Charge Differences to a Separate Account

Reason Code

R...	Short text	Long text	CorrT	C/D	Do not C...	Adv. Not...	
SEC	Security Deposit	Security Deposit Withheld		☐☐	☐	☐	▲

Figure 5.45 Define Reason Codes

Although the reason code is extremely important when optimizing your implementation, it is a configuration step most seem to miss. Take the time to carefully review this subsection. The key settings for a reason codes are listed here:

- ▶ **Reason Code**

  This is a three-digit identifier that is used to identify the reason code during payment processing.

- ▶ **Reason Code Short Text and Long Text**

  This is the text describing the reason code. The reason code long text gets copied to the residual line item.

- ▶ **Correspondence type**

  CorrT identifies the correspondence type that can be created with the specific reason code in case there are payment differences.

- ▶ **Charge off Mechanism (C)**

  This is the key to indicate that the difference will be charged off via a separate account.

- ▶ **Disputed (D)**

  Indicating whether the item is disputed.

- ▶ **Do not Copy**

  This can be used to define that the text does not get copied to the residual item.

Next you will learn how to prepare cross-company code clearing procedures.

Prepare Cross-Company Code Manual Payments

In this step, you can define the relationship of paying company codes and sending company codes. AUSGZAHL stands for outgoing payments and can be selected from a dropdown menu. The menu path is **IMG • Financial Accounting • Accounts Receivable and Accounts Payable • Business transactions • Outgoing payments • Manual Outgoing Payments • Prepare Cross-Company Code Manual Payments**. Figure 5.46 shows how you can set up cross-company codes for manual outgoing payments.

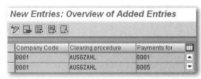

New Entries: Overview of Added Entries

Company Code	Clearing procedure	Payments for	
0001	AUSGZAHL	0001	▲
0001	AUSGZAHL	0005	▼

Figure 5.46 Defining Cross-Company Code Manual Payments

This **Company Code** in column 1 is the paying company code, and the company code in column 3 **Payments for** is the sending company code.

5.7.3 Configuring Outgoing Payments: Automatic Payments

In this section, you will learn to configure the key elements of automatic outgoing payments. Automatic outgoing payments are executed in AP by the payment run. Follow the menu path **IMG • Financial Accounting • Accounts Receivable and Accounts Payable • Business transactions • Outgoing payments • Automatic Outgoing Payments**.

Define Payment Method/Bank Selection for Payment Program

Figure 5.47 shows you the screen for the payment method and bank selection for the payment program. To set up company codes for payment transactions, use the menu path **IMG • Financial Accounting • Accounts Receivable and Accounts Payable • Business transactions • Outgoing payments • Automatic Outgoing Payments • Payment Method/Bank Selection for Payment Program • Set Up All Company Codes for Payment Transactions**, or Transaction OBVU.

Figure 5.47 Defining Payment Method and Bank Selection

Tip

A useful transaction code to access all the important substeps to configure payment method/bank selection is FBZP. After you execute it, you reach the submenus shown in Figure 5.47.

When you click on **All company codes**, you can define all of the company codes that are relevant for payment. Figure 5.48 shows how you can create a company code relevant for payment processing. Let's review these settings now:

▶ **Company Code**
Enter the company code that you want to be relevant for payment.

▶ **Sending and Paying company code**
These identify the sending and paying company codes for the identified company code in the previous step.

▶ **Separate payment per business area**
This allows you to separate the clearing of open items by business areas.

▶ **Payment method supplement (Pyt meth suppl)**
Check this box if you want to use payment method supplements. Payment method supplements are used to group payments together.

Figure 5.48 Payment Company Code and Sending Company Code

▶ **Cash discount and tolerance**
Here you can define the number of tolerance days (**Tolerance days for payable**) by which the payment can exceed the due date. You can also specify the lower limit of the percentage rate (**Outgoing pmt with cash disc. from**) with a discount deduction.

▶ **Maximum cash discount (Max. cash discount)**
This identifier always deducts the maximum cash discount applicable.

▶ **Sp. GL transactions to be paid**
Special GL indicators to be paid can be maintained for vendors and customers.

▶ **Sp. GL trans. for exception list**

Also the special GL indicators that should not be paid can be maintained in the exception list.

In the next section, you will maintain the parameters for the paying company code.

Set Up Paying Company Codes for Payment Transactions

Figure 5.49 shows the various settings that can be made when configuring the paying company code. The menu path is **IMG • Financial Accounting • Accounts Receivable and Accounts Payable • Business transactions • Outgoing payments • Automatic Outgoing Payments • Payment Method/Bank Selection for Payment Program • Set Up Paying Company Codes for Payment Transactions**.

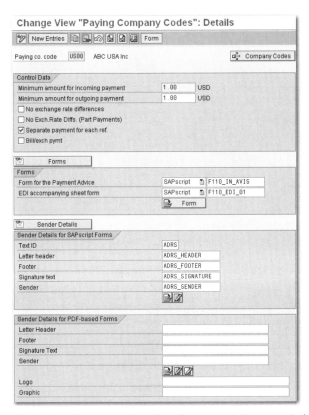

Figure 5.49 Figure 5.49: Detailing the Payment Company Code

One payment company code can pay multiple sending company codes. The key parameters to be configured are minimum amounts for incoming and outgoing payments. You can use the checkboxes to ensure that exchange rate differences are not applicable for the company code. Use the **Separate payment for each reference** checkbox to cut multiple checks for different invoices. The vendor invoice number is typically captured in the reference field. You can also customize your forms for the payment advice as well as the EDI communication that accompanies the payment. In addition, you can identify the sender details for SAPscript forms and PDF-based forms as shown in Figure 5.49.

Set Up Payment Methods Per Country for Payment Transactions

Figure 5.50 shows the payment method **C** that has been maintained for country USA. You can use the menu path **IMG • Financial Accounting • Accounts Receivable and Accounts Payable • Business transactions • Outgoing payments • Automatic Outgoing Payments • Payment Method/Bank Selection for Payment Program • Set Up Payment Methods per Country for Payment Transactions**.

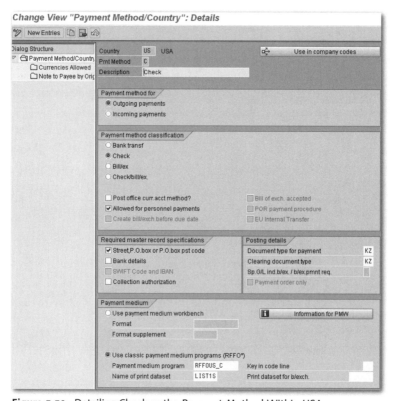

Figure 5.50 Detailing Check as the Payment Method Within USA

Note that the payment method identifies whether it is for outgoing or incoming payment. It can also be classified into a bank transfer, check, or a bill of exchange. Also you can tie the payment method to the document type for payment, clearing document type, and the master data specifications needed for the payment method.

Note that the payment medium program for check is *RFFOUS_C*, and the **Document type for payment** and **Clearing document type** is KZ. You can also specify the currencies allowed for a country and payment method by selecting the **Payment Method** and clicking on **Currencies Allowed**. This assignment is shown in Figure 5.51

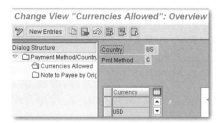

Figure 5.51 Defining Currencies per Payment Method and Country

Configure Payment Methods by Company Code

Figure 5.52 shows the settings that can be made to configure payment methods by company code. The menu path is **IMG • Financial Accounting• Accounts Receivable and Accounts Payable• Business transactions • Outgoing payments • Automatic Outgoing Payments • Payment Method/Bank Selection for Payment Program • Set Up Payment Methods per Company Code for Payment Transactions**.

Here you can define by company code and payment method the amount limits, the form that should be mapped to the payment method, and the company code. Multiple payment methods can be defined by making new entries in this screen.

Now that you have learned how to create a house bank, let's go back to completing the configuration for automatic payments. The next step is to configure the bank determination.

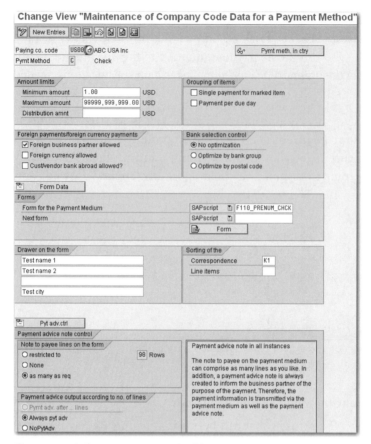

Figure 5.52 Defining Payment Method by Company Code

5.7.4 Bank Determination

Figures 5.53 to 5.57 shows the various settings that need to be made to map the bank to the automatic payment transactions. Figure 5.53 shows the ranking order of the payment method and house bank combination. Here you have maintained the Ranking Order of payment method **(P...)** along with the currency **(Crcy)**, **Rank. Order**, and house bank **(House Bk)**. You can follow the menu path **IMG • Financial Accounting • Accounts Receivable and Accounts Payable • Business transactions • Outgoing payments • Automatic Outgoing Payments • Payment Method/Bank Selection for Payment Program • Set Up Bank Determination for Payment Transactions**.

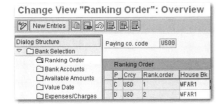

Figure 5.53 Defining the Ranking Order for Payment Method and House Bank

Figure 5.54 shows the bank accounts and the payment methods mapped by the paying company code.

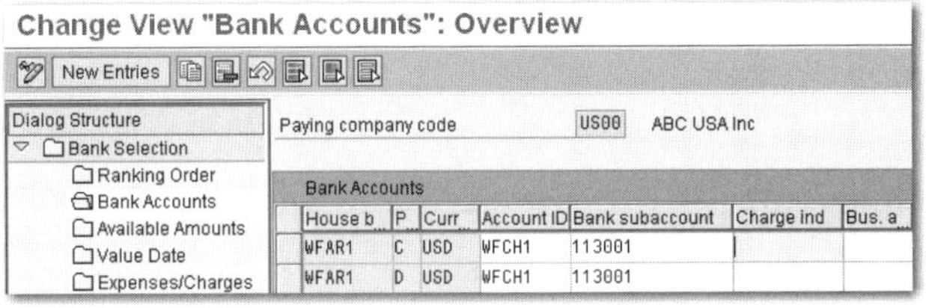

Change View "Bank Accounts": Overview

House b	P	Curr	Account ID	Bank subaccount	Charge ind	Bus. a
WFAR1	C	USD	WFCH1	113001		
WFAR1	D	USD	WFCH1	113001		

Paying company code US00 ABC USA Inc

Figure 5.54 Bank Accounts and Payment Methods

Figure 5.55 shows the maximum available amounts per house bank.

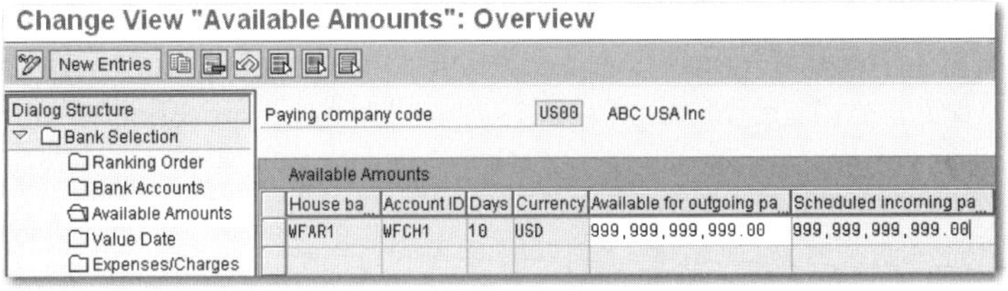

Change View "Available Amounts": Overview

Paying company code US00 ABC USA Inc

House ba	Account ID	Days	Currency	Available for outgoing pa	Scheduled incoming pa
WFAR1	WFCH1	10	USD	999,999,999,999.00	999,999,999,999.00

Figure 5.55 Define Available Amounts for House Banks

Figure 5.56 shows how you can manage the value date by house bank, payment method, and account ID.

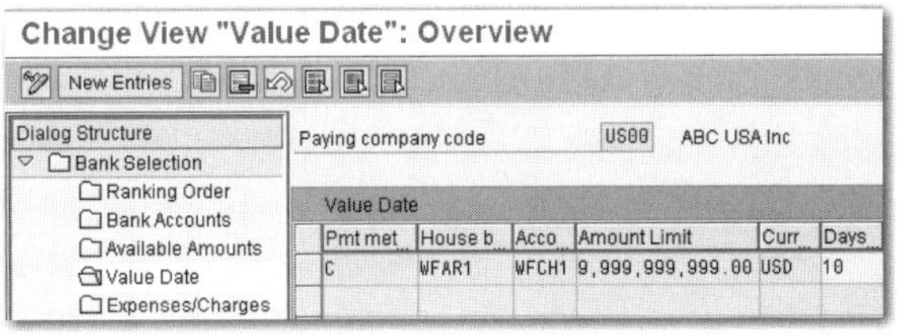

Change View "Value Date": Overview

Paying company code US00 ABC USA Inc

Pmt met	House b	Acco	Amount Limit	Curr	Days
C	WFAR1	WFCH1	9,999,999,999.00	USD	10

Figure 5.56 Define Value Date for Debit/Credit Memo from Bank and the Amount Limit

Figure 5.57 shows how you can map the expense charges to charge indicators, based on the amount limits. All these settings come predefined in the system and can be changed if required.

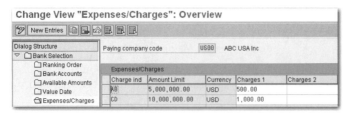

Figure 5.57 Define Bank Charges Based on Charge Indicators

Payment Media

The payment media configuration pertains to the forms and assignment of these forms to the appropriate payment methods and company codes. The menu path is **Automatic Outgoing Payments • Payment media • Make Settings for Classic Payment media Programs • Assign Payment Form for Payment Method in Company Code**.

Payment forms can either be created as SAPscript or via Smart Forms. In both cases, standard available forms should be used as a starting point and then modified to suit your requirements. The actual modification is done by your ABAP team. F110_US_AVIS is the form for US, which can be modified to suit the client requirements.

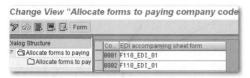

Figure 5.58 Assign Forms to Paying Company Code.

Figures 5.58 and 5.59 show the different ways of assigning the forms to company code and to company code and payment method.

Change View "Allocate forms to payment method in company code"
Form
Dialog Structure
Allocate forms to paying
Allocate forms to pay
Paying company code 0001
Pmt Method
Form for the payment transfer medium
Next form
C
F110_US_AVIS

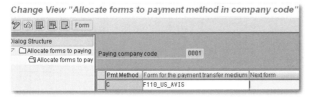

Figure 5.59 Assign Form to Company Code and Payment Method

In the next step, you will learn to assign the payment medium program to the payment method.

Assignment of Payment Method to Payment Media

Figure 5.60 shows the assignment of the payment method to the payment media. Follow the menu path **Automatic Outgoing Payments • Payment media • Make Settings for Classic Payment media Programs • Assign Payment medium Program to Payment method**.

Change View "Payment methods (Payment program)": Overview
Country Key US USA
Payment M... Program Name of the print dataset Print dataset for b/exch.
A RFFOM100 LIST3S
B RFFOUS_C LIST1S
C RFFOUS_C LIST1S
D RFFONO_D LIST3S
E
F
G RFFOUS_T LIST1S
H RFFOUS_C LISTIS
I RFFOEDI1
K RFFOEDI1
M RFFOUS_C LIST1S
O RFFOD__S LIST1S
P
S RFFOD__S LIST1S
T
U
V RFFOUS_C LIST1S
W RFFOD__W LIST2S
Z RFFOEDI1 LIST1S

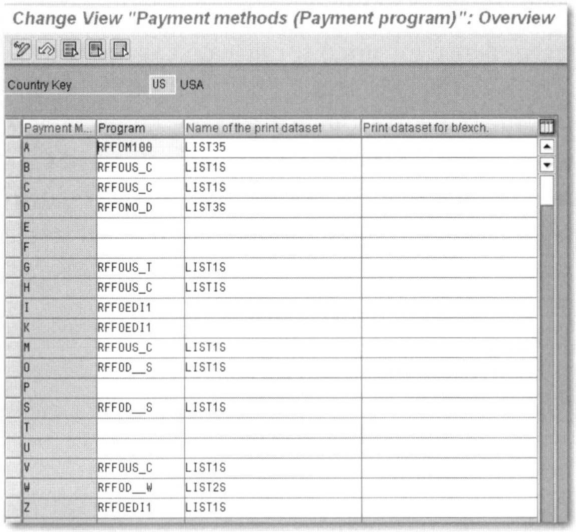

Figure 5.60 Assigning the Payment Media Program to Payment Method by Company Code

5.8 Interest Calculation

Generally, interest is calculated on customer debit balances. But the same functionality can be used to calculate interest if you have debit balances for vendors, particularly if you give loans and record them as advances/downpayments in AP. The interest calculation process can be segregated into the following steps:

1. The program identifies the items on which the interest should be calculated. You have the following options:

   ▶ Cleared or open items only

   ▶ All clearing transactions or only those with payment

   ▶ Credit or debit items or only debit items

2. The program identifies the number of days for which the interest needs to be calculated based on the calendar type. The following factors influence the calculation:

   ▶ Lower and upper limit of calculation period

   ▶ Date of last interest run

   ▶ Tolerance days for interest indicator

3. The program determines the amount on which the interest is to be calculated in local currency and if there is a minimum interest amount

4. The program reates correspondence for interest calculated above the minimum interest amount, with the details of the line items, interest rate, and suitable text describing the same. Follow **SAP Menu • Accounting • Financial Accounting • Accounts Receivable • Periodic Processing • Interest Calculation • Item Interest Calculation – Item Interest Calculation, Interest Run Display/ Arrears Interest – Without open items With open items, Without postings/Balance Interest**, or use Transactions FINT, FINTSHOW/F.2A, F.2B, F.2C, and F.24/F.26.

The following are the three options available for interest calculation:

▶ Item interest calculation

▶ Arrears interest calculation

▶ Balance interest calculation

Traditionally, after the interest (arrears and balance) gets calculated, then the system creates a batch input session. The batch input session posts the interest calculated to the GL, which updates accounting.

5.8.1   Enhancements in Items Interest Calculation

Interest calculation has been simplified a lot in the newer versions with the addition of functionality that allows the calculation of interest by items. Significant modification has been made in the philosophy and working of interest calculation via items.

Now the interest can be posted directly via Transaction FINT instead of posting it via batch. In the test run, the results can be seen before posting. If we choose update mode in FINT, then the interest is posted. The results of the interest calculation are now posted to two new tables: INTITHE and INTITHT. The new Transaction FINTSHOW can be used to view the interest runs, print interest runs, and reverse or report individual interest postings or entire interest runs. Interest on items can also be calculated for assigned vendors.

Branch and head office relationships are taken into account. However, calculation using interest calculation numerators is no longer supported.

5.8.2 Configuring Accounts Receivable: Interest Calculation

This section describes the configuration settings for interest calculation. The configuration of interest calculation can be divided into the following steps:

- Define global settings.
- Define interest calculation types.
- Define interest posting.
- Define settings for printing interest calculation remittances.

Figure 5.61 shows you the process for the interest calculation configuration. The menu path is **IMG • Financial Accounting • Accounts Receivable and Accounts Payable • Business Transactions • Interest calculation**.

Define Interest Calculation Type

This is the first step for configuring interest calculation. The interest calculation type is the basic building block for configuring interest. In this step, you will define the two-digit interest calculation identifier and identify the interest calculation type. The interest calculation indicator needs to be maintained in the customer master so that the system will calculate interest for a particular customer. You can follow **IMG • Financial Accounting • Accounts Receivable and Accounts Payable • Business Transactions • Interest Calculation • Interest Calculation Global Settings • Define Interest Calculation Types** or use Transaction OB46. Figure 5.62 shows the creation of an interest calculation indicator.

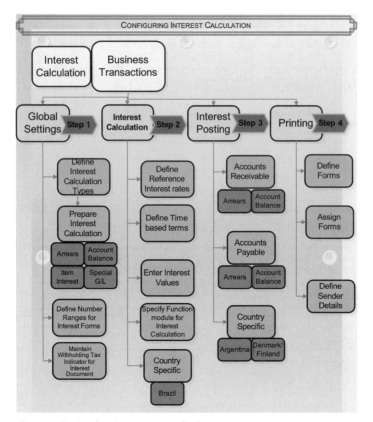

Figure 5.61 Configuring Interest Calculation Process

Settings for the Interest Calculation Indicator

You can define the properties of the two-digit interest indicator (Int ID). You can also check the account number as interest calculation indicator (Acct no. as IntCIcInd) to use the account number as an extended interest indicator in the interest terms. There are three types of interest calculation types that can be defined for an interest indicator:

Int ID	Name	Acct no. as IntClcInd	Int calc. type	Name
01	Standard itm int.cal	☐	P	Item Interest Calculatio
02	Standard bal.int.cal	☑	S	Balance Interest Calcula
03	Bal.int.calc.term 2	☐	S	Balance Interest Calcula
04	Item int.calc.term 2	☐	P	Item Interest Calculatio
05	Bal.int.calc.term 3	☐	S	Balance Interest Calcula

Change View "Interest Settlement (Calculation Type)": Overview

New Entries

Figure 5.62 Defining Interest Calculation Type

- ▶ **Indicator P**
  Item interest calculation or arrears interest calculation.
- ▶ **Indicator S**
  Balance interest calculation or scale interest calculation.
- ▶ **Indicator Z**
  Penalty interest calculation.

Define Number Ranges

In this step, you can define the number ranges for the document type that is selected for posting the interest. Use the menu path **IMG • Financial Accounting • Accounts Receivable and Accounts Payable • Business Transactions • Interest Calculation • Interest Calculation Global Settings • Define Number Ranges for Interest Forms** or Transaction FBN1. This is the same as defining the number range for any financial document. This number range is then assigned in the interest indicator.

Prepare Interest on Arrears Calculation

This interest indicator is used for interest on arrears calculation. Figure 5.63 shows the detailed settings for the interest calculation indicator. Follow the menu path **IMG • Financial Accounting • Accounts Receivable and Accounts Payable • Business Transactions • Interest Calculation • Interest Calculation Global Settings • Prepare Interest on Arrears Calculation**.

The different fields in the screen shown in Figure 5.63 are explained here:

- ▶ **Selection of items**
  The radio button allows you to configure which open due items are selected for interest calculation.
- ▶ **Open and all cleared items**
  This will select all the items that were past due even though the payment has already been made and the invoice cleared. This includes those invoices that were adjusted by credit memo, if they fall beyond the due date.
- ▶ **Open items and items cleared with a payment**
  This does not include open items that were adjusted by a credit memo. However, this includes all the open items and items that were cleared by payment, if the payment was made after the due date.

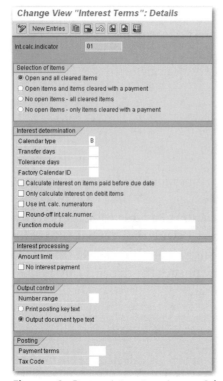

Figure 5.63 Prepare Interest on Arrears Calculation

- **No open items—all cleared Items**
  This does not include any open items. But all cleared items are selected for interest calculation.

- **No open items—only items cleared with payment**
  Open line items and line items cleared by any other method other than payment are ignored.

Interest determination includes the following:

- **Calendar type**
  This determines the number of days per period that interest is calculated. The various calendar types are:

  - **B (Bank Calendar):** 30 days/month and 360 days/year: 30/360.

  - **F (French calendar):** Exact number of days in each month and 360 days/year: 28 or 29 or 30 or 31/360.

  - **G (Gregorian calendar):** Exact number of days in each month and 365 days/year: 28 or 29 or 30 or 31/365.

  - **J (Japanese calendar):** 30 days/month and 365 or 366 (if it is leap year) days/year; 30/365 or 366.

▶ **Transfer days**
Represents the float time between the time the customer sends the check and you actually receive it. This is especially useful in scenarios if your organization uses lock box functionality (US only), and the customer sends the checks to the bank directly.

▶ **Tolerance days**
This is the grace period that is subtracted from the overdue dates to determine if you need to calculate interest.

▶ **Calculate interest on items paid before due date**
If this indicator is checked, then the items paid earlier also calculate a credit interest that reduces the overall customer balance. It is like giving a cash discount for paying early.

▶ **Only calculate interest on debit items**
If this indicator is checked, then interest is only calculated on debit items. If you do not set this indicator, then credit interest gets calculated on credit items offsetting the debit interest.

▶ **Use int. calc. numerators and Round-off int.calc. numer.**
These are typically not set.

▶ **Function module**
If the standard function module calculation does not meet your requirements, then you can define a new function module to calculate interest, and the name of the function module needs to be entered here.

Under **Interest processing**, you will find:

▶ **Amount limit**
Enter the minimum and maximum amount limit at which the system should not calculate any interest. This allows you to catch outliers and not post insignificant amounts as interest that are, for example, less than $5.

▶ **No interest payment**
If the system is allowed to calculate interest on credit items, then this indicator is checked to ensure that you are not paying the customer if the credit interest is more than the debit interest.

Under **Output Control**, there are the following:

▶ **Number range**
Here you update the number range for the reference document of the posting.

▶ **Print posting key text**
This indicator updates the posting key text on the interest form.

▶ **Output document type text**
This indicator updates the document type text in the line item that is created as a result of interest calculation posting.

Under **Posting**, you will find:

▶ **Payment terms**
This is used to update the payment terms of the interest document posted.

▶ **Tax Code**
This is the tax code indicator used by the system when posting the interest calculation document.

In the next section, you will learn more about the item interest calculation.

Prepare Item Interest Calculation

This is the new AR functionality that has simplified the interest calculation process. Follow the menu path **IMG • Financial Accounting • Accounts Receivable and Accounts Payable • Business Transactions • Interest Calculation • Interest Calculation Global Settings • Prepare Item Interest Calculation**. Figure 5.64 shows the settings for item interest calculation.

In this section, you will learn the delta settings from the previous configuration of interest calculation on arrears.

Configuration Added/Changed in Comparison to Arrears Interest Calculation

Many items that were part of the actual interest calculation transaction have been moved to configuration, and new configuration objects have been added as listed here. Under Item selection, you have the following:

▶ **Item Selection**
The radio button has now been made more intuitive by breaking into two sections. It allows better understanding of the selection of open and cleared Items

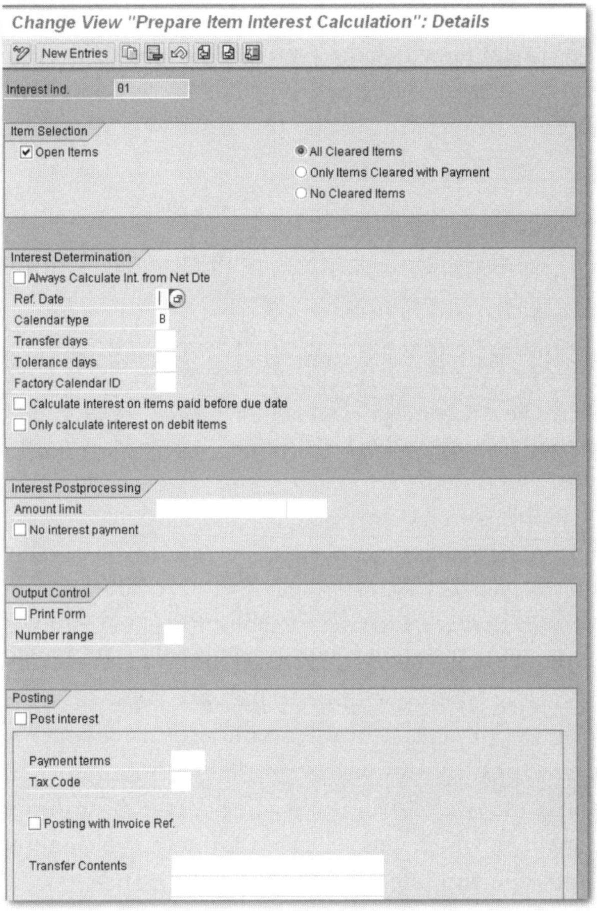

Figure 5.64 Prepare Interest on Item Calculation

Under **Interest Determination**, you have:

▶ **Always Calculate Int. From Net Dte**
Checking this indicator means that the interest always gets calculated as of the due date of the payment. Otherwise, interest gets calculated from the last interest run date maintained in the customer master.

▶ **Ref. Date**
This is the FI item interest calculation interest date and can be set as one of the following: value date or baseline date for net payment, document date or posting date, or payment baseline date.

▶ **Factory Calendar ID**
This addition can be used to define which days are nonworking. If the due date is on a nonworking day, then the next working day is considered the due date.

Under **Output Control**, you have the following:

▶ **Print Form**
Checking this indicator ensures that the form is printed when item interest calculation is run.

Tip
The forms for interest calculation using items can now be created using Smart Forms. Earlier the forms had to be created using SAPscript.

Under **Posting:**

▶ **Post interest**
Setting this indicator causes the interest to be posted. In the new interest item program, the posting happens when the program is set as an update run.

▶ **Posting with Invoice Ref.**
If you set this indicator, interest receivables are posted with reference to the invoice for which interest is calculated. Checking this indicator creates one document per invoice, which gets selected for interest calculation with the resulting document having the original invoice reference.

▶ **Transfer Contents**
Several fields from the customer invoice can be transferred to the interest posted. Some of the available fields that can be transferred include Branch account, product type, business area, contract number, contract type, reference, assignment, and payment terms. Enhancements can be made by using RFINTITUSEREXT.

These settings are similar to arrears interest calculation: calendar type, transfer days, tolerance days, calculate interest on items paid before due date, calculate interest on debit items, amount limit, no interest payment, number range, payment terms, and tax code. These have been removed in comparison to arrears: use interest calculation numerators, round-off interest calculation numerators, function module, print posting key text, and output document type text.

Now that you know the key configuration settings for arrears and item interest calculation, let's take a look at account balance interest calculation.

Prepare Interest Calculation on Account Balance

In this section, you will learn the key settings for account balances. You can follow the menu path **IMG • Financial Accounting • Accounts Receivable and Accounts Payable • Business Transactions • Interest Calculation • Interest Calculation Global Settings• Prepare Account Balance Interest Calculation**. There are some additional configuration settings in account balance interest calculation under Period Determination:

▶ **Interest calc. freq.**
This defines how many times interest is calculated (01: Monthly, 12: Yearly).

▶ **Settlement day**
This is the settlement day for interest calculation and is used in conjunction with **Last Run date** and **Frequency** to determine the upper limit of the interest calculation period.

Figure 5.65 illustrates the configuration details for interest calculation on account balance.

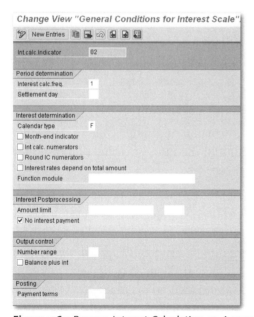

Figure 5.65 Prepare Interest Calculation on Account Balance

Prepare Interest Calculation for Special GL Transactions

In this section, you will learn the settings for configuring special GL transactions. You can follow the menu path **IMG • Financial Accounting • Accounts Receivable and Accounts Payable • Business Transactions • Interest Calculation • Interest Calculation Global Settings • Prepare Special GL Transaction Interest Calculation**. Figure 5.66 shows the settings for maintaining the interest calculation indicator for interest calculation for special GL indicator transactions.

Figure 5.66 Prepare Interest Calculation for Special GL Transactions

One of the important settings is the new interest calculation indicator **(New IntCalc.Ind):** This is required so that you can process GL transactions separately using outgoing and incoming interest scale reports. You need to assign the new interest calculation indicator to an interest indicator, account type, and special GL indicator.

Next you will learn to configure the interest calculation settings.

Configuring Interest Calculation: Interest Calculation

Now that you have the base interest calculation indicator, you can define the interest rates that you will be assigning to the interest calculation indicator previously defined. For this, follow these steps:

1. Define reference interest rates

Determine the rate for calculation. This rate can be fixed or variable. If this rate is fixed, then you do not need to define a reference rate. But if you want the interest rate to vary according to a mutually agreed benchmark such as LIBOR or U.S. Treasury rates, then those need to be defined in this step. Figure 5.67 shows the screen where you can maintain your reference interest rates. The menu path is **IMG • Financial Accounting • Accounts Receivable and Accounts Payable • Business Transactions • Interest Calculation • Interest Calculation • Define Reference Interest Rates**, and the Transaction is OBAC.

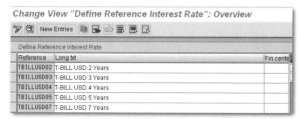

Figure 5.67 Define Reference Interest Rates

Figure 5.68 shows the details of the reference interest rate. Here the T-Bill of the United States has been defined as TBILLUSD02 for the duration of 2 years. It is very important to correctly identify an interest rate that is agreed upon mutually by customers and the organization.

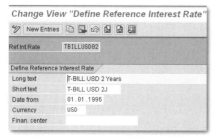

Figure 5.68 Define Reference Interest Rates (Continued)

Tip
For reference interest rate settings, you need to enter the long text, short text, and the effective from date as well as the currency for which this is valid. If a particular financial center is used, then that also needs to be entered. This is required when using the treasury module.

2. **Define time-based interest terms**

   Assign the interest indicator to the reference interest rate. The menu path is **IMG • Financial Accounting • Accounts Receivable and Accounts Payable • Business Transactions • Interest Calculation• Interest Calculation • Define Time Based Interest Rates**, and the Transaction is OB81. Using this configuration, you can assign the same interest indicator a different reference interest rate if the organization so chooses. Figure 5.69 shows you the process of defining the time-based interest rates and marrying it to the interest calculation indicator. There are some settings for time-based interest indicators:

▶ **Int. calc. indicator**
Enter the interest calculation indicator that is to be used.

▶ **Currency Key**
Enter the currency key identifier.

▶ **Eff. from**
This is the date from which the interest rate term is valid.

▶ **Sequential number**
For arrears, this is always 1 or can be left blank. But for account balance calculation, this field, along with the **Amount from** field, can be used to propose a different rate depending on the balance on which the interest is being calculated.

▶ **Term**
This needs to be selected from the dropdown and determines the function module that is used to calculate interest in the next step.

▶ **Ref. Interest Rate**
Enter the reference interest rate defined earlier.

▶ **Premium**
If you want to charge an additional percentage over the reference interest rate, then that needs to be entered here.

▶ **Amount from**
This is valid only for account balances and is used to identify different interest rates for different amounts only in the case of the account balance type interest indicator.

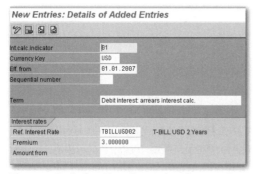

Figure 5.69 Define Time-Dependent Interest Rates

3. Define interest rate values
You can directly enter the interest rate values for reference rates as and when they change. Figure 5.70 shows how you can maintain the interest

rate values. The menu path is **IMG • Financial Accounting • Accounts Receivable and Accounts Payable • Business Transactions • Interest Calculation • Interest Calculation • Define Interest Rate Values,** and the Transaction is OB83. You need to maintain the rate with an effective from date (**Eff. from**).

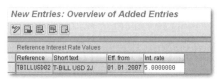

Figure 5.70 Define Reference Interest Rate Values

4. Specify function module for interest rate determination

AR has four standard function modules for interest rate calculation. In this step, you can define your own function module for interest rate determination. Follow the menu path **IMG • Financial Accounting • Accounts Receivable and Accounts Payable • Business Transactions • Interest Calculation • Interest Calculation • Specify Function Module for Interest Rate Determination**.

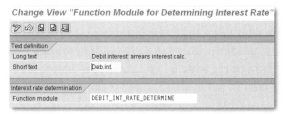

Figure 5.71 Define Function Module by Calculation Type

Figure 5.71 shows the screen where you have maintained the function module **DEBIT_INT_RATE_DETERMINE** for the **Debit interest: arrears interest calc.**

5. Configuring interest calculation: Interest posting

The final step in interest calculation configuration is to configure how the calculation procedure and interest rate definition actually posts to accounting. The interest calculation program does not use automatic the account determination procedure typically followed by other modules such as MM-FI-AP or SD-FI-AR. The configuration of this step is very similar to the bank accounting configuration. There are three components that are maintained by the interest calculation application:

> ► **Account Symbols**
> These represent business transactions; for example, 1000 represents customers.

> ► **Account Determination**
> In this step, you can assign account symbols to GL accounts.

> ► **Posting Specifications**
> In this step, you assign account symbols to business transactions by interest indicator. The business transactions are 1000 for interest received and 2000 for interest paid. You also need to define the posting keys appropriately.
>
> It is best to start from standard settings and then copy those to create a new one for your interest indicator. In all these components, the wildcard is defined by entering "+".

Note

This configuration is not very intuitive and standard to other modules. So it is important for you to play around with it a bit more and then understand the concept behind the configuration.

---

6. **AR calculation account assignment of interest rates on arrears**
   Figure 5.72 shows you the account determination (posting specifications) settings for arrears that come out of the box. If you click on **Symbols,** you will reach the next screen shown in Figure 5.73. The menu path is **IMG • Financial Accounting • Accounts Receivable and Accounts Payable • Business Transactions • Interest Calculation • Interest Postings • A/R: Calculation of Interest on Arrears,** and the Transaction is OBV1.

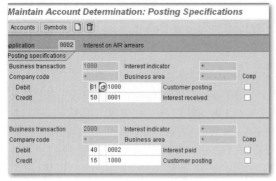

Figure 5.72 Maintain Account Determination for AR Calculation

Figure 5.73 Define Account Symbols

If you click on **Accounts**, you can maintain the GL account to the account symbols (see Figure 5.74).

Figure 5.74 Assign GL Accounts to Symbols

Tip

You can also maintain similar settings for vendors using the next setting in the menu path.

The menu path is **IMG • Financial Accounting • Accounts Receivable and Accounts Payable • Business Transactions • Interest Calculation • Interest Postings • Interest on Arrears Calculation (Vendors)**, and the Transaction is OBV9.

7. **AR balance interest**

Figure 5.75 shows the default settings for interest calculation balances on customers. Follow the menu path **IMG • Financial Accounting • Accounts Receivable and Accounts Payable • Business Transactions • Interest Calculation • Interest Postings • Prepare Interest on Balances (Customers)**, or use Transaction OBV5.

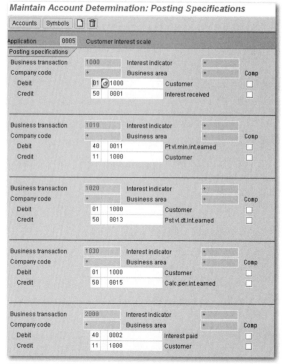

Figure 5.75 Posting Specifications for Customers: Balances

Figure 5.76 shows some of the account symbols predefined for customer interest scale.

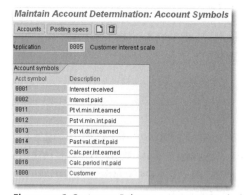

Figure 5.76 Customer Balances: Account Symbols

Figure 5.77 shows how you can assign the customer account symbols to the GL account.

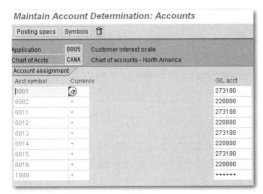

Figure 5.77 Customer Balances: Maintain GL Accounts

This completes the settings pertaining to the customer interest calculation determination. In the next section, you will learn how to configure the interest calculation for printing.

Configuring Interest Calculation: Printing

Here you can define the interest forms you want to print and then assign them to the calculation indicator, as well as define details. Let's begin with defining the forms:

▶ **Define interest forms**
Using the menu path, you can define your own forms for interest calculation. This entails outlining the format for the form that will be printed. The menu path is **IMG • Financial Accounting • Accounts Receivable and Accounts Payable • Business Transactions • Interest Calculation• Print • Define Interest Forms (with SAPscript),** and the Transaction is SE71.

▶ **Assign form to interest calculation indicator**
In this setting, the interest calculation indicator is assigned the form that has been defined in the previous step. In SAP ERP 6.0, you can assign a Smart Form and an Adobe Acrobat PDF form as well. You will need to follow the menu path **IMG • Financial Accounting • Accounts Receivable and Accounts Payable • Business Transactions • Interest Calculation• Print • Assign Forms for Interest Indicators**.

Figure 5.78 shows how you can assign the forms to the company code and interest calculation indicator.

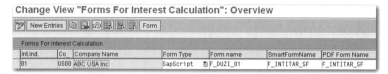

Figure 5.78 Assign the Form to the Interest Indicator

▶ **Define sender details for forms**
You define the sender details, such as header text, footer text, and signature text, along with the sender user ID, logos, and any additional identification information that should be part of the communication. This setting can be defined for both dunning and interest calculation by dunning area and company code. You can follow the menu path **IMG • Financial Accounting • Accounts Receivable and Accounts Payable • Business Transactions • Interest Calculation• Print • Define sender details for forms**.

This completes the settings pertaining to interest calculation. In the next section, you will learn about the settings for dunning.

5.9 Dunning

Dunning is the process by which customers are reminded of their open items and are sent correspondence about these items. The process of dunning can be configured to occur automatically per the business rules defined. The dunning process sequence consists of the following steps:

1. Selects overdue open items for a particular customer.

2. Determines the level of dunning.

3. Creates a dunning notice for the open items that are due.

4. Updates the dunning data for the items and accounts affected.

Let's now move on to how it works.

5.9.1 Dunning Program Execution

Executing the dunning program in SAP ERP Financials involves these steps:

1. Create the dunning proposal.

2. Edit the dunning proposal.

3. Print the dunning notices.

4. Mail the dunning notices to customers.

The overall structure of the dunning program is very similar to the payment program (see Figure 5.79). The menu path is **SAP Menu • Accounting • Financial Accounting • Accounts Receivable• Periodic Processing• Dunning,** and the Transaction is F150.

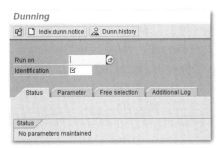

Figure 5.79 Dunning Transaction in SAP

You need to enter the correct parameters, which can be copied from a previous dunning run, and you can just modify the run date. During the dunning run, the system chooses the accounts and checks them for items that are overdue. It also checks whether dunning notices need to be sent and which dunning level needs to be assigned. All this data is stored in the dunning proposal. The dunning proposal can be edited, deleted, and recreated until you are satisfied with the output. This step is typically performed while initially setting up dunning for a particular group of customers and can be skipped altogether. The dunning notices can be printed immediately and analyzed for errors. The same also updates all the dunning-related master data and associated documentation.

5.9.2 Configuring Dunning

Here you will learn about the various settings for dunning and how you can customize dunning to your requirements. The process for dunning is shown in Figure 5.80. The menu path is **IMG • Financial Accounting • Accounts Receivable and Accounts Payable • Business Transactions • Dunning.**

Notes

▶ Most of the configuration pertaining to dunning can also be done from the user side of the application.

▶ Use Transaction F150, and then access **Environment• Display Configuration or Change Configuration**.

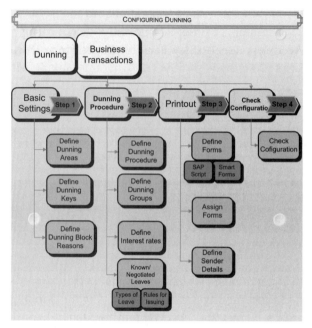

Figure 5.80 Outlining Dunning Configuration Process Steps

Let's take a look at the basic settings that you need to make for dunning.

Dunning Basic Settings

The basic settings for dunning include the following:

Note
If you are defining the dunning area for the first time, make sure that you assigned the company code as relevant for dunning by using Transaction OBVU

- ▶ **Define Dunning Area**

  The dunning area is defined so that you can segregate dunning one level below the company code. All the dunning activities are performed in a dunning area. Figure 5.81 shows how you can maintain your dunning area **DU** for company code **US00**. The menu path is **IMG • Financial Accounting • Accounts Receivable and Accounts Payable • Business transactions • Dunning • Basic Settings for Dunning • Define Dunning Areas**.

Figure 5.81 Define Dunning Area

- **Define Dunning Keys**
  Dunning keys specify that the line item can be dunned only with restrictions or is to be displayed separately on a dunning notice. Figure 5.82 shows you the **Dunn.key 1**, **2**, and **3** with the corresponding **Max. levels** of **1**, **2**, and **3**. The menu path is **IMG • Financial Accounting • Accounts Receivable and Accounts Payable • Business transactions • Dunning • Basic Settings for Dunning • Define Dunning Keys**.

Change View "Dunning Keys": Overview

New Entries

Dunn.key	Max.level	Print sep	Text
1	1	☐	Triggers maximum dunning level 1
2	2	☐	Triggers maximum dunning level 2
3	3	☐	Triggers maximum dunning level 3

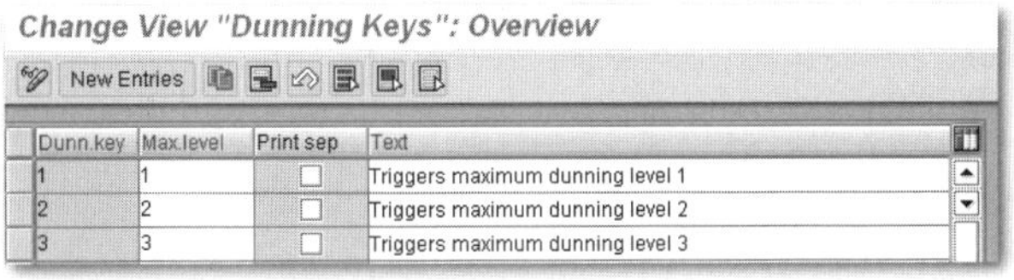

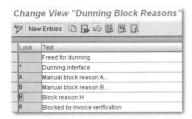

Figure 5.82 Define Dunning Keys

- **Define Dunning Block Reasons**
  In this configuration, you can define the block reasons for dunning. Figure 5.83 shows you the dunning block reasons, and you can also define your own reasons in this screen. The menu path is **IMG • Financial Accounting • Accounts Receivable and Accounts Payable • Business transactions • Dunning • Basic Settings for Dunning • Define Dunning Block Reasons**.

Change View "Dunning Block Reasons"

New Entries

Lock	Text
	Freed for dunning
*	Dunning interface
A	Manual block reason A...
B	Manual block reason B...
H	Block reason H
R	Blocked by invoice verification

Figure 5.83 Define Dunning Block Reason

Dunning Procedure

The dunning procedure controls how dunning is actually carried out. Every account must have a dunning procedure maintained in its master for it to be relevant for automatic dunning. The dunning process can use standard and/or special GL transactions. Follow the menu path **IMG • Financial Accounting • Accounts Receivable and Accounts Payable • Business transactions • Dunning • Dunning Procedure • Define Dunning Procedure**. Figure 5.84 shows you the screen for defining your dunning procedure.

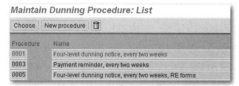

Figure 5.84 Define Dunning Procedure: List

The main dunning program configuration menu has links to all the other subareas. Click on the dunning procedure to learn about the key settings of the dunning area. Figure 5.85 shows you the various parameters that can be maintained by the dunning area.

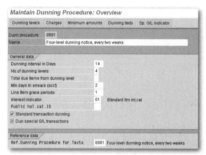

Figure 5.85 Define Dunning Procedure: Overview

The dunning procedure field definitions are provided here:

▶ **Dunn. procedure**
Enter the key for the dunning procedure.

▶ **Name**
Description of the dunning procedure.

▶ **Dunning Interval in Days**
This defines the time gap between two dunning notices. A new notice cannot be created if the dunning interval time has not passed from the last dunning run.

▶ **No. of dunning levels**
This identifies how many different types of communications are generated. The number here denotes the highest dunning level

▶ **Min. days in arrears (acct)**
This is the minimum number of days after the due date that at least one item in the account should have, which would trigger a dunning notice.

▶ **Line item grace periods**
This identifies how many days of a grace period is allowed per line item. If a particular item is within the grace period, then it is not dunned.

▶ **Interest indicator**
This denotes the interest calculation indicator for dunning interest.

Dunning Levels

Figure 5.86 shows the levels applicable for a dunning procedure.

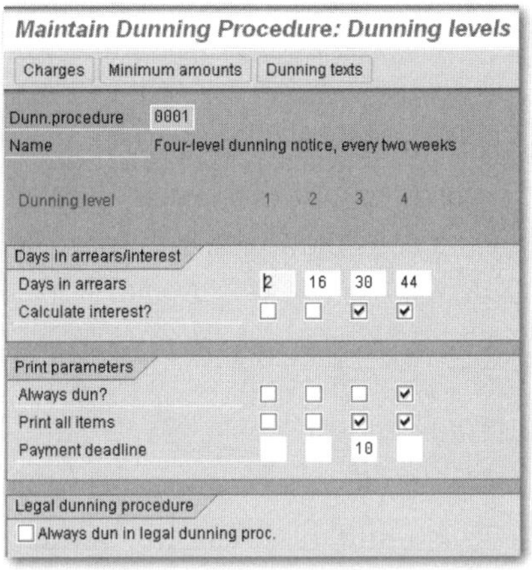

Figure 5.86 Define Dunning Procedure: Dunning Levels

The dunning level field definitions are provided here:

▶ **Days in arrears for different dunning levels**
Dunning level 1 has the earlier setting of minimum number of arrears prepopulated. You can define the past due number of days for level 2 (16), level 3 (30), and level 4 (44).

▶ **Calculate interest?**
If you check this, interest will be calculated for that dunning level.

▶ **Always dun?**
If this checkbox is selected, the dunning notice will always be printed, without any change in any of the past due items.

▶ **Print all items**
Checking this box ensures that all the line items will be printed, even if they are not due.

▶ **Payment deadline**
This specifies the number of days added to the payment run and will be printed as the deadline date for payment.

▶ **Always dun in legal dunning proc.**
This can be checked to always dun in legal procedures.

Define Dunning Charges

Figure 5.87 shows how you can maintain the settings for charges pertaining to dunning.

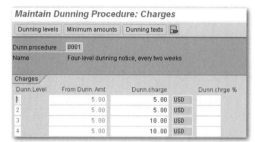

Figure 5.87 Define Dunning Procedure: Charges

Dunning charges field definitions are shown here:

▸ **Dunn.Level**
This helps segregate the Charges by dunning level.

▸ **From Dunn. Amt**
This is the minimum customer balance due amount at which the dunning charges will be levied.

▸ **Dunn. charge**
This can be maintained either as a fixed amount or as a fixed percentage of the dunned amount. This is maintained by dunning level.

Define Minimum Amounts

Figure 5.88 shows how you can maintain the settings for minimum amounts and percentages that are applicable for dunning. You can reach this screen by clicking on **Minimum amounts**.

Figure 5.88 Define Dunning Procedure: Minimum Amounts

Tip
Enter the minimum amount or percentage applicable for dunning as well as the minimum interest applicable for dunning interest calculation. These are also maintained by dunning level.

Maintain Company Codes by Dunning Area

Figure 5.89 shows how you can maintain the company code applicable for the dunning area.

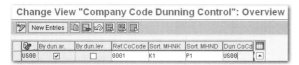

Figure 5.89 Define Dunning Procedure: Company Code Data

Maintain Dunning Texts

Figure 5.90 shows you how to maintain the dunning texts by dunning area and company code. You can get here by clicking on **Dunning texts** on the previous screen.

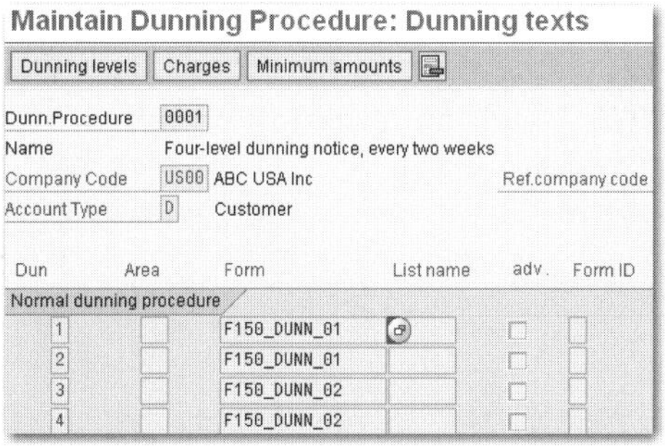

Figure 5.90 Define Dunning Procedure: Dunning Texts

The dunning text defines the layout of the form that is used for dunning. The form's key is entered here, which is defined in SAPScript or via a SAP Smart Form. Multiple forms can be generated by the dunning program.

Define Special GL Indicators Applicable for the Dunning Procedure

Figure 5.91 shows how you can maintain special GL transactions for a dunning procedure.

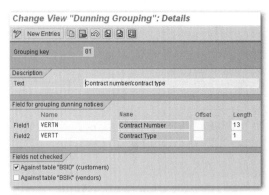

Figure 5.91 Define Dunning Procedure: Special GL Indicator

This identifies the list of special GL indicators that is relevant for the dunning notice. All these settings pertain to a particular dunning area.

Define Dunning Groups

This helps define how dunning notices can be grouped together. The menu path is **IMG • Financial Accounting • Accounts Receivable and Accounts Payable • Business transactions • Dunning • Dunning Procedure • Define Dunning Groupings**. Figure 5.92 shows the dunning groups; if the invoices pertain to the same contract number and contract type, they are grouped together.

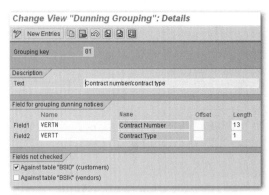

Figure 5.92 Define Dunning Groupings

Define Interest Rates

Interest rates need to be maintained if you are charging interest on overdue items. The menu path is **IMG • Financial Accounting • Accounts Receivable and Accounts Payable • Business transactions • Dunning • Dun-**

ning Procedure • Define Interest Rates. Figure 5.93 shows how you can maintain the interest rates for dunning.

Change View "Interest Rates": Overview

Int ID	Crcy	Valid from	Debit %	Cred. %
01	ATS	01.01.1991	9.250	6.00
01	DEM	01.01.1991	9.250	6.00
01	ESP	01.01.1991	9.250	6.00
01	EUR	01.01.1991	9.250	6.00
01	FRF	01.01.1991	9.250	6.00
01	INR	29.01.2006	5.000	5.00
01	ITL	01.01.1991	9.250	6.00
01	JPY	01.01.1991	9.250	6.00
01	NLG	01.01.1994	9.000	6.00
01	USD	14.10.2006	10.000	10.00

Figure 5.93 Define Interest Rate for Dunning

Here you can specify the interest rates for calculating dunning interest. Next you will learn to make settings for printing dunning notices:

▶ **Dunning printing**
This is where you make appropriate settings for assigning dunning forms to dunning areas.

▶ **Assign dunning form to dunning area**
In this configuration, you can assign appropriate dunning forms by dunning procedure, company code, and account type. Each dunning level can be assigned a dunning form. Follow the menu path **IMG • Financial Accounting • Accounts Receivable and Accounts Payable • Business transactions • Dunning • Printout • Assign Dunning Forms**.

Figure 5.94 shows how you can assign the dunning forms for a particular **Company Code (US00)**, **Dunn. procedure (0001)**, and **Account type (D)** by dunning levels (**1** to **4**). You can choose to assign legal and normal dunning forms separately as well.

Display View "Forms for normal dunning procedure": Overview

Dialog Structure	Dunn.Procedure	0001	Ref.Dunning Procedure for Texts	0001
▽ ☐ Dunning procedure	Company Code	US00	Ref.company code	0001
☐ Forms for normal dui	Account type	D		
☐ Forms for legal dunn				

Dunning Area	Dunning le	Form	List name
	1	F150_DUNN_01	
	2	F150_DUNN_01	
	3	F150_DUNN_02	
	4	F150_DUNN_02	

Figure 5.94 Assign Dunning Form to Dunning Procedure

Check Dunning Configuration

In this step, you can check the configuration for a particular company code and dunning area. This allows you to go back and maintain any missed settings. This is important to ensure that all of the configuration has been carried out accurately and to able to change any settings that need modification. You can follow **IMG • Financial Accounting • Accounts Receivable and Accounts Payable • Business transactions • Dunning • Generate List for Dunning Program Configuration** or use Transaction OBL6.

In the next section, you will learn to make settings for credit management from the financial perspective.

5.10 Credit Management

Credit management (FI-AR-CR) is used to minimize the credit risk by defining a credit limit for individual customers. Defining credit limits helps ingrain the understanding of risk in the AR department. This is especially important if a particular industry is entering a recession or facing downward pressures. Helping define limits gives you a headstart to focus your efforts and reduce the overall percentage of bad debts. Credit management is a powerful tool if both SD and AR are implemented. The menu path is **SAP Menu • Accounting • Financial Accounting • Accounts Receivable• Credit Management**. The following features are available in FI-AR-CR in conjunction with an SAP SD module:

▶ Ability to define automatic credit checks according to a company-defined parameter

▶ Ability to know the credit situation at the time of sales order processing

▶ Ability to define credit limits according to the risk category

---

Note

New SAP ERP releases will focus on developing credit management as a tool for Financial Supply Chain Management (FSCM), and eventually FIN-FSCM-CR will replace FI-AR-CR or SD-BF-CM. This will change the way you manage the credit from typically an internal SAP ERP Financials perspective to an external perspective. FSCM-CR will allow you to combine the credit information across disparate systems, thus helping to create one definition of the credit exposure for a particular customer.

5.10.1 Configuring Credit Management

In this section, you will learn about the various configuration settings for credit management. This includes Financials-Accounts Receivable Credit Management.

Credit Control Account

In the credit control account area, you make the settings for the following areas:

▶ **Define permitted credit control areas to company code**
The menu path is **IMG • Financial Accounting • Accounts Receivable and Accounts Payable • Credit Management • Credit Control Account • Assign Permitted Credit Control Areas to Company Code**.

▶ **Define preliminary settings for credit management**
The menu path is **IMG • Financial Accounting • Accounts Receivable and Accounts Payable • Credit Management • Credit Control Account • Define Preliminary Settings for Credit Management**.

Figure 5.95 Assign Credit Control Area to Company Code

Figure 5.95 shows you the assignment of the company code to the credit control area. Figure 5.96 shows the settings that can be made during this step.

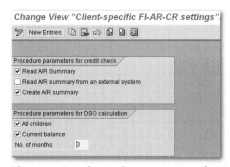

Figure 5.96 Define Preliminary Settings for Company Code

▶ **Read A/R Summary**
If you set this indicator, during credit checks, the checks conducted by the system read the AR summary data and not the current database.

▶ **Read A/R summary from an external system**
This allows you to establish the RFC during credit check.

▶ **Create A/R summary**
This indicator is set in clients where the AR summary needs to be created, and the central financial accounting is run.

Be sure to consider all three settings together when defining your scenario for credit management. The next settings identify the parameters for days of sales outstanding (DSO):

▶ **All children**
This ensures that all the customers tied to the parent customer credit account are included in the calculation.

▶ **Current balance**
Setting this indicator allows you to use the current balance to show DSO calculation instead of the usual average balance outstanding.

▶ **No. of months**
You can enter the number of months here to specify how far the system will go to calculate the balance and sales per day.

Credit Management and Risk Categories

You can define credit groups to categorize your customers. After you define these groups, you need to identify each of your customers by these groups. The menu path is **IMG • Financial Accounting • Accounts Receivable and Accounts Payable • Credit Management • Credit Control Account • Define groups**. Figure 5.97 shows how you can maintain the settings for defining new text IDs.

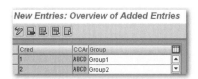

Figure 5.97 Define Credit Groups

You will also need to define risk categories so that you can categorize your customers according to risk. The menu path is **IMG • Financial Accounting • Accounts Receivable and Accounts Payable • Credit Management • Credit Control Account • Define groups**. Figure 5.98 shows how you can maintain the settings for defining new risk categories.

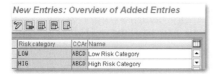

Figure 5.98 Define Risk Categories

After you define the risk categories, you need to maintain the risk categories to individual customers. The menu path is **IMG • Financial Accounting • Accounts Receivable and Accounts Payable • Credit Management • Credit Control Account • Define Credit Representative Group**. Figure 5.99 and Figure 5.100 shows how you can define new credit representative groups and credit representatives.

Figure 5.99 Define Credit Representative Groups

Credit representative groups are defined by the credit control area.

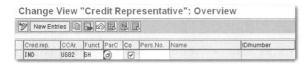

Figure 5.100 Define Credit Representative

Credit representative is assigned to a credit representative group, credit control area, partner function, partner counter (if the same customer has multiple partner functions), an indicator to copy the credit representative to the sales document, and the personnel number of the credit representative.

5.10.2 Business Transactions-Credit Monitoring

In this section, you will learn about the settings that you can make for business transactions. Let's review these now:

▶ **Define Reconciliation Accts without Credit Management Update**
In this step, you can choose to exclude reconciliation accounts from credit management. Figure 5.101 shows you the settings that you can maintain by reconciliation account. You can follow the path: **IMG • Financial Ac-**

counting • **Accounts Receivable and Accounts Payable** • **Credit Management** • **Business Transaction: Credit Monitoring** • **Define Reconciliation Accts without Credit Management Update** or use Transaction AKOF.

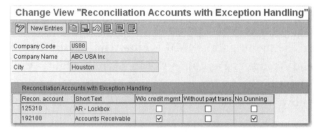

Figure 5.101 Figure 5.101 Define Reconciliation Accounts Without Credit Management Update

▶ **Exclude Reconciliation Account from Credit Management**
You can choose to exclude this, without payment transactions, and choose not to activate dunning for a particular reconciliation account. Figure 5.102 shows how you can maintain up to five different intervals to outline your days of arrears in credit management. This setting is used to define different intervals for days in arrears of open items. You can use **the RfDte (Reference Date)** field to specify whether the due date for net payment or the cash discount 1 date is used for calculating the number or days in arrears. The menu path is **IMG** • **Financial Accounting** • **Accounts Receivable and Accounts Payable** • **Credit Management** • **Business Transaction: Credit Monitoring** • **Define Intervals for Days in Arrears in Credit Management,** and the Transaction is OB39.

Change View "Interval for Days in Arrears": Overview

Int.	Name	RfDte	Day	Day	Day	Day	Day	
R01N	Net 15/30/45	2	15	30	45			
R01S	Cash discount 15/30/45	1	15	30	45			
R02N	Net 10/20/30/40/50	2	10	20	30	40	50	
R02S	Cash discount 10/20/30/40/50	1	10	20	30	40	50	

Figure 5.102 Figure 5.102 Define Intervals for Days in Arrears

5.11   Integration

Throughout this chapter, you learned about the integration of AP and AR. Now let's examine some of the key findings by looking at AP and AR integration with other financial and nonfinancial modules.

5.11.1 Accounts Payable

AP is heavily integrated with SAP MM and feeds into the GL for financial statement preparation. In addition, if a customer is also created as a vendor, then AP can be used to clear the balances of both customer and vendor together. At this point, you can review the integration touch-points of AP with the MM module. Figure 5.103 shows the purchase requisition to cash cycle, which was discussed earlier as well.

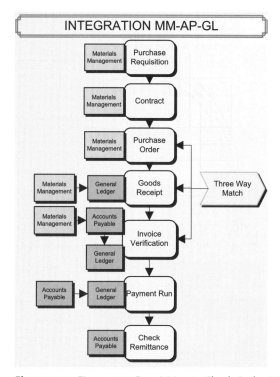

Figure 5.103 Figure 5.103 Requisition to Check Cycle: AP Integration

As you know the AP and MM integration happens primarily during the invoice verification where the material invoice is matched against the purchase order and the goods receipt. As a result of this verification, an invoice verification document creates a material vendor invoice document, which can then be paid using the payment run. The payment run is executed in AP, which updates the GL accounts.

5.11.2 Accounts Receivable

AR is integrated heavily with logistics (SD) and feeds into GL for financial statement preparation. The process flow for AR and SD integration is shown in Figure 5.104.

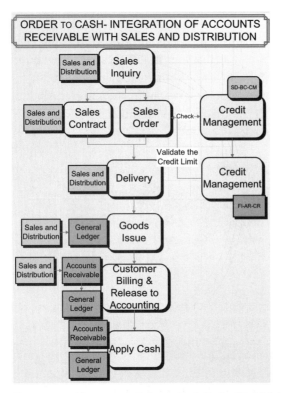

Figure 5.104 Figure 5.104 Order to Cash Cycle: SD-AR Integration

As you can see, the AR from an accounting perspective is linked to SD when you perform the customer billing in SD and release the documents to accounting. However, credit management is also linked to SD from the moment the sales order is created. A validation occurs when the system compares the credit limit against the credit limit maintained in the AR module.

Next you will learn some of the key trends that are emerging in AP and AR.

5.12 Business Trends in Accounts Payable and Accounts Receivable

The focus for AP and AR is on driving efficiency. Per a recent ASUG SAP Benchmarking survey in the United States, AP and AR represent significant chunks of transactional activities but are at the low end of the food chain of financials. Organizations focus on extracting the most efficiency from these departments. Figure 5.105 shows the categorization of financial activities.

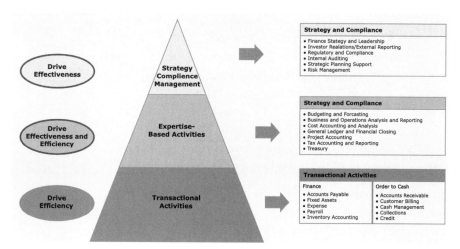

Figure 5.105 Figure 5.105 Benchmarking Study Model: 2006 ASUG SAP Benchmarking Study (Source: SAP Insight, Katherina Mullers-Patel)

A large percentage of costs in Financials is due to personnel costs, so organizations are trying to outsource functions to reduce costs. See Figure 5.106, which shows the breakdown of total costs incurred by a financial organization

Payroll and taxes were wave 1 of outsourcing the financial applications to third parties such as Ceridean. The next wave is for general accounting, AP/expense, fixed asset management, and project accounting. Revenue accounting (Order to Cash), though typically not outsourced, is slated to move in the outsourcing bucket very soon.

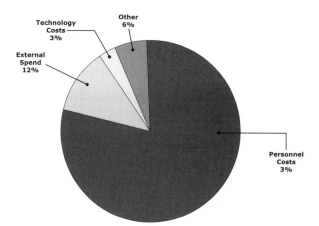

Figure 5.106 Figure 5.106 Breakdown of Average Financial Organization Spending (Source: SAP Insight, Katherina Mullers-Patel)

> **Note**
>
> SAP ERP is also planning to introduce an enhancement pack that details the shared services organization and how it integrates with SAP ERP's other modules.

The only key financial functions that will remain within an organization are treasury, internal controls, and financial strategy and planning. So both AP and AR functions are increasingly handled by outsourced vendors who manage the cash collection as well as vendor payments.

With the move toward shared services and outsourcing, cost incurred by the finance department is coming down as a percentage of revenues of the organization. So organizations have one place where all the AP functions are performed. This has not yet happened with AR, which focuses more on a regional approach so that the organization can listen more to customers. But significant savings can be achieved by sharing people and expertise across multiple divisions for the same function, and organizations are moving aggressively in that direction.

5.13   Summary

In this chapter, you learned about the AP and AR subledgers of financial accounting. You were introduced to some global document settings that can help you achieve standardization and rationalization of your reporting. According to SAP, the key highlights and takeaways of using SAP ERP AP are the following:

- ▶ Direct automatic posting of the GL from AP and AR
- ▶ Effective credit management using collected data and minimizing risk
- ▶ Grouping, expediting, and evaluating purchase orders, deliveries, and invoices to improve purchasing management
- ▶ Settling outstanding payables while taking maximum cash discount.

You also learned about some new functionality such as item interest calculation, downpayment chains, outgoing payments, dunning, and key trends and focuses of SAP ERP going forward. You also gained an understanding of house banks and their integration with AP in relation to the payment process.

Now let's move on to Chapter 6 where you will learn about bank accounting.

In this chapter, you will learn to implement and optimize Bank Accounting. You will learn how to configure banking master data along with the payment transactions. You will also discover some of the key features and uses of the cash journal.

6 Optimizing Financial Business Processes: Bank Accounting Implementation

During banking implementation, it is very important that you finalize the banking formats early and pay special attention to the EDI formats that form the basis of your exchanges with banks. Chapter 5 introduced the concept of the house bank. This chapter outlines the tools and techniques to implement and optimize the Bank Accounting submodule of SAP ERP Financials. In addition, you will learn how to configure and implement the cash journal. It is assumed that your implementation is already done, and now you need to optimize your financial business processes.

SAP Bank Accounting Not SAP Banking

The functions that a typical nonfinancial services organization needs to perform highlight the key interaction points with a financial services company (bank). SAP Banking is a separate module that focuses on the functions that a financial services firm performs.

Most organizations do not need the advanced functionalities that are available in SAP Banking. Using the basic banking functionality described in this chapter, you can cut down your monthly bank reconciliation effort drastically and reduce your working capital and cash flow requirements. After you have implemented these basic functionalities, you can use some of the advanced functionalities to fulfill your business requirement. But implementing these basic functionalities will allow any typical organization to achieve significant cost savings.

You will learn about the key configuration entities in Bank Accounting along with the configuration process diagram and the key configuration steps, illustrated in Figure 6.1.

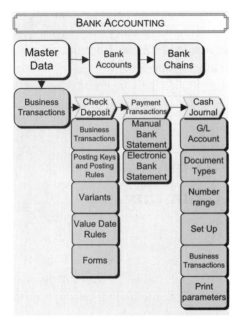

Figure 6.1 Bank Accounting Learning Path

6.1 Bank Accounting: Introduction

Bank Accounting is the submodule that handles the financial interactions with banks and helps maintain the bank structure and the associated relationship with banks. It is also used to define the procedures related to bank reconciliation and handles the transactions pertaining to banking.

Generally during your first wave of implementation, a lean version of Bank Accounting gets implemented. In this chapter you will be introduced to the basic version of Bank Accounting and how you can enhance your implementation with additional features such as the cash journal and electronic bank statements.

Tips

▸ Banking does not have much configuration behind it except the automatic account determination. You just need to understand how to post the master data and the transaction data associated with it.

▸ Banking has automatic transactions that happen based on the import export process between your company and the banking institution. Learn the manual processes first, and then try and master the electronic processing of those functions. Otherwise, you will learn the technical details but miss the overall picture.

6.2   Master Data

The key master data elements of banking data are the basic building blocks of banking. It is very important that you identify these master data elements in detail and ensure that they are in sync with your financial banking partner. Most of configuration and checks in banking are based on master data elements. Let's start with bank directories.

> **Note**
>
> Although it is important that you understand the basic details of how banking is structured, most banking transactions are dependent on your banking partner and their format. So it is important to establish an electronic means of communicating with your bank and to ensure that your system recognizes their formats and vice versa.

6.2.1   Bank Directories

A bank directory is a list of all of the banks that you require for payment transactions with your business partners. This includes the banks of your business partners. Basic things that you will need to maintain in a bank directory are the bank address data and control data such as the SWIFT Code and bank groups. You can either import the bank data automatically using RFBVALL_0 from an ASCII file, or you can manually create the bank master data using the path **SAP Menu • Accounting • Financial accounting • Banks • Master data • Bank master record • Create**. You can also use Transaction FI01. The bank directory is typically uploaded by country and is available from most financial institutions.

6.2.2   House Banks

House banks are the banks in which you have your bank accounts. These are needed so that the payment program can automatically determine the bank details when posting outgoing payments. Setting up house-banks was discussed earlier in AP configuration in Chapter 5.

6.2.3   Business Partner Banks

As you saw earlier when defining vendor and customer master, you can define your business partner's bank details in the customer or vendor master record by entering the bank country, the bank key (equivalent to bank number), and the bank account number. The payment program uses these details to determine the bank address and bank account number for credit transfer forms.

Note

Master data maintenance reaps big dividends. Some of the organizations keep Bank Accounting and AP and AR in silos, which is a cardinal sin. The only way to improve your cash management cycle is by ensuring that all of the vendor masters and customer masters have the correct bank account maintained in the system. These need to be continuously updated as well whenever the business partner's bank account changes.

6.2.4 Checks for Bank Master Data

You can specify different checks and control points that must be applied on a bank master data by country. You can specify the length of the bank account numbers, whether the entry is numeric or alphanumeric, and other details per your requirements. This ensures that the master data is clean and usable.

6.2.5 Bank Chains

Bank chains are also known as multistage payment methods Bank chains are used to make payment via more than one bank. This feature was introduced recently; before that, you had to rely on your house bank and business partner's bank when processing payments, so your payment cycle ended at your house bank.

Bank chains allow you to extend this linkage beyond your original house bank. Using bank chains, you can reduce the payment transaction time and achieve considerable savings via reduced bank charges.

Typical entities that form part of a bank chain are correspondence banks, intermediary banks, or recipient banks. Setting up bank chains in SAP ERP Financials is very simple and is described next.

6.2.6 Configuring Bank Chains

Figure 6.2 shows how you can get to the screen for configuring bank chains. You can use the menu path **IMG • Financial Accounting (New) • Bank Accounting • Bank Chains**.

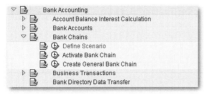

Figure 6.2 Configuring Bank Chains

Bank chains can be configured by following the upcoming instructions:

1. Define the scenario, which is the way in which the bank chain is to be determined. Following are the possible scenarios:

   ▸ Independent of recipient bank (general bank chain)

   ▸ Dependent on recipient bank

   ▸ With which fields and in which order

2. Figure 6.3 shows you the process of defining the scenario. The following activities are part of this configuration step:

   ▸ Check whether the predefined scenarios can be used.

   ▸ Define a new scenario if required.

   ▸ Select **Gen. Search** if payments to be made are not dependent on the partner's bank details. Select **Rec. Search** if the payments are dependent on the bank details.

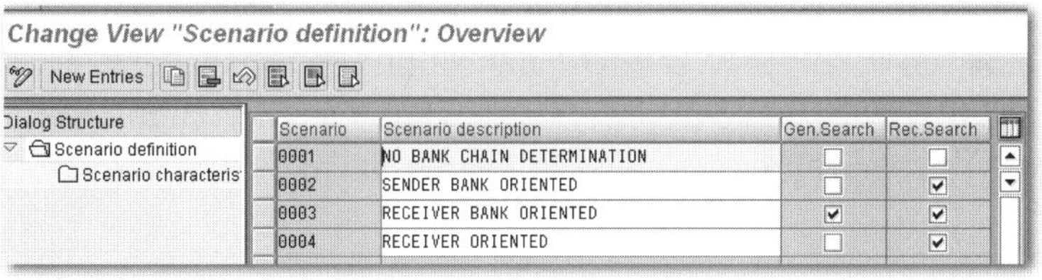

Scenario	Scenario description	Gen.Search	Rec.Search	
0001	NO BANK CHAIN DETERMINATION	☐	☐	
0002	SENDER BANK ORIENTED	☐	☑	
0003	RECEIVER BANK ORIENTED	☑	☑	
0004	RECEIVER ORIENTED	☐	☑	

Change View "Scenario definition": Overview
New Entries
Dialog Structure
▽ Scenario definition
   Scenario characteris

Figure 6.3 Define a Scenario

Figure 6.4 shows the various settings that can be maintained to define which attribute is used to outline the scenario characteristics. You can maintain the rankings of the sender bank, recipient country, receiving bank, and currency, which can be chosen in an appropriate order to reflect the scenario that you want to create for the bank chain. Follow these steps:

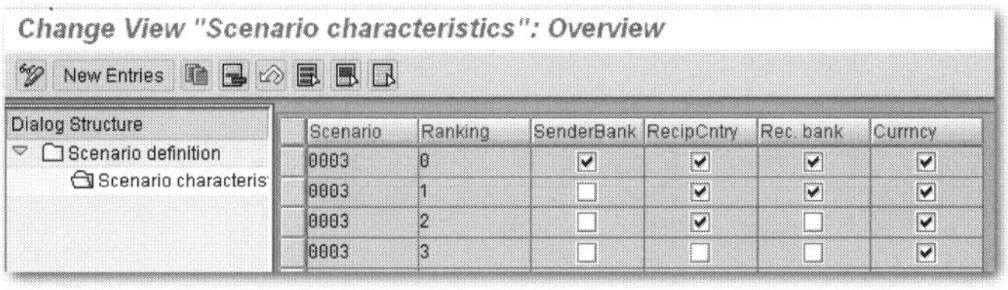

Scenario	Ranking	SenderBank	RecipCntry	Rec. bank	Currncy
0003	0	☑	☑	☑	☑
0003	1	☐	☑	☑	☑
0003	2	☐	☑	☐	☑
0003	3	☐	☐	☐	☑

Change View "Scenario characteristics": Overview
New Entries
Dialog Structure
▽ Scenario definition
   Scenario characteris

Figure 6.4 Define Scenario Characteristics

1. Activate the bank chain, where you specify the bank chain scenario defined in the previous step is to be used for payment (see Figure 6.5).

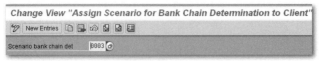

Figure 6.5 Bank Chain Determination

2. Create the general bank chain by defining settings related to bank chains independent of the recipient bank.

3. Define the sequence of steps and the accounts from which the payments are made. Figure 6.6 shows the screen where you can maintain these settings.

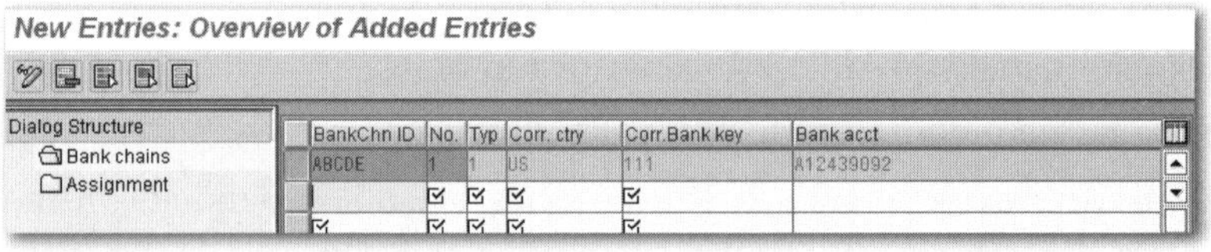

Figure 6.6 Add a New General Bank Chain

For a selected step, you can then define the bank chain to be used for a predefined combination of currency, sender bank country, sender bank key, recipient bank country, recipient bank key, and payment method supplement. Figure 6.7 shows the screen where you can further detail the parameters of a bank chain.

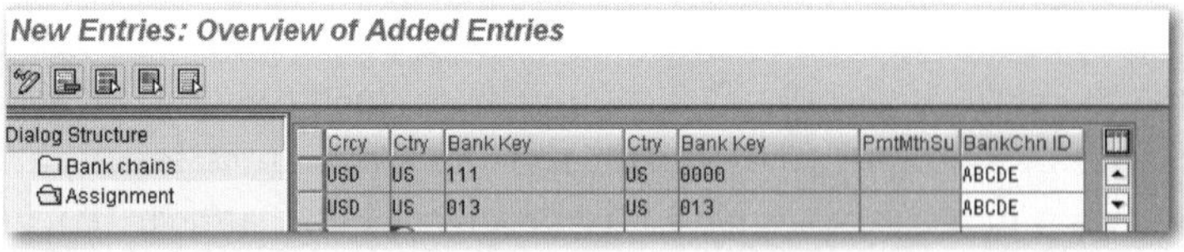

Figure 6.7 Assigning a Bank to a General Bank Chain

Now let's take a detailed look at the transaction data associated with banking.

6.3 Check Deposit

In this section you will learn about the check deposit functionality available in Bank Accounting to enter the checks that you received in the system.

Thousands of checks are deposited that need to clear outstanding AR for the customer. The check deposit functionality helps in the automatic clearing of AR items when you deposit the checks in the system.

Check deposit is used to record the checks received. The manual check deposit is a fast entry tool that reduces the manual effort while entering the checks in Bank Accounting. Only checks received need to be entered. The posting in accounting happens separately either immediately or as a batch job. The system automatically makes the posting to bank clearing and the customer account. A check deposit list can also be handed over to the bank for all of the checks that are entered using this method.

6.3.1 Recording a Check Deposit

The steps in the check deposit process in Bank Accounting are as follows:

1. Enter the checks received.

2. Run the subledger session posting to bank clearing (incoming checks) and customer account.

3. Print the check deposit list, and give it to the bank.

4. Import the bank statement with the bank postings.

The menu path (illustrated in Figure 6.8) is **SAP Menu • Accounting • Financial accounting • Banks • Incomings • Check Deposit • Manual entry**. You can also use Transaction FF68.

Figure 6.8 Check Deposit Transactions in SAP

Next, let's discuss the parameters you need to enter when the bank can be automatically determined either by using the external bank key that is maintained in the customer master or via the house bank setup.

Bank Determination Using Bank Key and Account Number

Figure 6.9 shows the bank determination by using the **Bank Key** and Bank **Account**.

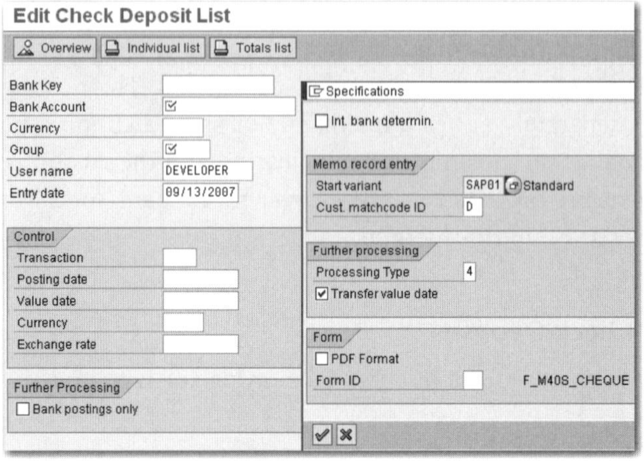

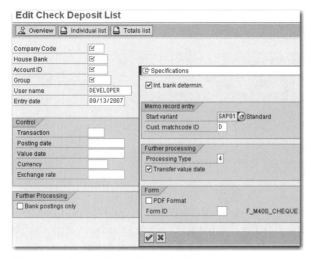

Figure 6.9 External Bank Determination

Internal Bank Determination

Now you check the internal bank determination box (**Int. bank determin.**) on the popup as shown in Figure 6.10. You can use the House Bank and other internal bank details to determine where you are posting your cash deposit.

Figure 6.10 Internal Bank Determination

You can print the list of check deposits by clicking the **Overview** button as shown in Figure 6.10. This list also shows the check deposits made and their processing statuses: posted in full, incomplete postings, or created.

At this point, you might have lots of questions about the check deposit functionality. It is always best to know a little bit about how the transaction looks from the user side and then go back to the configuration to see how you can tweak it. The configuration of the check deposit functionality is covered next to answer any questions you might have.

6.3.2   Configuring Check Deposit

Figure 6.11 shows you how to get to the screen where you can configure check deposits. This is the menu path you will need to follow: **IMG • Financial Accounting • Bank Accounting • Business Transactions • Check Deposit**.

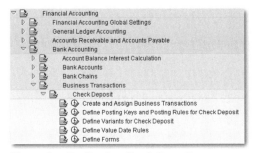

Figure 6.11 Configuring Check Deposit

Review Figure 6.11 and then follow these steps:

1. Select **Create and Assign Business Transactions**. Create and assign business transactions for check deposit. Use the menu path **IMG • Financial Accounting • Bank Accounting • Business Transactions • Check Deposit • Create and Assign Business Transactions** or Transaction OT53.

2. Define transaction indicators.

3. Assign the transaction indicators to **Posting Rules.**

4. Review Figure 6.12 for how to maintain these transaction indicators:

   ▶ **Tran**: The first column identifies the transaction indicator.

   ▶ **+ or −** : Indicates the sign of the incoming amount.

   ▶ **Post. rule**: Helps determine the posting procedure for GL and the subledger.

▶ **Acct mod**: Determines the account assignment to be used for a bank subaccount.

▶ **Text**: Here you can maintain the text for the transaction indicator.

▶ **Trans.**: Determines bank terms and controls the automatic determination of value dates in a check deposit list. If this is blank, then the post date is used to determine the value date.

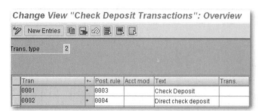

Figure 6.12 Defining Transaction Indicators

5. Select **Define Posting Keys and Posting Rules for Check Deposits**. In this step, the posting rules and posting keys are defined for the various scenarios of check deposit. Before you can define posting rules, you need to select a chart of accounts that you will use for these configuration settings.

The following steps define the posting rules for check deposits:

1. Create account symbols.

2. Assign accounts to account symbols.

3. Create keys for posting rules.

4. Define posting rules.

Use the menu path **IMG • Financial Accounting• Bank Accounting • Business Transactions • Check Deposit • Define Posting Keys and Posting Rules for Check Deposit**. Posting rules represent the business transactions typical of check deposits such as check clearing to customer, bank to incoming check, and incoming check to check clearing. Figure 6.13 shows some of the account symbols that you can use for the check deposit.

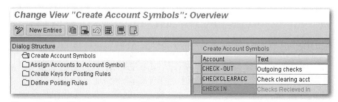

Figure 6.13 Create Account Symbols

Figure 6.14 shows the assignment of the GL accounts to the account symbols.

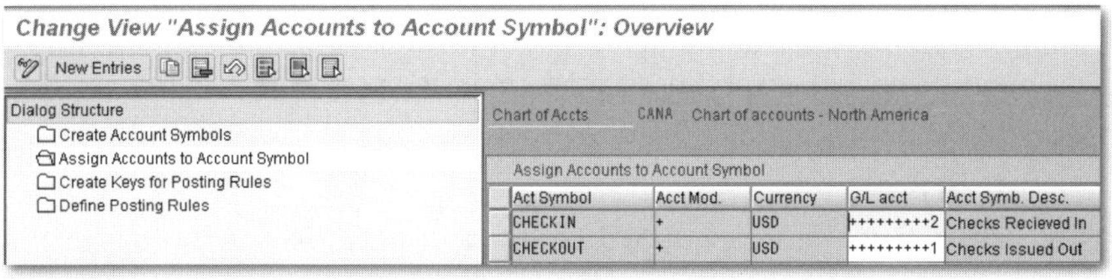

Figure 6.14 Assign Accounts to Account Symbols

The wildcard is indicated by **++++**. So in Figure 6.14, the **CHECKIN** account symbol identifies that the GL account can end in **2**. Figure 6.15 shows how to create keys for defining the posting rules.

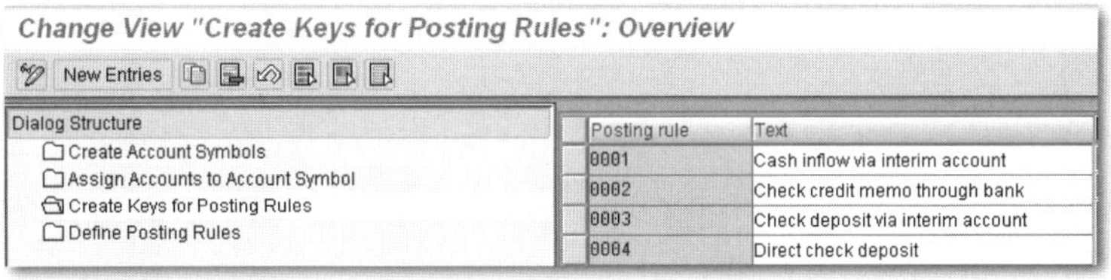

Figure 6.15 Create Keys for Posting Rules

Now that you have defined the account symbols and posting rules, and assigned GL accounts to account symbols, you are ready to define your rules for posting. Figure 6.16 shows the various posting rules available for use.

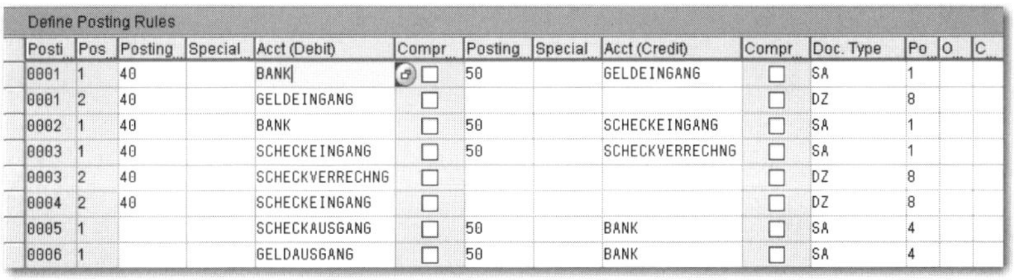

Define Posting Rules

Posti	Pos	Posting	Special	Acct (Debit)	Compr	Posting	Special	Acct (Credit)	Compr	Doc. Type	Po	O	C
0001	1	40		BANK	☐	50		GELDEINGANG	☐	SA	1		
0001	2	40		GELDEINGANG	☐				☐	DZ	8		
0002	1	40		BANK	☐	50		SCHECKEINGANG	☐	SA	1		
0003	1	40		SCHECKEINGANG	☐	50		SCHECKVERRECHNG	☐	SA	1		
0003	2	40		SCHECKVERRECHNG	☐				☐	DZ	8		
0004	2	40		SCHECKEINGANG	☐				☐	DZ	8		
0005	1			SCHECKAUSGANG	☐	50		BANK	☐	SA	4		
0006	1			GELDAUSGANG	☐	50		BANK	☐	SA	4		

Figure 6.16 Define Posting Rules

Here are some rules for the **Posting Rule** field definition:

- **Posting Rule**
  Identifier for the posting rule.
- **Posting Area**
  Options here are 1: bank accounting; 2: subledger accounting.

- ▶ **Posting key (D)**
  Describes the type of line item entered in the posting rule, and controls whether it is a GL or a subledger. This identifies the debit posting key.

- ▶ **Special G/L Indicator (D)**
  This would have the special GL indicator if applicable for the posting rule.

- ▶ **Acct (debit)**
  This defines the account symbol defined in account determination for the debit side.

- ▶ **Compression**
  If this checkbox is selected, then items are compressed automatically before posting.

- ▶ **Posting key (D)**
  This describes the type of line item entered in the posting rule. This controls whether it is a GL or a subledger. This identifies the credit posting key.

- ▶ **Special G/L Indicator (C)**
  This would have the special GL indicator if applicable for the posting rule. This is the indicator on the credit side.

- ▶ **Acct (credit)**
  This defines the account symbol defined in account determination for the credit side.

- ▶ **Compression (C)**
  If this checkbox is selected, then items are compressed automatically before posting.

- ▶ **Document Type**
  This denotes the document type for posting.

- ▶ **Posting Type**
  Figure 6.17 details different posting types.

Figure 6.17 Posting Types

▶ **On account posting**
This defines the posting key.

▶ **Reversal reason**
This identifies the Reversal reason.

Now you will learn how to define variants for the check deposit.

1. Define Variants for Check Deposit. In this configuration setting, you can define custom screen variants for data entry. Follow the menu path **IMG • Financial Accounting • Bank Accounting • Business Transactions • Check Deposit Define Variants for Check Deposit,** or use Transaction OT45. Figure 6.18 shows the standard variant that comes up when you make your settings for specifications.

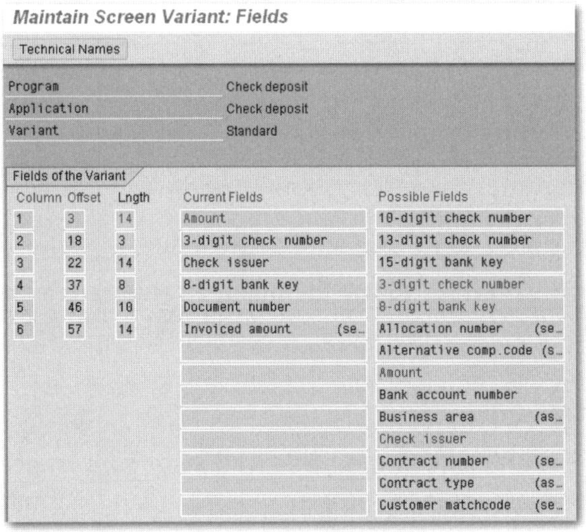

Figure 6.18 Define Variant for Check Deposit

2. You can choose to modify this to define a variant that makes sense for your organization.

3. Define value date rules, which are defined by house bank, account ID, and transaction type. The key determination factors are:

   ▶ Reference date

   ▶ Factory calendar

   ▶ Deviation

Tip

Separate settings can be done by company code.

4. Define forms, which is defined for the manual check deposit that is handed over to the bank along with the checks.

This completes the settings for the check deposit functionality. Next, you will learn more about the payment transaction in Bank Accounting.

6.4 Payment Transactions

The following important payment transactions are available in SAP ERP Financials Bank Accounting:

- ▶ Payment request
- ▶ Payment handling
- ▶ Online payments
- ▶ Manual bank statement
- ▶ Electronic bank statement
- ▶ Lockbox
- ▶ Payment authorization procedure
- ▶ Orbian payments

For these transactions to occur, you need to use the manual bank statement and electronic bank statement.

6.4.1 Manual Bank Statement

Even in this Internet and electronic era, some banks still send bank statements by mail. Manual bank statement is the process of entering the manual statement in Bank Accounting by using the fast entry tool. The reason you should learn the manual statement is to ensure that you understand the rationale for the bank statement upload.

The account assignment process and the associated configuration are very similar to check deposit. You only need to enter the bank statement items and not the posting records. You can then choose to post it immediately or as a batch process. The steps in the manual bank statement process are as follows:

1. Enter the bank statement received.

2. Run the subledger session posting to bank clearing (incoming or outgoing checks) and customer and vendor accounts.

Figure 6.19 shows you the screen for entering the manual bank statement, which is arrived at by using Transaction FF67. You can also use **SAP Menu •
Accounting • Financial Accounting • Banks • Incomings • Bank Statement • Manual Entry**.

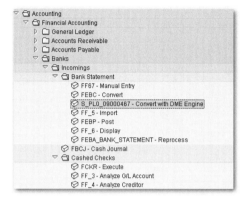

Figure 6.19 Bank Statement Transactions

Figure 6.20 shows you the screen for entering the manual statement with internal bank determination (**Int. bank determin**. is checked in the **Specifications** box). The key parameters that you need to enter in this case are the following:

▸ **Company Code**
▸ **House bank**
▸ **Account ID**
▸ **Statement number**
▸ **Statement date**

You can also maintain the **Beginning balance**, **Ending balance**, and **Posting date** as shown in Figure 6.20.

Figure 6.21 shows you the screen for entering the manual statement without internal bank determination (**Int. bank determin**. is unchecked). Here the bank determination is done by the **Bank Key** and **Bank Account Number**. The remaining parameters, such as **Statement number**, **Statement date**, **Beginning balance**, **Ending balance,** and **Posting date,** are the same as the previous entry with internal bank determination.

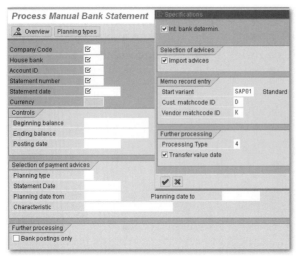

Figure 6.20 Processing Manual Bank Statement: With Internal Bank Determination

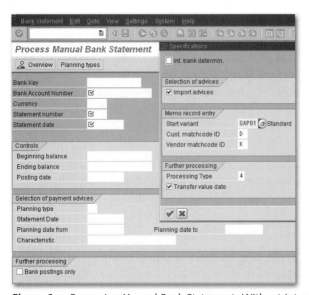

Figure 6.21 Processing Manual Bank Statement: Without Internal Bank Determination

6.4.2 Configuring the Manual Bank Statement

Configuring the manual bank statement is very similar to check deposit configuration. The menu path is **IMG • Financial Accounting • Bank Accounting • Business Transactions • Payment transactions • Manual Bank Statement**.

The configuration menu path for the manual bank statement is shown in Figure 6.22.

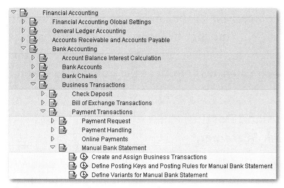

Figure 6.22 Configuring Manual Bank Statement

The steps for configuring the manual statement (seen in Figure 6.22) are as follows:

1. **Create and Assign Business Transactions**
2. **Define Posting Keys and Posting Rules for Manual Bank Statement**
3. **Define Variants for Manual Bank Statement**

These three configuration objects were covered in Section 6.3.2 when you were learning about the check deposit transactions. However, you will learn the variations in this section for configuring the manual bank statement.

6.4.3 Create and Assign Business Transactions

Now let's learn about the business transactions and how these can be assigned to the posting rules for configuring manual bank statement. The menu path is **IMG • Financial Accounting • Bank Accounting • Business Transactions • Payment transactions • Manual Bank Statement • Create and assign Business Transactions**. Figure 6.23 shows the manual bank statements transactions defined.

Change View "Manual Bank Statement Transactions"

New Entries

Trans. type   1

Tran	+-	Post. rule	Acct mod	Int algt...	Text
0001	+	0001			Credit memo
0001	-	0001			Credit memo
0002	+	0002			Check credit memo
0002	-	0002			Check credit memo

Figure 6.23 Defining Manual Bank Statement Transactions

The only addition in this in comparison to the check deposit configuration is the interpretation algorithm field (**Int algt** in Figure 6.23), which will be discussed in detail when the electronic bank statement is covered later in this chapter. This specifies the search mechanism to clear the initial transaction.

6.4.4 Define Posting Keys and Posting Rules for the Manual Bank Statement

This is similar to the configuration of the check deposit with the only difference being that the transaction types are specific to manual bank statement processing. The menu path is **IMG • Financial Accounting • Bank Accounting • Business Transactions • Payment transactions • Manual Bank Statement • Define posting keys and posting rules for manual banks statement**.

6.4.5 Define Variants for Manual Bank Statement

This is similar to the configuration of check deposit. You can use the menu path **IMG • Financial Accounting • Bank Accounting • Business Transactions • Payment transactions • Manual Bank Statement • Define variants for manual bank statement** or Transaction OT43.

Now, let's take a look at processing electronic bank statements.

6.4.6 Electronic Bank Statement

This section details the process of importing bank statements electronically from house banks. Electronic bank statement processing in Bank Accounting is based on the multicash format, but the SWIFT MT940 or BAI are also supported.

> **Note**
>
> BAI is the most common file format for the bank statement used in the United States. Although it is regulated by the Bank Administration Institute, the format is loosely interpreted by most banks and can vary significantly from bank to bank. You might need to customize the format to suit your exact requirements.

Figure 6.19 showed you the menu path for the electronic bank statement processing. Use menu path **SAP Menu • Accounting • Financial Accounting • Banks • Incomings • Bank Statement • Convert/Convert with DME Engine/Import/Post**, or Transactions FEBC/S_PL0_09000467/FF_5/FEBP.

The process of importing and processing electronic bank statement is outlined next.

Converting Data to Multicash Format

If the data format is other than multicash, then these can also be converted to multicash using Transaction FEBC. Figure 6.24 shows some of the programs that can be used to convert the various other banking formats to multicash formats. Therefore, **RFEBBE00** can be used to **Convert Belgium Bank Statement to Multicash Format** as shown in Figure 6.24.

```
Select Program: Generate Multicash format

 Choose

Program title                                                       Program

CODA - Convert Belgium Bank Statement to Multicash Format           RFEBBE00
Convert Bank Statement to Multicash Format (Denmark)               RFEBDK00
Bank statement Spain - conversion to MultiCash format              RFEBESCSB00
Bank Statement  Finland Reference Payments - Convert to MultRFEBFI00
Bank Statement Finland - Conversion to Multicash Format            RFEBFILUM00
Convert Norwegian Bank Statement to MultiCash Format               RFEBNO00
Read EDIFACT Files/Convert into MultiCash Format (Norway)          RFEBNORDIC
Convert Swedish Bank Statement to MultiCash Format                 RFEBSE00
Dunning (Sweden): Convert to MultiCash Format                      RFIDSE_DUNN_EBPOST
```

Figure 6.24 Convert Bank Statements to Multicash Format

Converting Data Using the DME Engine

The DME (distributed management environment) engine can also be used to convert files. The input parameters for the DME engine are shown in Figure 6.25. As you can see, there is not much business input required in the selection parameters. Most of the information relates to technical details as listed here:

▶ **Tree Type**
Determines the transfer structures used when the DMEE format tree is called, which then selects the possible source fields that you can use when you define a DMEE format tree.

▶ **Format Tree**
Used to uniquely identify a format tree in combination with **Tree Type**.

▶ **Read from Local File** or **Read from Application Server**
Allows you to choose the source of the file.

You can also indicate the location where the output file will be stored and then transfer the file in a report form.

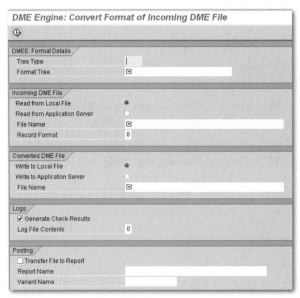

Figure 6.25 Using the DME Engine

After you convert the data in a format that is mutually understandable by the bank, you need to import the data in Bank Accounting, which is described next.

6.4.7 Importing Data in Bank Accounting

After converting the data to a format that your bank recognizes, you need to import the data in Bank Accounting. Keep these points in mind:

▶ Data is imported in Bank Accounting using Transaction FF_5 as shown in Figure 6.26.

▶ Data is imported to a temporary data set in Bank Accounting.

▶ For the data to be imported, the incoming data should be segregated into STATE.TXT and ITEM.TXT files using program RFEBKATX. During implementation of the electronic account statement, this will help with customizing and give you a feel for the options available in the electronic account statement.

The various parameters in Figure 6.26 are explained here:

▶ **Import data** needs to be checked to import the Bank Accounting data in SAP ERP.

Figure 6.26 Importing Bank Statement Data in Bank Accounting

▶ **Elect. Bank Statement Format** are as follows:

  ▶ M: Multicash.

  ▶ A: BAI format primarily used in the United States.

  ▶ I and S: SWIFT MT940 international format.

▶ **Statement file** contains the header level information.

▶ **Line item file** contains the line item information.

▶ **Workstation upload** needs to be checked if you are uploading the file from your local workstation.

▶ **Posting parameters** can be set up as **Post Immediately**, **Generate Batch Input**, or as **Do not post**.

▶ You can use **Assign value date** to transfer the value date to the account.

You can also make settings related to **Cash management**, **Algorithms** for selecting document numbers, and reference numbers within a document number. **Output controls** is used to specify printing details.

Bank Statement Posting

After importing the bank statement in Bank Accounting in the previous step, you can post the bank statement clearing the checks deposited and checks that have been cashed by business partners. Keep the following in mind:

▸ Data can be posted either via batch or immediately into bank clearing transactions and subledger transactions. Transaction FEBP is used for posting and is shown in Figure 6.27.

▸ The system determines how the data will be posted using the **Note to payee** field in the bank statement. The **Note to payee** field contains the document number or the invoice number that was cleared.

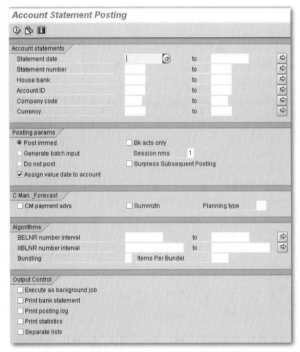

Figure 6.27 Account Statement Posting (Transaction -FEBP)

Postprocessing Functions

After posting your bank statements, you might need to modify or update some of the line items because they did not get posted correctly. The earlier Transaction FEBA for postprocessing is replaced by Transaction FEBAN. Using this, you can correct the items not yet posted electronically in less time. The new Transaction's selection parameters are shown in Figure 6.28.

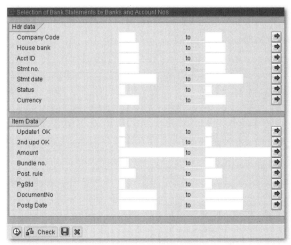

Figure 6.28 Postprocessing Bank Statements Using FEBAN

As shown in Figure 6.28, you can use the selection parameters at header level, such as **Company Code**, **House bank**, **Acct ID** (Account ID), **Stmt no.**(Statement number), **Stmt date** (Statement date), **Status,** and **Currency**. At the item level, you can use the update numbers (**Update 1 OK, 2nd upd OK**), the currency **Amount,** and posting rules (**Post. rule**) to go back into the posted transactions and correct them.

> **Note**
>
> The batch report RFEBKA00 imports account statements into the banking module and then creates batch input sessions for updating the GL and any applicable subsidiary ledgers.

Now that you understand the sequence of steps for processing electronic bank statements, let's discuss how to configure the electronic bank statement.

6.4.8   Configuring the Electronic Bank Statement

The menu path for this configuration is **IMG • Financial Accounting • Bank Accounting • Business Transactions • Payment transactions • Electronic Bank Statement**. See Figure 6.29 for the screen for Configuring Electronic Bank Statements.

The objective for customizing the electronic bank statement is that all of the business transactions communicated by the external bank are interpreted correctly and subsequently posted correctly.

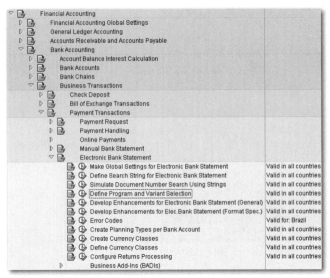

Figure 6.29 Configuring the Electronic Bank Statement

> **Note**
>
> Testing bank statements is very important. Whenever you have a third part invol-ved (in this case, a bank), it is very important that you perform a thorough testing to ensure that the bank understands your file and acts on it, and that you under-stand the bank's file.

Transaction types are used to group together similar types of external transac-tions, which are then assigned to posting rules that determine the appropriate account assignment.

Define Global Settings for the Electronic Bank Statement

The global settings are very similar to the manual bank statement. The po-sting rules detailed earlier in the check deposit follow the same structure here. Additional configuration in the electronic bank statement includes the assignment of transaction types to posting rules and the assignment of bank accounts to transaction types. The menu path is **IMG • Financial Accoun-ting • Bank Accounting • Business Transactions • Payment transactions • Electronic Bank Statement • Make global settings for electronic bank statement**. Figure 6.30 illustrates the various settings that you can maintain for configuring the electronic bank statement.

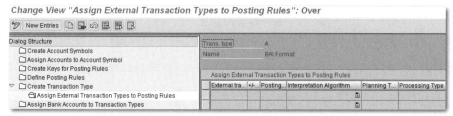

Figure 6.30 Global Settings for Electronic Bank Statement

The interpretation algorithm determines how the system interprets the Note to payee information and then uses it to clear open items automatically. These algorithms can identify pertinent data and then perform the postprocessing. The list of interpretation algorithms is shown in Figure 6.31.

You can define your own interpretation algorithms from **901** to **909** so that you can communicate with your bank correctly. All of the other key parameters for configuring electronic bank statements are similar to the manual bank statement.

> **Tips**
>
> ▶ Functional enhancement FEB0001allows you to change the way the electronic statement is processed.
> ▶ Use the Electronic Statement Implementation Tool (RFEBKATX).

The quick and efficient installation of the electronic account statements has some obstacles:

▶ Creating the files UMSATZ.TXT and AUSZUG.TXT is a complex process. Typically, implementation errors arise from incorrect creation (format errors) of these files. Also the files from the bank are usually very big and difficult to manage.

▶ Open items to be found and cleared using the electronic account statement must usually be entered into the (test) system manually and with correct clearing information. This information must also exist in the correct fields in the individual line items in the UMSATZ.TXT file (for example, in the Note to payee fields).

You can use the program RFEBKATX to create open items in a company code and the related (MULTICASH) account statement files for a house bank account. You can import this directly using program RFEBKA00, so test both your customizing settings and the general functions provided by program RFEBKA00.

Interpret. algrt...	Short text
000	000: No interpretation
001	001: Standard algorithm
011	011: Outgoing check: check no. different from pymt doc.no.
012	012: Outgoing check: check number same as payment doc.no.
013	013: Outgoing check: check number = or <> payment doc.no.
015	015: Clearing transaction: selection using assignment
019	019: Reference no. (DME management)
020	020: Document number search
021	021: Reference document number search
022	022: Bank transfer method (Germany only) with doc.numbers
023	023 Bank transfer method (Germany only) with ref.numbers
024	024: Reserved
025	025: Invoice list
026	026: Ref.doc.no. - Search with preceding zeroes if <10
027	027: Reference number (TITO)
028	028: Reference number using MULTICASH conversion programs
029	029: Payment order number
030	030: Brazilian search using BELNR, GJAHR, and BUZEI
031	031: Document number search (customer number from doc.line)
032	032: Look for EDI payment advice
033	033 Search for Payment Advice Notes
034	034 Finland Reference Number for Payment Order with RFFOFI_A
035	035 Search for structured payment notes -> SAP Note 555352
050	050: REAL ESTATE: First standard, then rental agrmt search
051	051: REAL ESTATE: Rental agreement search, then standard
120	120 Document Number Search Without Test Read
121	121 Reference Document Number Search Without Test Read
901	901: Customer-Specific Interpretation Algorithm 1
902	902: Customer-Specific Interpretation Algorithm 2
903	903: Customer-Specific Interpretation Algorithm 3
904	904: Customer-Specific Interpretation Algorithm 4
905	905: Customer-Specific Interpretation Algorithm 5
906	906: Customer-Specific Interpretation Algorithm 6
907	907: Customer-Specific Interpretation Algorithm 7
908	908: Customer-Specific Interpretation Algorithm 8
909	909 Customer-Specific Interpretation Algorithm 9

Figure 6.31 Interpretation Algorithms

Receiving Account Statements Using Electronic Data Interchange

You can send and receive your statements via EDI to speed up the communication and automate the reconciliation process. The process flow while processing account statements via EDI occurs in three stages:

1. Data is automatically imported into the system, where it is stored in the bank data storage or in the payment advice database. The formats and the other details are the same.

2. Schedule the report program RFEBKA30 to generate financial postings from the electronic account statement.

3. Process the account statement using the postprocessing Transaction FEBAN.

Tip
Bank Accounting provides you with enhancement FEDI0005, which has user exits EXIT_SAPLIEDP_201 and EXIT_SAPLIEDP_202, to read and modify the data set when processing the FINSTA01 type interim documents.

Now that you are familiar with the manual and electronic bank statements, you will learn about cash journal in the next section. Cash journal can save time while recording your cash transactions.

6.5 Cash Journal

The cash journal is a subledger of the banking module that was created to keep a tab on cash transactions. It shows the opening balance and closing balance of cash and represents the cash GL account. You need to implement the cash journal only if you have a huge volume of repetitive incoming payments.

6.5.1 Cash Journal Process

Some of the salient features of the cash journal are as follows:

▶ It is used to manage a company's cash transactions.

▶ A separate cash journal should be created for each currency.

▶ Multiple cash journals can be run in the same company code.

▶ Cash journal entries are processed in two steps:

  ▶ Create the cash journal entries.

  ▶ Transfer the cash journal entries to financial accounting.

▶ Cash journal is a single-screen transaction.

From SAP R/3 release 4.6C onward, checks can also be received in the cash journal. The menu path is **SAP Menu • Accounting • Financial Accounting • Banks • Incomings • Cash Journal**, and the Transaction is FBCJ. Figure 6.32 shows you the screen you arrive at after following that path or code.

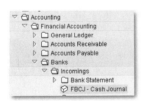

Figure 6.32 Cash Journal Menu Path

On executing the transaction, you reach a screen where you can maintain the cash journal transactions. Remember, the cash journal is a one-screen transaction. Figure 6.33 shows the cash journal transaction screen, which shows the **Cash payments** tab. As shown in the figure, you can always see the

Opening balance, **Total cash receipts**, **Total check receipts**, and **Total cash payments**. A combination of all of these transactions gives you the **Closing balance**. This is especially useful from a cashier's perspective.

As you can see, you just need to make single line entries of the actual reason you are receiving the cash, and the system automatically makes the offsetting entry to the cash GL account when you transfer the transactions to accounting.

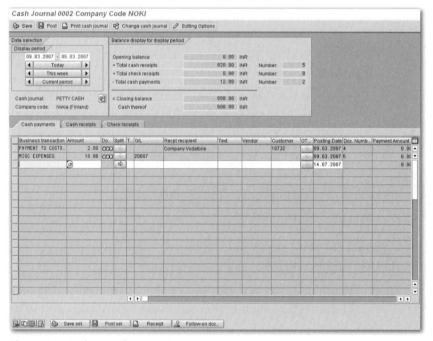

Figure 6.33 Cash Journal Transaction Screen

Figures 6.34 and 6.35 show the cash receipts and check deposit screens respectively.

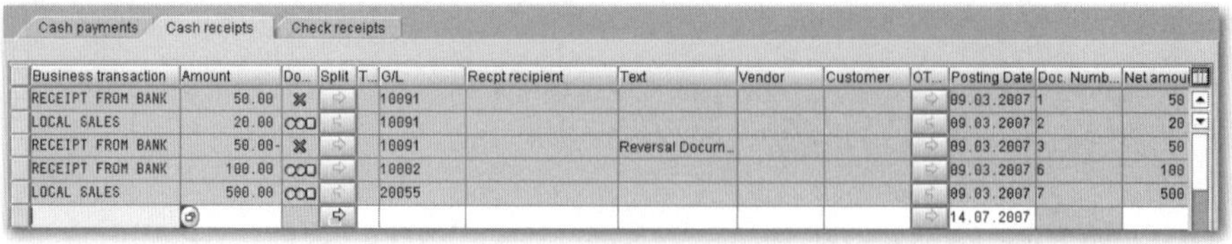

Figure 6.34 Cash Receipts

The cash journal is saved locally and then transferred to accounting every day. You can do all of the cash-related transactions on one screen. The cash journal entries can be entered, changed, and displayed from the same screen. The entries can also be printed along with the posted cash journal entries.

From SAP R/3 4.7 onward, one cash journal document can have multiple tax codes and/or controlling object assignments. Thus, one cash journal document can have multiple lines with different tax codes and controlling object assignments. This gets transferred to FI as one document.

Figure 6.35 Check Receipts

> **Note**
>
> When posting to one-time accounts, record the address of the customer and vendor when you are recording the cash transaction.

6.5.2 Configuring the Cash Journal

This section describes the configuration and setup of the cash journal in banking. The menu path is **IMG • Financial Accounting • Bank Accounting • Business Transactions • Cash Journal**. The screen for configuring the cash journal is shown in Figure 6.36.

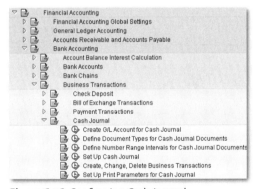

Figure 6.36 Configuring Cash Journal

The process for configuring a new cash journal in a company code requires the following activities:

▶ Define the cash journal identifier.

▶ Define the GL accounts for posting cash journal transactions.

- ▶ Identify the currency for cash journal.
- ▶ Identify the document types for the following:
    - ▶ GL account postings
    - ▶ Outgoing payments to vendors
    - ▶ Incoming payments from customers
    - ▶ Outgoing payments to customers
    - ▶ Incoming payments from vendors

Sequentially, the activities discussed in the following subsections need to happen in the configuration.

Create GL Account for Cash Journal

In this step, a GL account is created for the cash journal. Use the menu path **IMG • Financial Accounting • Bank Accounting • Business Transactions • Cash Journal • Create General ledger Account for Cash Journal,** or use Transaction FS00. Keep these caveats in mind while creating the GL record:

- ▶ The general account so chosen can only be posted automatically and displays a unique account currency.
- ▶ If multiple cash journals with different currencies point to this GL account, then make sure that the balances in local currency indicator is not set in the GL master, and the account currency is the same as company code currency.

Other than these, the GL account creation is the same as creating any other GL account.

Define Document Types for Cash Journal Documents

This is also the same as defining a new document type, which was discussed in Chapter 5. The menu path is **IMG • Financial Accounting • Bank Accounting • Business Transactions • Cash Journal • Define Document Types for Cash Journal Documents**. The Transaction is OBA7. The document types should have already been defined. You can just pick the appropriate ones that have the right subledgers (GL Account, Vendor Account, Customers, etc.) defined.

Define Number Range Intervals for Cash Journal Documents

This is also similar to defining number ranges for the financial documents. However, it is specific to cash journal documents only. The number range is defined by company code. You can use the menu path **IMG • Financial**

**Accounting • Bank Accounting • Business Transactions • Cash Journal •
Define Number Range Intervals for Cash Journal documents** or Transaction FBCJC1. Figure 6.37 shows the screen where you can maintain the cash journal documents' number ranges.

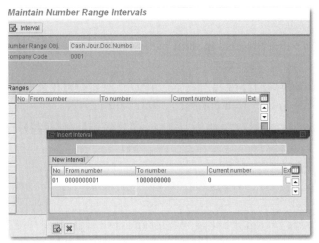

Figure 6.37 Maintain Number Range Intervals for Cash Journal Documents

Set Up Cash Journal

The menu path for setting up the cash journal is **IMG • Financial Accounting • Bank Accounting • Business Transactions • Cash Journal • Set Up Cash Journal**. You can also use Transaction FBCJC0. Setting up a new cash journal requires the definition of the following fields as illustrated in Figure 6.38:

▶ **Company Code**
The company code relevant for cash journal transaction.

▶ **Number**
This uniquely identifies a cash journal within a company code.

▶ **G/L Account**
The GL account to which the cash journal is eventually posted. This is typically the petty cash account.

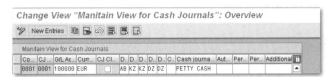

Figure 6.38 Setting Up Cash Journal

▶ **Currency**
The currency for the cash journal. Several cash journals with different currencies can correspond to the same GL account. However, to define different cash journals in the same currency in the same company code, you need to define new GL accounts.

▶ **Cash Journal Closed**
This identifier indicates that the cash journal has been closed.

▶ **Document Types**
This identifies the document types for GL account postings, that is, outgoing and incoming payments from customers and vendors.

▶ **Name**
The cash journal identification name.

▶ **Authorization Group**
Used to define authorizations and control access for a particular cash journal.

▶ **Person 1, Person 2**
These identify the names of important people for the cash journal, such as the cashier and the manager for the cashier.

▶ **Text**
Additional information regarding cash journal can be maintained here.

Create, Change, Delete Business Transactions

In this step, the business transactions relevant for the cash journal are configured. The menu path is **IMG • Financial Accounting • Bank Accounting • Business Transactions • Cash Journal • Create, Change, Delete Business Transactions**. The screen for defining the business transactions is shown in Figure 6.39.

New Entries: Overview of Added Entries

Maintain View for Cash Journal Transaction Names

Co...	Tra...	B	G/L Accoun...	T...	Cash journal business...	BusTraBlkd	Acct Mod.	Tax Mod.
0001	1	E	476000	V1	OFFICE SUPPLIES	☐	☑	☑
0001	2	C	300050		RECEIPT FROM BANK	☐	☐	☐
0001	3	R	300050		LOCAL SALES	☐	☐	☐
0001	4	E	300050		MISC EXPENSES	☐	☐	☐

Figure 6.39 Defining Cash Journal Business Transactions

The following fields need to be defined for configuring business transactions within a cash journal:

▶ **Company Code**
This is the company code in which the business transaction is created.

▸ **Business Transaction Number**
This is a random number that uniquely identifies the business transactions.

▸ **Business Transaction Type**
The following categories of business transaction types have been predefined, and these link to the document types:

- ▸ **E**: Expenses
- ▸ **R**: Revenue
- ▸ **B**: Cash transfer cash journal to bank
- ▸ **C**: Cash transfer bank to cash journal
- ▸ **D**: Customers incoming and outgoing payments
- ▸ **K**: Vendors incoming and outgoing payments

▸ **G/L Account**
Here you need to maintain the expense or revenue account for the offsetting posting of GL account postings. No entries are needed for business transactions D and K because the GL account automatically gets determined from the vendor master or customer master.

▸ **Tax Code**
This determines the business transaction control. You need to make this entry only for expenses (E) and revenue (R).

▸ **Cash Journal Business Transaction**
This describes the business transaction.

▸ **Business Transaction Block**
If you check this indicator, it prevents any further postings to the business transaction.

▸ **Account Modifiable during Document Entry**
This indicator, if checked, allows you to modify the GL account during document entry.

▸ **Tax Code Modifiable during Document Entry**
This indicator, if checked, allows you to modify the tax code during document entry. The tax code defined is a default value that can be changed later.

Now you will learn how to set up print parameters for the cash journal.

Set Up Print Parameters for the Cash Journal

This is used to set up print parameters for printing the cash journal and cash journal receipts. These settings are not relevant for Brazil, Canada, the United States and India, and are made by company code. The print program to be used for the cash journal is RFCASH00. The report variants to be used are FI_CASH_BB (opening balance text), FI_CASH_EB (closing balance text), FI_CASH_CF (carry forward text), and FI_CASH_SI (signature text).

For the cash journal receipts, specify the correspondence type and the indicator **Accounting documents,** which, if set, means that the receipts are printed based on accounting documents. If you do not set this indicator, then all of the receipts in the cash journal can be printed. The menu path is **IMG • Financial Accounting • Bank Accounting • Business Transactions • Cash Journal • Set Up Print Parameters for Cash Journal**. Figure 6.40 shows how you can maintain the print parameters (**Program, Variant, and Correspondence Type**) by **Company Code (Co...)**.

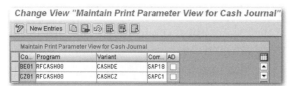

Figure 6.40 Setting Up Print Parameters for the Cash Journal

6.6 Summary

In this chapter, you learned about Bank Accounting, including master data and key business transactions, which include the manual bank statement, the electronic bank statement, and the check deposit. You were also introduced to the cash journal, which can be used to record petty cash transactions within a very short time frame.

In addition to the topics that you learned in this chapter, SAP ERP has structured more advanced web integration of financial transactions in Financial Supply Chain Management (FSCM), which can be used to manage your banking transactions in a more flexible and customizable fashion. Also SAP ERP now offers a new enhancement for banking relationship management that takes away some of the pain that organizations have when configuring and implementing Bank Accounting. In banking relationship management, you can use the SWIFT adaptor, which can help integrate your organization to the banking system.

Now that you've learned how to manage your relationship with banks, you can proceed to Chapter 7, where you will learn more about asset accounting, which is used to manage your fixed assets.

*Asset Accounting allows you to manage your fixed assets by perform-
ing all of the routine business transactions, such as asset acquisition,
asset transfers, asset retirement, and period-end activities, including
depreciation run and balance carryforward. The Asset Accounting
module is a statutory reporting module that allows you to ensure
compliance to GAAP principles by country.*

7 Optimizing Financial Business Processes for Asset Accounting

Asset Accounting (FI-AA) is the SAP ERP Financials submodule that records
fixed asset-related transactions. It is a subledger for the SAP ERP Financials
GL and provides functionality for processing fixed asset-related transactions.
Asset Accounting rules are driven by GAAP standards, which can vary across
countries. However, SAP Asset Accounting comes preconfigured with the
basic structure ready to implement Asset Accounting across countries.

Asset Accounting receives input from MM especially in the procurement
cycle when you buy an asset. From the Plant Maintenance (PM) module, the
plant maintenance activities that require capitalization can be directly passed
to Asset Accounting. In this chapter, you will learn how you can configure
the system to integrate with these logistics components, and you will learn
the key configuration entities along with their detailed configuration process
diagrams. You can review the Asset Accounting process in Figure 7.1, which
is also the path this chapter will follow.

7.1 Asset Organization Elements and Structure

Asset Accounting maps the organization structure by using assignments to
other enterprise organization entities. The chart of depreciation and the depreciation area are organization entities created specifically for assets. The
chart of depreciation can differ by company codes, so they are assigned at
a company code level. The chart of depreciation is used to manage the legal
requirements for valuation and reporting of assets. Asset Accounting can be
used to manage the value of assets in parallel (up to 99 depreciation areas).

The chart of depreciation is a directory of depreciation areas combined together. A depreciation area is always assigned to one chart of depreciation.

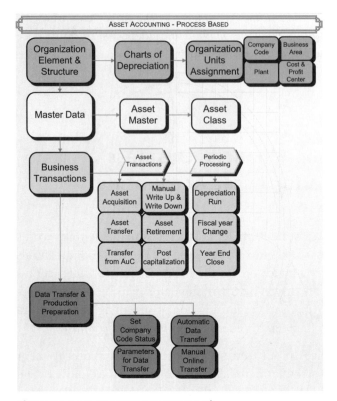

Figure 7.1 Asset Accounting Learning path

A company code can be assigned to only one chart of depreciation. And a company code can be assigned to only one chart of accounts. However, several company codes can have the same chart of depreciation but different charts of accounts and vice versa. Figure 7.2 shows the relationship of **Operating Chart of Accounts**, **Chart of Depreciation**, and **Company Code**.

An asset can be assigned to multiple organization units in the asset master. However, you have to make some basic assignments in Asset Accounting to configure asset management. These are discussed next.

7.1.1 Company Code Assignment

It is important to define company codes relevant for Asset Accounting. The following asset-related settings are done at a company code level:

- Chart of depreciation
- Depreciation area
- Number range assignment for asset masters
- Fiscal year variant
- Depreciation area for net worth tax
- Document type for posting depreciation

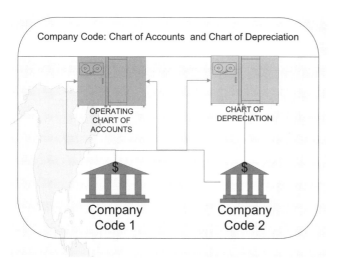

Figure 7.2 Charts of Depreciation and Charts of Accounts

7.1.2   Business Area Assignments

If a business area balance sheet is required, then assets require a mandatory business area assignment.

7.1.3   Plant and Location Assignments

The plant and location are used to generate reports regarding the physical location of assets. This assignment does not have any accounting significance. These assignments can be made in a time-dependent fashion.

7.1.4   Cost Center and Profit Center Assignments

These assignments are made so that you can record the Controlling postings per the internal reporting requirements when the depreciation run is executed. This assignment is also time-based.

> **Note**
>
> When assigning a chart of depreciation to a company code, make sure that the following entries have been maintained for the company code: currency, chart of accounts, fiscal year version, and input tax indicator for nontaxable transactions. The last one is easy to forget. You can perform the last setting using Transaction OBCL.

Now that you understand the basic structure of Asset Accounting let's take a detailed look at the asset master.

7.2 Asset Master

You need to understand assets from three different perspectives that translate effectively to the hierarchical levels at which you can delineate the asset master:

- **Balance Sheet Level**
  This starts from how you will represent fixed assets in the balance sheet that is generated for the company code. The sublevels at this stage are: financial statement version, balance sheet item, and GL accounts with increasing level of detail. This level is used to group similar asset classes together and is used in statutory reporting. This is the book-keeping structure that is kept for assets.
- **Classification Level**
  These are asset classes that typically correspond to GL accounts. But these can be defined to be more granular than the GL accounts.
- **Asset Related Structure**
  This is at the asset master level where the classification is group number, main asset number, subnumber, and line items. Simple asset has a subnumber of 0000, whereas complex asset with components can have one asset number with multiple subnumbers. Group asset is represented by a separate number in the system and is used to group together assets so that all of them can be depreciated together instead of individually.

It is important to understand these levels of assets before undertaking any asset implementation. There are many opportunities to simplify and rationalize the asset structure when you transfer assets from legacy systems.

> **Note**
>
> The asset class is the most important means of structuring assets because it typically has one-to-one correspondence with the GL account setup.

7.2.1   Creating an Asset Master

As you follow the process of creating an asset master, you will also understand the features of the asset master. The menu path you will need to follow is **SAP Menu Accounting • Financial accounting • Fixed Assets • Asset • Create • Asset**, and the Transaction is AS01. On executing Transaction AS01, the screen shown in Figure 7.3 comes up.

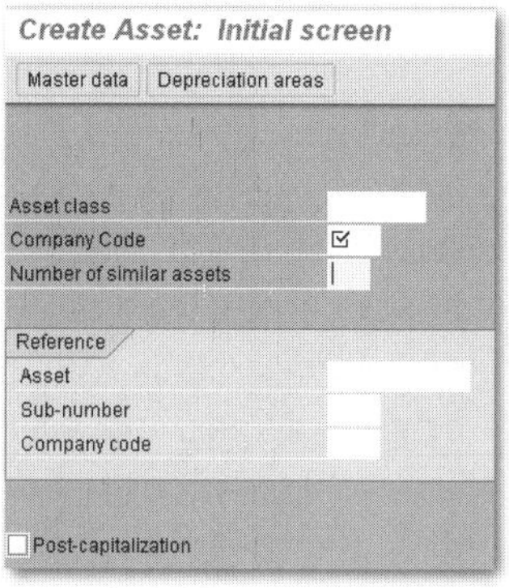

Figure 7.3 Creating a New Asset: Initial Screen

If you want, you can either enter the asset class or a reference asset whose asset class gets used for the new asset. For example, if you enter the machinery asset class and press Enter, you can maintain parameters in various tabs.

General Data Tab

In this tab, you can enter the **Description**, **Serial number**, **Inventory number**, and **Quantity** with its unit of measure in the **General data** tab. In addition, you can maintain the posting information of the capitalization date.

> **Note**
>
> The capitalization date is the most important field for the depreciation run.

Time-Dependent Tab

After you maintain the general parameters, you can move on to maintain the account assignment parameters. Here you can maintain the account assignments (Cost Center, Plant, Business Area, Location, Fund, Functional Area, Grant, Funds Center, etc.) which are tied to the asset master.

Allocation Tab

After you maintain the account assignments, you can maintain the evaluation groups. These can be customized to include your legacy data per your requirements, however, you are restricted to four characters for four of the five evaluation groups. The fifth evaluation group can have eight characters. You can also maintain the asset super number if applicable. In addition, you can integrate assets and plant maintenance equipment creation using the same tab.

Origin Tab

In this tab, you can maintain the original vendor for the asset and the manufacturer. You can also specify whether the asset is a brand new or a used asset. You can specify the asset type that can be used to categorize assets per your requirements. In addition, you can maintain the original acquisition year and original value along with the percentage of the asset that was created in house. Also you can assign an investment order to this investment.

Leasing Tab

In this tab, you can maintain the parameters for leasing. First you need to identify whether it is a capital lease or operational lease. Then you can enter the **Base value as new**, the **Purchase price**, the number of lease payments, and the amount of lease payment. You can also specify whether the lease payment has to be made as an advance payment at the beginning of the month. This changes the way net present value is calculated for the lease amount.

Depreciation Areas Tab

In this tab, you can maintain the depreciation areas. Generally, you do not have to change anything on this tab because the data defaults from the asset class configuration. But you can choose to change the useful life and other details if you so choose depending on the asset master.

After saving, you get a new asset number. Now that you are familiar with the asset master from the user's perspective, you will learn the configuration of the asset master.

7.2.2 Configuring Asset Master Data

The screen for configuring asset master data is shown in Figure 7.4. Follow **IMG • Financial Accounting • Asset accounting • Fixed Assets • Master Data**.

Broadly, the configuration of the asset master data can be divided into the headings described in the following subsections.

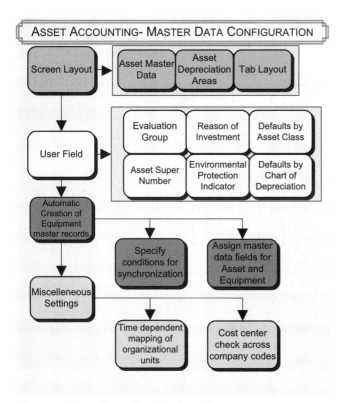

Figure 7.4 Asset Master Data Configuration

Screen Layout

First you need to customize the way the user fields are displayed in the asset master. For this you will need to follow **IMG • Financial Accounting • Asset accounting • Fixed Assets • Master Data • Screen Layout**. The screen layout definition consists of identifying the logical field groups and then defining whether the individual fields are required, optional, or display only. For defining the screen layout the menu path is **IMG • Financial Accounting • Asset accounting • Fixed Assets • Master Data • Screen Layout • Define Screen Layout for Asset Master Data**. Figure 7.5 shows the parameters you can maintain for a screen layout: **Logical field groups** and **Field group rules**.

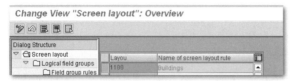

Figure 7.5 Define Screen Layout for Asset Master Data

Screen layouts for assets are typically created by asset classes. Figure 7.6 shows how you can detail out the logical field groups. These identify the list of tabs that will appear for the screen layout.

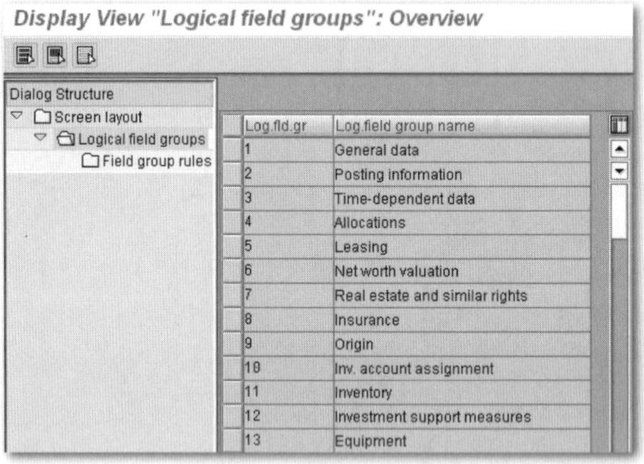

Figure 7.6 Logical Field Groups within an Asset Screen Layout

Figure 7.7 shows the **Field group rules** setting for the **Logical fld grp** Posting information.

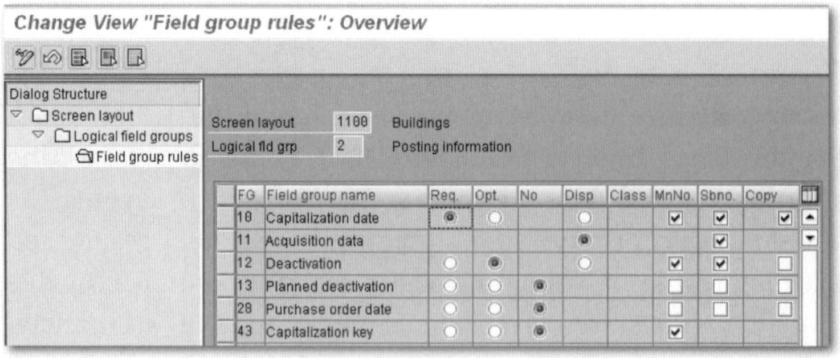

Figure 7.7 Field Groups rules within Logical Field Groups

The Field group rules definition attributes include the following:

▸ Fields are identified as Required (**Req.**), Optional (**Opt.**), Suppressed (**No**), or Display (**Disp**).

- ▶ If the **Class** checkbox is selected, then entry is allowed in the asset class.

- ▶ If the **MnNo.** checkbox is checked, then the entry for the field in the main number is transferred to the subnumber.

- ▶ If **SbNo.** is checked, then the entry for the field can also be made in the subnumber of the asset.

- ▶ If the **Copy** field is checked, then the field gets copied if you create an asset with reference to any asset.

Define the Screen Layout for Asset Depreciation Areas

Here you define the screen layout for the asset depreciation areas. The menu path is **IMG • Financial Accounting • Asset accounting • Fixed Assets • Master Data • Screen Layout • Define Screen Layout for Asset Depreciation Areas**. The Transaction is AO21. Figure 7.8 shows the screen layout for the depreciation areas.

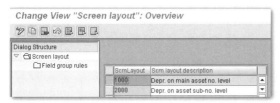

Figure 7.8 Defining Screen Layout for the Asset Depreciation Areas

Figure 7.9 shows how you can define the field group rules by screen layout. The settings you see in this figure are similar to the ones we discussed in the previous step.

Define the Tab Layout for Asset Master Data

Here you can customize the tab layouts per your requirements. For simplicity and ease of understanding, take a look at the preconfigured standard layouts. For this you should follow the menu path **IMG • Financial Accounting • Asset accounting • Fixed Assets • Master Data • Screen Layout • Specify Tab Layout for Asset Master Record • Define Tab Layout for Asset Master Data**, or use Transaction AOLA. Figure 7.10 shows the initial screen with the standard layouts for the tabs.

Figure 7.11 shows the **Tab Pages** titles that can be maintained for one of the tab layouts.

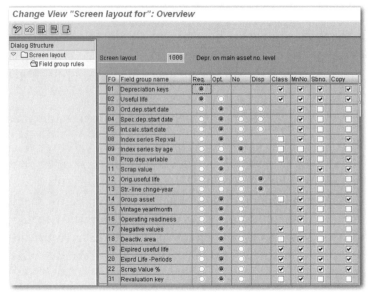

Figure 7.9 Defining Field Group Level data for Asset depreciation Area screen layout

Figure 7.10 Define the Tab Layout for the Asset Master data

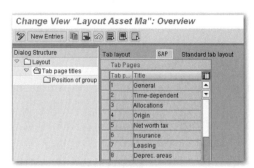

Figure 7.11 Define Tab Page Titles

Figure 7.12 shows the **Position of Groups** for the **General** tab page title.

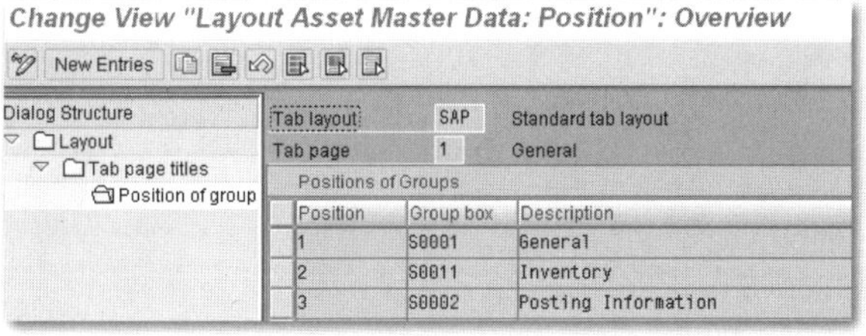

Figure 7.12 Define Position of Groups Within Tabs

You can change the position of these tabs if required to make sure that the important tabs are in the front when you are creating an asset master.

Assign Tab Layouts to Asset Classes

Here you can assign the tab layouts defined in the previous step to asset classes. Follow the menu path **IMG • Financial Accounting • Asset accounting • Fixed Assets • Master Data • Screen Layout • Specify Tab Layout for Asset Master Record • Assign Tab Layouts to Asset Classes**, or use Transaction AOLK. Figure 7.13 shows the process of assigning the asset classes to tab layouts.

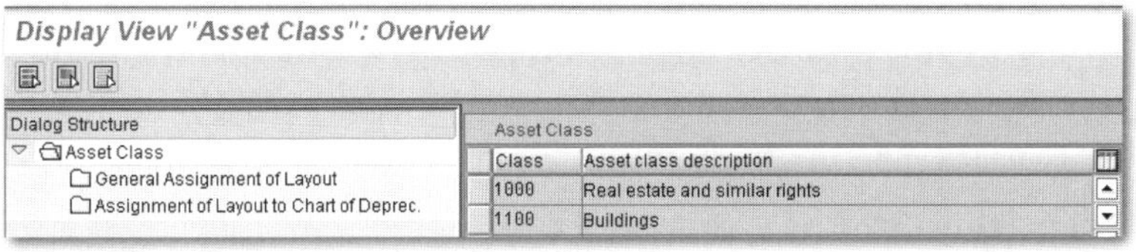

Figure 7.13 Assign Tab Layouts to Asset Classes

After you select an **Asset Class** and click on **General Assignment of Layout** in the left pane, you can assign appropriate general tab layouts to asset classes as shown in Figure 7.14.

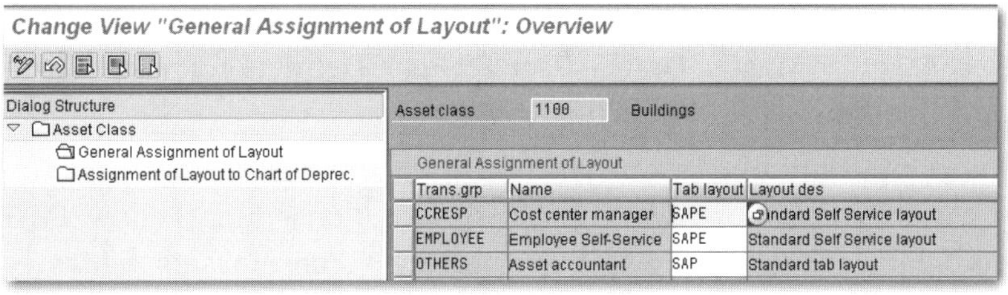

Figure 7.14 General Assignment of Layout

Figure 7.15 shows the assignment of layout to chart of depreciation.

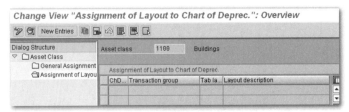

Figure 7.15 Assignment of Layout to Chart of Depreciation

Next, you will learn how to process the selection criterion by following the steps below:

1. **User Fields**

   User fields can be used to define your method of classifying assets. User fields are not tied to any functionality per se but can be used for reporting purposes.

2. **Change Key words in evaluation group**

   This allows you to change the way evaluation groups are displayed in the asset master. In this step, you can define your own names for evaluation groups. The evaluation group ID will start appearing as a heading in the previous step. The menu path is **IMG • Financial Accounting • Asset accounting • Fixed Assets • Master Data• User Fields • Change Key Words in the Evaluation Groups • Change key words for evaluation group 1, 2, 3,4,5**. The Transactions that can be used are OACB, OACC, OACD, OACE, OACF respectively for each of the evaluation groups.

3. **Define Evaluation Groups 4 characters**

   Evaluation groups can be used to classify assets per user-defined criteria. These can then be used when generating asset-related reports for classifying purposes. As discussed earlier, there are two types of evaluation groups: four characters and eight characters. Let's first take a look at the four characters evaluation group. Only four evaluation groups of four characters can be defined. These can then be populated in the asset master record. Follow the path **IMG • Financial Accounting • Asset accounting • Fixed Assets • Master Data • User Fields • Define 4-Character Evaluation Groups**, or use Transaction OAVA.

4. **Define evaluation groups 8 characters**

   Here you can define the eight-character evaluation group. Follow **IMG • Financial Accounting • Asset accounting • Fixed Assets • Master Data• User Fields • Define 8-Character Evaluation Groups**, or use Transaction OAV8. Figure 7.16 shows the screen where you can enter the evaluation group after defining **Asset Bar Code #** as the heading of your evaluation group.

Figure 7.16 Define Evaluation Groups

5. Define reason for investment

This is used to define the reason for investing in the asset and can be used for reporting purposes. The menu path is **IMG • Financial Accounting • Asset accounting • Fixed Assets • Master Data • User Fields • Define Reason for Investment**. The Transaction is OAW1. Some of the predefined reasons of investment are **Replacement, Rationalization, Enhancement, Environmental protection**, and so on. You can choose to define your own investment reasons. In the next step, you will learn to define the environmental protection indicator:

6. Define Environmental Protection Indicator

This is used in case you brought an asset to ensure that you meet your organization's environmental policy. This indicator is used to generate reporting related to the investments made for environmental reasons. This is especially becoming important as the focus is on preserving the environment and minimizing the pollution caused by operations of the organization. Traditionally, this was used by oil companies and organizations in chemical industries. Some typical environmental indicators that can be maintained are waste management, protection of water reserves, noise reduction, and so on. You can define additional environment protection indicators if needed. The menu path is **IMG • Financial Accounting • Asset accounting • Fixed Assets • Master Data • User Fields • Define Environmental Protection Indicator**.

7. Define Asset Super Number

Asset super numbers allow you to group together assets according to any user-defined criterion. This number can then be entered in the asset master. Follow **IMG • Financial Accounting • Asset accounting • Fixed Assets • Master Data • User Fields • Define Asset Super Number**.

8. Enter your User Fields in Asset Class

Define the default assignment of the evaluation groups and asset super number to an asset class. The menu path is **IMG • Financial Accounting • Asset accounting • Fixed Assets • Master Data • User Fields • Enter Your User Fields in Asset Class**.

9. Enter Charts of Depreciation–Dependent User Fields in Asset Class

Define your fields and assign them by chart of depreciation. This is used to further refine your defaults by chart of depreciation. Follow the menu path **IMG • Financial Accounting • Asset accounting • Fixed Assets • Master Data • User Fields • Enter Chart-of-Deprec.-Dependent User Fields in Asset Class**, or use Transaction ANK2.

This completes the settings that you can make on the basis of your custom definition. Now you can do the following settings for integrating assets with plant maintenance equipment:

1. Automatically create equipment master records

This ensures that the creation and changing of master data in FI-AA and PM is linked and synchronous. The following settings are done in Asset Accounting:

2. Specify conditions for synchronization of master data

In this step, you can specify the conditions for synchronization of master data. Follow the menu path **IMG • Financial Accounting • Asset accounting • Fixed Assets • Master Data • Automatic Creation of Equipment Master Records • Specify Conditions for Synchronization of Master Data**. Figure 7.17 shows the settings that can be made for synchronization of master data between AA and PM.

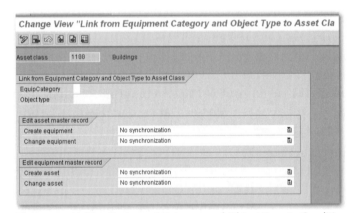

Figure 7.17 Linking Equipment Category and Object Type to Conditions for Synchronization

You can specify the equipment type category to distinguish the technical objects according to their usage, such as machinery, device, and customer equipment. Further classification can be made by using the **Object type**, which describes the type of technical object. In addition, you can set up rules by which you specify how PM equipment management is integrated with the asset class for a specific equipment category and object type. The following options can be used for synchronization:

▶ No synchronization

▶ Saving triggers a workflow

▶ Direct synchronization after saving

▶ Direct synchronization plus workflow

Assign Master Data Fields for Asset and Equipment

Now you need to perform the mapping of Asset Accounting (FI-AA) fields to PM fields. The menu path you need to follow is **IMG • Financial Accounting • Asset accounting • Fixed Assets • Master Data • Automatic Creation of Equipment Master Records • Assign Master Data Fields of Assets and Equipment**. Figure 7.18 shows the field assignment that allows you to transfer data between the FI-AA and PM.

Change View "Field Assignment between FI-AA and PM"

New Entries

Field Assignment between FI-AA and PM

S...	AA fld	Description	PM fld	Description
5	BUKRS	Company Code	BUKRS	Company Code
10	TXT50	Description	EQKTX	?
15	INVNR	Inventory number	INVNR	Inventory number
20	KOSTL	Cost Center	KOSTL	Cost Center
25	WERKS	Plant	SWERK	Maintenance plant
30	STORT	Location	STORT	Location
35	GSBER	Business Area	GSBER	Business Area
40	LIFNR	Vendor	ELIEF	Vendor
45	HERST	Manufacturer	HERST	Manufacturer
50	LAND1	Country of origin	HERLD	Country of manufact.

Figure 7.18 Field Assignment Between Asset Management and Plant Maintenance

This helps in copying data entered while creating master data in assets or in PM and maps it to the corresponding field entered in the preceding configuration. You can also use enhancements to further integrate asset management and PM. The following settings are also important.

Specify Time-Independent Management of Organization Units

This is an indicator, by company code, which ensures that the organization units of business area, cost center, and profit center are not dependent on time. Any change to the organization units generates a transfer posting document. If this indicator is not set, then any change to the business area cost center or profit center requires you to create a new asset master and manually transfer the asset. The menu path is **IMG • Financial Accounting • Asset accounting • Fixed Assets • Master Data • Specify Time-Independent Management of Organiz. Units**.

Cost Center Check Across Company Codes

This indicator allows you to enter a cost center that does not belong to the company code entered in the asset master. The standard setting is that you are not allowed to post to a cost center that belongs to a different company code from the asset transaction. The menu path is **IMG • Financial Accounting • Asset accounting • Fixed Assets • Master Data • Specify Cost Center Check Across Company Codes**, and the Transaction is AOCO.

> **Best Practice**
>
> It is always a good idea *not* to check this box. One of my favorite interview questions is whether you can restrict the posting of cost centers within a company code.

7.3   Asset Class

The asset class forms the backbone of automatic account determination and integration of FI-AA with the GL. Asset classes are used as a template that drives the structure of the asset master data. The asset class helps in driving the organization toward standardization because asset class definitions are common across company codes.

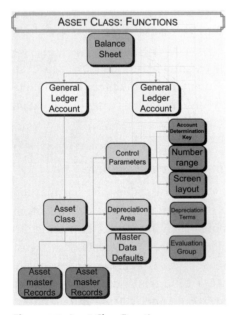

Figure 7.19 Asset Class Functions

Figure 7.19 shows the various functions of the asset class. As we discussed earlier, the asset class is the lowest level that defines the control parameters, depreciation area settings, and master data defaults. Control parameters link to the account determination key, number range, and screen layout. The account determination key is the integration between FI-AA and FI-GL. All these settings were discussed in the previous section where you explored the asset master configuration.

The asset class wizard (Transaction ANKL) lets you quickly configure asset classes as illustrated in Figure 7.20. If you look at the settings, they are a repetition of the previous section except that they are strung together in a sequence making it easier to understand.

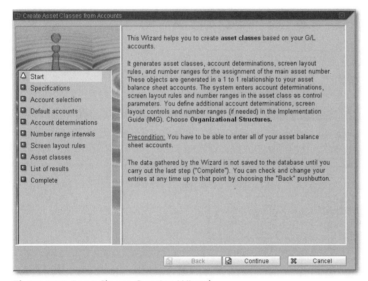

Figure 7.20 Asset Classes Creation Wizard

> **Best Practice**
>
> Use the wizard to create your asset classes because it allows you to think through the various interdependencies.

7.4 Business Transactions

An asset goes through multiple phases in its useful cycle as shown in Figure 7.21. You first acquire an asset either via **Transfer from Asset under**

Construction (AuC) or directly acquire through **Asset Acquisition**. During its lifecycle, the asset can be transferred to other locations via asset **Transfer**. You can increase or decrease its value using **Manual Write Up and Write Down**. In addition, you can perform **Post Capitalization,** which increases the value of an asset. At month end, you need to execute **Depreciation Run,** which calculates the depreciation per the asset master parameters. You need to also perform some special fiscal year change transactions. When the asset is no longer in service, you can retire it using **Asset Retirement**.

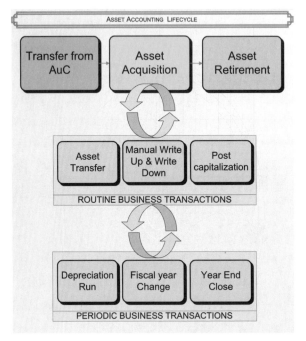

Figure 7.21 Lifecycle and Business Transactions for Fixed Assets

Before delving into business transactions, you should understand the concept of *transaction types,* which is unique to Asset Accounting. A transaction type has to be entered for each transaction that affects an asset. Transaction types specify which of these are updated:

▶ Asset balance sheet accounts

▶ Depreciation areas

▶ Value fields

Each transaction type is assigned to a particular *transaction type group*. These groups are then pulled into various Asset Accounting statutory reports, which is particularly important in the Asset History Sheet Report. Asset transaction groups represent business transactions and are classified as the following:

▶ Acquisitions, Transfers, Retirements, Postcapitalization

▶ Downpayments

▶ Investment Support measures

▶ Manual Depreciation

▶ Write Ups

> **Note**
>
> An asset history sheet is the most important statutory report that needs to be generated and reconciled every month.

Groups are predefined in the system and cannot be changed. However, new transaction types to reflect business needs can be defined. Following is the Transaction Type Group Series:

▶ 1 series: Acquisitions

▶ 2 series: Retirement

▶ 3 series: Transfers

Now let's take a look at the important asset transactions.

7.4.1   Asset Acquisition

Asset acquisition is the process of recognizing a new asset in the balance sheet either via purchase of assets or capitalization of in-house produced goods or services. Asset acquisition can have two phases: asset under construction and asset capitalization.

An asset can be capitalized immediately, but an asset under construction needs to be recorded either as a separate asset classified as **Asset under Construction (AuC)** and then settled to an asset, or recorded as an investment measure in CO-IM (Investment Management). There are some assets that can be immediately capitalized and do not have the phase of AuC. So you can acquire an asset either directly or via settlement of AuC to an asset, which is shown in Figure 7.22.

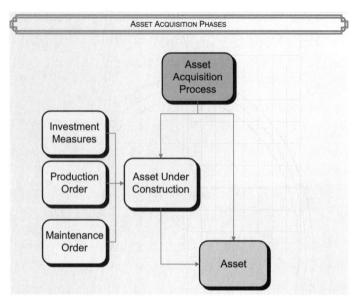

Figure 7.22 Asset Acquisition Phases

There are two types of asset acquisition: external or internal (see Figure 7.23).

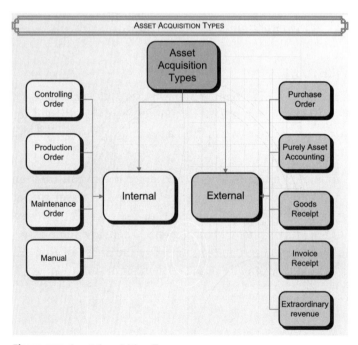

Figure 7.23 Asset Acquisition Types

External Asset Acquisition

This is an acquisition from an external business partner. This can be done via the following modes:

▸ **Via a purchase order**
This requires creating a purchase order with an account assignment category of "A". This requires you to enter the asset number in the purchase order.

▸ **Purely in asset accounting**
With an offsetting posting to a clearing account.

▸ **Via goods receipt or invoice receipt**
Depending on whether the goods receipts (GR) is valuated or nonvaluated, asset value can be updated at either the time of GR or at the time of invoice receipt (IR). If the GR is valuated, any differences between the GR and IR can be posted to assets at the time of invoicing. Otherwise, the asset value gets updated at the time of invoicing.

An asset can be created from the department that is primarily responsible for the business transaction.

Internal Asset Acquisition

An internal acquisition can occur when you transfer costs from the following:

▸ Production order

▸ Maintenance order

To capitalize the costs you settle the production or maintenance order to an asset. It is also possible to capitalize the asset via creating a controlling order and subsequent settlement of the same to the asset. You can also manually post an internal asset acquisition. The system posts to the asset, and the offsetting entry goes to a clearing account, which should also be open-item managed.

Tip
Manual posting should only be used to take care of timing differences between the invoice receipt and the actual asset receipt.

A subsequent acquisition is an addition to the capitalized asset in the same fiscal year. An acquisition from extraordinary revenue is an asset acquisition that is posted to Asset Accounting without any reference to a GR or IR. This might be necessary if:

▸ You found the asset during the process of taking physical inventory.

▸ The asset was a gift from outside.

If we use a stockable item from the warehouse as a replacement part for an existing asset, then that also needs to be added to the value of the asset. The movement type to perform such a transaction is 241.

> **Tip**
>
> The posting date and the asset value date should be in the same fiscal year.

The following data automatically get updated to the asset master record at the time of the first acquisition for the asset:

▸ Date of asset capitalization (derived from the asset value date)

▸ Date of initial acquisition (derived from the asset value date)

▸ Acquisition year and acquisition period (derived from the posting date)

> **Note**
>
> If we enter an asset data from AP, the vendor is automatically populated in the asset's origin field.

The transaction types for asset acquisition are in the 1 series:

▸ 100: External Acquisition

▸ 110: In House Production Acquisition

> **Note**
>
> Program SAPF181 (executed using Transaction SE38) is used to correct cash discounts, which are either wrongly calculated or need to be reversed or adjusted.

7.4.2 Transfer from Asset Under Construction (AuC) to Asset

A fixed asset can have two stages: the construction phase followed by the useful life phase. If the asset is in construction phase, then it needs to be represented in a different balance sheet account, which is referred to as an asset under construction (AuC). This subsection describes the conversion process from an AuC to an asset. An AuC can be either created as a normal asset record or as a master record with a line item. Multiple normal asset records created as AuCs can be transferred to one capitalized asset. For line items, you can have the actual transactions recorded, such as purchase order line item receipt, internal order, stock material, and so on. Depending on how the AuC is created, you could have multiple ways to transfer to an asset. If the AuC is created as an asset, you can transfer from the sender AuC asset to the receiver asset.

Otherwise, you can perform the line-item settlement of the AuC to the receiver asset. To perform the line-item settlement, you need to create distribution rules that contain a distribution key and a receiver. The distribution key can be either a percentage or an amount. You will learn more about setting in internal order settlement, but the process is the same in assets as well.

7.4.3 Asset Transfers

As you know, an asset is tied to a location. If you have a physical movement of an asset, then you need to transfer the asset from the sender (original) to the receiver asset. Asset transfer can be classified broadly in two types as described next.

Intracompany Asset Transfer

You might want to transfer an asset within a company code if the asset class is wrong, you split up an asset, or you settle an AuC and transfer it to an asset.

> **Notes**
>
> ▶ Transferring an asset within the same company code is simple as long as the depreciation area settings are consistent in the sending asset and receiving asset.
>
> ▶ Distinguish between prior year and current year transfers when making the transfer. The standard system uses variant 4 for intracompany transfers

Intercompany Asset Transfer

This needs to be performed if you transfer to a different company code due to business restructuring or due to a physical move of the asset. This can have the following flavors:

▸ **Within one client**
A retirement transfer from the sending company code and an acquisition transfer from the receiving company code can be done in a single step.

▸ **Across clients**
You can use the application link enabling (ALE) scenario to configure the transfer from one company code to another. You can also transfer assets across clients by manually performing two transactions (transfer and acquisition).

The transaction types for retirement/acquisition transfer are:

▸ **350/360**: Previous Year

▸ **370/380**: Same Year

7.4.4 Postcapitalization

This represents any additions to an already capitalized asset to correct the acquisition value of the asset. This transaction not only readjusts the book value but also recalculates the depreciation on past periods based on the asset capitalization date. The system then updates the accumulated depreciation as well for the asset. You might have to create a new asset number and sub-number to record the postcapitalization in cases where:

▸ The complete asset was not capitalized earlier.

▸ The postcapitalization date is different from the capitalization date of the previous asset.

You can use Transaction types 400 or 401 for postcapitalization. Transaction type 401 is used if you want the depreciation to start from the beginning of the fiscal year, regardless of the asset value date.

7.4.5 Manual Write Up or Write Down

Write ups and write downs affect the book value of the asset. The change might be needed for recognizing missed capitalizations for a particular asset after a fiscal year has been closed. Sometimes you might recognize that the asset book value has gone up or down considerably due to changing market conditions.

This is typically done using postcapitalization. Postcapitalization affects the acquisition value of the asset. However, it is possible to change the book value by changing the depreciation posted as well. Write ups and downs can be posted to ordinary depreciation, manual depreciation, unplanned depreciation, special depreciation, or transferred reserves. The transaction types for write ups are in the 7 series. It is important to use the correct transaction type so that the depreciation area is automatically determined.

7.4.6 Unplanned Depreciation

Instead of the system calculating depreciation, you can also manually enter depreciation in the system. The transaction type for manual depreciation for prior year acquisitions is 640. The system does not automatically generate the financial document when you enter the manual depreciation. When you execute the depreciation run, the system then posts the unplanned depreciation. Let's now consider the periodic processing transactions in Asset Accounting.

7.4.7 Asset Retirement

Accounting wise, asset retirement is the process of reducing the asset value by doing the following:

▶ Completely retiring the asset

▶ Partially retiring the asset

▶ In addition, the different types of asset retirements are the following:

▶ Sale (with revenue)

  ▷ Linked with a customer

  ▷ Without a customer

▶ Scrapping (without revenue)

> **Note**
>
> The field status variant for the sales revenue account should have the asset retirement field as optional or required if you are retiring an asset with a sale to a customer.

Figure 7.24 shows the different types of asset retirements described earlier.

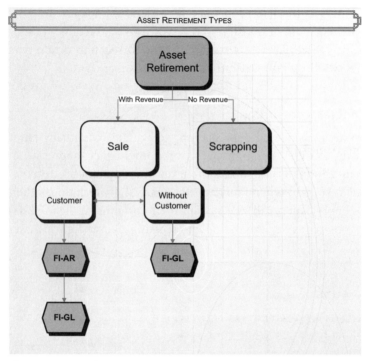

Figure 7.24 Asset Retirement Types

7.4.8 Gain/Loss on Retiring an Asset with Revenue

The system automatically determines any gain or loss by calculating the difference between the sale value of the asset and the book value of the asset (after incorporating the calculated depreciation). For scrapping, there is no revenue recorded, and the net book value is noted as a loss from the asset retirement. It is important to correctly identify the transaction type for the current year retirements as well as the previous year retirements. Also Asset Accounting allows you to mass-retire assets in business scenarios where a particular division or plant is sold. To perform mass retirement, follow these steps:

1. Identify the list of assets to be retired.

2. Create a worklist for the assets to be retired.

3. Identify whether it is a sale or scrapping transaction.

4. Enter the revenue distribution if it is a sale.

5. Process the worklist after releasing it.

7.5   Periodic Processing in Asset Accounting

This section covers some business transactions for periodic processing. You will first learn about the depreciation run. The menu path you will need to follow is **SAP Menu • Financial Accounting • Fixed Assets• Periodic Processing**.

7.5.1   Depreciation Run

Before delving into the depreciation run, let's go over the mechanics of depreciation. The system supports the following types of depreciation posting:

▸ **Ordinary Depreciation**
The planned depreciation in the asset due to normal wear and tear.

▸ **Special Depreciation**
A tax-based type of depreciation for wear and tear that is dependent on tax concessions and tax rules.

▸ **Unplanned Depreciation**
The type of depreciation related to damage to the asset or some unusual circumstance that leads to a permanent reduction in the value of the asset.

▸ **Unit of Production Depreciation**
Allows you to take into account the actual usage of the asset and depreciation according to the usage. For example, based on the number of miles driven in a car, you can choose to depreciate 10% of the value for each 10,000 miles driven.

In addition, you need to define the calculation methods that are assigned to a depreciation key, which determine how the depreciation gets calculated. The following are the calculation methods for depreciation:

▸ Base method
▸ Declining balance method
▸ Maximum amount method
▸ Multilevel method
▸ Period control method

Based on the depreciation key and the useful life, the system calculates the depreciation. Changing the depreciation key, however, does not update the depreciation. You have to run the recalculate depreciation program for the system to post a different depreciation. The depreciation run can be executed for planned or unplanned depreciation. The menu path for executing a depreciation run is **SAP Menu • Financial Accounting • Fixed Assets• Periodic Processing • Depreciation Run • Execute**, and the Transaction you can use is AFAB. Figure 7.25 displays the screen where you can maintain the parameters for executing the depreciation run.

Figure 7.25 Depreciation Run

You first need to enter the company code, fiscal year, and posting period. Then you need to select the reason for the posting run.

> **Note**
>
> With SAP ERP 2005, depreciation can now be posted directly. Earlier you had to execute depreciation only via the batch input program.

The reasons for the posting run are the following:

▶ **Planned posting run**
The depreciation is posted per the schedule and the next period per the posting cycle.

▶ **Repeat posting run**
This results in the posting depreciation for the last posting run already executed. This might be needed if the depreciation terms are changed in

the asset master data. The system only posts the delta between the previous posting run and the repeat posting run.

► **Restart**
If the posting run terminates because of user error or some technical reason, you can restart the posting run. This affects only those assets that were not successfully executed in the previous run.

► **Unplanned posting run**
This posts the unplanned depreciation to accounting.

You should always first run the posting in the test mode and then execute it. In the test mode, the system simulates the posting with all the necessary documents and checks the account assignments as well as various configuration settings.

> **Note**
>
> From SAP ERP 2005, the Depreciation Calculation Program (DCP) provides a new way of calculating depreciation. It is a backend solution that does not require any configuration. You can also use BADIs to modify the calculation to suit your specific requirements. This new functionality allows you to manage the myriad rules of depreciation that are valid in different countries.

The architecture of the new depreciation program is shown in Figure 7.26. The Depreciation Calculation Program (DCP) consists of two parts: the business-oriented application-specific part and the evaluation engine that calculates the depreciation per the calculation logic.

The application-specific part gets the data from the Asset Accounting module, taking into account the configuration of depreciation areas and depreciation keys. The data is then transferred from the asset tables to a data buffer. In addition, you can get the values from the various transactions, which are part of the interfaces box in Figure 7.26.

After you input all this data to the system, the system transfers all the information in its internal structures and applies the logic from the evaluation engine. The evaluation engine then performs various calculations as defined in the business rules. Then the engine feeds the data back to the application-specific part where the values are stored. The new functions available in DCP include the following:

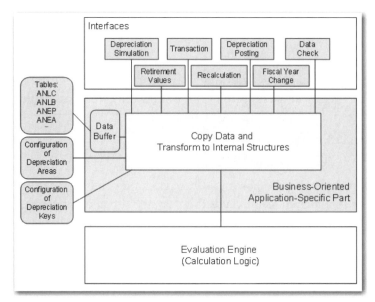

Figure 7.26 Architecture of the New Depreciation Calculation Program

► **Period-based calculation**
The calculation of depreciation is now based on periods rather than the individual transactions. The system groups similar transactions for a particular period together. The system then assigns each transaction to a calculation period, which is determined by the asset value date and the period control group of the transaction type group. Based on the periods determined, the system then calculates depreciation.

► **Time-dependent depreciation terms**
You can now make mid-year changes in depreciation terms of asset master data, and the system considers those when depreciation is run again. Time-dependent depreciation terms include useful life, depreciation key, scrap value, and variable depreciation portion. This allows you to change your depreciation terms mid-year without any extra effort. You can calculate depreciation for the first half of a fiscal year with a different depreciation rate than the second half of the fiscal year. The special feature of this development is that only six months are used as the basis for calculating the depreciation for the first half. Previously, you had to do a workaround by creating a new asset and transfering your assets to the new asset to be able to change depreciation terms.

► **Mid-year period-dependent changeover**
You can change depreciation methods (base to double declining, etc.) mid-year instead of affecting the change on an annual basis, which was what

previous depreciation runs allowed. The BADI available in DCP is FAA_DC_CUSTOMER BADI.

7.5.2 Year-End Closing Transactions

The key transactions for year-end closing are the following:

- Fiscal year change
- Reconcile FI-AA with FI-GL
- Year-end closing
- Undo year-end closing: By company code
- Undo year-end closing: By depreciation area

The fiscal year change program opens new annual value fields for each asset and represents the opening of a new fiscal year for assets.

> **Note**
>
> Only Asset Accounting's fiscal year needs to be opened or closed. All other subledger's year open or close is controlled via the GL.

The asset values from the previous year are carried cumulatively to the next year. Here are the prerequisites to run this year-end program:

- You are in the last posting period of the fiscal year.
- You want to execute this for the whole company code.
- The previous fiscal year should be closed to open the new fiscal year.

This program is different from the year-end closing and should not be confused with the same. The menu path for a fiscal year change is **SAP Menu • Financial Accounting • Fixed Assets • Periodic Processing • Fiscal Year Change**. The Transaction is AJRW. After executing the transaction code, enter the company codes and the new fiscal year, and then click **Execute**. This should be run in the background.

Account Reconciliation FI-AA Versus FI-GL

This reconciliation program is run so that Asset Accounting is in sync with GL Accounting. This program helps identify the list of GL accounts that show a difference. Follow the menu path **SAP Menu • Financial Accounting • Fixed Assets • Periodic Processing • Year End Closing • Account Reconciliation**, or use Transaction ABST2. Figure 7.27 shows the selection screen for FI-AA and FI-GL reconciliation reporting.

Figure 7.27 FI-AA and FI-GL Reconciliation Program

You can execute the transaction by company code to run the program and find the list of GL accounts that show differences.

Year-End Closing Execution

This is used to close the Asset Accounting for a company code so that you can no longer post or change values within Asset Accounting. Follow the menu path **SAP Menu • Financial Accounting • Fixed Assets • Periodic Processing • Year End Closing • Execute**. You can also use Transaction AJAB. Figure 7.28 displays the screen where the selection parameters for year-end closing in Asset Accounting are maintained.

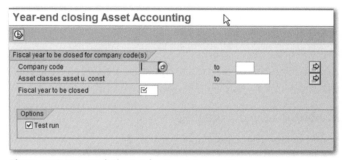

Figure 7.28 Year-End Closing for Asset Accounting

This transaction helps in preparing the full fiscal close for a company code. The fiscal year that is closed is always one year less than the current year. The system can perform year-end closing only if:

▸ There are no errors during depreciation calculation.

▸ Planned depreciation has been posted to the GL.

▸ All acquired assets have been capitalized.

▸ All incomplete asset masters have been completed.

Undo Year-End Closing

You can also undo the year-end closing by the following transactions. It can be undone either for a company code or for a depreciation area within a company code as seen here.

▶ **By Company Code**
Shown in Figure 7.29, the menu path is **Accounting • Financial Accounting • Fixed Assets • Periodic Processing • Year End Closing • Undo • Entire Company code**, and the Transaction is OAAQ.

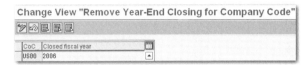

Figure 7.29 Undo Year-End Closing By Company Code

▶ **By Depreciation Area**
Shown in Figure 7.30, the menu path is **Accounting • Financial Accounting • Fixed Assets • Periodic Processing • Year End Closing • Undo • By Area**, and the Transaction is OAAR.

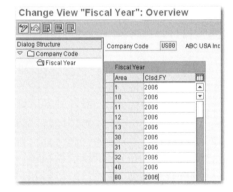

Figure 7.30 Undo Year-End Closing By Depreciation Area

7.6 Configuring Business Transactions in Asset Accounting

The overall learning path for configuring Asset Accounting transactions is shown in Figure 7.31. First you need to define the integration of Asset Accounting with the GL. Then you need to define the parameters for valuation. After that, you will learn about the configuration related to depreciation before going on to learn about the settings for routine business transactions.

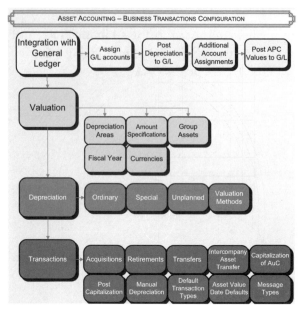

Figure 7.31 Asset Accounting: Configuration Areas

7.7   Integrating Asset Accounting with the General Ledger

You can see the screen for configuring integration with the GL in Figure 7.32. Integrating Asset Accounting with the GL has many advantages, not the least of which is smoother functioning of your SAP ERP Financials implementation. The menu path for integrating with the general ledger is **IMG • Financial Accounting • Asset Accounting • Integration with the General Ledger**.

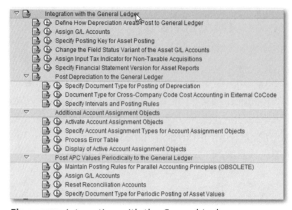

Figure 7.32 Integration with the General Ledger

You will learn about some of the important settings that need to be made to ensure that you can post Asset Accounting to the GL. The first step as shown in Figure 7.32 is to **Define How Depreciation Areas Post to General Ledger** and the manner in which it gets updated.

7.7.1 Define How Depreciation Areas Post to the General Ledger

The menu path for defining depreciation areas post to the GL is IMG • **Financial Accounting** • **Asset Accounting** • **Integration with the General Ledger** • **Define how Depreciation areas post to General Ledger**. The Transaction is OADX. The depreciation areas can be configured to post to the GL per one of the following options:

▶ **0**
Areas does not post.

▶ **1**
Areas post in real time.

▶ **2**
Area posts acquisition production cost (APC) and depreciation on a periodic basis.

▶ **3**
Area posts depreciation only.

▶ **4**
Area posts APC directly and depreciation.

▶ **5**
Area posts APC only.

▶ **6**
Area posts only APC directly.

Figure 7.33 shows how depreciation areas post to the GL. For Chart of depreciation (**Chart of dep.) 1US**, the depreciation area (**Ar.) 1** is assigned as the depreciation area that posts in real time via option **GL 1**. On the other hand, depreciation area **10** is shown as not posting to GL via option **0**.

Typically, book depreciation posts to GL in real time, whereas rests do not post at all to the GL. But you might have different business scenarios that require you to choose the options described earlier.

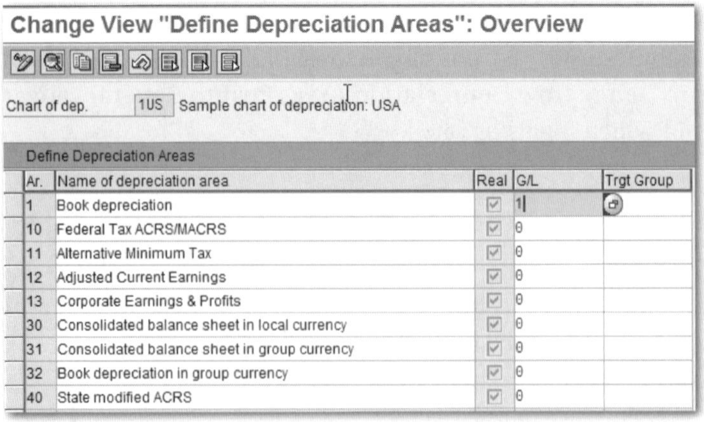

Figure 7.33 Define How Depreciation Areas Post to the General Ledger

7.7.2 Assign GL Accounts

In this configuration, you will learn how the system automatically determines the GL account based on the business transaction. The menu path is **IMG • Financial Accounting • Asset Accounting • Integration with the General Ledger • Assign GL accounts**, and the Transaction is AO90. Figure 7.34 shows how you can assign GL accounts by chart of depreciation and chart of accounts.

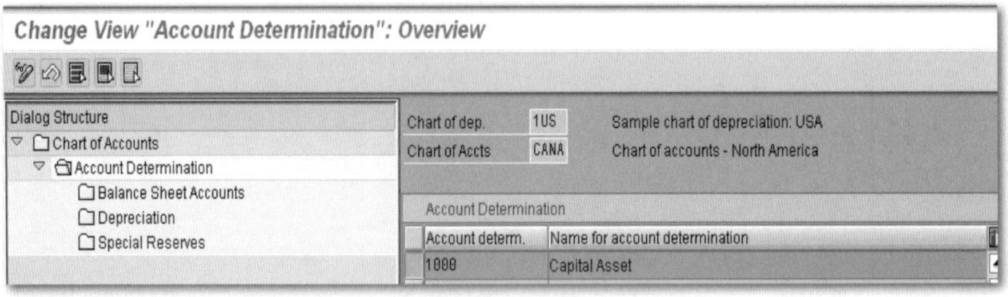

Figure 7.34 Account Determination Overview

After selecting the account determination for which you want to set up the GL accounts, you need to double-click **Balance Sheet Accounts, Depreciation,** or **Special Reserves** shown on the left side of Figure 7.34. This allows you to configure an appropriate GL account as shown in the Figure 7.35, which summarizes the integration of GL with AA.

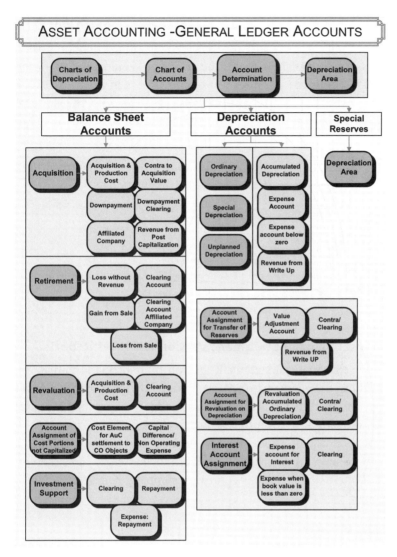

Figure 7.35 Integration of General Ledger with Asset Accounting

7.7.3 Specify the Posting Key for Asset Postings

You can specify the posting key for asset postings. Posting keys for assets are 70 (debit) and 75 (credit) for asset postings and 40 (debit) and 50 (credit) for GL postings. The transaction key for asset posting keys is ANL; for GL accounts, it is ANS. The menu path is **IMG • Financial Accounting • Asset Accounting • Integration with the General Ledger • Specify Posting Key for Asset Postings**, and the Transaction is OBYD.

7.7.4 Assign Input Tax Indicator for Nontaxable Acquisitions

This indicator is used for automatic postings of acquisitions that are posted to tax-relevant GL accounts. This avoids the error you would get if you tried posting to a GL account that requires a tax code. The menu path is **IMG • Financial Accounting • Asset Accounting • Integration with the General Ledger • Assign Input Tax Indicator for Non-Taxable Acquisitions**, and the Transaction is OBCL.

Figure 7.36 shows how to set up the default **Input tax** indicator, **Output tax** indicator, and **Jurisdiction code** for nontaxable acquisitions.

Change View "Allocate Co.Cd. -> Non-Taxable Transactions"

Co.	Company Name	City	Input ta	Output t	Jurisdict. c
US00	ABC USA Inc	Houston	I0	O0	

Figure 7.36 Assign Input Tax Indicators for Nontaxable Acquisitions

7.7.5 Specify a Financial Statement Version for Asset Reports

This helps define the financial statement version by depreciation area. You will need to follow the menu path **IMG • Financial Accounting • Asset Accounting • Integration with the General Ledger • Specify Financial Statement Version for Asset Reports**. You can also use Transaction OAYN. Figure 7.37 shows how you can assign the financial statement version to a depreciation area and company code. By default, the system assigns the version BAUS to all the depreciation areas for U.S. company codes.

Change View "Assign financial statement version": Overview

Company Code US00 ABC USA Inc

Ar.	Name of depreciation area	FS Vers	Financial Statement Version Name
01	Book depreciation in local currency	BAUS	Financial Statement (USA)
10	Federal Tax ACRS/MACRS	BAUS	Financial Statement (USA)
11	Alternative Minimum Tax	BAUS	Financial Statement (USA)
12	Adjusted Current Earnings	BAUS	Financial Statement (USA)
13	Corporate Earnings & Profits	BAUS	Financial Statement (USA)
30	Consolidated balance sheet in local curre	BAUS	Financial Statement (USA)
31	Consolidated balance sheet in group curr	BAUS	Financial Statement (USA)
32	Book depreciation in group currency	BAUS	Financial Statement (USA)

Dialog Structure
▽ ☐ Company code selection
   ☐ Assign financial state

Figure 7.37 Assign Financial Statement Version by Company Code and Depreciation Area

7.7.6 Post Depreciation to General Ledger

In this section, you will learn to make appropriate settings for posting depreciation to the GL.

Specify Document Type for Posting Depreciation

This configuration defines the document type that is posted when the system posts the depreciation. Figure 7.38 shows how you can define the document type for posting depreciation. Follow **IMG • Financial Accounting • Asset Accounting • Integration with the General Ledger • Post Depreciation to the General Ledger • Specify Document type for posting depreciation**. The Transaction is AO71.

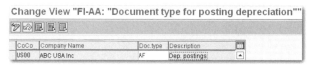

Figure 7.38 Define Document Type for Posting Depreciation

The standard document type that the system assigns is AF. However, this can be changed if desired. The document type so defined should be enabled for batch input and must be defined with an external document number assignment.

So, is it necessary to define the depreciation with the batch input, now that you can post depreciation in the foreground as well from ERP 2005?

Specify Document Type for Cross-Company Code Cost Accounting in External Code

This is only necessary if you use cross-company code cost accounting. You need to define the document type by transaction type for cross-company code cost accounting. The menu path is **IMG • Financial Accounting • Asset Accounting • Integration with the General Ledger • Post Depreciation to the General Ledger • Document type for Cross Company Code Cost Accounting in External CoCode**. Figure 7.39 shows the screen where you can define the document type for cross-company code cost accounting.

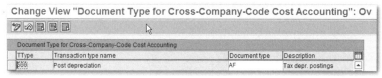

Figure 7.39 Define the Document Type for Cross-Company Code Posting

Specify Intervals and Posting Rules

In this setting, you define the intervals and the posting rules for the depreciation areas. Figure 7.40 shows the screen where you can define the interval and posting rules. The menu path is **IMG • Financial Accounting • Asset Accounting • Integration with the General Ledger • Post Depreciation to the General Ledger • Specify Intervals and Posting Rules**. The Transaction is OAYR.

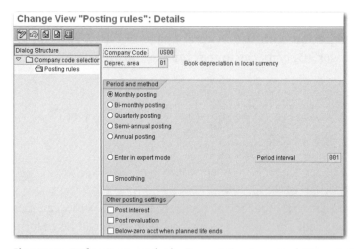

Figure 7.40 Define Posting Rules by Depreciation Area: Book Depreciation

The following settings are made in this configuration:

- **Period**
  How frequently the posting happens: monthly, bimonthly, quarterly, semi-annually, or annually.

- **Smoothing**
  If you set this indicator, the system posts the depreciation remaining by distributing it equally among the remaining time intervals for the fiscal year.

- **Post interest**
  If you set this indicator, the cost accounting interest is also posted in addition to depreciation.

- **Post revaluation**
  This is set if you want the revaluation of accumulated depreciation to also post to the GL during the depreciation posting.

- **Below-zero acct when planned life ends**
  If you set this indicator, the system posts the depreciation even after the

useful life has ended to the account specified in the account determination.

For cost accounting depreciation area (20), **Smoothing** and **Post revaluation** are checked. However, for investment support posted to liabilities (depreciation area 51), only **Smoothing** is checked.

7.7.7 Additional Account Assignment Objects

In this section, you will learn about the account assignment elements for Asset Accounting. You will have to first activate the account assignment object and then assign the account assignment type for the account assignment objects.

Activate the Account Assignment Objects

You can choose to activate the account assignment objects for Asset Accounting. Figure 7.41 shows the typical account assignment objects that can be activated. The menu path is **IMG • Financial Accounting • Asset Accounting • Integration with the General Ledger • Additional Account Assignment Objects • Activate Account Assignment objects**.

AcctAsgnOb	Account Assignment Object Name	Active	Bal. sheet	Agreement	
CAUFN	Internal Order	☑	☐	☐	
EAUFN	Investment Order	☑	☐	☐	
FISTL	Funds Center	☐	☑	☑	
FISTL2	Funds Center for Investment	☐	☑	☑	
FKBER	Functional Area	☐	☑	☑	
FKBER2	Functional Area for Investment	☐	☑	☑	
GEBER	Fund	☐	☑	☑	
GEBER2	Fund for Investment	☐	☑	☑	
GRANT_NBR	Grant	☐	☑	☑	
GRANT_NBR2	Grant for Cap. Investment	☐	☑	☑	
IAUFN	Maintenance Order	☑	☐	☐	
IMKEY	Real Estate Object	☐	☐	☐	
KOSTL	Cost Center	☑	☐	☑	
LSTAR	Activity Type	☑	☐	☐	
PS_PSP_PNR	WBS Element of Investment Project	☑	☐	☐	
PS_PSP_PN_	WBS Element	☐	☐	☐	

Figure 7.41 Define Account Assignment Elements for Asset Accounting

The first two fields identify the account assignment object. The other three fields help define the account assignment object as follows:

- ▶ **Active**

  If checked, this means that the account assignment object is available for entry in asset master record.

- ▶ **Bal. sheet**

  If checked, this means that the object is relevant to the balance sheet. This also means that this object cannot be changed directly in the asset master if the asset has been capitalized. You need to transfer this asset to make the requisite change.

- ▶ **Agreement**

  If checked, this means that the object during posting should match or agree with the object in the asset master record.

Specify Account Assignment Types for Account Assignment Objects

You need to define the account assignment object to the account assignment type. Figure 7.42 shows how you can assign the account assignment type to account assignment objects. These assignments are dependent on company code, depreciation area, and transaction type. The menu path is **IMG • Financial Accounting • Asset Accounting • Integration with the General Ledger • Additional Account Assignment Objects • Specify Account Assignment Types for Account Assignment Objects**, and the Transaction is ACSET.

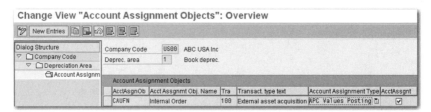

Figure 7.42 Define Account Assignment Types for Account Assignment Objects

You can make the **account assignment type** either as an account assignment for depreciation or for periodic posting. You can also choose to activate the account assignment by checking the *ActAssgnt* checkbox. If not, then the account assignment object will not be active.

7.7.8 Process Error Table

This setting is only required for those account assignment objects that have been set up the status of agreement in the preceding configuration. Figure

7.43 shows the screen for maintaining the error messages. Follow the menu path **IMG • Financial Accounting • Asset Accounting • Integration with the General Ledger • Additional Account Assignment Objects • Process Error Table**.

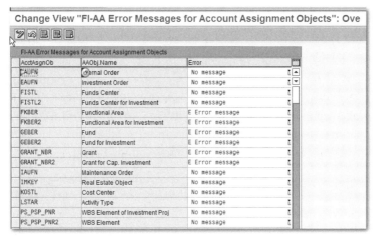

FI-AA Error Messages for Account Assignment Objects		
AcctAsgnOb	AAObj.Name	Error
CAUFN	Internal Order	No message
EAUFN	Investment Order	No message
FISTL	Funds Center	No message
FISTL2	Funds Center for Investment	No message
FKBER	Functional Area	E Error message
FKBER2	Functional Area for Investment	E Error message
GEBER	Fund	E Error message
GEBER2	Fund for Investment	E Error message
GRANT_NBR	Grant	E Error message
GRANT_NBR2	Grant for Cap. Investment	E Error message
IAUFN	Maintenance Order	No message
IMKEY	Real Estate Object	No message
KOSTL	Cost Center	No message
LSTAR	Activity Type	No message
PS_PSP_PNR	WBS Element of Investment Proj	No message
PS_PSP_PNR2	WBS Element	No message

Figure 7.43 Define Messages for Account Assignment Objects

The account assignment entered in the asset master is copied, and the one in the posting is ignored. In this configuration, you have four choices regarding the message: no message, information message, warning message, or error message.

7.7.9 Display of Active Account Assignment Objects

This is the report that lists the active account assignment objects in an ALV list form by executing against the parameters of company code, depreciation area, account assignment object, account assignment type, and transaction type. You can follow the menu path **IMG • Financial Accounting • Asset Accounting • Integration with the General Ledger • Additional Account Assignment Objects • Display of Active Account Assignment Objects**, or use Transaction AACCOBJ.

7.7.10 Post APC Values Periodically to the General Ledger

Now you can make settings that allow you to post APC values to the GL.

Reset Reconciliation Accounts

Here you can define the reconciliation accounts in Asset Accounting as normal accounts that can be posted directly. However, this is possible only for those company codes that are not in production status. The menu path is **IMG • Financial Accounting • Asset Accounting • Integration with the General Ledger • Post APC Values Periodically to the General Ledger • Reset Reconciliation accounts**, and the Transaction is OAMK.

This step is only used when you are transferring the data from legacy assets, or you discover an error in account assignments between Asset Accounting and the GL. You can perform this setting by company code. The Set Reconciliation Ind. for all accounts button allows you to set reconciliation indicators for all accounts, whereas Delete Reconciliation Ind. for all accounts deletes the reconciliation indicator and allows you to make manual entries.

Tip
Only use this in legacy asset data transfer.

7.7.11 Specify Document Type for Periodic Posting of Asset Values

This is used to define the document type for the periodic posting of asset balance sheet values (not depreciation). Figure 7.44 shows the screen where you can enter the document type by company code. This document type is used by the periodic posting program RAPERB2000. The menu path is **IMG • Financial Accounting • Asset Accounting • Integration with the General Ledger • Post APC Values Periodically to the General Ledger • Specify Document Type for Periodic Posting of Asset Values.**

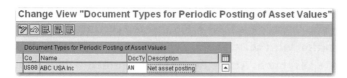

Figure 7.44 Define Document Type for Periodic Processing

7.8 Valuation

This section details the configuration regarding valuation of fixed assets. First you will learn about setting up depreciation areas and how you can set up parallel valuation in Asset Accounting. You will also learn the setting where you can maintain the maximum amount for low-value assets. The last step is the definition of the fiscal year for Asset Accounting. You will also learn about defining shortened fiscal years for Asset Accounting. Follow **IMG • Financial Accounting • Asset Accounting • Valuation**.

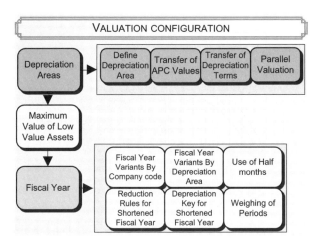

Figure 7.45 Valuation Configuration Steps

Figure 7.45 shows the configurations steps for valuation in a schematic form. So let's discuss how you can configure the valuation settings. Before you begin your configuration activities, you need to identify the chart of depreciation that must be configured. This depreciation area then gets defaulted in all the settings that you will be making in this section. For illustrative purposes, let's take a look at the preconfigured depreciation area **1US**. Follow **IMG • Financial Accounting • Asset Accounting • Valuation • Set chart of depreciation**, or use Transaction OAPL.

7.8.1 Define Depreciation Area

In this step, you can define a new depreciation area within a chart of depreciation either by copying an existing depreciation area or creating an entirely new one. Figure 7.46 shows the screen for maintaining depreciation area within your chart of depreciation **1US.** The menu path you can use to define the depreciation area is **IMG • Financial Accounting • Asset Accounting • Valuation • Depreciation Areas • Define Depreciation Area**.

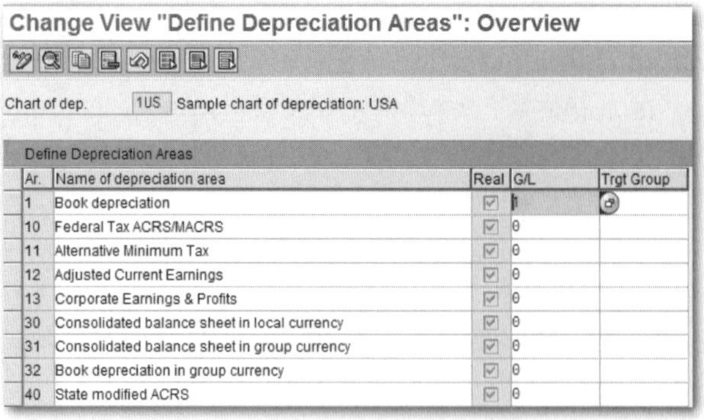

Figure 7.46 Define Depreciation Area

After defining this, you can define the area type using Transaction **OADC**.

7.8.2 Specify Transfer of APC Values

In this step, you define the transfer rules for posting values of depreciation areas. Figure 7.47 shows the screen where you can specify the rules for value takeover in your depreciation area. This is only necessary if you are posting values from a depreciation area other than 01. Follow **IMG • Financial Accounting • Asset Accounting • Valuation • Depreciation Areas • Specify Transfer of APC Values**, or use Transaction OABC.

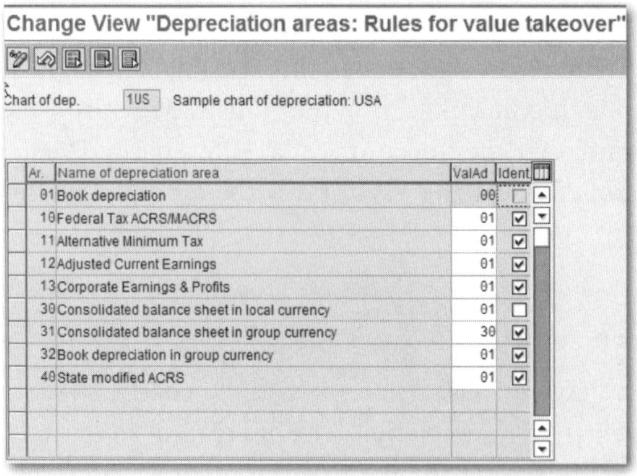

Figure 7.47 Define Depreciation Area- Specify transfer of APC values

In the **ValAd** field, you specify the adoption of values from the depreciation area. The system transfers the posting amounts of any transactions to the dependent area. The **Ident** field, if set, does not allow any change in the values from the transferring area.

> **Note**
>
> A depreciation area can only adopt from an area that has a smaller key than itself. You cannot transfer to area 01.

7.8.3 Specify Transfer of Depreciation Terms

In this step, you can define the transfer rules for posting values of depreciation terms of the depreciation areas. This allows you to copy depreciation terms from one area to another. Figure 7.48 shows the screen where you can maintain these settings. The menu path is **IMG • Financial Accounting • Asset Accounting • Valuation • Depreciation Areas • Specify Transfer of Depreciation Terms**, and the Transaction is OABD.

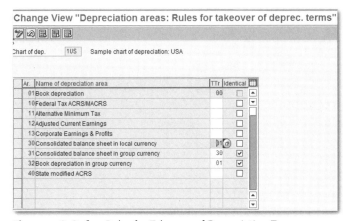

Figure 7.48 Define Rules for Takeover of Depreciation Terms

TTr identifies the depreciation terms transfer from depreciation area. This allows you to specify depreciation term in one area and then adopt the same in other depreciation areas using this field. Setting the **Identical** checkbox does not allow you to change the depreciation terms. If you do not check this field, then you can change the proposed depreciation terms in the asset master record.

7.8.4 Set Up Areas for Parallel Valuation

This setting is used in conjunction with the new GL so that you can set up parallel valuation in a new GL. Keep in mind that the new GL and the master depreciation should have been set up already. Figure 7.49 shows the steps graphically. Follow **IMG • Financial Accounting • Asset Accounting • Valuation • Depreciation Areas • Set up Areas for Parallel Valuation**. You can also use Transaction OADB_WZ. Let's review the steps for setting up areas for parallel valuation now:

1. **Assign Master Area to Ledger Group**

   You assign the master depreciation area to the leading ledger group.

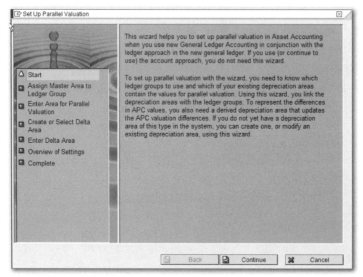

Figure 7.49 Setting Up Parallel Valuation Wizard

2. **Enter Area for Parallel Valuation**

   You select another depreciation area and another ledger group.

3. **Create or Select Delta Area**

   You can either choose to create a new area or an existing area as the delta area.

4. **Enter Delta Area**

   If you choose new depreciation area, then you can create the new depreciation area and choose the ledger group to which you want to assign it. In addition, you can choose the various options for posting APC values directly, not at all, and so on.

5. **Overview of Settings**

   You are shown the various settings that you made. If you are happy with what you see, then go on to the next step and complete the setup for parallel valuation.

6. Complete

The modifications that you selected are made in the background when you select **Complete**. In certain cases, it might be necessary to change the intervals for depreciation posting and the other posting settings (Transaction OAYR) of the depreciation area for parallel valuation. In addition, you can also use Transaction AACCOBJ to check whether the account assignment types are maintained as you want for both depreciation areas.

7.8.5   Specify Low Value Asset Classes

In this step, you define which of the asset classes have low value asset checks and on the basis of what parameters. The first step is to identify the low value asset classes. The menu path is **IMG • Financial Accounting • Asset Accounting • Valuation • Amount Specifications (Company Code/Depreciation Area) • Specify Maximum Amount for Low Value Assets + Asset Classes • Specify LVA Asset classes**, and the Transaction is OAY2. Figure 7.50 shows the screen where you can specify the low-value asset class. There are three options from which you can choose:

▶ **0**
No maximum amount check.

▶ **1**
Value based maximum amount check.

▶ **2**
Check maximum amount with quantity.

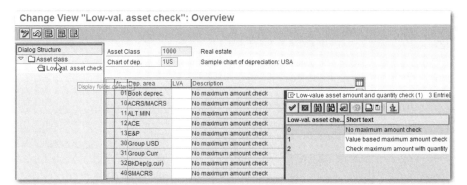

Figure 7.50 Setting Up Low-Value Asset Check by Asset Class

7.8.6 Specify the Maximum Amount for Low-Value Assets

In this step, you define the amount that qualifies an asset as a low-value asset. However, this setting is applicable only if you chose option 1 or 2 in the previous step. Follow the menu path **IMG • Financial Accounting • Asset Accounting • Valuation • Amount Specifications (Company Code/ Depreciation Area) • Specify Maximum Amount for Low Value Assets + Asset Classes • Specify amount for low value assets**, or use Transaction OAYK. Figure 7.51 shows the screen for maintaining the amount per depreciation area.

Change View "Amount for low-value assets": Overview

Dialog Structure	Company Code	US00	ABC USA Inc			
▽ ☐ Company code selection						
☐ Amount for low-value	Ar.	Name of depreciation area	LVA amount	MaxLVA pur	Crcy	
	01	Book depreciation in local currency	500.00	550.00	USD	
	10	Federal Tax ACRS/MACRS	500.00	550.00	USD	
	11	Alternative Minimum Tax	500.00	550.00	USD	
	12	Adjusted Current Earnings	500.00	550.00	USD	
	13	Corporate Earnings & Profits	500.00	550.00	USD	
	30	Consolidated balance sheet in local cu	500.00	550.00	USD	
	31	Consolidated balance sheet in group c	500.00	550.00	USD	

Figure 7.51 Defining the Amount for Low Value Assets

7.8.7 Fiscal Year Variants

Fiscal year variant defines how the fiscal year is structured in comparison to the calendar year, whether it is April to March or January to December, for reporting the balance sheet to external authorities.

> **Note**
>
> You will learn more about defining a fiscal year variant in the GL accounting and financial accounting global settings.

Specify Other Versions on the Company Code Level

Here you can define a fiscal year variant for Asset Accounting that is different from that of the GL accounting at a company code level. The menu path is **IMG • Financial Accounting • Asset Accounting • Valuation • Fiscal Year • Fiscal Year Variants • Specify other versions on Company Code Level**. Figure 7.52 shows the screen where you can maintain the fiscal year variant by company code. Typically this step is not required because the GL fiscal year variant flows to Asset Accounting, and organizations keep the fiscal year variant the same for GL and Asset Accounting. So the settings would be blank here.

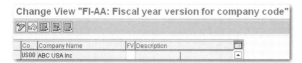

Figure 7.52 Define the Fiscal Year Version for Assets by Company Code

Specify Other Versions on Depreciation Area Level

In this step, you define a fiscal year variant for Asset Accounting that is different from that of GL accounting at a depreciation area level. Figure 7.53 shows the screen where you can maintain the fiscal year variant for the depreciation area. Follow the menu path **IMG • Financial Accounting • Asset Accounting • Valuation • Fiscal Year • Fiscal Year Variants • Specify other versions on Depreciation Area Level**.

Figure 7.53 Define Fiscal Year Version by Depreciation Area

Best Practice

Keep the fiscal year variant the same across Asset Accounting and the GL.

7.8.8 Shortened Fiscal Year

The shortened fiscal year is described in detail in the GL in Chapters 8 and 9. In this section, you will learn about the settings that need to be made in Asset Accounting. One scenario for the shortened fiscal year is when data is transferred from a merger or acquisition of the company to a different company that has a different fiscal year, so that the fiscal years now align with each other. You need to make the following settings so that the depreciation is calculated correctly for the remaining portion of the fiscal year.

Define Reduction Rules for Shortened Fiscal Years

Reduction rules are used to reduce the length of the fiscal year by the duration of the reduction in a fiscal year. Figure 7.54 shows the screen where you can maintain the reduction rules for the shortened fiscal year. The menu path is **IMG • Financial Accounting • Asset Accounting • Valuation • Fiscal Year • Shortened Fiscal Year • Define Reduction Rules for Shortened Fiscal Years**, and the Transaction is OAYP.

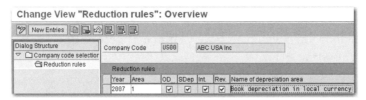

Figure 7.54 Define the Reduction Rule for a Shortened Fiscal Year

You need to enter the fiscal year that you want to be reduced. In addition, you need to specify the depreciation area for which you want to make the settings. For a combination of fiscal year and depreciation area, you can define that the ordinary depreciation, special depreciation, interest calculated for depreciation, and revaluation are reduced in proportion to the reduced fiscal year that is defined in the fiscal year variant. After making these settings, depreciation is calculated only for the reduced fiscal year. Otherwise, the system calculates depreciation for the complete duration of the fiscal year, even though you have reduced the fiscal year.

Maintain Depreciation Key

You can make settings in the depreciation key that overrule the reduced depreciation calculation. This helps you in depreciating some of the assets per the original plan. These settings are required when in certain legal situations you have to depreciate fully even in a reduced fiscal year, when using certain depreciation methods such as fixed-percentage reduction per year. Figure 7.55 shows the settings that can be made for a chart of depreciation and depreciation key. The menu path is **IMG • Financial Accounting • Asset**

Accounting • Valuation • Fiscal Year • Shortened Fiscal Year • Maintain Depreciation Key, and the Transaction is AFAMA.

Change View "Depreciation Key": Details

Chart of dep.	1US
Description	Sample chart of depreciation: USA
Dep. key	6L20 Buildings straight-line 2%
Status	Active

Maximum amount	
Cutoff val. key	

No ordinary dep. with special dep.	☐
No interest if no deprec. is planned	☐
Period control according to fiscal years	☐
Dep. to the day	☐
No reduct. in short year	☑

Acq.only allowed in capitalization year	No
No. of places	

Figure 7.55 Depreciation Key Override of Depreciation Reduction

Mark **No reduct. in short year** to indicate that the full depreciation goes through for this specific depreciation key.

7.8.9 Use of Half Months in the Company Code

This setting allows you to work with 24 periods instead of 12 normal periods. Half periods are used to represent the mid-quarter/month rule, which is widely used in the United States where depreciation gets calculated depending on when the acquisition happened (in the first half or in the second half). Figure 7.56 shows that for company code US00 you have maintained 15 as the mid-month identifier. The menu path you will need to follow is **IMG • Financial Accounting • Asset Accounting • Valuation • Fiscal Year • Use of Half Months in the Company Code**.

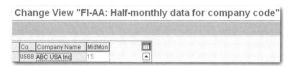

Change View "FI-AA: Half-monthly data for company code"

Co	Company Name	MidMon	
US00	ABC USA Inc	15	

Figure 7.56 Define Half Monthly Day of the Month

7.8.10 Define Weighting of Periods

To define the weighting of periods, you apply the depreciation area and then define the weighting percentages by fiscal year variant. Depending on the weighting percentages defined in the fiscal year variant, the system calculates the depreciation per the relative weight. Figure 7.57 shows the screen for maintaining the weighting indicator by depreciation area and company code. The menu path is **IMG • Financial Accounting • Asset Accounting • Valuation • Fiscal Year • Define Weighting of Periods**, and the Transaction is OAYL.

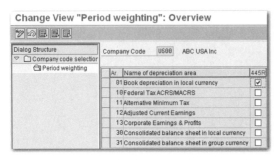

Figure 7.57 Define Period Weighing by Depreciation Area

This affects retirements and transfers as well. After defining which area you need to define as relevant for weighing, you need to detail out the fiscal year variant and assign appropriate weights using Transaction OA85. For each fiscal year and period, you need to maintain the weighing factor.

We have completed our discussion of the important configuration settings for valuation. Now you will learn about the depreciation settings.

7.9   Depreciation

This section details the configuration regarding depreciation of fixed assets. First you need to define the depreciation area and detail the depreciation calculation method. Then you need to define the depreciation key followed by the period controls and the miscellaneous settings for cutoff value and maximum base value. The menu path is **IMG • Financial Accounting • Asset Accounting • Depreciation**.

As you can see, the configuration is first divided by the type of depreciation. So you can configure ordinary depreciation, special depreciation, and unplanned depreciation separately (see Figure 7.58). In this setting, you need to define the depreciation areas that need to have the applicable depreciation. In addition, you can specify the general accounts for each depreciation type. Further, there are specific settings that need to be made for different depreciation types.

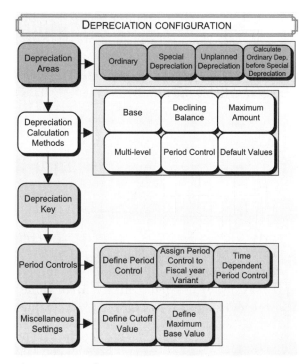

Figure 7.58 Configuring Depreciation

7.9.1 Defining Depreciation Areas

Table 7.1 gives you the menu path and transaction codes for the types of depreciation areas.

Type of Depreciation	Menu Path	Transaction Code
Ordinary Depreciation	IMG • Financial Accounting • Asset Accounting • Depreciation• Ordinary Depreciation • Determine Depreciation Areas	OABN
Special Depreciation	IMG • Financial Accounting • Asset Accounting • Depreciation • Special Depreciation • Determine Depreciation Areas	OABS
Unplanned Depreciation	IMG • Financial Accounting • Asset Accounting • Depreciation • Unplanned Depreciation • Determine Depreciation Areas	OABU
Unit of Production Depreciation	IMG • Financial Accounting • Asset Accounting • Depreciation • Ordinary Depreciation • Determine Unit of Production Depreciation	AO25

Table 7.1 Specify Depreciation Areas for Types of Depreciation

By checking **Ord. depr.** as shown in Figure 7.59, you can specify that this depreciation area is relevant for ordinary depreciation.

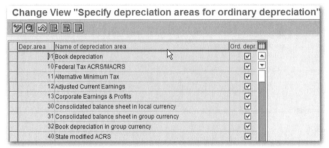

Figure 7.59 Specify Depreciation Areas for Ordinary Depreciation

The settings for special depreciation and unplanned depreciation follow the same logic. However, for special depreciation, you get to choose the following options: **Special depreciation not desired, Only positive values and zero allowed, Only negative values and zero allowed,** or **All values allowed**.

Calculate Ordinary Depreciation Before Special Depreciation

The menu path for calculating ordinary depreciation before special depreciation is **IMG • Financial Accounting • Asset Accounting • Depreciation • Special Depreciation • Calculate Ordinary Depreciation before Special Depreciation**. The Transaction is AOBK. The system has a sequence of determining depreciation, which is typically the following:

1. Transferred reserves
2. Special depreciation
3. Ordinary depreciation
4. Unplanned depreciation

You cannot change 1 and 4. However, using the setting shown in Figure 7.60, you can change the order of 2 and 3 by depreciation area.

Now that you understand some of the key settings for types of depreciation, let's take a look at the depreciation calculation methods.

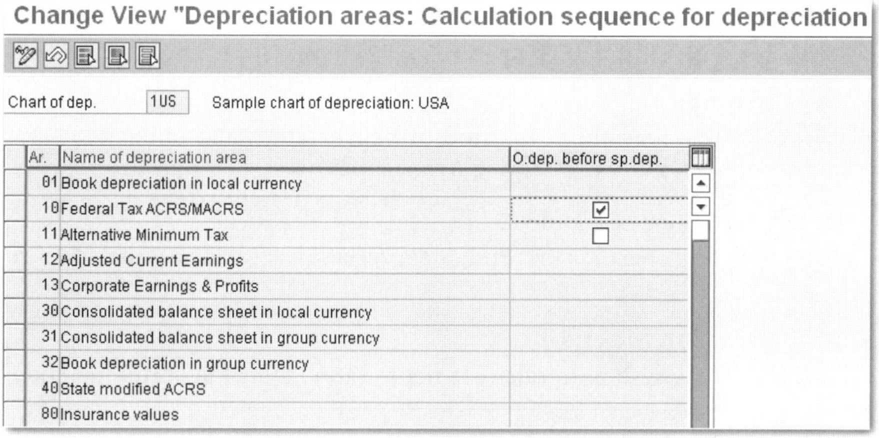

Figure 7.60 Specify Calculation Sequence for Depreciation

7.9.2 Depreciation Calculation Methods

The most important settings that you need to make pertain to the depreciation key, which defines the calculation methods for depreciation. Now you can define the calculation methods that are assigned to the depreciation key. First you will learn to define the base method and then to define the parameters for declining balance method.

To define the base method, follow the menu path **IMG • Financial Accounting • Asset Accounting • Depreciation • Valuation Methods • Depreciation Key • Calculation Methods • Define Base Methods**. This is when you define the base methods that are valid across charts of depreciation. Let's take a look at one of the base methods, 001–Sum of Years digits. The various fields that form a base method are enumerated here and shown in Figure 7.61:

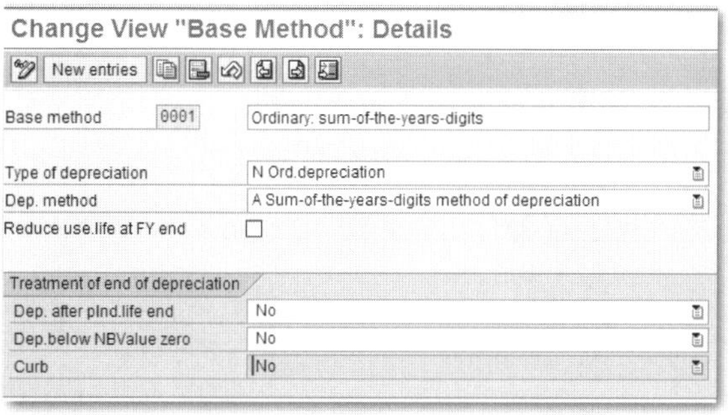

Figure 7.61 Define Base Method

▶ **Type of depreciation**
Options are **N**: Ordinary, **S**: Special, and **Z**: Interest.

▶ **Dep. method**
A **Sum-of-the-years-digit-method of depreciation** and others (U, D, G, P, M, S, T, L, J, K, C, V, X, Y, Z, N, H, and 1 to 9).

▶ **Reduce use.life at FY end**
This, if checked, ensures that end of depreciation coincides with fiscal year end.

▶ **Dep. after plnd.life end**
This allows the system to calculate depreciation after the useful life ends.

▶ **Dep.below NBValue zero**
This allows the depreciation to continue even after the book value becomes zero.

▶ **Curb**
This allows you to calculate depreciation beyond the useful life using the percentage rate resulting from the effective useful life and is used to define the declining balance method.

Next you will learn how to define the declining balance method. The menu path is **IMG • Financial Accounting • Asset Accounting • Depreciation • Valuation Methods • Depreciation Key • Calculation Methods • Define Declining Balance Method**, and the Transaction is AFAMD:

▶ **Dec. factor:** This represnt the depreciation percentage rate. The system multiplies the percentage rate resulting from the total useful life by this factor:

▶ **Max. perc.:** Upper limit for the depreciation percentage rate

▶ **Min. Perc.:** Lower limit for the depreciation percentage rate

Figure 7.62 shows the settings that can be made for the declining balance method.

Change View "Declining-Balance Method": Overview

New entries | Usage | Copy method

Chart of dep.　1US　Sample chart of depreciation: USA

Decl.-bal.	Description of the method	Dec.factor	Max.perc.	Min.Perc.
001	0.00x / 0.0000% / 0.0000%			
002	2.00x /20.0000% / 0.0000%	2.00	20.0000	
003	1.50x /0.0000% / 0.0000%	1.50		
004	2.00x / 0.0000% / 0.0000%	2.00		
005	1.50x /42.0000% / 0.0000%	1.50	42.0000	
006	1.75x /17.5000% / 0.0000%	1.75	17.5000	

Figure 7.62 Define Double Declining Balance Method

The menu path for defining the maximum amount is **IMG • Financial Accounting • Asset Accounting • Depreciation • Valuation Methods • Depreciation Key • Calculation Methods • Define Maximum amount Method**. This is used to define the maximum amount that is not allowed to be exceeded within a calendar date. If the depreciation exceeds the maximum amount, then the system overrides it with the maximum allowed amount. The following parameters need to be defined for the maximum amount method (see Figure 7.63):

▸ Maximum amount (**Max. amount**)

▸ **Currency** for the amount

▸ Validity date (**Valid To**)

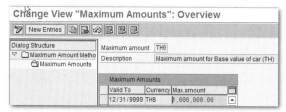

Figure 7.63 Define Maximum Amount Method

Now you will need to define multilevel methods. The menu path for defining the multi level is **IMG • Financial Accounting • Asset Accounting • Depreciation • Valuation Methods • Depreciation Key • Calculation Methods • Define Multi Level**. The Transaction is AFAMS. Each level represents a validity period for a given percentage rate. The steps to define a multilevel method include the following:

▸ Enter the multilevel method and description.

▸ Enter the characteristics of the multilevel method:

  ▸ **Valid to Vintage Year** is the acquisition year to which the entry is valid.

  ▸ **Validity Period in years** is the validity in number of years.

  ▸ **Validity period** in calendar months for a percentage rate.

  ▸ **Base Value Key** for depreciation calculation.

  ▸ **Percentage rate** for depreciation calculation.

  ▸ Indicator to calculate percentage from **remaining useful life**

  ▸ **Reduction of Base value** by the percentage rate.

A sample multilevel method is shown in Figure 7.64.

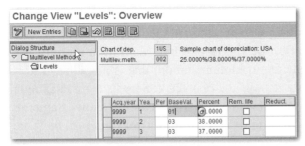

Figure 7.64 Define Multiple Levels Method

Using period control methods, you can define the day of the month depreciation begins for acquisitions (**Acq**), additions (**Add**), retirements (**Ret**), transfers (Trn), revaluation (**Rev.**), investment support (**InvS**), unplanned depreciation (**UpDp**), and write ups to reserves (**WupR**). Figure 7.65 shows the appropriate settings. The menu path is **IMG • Financial Accounting • Asset Accounting • Depreciation • Valuation Methods • Depreciation Key • Calculation Methods • Maintain Period Control Methods**. The Transaction is AFAMP.

Change View "Period Control": Overview

New entries   Usage   Copy method

Chart of dep.   1US   Sample chart of depreciation: USA

Period Control

Prd.c.meth	Description	Acq	Add	Ret	Trn	Rev.	InvS	UpDp	WUpR
001	01/01/02/02	01	01	02	02				
002	03/06/02/02	03	06	02	02				
003	06/06/06/06	06	06	06	06				
004	07/07/07/07	07	07	07	07				
005	09/09/09/09	09	09	09	09				
006	03/03/03/03	03	03	03	03				
007	04/06/02/02	04	06	02	02				
008	01/06/02/02	01	06	02	02				
009	06/06/02/02	06	06	02	02				
010	03/03/03/06	03	03	03	06				
011	07/07/07/06	07	07	07	06				

Figure 7.65 Define Period Control

The menu path for proposing values for the depreciation areas and company codes is **IMG • Financial Accounting • Asset Accounting • Depreciation • Valuation Methods • Depreciation Key • Default Values • Propose Values for Depreciation Areas and Company Codes**, and the Transaction is AFAM_093B. This is used to default the depreciation key parameters for a particular company code and depreciation area. Figure 7.66 shows the settings made for company code **US00** and the **01** depreciation area.

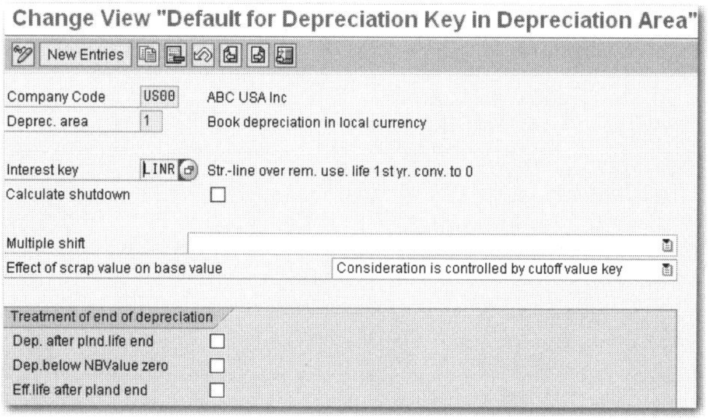

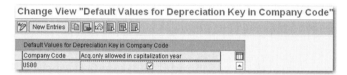

Figure 7.66 Define Default Values for Depreciation Area and Company Code

By this setting, acquisition is only allowed in the capitalization year for the company code (see Figure 7.67). The menu path for this is **IMG • Financial Accounting • Asset Accounting • Depreciation • Valuation Methods • Depreciation Key • Default Values • Propose Acquisition only in Capitalization Year for Company**, and the Transcation is AFAM_093C.

Figure 7.67 Propose Acquisition Only in the Capitalization Year of the Company Code

7.9.3 Depreciation Key

The depreciation key ties all these elements for calculation of depreciation together. The menu path for maintaining the depreciation key is **IMG • Financial Accounting • Asset Accounting • Depreciation • Valuation Methods • Depreciation Key • Maintain Depreciation Key**. The Transaction is AFAMA. Using this configuration, you can assign calculation methods and the other parameters pertaining to the depreciation key and control indicators. Figure 7.68 shows the various settings that can be done by the depreciation key.

First you need to define a depreciation key identifier, and then you need to maintain it per the chart of depreciation. The following are the key parameters for a depreciation key:

▸ **Depreciation type**
This can be ordinary, special, or interest.

▸ **Phase**
This can be from the start of depreciation, changeover within planned life, or changeover after the end of the useful life.

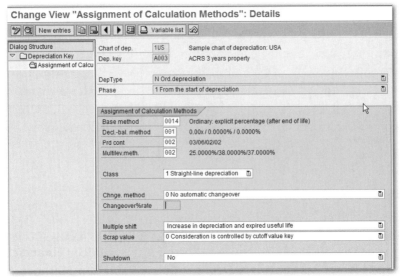

Figure 7.68 Assignment of Depreciation Key to Calculation Method

▶ **Assignment of calculation methods**

These can be the following:

▶ **Base method**: This defines the base method associated with the depreciation key.

▶ **Declining balance method**: This identifies the declining balance method associated with the key.

▶ **Period control**: This identifies the period control.

▶ **Multilevel method**: This identifies the multilevel method.

▶ **Class:** This identifies whether it is straight-line depreciation, declining balance depreciation, or another depreciation method; it is also a classification of ordinary depreciation.

▶ **Changeover method**: This identifies the changeover method.

▶ **Changeover %age rate**: This is the changeover rate.

▶ **Multiple shift:** This captures how useful life affects the change in depreciation.

▶ **Scrap value**: This identifies the impact of scrap value on the base value and the cutoff value.

▶ **Shutdown**: This identifies whether the depreciation can be reduced or shut down if there are settings pertaining to these in the asset master record.

7.9.4 Period Control

In this configuration, you define when the depreciation starts or ends depending on the asset value date of the transaction. This is just identifying the list of period controls. Follow this menu path to maintain period control: **IMG • Financial Accounting • Asset Accounting • Depreciation • Valuation Methods • Period Control • Maintain Period Control**. You can also use Transaction OAVS. Two of the period controls that can be defined follow:

▶ **01**
Pro rata at period start date.

▶ **02**
Pro rata up to mid-period at period start date.

The menu path for defining calendar assignments is **IMG • Financial Accounting • Asset Accounting • Depreciation • Valuation Methods • Period Control • Define Calendar Assignments**. You can also use Transaction OAVH. In this configuration, you link the fiscal year variant to the period control defined in the pervious step. This configuration helps outline when the depreciation should start. Figure 7.69 shows the period control maintained by the fiscal year variant.

Here you define how time-dependent period controls are assigned to the depreciation key and company code. The menu path is **IMG • Financial Accounting • Asset Accounting • Depreciation • Valuation Methods • Period Control • Define Time Dependent Period Controls • Assign Time Dependent Period Controls to Depreciation Keys**.

FV	Per.co.	Name for period control	Year	Mo	Dy	Period	MidMon
K3	01	Pro rata at period start date	0	0			☐
K3	02	Pro rata upto mid-period at period start date	1	15			☐
K3	02	Pro rata upto mid-period at period start date	2	15	1		☐
K3	02	Pro rata upto mid-period at period start date	3	15	2		☐
K3	02	Pro rata upto mid-period at period start date	4	15	3		☐
K3	02	Pro rata upto mid-period at period start date	5	15	4		☐
K3	02	Pro rata upto mid-period at period start date	6	15	5		☐
K3	02	Pro rata upto mid-period at period start date	7	15	6		☐
K3	02	Pro rata upto mid-period at period start date	8	15	7		☐
K3	02	Pro rata upto mid-period at period start date	9	15	8		☐
K3	02	Pro rata upto mid-period at period start date	10	15	9		☐
K3	02	Pro rata upto mid-period at period start date	11	15	10		☐
K3	02	Pro rata upto mid-period at period start date	12	15	11		☐

Figure 7.69 Define Period Control Within a Fiscal Year Variant

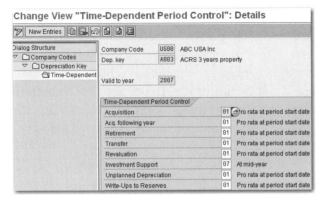

Figure 7.70 Define Time-Dependent Period Controls

Figure 7.70 shows the time-dependent period controls for **US00**.

7.9.5 Defining the Cutoff Value Key

This stops depreciation when a cutoff value is reached. The menu path is **IMG • Financial Accounting • Asset Accounting • Depreciation • Valuation Methods • Further Settings • Define the cutoff value key**, and the Transaction is ANHAL. Figure 7.71 shows the screen where you can maintain the keys for cutoff values.

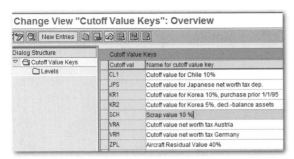

Figure 7.71 Define Cutoff Value Keys

Figure 7.72 shows the details of the cutoff value key **SCH**.

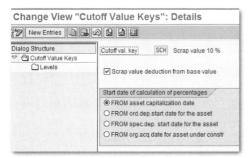

Figure 7.72 Define Cutoff Value Keys: Details

Figure 7.73 shows the screen where you can maintain the levels of the cutoff keys.

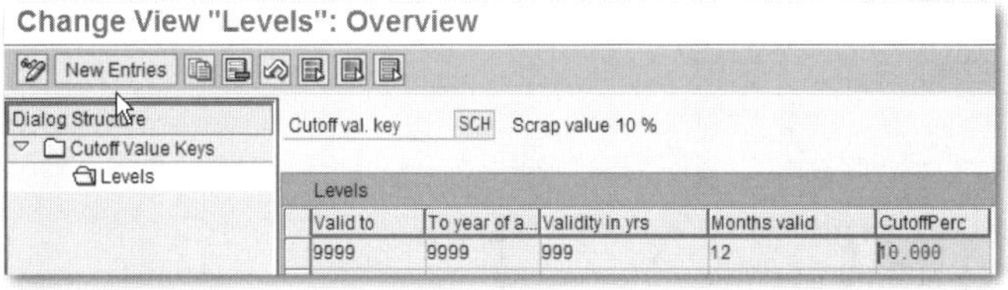

Change View "Levels": Overview

Valid to	To year of a...	Validity in yrs	Months valid	CutoffPerc
9999	9999	999	12	10.000

Figure 7.73 Define Cutoff Value Keys

7.9.6 Define Maximum Base Value

This defines the maximum base value that can be depreciated within a year. So if an asset has a value that is larger than the maximum value specified here, depreciation is calculated on the basis of this maximum value. The menu path is **IMG • Financial Accounting • Asset Accounting • Depreciation • Valuation Methods • Further Settings • Define the maximum Base Value**, and the Transaction is OAW2. Figure 7.74 shows how you can maintain the settings for a company code, asset class, and depreciation area.

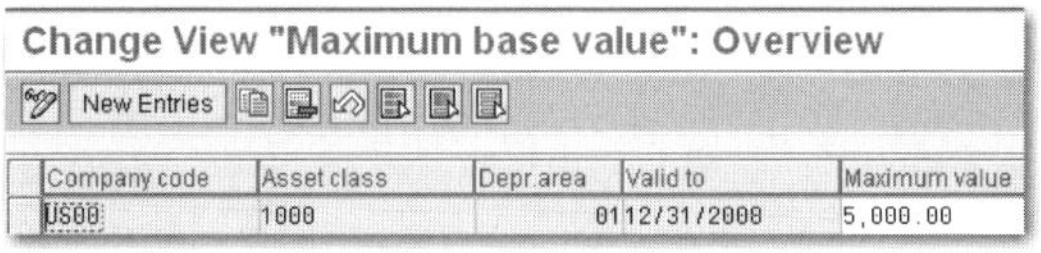

Change View "Maximum base value": Overview

Company code	Asset class	Depr.area	Valid to	Maximum value
US08	1000	01	12/31/2008	5,000.00

Figure 7.74 Define Maximum Base Value

7.10 Configuring Asset Accounting Business Transactions

The configuration menu path of business transactions is shown in Figure 7.75.

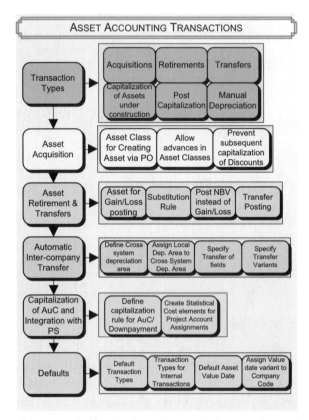

Figure 7.75 Configuring Asset Accounting Business Transactions

7.10.1 Define Transaction Type

For all the business transactions in Asset Accounting, you need to define a transaction type. The transaction type controls the following settings:

▶ **Transaction Type Group**
Each transaction type is assigned to a transaction type group. This is used to control the posting parameters.

▶ **Account Assignment**
Here you can define the following parameters:

▸ **Credit or Debit transaction:** This allows you to define whether the transaction posted with this transaction type is posted as default credits or debits.

▸ **Capitalize fixed asset** or Decapitalize fixed asset: If you set this indicator, the system will capitalize (or decapitalize) the asset when you post using this transaction type.

▸ **Deactivate fixed asset:** If you set this indicator, the asset will be deactivated if the acquisition value of the asset becomes zero. This will automatically set up the asset retirement date as well.

▸ **Document type**: Here you can specify the document type that will be used for posting the transaction type.

▸ **Retirement/Transfer/Current Year Acquisition**
Here you can define the following parameters:

▸ **Retirement with Revenue**: This indicator if set requires that you must enter revenue during retirement posting.

▸ **Transfer adopting depreciation start date:** This allows you to transfer the historical depreciation start date and capitalization date when you transfer this to a new asset.

▸ **Repay investment support**: This indicator if set will trigger the repayment of investment support at the time of retirement, if the investment support was claimed earlier.

▸ **Post gain/loss to asset**: This if set posts the gain or loss to an asset instead of a profit and loss account. This will be discussed later in more detail.

▸ **TTY offsetting entry:** This allows you to maintain the reciprocal history of transfers and acquisitions for offsetting entries.

▸ **Transaction type for acquisition in the same year**: If you are retiring an asset in the same year in which you acquired it, you need to report it separately.

▸ **Posting Type**
Note that the two groups (Affiliated versus No Affiliated and **Post Gross** versus **Post Net**) of these parameters work in tandem to identify the correct transaction type for transfers. Here you can define the following parameters:

▸ **Post to affiliated company**: You need to set this indicator if the transaction type is for transfer between affiliated countries.

411

> ▶ **Do not post to affiliated co.**: This indicates that this transaction type does not involve any affiliated companies.

> ▶ **Post Gross:** If you set this indicator, the system posts the acquisition transaction type to a transfer transaction type when you post to an affiliated company.

> ▶ **Post Net:** Choosing this indicator does not post the adjustment values and only posts the APC (Acquisition and Production Cost).

▶ **Cannot be Used Manually**
This ensures that the transaction can only be used for automatic postings.

▶ **Consolidation transaction type**
This identifies the consolidation transaction type that allows you to summarize your variations of transaction types that need to be created for reporting purposes. It represents the legal accounting view and allows you to group together transactions from a similar legal perspective.

▶ **Asset History Sheet Group**
Each transaction type needs to be assigned to an asset history sheet group so that these can be reported per legal reporting requirements. For example, all the asset acquisition transaction types are assigned to asset history sheet group **10**.

▶ **Set Changeover Year**
This indicator sets a changeover year whenever an appropriate asset acquisition is posted and triggers the recalculation of depreciation based on the changeover year.

▶ **Call up Individual Check**
If you set this indicator, the system looks for your custom check defined in a user exit when posting with this transaction type.

For illustrating transaction types and the functionality behind it, let's take a look at the process of defining a transaction type for acquisitions and how you can restrict it for a particular depreciation area. The menu path is **IMG • Financial Accounting • Asset Accounting • Transactions • Acquisitions • Define Transaction Types for Acquisitions • Define Transaction Types for Acquisitions**, and the Transaction is AO73. In this step, transaction types for acquisitions are defined. Figure 7.76 shows the Transaction type 020.

After you define the transaction type, you can restrict it by depreciation area so that it can only be used for the specific depreciation area as shown in Figure 7.77. The menu path is **IMG • Financial Accounting • Asset Accounting • Transactions • Acquisitions • Define Transaction Types for**

Acquisitions • Limit Transaction Type for Depreciation Area, and the Transaction is OAYA.

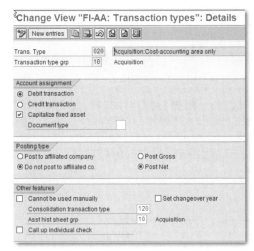

Figure 7.76 Define the Transaction Type for Asset Acquisition

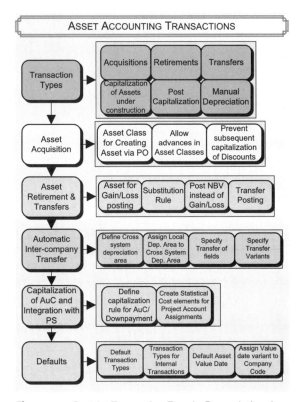

Figure 7.77 Restrict Transaction Type in Depreciation Area

Table 7.2 shows the menu paths and transaction codes for all the business processes in Asset Accounting for defining the transaction types, and Table 7.3 gives you the menu paths and transaction codes for restricting these transaction types within a depreciation area.

Business Process	Menu Path	Transaction Code
Acquisition	IMG • Financial Accounting • Asset Accounting • Transactions • Acquisitions • Define Transaction Types for Acquisitions • Define Transaction Types for Acquisitions	AO73
Retirement	IMG • Financial Accounting • Asset Accounting • Transactions • Acquisitions • Define Transaction Types for Retirements • Define Transaction Types for Retirements	AO74
Write Up due to Gain/Loss	IMG • Financial Accounting • Asset Accounting • Transactions • Retirements • Gain/Loss Posting • Define Transaction Types for Write Ups due to Gain/Loss	AO82
Retirement Transfers	IMG • Financial Accounting • Asset Accounting • Transactions • Transfers • Define Transaction Types for Transfers • Define Transaction Types for Retirement Transfers	AO76
Acquisition Transfers	IMG • Financial Accounting • Asset Accounting • Transactions • Transfers• Define Transaction Types for Transfers • Define Transaction Types for Acquisition Transfers	AO75
Capitalization of Assets Under Construction	IMG • Financial Accounting • Asset Accounting • Transactions • Capitalization of Assets Under Construction• Define Transaction Types	OAXG
Post Capitalization	IMG • Financial Accounting • Asset Accounting • Transactions • Define Transaction Types for Post Capitalization • Define Transaction Types for Post Capitalization	AO77
Unplanned Depreciation	IMG • Financial Accounting • Asset Accounting • Transactions • Define Transaction Types for Manual Depreciation • Define Transaction Types for Unplanned Depreciation	AO78

Table 7.2 Menu Paths and Transaction Codes for Asset Accounting Business Transactions Types

Business Process	Menu Path	Transaction Code
Acquisition	IMG • Financial Accounting • Asset Accounting • Transactions • Acquisitions • Define Transaction Types for Acquisitions• Limit Transaction Type for Depreciation Area	OAYA
Retirement	IMG • Financial Accounting • Asset Accounting • Transactions • Retirements • Define Transaction Types for Retirement • Limit Transaction Type for Depreciation Area	OAXB
Transfers	IMG •Financial Accounting • Asset Accounting • Transactions • Transfers • Define Transaction Types for Transfers • Limit Transaction Types to Depreciation Area	OAXC
Capitalization of Assets under Construction	IMG • Financial Accounting • Asset Accounting • Transactions • Capitalization of Assets under Cost • Allow Transaction Types for Asset Classes	OAYB
Post Capitalization	IMG • Financial Accounting • Asset Accounting • Transactions • Define Transaction Types for Post Capitalization • Limit Transaction Types to Depreciation Areas	OAXD
Manual Depreciation	IMG • Financial Accounting • Asset Accounting • Transactions • Define Transaction Types for Manual Depreciation • Limit Transaction Types to Depreciation Areas	OAXE

Table 7.3 Menu Paths and Transaction Codes for Restricting Transaction Types by Depreciation Area

7.10.2 Optimization Settings for Asset Acquisitions

Let's now learn about some key settings that allow you to optimize and integrate Asset Accounting across nonfinancial SAP ERP components. You can follow the menu path **IMG • Financial Accounting • Asset Accounting • Transactions • Acquisitions • Specify Asset Class for Creating Asset from Purchase Order**, or use Transaction OMQX.

You can directly create an asset from purchasing transactions for creating purchase orders with account assignment category **A**. In this step, you identify the asset class for the asset that can be directly created from the purchase order. The assignment of asset class is done by material group. Figure 7.78

415

shows the assignment of the material group to the asset class. Material group
(**Mat. Grp**) **01** has been assigned to Asset Class (**Class**) **2000**.

Change View "Default Asset Class": Overview

Mat. Grp	Mat. Grp Descr.	Class	Short Text
01	Material group 1	2000	Machinery
02	Material group 2	3200	DP / Hardware

Figure 7.78 Define Default Asset Class by Material Group

The menu path for allowing downpayment transaction types in the Asset
Class is: **IMG • Financial Accounting • Asset Accounting • Transactions •
Acquisitions • Allow Downpayment transaction types in Asset Class**. The
Transaction is OAYB. You define the asset classes for which downpayments
can be made. Figure 7.79 shows the asset classes (**Class**) **4000** and **4001**,
which can be given a downpayment (**Trans. Type grp.** as **15**) for **Chart of
dep. 1US**.

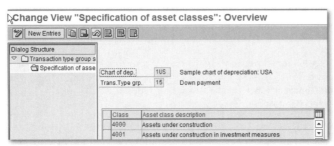

Figure 7.79 Define Specification of Asset Class

The menu path is **IMG • Financial Accounting • Asset Accounting • Transactions • Acquisitions • Prevent Subsequent Capitalization of Discounts**.
In AP, you can deduct the cash discount at the time of invoicing, and if AP is
integrated with Asset Accounting, the same gets passed to the asset. However,
if the actual cash discount to be deducted from the vendor is different from
the one deducted at the time of invoice, then the same can be adjusted at the
time of payment run. You can pass on any deltas between the invoicing and
the payment run to the asset by running a batch program in GL accounting
(**Closing. • Regroup • Profit and Loss Adjustment**). This setting prevents
any subsequent discounts (after invoicing) from passing on to the assets. Figure 7.80 shows the settings that have been made for company code **US00**.

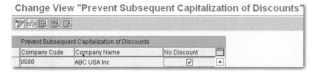

Figure 7.80 Prevent Subsequent Capitalization of Discounts

The menu path is **IMG • Financial Accounting • Asset Accounting • Transactions • Acquisitions • Define Validation**. In this configuration, you define whether any validation needs to be done by the transaction type group that represents the business transaction (e.g., **10** represents **Acquisition**, whereas **20** represents **Retirement**). Using this, you can use various conditions to instill some discipline in the validation of posting in Asset Accounting. For example, certain transactions can only be posted to a specific asset class.

7.10.3 Country-Specific Settings for Asset Retirement

For asset retirement and transfers, you can make the following settings to customize the business processes per country-specific requirements. You can make the following settings which are country specific:

▸ Determine assets for gain/losss posting per asset class

▸ Determine asset for gain/loss individually using substitution rules

▸ Post net book value instead of gain/loss

▸ The first two are specific to USA while the last one is specific to France.

First let us learn how to define the assets for gain/loss posting per asset class. You need to follow the menu path **IMG • Financial Accounting • Asset Accounting • Transactions • Retirements • Gain/Loss Posting • Determine Assets for Gain/Loss Posting per Asset Class**, or use Transaction OAKB.

You need to maintain this setting if you do not collect the gain/loss to profit and loss accounts but want to transfer to collect these in assets. In this setting, you can define the asset number that can be used to post the gain or loss posting by asset class.

In cases where you want the posting to happen to assets instead of to profit and loss accounts, you can define substitution rules to define them at a more granular level. Substitution rules allow you to determine the assets to which gains or losses should be posted. Asset retirement substitution rules can be maintained by company code. The menu path for defining substitution rules is **IMG •Financial Accounting • Asset Accounting • Transactions • Re-**

tirements • Gain/Loss Posting • Determine Asset for Gain/Loss Individually (Substitution), and the Transaction is OA01. Once you execute the transaction, you need to click on the **Substitution** button, and you can easily define a substitution rule that helps you determine the asset for gain/loss posting.

Next you will post the retiring asset's net book value to a balance sheet account such as the **Clearing of Revenue from Sales of Assets** account. This ensures that no profit or loss from the sale of the asset is posted. The menu path is **IMG •Financial Accounting • Asset Accounting • Transactions • Retirements • Gain/Loss Posting • Post Net Book Value instead of Gain/ Loss**, and the Transaction is AO72.

Figure 7.81 shows how you can choose to **Post net book value** instead of gain or loss, by company code.

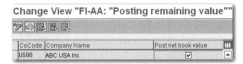

Figure 7.81 Define Posting Remaining Value

7.10.4 Optimization Settings for Asset Transfers

In this step, you can define whether you are going to transfer APC (Acquisition and Production Cost) or APC with subsequent value adjustments over the life cycle of the asset while retiring. The menu path is **IMG • Financial Accounting • Asset Accounting • Transactions • Transfers • Specify Posting Variant for Retirement Transfers**, and the Transaction is OAY1.

Figure 7.82 shows the screen where you can maintain the posting variant for retirement transfers. Checking the indicator Trans. APC only allows you to transfer only the acquisition value. If you do not check the indicator, then you can also transfer proportional value adjustments. This setting can be made by depreciation area within a chart of depreciation and transaction type.

> **Note**
>
> Most countries require that you transfer APC and subsequent adjustments. However, in the United States, for group assets, you need to transfer APC only.

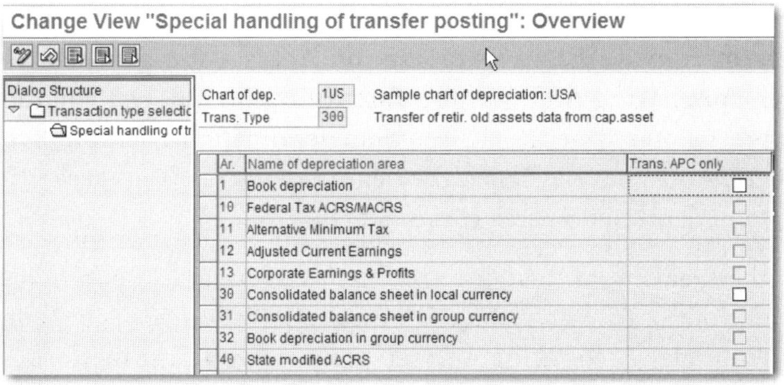

Figure 7.82 Define Special Handling of Transfer Posting

7.10.5 Optimization Settings for Intercompany Asset Transfers

You can set up automatic intercompany transfers using the settings described in this subsection. So the acquisition in the receiving company code and the transfer from the sending company code are completed in one step. The first step in defining automatic intercompany asset transfer is to define the cross-system depreciation area (see Figure 7.83).

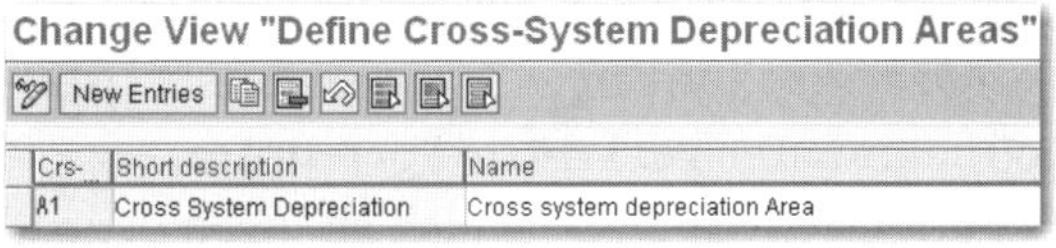

Figure 7.83 Define Cross-System Depreciation Areas

Cross-system depreciation areas allow you to assign a common meaning across multiple chart of depreciation. For each cross-system depreciation area, you can define your own transfer methods by defining new transfer variants. The menu path you will need to follow is **IMG • Financial Accounting • Asset Accounting • Transactions • Intercompany Asset Transfers • Define Cross System Depreciation Areas • Define Cross-System Depreciation Areas**.

> **Note**
>
> Define cross-system depreciation areas only if you use multiple charts of depreciation that have different purposes and meanings across the system for the same depreciation area key.

After defining the cross-system depreciation area, you need to assign local depreciation areas to these. To do this follow the menu path **IMG •Financial**

Accounting • Asset Accounting • Transactions • Intercompany Asset Transfers • Define Cross System Depreciation Areas • Assign Local to Cross-System Depreciation Areas, or use Transaction OATB. Then you can assign your depreciation area to the cross-system depreciation area as shown in Figure 7.84. Here you have assigned the depreciation area (**Dep.area**) **10** to the cross-system depreciation area (**Crs-sys.ar**) **A1**.

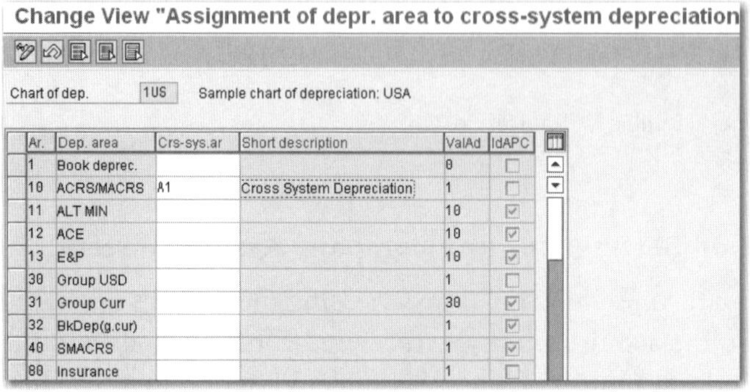

Change View "Assignment of depr. area to cross-system depreciation

Chart of dep.   1 US   Sample chart of depreciation: USA

Ar.	Dep. area	Crs-sys.ar	Short description	ValAd	IdAPC	
1	Book deprec.			8	☐	
10	ACRS/MACRS	A1	Cross System Depreciation	1	☐	
11	ALT MIN			10	☑	
12	ACE			10	☑	
13	E&P			10	☑	
30	Group USD			1	☐	
31	Group Curr			30	☑	
32	BkDep(g.cur)			1	☑	
40	SMACRS			1	☑	
80	Insurance			1	☐	

Figure 7.84 Assignment of Depreciation Area to Cross-System Depreciation Area

This allows you to define which fields should be captured from the transferred asset to the target asset in the new company code. The menu path is **IMG • Financial Accounting • Asset Accounting • Transactions • Intercompany Asset Transfers • DefineTransfer Variants • Specify Transfer of Fields**. Figure 7.85 shows the field transfer structure, which has been defined in the transfer variant (**Transfer var.**) as **1 Gross method**. The transfer variant identifies the field group (**Field grp**), which should be copied for the particular transfer variant.

The menu path is **IMG • Financial Accounting • Asset Accounting • Transactions • Intercompany Asset Transfers • Define Transfer Variants • Define Transfer Variants**. Figure 7.86 shows the screen for maintaining the transfer variant **Gross method**.

Figure 7.85 Define Field Transfer Rules for Field Groups

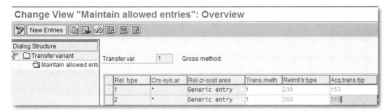

Figure 7.86 Define Minimum Allowed Entries

The fields in this screen are listed here:

▶ **Rel. type**
This identifies the relationship type of the two company codes. **1** denotes legally independent units; **2** denote one legal unit.

▶ **Crs-sys ar**
This identifies the cross-system depreciation area.

▶ **Trans. Meth**
This identifies the transfer method applicable.The following standard options are available:

  ▶ **1** Gross method without transfer of values to dependent areas

  ▶ **2** Net method with transfer of values to dependent areas

  ▶ **3** New value method with transfer of values to dependent areas

> ▶ **4** Gross method with transfer of values to dependent areas

▶ **Retmt tr. type**
This identifies the retirement transaction type that will be used in the sender company code.

▶ **Acq. Trans. typ**
This identifies the acquisition transaction type that will be used in the target company code.

Now let's discuss the settings needed for capitalization of AuC.

7.10.6 Optimization Settings for Capitalization of Assets Under Construction

You can control the settlement process while capitalizing an asset from an AuC focusing on the advances given in the previous year. This allows you to represent downpayments from previous years in the asset history sheet according to your requirements. Follow the menu path **IMG • Financial Accounting • Asset Accounting • Transactions • Capitalization of Assets under Transaction • Specify Capitalization Rule of AuC/Downpayment**, or use Transaction OAYU.

Figure 7.87 shows the screen where you can maintain the capitalization rule by depreciation area and company code for AuC and downpayments.

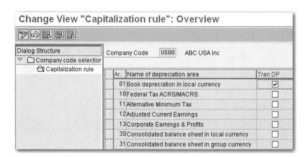

Figure 7.87 Define Capitalization Rule for AuC/Downpayment

If you set the **Tran DP** indicator, the system ignores the downpayments during the line-item settlement of AuC. If you do not set the indicator, the system considers the downpayment date and whether it is in a different year, and then system just transfers the difference between the invoice and the downpayment per the invoice date. However, the downpayment amount is transferred as an old acquisition in the previous year.

> **Note**
>
> This setting is only significant if the posting date of the downpayment and the invoice are in two different fiscal years.

7.10.7 Optimization Setting for Integrating Asset Accounting with Project Systems

In this sub-section you will learn how you can integrate project systesm and asset accounting from budgeting perspective. These settings only need to be maintained if you want to monitor the actuals against the budgeted and commitment values. To enable the integration of FI-AA with PS for budgeting purposes, post the real cost object to the asset during acquisition, while a statistical entry is also posted to a WBS element or an internal order. This can be accomplished by creating a statistical cost element for each of your asset balance sheet accounts. These settings are only used if the transaction type for acquiring assets is marked as relevant for budget. The menu path for creating statistical cost elements is **IMG • Financial Accounting • Asset Accounting • Transactions • Budget Monitoring with Statistical Orders/ WBS Elements • Create Cost Elements for Project/Order Acccount Assignment**, and the Transaction is OAK7.

On executing the transaction, you need to enter the Controlling area along with validity dates. Executing this transaction automatically creates statistical cost elements for controlling area US00 based on the GL accounts that were used in assets. You can run the transaction in test mode as well.

7.10.8 Optimization Setting for Defaults in Asset Accounting Business Transactions

In this subsection, you will learn about setting defaults in Asset Accounting. First, you will learn how to specify default transaction types. To specify default transaction types follow **IMG • Financial Accounting • Asset Accounting • Transactions • Specify Default transaction types**.

You can assign default transaction types for each of the Asset Accounting posting transactions such as asset acquisition, asset retirement, and so on. Typically, these come prepopulated, but if you have defined custom Z transaction types, then those should be assigned as the default transaction types by business transactions. To determine transaction types for internal transactions you will need to follow **IMG • Financial Accounting • Asset Accounting • Transactions • Determine Transaction Types for Internal Transactions**.

Figure 7.88 shows the default transaction types for internal asset transactions that are initiated in nonfinancial modules and are triggered automatically. Typical examples are **Gain/loss on retirement (770)**, **Acquisition from goods receipt (120)**, and so on. These are also prepopulated and need to be maintained only if you have defined a Z transaction type that should be used in these processes.

Change View "Default transaction types": Overview		
Transaction name	Tra	Transaction type name
Balance from AuC at partial settlement	342	Bal.forward AuC after partial settlement old da.
Gain/loss on retirement	770	Write-up from gain/loss
Acquisition from invoice receipt	100	External asset acquisition
Acquisition from invoice receipt (affil. co.	152	Acquisition from affiliated company -net
Follow-up discount postings	165	Calc. of cash discount recvd/lost in prior year?
Transfer to affil.co.	350	Transfer old assets data to affiliated company
Input tax correction foll. fiscal year	160	Credit memo in following year
Input tax correction current fiscal year	160	Credit memo in following year
Transfer from affil.co.	360	Transfer old assets data from affiliated comp.
Withdrawal from stock	130	Withdrawal from stock
Acquisition from goods receipt	120	Goods receipt
Goods receipt completed order	121	Goods receipt for production order
Acquisition from goods receipt (affil. co.)	122	Goods receipt from affiliated company (net)
External asset acquisition	100	External asset acquisition

Figure 7.88 Default Transaction Types for Internal Asset Transactions

The menu path is **IMG • Financial Accounting • Asset Accounting • Transactions • Specify how default asset value date is determined • Define variant for determining default asset value date**. Figure 7.89 shows the screen for maintaining the default asset value date by business transactions. You can define a primary rule **(Prim.rule)** and an alternate rule **(Alt.rule)** for each type of transaction.

The posting rules that can be maintained for defaulting the asset value date are as follows:

- **01:** To be entered manually
- **02:** Posting date
- **03**: Document date
- **04**: Earlier of either document or posting date (if different fiscal year then posting date)
- **05:** First day of period
- **06:** First day of Fiscal year
- **07:** User-specified fixed date
- **08:** Current date

Change View "Business Transactions": Overview

Variable list | Set defaults

Dialog Structure
- Variants
  - Business Transactio

Variant SAP_DEFAULT Used when no variant assigned to company code

Name of transaction	Prim.rule	Alt.rule
Current-value depreciation	9	4
Retirement	1	
Settlement of AuC	2	
Down payment	2	
Settlement of order	2	
Revaluation	14	6
Acquisition posting for settlement of AuC	2	2
Credit memo related to invoice	12	2
Investment support	9	4
Manual transfer of reserves	9	4
Subsequent retirement costs	10	2
Post-capitalization	6	
Subsequent revenue	10	2
Manual ordinary depreciation	9	4
Manual special depreciation	9	4
Intracompany transfer	1	
Acquisition from settlement	2	
Invoice receipt for purchase order	12	2
Invoice receipt w/o purchase order	9	4
Acquisition	9	4
Write-up	6	

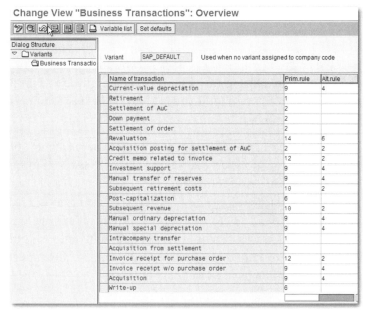

Figure 7.89 Define Determination Rule of Default Asset Value Date

- **09**: Capitalization date
- **10**: Date of last retirement
- **11**: First day after last retirement
- **12**: Posting date of goods receipt
- **13**: Date of revaluation measure

As you can see, many variations can be used to default the asset value date. To assign a value date variant to the company code, follow the menu path: **IMG • Financial Accounting • Asset Accounting • Transactions • Specify how default asset value date is determined • Assign value date variant to company code**. Figure 7.90 shows the screen for assigning the asset value date variant to a company code. If you do not maintain this setting, then SAP_DEFAULT is used, which was described in the previous step.

Change View "Assign value date variants to company codes"

Variable list

CoCd	Company Name	Variant	Variant description
US00	ABC USA Inc	SAP_DEFAULT	Used when no variant assigned to company coc

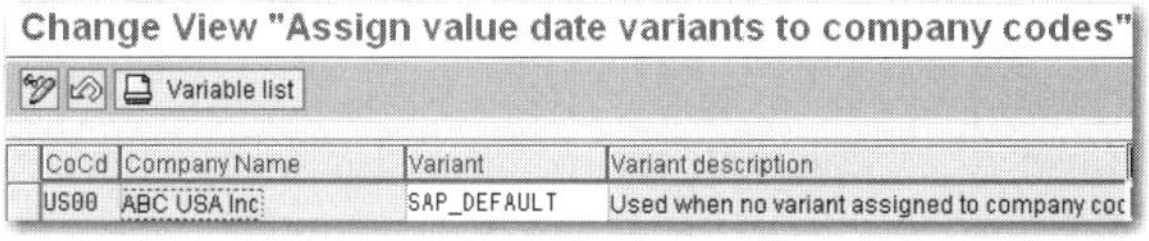

Figure 7.90 Assign Value Date Variants to Company Code

7.11   Legacy Data Transfer

Legacy data transfer is the first step in implementing Asset Accounting, which involves transferring data from your legacy Asset Accounting system to the new Asset Accounting system. During the realization phase of the SAP ERP Financials implementation, it is important that you identify the business rules for transferring legacy data in Asset Accounting.

The toughest part of Asset Accounting is legacy data transfer because most of the other Asset Accounting functions do not require a major customization. So make sure that you plan your asset transfer methodically and test all your legacy data for correctness before importing in Asset Accounting. It is very important that you conduct dry runs before importing the data in production. This task involves transferring the asset master records and transactions from the start of the fiscal year to the date of the go-live. Following are the important factors when performing the legacy asset data transfer:

▸ **Time of transfer**
This is the day when you cutover the Assets. There are two broad possibilities:

  ▸ **End of the last fiscal year** (e.g., for a January to December fiscal year, this would be December 31st)

  ▸ **During the fiscal year** (e.g., for a January to December fiscal year, this would be July 1st)

▸ **Transfer parameters**
These specify whether the data from legacy will be modified and the parameters that affect the modification. The following are the key parameters that can be set up in legacy data transfer:

  ▸ Transfer date

  ▸ Last period posted in previous system

  ▸ Entry of net book value versus cumulated depreciation

  ▸ Recalculate depreciation for previous year

  ▸ Transfer foreign currency areas

▸ **Transfer of Auc**
You also need to understand how you will be moving the AuC. The key aspects to be considered here are the transfer of line items and how advances need to be treated for these items.

▶ **Reconciliation of balances with the GL**
As mentioned earlier, the reconciliation between FI-AA and FI-GL from legacy data does not happen automatically. The folowing reports can be used to validate that the balances tie in: AA (RABEST01) and GL (RFSSLD00). For reconciling the transactions within a fiscal year, the asset history sheet is used to match GL with AA.

▶ **Transfer after Asset Accounting is already productive**
This is a special scenario, and ideally you should not be using the legacy data transfer but the asset acquisition process to upload new assets. This ensures the continuity of asset balances.

Let's review the methods for data transfer next.

> **Note**
>
> In all these transfers, GL accounts are not updated. So reconciliation of GL accounts is a subsequent step after the data has been loaded into the system. Do not forget to reconcile the GL with Asset Accounting.

7.11.1 Manual Legacy Asset Data Transfer

This is the same as creating assets with the additional functionality pertaining to the takeover of asset values and transactions in the current year. The following are the key consideration points while performing manual legacy data transfer:

▶ **Master data**
Capitalization date is always a required entry. Time-dependent data can only be transferred with the current values. Useful life is a required entry when a depreciation key for automatic depreciation calculation is entered.

▶ **Asset Values**
Historical acquisition costs need to be entered along with all the active depreciation areas for the asset. For transfer during the fiscal year, the depreciation for the current year should also be entered.

▶ **Transactions**
To transfer transactions, the asset value date and the transaction type are required.

7.11.2 Legacy Data Transfer Using Microsoft Excel

The transfer limitation for this method is due to the number of rows in Excel that can be populated. The maximum number that can be transferred using Excel is about 5,000 asset records. In this method, record types are used for the interpretation logic by SAP Asset Accounting from Excel. The first five rows are used to capture the header information that identifies which column corresponds to which Asset Accounting field according to the record type. The following are the record types that are entered in row A of the Excel sheet:

▶ **Record Type 0**
This corresponds to the legacy asset number.

▶ **Record Type 1**
This can be used for asset master data, general data, and inventory data.

▶ **Record Type 2**
This pertains to posting information and time-dependent data.

▶ **Record Type 3**
This captures the depreciation areas, cumulative values, and posted values.

▶ **Record Type 4**
This corresponds to transactions for the asset master.

This can be run in the test run mode, which helps you identify any errors before you actually execute the legacy data transfer.

7.11.3 Automatic Data Transfer

This involves transferring legacy data using a sequential file and then using one of the two reports: RAALTD01 or RAALTD11. The following steps are needed for automatic data transfer:

1. Identify relevant fields using AS91.
2. Analyze the transfer structure.
3. Modify the standard available structures: BALTD (master data and values) and BALTB (transactions).
4. Create the sample data transfer file.
5. Test the transfer program.
6. Analyze the legacy data.
7. Assign the fields.

8. Code the conversion program.

9. Prepare the legacy system.

10. Test the transfer program.

11. Perform the transfer.

7.11.4 Configuring Legacy Data Transfer: Asset Accounting

Figure 7.91 shows the process of configuring the legacy data transfer in Asset Accounting.

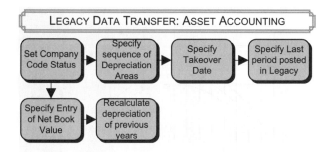

Figure 7.91 Configuring Legacy Asset Data Transfer

The first step in legacy data transfer for Asset Accounting is to make sure that you have correctly set the status of the company code. In addition, you also need to specify the sequence in which the depreciation area gets populated. The takeover date identifies the date when you transfer all your asset data to SAP ERP Financials. You also need to specify the last period for which depreciation was posted if you are taking over your data midway in a fiscal year.

You can choose to only enter the net book value and not to capture all the business transactions that happened on an asset using **Specify Entry of Net**

Book Value. You also have the option to **Recalculate depreciation of previous years** if you want to start fresh altogether if your legacy Asset Accounting had a large amount of errors. The menu path is **IMG • Financial Accounting • Asset Accounting • Asset Data Transfer • Set Company code Status**. Figure 7.92 shows how you can maintain the status of a company code as far as asset data transfer is concerned. Following are the available options, seen in Figure 7.92:

- ▸ **0**: **Asset data transfer completed**
- ▸ **1**: **Asset data transfer not yet completed**
- ▸ **2**: **Test company code with data transfer always allowed**
- ▸ **3**: **Company code deactivated**

It is important that the status should be 1 or 2 for the system to allow legacy data transfer. Follow the menu path **IMG • Financial Accounting • Asset Accounting • Asset Data Transfer • Specfiy Sequence of Depreciation Areas**. You can also use Transaction OAYE.

Change View "FI-AA: Set status of the company code": Overview

Co...	Company Name	Status	Status details
FI01		2	Test company code with data transfer always allo
FR01		2	Test company code with data transfer always allo
IT01		2	Test company code with data transfer always allo
MX01		2	Tes
MY01		2	Tes
RU01		2	Tes
SG01		1	Ass
US01		1	Ass

Staus of asset data transfer in the company code (2)   4 Entries found

Status company co...	Short text
0	Asset data transfer completed
1	Asset data transfer not yet completed
2	Test company code with data transfer always allowed
3	Company code deactivated - later reporting allowed

Figure 7.92 Set Status of the Company Code

Figure 7.93 shows the sequence of populating the depreciation area by company code. **No** identifies the sequence, and **Ar.** denotes the depreciation area. You should keep the dependent depreciation areas as the last number of the sequence. If there are no dependencies, then this step does not matter. This affects the performance of data transfer during automatic data transfer. The first depreciation area that is typically transferred is the **Book depreciation in local currency**.

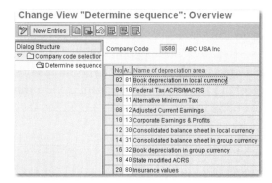

Figure 7.93 Determine Sequence of Populating the Depreciation Area

Next you will learn to configure the date settings for asset data transfer. The menu path for specifying the transfer date is **IMG • Financial Accounting • Asset Accounting • Asset Data Transfer • Parameters of Data Transfer • Date Specifications • Specify Transfer Date/Last Closed Fiscal Year**. Figure 7.94 shows the **Take-over date** for **Company code US00** as **12/31/2006**. The take-over date identifies when you will transfer all your asset data to SAP ERP Financials. This also identifies in the system whether the transfer is within a fiscal year or during a fiscal year.

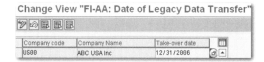

Figure 7.94 Identify Date of Legacy Data Transfer

If the date is anything other than the last of the fiscal year, you are allowed to make the next setting where you specify the last period posted in the previous system. The menu path is **IMG • Financial Accounting • Asset Accounting • Asset Data Transfer • Parameters of Data Transfer • Date Specifications • Specify Last Period Posted in Prv.System (Transf.During FY)**, and the Transaction is OAYC.

You can define the last period that was posted in the legacy system by company code and depreciation area. If you are taking over in July 2007, then the last period would be June 2007. This setting is only relevant if you are taking over during a fiscal year. The menu path is **IMG • Financial Accounting • Asset Accounting • Asset Data Transfer • Parameters of Data Transfer • Options • Specify Entry of Net Book Value**.

Here you can define that you only want to transfer the net book value from legacy rather than the original acquisition value and accumulated depreciation. This is useful if your legacy system does not have the original acquisition value maintained. Figure 7.95 shows how you can define the parameters of entry for net book value. By checking the **Enter net bkval** box, you can specify that you are transferring net book value.

> **Note**
>
> Net book values can only be transferred using manual take-over transactions and cannot be transferred using batch input transactions.

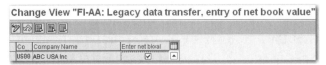

Figure 7.95 Define the Parameter of Entry for Net Book Value

The menu path is **IMG • Financial Accounting • Asset Accounting • Asset Data Transfer • Parameters of Data Transfer • Options • Recalculate Depreciation for Previous Years**. If you set the indicator, then the system recalculates the depreciation previously calculated in the legacy systems. This can be used if you have defined a new depreciation area, or you want the depreciation to be recalculated for specific asset classes. The system recalculates the depreciation by assuming that the total asset value was capitalized on the capitalization date; this is why many times the calculated depreciation does not match the legacy depreciation. Figure 7.96 shows how you can use the **Calcul.** box to recalculate depreciation for the book depreciation of **Company Code US00** for previous years.

> **Note**
>
> Typically this indicator is not set because you want to bring over the depreciation calculated in your legacy system. If you set this indicator, there can be huge variations between what your legacy system calculated and what SAP ERP Financials calculates per the depreciation key settings. That might require a restatement of previously published financial statements and require a note to auditors about the change in depreciation method going forward. So conservative accounting departments usually do not want a recalculation.

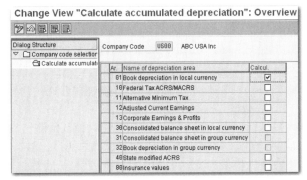

Figure 7.96 Set the Parameter for Entering Cumulative Depreciation

7.12 Summary

In this chapter, you learned about the structure and configuration of the asset master along with the organization entities of Asset Accounting. In addition, you learned about the typical business transactions performed in Asset Accounting, such as acquisition, transfer, and retirement. Period-end activities were introduced with a detailed discussion of the depreciation run and the new depreciation calculation method. And, you learned about the configuration elements of the business transactions and how you can customize Asset Accounting to your needs. Lastly, you learned about the legacy asset data transfer and its key settings. This completes the various subledgers of financial accounting.

In Chapter 8, you will be introduced to the global settings of financial accounting that will help launch you into the general ledger discussion.

Financial accounting global settings are common to all of the SAP ERP Financials modules and are key to understanding the SAP ERP Financials structure. Recently, many new global settings have been added for the new General Ledger (GL).

8 Financial Accounting Global Settings

Earlier you were introduced to AP, AR, Bank Accounting, and Asset Accounting. This chapter outlines the configuration pertaining to Financial Accounting global settings, which are common to all of these financial subledgers. However, these settings are of major significance to GL accounting. Overall, it is very important for you to fully understand that these settings are the building blocks of Financial Accounting in SAP ERP.

Most of these settings relate to the GL, and the menu paths have changed because of the introduction of the new GL. You will get the new global settings in the IMG when you choose to implement the new GL. Otherwise, you will continue seeing the previous global settings. We will point out the key differences between release 4.7 and ERP 2005 in terms of financial accounting global settings. Let's first get an idea about the global settings for SAP ERP Financials.

Financial global settings are common across all the financial modules and pertain to the configuration of the company code global parameters, document settings, ledgers (5.0 onward), taxes, correspondence, and financial configuration tools. Figure 8.1 displays the global settings for ERP 2005 6.0, whereas Figure 8.2 shows the global settings for version 4.7. All releases prior to 4.7 have the same set of global settings shown in Figure 8.2. The menu path is **Financial Accounting • Financial Accounting (New) • Financial Accounting Global Settings (New)**, and the Transaction is OXK3.

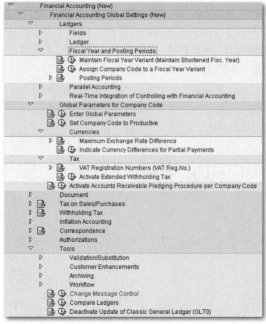

Figure 8.1 Global Settings SAP ERP 6.0

Differences Between 4.7 and 6.0

The key additions from ERP 2005 version 5.0 onward are the configuration of ledgers and the addition of nodes for tools, which include validation, substitution rules, and message control. In addition, you have new nodes for parallel accounting, and real time integration with controlling and FI.

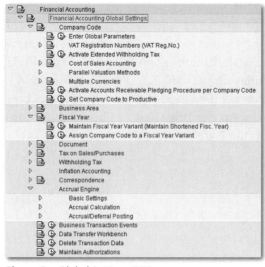

Figure 8.2 Global Settings ECC 4.7

The document and correspondence settings are the same as for AP, so they are not covered in this chapter. For the sake of simplicity, the focus of this chapter is on the settings for SAP ERP 6.0.

8.1 Financial Accounting Global Settings: Company Code

The Company Code is the building block for FI enterprise organization structure. Let's discuss how to define the parameters for the global settings pertaining to the company code. Figure 8.3 shows the menu path for defining the global settings for the company code.

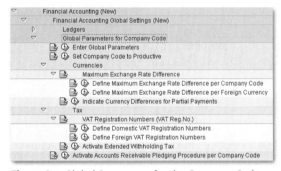

Figure 8.3 Global Parameters for the Company Code

8.1.1 Enter Global Parameters

Let's learn about the global parameters of company code. Figure 8.4 shows you the **Global Parameters for Company Code**. To enter the global parameters follow this menu path: **Financial Accounting • Financial Accounting Global Settings (New) • Global Parameters for Company Code • Enter Global Parameters**. The Transaction is OBY6.

These were also discussed in Chapter 3 when you learned about the enterprise structure. It is very important to understand what is possible in a company code, so memorize Transaction OBY6. The following entries need to be defined in the beginning when you are defining the enterprise structure:

▶ **Country key**
The country where the company code is based.

▶ **Currency**
Identifies the currency of the company code.

437

▸ **Language**
The language of the company code.

The following are the key data entry fields for the company code global parameters, which can be maintained in **Accounting organization**:

▸ **Chart of Accts**
This is the four-digit identifier of the chart of accounts relevant for this company code.

▸ **Country Chart/Accts**
This identifies the country chart of accounts if applicable.

▸ **FM Area**
FM Area is the financial management area used for the funds management module.

▸ **Credit control area**
This controls the credit limit and tolerances for the customers.

▸ **Fiscal Year Variant**
This is the fiscal year identifier that identifies the fiscal year calendar for the company code.

▸ **VAT Registration No**.
Here you can enter the VAT registration number. This is more relevant in Europe.

▸ **Company code is productive**
This prevents the data from being deleted accidentally. This needs to be checked after the company code has gone live.

▸ **Ext. co. code**
You can check this indicator of external company code, if you are going to import data to this company code using ALE (application link enabling).

▸ **Global Cocde**
This is only required to be maintained for a global company code, if you have an ALE distribution scenario.

You can also define the **Processing parameters**:

▸ **Field status variant**
This controls which field status groups are assigned to the company code.

▸ **Pstng period variant**
Posting period variant controls how you would open and close the posting periods in the GL.

▶ **Busines area fin. statements**

If you want to generate business area statements, then you should check this box. This box makes the business area ready for input for the company code, regardless of the field status group. Business area becomes a mandatory entry in controlling, MM, and SD.

Change View "Company Code Global Data": Details

| Additional Data | ◀ | ▶ | 🖨 |

Company Code	US00	ABC USA Inc		Houston	
Country key	US	Currency	USD	Language Key	EN

Accounting organization

Chart of Accts	CANA	Country Chart/Accts	CANA	
Company	US01	FM Area	ABCI	
Credit control area	US02	Fiscal Year Variant	K4	
Ext. co. code	☐	Global CoCde		
Company code is productive	☐	VAT Registration No.		

Processing parameters

Document entry screen variant		☐ Business area fin. statements	
Field status variant	0001	☐ Propose fiscal year	
Pstng period variant	0001	☐ Define default value date	
Max. exchange rate deviation	%	☐ No forex rate diff. when clearing in LC	
Sample acct rules var.		☐ Tax base is net value	
Workflow variant		☐ Discount base is net value	
Inflation Method		☐ Financial Assets Mgmt active	
Crcy transl. for tax		☐ Purchase account processing	
CoCd→CO Area	2		
Cost of sales accounting actv.			
☐ Negative Postings Permitted		☐ Enable amount split	
☐ Cash Management activated			

Figure 8.4 Company Code Global Parameters

▶ **Propose fiscal year**

If you check this box, then the fiscal year is defaulted for the company code whenever you display a document.

▶ **Document entry screen variant**

For most of the company codes, this should be blank. However, you need to choose 1 for Austria and Switzerland, 2 for France and countries with extended withholding tax, and 3 for countries with classic withholding tax.

▶ **Max. exchange rate deviation**

Here you can enter the maximum percentage exchange rate deviation that is allowed for the company code.

▶ **Sample acct rules var.**

Here you can maintain the rules for copying the sample account to the actual GL account.

▶ **Workflow variant**
In this configuration, you maintain the workflow variant to group together company codes.

▶ **Inflation Method**
This is only used if the company code uses inflation accounting. Here you need to enter the inflation ID.

▶ **Crcy transl. for tax**
The default setting for currency translation for tax is blank, which means that the currency translation is handled per the document header. You can maintain other settings, which indicate that manual entry is possible, and exchange rate is dependent on the posting date, on the document date, or on the posting date with distribution of differences.

▶ **CoCd → CO Area**
The assignment setting of the company code to the controlling area is automatically derived from the assignment you made in the controlling area to the company code assignments. 1 means that there is a one-to-one relationship between company code and controlling area. 2 means that the controlling area can be assigned multiple company codes.

▶ **Cost of sales accounting actv**
Blank indicates inactive, 1 indicates that it is in preparation, and 2 indicates that cost of sales accounting is active for the company code.

▶ **Negative Postings Permitted**
This, if checked, reduces the overall debit and credit balances if a document is reversed.

▶ **Cash Management activated**
This indicator, if checked, indicates that cash management and forecast are active.

▶ **Define default value date**
If this is checked, then the current date is used as the default value of the value date.

▶ **No forex rate diff. when clearing in LC**
This indicator controls how foreign exchange differences are posted when you clear a foreign currency item with an item that is in local currency. If you set this indicator, then no difference is posted if you match the historically posted exchange rate. However, if you do not set this indicator, then the system considers the current rate and posts the difference between the current and the historical exchange rate as a difference to the exchange rate account.

▶ **Tax base is net value**
If you set this indicator, then the base amount is reduced by the discount amount. So if you give a discount or receive a discount, then tax is calculated after the discount.

▶ **Discount base is net value**
If you set this indicator, then the discount base is after the calculation of net value. In this case, you calculate the discount after you have reduced or added the tax amount.

> **Note**
>
> Both these indicators (**Tax base is net value** and **Discount base is net value**) can be used in conjunction, and it is important to understand what will happen in various combinations of these scenarios.

▶ **Financial Assets Mgmt active**
This, if set, activates the financial assets management.

▶ **Purchase account processing**
If you set this indicator, then purchasing account management is activated. This ensures that whenever you purchase something, extra entries are made to record the purchase of the same along with its offsetting.

▶ **Enable amount split**
This allows you to split an invoice or credit memo final amount per different withholding information.

8.1.2 Define Maximum Exchange Rate Difference per Foreign Currency

Earlier in the company code definition, you defined the maximum exchange rate difference, which was allowed for the company code. However, in case of hyper-inflation in some countries, the exchange rate might fluctuate widely for specific currencies. In this setting, you can specify the maximum exchange rate percentage difference between exchange rates for the foreign currency and local currency. The menu path to follow is **Financial Accounting • Financial Accounting Global Settings (New) • Global Parameters for Company Code • Currencies • Maximum Exchange Rate Difference • Define Maximum Exchange Rate difference per Foreign Currency**. The Transaction is OBBF.

Figure 8.5 shows the screen where you can maintain the maximum exchange deviation for a foreign currency and local currency. Here you have maintained Mexican peso **MXN** as foreign currency **(For. Curr.)**, whereas **USD** is maintained as Local currency **(Loc. Curr.)** with the maximum exchange deviation **(Max.ex.dev.)** of **30%**.

Figure 8.5 Defining Maximum Exchange Rate Difference per Foreign Currency

8.1.3 Indicate Currency Differences for Partial Payments

This indicator activates the calculation of currency differences for partial payments. If you set this indicator, then the system compares the exchange rate at the time of invoicing and at the time of payment. At the time of partial payment and subsequent payments, the system posts the exchange rate differences of partial payments to the document type identified in this step. The menu path is **Financial Accounting • Financial Accounting Global Settings (New) • Global Parameters for Company Code • Currencies • Indicate Currency Difference for Partial Payments**, and the Transaction is IDPH1. Figure 8.6 shows you the screen where you can ensure that the currency differences for partial payments **(E/rte dif.pt py)** by period are activated for the document type **(T...) AB**.

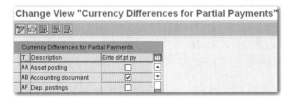

Figure 8.6 Indicate Currency Differences for Partial Payments

8.1.4 Activate Extended Withholding Tax

SAP ERP has always provided the functionality to support withholding tax, which needs to be deducted whenever you pay your vendor according to legal regulations in some countries. However, over time, the functionality has evolved. The earlier functionality was known as standard, whereas the new functionality is called *extended withholding tax*.

Standard functionality allowed you to calculate withholding tax in AP. In standard functionality, tax was applied at the time of payment and per vendor line item. However, using extended withholding tax, you can apply withholding tax for partial payments and by customer and vendor line item. In addition, the reporting capability of extended withholding tax is also vastly improved over the standard functionality. The menu path is **Financial Accounting • Financial Accounting Global Settings (New) • Global Parameters for Company Code • Activate Extended Withholding tax**.

Figure 8.7 shows you the process of activating the extended withholding tax by company code. Typically, extended withholding tax is activated by clicking (on the **Ext. w/tax**) for UK **GB01** and for Spain **ES01** as shown in the Figure 8.7.

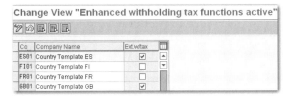

Figure 8.7 Activate Extended Withholding Tax

8.2 Financial Accounting Global Settings: Ledger

Figure 8.8 shows you the screen for configuring ledgers. The key configuration settings enable you to customize your GL implementation per your requirements. You will become familiar with the following aspects in this section:

▶ **Asset Transaction Types of Consolidation and Assignment**
Here you will learn about the definition of asset transaction types relevant for Asset Accounting and how you can assign these to Asset Accounting business transactions.

▶ **Functional Area and Cost of Sales Accounting**
This subsection details the concept of the functional area and how it can be leveraged to implement cost of sales accounting.

▶ **Customer Fields**
Here you will learn to add custom fields in your accounting ledger.

▶ **Field Status Variants and Field Status Groups**
You will learn about defining field status variants and groups and understand the difference between the two.

▶ **Ledgers**
This details the definition of your main ledger, representative ledger, and leading ledger. You will also learn how to define currencies for your ledgers.

- **Fiscal Year Variants and Posting Period Variants**

  In this subsection, you will learn how to define a fiscal year calendar and how you can control the opening and closing of the GL.

- **Parallel Valuation**

  This identifies the key settings that need to be made to support parallel valuation in the new GL.

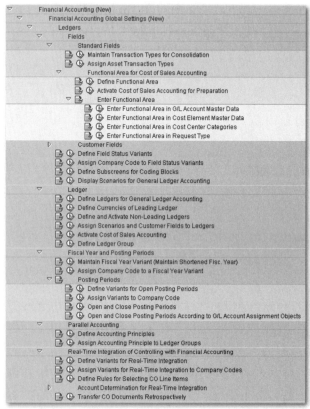

Figure 8.8 Global Settings—Ledgers

8.2.1 Asset Accounting: Transaction Types for Consolidation and Assignment

In Chapter 7, you learned about Asset Accounting and how the transaction types control the business transactions in asset transactions. We take this one step further by discussing how this comes together in groupwide corporate reporting.

Maintain Transaction Types for Consolidation

You need to define consolidation transaction types to outline how your group level balance sheet will look. At a consolidation level, you do not need the various hues that are captured at the business transaction level. So you can define one transaction type for asset acquisition that represents all the types of asset acquisitions possible in the system. Figure 8.9 shows the screen where you can define the details of the transaction types relevant for consolidation. You can follow this path: **Financial Accounting • Financial Accounting Global Settings (New) • Ledgers • Fields • Standard Fields • Maintain Transaction Types for Consolidation**. You can also use Transaction OC08.

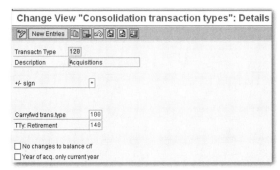

Figure 8.9 Maintain Consolidation Transaction Types

In this setting, you define the transaction type along with the description of the transaction type. The following are the other settings in this configuration:

▸ **+/– sign**
Indicates the default sign of the posting.

▸ **Carryfwd trans. type**
Specifies how the transaction type will be carried forward in the next period. Acquisition gets carried forward as opening balance.

▸ **TTy: Retirement**
The transaction type that will be used for posting retirement transactions.

▸ **No changes to balance c/f**
If this parameter is selected, you cannot add more data.

▸ **Year of acq. only current year**
If checked, this ensures that all the acquisitions occur in the current year.

Assign Asset Transaction Type to Consolidation Transaction Type

After you have defined your consolidation transaction type, you need to assign the asset transaction types that you learned in Chapter 7 to the consolidation transaction type. This allows you to perform a many-to-one mapping to consolidation transaction types. The menu path is **Financial Accounting • Financial Accounting Global Settings (New) • Ledgers • Fields • Standard Fields • Maintain Transaction Types for Consolidation**.

Figure 8.10 shows you the assignment of the asset transaction type to the corresponding asset transaction type. **Trans Type 020, 100, 101** and others have been assigned to **Cons TType** 120, which was defined in the previous step.

Change View "Asset transaction types -> Consolidation": Overv

Trans. Type	Transaction type name	Cons TType
000	Formal transctn type for migration (000,398,399)	
020	Acquisition:Cost-accounting area only	120
030	Acquisition in group area only	120
100	External asset acquisition	120
101	Acquisition for a negative asset	120
103	Incidental costs, non-deduct. input tax (fol.yrs)	100
105	Credit memo in invoice year	120
106	Credit memo in invoice year to affiliated company	125
110	In-house acquisition	120

Figure 8.10 Assign Asset Transaction Type to Consolidation Transaction Type

> **Tip**
>
> No changes need to be made to the existing predefined assignments. However, if new asset transaction types are defined in Asset Accounting, then those need to be assigned in this step.

As you learned in Chapter 7, transaction types are used for creating the asset history sheet, which is a legal requirement that needs to be presented to your auditors. Using the preceding settings, you can design your corporatewide asset history sheet, which takes a group view of your fixed assets.

In the next section, you will learn about the functional area and cost of sales accounting.

8.2.2 Functional Area for Cost of Sales Accounting

As you learned in Chapter 3, the functional area allows you to group your organization in a departmental fashion, such as marketing, production, administration, and so on. Here you will learn the process of activating cost of sales accounting.

Figure 8.11 shows you the sequence of activities to activate cost of sales accounting by defining the functional area and then activating cost of sales accounting by company code. In the last step, you can enter the functional area by GL account, cost center categories, cost element, or internal order.

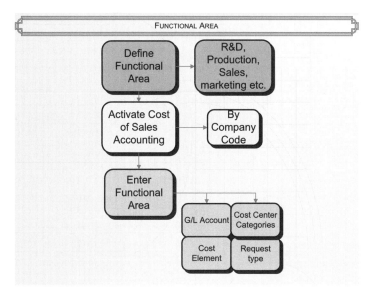

Figure 8.11 Functional Area Definition and Assignment

8.2.3 Customer Fields

Prior to the introduction of the new GL, you could not add your own fields in the GL. The tables were predefined, and you could not change them without incurring the wrath of your standardization architecture guru. However, with the introduction of the new GL, you can add fields that you would have loved to have added in the GL (You are probably already making a mental list of fields that you want to add such as plant). In this subsection, you will learn how to add your own customer fields. We will begin our exploration of this area by adding fields in the coding block.

Edit the Coding Block

The coding block identifies the set of account assignment fields together (Account Assignment tab). In this configuration setting, you can define new fields in the coding block. The menu path is **Financial Accounting • Financial Accounting Global Settings (New) • Ledgers • Fields • Customer Fields • Edit Coding Block**. After you add fields in the coding block, they can be used in FI-GL, MM-Inventory Management, and MM-Purchasing as well. All the fields added in the coding block are updated during the automatic postings.

Tips
▶ It is very important that no users are in the system when the coding block is being modified.
▶ This is a client-independent setting, so it affects all the clients within a box.
▶ This is a very sensitive setting and should be carefully deliberated across teams to finalize the format and the field addition.

Figure 8.12 shows the user-defined coding block fields. You can add your field to **Customer-Defined Account Assignments** by adding new fields in **Customer APPEND Structures**. After you make the change, all the ABAP dictionary tables are also updated across all the clients.

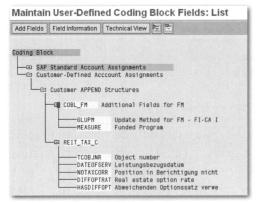

Figure 8.12 Edit the Coding Block

Include Fields in the Totals Table

In this setting, you can modify the GL totals table structure to include the customer fields added in the coding block in the previous step. The fields can be added to the SAP-supplied table FAGLFLEXT or to your own custom table. Each new field that you add in this table increases the overall volume of data and can affect the performance. Some of the typical fields that can be used are WBS Element or Plant. It makes sense to add customer indices as well to take care of performance issues. The menu path for including fields in the totals table is **Financial Accounting • Financial Accounting Global Settings (New) • Ledgers • Fields • Customer Fields • Include Fields in Totals Table**. You can also use Transaction FAGL_GINS. Figure 8.13 shows the customer enhancement (**Customer Include CI_FAGLFLEX04**) that can be used to add the new account assignment fields defined earlier in the totals table.

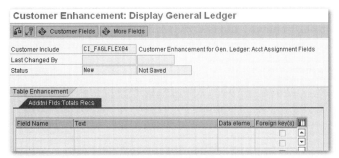

Figure 8.13 Include Fields in the Totals Table

Master Data Check

Prior to the new GL, to establish master data checks, you had to define validation rules. Using this setting, you can define the table against which the master data fields such as the GL account gets checked. This allows you to establish control procedures for valid combinations of integrated master data such as the GL account, cost center, cost element, and so on. Follow the menu path **Financial Accounting • Financial Accounting Global Settings (New) • Ledgers • Fields • Customer Fields • Master Data Check**, or use Transaction GLGCS1. If you notice, the new GL is more customizable and very similar to the special purpose ledger. Figure 8.14 shows you the screen for the master data check.

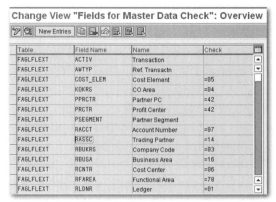

Figure 8.14 Define Fields for the Master Data Check

The fields shown in Figure 8.14 are shown here:

▸ **Table**
This identifies the totals table for the GL master data, which is used as the basis for defining the coding block.

▸ **Field Name** and **Name**
This is used for identifying the field within the totals table against which you would be setting up the master data check.

▸ **Check**
This identifies the user exit against which the master data check will be performed. The exit routine can be accessed by executing the program SAPLGUMD. You can also access this using Transaction SMOD and then entering the enhancement GLX_MD01.

Figure 8.15 details the settings for the master data check for the **PRCTR Profit Center** field. If you cannot find a user exit that has been defined, then you can perform master data checks using value table validations.

Note
The old GL table GLT0 has been replaced by FAGLFEXT

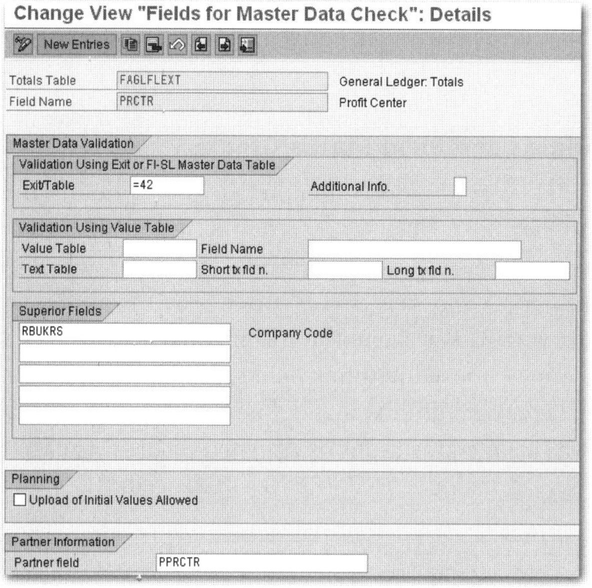

Figure 8.15 Defining the Settings for the Master Data Check

Include Customer Fields in Enjoy Transactions

SAP Enjoy transactions were introduced from the 4.6C release onward to allow users to perform the transaction entry in smoother fashion. In this setting, the customer fields (defined in the previous steps in this subsection) are assigned to the variants of the SAP ERP Enjoy transactions so that you can enter these in the Enjoy transactions. The menu path is **Financial Accounting • Financial Accounting Global Settings (New) • Ledgers • Fields • Customer Fields • Include Customer fields in Enjoy transactions**. Figure 8.16 shows the screen where you can assign the customer fields to the entry variants. You need to click on **New Entries** and then enter the column number in **Cm** and the actual field in the **Field Name**.

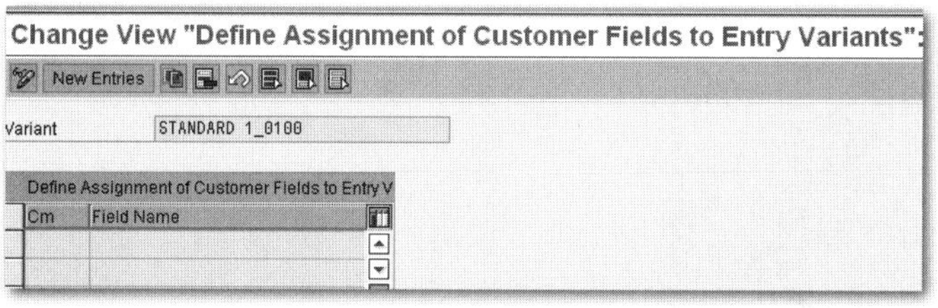

Figure 8.16 Define Assignments of Customer Fields to Entry Variants

Now that you understand how you can add your fields and display them in transactions and define validations for master data fields, we will move on to the field status variants and field status groups, which control the settings for the GL master record.

8.2.4 Field Status Variants and Field Status Groups

Field status variants and field status groups together help you define the checks that need to be made for the GL master record in terms of a required, optional, displayed, or suppressed entry for a particular field. The relationship of field status variants (FSV) and field status group (FSG) is as shown in Figure 8.17. Field status variant is assigned to a company code (refer to Figure 8.4). Field status group is housed within a field status variant. Within the field status group, you have various tabs that define the various facets of accounting transactions. The field status group is assigned to the GL master data. So schematically, the relationship is **FSV → FSG → GL account**.

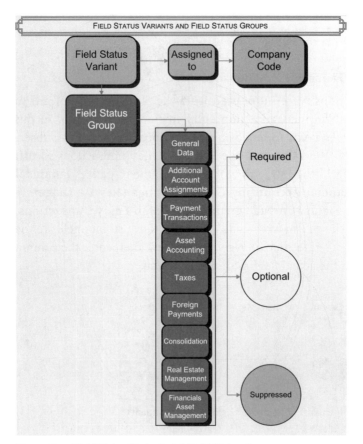

Figure 8.17 Field Status Variant and Field Status Group

You can follow **Financial Accounting • Financial Accounting Global Settings (New) • Ledgers • Fields • Define Field Status Variants**, or use Transaction OBC4. In this setting, you define the field status variants and further define the field status groups that identify which field is optional, required, or suppressed. Figure 8.18 shows you the **Field status variant 001** along with the **Field status groups G001** to **G011**.

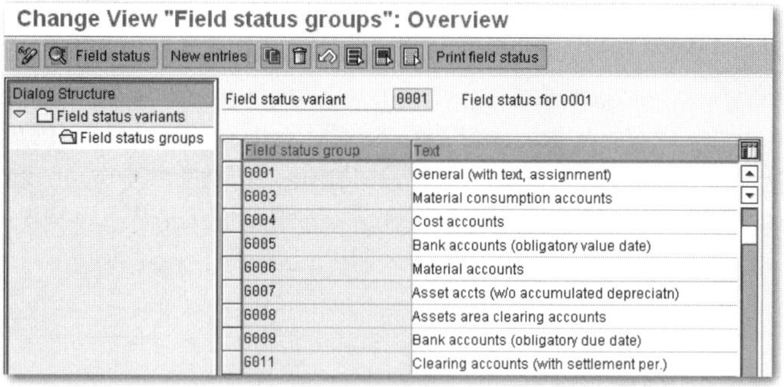

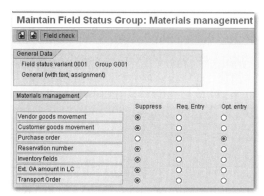

Figure 8.18 Field Status Variant Definition

Figure 8.19 shows you the screen where you can define the field status group **G001** in detail for the **Materials Management** tab. You have identified that except for Purchase order, which is an optional entry, all the other fields are suppressed. So when you enter this field status group (**G001**) in a GL master, you will see the purchase order as an optional entry field, but the reservation number will not even show up.

Figure 8.19 Field Status Group Definition

To assign the field status variant to the company code follow **Financial Accounting • Financial Accounting Global Settings (New) • Ledgers • Fields • Assign Field Status Variant to Company Code**. You can also use Transaction OBC5. Figure 8.20 shows the assignment of field status variant (**Fld stat.var.**) as **0001** to company code (**Co...**) **US00**. You can also do this directly using Transaction OBY6.

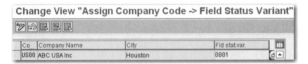

Figure 8.20 Assign Field Status Variant to Company Code

Tip

To maintain or change the field status variant for a lot of company codes in one go, use Transaction OBC5.

8.2.5 Configuring Ledgers

Ledgers, in accounting terms, are sets of books that contain all the relevant accounting transactions in the system. Prior to the new GL, there was only one GL, which came predefined in SAP ERP. However, with the introduction of the new GL, you can define multiple ledgers in the GL umbrella that allow you to meet multiple legal and management reporting requirements. You will be introduced to the new GL in detail in Chapter 9. In this subsection, you will learn how to configure new ledgers and the basic concepts behind defining new ledgers.

The configuration of ledgers comprises the steps shown in Figure 8.21. First you define the ledgers and then identify the leading ledger. After identifying the leading ledger, you need to define the currencies for the ledger. Every ledger that you create will automatically get assigned to a ledger group. If you have multiple ledgers, then you need to identify a representative ledger, which is confusing enough. So let's start by defining each step.

Defining Ledgers

In this step, you will be defining the attributes of a ledger such as the identifier, and the totals table, and you will indicate whether the ledger is a leading ledger or not. The leading ledger is integrated with all the other ledgers defined and is updated in all the company codes. To define ledgers for GL accounting follow this menu path: **Financial Accounting • Financial Accounting Global Settings (New) • Ledgers • Ledger • Define Ledgers for General Ledger Accounting**.

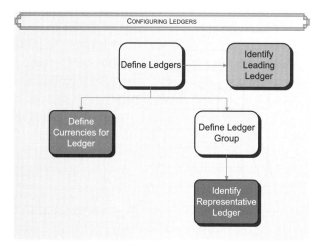

Figure 8.21 Configuring ledgers

Figure 8.22 shows you the steps for defining a ledger. In this step, you can define a ledger (**Ld**) as **LL,** give the name to the ledger (**Ledger Name**) as **Leading Ledger**, and identify the **Totals Table** (**FAGLFLEXT**) as well as indicate that the ledger is the leading ledger (**Leading**).

SAP recommends that you use the totals table FAGLFLEXT for defining your ledgers. As shown in Figure 8.22, you choose to define two ledgers **NL** (**New Ledger**) and **LL** (**Leading Ledger**). Now you can use the LL for your legal reporting, and you can use the NL to fulfill a country-specific reporting need or for management reporting.

Change View "Define Ledgers in General Ledger Accounting"

New Entries

Define Ledgers in General Ledger Accounting

Ld	Ledger Name	Totals Table	Leading	
LL	Leading Ledger	FAGLFLEXT	☑	
NL	New Ledger	FAGLFLEXT	☐	

Figure 8.22 Define Ledgers in GL Accounting

The menu path is **Financial Accounting • Financial Accounting Global Settings (New) • Ledgers • Ledger • Define and Activate Non-Leading Ledgers**. You can choose to update the nonleading ledger in specific company codes only. While defining your nonleading ledger, you have the option of defining your own currencies, fiscal year variant, and posting period variant.

Note

Only one ledger can be designated as the leading ledger.

Define Currencies of the Leading Ledger

As you learned earlier, you can define one currency for each company code using Transaction OBY6. In this step, you can define additional currencies of the leading ledger by company code. These currencies can then be used in parallel with the main currencies for the company code. This setting, if correctly made, can save you the implementation of one complete ledger as it allows you a maximum of three currencies by which you can valuate all the transactions in a company code. Make these settings after careful deliberation because you cannot change the currency types after a company code is productive. Figure 8.23 shows you the screen for maintaining the three currencies for company code MX01. The menu path for defining currencies of the leading ledger is **Financial Accounting • Financial Accounting Global Settings (New) • Ledgers • Ledger • Define Currencies of Leading ledger**. The Transaction is OB22.

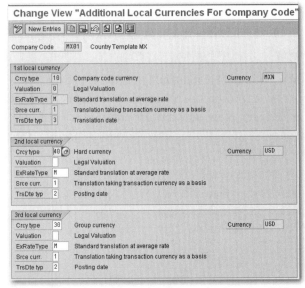

Figure 8.23 Define Additional Currencies for Company Code

▶ **Crcy type**
There are five types of currencies: company code currency, group currency, hard currency, index-based currency, and global company currency.

▶ **Valuation**
You can define the valuation as a legal valuation, group valuation, or profit center valuation.

▶ **ExRate Type**

You can also maintain the exchange rate type, which determines the exchange rate stored in the system. You need to enter the exchange rate per the exchange rate type using Transaction S_BCE_68000174.

▶ **Srce Curr**

This identifies the base currency for the translation.

▶ **TrsDte typ**

This identifies the date that should be used for translation (posting date, document date, or translation date).

Note that this was also available in the classic GL configuration but was mostly a hidden functionality that was rarely implemented. Now that you understand how to define the currencies for the leading ledger, you can define a ledger group.

Define Ledger Group

The ledger group is used to group together similar ledgers. It allows you to define different buckets in which the transactions should post. Defining the ledger group allows you to post GL transactions to the ledger group as a whole. This leads to simplification of the GL postings because now you just specify the ledger group and the posting happens to all the ledgers that are part of the ledger group. Follow this menu path: **Financial Accounting • Financial Accounting Global Settings (New) • Ledgers • Ledger • Define Ledger Group**.

> **Note**
>
> If you do not specify a ledger group, then the system posts to all the ledgers.

Then, you first define the ledger group, and then identify the representative ledger within the ledger group. The representative ledger determines and checks the posting period of the financial documents, which is discussed in detail in Section 8.2.6. Prior to the new GL, there was only one ledger, so you needed to specify the posting period as open or closed only once. Now that you have defined multiple ledgers, the representative ledger identifies whether the posting period is open or closed for a particular ledger group.

> **Tip**
>
> Only one ledger can be designated as the representative ledger.

After checking whether the posting period is open for the representative ledger, the system posts to all the other ledgers per their fiscal year variant.

> **Note**
>
> If the representative ledger's period is open, the system still makes the posting to all the other ledgers even if their posting period is closed.

Figure 8.24 shows the ledger group **LL,** which is also the leading ledger defined earlier.

Figure 8.24 Define Ledger Group

Figure 8.25 shows the assignment of ledgers to the ledger group. So, in our example, you have identified LL and NL ledgers as part of the ledger group LL. However, you need to select one of the ledgers as a representative ledger. **LL** is chosen as the representative ledger.

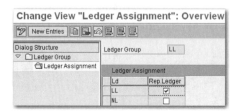

Figure 8.25 Define Representative Ledger of a Ledger Group

So even if **NL** ledger's posting period is closed, the system still allows you to post to NL if the posting period of the **LL** ledger is open. So in our example, **LL** is both the leading ledger and the representative ledger. This saves you time and effort to maintain the opening and closing of posting periods, which is discussed in the next subsection.

8.2.6   Fiscal Year Variant and Posting Period Variant

Opening and closing of posting periods is dependent on the definition of the fiscal year variant and the posting period variant. You can define a unique fiscal year variant (FYV) and assign the same to a company code. Similarly, the posting period variant (PPV) can be assigned to a company code. Together these define how you can open and close the posting period. Figure 8.26 outlines the relationship of the fiscal year variant and the posting period variant and how together these can be used to control the opening and closing of posting periods. These relationships will become clearer as you learn more about each individual setting.

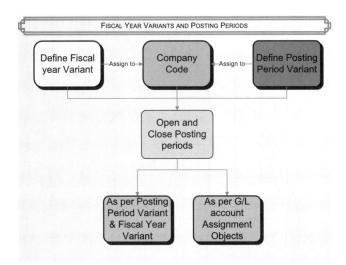

Figure 8.26 Defining Parameters for Opening and Closing Posting Periods and Link

You will learn first about the fiscal year variant.

Define the Fiscal Year Variant

The fiscal year variant identifies the fiscal year for your organization. For example, your fiscal year might be from April to March. So April 2008 would be represented as Period 1 of Fiscal Year 2008. You need to represent this in the system. The fiscal year variant allows you to map this in the system. The menu path to follow is **Financial Accounting • Financial Accounting Global Settings (New) • Ledgers • Fiscal Year and Posting Periods • Maintain Fiscal Year variant**, and the Transaction is OB29.

SAP ERP comes preconfigured with some of the common variations of the fiscal year variants. You should copy an existing variant to define a custom one if the standard ones do not meet your requirements. Most of the variants have the number of posting periods as 12 and special periods as 4. Figure

8.27 shows the screen where you can maintain the fiscal year variants. The right pane shows the **Fiscal year variants**, and the left pane shows the actions that detail the fiscal year variant further.

		Year-depend	Calendar yr	Number of posting	No.of special peri

Change View "Fiscal year variants": Overview

New Entries

Dialog Structure
▽ ⌂ Fiscal year variants
　　▢ Periods
　　▢ Period texts
　　▢ Shortened Fiscal Yea

Fiscal year variants

FV	Description	Year-depend	Calendar yr	Number of posting	No.of special peri
24	Half periods	☐	☐	24	
C1	1st period (calendar year	☐	☐	1	
K0	Calendar year, 0 spec. pe	☐	☑	12	
K1	Cal. Year, 1 Special Peric	☐	☑	12	1
K2	Cal. Year, 2 Special Peric	☐	☑	12	2
K3	Cal. Year, 3 Special Peric	☐	☑	12	3
K4	Calendar year, 4 spec. pe	☐	☑	12	4
R1	Shortened fisc.year Jan-S	☑	☐	12	4
V3	Apr.- March, 4 special per	☐	☐	12	4
V6	July - June, 4 special peri	☐	☐	12	4
V9	Oct- Sept, 4 special peri	☐	☐	12	4
WK	Calendar weeks	☑	☐	53	

Figure 8.27 Maintain Fiscal Year Variant

If a fiscal year follows the calendar year, then the **Calendar yr** flag should be checked. **Year-dependent** is checked if the fiscal year changes within a year. For instance, for calendar year 2006, the fiscal year for your organization was from January to December. But on September 30th, your organization decided to change it to October to September. In that case, 2006 Fiscal Year got shortened to nine months and you have 2007 Fiscal Year starting from October 1st. This situation leads to the shortened fiscal year as well, which is also discussed in this section.

First let's map your fiscal year in the system. To understand the settings for a fiscal year variant, let's take the example of **V3: Apr.-Match, 4 special per,** which has a shift in the calendar months and the fiscal year months. Figure 8.28 shows the fiscal year variant **V3: Apr.-Match, 4 special per** after you select **V3** and then click on **Periods** in the left pane. The columns in Figure 8.28 in the right hand pane are described here:

▸ **Month**
Calendar month 1 = January, 12 = December.

▸ **Day**
Maximum number of days in the calendar month.

▸ **Period**
This identifies the fiscal year period of the fiscal year.

▸ **Year shift**
This identifies how the fiscal year is different from the calendar year. −1

indicates that the fiscal year is one less than the calendar year, 0 means that the fiscal year is equal to the calendar year, +1 means that the fiscal year is one greater than the calendar year.

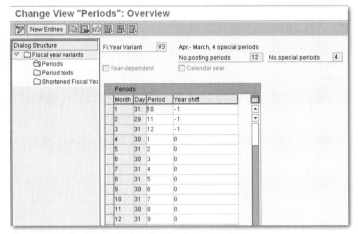

Figure 8.28 Define Periods of a Fiscal Year Variant

So Month **1,** which has been equal to January, is the period 10 of a fiscal year that is **one less** than the current Year. So in this example, January 2008 would be Fiscal Year 2007 Period 10. Likewise, February 2008 is fiscal year 2007 Period 11, March 2008 is Year 2007 Period 12, and April 2007 is Fiscal Year 2007 (**Year shift** "0" Period 1). Next, you can define the text of each period as shown in Figure 8.29. So Period **1** is **April**, Period **2** is **May,** and so on.

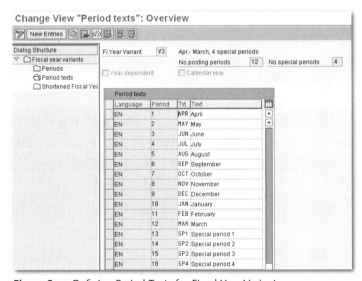

Figure 8.29 Defining Period Texts for Fiscal Year Variant

Let's now learn more about the shortened fiscal year.

> **Note**
>
> For a shortened fiscal year variant to be defined, mark the fiscal year variant as year dependent.

In the settings shown in Figure 8.30, the number of posting periods is defined by the fiscal year. **R1** is a preconfigured shortened fiscal year variant that has nine posting periods for the **Fiscal Year 1994**, as shown in Figure 8.30.

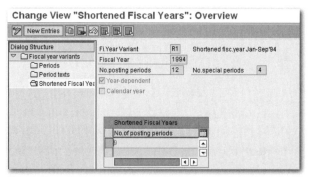

Figure 8.30 Defining Shortened Fiscal Year Variant

Assign a Company Code to a Fiscal Year Variant

Now that you have defined the fiscal year variant, you can assign a company code to the fiscal year variant. In this step, you assign the company code to a fiscal year variant defined in the previous step. This can also be done in the company code global settings (OBY6). Follow the menu path **Financial Accounting • Financial Accounting Global Settings (New) • Ledgers • Fiscal Year and Posting Periods • Assign Company Code to a Fiscal Year variant**, or use Transaction OB37.

Figure 8.31 shows the assignments of the company code (**Co...**) **US01** to the **Fiscal Year Variant K4**, which ties to the calendar year. The fiscal year starts in January and ends in December. Note that each of these variants also has four special periods that can be used to post retrospective accounting entries after the close has been completed.

Change View "Assign Comp.Code -> Fiscal Year Variant": Overvi

Co	Company Name	Fiscal Year Variant	Description
RECO	Sondereigentum (WEG)	K4	Calendar year, 4 spec. periods
REOB	Referenz Objektmandate	K4	Calendar year, 4 spec. periods
RERF	WEG Referenzbuchungskreis	K4	Calendar year, 4 spec. periods
RU01	Country Template RU	K4	Calendar year, 4 spec. periods
SE01	Country Template SE	K4	Calendar year, 4 spec. periods
SG01	SAP Asia	K4	Calendar year, 4 spec. periods
SK01	Country Template SK	K4	Calendar year, 4 spec. periods
TH01	Country Template TH	K4	Calendar year, 4 spec. periods
TR01	Country Template TR	K4	Calendar year, 4 spec. periods
TW01	Country Template TW	K4	Calendar year, 4 spec. periods
UA01	Country Template UA	K4	Calendar year, 4 spec. periods
US01	Country Template US	K4	Calendar year, 4 spec. periods
VE01	Country Template VE	K4	Calendar year, 4 spec. periods

Figure 8.31 Assigning Company Code to a Fiscal Year Variant

Define Variants for Open Posting Periods

This defines how you want to control the closing and opening of new posting periods. This allows you to define an identifier by which you can distinguish for which company codes you want the posting periods to be open or closed. The menu path is **Financial Accounting • Financial Accounting Global Settings (New) • Ledgers • Fiscal Year and Posting Periods • Posting periods • Define Variants for Open Posting Periods**, and the Transaction is OBBO. Figure 8.32 shows how you have defined the posting period variants (**Variant**) **0001** and **0002**. New posting periods can be defined by clicking on **New Entries** and then entering the **Variant** identifier along with the **Name** of the variant.

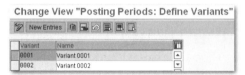

Change View "Posting Periods: Define Variants"

Variant	Name
0001	Variant 0001
0002	Variant 0002

Figure 8.32 Define Variants for Open Posting Periods

Typically, these are done by company code, so a new posting period variant is created for each company code. However, if the closing process is controlled centrally, then you can define one variant that controls the posting for all the company codes.

Assign a Company Code to a Posting Period Variant

In this step, you assign the company code a posting period variant, which was defined in the previous step. This can also be done in the company code global settings (OBY6). The menu path you will need to follow is **Financial Accounting • Financial Accounting Global Settings (New) • Ledgers • Fiscal Year and Posting Periods • Posting periods • Assign Company Code to Posting Period Variant**.

Figure 8.33 shows the screen where you can maintain the posting period variant by company code. So company code (**Co…**) **US01** has been assigned the posting period variant (**Variant**) as **0001**.

Change View "Assign Comp.Code -> Posting Period Variants"

Co	Company Name	City	Variant
TH01	Country Template TH	Bangkok	0001
TR01	Country Template TR	Turkey	0001
TW01	Country Template TW	Taipei	0001
UA01	Country Template UA	Ukraine	0001
US01	Country Template US	Houston	0001

Figure 8.33 Assign Company Code to the Posting Period Variant

Open and Close Posting Periods

In this step, you can open and close posting periods for a particular posting period variant. This allows you to close your accounting books and prevents any further entries to previous periods by mistake. This also controls which periods are open for entry as well. Only the current fiscal period can be posted at one point of time. The menu path is **Financial Accounting • Financial Accounting Global Settings (New) • Ledgers • Fiscal Year and Posting Periods • Posting periods • Open and Close Posting periods**, and the Transaction is OB52. Figure 8.34 shows the screen where you can maintain the posting periods that are open by posting period variants.

Change View "Posting Periods: Specify Time Intervals": Overview

Var.	A	From acct	To account	From per	Year	To period	Year	From per.2	Year	To peri	Year	AuGr
0001	+			1	2000	12	2010	13	2000	16	2010	
0001	A		ZZZZZZZZZZ	1	2000	12	2010	13	2000	16	2010	
0001	D		ZZZZZZZZZZ	1	2000	12	2010	13	2000	16	2010	
0001	K		ZZZZZZZZZZ	1	2000	12	2010	13	2000	16	2010	
0001	M		ZZZZZZZZZZ	1	2000	12	2010	13	2000	16	2010	
0001	S		ZZZZZZZZZZ	1	2000	12	2010	13	2000	16	2010	
0002	+			1	2000	12	2010	13	2000	16	2010	
V001	+			1	2000	12	2010	13	2000	16	2010	

Figure 8.34 Open and Close Posting Periods

The fields in this screen are explained here:

► **Var.**
This identifies the posting period variant. Remember that this can be assigned to a company code.

► **A**
This identifies the account group. **+** represents all the account groups. This field allows you to control the opening and closing to be done separately for GL accounts, vendors, customers, assets, and materials by using their respective account groups **S, K, D, A,** and **M.**

► **From acct** and **To account**
These represent a range of accounts per the identifier (whether it is a range of customers, a range of GL accounts, etc.).

► **From period, Year** and **To period, Year**
This represents the normal periods that are typically 1 to 12 and represent the fiscal periods applicable for the company code per the fiscal year variant.

► **From period, Year** and **To period, Year**
This represents the *special periods* that are typically 13 to 16, one for each quarter close.

► **AuGr**
This identifies the authorization group that can be used to control the access to this transaction code for a particular combination of posting period variant and account group The authorization object is F_BKPF_BUP.

Open and Close Posting Periods by Account Assignment:
New GL Functionality

As you learned earlier, you could control the opening and closing of posting periods in the GL by type of account and range of account groups. However, you can enhance this further in the new GL if you are implementing public sector funds management by defining additional account assignment objects that can be used to control the opening and closing of posting periods. In this step, you define the periods that are open for posting by posting period variant and account assignment object. The account assignment object should be updated in the table FMGLFLEXT, which is the public sector management totals table. The menu path is: **Financial Accounting • Financial Accounting Global Settings (New) • Ledgers • Fiscal Year and Posting Periods • Posting periods • Open and Close Posting periods according to G/L account assignment objects**.

Figure 8.35 shows how you can add fund (RFUND) as one of characteristics that can be used to control how periods are opened and closed. After you select the account assignment object, you can define the periods for which the postings are allowed by clicking on **Permitted Period,** which opens a screen similar to Figure 8.34.

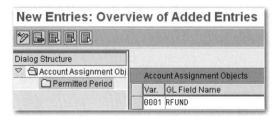

Figure 8.35 Open and Close Posting Periods by Account Assignment Objects

Now that you understand how you can control the opening and closing of posting periods, let's move on to parallel valuation global settings.

Parallel Valuation

Parallel valuation allows you to have multiple ledgers that can then be valuated per different accounting principles and different local country specific requirements. You will learn more about parallel valuation in Chapter 9 when we discuss GL accounting. In this section, you will define the accounting principles and the assignment of these to the ledger group. Figure 8.36 shows the steps to perform in a schematic form.

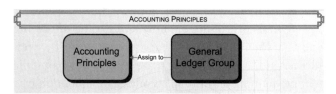

Figure 8.36 Accounting Principles and Assignment to the General Ledger Group

Figure 8.37 shows how you can define accounting principles by clicking on **New Entries** and then adding the accounting principle identifier (**Acc…**) as **GAAP** along with the **Name/Description of Accounting Principle** as **Generally Accepted Accounting Principles**. You will need to follow **Financial Accounting • Financial Accounting Global Settings (New) • Ledgers • Parallel Accounting • Define Accounting Principles**.

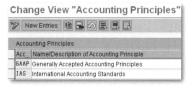

Figure 8.37 Defining Accounting Principles

Figure 8.38 shows how you can assign the accounting principle (**Accounting…**) **GAAP** to the ledger group (**Target Ledger Gr…**) **LL**. The menu path for assigning the accounting principle to the ledger group is **Financial Accounting • Financial Accounting Global Settings (New) • Ledgers • Parallel Accounting • Assign Accounting Principle to Ledger Groups**.

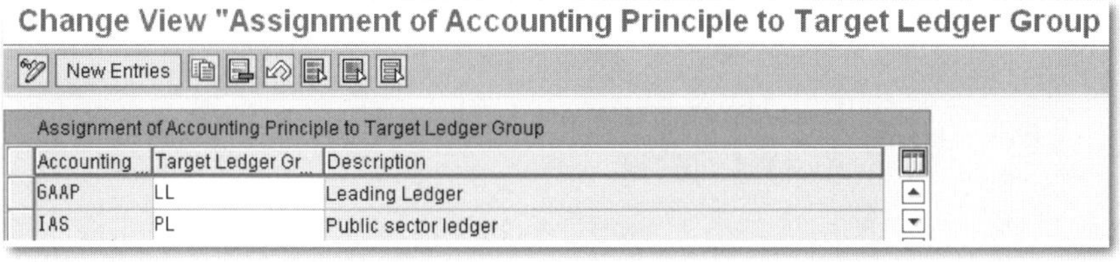

Change View "Assignment of Accounting Principle to Target Ledger Group

Accounting	Target Ledger Gr	Description
GAAP	LL	Leading Ledger
IAS	PL	Public sector ledger

Figure 8.38 Assigning Accounting Principles to the Ledger Group

8.3 Summary

In this chapter, you learned all about the company code global parameters, and about the settings you need to make for your ledgers in the new general ledger. You discovered how to define your ledgers, choose a leading ledger, define a ledger group, and identify a representative ledger. You explored traditional global settings and the differences among posting period variant, fiscal year variant, and field status variant. And you were also introduced to the settings for parallel valuation where you defined accounting principles and then assigned them to a ledger group.

All of these settings gave you a glimpse into the new GL, which you will learn more about in Chapter 9.

The general ledger became exciting with the introduction of the new General Ledger. Suddenly you could do things in the general ledger (GL) that you had only wished for. Now you have a special GL morphed into a new GL that is easier to implement and operate on an ongoing basis. Plus, you get interesting new features that ease the pain of working with the GL.

9 Improving General Ledger Management

In a mobile, ever-changing, and increasingly competitive business environment, general ledger (GL) accounting needs to meet at the convergence and standardization of accounting principles. A key emerging trend is the new era of shareholder activism and federal regulations, which aim at more transparency regarding statutory reporting. With increased disclosure requirements, it is crucial for various aspects of management reporting to be disclosed to investors. This has led to the convergence of financial and managerial accounting. In SAP-speak, Financial Accounting (FI) and Controlling (CO) need to be more tightly integrated.

Before SAP ERP ECC 5.0, FI was segregated from CO, and they were two entirely different consulting skill-sets. But then, SAP ERP introduced the new general ledger, which was a fundamental shift, and changed the way you looked at the GL.

In this chapter, you will learn about the new general ledger (GL) in detail, including its key functionalities that support the balance sheet, profit and loss preparation, parallel accounting, accrual accounting, and segment accounting. Normally the GL was used only for balance sheet and profit and loss statements. Everything else was taboo. A major shift in the mindset is needed in the minds of GL accountants to not only think about the balance sheet but other useful reporting, such as segment reporting, which has become an integral part of the published financial statements worldwide.

You will also learn key configuration tools and techniques, which will give you the tools you need to enhance GL management. The biggest impact of carefully managing and standardizing your GL is at month-end close. By using the new GL, you can significantly reduce your month-end closing process timeline, one of the key value drivers for an SAP ERP Financials implementation.

You will also learn the distinction between the old GL and the new GL. Most SAP ERP implementations were SAP R/3 4.6C and earlier, which did not have the new GL functionality. So it is an important case study of identifying the rationale and business case for upgrading to SAP ERP 2005.

9.1 General Ledger Accounting: Introduction

The new GL can be used not only for legal reporting but also for other modern accounting needs as listed here:

▶ **Segment Reporting**
The introduction of the segment as a dimension helps meet the GAAP and IFRS principles.

▶ **Module Integration Requirements**
GL is also integrated with FI-AA/AP/AR, CO, and NonFI (MM, HR) modules as well.

▶ **Integration of Legal and Management Reporting**
The new GL allows you to do internal management reporting in sync with the legal reporting. You can now generate balance sheets by profit center as well.

▶ **Parallel Reporting**
You can now manage several ledgers with different accounting principles.

▶ **Cost of Sales Accounting**
The new GL allows you to do cost of sales reporting without writing any substitution rules by populating the functional area directly in the GL master data.

The process for GL accounting is shown in Figure 9.1 and is described as follows:

▶ **Master Data**
GL master account, line item display, and balances.

▶ **Business Transactions**

This covers the posting of a GL entry, document splitting (the new GL functionality), cross-company code transactions, accruals, awards, parallel valuation, and so on.

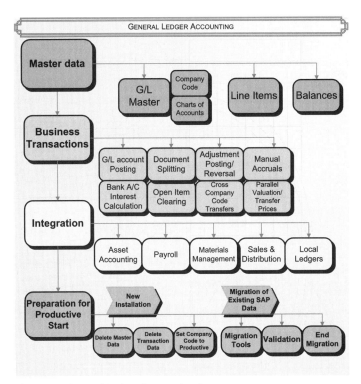

Figure 9.1 General Ledger Accounting Process

▶ **Periodic Processing**

This section details the period-end activities that typically happen at month end. The processes covered here are planning, statistical key figures, financial statements, check, valuate, roll up reclassification, allocate, and carryforward.

▶ **Integration**

This section covers how GL is integrated with other financial and nonfinancial modules.

▶ **Preparation for Productive Start**

This details the process of converting to the new GL either directly from a new GL installation or from pre-new GL scenarios when the classic GL was implemented.

Let's begin the discussion of the GL by looking at the master data that will guide your overall understanding of GL accounting.

9.2 General Ledger Accounting: Master Data

The GL master data is the lynchpin of GL accounting. Overall, the structure of the GL master data is derived from your financial statements (balance sheet and P&L statements). Then you need to divide that broad statement level understanding into individual subledgers. After you have identified your subledgers, you need to categorize how you want to present your financial reporting.

> **Best Practice**
>
> Never map your legacy GL master to the SAP ERP GL master one to one. Typically, in legacy systems, a lot of financial and nonfinancial reporting requirements are embedded in the GL master data numbering schema. However, when you switch to SAP ERP, you have reconciled subledgers that have their own reporting schemas and structures. So it is best to start from the preconfigured SAP ERP chart of accounts that already has this unique SAP ERP understanding built in. For example, for the United States, you should start from the chart of accounts CANA, which comes preconfigured with a list of relevant GL accounts.

Now that you understand the broad rationale for creating the GL master, let's consider the technical details of the GL. The GL master record can be created at two levels:

- ▶ Chart of accounts
- ▶ Company code

You can, however, create the master record centrally (Transaction FS00) for both the chart of accounts and for a particular company code using the same transaction code. You can also perform these two activities separately (FSP0 and FSS0). You can see how to get to the screen where these activities are performed in Figure 9.2.

> **Note**
>
> From SAP ERP 5.0 onward, the GL also treats the profit center as part of the GL.

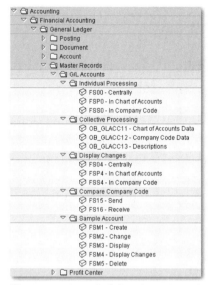

Figure 9.2 Menu Path for Maintaining GL Master Records

You can use the menu path **SAP Menu • Accounting • Financial Accounting • General Ledger • Master Records • G/L accounts • Individual Processing • Centrally/In chart of accounts/In company code** or Transactions FS00/FSP0/FSS0.

9.2.1 General Ledger Account: By Chart of Accounts

Let's first take a look at the data that you can enter at a chart of accounts level. Chart of accounts data is common for all the company codes. Figure 9.3 shows the screen where you can enter the chart of accounts data. The data you enter at the chart of accounts level is as follows:

► **Account Group**
Account group helps determine the screen layout of fields and drives most of the GL account master data configuration. This determines how the data will be displayed during the GL account master data creation time.

Note
Be sure you understand the distinction between *account group* and *field status group*, before going further.

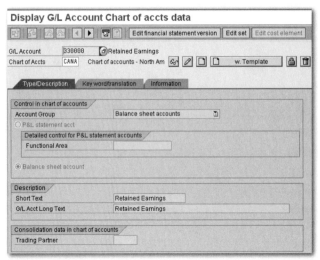

Figure 9.3 GL Account by Chart of Accounts

▸ **Functional Area**
From SAP ECC 5.0 onward, you can directly enter the functional area in the GL account master for profit and loss (P&L) accounts.

▸ **Type of account**
You can specify whether the account is a balance sheet account or a P&L account.

▸ **Short Text**
This is used to enter the short text for the GL account.

▸ **G/L Acct long text**
This is used to denote the long text of the GL account.

▸ **Trading Partner**
This is entered if applicable for consolidation-related activities.

Figure 9.4 shows the **Key word/translation** tab that can be used to maintain the text in multiple languages if applicable. This is extremely useful if you have one global chart of accounts across multiple countries. This allows you to clearly distinguish the GL accounts by country. The irony is that this tab is the least used tab as organizations slowly deviate from the common chart of accounts and start defining their own GL account numbers, which are their interpretations of the same GL account number across the continents.

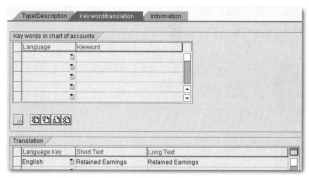

Figure 9.4 Key Word/Translation Tab

The other tab at the chart of accounts level is the **Information** tab, which captures when a GL account was created and by whom. It also houses all the changes for the GL account master and the GL text. This is shown in Figure 9.5. If you click on **Change documents**, you get a history of all the changes that happened in the GL account.

Figure 9.5 Information Tab in Chart of Accounts

9.2.2 General Ledger Account: By Company Code

Now that you understand the settings at the chart of accounts level, you are ready to explore the settings specific for a company code. Company code-specific settings help you use the same GL account number across company codes with different parameters. There are three tabs at the company code level, which are examined next.

Control Data Tab

Figure 9.6 shows the **Control Data** tab that has the fields described next:

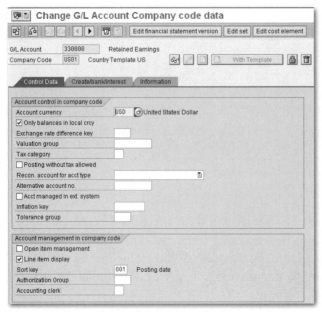

Figure 9.6 General Ledger Account Data by Company Code

▶ **Account currency**

This is typically the company code currency, but setting this to the company code currency still allows you to post to the account in different currencies.

> **Notes**
>
> ▶ If the Account currency is any other currency than the company code currency, the postings to the accounts are restricted to that currency.
>
> ▶ To change this setting and some others, make the balance in the GL account zero before making the change. It is important to deliberate carefully before making the currency of the GL account different from that of company code.

▶ **Only balances in local crcy**

This indicator means that the balances are managed only in the local currency. This indicator is typically set for GL accounts that are managed on an open-item basis, for example, GR/IR accounts.

▶ **Exchange rate difference key**

This is entered typically for accounts that are managed in foreign currency and helps in account determination of the gains and losses when converting to the local currency.

▶ **Valuation group**
This is freely definable and includes a group of GL accounts. With this, you can map the exchange rate gains and losses differently.

▶ **Tax category**
This indicator identifies the tax categories that can be posted using this account. The various options are the following:

- ▶ **–**: Only input taxes (sales and use tax paid by the company—vendor side)
- ▶ **+**: Only output TAXES (sales tax charged by company—customer side)
- ▶ *****: Both input and output taxes
- ▶ **<**: Input taxes on a tax account
- ▶ **>**: Output taxes on a tax account
- ▶ **–B**: Input tax – downpayments managed gross
- ▶ **+B**: Output tax – downpayments managed gross
- ▶ **E0**: AP sales tax, exempt
- ▶ **E1**: AP sales tax, taxable, posted to cost account
- ▶ **I0**: AP sales tax, exempt
- ▶ **I1**: AP sales tax, taxable, distributed to line items
- ▶ **O0**: AR sales tax, exempt
- ▶ **O1**: AR sales tax, taxable
- ▶ **S1**: AR sales tax, taxable
- ▶ **U0**: AP use tax, exempt
- ▶ **U1**: AP use tax, taxable, self assessed

▶ **Posting without tax allowed**
This allows you to post both taxable and nontaxable postings to the GL account. If you entered something in the tax category, then you cannot post nontaxable items unless you mark **Posting without tax allowed**.

▶ **Recon. account for acct type**
This identifies the account type for reconciliation. When you select an option, the GL account is recognized as a reconciliation account. A reconciliation account is typically not posted directly in the GL but via a subledger. The various subledger options include the following:

- ▶ Asset
- ▶ Customers

▸ Vendors

▸ Contract accounts receivable

Note

Contract accounts receivable is a new subledger introduced as part of Financial Supply Chain Management (FSCM).

▸ **Alternative account no.**
This is the GL account in the country chart of accounts that corresponds to this GL account.

▸ **Acct managed in ext. system**
Indicates whether the account is being maintained in an external system via ALE.

▸ **Inflation key**
This specifies the inflation key's ID and is used only when the particular GL account is managed for inflation. The actual adjustment is done in the appropriate subledger

▸ **Tolerance group**
These groups are used to define how you treat the differences resulting from the open-items clearing.

▸ **Open item management**
This box is selected if you want to manage the account with open-item management. Typical candidates for this setting are GR/IR clearing, bank clearing, payroll clearing, cash discounts clearing, and other clearing accounts. This allows you to see open items, cleared items, and balances in the account.

Best Practice

Bank accounts, raw material accounts, reconciliation accounts, P&L accounts, and tax accounts should not be open-item managed.

▸ **Line item display**
If checked, this allows you to see the line items posted to the GL account. In the new GL, this indicator does not make sense because all the items have the ability for line-item display. For the new GL, this posting is required if you want open-item management of the account because this entry was earlier a prerequisite to open-item management. Generally speaking, prior to the new GL, this was not set for accounts that have a huge amount of entries such as receivables, payables, tax accounts, and so on

- **Sort key**

  This determines what gets populated in the allocation field of the GL line item. The allocation field automatically gets determined by the system based on the sort key, or the user can manually enter it during posting. This is especially useful if you want to open-item manage an account, for example, the purchase order and line-item number is typically used as a sort key for the GR/IR account so that the account can be automatically cleared.

- **Authorization Group**

  This allows you to limit the personnel who can make changes to the GL account.

- **Accounting clerk**

  This can be used to assign the responsibility of the reconciliation of the account.

Now that you understand the **Control** tab, let's take a look at the **Create bank/interest** tab and what that allows you to manage from a GL accounting perspective.

Create/Bank/Interest Tab

Figure 9.7 shows the **Create/bank/interest** tab and is described here:

- **Field status group**

  This identifies which of the fields are required when you enter data for the GL account during posting. This controls the account assignments that are made to the account during posting. We discussed this in Chapter 8 when you learned about the distinction between a field status variant and a field status group.

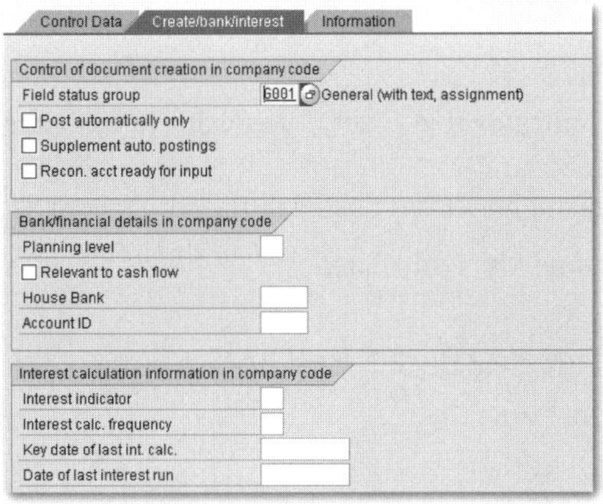

Figure 9.7 General Ledger: Company Code: Create/Bank/Interest Tab

▶ **Post automatically only**
If checked, this does not allow a direct GL posting. The posting can happen via the subledger and also per the automatic account determination settings.

▶ **Supplement auto. postings**
This allows you to manually update the account assignments that are generated automatically by the system.

▶ **Recon. acct ready for input**
This allows you to specify that the reconciliation account can be posted manually and is typically used to post acquisition values in asset accounting.

▶ **Planning level**
This is used to specify the cash management position and indicates how the system will update the cash position of the company.

▶ **Relevant to cash flow**
This indicator, if checked, indicates that the cash flow is affected and is then included in various cash management reports.

▶ **House Bank**
Here you can specify the house bank applicable for the GL account. This identifies a particular bank.

▶ **Account ID**
Account ID is used to further classify the relationship with the bank to the exact bank account number that you have with the house bank.

▶ **Interest indicator**
This is the interest calculation indicator that is set if you want to calculate interest on balances in this GL account.

▶ **Interest calc. frequency**
This identifies how frequently interest is calculated.

▶ **Key date of last int. calc.**
The system updates this field with the date on which the interest was last calculated.

▶ **Date of last interest run**
This identifies the date of the last interest run.

Information Tab

The **Information** tab captures the change information and GL account text at the company code level as shown in Figure 9.8. If you click on **Change documents**, you get a history of all the changes that happened in the GL account. This tab is your audit check for all the changes that happened in the GL account at the company code level.

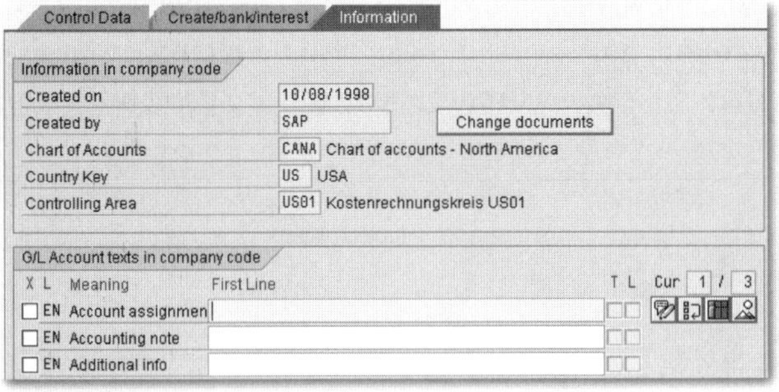

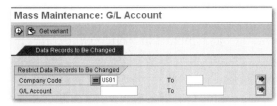

Figure 9.8 Information Tab for GL Master Data

One of the most important tasks in GL accounting is maintenance of the master data. In the next subsection, you will learn to quickly maintain master data in GL accounts.

9.2.3 Collective Processing of GL Accounts

Now you will learn how to change en-masse fields for a particular series of GL accounts. This is especially important if you have to change a particular parameter in a GL account across all the company codes. Also, you can use collective processing to manage the same change across a range of GL accounts. Use the menu path **SAP Menu • Accounting • Financial Accounting • General Ledger • Master Records • G/L accounts • Collective Processing • Chart of Accounts Data/ Company Code Data/ Descriptions**. The transaction codes are OB_GLACC11/OB_GLACC12/OB_GLACC13. Figure 9.9 shows the initial selection screen for changing the company code data en masse. You need to enter the **Company Code** US01 and the range of **G/L Account**.

Figure 9.9 Mass Maintenance GL Accounts By Company Code OB_GLACC12

After you execute this Transaction by pressing **F8** or clicking on the clock icon shown in Figure 9.9, you arrive at the screen where you can perform GL maintenance, shown in Figure 9.10. The top pane shows the new values that can be maintained for the range of GL accounts, and the bottom pane shows the old values of the GL accounts (e.g., company code (**Co...**in Figure 9.10): **US01, G/L Account: 111000, Short Text: Cash Desk,** and the parameters (**Fiel..** (Field Status Group): **G001**), which are part of the selected GL accounts. After you choose a new value in the top pane and save, all the GL accounts can be changed in one go. The values can also be filtered from this selection using the icon that looks like a funnel above the top pane (fifth icon from left) of Figure 9.10.

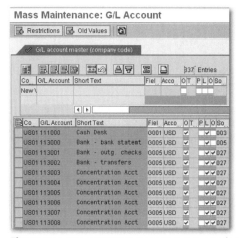

Figure 9.10 Mass Maintenance: Company Code Parameters

9.2.4 Compare Company Code

This functionality allows you to copy data from one company code to another. This allows you to transfer data across company codes and is one of the most important tools for synchronizing data across company codes. You need to first send the data from the origin company code and then receive the same in the receiver company code. Follow the menu path **Accounting • Financial Accounting • General Ledger • Master Records • G/L accounts • Compare Company Code • Send/Receive**, or use Transactions FS15/FS16.

So first you will learn how to send the batch input data. Sending the company code creates a batch input session that can then be executed to create the GL accounts in the receiver company code. Figure 9.11 shows the screen that is used for sending the GL master data. Here you need to enter the source company code for the GL master data. You can also choose to transfer blocking indicators and deletion flags if you so choose.

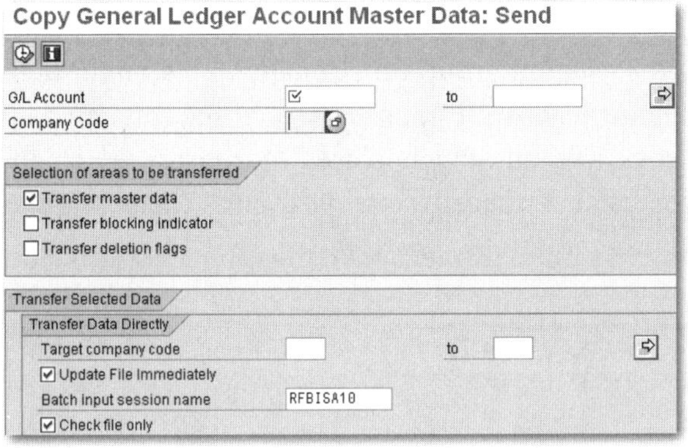

Copy General Ledger Account Master Data: Send

G/L Account	☑ to 🖼
Company Code	🖉

Selection of areas to be transferred
- ☑ Transfer master data
- ☐ Transfer blocking indicator
- ☐ Transfer deletion flags

Transfer Selected Data
Transfer Data Directly
- Target company code ___ to ___ 🖼
- ☑ Update File Immediately
- Batch input session name RFBISA10
- ☑ Check file only

Figure 9.11 Send GL Master Data (Transaction FS15)

Please note that this transaction does not upload the data in the target company code as the process of copying the general ledger accounts is a two step process. The first step is creating the send file, while the second step is to receive the sent file in the receiving company code. So in the previous step you created the send file. Now you need to receive that data in the target company code. Figure 9.12 shows the screen where you can receive the GL master data. You need to enter the **File Name** and the **Target Company Code** that will create another batch input session.

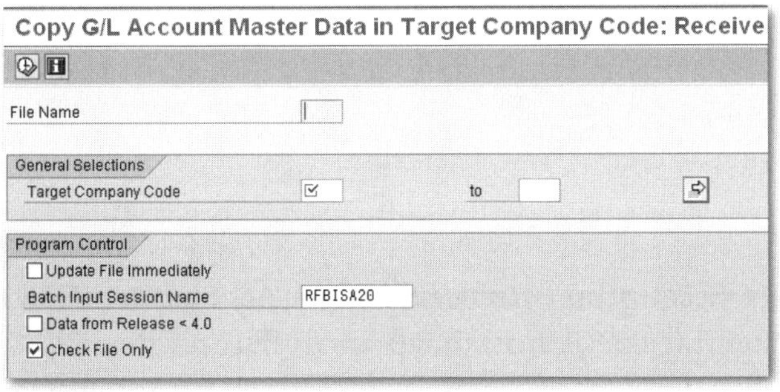

Copy G/L Account Master Data in Target Company Code: Receive

File Name	___

General Selections
- Target Company Code ☑ to ___ 🖼

Program Control
- ☐ Update File Immediately
- Batch Input Session Name RFBISA20
- ☐ Data from Release < 4.0
- ☑ Check File Only

Figure 9.12 Receiving the GL Account Master Data in Receiving Company Code (Transaction FS16)

You just need to run the batch input session created to transfer the GL master data to the target company code.

9.3   Configuration of General Ledger Master Data

You might want to customize the GL per your organization's requirements. This configuration is the responsibility of the GL accountant. For example, if you need to define your business rules for required versus optional fields, then you can do that using the account group functionality. This might help you in defining additional controls within your GL structure. You can also configure the retained earnings account, which is used to transfer the balances from P&L accounts to the balance sheet at fiscal year end. The configuration learning path of the GL master data is shown in Figure 9.13.

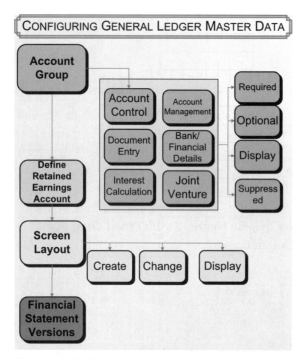

Figure 9.13 Configuring GL Master Data

The menu path is **IMG • Accounting • General Ledger Accounting (New) • Master Data** for configuring the GL master data and is illustrated in Figure 9.14.

9.3.1   Account Group

The first step in configuring the GL master record is to identify the broad segregation of the GL account numbers by account group. The menu path is

IMG • **Financial Accounting** • **General Ledger Accounting (New)** • **Master data** • **G/L accounts** • **Preparations** • **Define Account Group,** and the Transaction is OBD4. Figure 9.15 shows the settings that you can make for defining the account group.

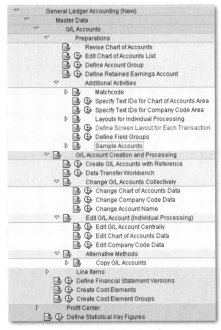

Figure 9.14 Menu Path for Configuring GL Account Master Data

Change View "G/L Account Groups": Overview

Chrt/Accts	Acct Group	Name	From acct	To account
CANA	BS	Balance sheet accounts	100000	399999
CANA	PL	Profit and loss accounts	400000	999999

Figure 9.15 Defining a New Account Group

In the previous example, you have defined two account groups: One each for **Balance sheet accounts** and for **Profit and loss accounts** with their number ranges. After you click on the **Acct Group BS** in Figure 9.15, you will reach the next screen (see Figure 9.16) where you can select the subgroup you want to update.

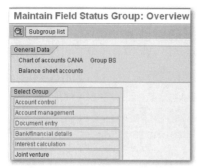

Figure 9.16 Selecting a Subgroup for an Account Group

In the screen shown in Figure 9.16, you need to select a subgroup. Selecting a subgroup (**Account control**) allows you to modify the settings of individual fields within the subgroup (**Account control**) as shown in Figure 9.17.

Maintain Field Status Group: Account control

Account control	Suppress	Req. Entry	Opt. entry	Display
Currency	○	○	◉	○
Tax category	○	○	◉	○
Reconciliation account	○	○	◉	○
Exchange Rate Difference	○	○	◉	○
Account managed in ext. system	○	○	◉	○
Only balances in local crcy	○	○	◉	○
Alternative account number	○	○	◉	○
Inflation key	○	○	◉	○
Tolerance group	○	○	◉	○

General Data
Chart of accounts CANA   Group BS
Balance sheet accounts
Page   1

Figure 9.17 Setting the Fields Within Account Subgroup as Required, Suppressed, Optional, or Display Only

On the screen shown in Figure 9.17, you can define whether a particular field is a required or optional entry and whether the field needs to be suppressed or if you need to just display the field. This allows you to define your control points for your GL master record. In the next section, you will learn about defining the retained earnings account.

9.3.2   Retained Earnings Account

Now you need to define the retained earnings account to which all the profit and loss accounts balances will get carried forward to, after you run the balance carried forward transaction. The menu path is **IMG • Financial**

Accounting • General Ledger Accounting (New) • Master data • G/L accounts • Preparations • Define Retained Earnings account. The transaction code is OB53.

Figure 9.18 shows the screen where you can maintain the retained earnings account. First you need to select the **Chart of Accounts** as **CANA**. The **Transaction BIL** gets defaulted automatically. In the **Account assignment** tab, you need to define the retained earnings **Account** per **P&L statmt** (profit and loss statement type). Generally, organizations define one retained earnings account. But if you want to maintain multiple GL accounts for retained earnings, then you need to define multiple P&L statement types and then maintain the same in these settings

Figure 9.18 Define Retained Earnings Account

> **Note**
>
> This setting is done by chart of accounts and is not by company code. You can configure multiple retained earnings account by defining a new P&L statement account type and then assigning a different GL account to each of them.

If you choose to identify multiple **P&L statmt**, then you also need to identify the same in the GL master record. X is defaulted if you do not maintain these for all the profit and loss accounts. In the next subsection, you will learn more about the screen layout of the GL master data.

9.3.3 Define Screen Layout

In this step, you can define the layout of the screens by activity: create, change, or display. This allows you to differentiate what needs to be a mandatory entry when you are creating a GL master record versus changing a GL master record. The menu path is **IMG • Financial Accounting • General Ledger Accounting (New) • Master data • G/L accounts • Preparations • Additional Activities • Define Screen Layout** for each transaction, and the transaction code is OB26.

Figure 9.19 shows the screen that you see when you execute this transaction. As you can see, there are three options in **Activity category**: **Display, Create, and Change**. These options allow you to modify the field selection by the transaction type of GL master, that is, whether you are displaying the GL master versus creating the GL master or changing the GL master, respectively.

Figure 9.19 Define Screen Layout

Figure 9.20 shows the screen for defining the activity category create and the subgroup level details of the same. Note that these subgroups directly correspond to the GL master tabs you saw in Section 9.2.

Figure 9.21 shows the definition by fields that can be made if you click on the **Account control** tab. You might choose to make the **Currency** field required when you are creating a GL master. This ensures that whenever someone creates a GL master, currency should be entered.

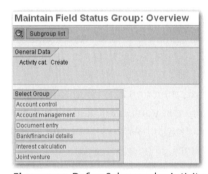

Figure 9.20 Define Subgroup by Activity Category: Create

Account control				
	Suppress	Req. Entry	Opt. entry	Display
Currency	O	O	◉	O
Tax category	O	O	◉	O
Reconciliation account	O	O	◉	O
Exchange Rate Difference	O	O	◉	O
Account managed in ext. system	O	O	◉	O
Only balances in local crcy	O	O	◉	O
Alternative account number	O	O	◉	O
Inflation key	O	O	◉	O
Tolerance group	O	O	◉	O

Figure 9.21 Define the Field Status Group of GL Master Create

9.3.4 Define Financial Statement Version

Now you can define the financial statement versions that are used to prepare and structure the balance sheet or profit and loss statement per your format. This allows you to create one global design of your financial statement. However, you can design multiple financial statements to fulfill local statutory reporting requirements. So if your company is based out of the United States but has operations in India, you can create one global version and one separate version per Indian requirements. This allows the Indian subsidiary to run both the versions and to ensure that they are in sync. The menu path is **IMG • Financial Accounting • General Ledger Accounting (New) • Master data • G/L accounts • Define Financial Statement Version**. You can also use Transaction OB58.

Figure 9.22 shows some of the sample financial statement versions available. It is best to start off by copying a version that pertains to your country and then modify the same to include your organization-specific attributes.

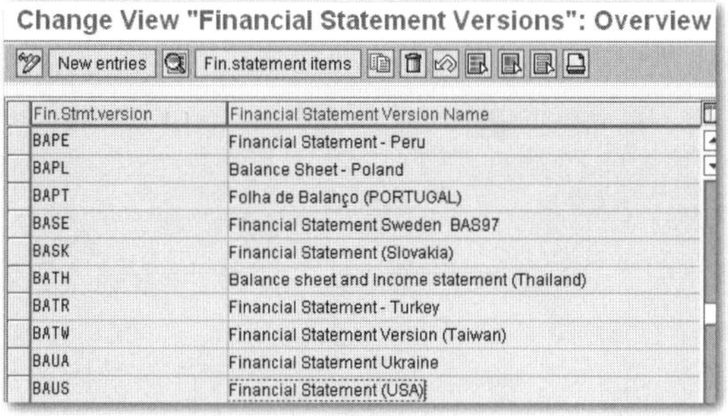

Figure 9.22 Financial Statement Version

As an example, let's take a look at the **BAUS** (the basic U.S. financial statement version). After you double-click on the **BAUS**, you will see the screen shown in Figure 9.23. Here you can define the maintenance language and chart of accounts. You can also choose to allow the group account numbers and functional areas to be entered in the financial statements. If you select the **Item keys auto.** checkbox, the system automatically generates an item key as you create your own version.

On each statement, you can create as many groupings as you want. The lowest level assignment is the GL account. In Figure 9.24, you have displayed the U.S. financial statement **BAUS** in further detail. The broad groupings are **ASSETS**, **LIABILITIES/EQUITY**, and **PROFIT & LOSS STATEMENT**. The subgroupings are also detailed. These are **Cash and Cash Equivalents** and **Petty Cash** under **ASSETS**, for instance. Finally, the GL master record **Cash Desk** is assigned under the **Petty Cash** heading.

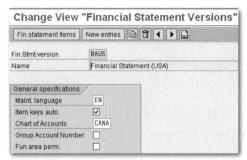

Figure 9.23 Defining the Financial Statement Version

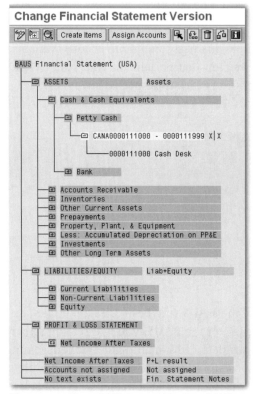

Figure 9.24 Financial Statement Version: BAUS

Click on all the buttons that you see on the top header. These allow you to configure your own financial statements by assigning GL accounts, deleting the assignments, or moving the GL account assignments. Most of these functions are self-explanatory. Experiment with them before you move on to the next topic.

9.4 The New General Ledger

The new general ledger (GL) has completely redefined the accounting function by providing one solution that fits multiple needs. It is the unified approach to GL accounting rather than the scattered approach previously propagated to ensure that the financial accounting (FI) was separated from management reporting (CO). Prior to the new GL, companies managed their accounting in multiple ledgers. The GL was primarily used for legal requirements. To fulfill other reporting requirements, there were ledgers for cost of sales accounting, profit center accounting, special-purpose ledger, industry-specific ledgers, and so on It was difficult to manage all these ledgers because there was extra effort involved in their reconciliation among themselves.

> **Note**
>
> The new GL offers many advantages by acting as a unified platform for all the ledgers and removing the reconciliation effort. So you have one interface to do multiple things. The new GL removes a lot of data redundancy because it is stored in one place only.

You learned about the global settings for the new GL in Chapter 8. It is important to understand some of the key concepts and new features of the new GL as described next.

9.4.1 Planning

As part of the new GL, the planning process has been modified to include the allocation cycles of assessment and distribution as well. Prior to the new GL, the planning process was very narrow. FSE5N and FSE6N were used to enter the plan for a particular ledger and then display the plan data, respectively. With the new GL allocation, functions are now possible for FI transactions as well. Now the good news is that the planning functionality built-in to the new GL uses the same user interface as the previous controlling allocation functions in cost center planning. So you see a smattering of controlling functionality is now part of the new GL. Now the financial planner can perform the planning for GL and Controlling. This is especially important for segment reporting, which requires that you perform allocations in GL to finalize your segment reporting.

9.4.2 Representative Ledger

Every ledger is also automatically created as a ledger group. However, there is exactly one representative ledger in each ledger group. This ledger controls and determines whether you can post to any of the ledgers defined in the new GL. If this ledger has the period as open, then only you can post a transaction in the GL. So this ledger inherits and controls the posting period in the new GL.

9.4.3 Tables in the New General Ledger

With the introduction of the new GL, the previous classic GL tables have changed. So let's take a look at the new tables in the new GL, as listed in Table 9.1.

Classic GL versus New GL Tables	Classic GL Tables	New GL Tables
Totals Table	GLT0	FAGLFLEXT
Line Item Actuals	BSEG	BSEG, BSEG_ADD, and FAGLFLEXA
Line Item Planned		FAGLFLEXP
Valuation of year end closing in parallel ledgers		BSEG_ADD

Table 9.1 New General Ledger Tables

These replace the GLT0 tables that used to store the table entries in the classic GL. You can define your own tables if the characteristics needed in ledgers are drastically different from the standard tables. This is only required in extreme cases when you are trying to use the GL for some nonconventional reporting. Some of these characteristics might be related to a product or some specific material attributes. The only caveat is that nonstandard tables do not augur well for Report Painter and Report Writer drill-down reports. It is best to add new fields in the existing ledgers if required to enable various reporting needs. Plant is one of the most common fields that you will want to add in your ledgers.

9.4.4 New General Ledger User Interface

The structure and user interface, however, still remains the same as the classic GL for all the ledgers defined in the new GL. The number ranges still post documents based on the financial document number range defined in the classic GL. However, if other ledgers have different fiscal years, system posts separate documents for those.

Any document posted in SAP ERP Financials now updates all the ledgers that have been defined in the new GL. Previously, you could make postings specific to one of the ledgers, but this is no longer possible. If you make one posting in the main GL, it updates all the ledgers. This helps in instantaneous reconciliation of all the ledgers involved. You can, however, choose to post only to a local ledger also by selecting only the local ledger while posting.

> **Note**
>
> The frontend of the new GL is similar to the classic GL. The backend is different and more customizable.

You will learn other new functionality available in the new GL, such as document splitting and FI allocations, next.

9.5 Business Transactions: General Ledger

Business transactions in GL correspond to journal entries or journal vouchers (JVs) that can be done only in the GL or in combination with various subledgers. These allow an accountant to post various JVs for intercompany postings, period-end adjustments, recognition of bank reconciliation postings, and so on. In this section, you will learn the routine business transactions possible in the GL. In addition, you will learn about the document splitting functionality in the new GL.

9.5.1 GL Posting

Performing a GL posting still remains the same as the classic GL for all the ledgers defined in the new GL (see Figure 9.25). The entry of the transactions, displaying the documents posted, and other visual interface remains the same. Prior to the new GL, the transaction code for posting JVs in SAP ERP Financials was FB50. However, if you have implemented the new GL, you can also post using the ledger view via Transaction FB50L instead of the usual FB50.

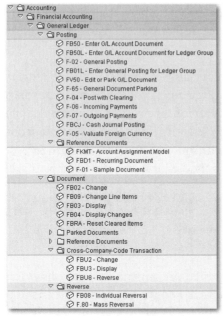

Figure 9.25 General Ledger Posting

The menu path is **SAP Menu • Accounting • Financial Accounting • General Ledger • Posting • Enter G/L account document for Ledger Group**, and the transaction code is FB50L. Figure 9.26 shows how you can make a posting in the leading ledger, which is also described here:

- In the **Basic data** tab, enter the header level data that is common across all the line items.
- Enter the **Document Date** as "08/15/2007".
- The **Company Code** automatically defaults to **US00** based on your user settings, whereas **Posting Date** defaults as "09/17/2007".
- Enter **Reference** text "GL POSTING IN LL" and document header text (**Doc. Header Text**) as "Posting in Leading Ledger".
- In the **Lower Grid**, enter the **G/L acct** "170070/125500/170010", **D/C** (Debit or Credit) "Debit/Credit/Credit", and **Amount in doc. curr.** "200/100/100".

Make sure that debits and credits are equal. Otherwise, you could only hold the document and would not be able to save it. After you save the document with these entries, you will get a document number that will be by company code and fiscal year.

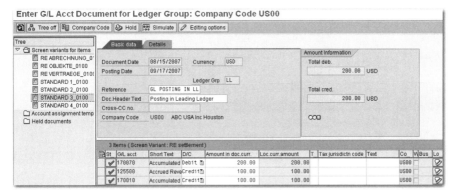

Figure 9.26 Leading Ledger Posting

Displaying a Posted Document

Here you will learn how to display a posted document. You can follow **Accounting • Financial Accounting • General Ledger • Document • Display** or use Transaction FB03. Figure 9.27 shows the default **Data Entry View** that is very similar to the classic GL view. You can use the icons **General Ledger View** and **Entry View** to alternate between the ledger view and the entry view.

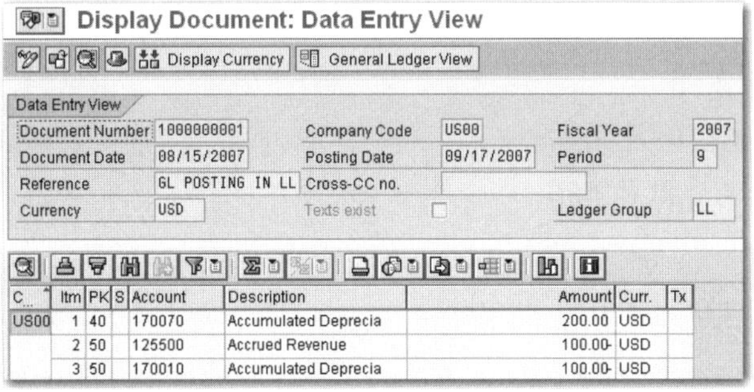

Figure 9.27 Data Entry View of a Posted Document in the New GL

Using the **General Ledger View** button, you can go to the ledger view as well. The **General Ledger View** is shown in Figure 9.28. However, now the icon **Entry View** is visible. You can click this button to go back to entry view.

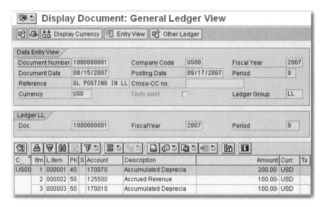

Figure 9.28 GL View of a Posted Document in the New GL

9.5.2 Document Splitting

This is used to split the account assignment items in the balance sheet GL account per the originating account assignments. The beauty of document splitting lies in the fact that you do not have to change the way you enter the data. Based on the rules defined, the system automatically generates a GL view that distributes the account assignment per the rules. So let's say you have the following vendor invoice:

- Cr Vendor: 1000
- Dr Expense GL 1 with CC1 and PC1: 600
- Dr Expense GL 2 with CC2 and PC2: 400

You enter this in the same format in the data entry view. However, the system splits this in the GL view as:

- Cr Vendor: With CC1 and PC1: 600-
- Cr Vendor: With CC2 and PC2: 400-
- Dr Expense GL 1: With CC1 and PC1: 600
- Dr Expense GL 2: With CC2 and PC2: 400

This ensures that you can generate balance sheet views by segments (cost centers or profit centers). Previously, it was very tough to generate this view unless you wrote custom reports that did the document splitting. You also had to define complex validation and substitution rules to accomplish the same level of sophisticated analytical reporting, but now document splitting is configurable per your business rule. You will learn more about configuring document splitting in Section 9.6.2.

9.5.3 Adjustment Posting/Reversal

After a document is posted, you cannot change the dollar amount and posting details. However, you can choose to reverse the posting document for the GL, which allows you to make corrections for wrong postings. Table 9.2 shows the reversal transaction codes.

Reversal Transaction Code	Action
FB08	Individual Reversal
F.80	Mass Reversal
FBU8	Reverse Intercompany Transactions
FBV6	Reject a Parked Document
FBRA	Reset Cleared Items

Table 9.2 Reversal Transaction Code

Figure 9.29 shows how you can perform an individual reversal of a financial document.

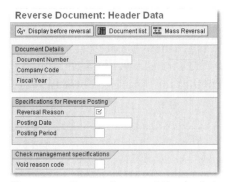

Figure 9.29 Reverse Document Header Data

Let's examine this in more detail now by reviewing these steps:

1. Enter the **Document Number**, **Company Code**, and **Fiscal Year.**

2. Enter the **Reversal Reason**, which can be reversal in current period or reversal in previous period.

3. Enter the **Posting Date**, which defaults to today's date unless the reason code is chosen to be in the previous month.

4. Enter the **Posting Period**, which is derived from the posting date.

5. Enter the **Void reason code** only if you are voiding a check and reversing the associated payment document.

Transaction FBRA is used to reset the cleared items before you can reverse them. As part of FBRA, you can also reverse a document. Figure 9.30 shows the settings needed for resetting cleared items.

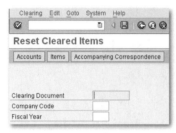

Figure 9.30 Reset Cleared Items

9.5.4 Manual Accruals

Accrual is the process of recognizing expenses in the correct period that they occur accounting wise. The GL module allows you to calculate and post accruals automatically. After you set up the accrual, then the system automatically posts the accrual per the setting made in the accrual engine.

The manual accrual functionality is based on the accrual engine whereby master data is entered in the manual accrual process, while transaction data is calculated and posted in the accrual engine. The accrual engine calculates and posts the accruals. It is the interim stage where the accrual documents are staged in the accrual engine and are then transferred to accounting for posting. Following is the sequence of activities for the accrual process:

▶ Maintain the accrual objects.

▶ Perform the periodic accrual run.

▶ Validate the accrual run.

Accruals can also be posted by the recurring entry functionality, which was the historical version of setting up accruals. The new accrual functionality offers the following advantages in comparison with the recurring entry:

▶ The entry of accruals is a one-time activity.

▶ The new functionality is more flexible in terms of amounts being posted. Recurring entry required that the posting amount was the same across the accrual periods.

▶ Complex calculation rules can be used in the accrual process.

The menu path of accruals and the various transactions associated with setting up and executing accruals is shown in Figure 9.31. You will need to follow the menu path **Accounting • Financial Accounting • General Ledger • Periodic Processing • Manual Accruals.**

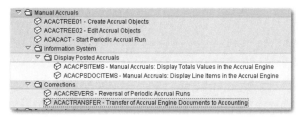

Figure 9.31 Manual Accrual Processes

Let's explore how you can create an accrual object. The accrual object houses all the relevant data required to accrue a business transaction. The menu path is **Accounting • Financial Accounting • General Ledger • Periodic Processing • Manual Accruals • Create Accrual Objects**, and the transaction code is ACACTREE01.

Figure 9.32 shows how an accrual object can be created As you can see, the primary details that need to be maintained for an accrual object are the amount to be accrued, the quantity to be accrued, and the life over which the amount needs to be accrued.

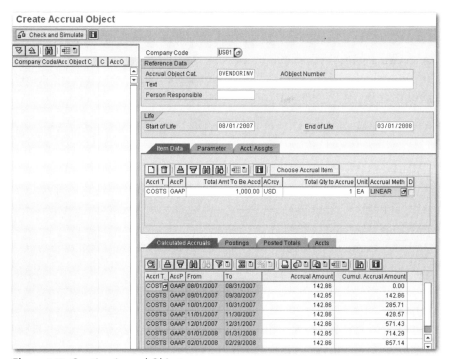

Figure 9.32 Creating Accrual Objects

In the accrual process, you need to define the following:

▶ **Life of accrual**
Time period of accrual: start date and end date.

▶ **Item Data**
Accrual type, which can be the following:

  ▶ **COSTS**: Cost accrual.

  ▶ **COSTSP**: Cost accruals, only periodic postings.

  ▶ **RVNUEP**: Revenue accruals, only periodic postings.

  ▶ **RVNUES**: Revenue accrual.

▶ **Accrual procedure**
This specifies the accounting principle: GAAP or IAS.

▶ **Amount to be accrued**
Enter the amount to be accrued.

▶ **Accrual currency**
Enter the relevant accrual currency.

▶ **Quantity to be accrued (optional)**
You can enter the accrual quantity if you need to track the accrual quantity as well.

▶ **Accrual method**
Linear method distributes the accrual equally across all the periods.

▶ **Account Assignments**
In this tab, you can define the account assignment such as cost center, profit center, WBS element, or business area.

After you calculate the accrual, the following appears in the results section at the bottom of the screen:

▶ **Calculated Accruals**
This shows the item data and the actual amount that will get accrued per accrual period.

▶ **Postings**
This shows the posted amount and the reference accounting document.

▶ **Posted Totals**
This shows the totals that have been posted.

▶ **Accts**
This can be used to define the accounts for opening posting, periodic posting, and closing posting.

You can use transaction codes ACACACT and ACACTREE02 to execute the accruals per the selection criterion or to edit an accrual object if required.

9.5.5 Cross-Company Code Transfers

Many JV transactions need to be recorded across company codes to ensure that the balance sheet and profit and loss statements can be segregated. In cross-company code transfers, you can post to multiple company codes. The system automatically posts to the interclearing accounts defined by the configuration of the same.

This generates an intercompany document number in addition to the two document numbers that get posted across the two company codes. Figure 9.33 shows the screen that details out the process of making an intercompany posting. When you are posting the second line item, you just need to select the appropriate company code (**New co. code**), which allows you to post to the other company code.

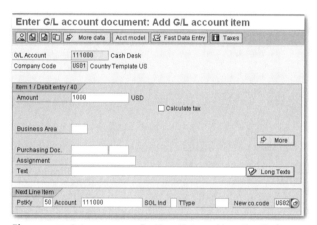

Figure 9.33 Intercompany Posting: Enter a New Co. Code

The intercompany document can be changed using Transaction FBU2, displayed using FBU3, and reversed using FBU8.

9.5.6 Bank Account Interest Calculation

The process for executing and configuring bank account interest calculation is very similar to the interest calculation for vendors and customers. The only difference is that you are applying the interest in this case on GL accounts instead of vendors and customers. This is especially important if your bank gives you interest on the balances in your GL account. You can use this interest calculation functionality to calculate the interest that should be paid by the bank.

The additional feature available in the GL interest calculation is cash pooling. This allows you to combine several bank accounts' debit and credit balances as long as they have the same currency. Follow the menu path **SAP Menu • Accounting • Financial Accounting • General Ledger • Periodic Processing • Interest Calculation • Balance Interest Calculation**, or use Transaction F.52.

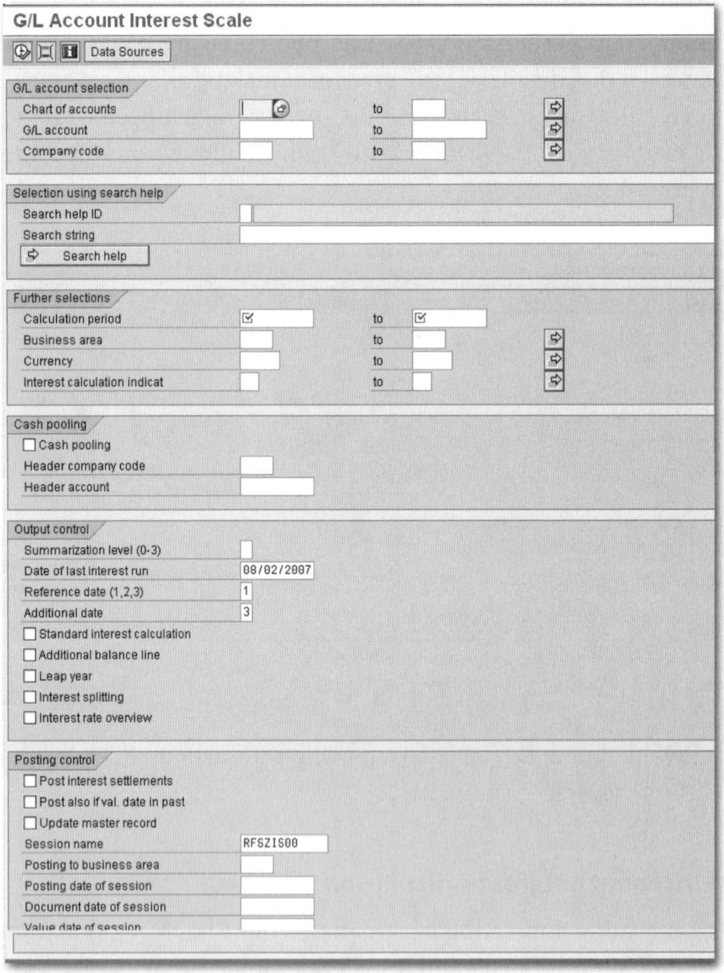

Figure 9.34 GL Account Interest Scale

Figure 9.34 shows the screen for interest calculation on GL balances. Here you can perform the cash pooling by checking **Cash pooling** and entering the **Header company code** and the **Header account**. All the other parameters are the same as that of interest calculation for customers and vendors. One of the most important indicators is the **Interest calculation indicator** along with the **Currency**.

9.5.7 Open-Item Clearing

Open-item clearing allows you to clear open GL line items such as GR/IR clearing, which balance each other out. After the open items are cleared, you can look at the balances that are open and need to be cleared. There are multiple ways to clear the GL accounts that have open-item management checked in their master record. Transactions F-03, F.13, or F.13E can be used to clear open GL items.

Manual Clearing of Open Items

Figure 9.35 shows the screen to clear open items using F.03. This is the process of cleaning the open items manually, but this provides you the maximum flexibility in terms of clearing open items.

Figure 9.35 Clear Open Items

You need to enter the GL account in **Account, clearing date,** and **Company Code,** and then click on **Process Open Items.** This allows you to select appropriate open items for the GL account and clear them. However, the biggest limitation of this transaction is that it is useful for clearing only one GL account.

Automatic Clearing Without Specifying the Clearing Currency

Using Transaction F.13, you can actually clear multiple GL accounts in one go. Also this transaction allows you to clear open items automatically per predefined rules that group together open items per account. If the open-item balances per the criteria is zero in local, foreign, or parallel currency, the items are cleared against each other.

> **Best Practice**
>
> Use automatic clearing instead of the manual clearing program.

You can define custom selection criteria to clear open items. This is especially important when you are clearing accounts that have a large number of open items. During automatic clearing, the system adds a clearing document number that ties all these open items together and marks them as cleared. For example, for clearing the open items in the GR/IR clearing account automatically, you can define the purchase order number and item number as an additional criteria for clearing open items. This criterion ensures that only goods receipt items and invoice items that belong to each other are cleared together.

Figure 9.36 shows the screen for automatic clearing, which can be used for vendors and customers. In this screen, you can perform automatic clearing without specifying a clearing currency. This forces the system to post any exchange rate differences automatically to exchange rate clearing accounts. The selection options in this case are **Company code, Fiscal year, Assignment, Document number** range, and **Posting date**, which can be used to narrow down your selection of open item clearing accounts.

One of the most important fields that you can use is **GR/IR account special process.** If the assignment of goods receipts to the corresponding invoice receipts using the purchase order number and item is not sufficient, (for example, in the case of scheduling agreements), you can set this. This has the effect that the assignment of documents to GR/IR accounts is not done using only the purchase order number and item but also using the material document, which is captured in the XREF3 field.

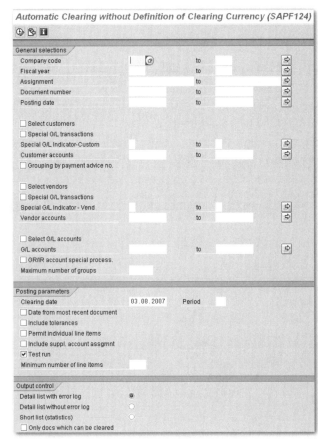

Figure 9.36 Automatic Clearing

Automatic Clearing with Clearing Currency Specified

Figure 9.37 shows the screen that can be used to clear GL items. In Transaction F13E, you can specify the clearing currency as well. This ensures that the system posts any exchange rate differences in clearing currency.

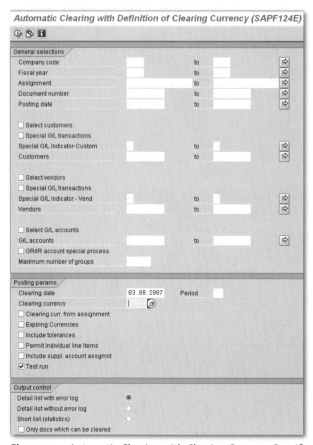

Figure 9.37 Automatic Clearing with Clearing Currency Specified

Now that you have learned some of the key GL business transactions, let's take a detailed look at configuring them.

9.6 Configuring Business Transactions: General Ledger

Configuring GL business transactions allows you to tailor the GL to your specific business scenarios. In this section, you will learn about the settings that can be made for GL postings, document splitting, cross-company code transactions, and accrual postings.

9.6.1 Configuring General Ledger Posting

The GL posting screens (refer to Figure 9.26 and Figure 9.27) are not configurable to a great extent. However, you can configure which document types are relevant for SAP Enjoy transactions (post SAP R/3 4.6C release).

You can also configure to include customer fields in Enjoy transactions. In addition, you can also specify the posting keys that should be used for the GL posting. SAP Enjoy transactions were introduced in the 4.6 C release, which allowed users to enter the transaction data in significantly less time. So instead of users entering posting keys, which was the norm previously, you can now enter debit and credit as shown in Figure 9.26. Figure 9.38 shows the settings that can be made in the GL.

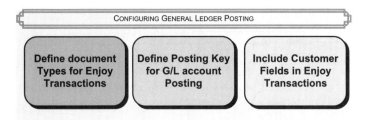

Figure 9.38 Configuring General Ledger Posting

Typically, all these are defaulted by SAP ERP. For example, the posting keys (which indicate debit and credit) default as 40 for debit and 50 for credit. It is advisable that you do not change any of these settings. So we would not go into the detail of these settings.

9.6.2 Configuring Document Splitting

You already know about the document splitting functionality. Now you will learn more about the process for configuring document splitting. You must activate document splitting to ensure that the segment characteristic is split consistently. It is also important to ensure that a *zero balance* is achieved for each document for the relevant entity. There are two stages of document splitting that can be implemented for an organization: basic document splitting and extended document splitting. The process flow of configuring basic document splitting is outlined in Figure 9.39.

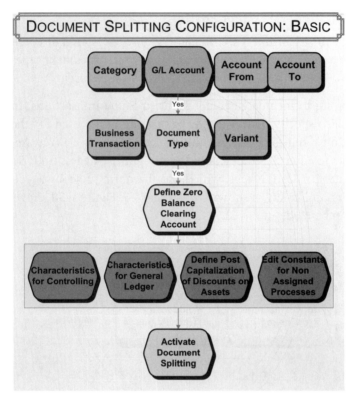

Figure 9.39 Document Splitting: Basic

As shown in Figure 9.39, you need to first assign a range of GL accounts to an item category. Then you assign the business transaction and variant to a document type. After that is done, you define the GL account that will be used for clearing the balance for GL accounts in cases where document-splitting rules do not derive the necessary assignments.

After defining these parameters, you need to detail the characteristics for controlling, GL, posting capitalization of discounts for assets, and defining constants for nonassigned processes. The last step is the activation of document splitting for the GL. You will learn in detail all these configuration settings in this section.

Let's look at the lean version of document splitting. You can also do enhancements that can be achieved in extended document splitting as shown in Figure 9.40. Extended document splitting includes additional configuration of the splitting method, splitting rule, and new business transaction variants per your requirements.

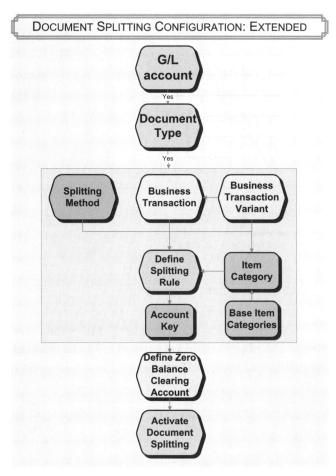

Figure 9.40 Document Splitting: Extended

Classify GL Accounts for Document Splitting

In this setting, you need to first select the chart of accounts and then enter the range of accounts along with the category of the document splitting. If you activate document splitting, each business transaction that is entered is analyzed (remains the same or is split) during the document splitting procedure. For document splitting to recognize how the individual document items are to be handled, you need to classify them by assigning them to an item category.

The item category is determined by the account number. In this IMG activity, you need to assign the revenue, expense, bank account/cash account, and balance sheet account. The following item categories are included in the system: Customer, Vendor, Cash discount offsetting, Asset, Material, Expense, and Revenue. You cannot change item categories. The menu path is **IMG • Financial Accounting (New) • General Ledger Accounting (new) • Business Transactions • Document Splitting • Classify G/L accounts for Document Splitting**. Figure 9.41 shows the settings that you made for the range of accounts from **500000** to **700000** as having an expense category.

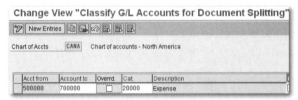

Figure 9.41 Classify GL Accounts for Document Splitting

Classify FI Document Types for Document Splitting

Now you need to assign the business transaction and the business transaction variant to the document type. Follow the menu path **IMG • Financial Accounting (New) • General Ledger Accounting (new) • Business Transactions • Document Splitting • Classify FI Document Type for Document Splitting**.

Figure 9.42 shows the screen where you can make the necessary settings. Enter the **Type** "AA/AB/AF/AN" (Document Type), **Transactn.** "0000" (Business Transaction), and **Variant** "0001" (Business Transaction Variant) All three combined together complete the assignment. Using this setting, you can create different rules for different document types.

Change View "Classify FI Document Type for Document Splitting"						
Type	Description	Transactn.	Variant	Description	Name	
AA	Asset posting	0000	0001	Unspecified posting	Standard	
AB	Accounting document	0000	0001	Unspecified posting	Standard	
AF	Dep. postings	0000	0001	Unspecified posting	Standard	
AN	Net asset posting	0000	0001	Unspecified posting	Standard	

Figure 9.42 Classify FI Document Type for Document Splitting

Define Zero Balance Clearing Account

When you need account assignments to have a zero balance, you define the clearing GL account, which gets hit when the balance is not zero. The menu path is **IMG • Financial Accounting (New) • General Ledger Accounting**

(new) • **Business Transactions** • **Document Splitting** • **Define Zero Balance Clearing Account**, and the transaction code is GSP_KD.

The first step is to define the **Posting Key** for the clearing account, which is **40** (debit) and **50** (credit) as shown in Figure 9.43. The item category **01001** zero balance posting (free balancing units) is defaulted in basic document splitting. In extended document splitting, you can define your own item categories.

Figure 9.43 Define Posting Keys Tied to Account Key

After the posting key definition, you specify the GL account in the next screen as shown in Figure 9.44. The **Account Key** is automatically defaulted to **000**.

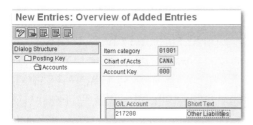

Figure 9.44 Define the GL Account for the Zero Balance Clearing Posting

Define Document Splitting Characteristics for General Ledger Accounting

In this configuration, you will identify the document splitting characteristics that are relevant for the GL. You will define the attributes for each of the characteristics. The menu path for detail characteristics for GL accounting is **IMG** • **Financial Accounting (New)** • **General Ledger Accounting (new)** • **Business Transactions** • **Document Splitting** • **Define Document Splitting Characteristics for General Ledger Accounting**.

Figure 9.45 shows the screen where you can maintain the GL characteristics. Here you can see that you have specified that **Segment**, **Business Area,** and **Profit Center** are the characteristics that are used in document splitting.

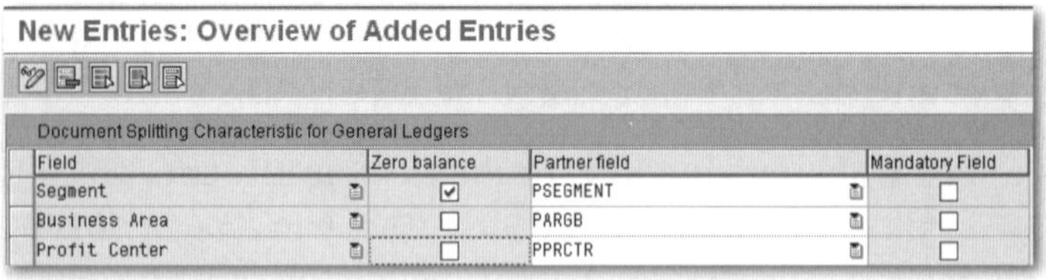

New Entries: Overview of Added Entries

Document Splitting Characteristic for General Ledgers

Field		Zero balance	Partner field		Mandatory Field
Segment	🖿	☑	PSEGMENT	🖿	☐
Business Area	🖿	☐	PARGB	🖿	☐
Profit Center	🖿	☐	PPRCTR	🖿	☐

Figure 9.45 Define Characteristics for GL Accounting

You can identify which characteristic should be checked:

▸ **Zero balance**
If checked, the system ensures that the balance for the characteristic is zero during the posting.

▸ **Mandatory Field**
If checked, this requires an entry for document splitting.

Define Document Splitting Characteristics for Controlling

In this setting, you define additional cost assignment objects as relevant for splitting. These settings are not relevant for GL accounting. Instead, these settings are relevant for controlling documents that get transferred from GL accounting. You can follow the menu path **IMG • Financial Accounting (New) • General Ledger Accounting (new) • Business Transactions • Document Splitting • Define Document Splitting Characteristics for Controlling**. Figure 9.46 displays the screen where you can add the controlling characteristics. Here you have maintained the **Cost Center, Cost Object, Counter, Network,** and other important controlling attributes as relevant for document splitting.

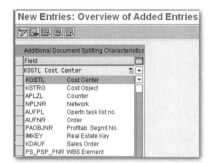

Figure 9.46 Define Document Splitting Characteristics for Controlling

> **Note**
>
> Controlling account assignments are only transferred when the account has also been set up as a cost element.

Define Postcapitalization of Cash Discount to Assets

If this setting is made, then the cash discount amount is posted to the asset instead of the cash discount expense account. For example, let's say that you received a vendor invoice. At the time of invoice, the accounting entries are the following:

▸ Credit Vendor: 100 USD

▸ Debit Asset: 100 USD

Now at the time of payment, you get a cash discount of 5% because you paid it earlier. So now the payment accounting entry if you activate this indicator is as follows:

▸ Debit Vendor: 100 USD

▸ Credit Bank: 95 USD

▸ Credit Asset: 5 USD

So in this case, the cash discount that you got gets transferred to the asset. The menu path is **IMG • Financial Accounting (New) • General Ledger Accounting (new) • Business Transactions • Document Splitting • Define Post-Capitalization of Cash Discount to Assets**. Figure 9.47 shows the setting, which transfers any postcapitalization discount to assets. In this setting, you just add the asset field **ANLN1 Asset**, which ensures that any postcapitalization discount gets transferred to the asset.

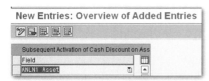

Figure 9.47 Define Postcapitalization of Cash Discount to Assets

Edit Constants for Nonassigned Processes

In this step, you define the default account assignments when it is not possible to derive the account assignments (e.g., a default segment). This is the case if the required information is not yet available when the posting occurs. For example, if you are receiving cash, you want to get this in the system as soon as possible so that you can send it to the bank. So you record the cash receipt without any reference to customer. At this time, the default segment that you have defined as a constant is used. However, when you clear the cash with the correct customer, the appropriate segment is derived. The menu path is **IMG • Financial Accounting (New) • General Ledger Accounting (new) • Business Transactions • Document Splitting • Edit Constants for Non-assigned Processes**.

Activate Document Splitting

In this step, you activate document splitting. Without this, all the previous settings are not valid. After you activate document splitting, you can start using the document splitting functionality. You can follow the menu path **IMG • Financial Accounting (New) • General Ledger Accounting (new) • Business Transactions • Document Splitting • Activate Document Splitting**. Figure 9.48 shows the screen where you activate document splitting.

Figure 9.48 Activate and Deactivate Document Splitting

▶ **Activate Document Splitting**
To activate document splitting, check the **Document Splitting** checkbox and you need to save the setting.. This will activate document splitting for all company codes.

▶ **Level of Detail**
There are two options in document splitting. Either use the characteristics that you identified in document splitting earlier or use the default account assignments. These can be achieved by using the **Inheritance** and **Standard A/C Assgnmt** checkboxes, respectively. With account assignment inheritance, the characteristics for GL accounting are transferred to lines that do not have any assignments. The other indicator, **Standard A/C**

Assgnmt, allows you to activate the standard account assignment in the nonassigned lines. If you have used standard account assignments, then you also need to define the **Constant** that gets derived for nonassigned GL lines.

Document splitting gets activated for all company codes. You can choose to deactivate it for specific company codes by using the left pane as shown in Figure 9.48.

9.6.3 Extended Document Splitting

Now that you know the settings for document splitting, let's take a look at extended document splitting. This is only needed if the standard settings available in document splitting are not sufficient for your needs, and you want to make some enhancements in document splitting. For example, you might need to tweak the way the vendor invoice needs to be split for a particular item category, which is different from the SAP ERP delivered rules.

Extended document splitting allows you to define your own rules for document splitting. In a subsequent discussion, you will learn more about the splitting methods, splitting rule, assigning splitting methods, and details about the business transaction variant.

> **Tip**
>
> You cannot use partial standard and partial extended document splitting.

Define Document Splitting Method

In this step, you will learn about the document splitting methods. A splitting method contains the rules governing how the individual item categories are dealt with. The menu path is **IMG • Financial Accounting (New) • General Ledger Accounting (new) • Business Transactions • Document Splitting • Extended Document Splitting • Define Document Splitting Method**. Figure 9.49 shows the document splitting methods that SAP ERP comes prebuilt with, and these must not be changed. So you have splitting method **0000000001** for **Splitting: Customer, Vendor, Tax.**

Figure 9.49 Define Document Splitting Method

If the functions delivered in the SAP ERP standard system are not sufficient, you have to create your own splitting method in this activity. If you want, you can copy a method, and create your own document splitting method by entering a name and description for your method.

Define Document Splitting Rule

In this step, you can define the rules for document splitting that allow you to customize how the characteristics will flow in documents. It is recommended that you copy the delivered default settings to the splitting method you define and then make changes to those settings. You can follow the menu path **IMG • Financial Accounting (New) • General Ledger Accounting (new) • Business Transactions • Document Splitting • Extended Document Splitting • Define Document Splitting Rule**.

Figure 9.50 shows a sample document splitting rule at the lowest level where you see the base item categories. The document splitting rule , as you can see in Figure 9.50, is a combination of the following:

- **Splitting Method: 0000000001 Splitting: Customer, Vendor, Tax**
- **Business Transaction: 0300 Vendor Invoice**
- **Business Transaction: 0001 Standard** (identifies the business transaction variant)
- **Item category: 03000 Vendor**
- **Base Item Category** (Cat. in Figure 9.50): **01000 Balance Sheet Account**

By combining these parameters, you specify how the posting will happen for document splitting. All these updates split into tables, which then updates the actual line items and subsequently the GL totals table.

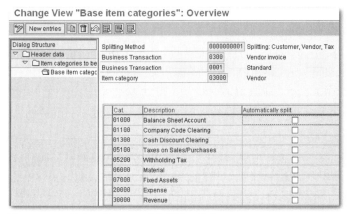

Figure 9.50 Define Document Splitting Rule

If you set the **Automatically split** indicator, the item category is only applied for the split when splitting happens automatically, for example, for clearing, partial clearing, and reversal processes.

Assign Document Splitting Method

The screen for maintaining the extended document splitting method is similar to activating basic document splitting. You can only assign a custom document splitting method, if you have activated basic splitting. Here you can modify the standard delivery splitting method and replace it with your custom splitting method. The menu path is **IMG • Financial Accounting (New) • General Ledger Accounting (new) • Business Transactions • Document Splitting • Extended Document Splitting • Assign Document Splitting Method**.

Define Business Transaction Variants

The menu path for defining this variant is **IMG • Financial Accounting (New) • General Ledger Accounting (new) • Business Transactions • Document Splitting • Extended Document Splitting • Define Business Transaction Variants**. This is where you can define the business transaction variant for the document split business transactions, which makes up the splitting rule. This is important from the following perspectives:

▶ Business transaction is exactly tied to the item categories that can be posted. With a business transaction variant, you can restrict the business transaction further by excluding item categories. When you post a document, the system can check, using the business transaction variant, whether the posting is permitted. If an item category is not permitted, the system rejects the posting.

▶ For each business transaction variant, you can define the document splitting rule. If you also want to split individual documents for one business transaction according to different rules, you have to define the required number of business transaction variants.

Figure 9.51 shows the standard business transaction variants and the categories that are assigned to the business transaction, such as vendor invoice, customer invoice, and so on. As shown in Figure 9.51, certain item categories can be forbidden (**Forbidd.**) or made **Required** for the business transaction variant.

Change View "Assigned item categories": Overview

Cat.	Description	Forbidd.	Required	Only once
01000	Balance Sheet Account	☐	☐	☐
01100	Company Code Clearing	☐	☐	☐
01300	Cash Discount Clearing	☐	☐	☐
03000	Vendor	☐	☑	☐
03100	Vendor: Special G/L Transaction	☐	☐	☐
05100	Taxes on Sales/Purchases	☐	☐	☐
05200	Withholding Tax	☐	☐	☐
06000	Material	☐	☐	☐
07000	Fixed Assets	☐	☐	☐
20000	Expense	☐	☐	☐
30000	Revenue	☐	☐	☐
40200	Exchange Rate Difference	☐	☐	☐
80000	Customer-Specific Item Category	☐	☐	☐

Figure 9.51 Define Business Transaction Variant

▶ **Forbidd.**

If you set this indicator, the item category is not permitted for this business transaction category. You should prohibit the item categories that are not to be used for this business transaction variant. For example, in an asset invoice, only the item category asset is to be posted; the expense is not to be posted.

▶ **Required**

If you set this indicator, this item category must exist when you post a document. Set the item categories as required if the business process and/ or its logic requires this item category. For example, a vendor invoice must contain a vendor because subsequent processing might happen based on the initial derivation of vendor.

▸ **Only once**
If you set this indicator, the item category must only appear once in the business transaction specified.

> **Note**
>
> Although you cannot define your own business transactions, you can define your own business transaction variants that restrict the business transactions further.

This completes the settings related to document splitting. Document splitting is a great help to auditors as well because now the account assignments are more granular, and you can track any transfer to the balance sheet that occurred by the identified characteristics, which makes financial postings easier to trace.

9.6.4 Configuring Cross-Company Code Transactions

This section details the configuration pertaining to cross-company code GL transactions, which was discussed earlier in Section 9.5.5. The menu path is **IMG • Financial Accounting (New) • General Ledger Accounting (new) • Business Transactions • Prepare Cross Company Code Transactions,** and the transaction code is OBYA.

During this configuration, you first need to identify the pair of company codes that will have intercompany transactions. After that, you just need to configure the GL clearing accounts for receivable and payable transactions. The posting key for credit is 50, and the debit posting key is 40. Both sides of the pairs need to be configured. Typically, the GL accounts are chosen to be the same in both sides to reduce the number of GL accounts. Figure 9.52 shows the setup for company code **US01** and **CA01**. Enter the **Account debit** and **Account credit** for the **Receivable** and the **Payable** side along with the **Debit posting key** and the **Credit posting key**.

Maintain FI Configuration: Automatic Posting - Clearing Accounts

Transaction	BUV	Clearing between company codes

Company Code 1

Posted in	US01
Cleared against	CA01

Receivable		Payable	
Debit posting key	⊘	Credit posting key	
Account debit		Account credit	

Company Code 2

Posted in	CA01
Cleared against	US01

Receivable		Payable	
Debit posting key		Credit posting key	
Account debit		Account credit	

Figure 9.52 Cross-Company Code GL Account Determination

9.6.5 Configuring Open-item Clearing

This section details the flow for configuring open-item clearing, which was discussed in Section 9.5.7. The configuration process diagram for open-item clearing is shown in Figure 9.53. The detailed configuration was covered in Chapter 5. You will learn the last step of **Preparing Automatic Clearing** next.

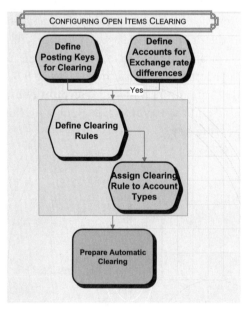

Figure 9.53 Process Flow for Configuring Open-Items Clearing

9.6.6 Prepare Automatic Clearing

In this step, you can define additional rules that help in structuring the automatic clearing process. Remember that you can configure up to four additional criteria to help you with automatic clearing. The menu path is **IMG • Financial Accounting (New) • General Ledger Accounting (new) • Business Transactions • Open Item Clearing • Prepare Automatic Clearing**.

Figure 9.54 shows the rules that you can maintain for automatic clearing. Note that you can maintain the clearing rules by chart of accounts, account type, and range of accounts. For each of these parameters, you can define the criteria by which the system will be clearing the GL accounts.

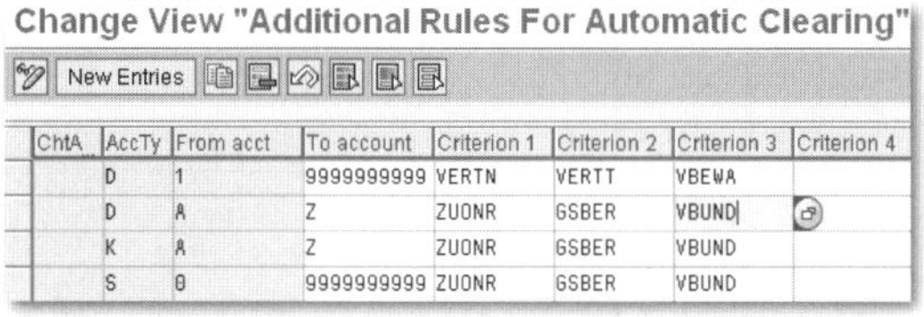

Change View "Additional Rules For Automatic Clearing"							

ChtA	AccTy	From acct	To account	Criterion 1	Criterion 2	Criterion 3	Criterion 4
	D	1	9999999999	VERTN	VERTT	VBEWA	
	D	A	Z	ZUONR	GSBER	VBUND	
	K	A	Z	ZUONR	GSBER	VBUND	
	S	0	9999999999	ZUONR	GSBER	VBUND	

Figure 9.54 Prepare Automatic Clearing

> **Note**
>
> ZUONR is the technical name for the allocation field and is one of the most common methods by which you can clear accounts automatically. You can identify what gets populated in the allocation field by using the *sort key*. So you need to make sure that for the GR/IR account, if you define the sort key as purchase order and purchase order item number, then the same must get populated in the allocation field. Using the preceding rule, you can clear the GR/IR account.

9.6.7 Configuring Accruals

This section details the flow for configuring manual accruals, which was discussed in Section 9.5.4.

Figure 9.55 shows the screen with the configuration elements for manual accruals, and Figure 9.56 shows the configuration process flow diagram for manual accruals, which contains the sequence of steps you need to perform for configuring accruals. The important configuration steps are described here:

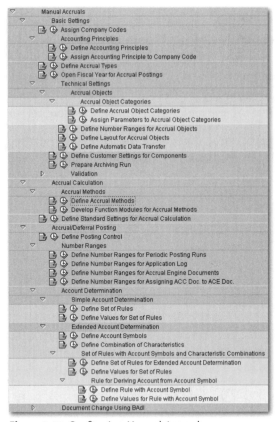

Figure 9.55 Configuring Manual Accruals

1. Basic Settings

You can perform the following steps:

- Assign a company code as applicable for accrual.
- Open a fiscal year for accrual.
- Define the accounting principles (GAAP, IAS, etc.), and assign them to a company code.
- Define accrual types.

2. Accrual Objects

You can perform the following steps:

- Define number ranges for accrual objects.
- Define accrual object categories.
- Assign parameters to accrual object categories.

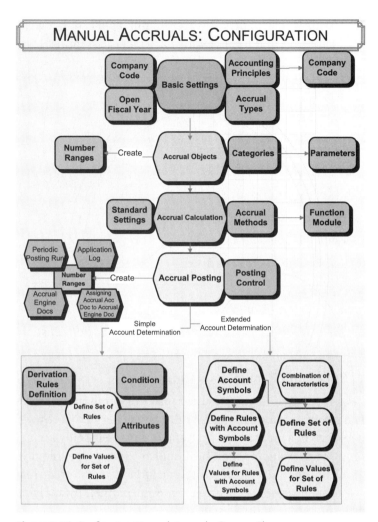

Figure 9.56 Configuring Manual Accruals: Process Flow

3. Accrual Calculation

Here you can do the following:

▶ Define standard settings.

▶ Define accrual methods.

▶ Assign a function module to an accrual method for defining your own complex calculation.

4. Accrual Posting

Here you can do the following:

▶ Define number ranges for the periodic posting run, application log, accrual engine documents, and for assigning an accrual accounting document to the accrual engine document.

▶ Define posting control.

5. Account Determination

Here you can do the following:

▶ Simple account determination:

  ▶ Define a set of rules.

  ▶ Define values for a set of rules.

▶ Extended account determination:

  ▶ Define account symbols.

  ▶ Define a combination of characteristics.

  ▶ Define a set of rules.

  ▶ Define values for a set of rules.

In the next section, you will learn about transfer prices and parallel valuation.

9.6.8 Transfer Prices and Parallel Valuation

A transfer price is a price used to valuate the transfer of goods and services between independent organizational units. As the raw material gets converted to semifinished, then to a finished product, and is ultimately sold, it might cross multiple profit centers and/or multiple company codes. This requires you to valuate and track the price at which the material is transferred from one legal entity to another or from one profit center to another, by applying appropriate transfer pricing at multiple stages.

You can have multiple parallel valuations in the new GL. The entire value chain from purchase to sale is integrated with the parallel valuation approach, which helps in providing additional reporting capability regarding transfer pricing. Transfer pricing was introduced for the first time in Profit Center Accounting (PCA). But now with the merger of PCA functionality in the new GL, it becomes much more significantly integrated with the legal view. Functionally speaking, there can be three viewpoints of transfer prices that you can use:

▶ **Groupwide View**

If you want to understand the costs from the organization as a whole, then groupwide view should be used. For example, production costs need to be looked at from an overall product group perspective.

▶ **Profit Center View**
If your objective is to assess the performance of decentralized responsibility areas, then the profit center view should be used. For example, the management price needs to be looked at by whomever is managing the profit center.

▶ **Legal View**
If you have independent legal companies, then you need to look at the transfer prices from a legal view. For example, sales and purchase prices across subsidiaries operating in different countries may need to be looked at from a legal view. This is especially important if you are crossing legal country limits.

> **Note**
>
> The overall viewpoint dictates the methodology of transfer pricing.

The most common acceptable methods of transfer pricing are the following:

▶ **Cost plus method**
Charging cost plus profit margin. In this method, whenver you have a transfer pricing situation, you add a profit margin and use that to transfer the product to the reciever. However, it is very important that you add a reasonable profit margin that is acceptable to the reciever.

▶ **Comparable arm's length price method**
This is determined by using what a third party would pay for the service rendered. This is the most objective way of assessing the transfer price. However, this might impact the ability to act as one organization.

Variations of these two methods are also used to determine the appropriate transfer price for transactions. The configuration process flow for transfer pricing is detailed in Figure 9.57: As you can see, the first step is defining the condition tables. After defining condition tables, you need to maintain the access sequence, condition types, and pricing procedure. All this determines the transfer price that will be used. As you can remember, this is very similar to the SD: price determination procedure.

Define Condition Tables

The condition table is the beginning point of configuring transfer pricing. In this step, you can define the condition tables and identify the fields relevant for transfer pricing. The menu path is **IMG • Financial Accounting (New) • General Ledger Accounting (new) • Business Transactions • Parallel Valuation Approaches/Transfer Prices • Advanced Settings for Prices**

• **Define Price Dependencies (Condition Tables)** • **Maintain Condition Tables**. The transaction code is 8KEA.

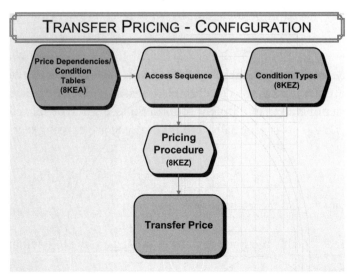

Figure 9.57 Transfer Pricing: Configuration Process Flow

Figure 9.58 shows how you can maintain the settings for defining the condition tables for transfer pricing. The figure shows **Table 141**, which has fields that identify the parameters of material and receiver profit center. The fields on the left can be selected to be processed later in the definition of access sequences in the next step. When you double-click a field in **Field Catlg,** it moves to the left side as a **Selected field.**

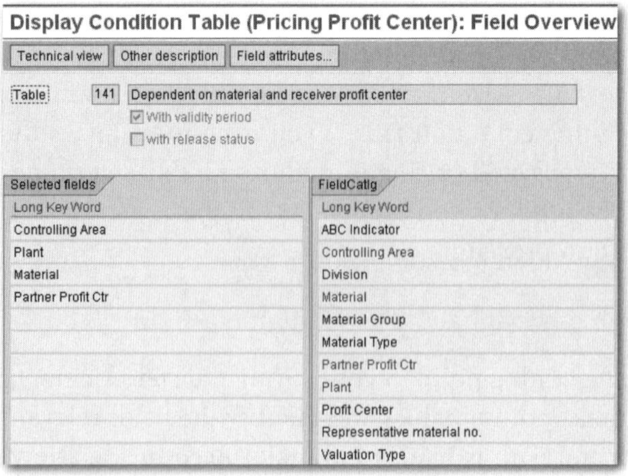

Figure 9.58 Display Existing Condition Table

Define Access Sequence

In this step, you can define the access sequence in which the system looks for valid condition records for a condition type. The starting point is the condition table and then within that table you can identify the sequence of fields. This helps you in defining multiple methods of price determination by moving from the most specific attribute combination to the general attributes. You can follow the menu path **IMG • Financial Accounting (New) • General Ledger Accounting (new) • Business Transactions • Parallel Valuation Approaches/Transfer Prices • Advanced Settings for Prices • Define Access Sequence**.

Figure 9.59 shows the access sequence for transfer pricing which then picks up the fields and the sequence in which they are used to determine the pricing schema for transfer pricing. For **Access Sequence TP00 10** and the selected **Table 141**, you can maintain the appropriate fields, such as **Controlling Area, Plant, Material,** and **Partner Profit Ctr**.

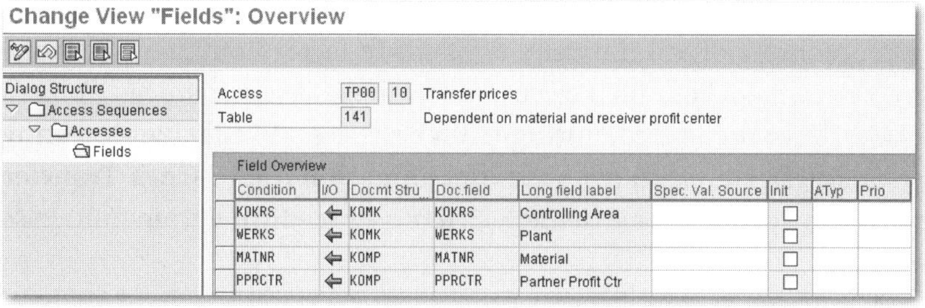

| Change View "Fields": Overview | | | | | | | | |

Dialog Structure	Access	TP00	10	Transfer prices				
▽ ☐ Access Sequences	Table	141		Dependent on material and receiver profit center				
▽ ☐ Accesses								
☐ Fields								

Field Overview								
Condition	I/O	Docmt Stru	Doc.field	Long field label	Spec. Val. Source	Init	ATyp	Prio
KOKRS	⇐ KOMK		KOKRS	Controlling Area		☐		
WERKS	⇐ KOMK		WERKS	Plant		☐		
MATNR	⇐ KOMP		MATNR	Material		☐		
PPRCTR	⇐ KOMP		PPRCTR	Partner Profit Ctr		☐		

Figure 9.59 Display Access Sequence

Define Condition Types

Condition types are used to indicate the transfer price values and can be used to build up your overall pricing procedure. In this step, we identify and create condition types that are relevant for transfer pricing. The menu path is **IMG • Financial Accounting (New) • General Ledger Accounting (new) • Business Transactions • Parallel Valuation Approaches/Transfer Prices • Basic Settings for Pricing**. The transaction code is 8KEZ.

Figure 9.60 shows how you can maintain the condition type for a particular pricing procedure. You have to click on the **Create** button on the left hand side and then define the transfer pricing **Condition Type**. After you have defined the condition types, you need to select the **Access Sequence** in which this is valid. You also need to select whether the condition type denotes the

base condition type for costing or material ledger. You can also choose a
Fixed Price, Percentage Overhead, or **Other Condition Types**.

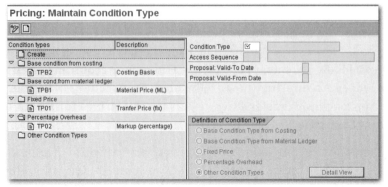

Figure 9.60 Maintain Condition Type for Transfer Pricing

Define Pricing Procedure

Now you will learn to define the pricing procedure for transfer pricing. The
pricing procedure pulls all the definitions made in previous steps into one
coherent structure that can then be customized to your requirements. You can
follow **IMG • Financial Accounting (New) • General Ledger Accounting
(new) • Business Transactions • Parallel Valuation Approaches/Transfer
Prices • Basic Settings for Pricing • Pricing Procedure Submenu** or use
Transaction 8KEZ.

Figure 9.61 shows the screen for maintaining the pricing procedure. In pricing procedure **TP0001**, you have defined that the condition type **TP01** is
part of the pricing procedure. The pricing procedure will be defined by the
MM consultant, but you should be aware of these settings as well.

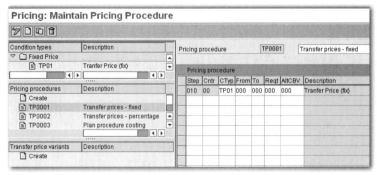

Figure 9.61 Defining a Pricing Procedure

This is a combination of access sequence and condition types so that you can define a pricing procedure for transfer pricing. Pricing procedure controls how the postings will happen in the material ledger when you transfer any materials from one company to another.

> **Note**
>
> To configure transfer pricing, first define your business scenario and then map it in the system. The settings described are rudimentary to explain the concept behind the configuration process flow.

Now let's explore GL integration issues.

9.7 Integration with General Ledger

The basic premise of implementing SAP ERP is to integrate all the applications so that you can get to one truth for the organization. The GL allows you to integrate with all the other components of SAP ERP. In this section, you will learn the integration of the GL to other financial applications, as well as nonfinancial applications that impact the company SAP ERP Financials. This is the part of the GL configuration where you can specify how other applications are integrated with the GL. Figure 9.62 shows the various integration aspects that you will learn in this section.

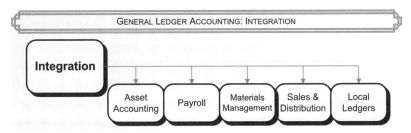

Figure 9.62 Integration with Other Modules

The menu path is **IMG • Financial Accounting (New) • General Ledger Accounting (new) • Periodic Processing • Integration**. Figure 9.63 illustrates the menu path of configuring the settings pertaining to account determination across many business processes pertaining to **Asset Accounting, Materials Management, Payroll, Sales and Distribution, and Local Ledgers.**

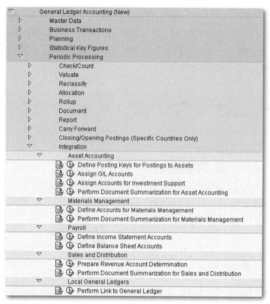

Figure 9.63 Integration with General Ledger: IMG View

9.7.1 Integration with Asset Accounting

Asset Accounting is used to manage your fixed assets. The integration with Asset Accounting is represented by the configuration process diagrams shown in Figure 9.64. The first step is to **Define Posting Keys for Asset Postings,** and then you can define the GL accounts for asset transactions, including accounts for investment support and document summarization. For assets, the posting keys are 70 (debit) and 75 (credit); they should not be changed.

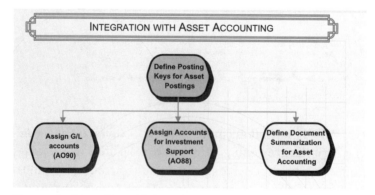

Figure 9.64 Integration with Asset Accounting

GL accounts can be assigned by business transaction and for a combination of charts of depreciation, chart of accounts, account determination, and depreciation area. Discover more details about asset management accounts in Figure 9.65 and also by reviewing Chapter 8.

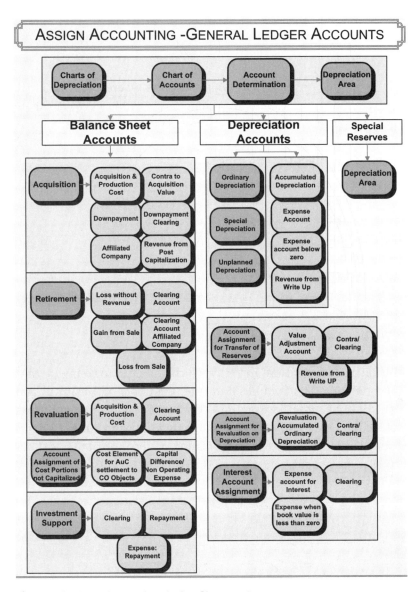

Figure 9.65 Asset Accounting: Assign GL accounts

9.7.2 Integration with Materials Management

The assignment of GL accounts for MM is done using Transaction OBYC or OMWB. If you use OMWB, then the screen shown in Figure 9.66 appears.

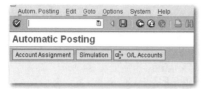

Figure 9.66 Materials Management: Transaction OMWB

OMWB allows simulation functionality and also the where–used list of GL accounts. OBYC is just the Account Assignment tab within OMWB. Figure 9.67 shows the **Account assignment** screen where you can define your account assignments. The transaction key is **GBB,** which is used to capture the **Offsetting entry for inventory posting**.

Display FI Configuration: Automatic Posting - Accounts

Chart of Accounts	CANA	Chart of accounts - North America
Transaction	GBB	Offsetting entry for inventory posting

Account assignment

Valuation	General m	Valuation class	Debit	Credit
0001	VB0	7900	500000	500000
0001	VB0	7920	500000	500000
0001	VBR	3000	510000	510000
0001	VBR	3030	510060	510060

Figure 9.67 Configuring MM Account Determination

Figure 9.68 illustrates the various fields by which you need to configure MM account determination. First, you need to enter the **Chart of Accounts**, and then you need to select the **Transaction Key** that identifies the transaction group. You can then maintain the GL accounts by **Valuation Area, General Modifier,** and **Valuation Class**. A combination of these attributes defines how a particular movement type posts to the GL.

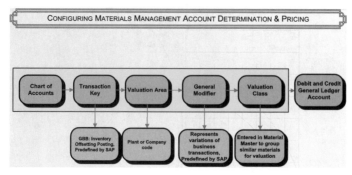

Figure 9.68 Process Flow for MM Account Determination

To understand it better, let's take a look at Transaction GBB, which is used to define the offsetting entry for inventory posting as shown in Figure 9.69. You reach this screen when you click on **Procedures** in Figure 9.67, shown earlier. Note the parameters that describe how the accounts are determined. If you uncheck the parameters, they are not used for account determination. For example, if you uncheck **Debit/Credit,** then the same account will be applicable for both debit and credit. This will reduce your maintenance activities pertaining to account determination if you plan to choose the same account for debit and credit.

Figure 9.69 Posting Rules for Automatic GL Determination

If you click on **Posting Key** in Figure 9.69, you will see the next screen as shown in Figure 9.70. Here you can maintain the **Posting Keys** for **Debit** and **Credit**. For **GBB**, the **Posting Key** tab shows the **Debit** key as **81** and the **Credit** key as **91**. So all the material movements will get posted to SAP ERP Financials using these posting keys.

Figure 9.70 Posting Keys for Transaction Keys

In the next subsection, you will learn about the integration of payroll with the GL.

9.7.3   Integration with Payroll

As you learned in Chapter 4, payroll processes are run separately from accounting. However, after the payroll calculation is done, you need to transfer the payroll data to accounting. In this subsection, you will learn the settings that enable the payroll process to talk to financial accounting. The assignment of GL accounts for payroll is done using Transactions OBYE (income statement accounts) and OBYG (balance sheet accounts). Figure 9.71 shows the parameters that can be used for determining the GL accounts for payroll.

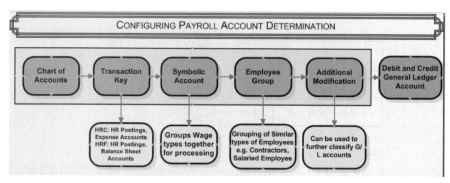

Figure 9.71 Process Flow for Payroll Account Determination

The parameters for determining GL accounts for payroll are the **Symbolic Account** (which groups together the common wage types for processing), the **Employee Group** (grouping of similar types of employees), and the **Additional Modification** (this field can be used to further enhance the GL and payroll mapping per your requirements). Integration of payroll with the GL for expense accounts is shown in Figure 9.72. Note that the **Transaction** key for expense accounts is **HRC**, which is automatically determined by SAP ERP. In the figure, **Symbolic a…** (symbolic accounts) **1100** and **Employee group 1** and **2** are assigned to **Accounts 611030** and **611000**, respectively.

Maintain FI Configuration: Automatic Posting

Posting Key	Rules

Chart of Accounts	CANA	Chart of accounts - North America
Transaction	HRC	HR postings, expense accounts

Account assignment		
Symbolic a	Employee group	Account
1100	1	611030
1100	2	611000

Figure 9.72 Defining the GL Account for Expenses (OBYE)

The assignment of balance sheets is shown in Figure 9.73. Note that the **Transaction** key for the balance sheet accounts is **HRF**, which is automatically determined by SAP ERP. In the figure, **Symbolic a...** (symbolic accounts) **1221** and **1310** are assigned to **Account**s **215160** and **215030**, respectively. You have flexibility to do the assignments by just symbolic accounts and not distinguish them by other parameters identified earlier in Figure 9.71.

Figure 9.73 Defining GL Accounts for the Balance Sheet (OBYG)

9.7.4 Integration with Sales and Distribution

The assignment of the GL account for SD is done using Transaction VKOA. Account assignment in SD is different from the ones that we discussed until now for MM, fixed assets, and payroll. It is dependent on condition tables and the access sequence structure of pricing. Figure 9.74 shows the screen where you can define the condition tables and its parameters.

Figure 9.74 Assign GL Accounts (Transaction VKOA)

You can also define your own tables and then define a particular access sequence. The most specific condition table is put in the beginning so that the correct GL account can be determined. So in the example shown in Figure 9.74, the assignment of the GL account with the customer group (**Cust. Grp**), material group (**Material Grp**), and account key (**Acct Key**) combination is checked first, the **Cust. Grp/Account Key** combination is checked next, and the **Material Grp/ Acct Key** combination is checked after that. If the conditions are not met, then it goes into the next level, which is broader than the previous one.

If the access sequence number **1** does not have any entries maintained for the table, then it goes to access sequence number **2,** and so on. This sequence is used to determine the GL account while processing which sales account should be hit for the condition type. Figure 9.75 shows the schematic of configuring the SD account determination and how it integrates with pricing. You learned about the transfer pricing earlier. This bears a striking resemblance to transfer pricing with additional components and differences accounted for SD.

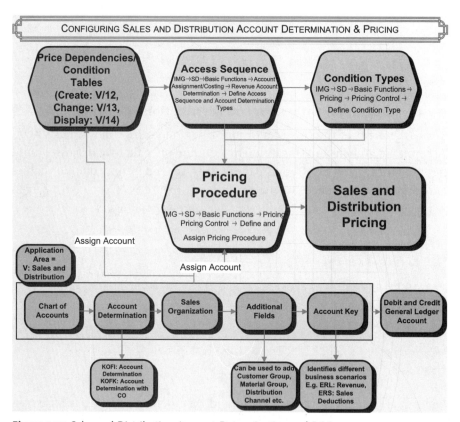

Figure 9.75 Sales and Distribution Account Determination and Pricing

Overall, you need to assign GL accounts by **Chart of Accounts, Account Determination, Sales Organization,** any **Additional Fields (Customer Group, Material Group,** and other parameters that need to be selected in the access sequence outline in Figure 9.74), and **Account Key** (which represent the different sales scenarios such as **Revenue, Deductions**, etc.). For SD, you have greater flexibility in defining your pricing procedure by defining your own pricing condition tables that can then be mapped to the access sequences. This enables you to map complex pricing arrangements with your customers. **Account Key** is derived from the condition type that identifies the business transaction.

As shown in Figure 9.75, the account determinations to be used are either **KOFI** or **KOFK** (with controlling assignments). Figure 9.76 shows the account assignment details for the **Cust.GrMaterialGrp/Acct key** combination. You can define your GL account here to assign this combination a sales account.

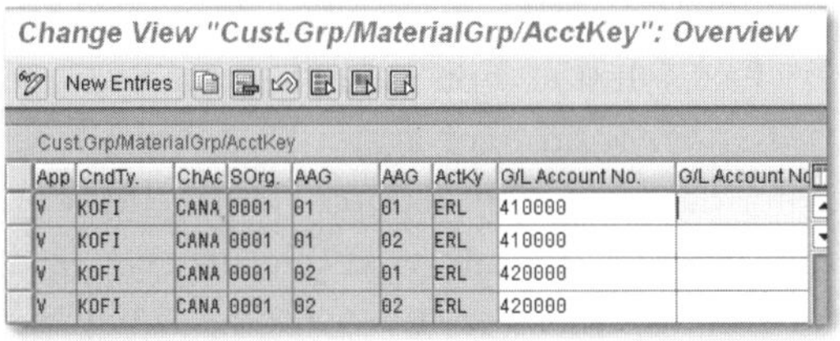

App	CndTy.	ChAc	SOrg.	AAG	AAG	ActKy	G/L Account No.	G/L Account No
V	KOFI	CANA	0001	01	01	ERL	410000	
V	KOFI	CANA	0001	01	02	ERL	410000	
V	KOFI	CANA	0001	02	01	ERL	420000	
V	KOFI	CANA	0001	02	02	ERL	420000	

Figure 9.76 Assign GL Accounts by Customer Group/Material Group/ Account Key

This completes the settings that you need to make as an SAP ERP Financials consultant. Typically, you will be making the GL account settings in Figure 9.76 and will be consulted while designing the access sequences in Figure 9.74 and the overall sales pricing procedure.

9.7.5 Integration with Local Ledgers

You need to integrate the postings that occur in non-SAP systems or in other SAP ERP applications that are not integrated online. To interpret those postings in the GL, you need to indicate the debit and credit indicators for the local ledgers. Using Transaction OBBT, you can define the posting keys as 40 (debit) and 50 (credit) for local ledgers. The transaction key is GLU.

This covers all the important settings that you need to make to ensure that your financial statements are consistent and online. It is very important that you interact with your logistics implementing team during the definition and design of their accounts. Otherwise, you might be saddled with complex workarounds for your financial statements

Next you will learn about some of the key tools and techniques to help you during the migration from your legacy systems to the new GL.

9.8 Preparation of Productive Start

Productive start is the culmination of all your hard work when you actually go-live with SAP ERP. The production preparation or cutover phase is typically when you burn the midnight oil in getting the system ready for live operation. SAP ERP arms you with important tools that will help you in the installation preparation. In this section, you will learn the tools for activating the new GL on a new installation or converting the classic GL to the new GL. Let's first take a look at a new installation, which does not have the classic GL implemented.

9.8.1 New Installation

When you are installing a new SAP ERP solution, you might need to practice your data loads and transaction loads over and over again. SAP ERP allows you to quickly delete all your master data and transaction data. In addition, SAP ERP provides a data transfer workbench that allows you to manage your data migration activities. The discussion of data migration activities is beyond this book. Refer to other SAP PRESS books for a more detailed understanding of data migration activities. You can see the screen for executing these transactions in Figure 9.77. You can follow the menu path **IMG • Financial Accounting (New) • General Ledger Accounting (new) • Prepare for Productive Start • New Installation**.

Figure 9.77 New Installation Toolset for the New GL

We will discuss these transactions in detail in this section. First let's take a look at transactions to delete the GL master data.

Delete the GL account

Using this transaction code, you can delete the GL master data from the system. The transaction is shown in Figure 9.78. The menu path is **IMG • Financial Accounting (New) • General Ledger Accounting (new) • Pre-**

pare for Productive Start • New Installation • Delete Test Data • Delete Master Data • Delete G/L Account, and the transaction code is OBR2.

The selection parameters for the transaction are shown in Figure 9.78. As you can see, you can delete the GL accounts by selecting the **Delete G/L accounts** checkbox. You can choose to enter a particular range also if you want to delete only a particular range of GL accounts. You can also maintain the **Deletion depth.** You can choose to delete the GL master data only for a particular company code or for a particular chart of accounts by entering the appropriate chart of accounts and company codes respectively by checking the option **Only general master data** or **With general master data..**

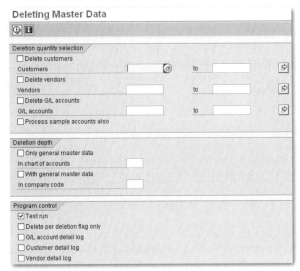

Figure 9.78 Delete GL Account, Customers, and Vendors

Delete Chart of Accounts

The chart of accounts can also be deleted by following the menu path **IMG • Financial Accounting (New) • General Ledger Accounting (new) • Prepare for Productive Start • New Installation • Delete Test Data • Delete Master Data • Delete Chart of Accounts** or by using Transaction OBY8. Before deleting the chart of accounts, you can also check the **Deletion Capability.** This allows you to check whether it is possible to delete the chart of accounts.

Now that you understand how you can delete the GL master data, let's take a look at the tools that enable you to reset the transaction data. First you learn how to annihilate data in a company code.

Delete Company Code Data: Transaction OBR1

Using this transaction code, you can delete all the company code data. This allows you to not only test and test again by generating new data, but it also is a lifesaver if somehow the wrong file gets loaded or a partial file gets loaded and you want to start fresh instead of finding the records that did not get loaded.

Figure 9.79 shows the selection parameters for deleting the data in a company code. You need to enter the **Company code**, identify the parameters for deletion, and then click the execute button (the icon which looks like a clock). It is always prudent to use **Test run** at least a couple of times to see whether everything is okay for you to delete the data.

Note

Back in the day, **Suppress repetitive warnings** (see Figure 9.79) was not available, so we used *quarter technology* (insert a quarter between your Enter button on your keyboard so that Enter remains pressed, and go get your coffee or tea) to automatically press Enter when the next screen came up.

Figure 9.79 Delete Company Code Data

Real-World Example

One day before go-live, I loaded a file with 20,000 records in a company code in production. Unfortunately, the debit and credit signs in the file were wrong. So, while all my numbers matched to the penny, the signs were wrong. The only solution was to use the delete company code data transaction and obliterate everything, start fresh, and load the file again with the correct signs. This is a huge lifesaver, if you know how to use it. However, there have been instances when someone used this transaction and deleted everything, causing huge problems. So use this very carefully in situations that make sense.

Delete Transaction Data from Ledgers

Using Transaction GLDE, you can delete the data from all the ledgers. Now this transaction was earlier used only in the perspective of the special purpose ledger. However, with the introduction of the new GL, this has become more significant and useful. Figure 9.80 shows the selection parameters for deleting transaction data along with the deletion scope and processing options. So you can delete by **Ledger, Record Type, Version Company Code**, **Reference Transact.**, **Business Transaction**, **Fiscal Year,** and **Period**. You can choose to delete the **Totals records**, **Actual line items,** or **Plan Line items**. You can also run the program in **Test run** before executing it for real.

Figure 9.80 Delete Transaction Data by Ledgers

Set Company Code to Productive

This is one of the most important settings that should be part of the cutover checklist. As part of the cutover, after the data is successfully loaded, it is very important to ensure that no mass deletions of data occur. After you have gone live, you need to set the company code as productive to prevent you from accidentally deleting any data. So this is the opposite of what you were trying to accomplish in the previous steps. The menu path is **IMG • Financial Accounting (New) • General Ledger Accounting (new) • Prepare for Productive Start • New Installation • Set Company Code to Productive**.

Now that you understand some of the key tools and techniques that help you in smoothing wrinkles during go-live, let's take a look at how you can implement the new GL if the classic GL is already implemented.

9.8.2 Migrating the Old GL to the New GL

The new GL was introduced only from ERP 2004 onward. Most of the existing installations are on the classic GL, so you can use a set of utilities to transition from the classic ledger to the new ledger. In this subsection, you will learn about these utilities along with the typical structure of a new GL implementation. The new GL implementation should be treated like an upgrade project, which has the same set of stages as a normal SAP ERP upgrade project from project preparation to go-live and support. The key aspects and phases of implementing the new GL are listed here:

1. Identify requirements from document splitting perspective as part of the business blueprint phase.

2. Decide whether to include document splitting in phase 1 of the project.

3. Finalize the ledgers of originating balances. It is important to correctly identify from which ledger the balances are transferred to the new GL. Ensure that you have reports to validate that the data from the old GL and the new GL matches.

4. Analyze the dimensions that need to be added in the new GL. Also determine the source of these dimensions. Identify the approach to load dimensions in scenarios where dimensions are not available in existing ledgers.

5. Transition to the new GL by converting all the previous balances and run the old GL in parallel until the end of the fiscal year. Activation of the new GL is done at this stage.

6. Compare the old GL to the new GL in the parallel period, analyze any differences between them, and reconcile them.

7. Switch off the old GL at the end of the fiscal year.

This process outlines some of the important aspects of migrating to the new GL from the classic GL. Next, you will learn about the toolkit that you can use to help you plan the migration effort.

Migrating Old GL to New GL Project Plan Cockpit

SAP ERP comes prebuilt with the project plan to manage your new GL upgrade using the closing cockpit (Transaction CLOCO_MIG). You will learn about closing cockpit more in Chapter 10 when we discuss month-end close. The closing cockpit can be used to retrieve the migration plan with or without document splitting. Figure 9.81 shows the screen where you can choose the migration plan with or without document splitting. If you choose to implement document splitting, choose **Migration Plans with Document Splitting**.

Figure 9.81 Migration Plan Selection With or Without Document Splitting

After you execute this, click on **Template/Task List,** click on **Other Template/Task List,** and then select **0_MIG_MBA1** as the task list with document splitting. **0_MIG_OBA1** is the one without document splitting. Figure 9.82 shows the closing cockpit for migration with document splitting. The left pane shows the organizational structure, whereas the right pane shows the details of the tasks along with the timelines.

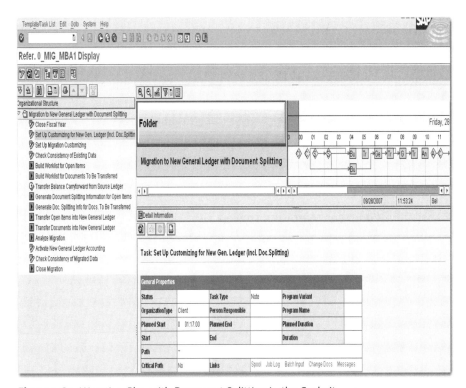

Figure 9.82 Migration Plan with Document Splitting in the Cockpit

Because you cannot read through the list of tasks (shown in Figure 9.82) that need to be executed for the new GL, conversion with document splitting is shown separately in Figure 9.83.

Figure 9.83 List of Tasks for New General Ledger Migration Plan: With Document Splitting

The task list without document splitting is detailed in Figure 9.84.

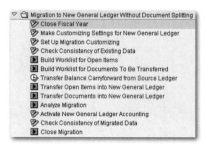

Figure 9.84 List of Tasks for the New General Ledger Migration: Without Document Splitting

Transaction Codes for Migrating to New GL

Table 9.3 gives you the list of transaction codes by migration activity along with their descriptions. You can use these as and when you need, depending on your company's requirements.

Migration Activity	Transaction Code	Transaction Code Description
Worklist	FAGL_MIG_OPFILL	Create worklist for creating open items
Worklist	FAGL_MIG_RPFILL	Create worklist for documents
Open items from previous years	FAGL_MIG_CRESPLIT	Process document splitting information for open items
Open items from previous years	FAGL_MIG_RE-POST_OP	Create Gl line items and balance carryforward
Document transfer from current year	FAGL_CHECK_AC-COUNT:	Check GL accounts for document splitting
Document transfer from current year	FAGL_CHECK_DOC_TYPE:	Check document types for document splitting
Document transfer from current year	FAGL_CHECK_LINE-TYPE:	Check business transaction assignment for migration documents
Document transfer from current year	FAGL_MIG_SPLIT:	Build document splitting information
Document transfer from current year	FAGL_MIG_REPOST:	Transfer documents to new GL accounting
Balance carryforward	FAGL_UPL_CF	Transfer balance carryforward
Balance carryforward	FAGL_MIG_REPORT_SUM	Display log of balance carryforward
Balance carryforward	FAGL_DEL	Reset balance carryforward
Balance carryforward	FBB1	Repost balance carryforward manually
Evaluation of migration	FAGL_MIG_STATUS	Display migration status
Evaluation of migration	GCAC:	Compare ledgers
Evaluation of migration	FAGL_MIG_ADJUST	Display log of migration specific document adjustment
Evaluation of migration	FAGL_MIG_SHOW_SPL	Display document splitting results
Evaluation of migration	FAGL_MIG_SIM_SPL	Simulate document splitting
End migration	FAGL_MIG_FINISH	Complete migration
Reset migration plan	FAGL_MIG_RE-STORE_ALL	Reset migration plan

Table 9.3 Transaction Codes for New GL Migration

9.9 Summary

In this chapter, you learned about one of the most important parts of Financial Accounting: the GL. You learned how you can use the new and improved GL to support statutory and management-level reporting. In addition, you learned how to optimize your financial reporting and to reduce the number of ledgers by using new functionalities.

An SAP ERP Financials perspective is needed to understand the end-to-end business scenario, which is typically missing from the logistics team. So this chapter introduced you to GL integration with MM, SD, AA, and payroll and how to play the important role of integrating all the process requirements together for account determination. You were also introduced to the general master data and how to use the GL structure to generate customized financial statements to fulfill local versus global consolidation requirements.

Finally, the steps for undertaking a transition from the classic GL to the new GL were detailed. Prior to the new GL, there were multiple versions of the same information that required time and effort to reconcile. The new GL gives you one integrated platform, getting rid of scattered ledgers such as cost of sales and other custom ledgers that you might have had to create. Despite all these enhancements, the new GL has the same interface, which allows the end user to see minimal change.

In Chapter 10, you will learn how to use these tools along with some new techniques to achieve faster closes in SAP ERP Financials.

Month-end close is fraught with many connotations. Most accountants consider it a curse that repeats month after month without fail, and then just to add to the fun, it becomes complex during quarters and then even more complex during year end. Just when you finish one month-end, here comes another. Fortunately, the SAP General Ledger (GL) can help alleviate the pain and smooth it out over the month. You also get access to fun tools such as the closing cockpit, which helps you apply a method to the madness.

10   Achieving Faster Closes

Your company's ability to survive is tested daily in this ever-competitive marketplace. However, your quarterly report card might make or break your company's executive management. One of the key value drivers of an SAP ERP Financials implementation is to achieve faster closes. Take a look at any business case, and you will find that a faster close is what everybody wants. Closing books earlier and faster enables the executive management to understand the ground realities earlier and allows them to plan and maneuver the company in the right direction. It also allows you to establish an earlier dialogue with your shareholders. SAP ERP Financials allow you to achieve faster closes, facilitated by the integrated nature of SAP ERP. In many implementations, the month-end close process has been reduced from close to 10 days to 2 or 3 days, and that is what gives an accountant a high.

This chapter describes the tools and techniques to achieve faster closes using SAP ERP Financials. First you will learn about the month-end closing checklist in general, and then you will learn the importance of segregating these into daily, monthly, or periodic activities. After becoming familiar with typical month-end activities, you will learn about the toolkits available in SAP ERP Financials to optimally manage your month-end processes. Now all the period end closing activities across all the modules can be managed in one place using the closing cockpit. The closing cockpit replaces all the available Excel sheets that you so arduously made in painstaking detail. But the rigor and discipline is still required to manage your month-end closing process. After you are familiar with the tools, you will learn the functionalities that need to be managed on a monthly basis.

First let's learn about the SAP ERP Financials month-end closing checklist.

10.1 Month-End Closing Checklist

The month-end process is the administrative process of closing the financial books of a company. Key to evolving a month-end process is to identify the month-end closing checklist. Before we go into the month-end closing process, let's understand the root cause of why the month-end close is so hard. It typically suffers from the following problems:

▸ More time is spent in collecting information rather than analyzing information.

▸ There is no well-defined month-end process.

▸ No well-defined roles are identified.

As more and more organizations are geographically dispersed across continents, it becomes very difficult to manage the overall month-end process if problems are not discovered earlier and fixed earlier. Other key administrative issues that result in an elongated month-end are the following:

▸ Too many manual processes.

▸ Duplicated data across different modules and systems.

▸ Lack of standardization across global reporting.

▸ Lack of clock work precision in closing processes.

▸ More effort needed to get data rather than analyze information.

▸ No clear understanding of the status of the month-end by all participants.

All these issues can be resolved by doing the following:

▸ Communicating common process standards by identifying applicable accounting principles and disbursing common templates and sufficient documentation at each process step.

▸ Having a central status information on month-end process.

▸ Constantly monitoring the closing process and identifying any scope of improvement.

You can also make a conscious decision to steer the organization in the right direction by doing the following:

▸ Reduce the flux in reporting by following common accounting principles across the organization.

▸ Use ECCS or BW to enable central administration of the closing data.

- Reduce the time taken by stacking the closing activities throughout the month instead of the last week.

- Automate as many processes as possible per a schedule in a batch job. This takes the manual intervention away and helps focus the group toward common goals.

The month-end process identifies the operating rhythm of the financial organization by identifying the following:

- SAP ERP Financials transactions (reports, programs, batch jobs, variants, etc.).

- Interfaces to and from the legacy system.

- Sequence and interdependencies.

Typically, in every implementation, you need to come up with a master Excel sheet that is the gospel for the financial processes on a daily, weekly, and monthly basis. The most important thing is the assignment of roles to each task. These assignments can be uploaded via Excel or loaded as favorites.

10.1.1 Daily Review and Audit

You need to focus more on quality control that does not have to wait until the month-end to clean up. Month end essentially is an ongoing activity that can happen throughout the month, and ideally should start at the first of the month. Don't wait for things to happen during the month and then clean them up at month-end. It is important that month-end is driven by processes and not dependent on consultant support. To ensure a smooth month-end, it is very important to operationally (transaction codes are in parentheses) do the following:

- Identify the list of batch jobs daily, weekly, and monthly, and whether they actually ran as scheduled.

- Improve nonfinancial processes.

- Check the GR/IR (goods received/invoices received) account and other clearing accounts for items that have not yet been cleared.

- Make sure accounts that are automatically posted only do not get any manual postings.

- Identify documents blocked for billing (V. 23) or invoices (MRBR).

- Identify documents that have not been transferred to accounting (VFX3).

- Identify credit blocks on a daily basis (VKM1).

- Identify noted items and parked documents that have not been posted (FV65).

- Identify any special GL transactions in AP and AR.

- Identify any additional rollups that are supposed to happen for consolidation and other ledgers.

The idea is to make the schedule for month-end operational at a task level. The next step is to identify a process owner for each task. This is especially important in an integrated environment where organizations cross over multiple SAP ERP modules.

Tips

- Communicate what the AP department owns versus what the purchasing department owns.

- Appoint an overall month-end process owner who monitors all the tasks and is typically the person who manages the consolidation functions.

10.1.2 Month-End Processes

The typical tasks for a month-end process checklist include the following:

- Opening of new posting period by vendor, customer, assets, and GL
- Final goods issue
- Final invoice posting
- Depreciation run
- Settlement of assets under construction (AuC) to assets
- Cost assessments and distributions
- Accruals and provisions
- Salary journals
- Currency revaluation
- Reconcile ledgers
- Consolidation activities
- Budgetary cycle administration

SAP ERP provides multiple tools such as schedule manager and closing cockpit to support the month-end process and design the month-end checklist. You will learn in detail about the closing cockpit as it is more attuned to the closing process per se and is an extension of the schedule manager Figure

10.1 illustrates the process of configuring the closing cockpit along with the special closing processes that need to be executed at month-end.

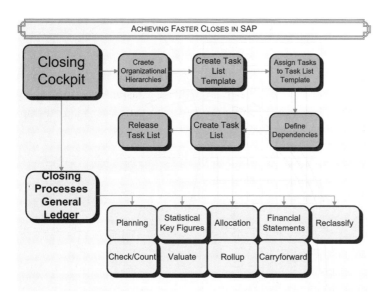

Figure 10.1 Achieving Faster Closes in SAP

You will first learn the process of defining your own closing cockpit, which is the latest functionality introduced in SAP ERP

10.2 The Closing Cockpit

In the previous section, you learned that one of the basic problems in existing month-end processes is disaggregated processes that are geographically dispersed. The closing cockpit in SAP ERP allows you to optimally structure your closing process by providing the following:

▶ One common status tracking mechanism

▶ Common templates and guidelines that everyone can use

▶ Ability to assign roles and responsibilities for each task

▶ Dependency information related to closing process

10.2.1 Configuring Closing Cockpit

The closing cockpit can be configured directly from the SAP ERP user menu as shown in Figure 10.2. The menu path is **SAP Menu • Accounting • Financial Accounting • General Ledger • Periodic Processing • Closing •**

Closing Cockpit (Manage Templates and Task Lists), and the Transaction is CLOCOC.

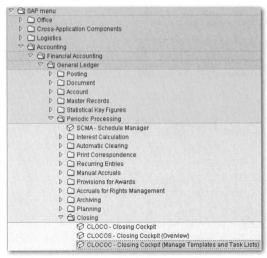

Figure 10.2 Configuring the Closing Cockpit

The various structural objects available in the closing cockpit to support the closing process are as follows:

▶ **Hierarchies**

This is used to display the organizational objects involved in the closing process. For example, relevant company code, controlling area, and operating concern need to be identified for the month-end processes.

▶ **Task List Template**

You can use the preconfigured templates, one for month-end and one for year end, to create your own templates for the task lists. However, you need to define your own custom templates tailored to your needs.

▶ **Task Lists**

This is derived from the template and is extremely crucial for the successful definition of month-end close. Task lists identify the task, such as executing depreciation run, run allocation cycles, and so on.

▶ **Monitor**

This shows visually the dependencies between various tasks and when they are supposed to begin and end. Monitor allows you to sequence the tasks and identify the window in which you need to perform your month-end activities. This is the dashboard of all the tasks that need to be executed and provides you with a status of the individual tasks in a visual form.

▶ **Detailed Information**

This can be used to add relevant information pertaining to background jobs, spool information, and so on. Any documentation and other details can also be captured here.

▶ **Dependencies**

Here you can define the dependencies between the tasks. This is the key to building an effective month-end process by identifying when you will be executing each of these individual tasks.

> **Note**
>
> You need to come up with your own template for month-end close. However, it is important that you capture all the broad elements of the standard template because this has been prepared by SAP AG based on the best practices associated with month-end closing processes and contains the breakdown of all the month-end processes by application areas.

10.2.2 Standard Templates and Closing Cockpit

Let's take a look at the standard templates and closing cockpit after you execute CLOCOC:

1. Choose the template you want to use for your closing process.

2. Click on **Template/Task List**.

3. Choose **Other Template or Task List**.

4. Find the templates as shown in Figure 10.3.

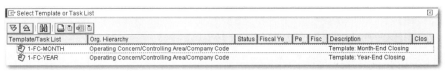

Figure 10.3 Templates Available in SAP

Let's take a look at the monthly template first. The structure of the closing cockpit can be divided in following sections, as shown in Figure 10.4:

▶ **Organizational Structure** along with the transaction and task list

▶ List display of the task selected in **Organizational Structure**

▶ Monitor to show the dependencies

▶ **Detail information**, which shows the **Person Responsible**, **Planned Duration**, and links to **Spool**, **Batch Input**, and so on

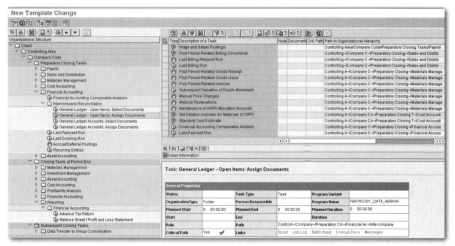

Figure 10.4 Closing Cockpit: Defining a New Template

Figure 10.4 shows the details of the organization structure on the left pane. As you might have noticed, this follows the SAP User menu. However, you can see the typical activities such as **Intercompany Reconciliation** with task level details of **General Ledger—Open items: Assign Documents**. Figure 10.5 shows you details of the left pane you saw in Figure 10.4.

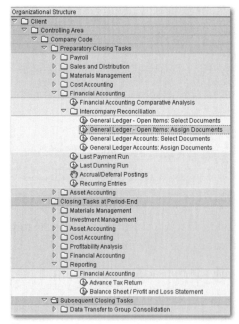

Figure 10.5 Identifying Tasks to the Template

As you can see from Figure 10.5, first you see the organizational hierarchy starting from **Client** to **Controlling Area** to **Company Code**. After that, the month-end tasks are divided into the following groups:

▸ Preparatory Closing Tasks

▸ Closing Tasks at Period-End

▸ Subsequent Closing Tasks

> **Note**
>
> It is very important to define preparatory closing tasks carefully so that you can minimize the workload during month-end. For example, if you schedule your payment run every Friday, and the month-end closing happens to be on Friday, it would make sense to schedule the payment run earlier so that you are not saddled with too many routine activities during the month-end time frame. In addition, if you make sure that you perform a daily audit, then you can catch any accounting glitches early and resolve them earlier. Otherwise, those things keep piling on.

Figure 10.6 shows the detailed task view in the task list which was shown in the right-hand pane in Figure 10.4.

Type	Description of a Task	Note	Document	Crit. Path	Path in Org. Hierarchy	Task	Variant	Processor	Person Responsible	Role	Offst/Time
	Wage and Salary Postings				Controlling Area/Company C						0 00:00:00
	Post Period-Related Billing Documents				Controlling-/Company C-/P						0 00:00:00
	Last Billing Request Run				Controlling-/Company C-/P	DP95					0 00:00:00
	Last Billing Run				Controlling-/Company C-/P	RV60SBT1					0 00:00:00
	Post Period-Related Goods Receipt				Controlling A-/Company C-/	MIGO					0 00:00:00
	Post Period-Related Goods Issue				Controlling A-/Company C-/	MIGO					0 00:00:00
	Post Period-Related Invoices				Controlling A-/Company C-/	MIRO					0 00:00:00
	Subsequent Valuation of Goods Movement				Controlling A-/Company C-/	RM07MWBU					0 00:00:00
	Manual Price Changes				Controlling A-/Company C-/	MR21					0 00:00:00
	Material Revaluations				Controlling A-/Company C-/	MR22					0 00:00:00
	Maintenance of GR/IR Allocation Accounts				Controlling A-/Company C-/	MR11					0 00:00:00
	Set Deletion Indicator for Materials (CO/PP)				Controlling A-/Company Co-						0 00:00:00
	Standard Cost Estimate				Controlling A-/Company Co-						0 00:00:00
	Financial Accounting Comparative Analysis				Controlling A-/Company C-/	SAPF190					0 00:00:00
	Last Payment Run				Controlling A-/Company C-/	SAPF110S					0 00:00:00
	Last Dunning Run				Controlling A-/Company C-/	SAPF150S					0 00:00:00

Figure 10.6 Detailing a Task in the Task List

The following aspects need to be populated for a task in the task list:

▸ Task type

▸ Description of the task

▸ Notes

▸ Documentation pertaining to the task

▸ Critical path applicability

▸ Path in organization hierarchy

▸ Task program/transaction code

- ▶ Variant
- ▶ Task processor
- ▶ Person responsible
- ▶ Authorization role
- ▶ Time of the task

You can toggle between the task list and the monitor by clicking on **Go To • Toggle between Monitor and List Display**. The monitor is displayed in Figure 10.7.

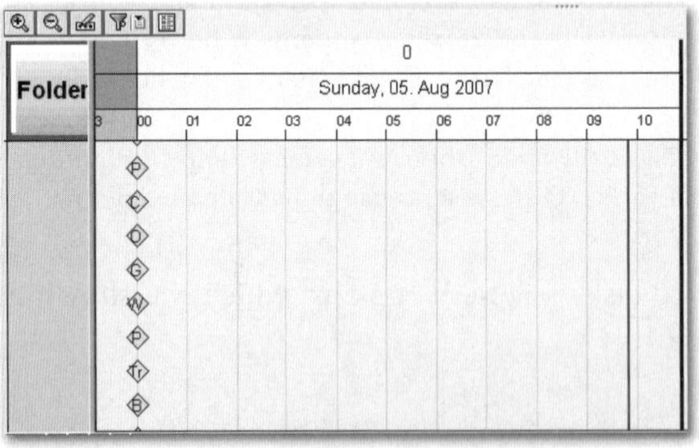

Figure 10.7 Displaying the Monitor and the TimeLine

The details of a particular task list (**General Ledger—Open Items: Select Documents**) can be modified by changing the same in the detail information grid shown in Figure 10.8. The key things that you will want to add to this can be added by detailing the tasks while creating the task list.

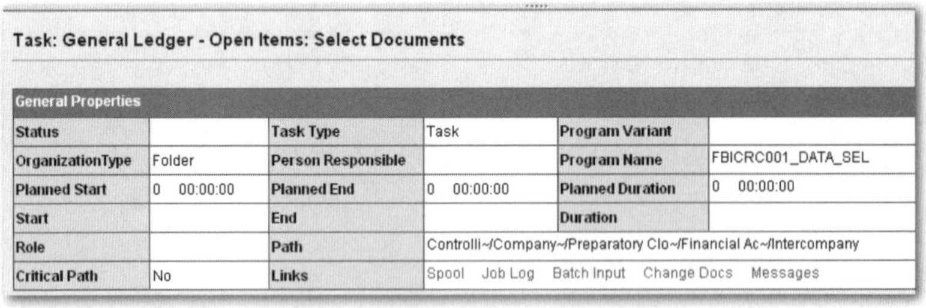

Task: General Ledger - Open Items: Select Documents

General Properties					
Status		Task Type	Task	Program Variant	
OrganizationType	Folder	Person Responsible		Program Name	FBICRC001_DATA_SEL
Planned Start	0 00:00:00	Planned End	0 00:00:00	Planned Duration	0 00:00:00
Start		End		Duration	
Role		Path	Controlli~/Company~/Preparatory Clo~/Financial Ac~/Intercompany		
Critical Path	No	Links	Spool Job Log Batch Input Change Docs Messages		

Figure 10.8 Adding Details to a Task

> **Note**
>
> You can register new transactions and programs in the cockpit via the schedule manager tables: SCMAPROGRAMS for programs and SCMATRANSACT for transactions.

You can create a task plan by defining the following:

▸ Key date

▸ Closing type: month-end, quarter end, year end, or special closing

▸ Fiscal year and posting period

Tasks can be categorized and tracked per the task types and processing statuses shown in Figure 10.9.

Figure 10.9 Task Types and Processing Status of Each Task, Including Symbols

The next step is to define the dependencies between the various tasks by clicking on the **Dependencies** button just below the detail information shown in Figure 10.10.

Figure 10.10 Defining Dependencies

You can just drag and drop tasks that should happen first or are linked to the task that you are detailing. To create a task list and assign it to a task list template, go to change template via **Edit • Display or Change**. You can add tasks by clicking on **Template/Task List • Create Task List**. This allows you to enter parameters related to a fiscal year variant, key date, and posting period for the **Task List** as shown in Figure 10.11.

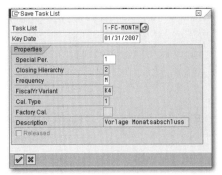

Figure 10.11 Creating a New Task List within a Template

Similarly, you can also create a new task plan that houses the task list as shown in Figure 10.12. You have to release this task list so that it can be used in the closing cockpit.

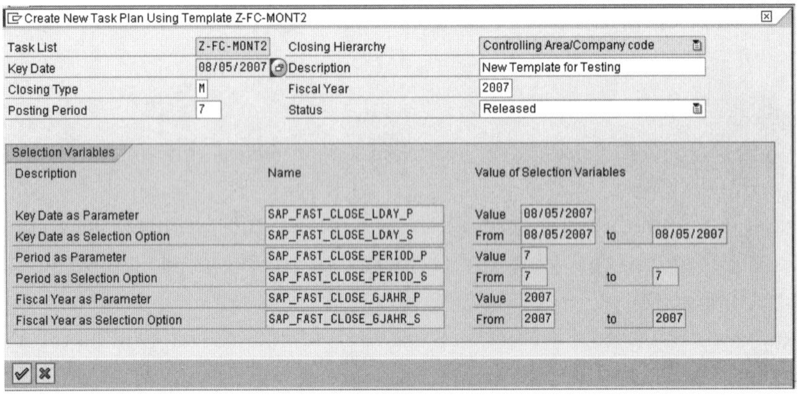

Figure 10.12 New Task Plan for creating Task List

After you set the status of the task list as released, you can see it in CLOCO (the closing cockpit transaction). Figure 10.13 shows you the cockpit after the task list has been released.

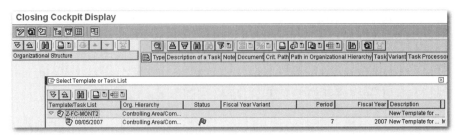

Figure 10.13 Closing Cockpit Display After the Task List Has Been Released

The most important aspect of the closing cockpit is to be able to identify the progress of the closing process in one place. So instead of Excel sheets that tracked the sequence and list of activities, you can now use the closing cockpit to organize, sequence, communicate, and monitor all the month-end closing processes.

Next, you will learn about the closing processes that are processed only in the GL.

10.3 Closing Processes

Multiple personnel are responsible for the closing processes across the Finance department and nonfinance departments as well. For instance, AP will own the vendor balance carryforward process in the year-end close. However, the closing processes are the responsibility of the owner of the GL who ensures that all the activities are executed according to the plan. The focus of this section is to learn the period-end activities that are part of the GL close.

10.3.1 Planning Process

As part of the new GL, the planning process has been modified to include the allocation cycles of assessment and distribution. Allocation cycles will be covered separately. Prior to the new GL, the planning process was very narrow. FSE5N and FSE6N were used to enter the plan for a particular ledger and then display the plan, respectively. However, with the new GL, the scope of planning has expanded. Planning can be used to generate additional reporting related to budgeting and forecasts. Follow this menu path: **Accounting • Financial Accounting • General Ledger • Periodic Processing • Planning**. Figure 10.14 shows you a list of the transaction codes that can be used for planning in the GL.

Figure 10.14 Planning Process

The planning process for the GL is shown in Figure 10.15.

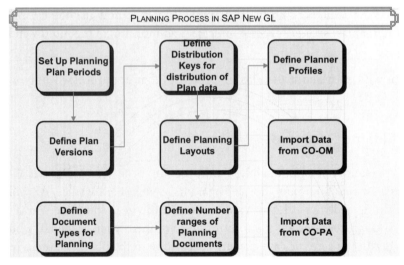

Figure 10.15 Defining Planning Process in the New GL

The following are the key aspects of planning in GL:

- Periods must be stored in planning and should follow a similar structure as actuals.
- Multiple versions can be specified in GL planning, similar to controlling. Actuals are maintained in version 0.
- Define the distribution keys for the distribution of plan data.
- The define planning layouts details the content structure in the planning screen.
- SAPFAGL is the standard planning profile. This defines which layouts are available in the profile.
- For define planning document types, you must define a separate document category for the planning process.

You can also transfer the data directly from CO-OM and CO-PA to transfer the planning process to the new GL.

10.3.2 Statistical Key Figures

Statistical key figure (SKF) is a functionality that was only used in Controlling to allocate costs. However, with the introduction of segments in the new GL, the same functionality has been extended to the GL. However, the user interface for maintaining the SKF is still similar to controlling. SKF provides information about the nonmonetary data of an organization that influences the planning process and is used in the allocation step as well. Typical examples for an SKF are the following:

- Employee headcount
- Number of laptops and desktops
- Square meters of office space

These can be used in reporting controlling information such as sales per employee, personnel costs per employee, and so on. In addition, the more common use is in assessment and distribution cycles. The master data of SKF is set up in cost center accounting and requires controlling area, unit of measure, and identification whether it represents a fixed value or total values.

Using this, you can plan how many employees you will be having six months from now and what that means as far as administrative expenses are concerned. So you can plan the expenses as well as allocate them by department.

10.3.3 Allocation

Prior to the new GL, allocation was restricted to Controlling only. Traditionally, allocation is defined as the assessment or distribution of costs from one cost object to another cost object per predefined rules. However, from ERP 2005 onward, the new GL can also be used for allocation among segments, which is an additional dimension that has been introduced with the new GL. This allows you to represent the correct values by segment.

Note
Although you can do cost center allocations from the GL, it should be used for allocations for profit center and segment only because the new GL allocations do not take care of complex scenarios.

Allocations are used to allocate values from one or more senders to one or more receivers. This can be done in the actuals and/or plan as well. For example, let's say that you incurred 10,000 USD on administration costs. At the time of recording these costs, you entered a default segment that collected all the costs. Now to understand the true profitability of a business segment, these costs should be allocated to the correct segments by some business rule such as the number of employees in department (SKF) or some formula that makes sense. So you can use allocations to divide this 10,0000 USD into five business units per the total employees that belong to those five units.

The difference between assessment and distribution is the same as the terminology in controlling allocation cycles. Distribution is posted with the original account without any aggregation. In assessment, you aggregate the costs to an assessment account and then the costs are allocated to the receivers. In distribution, the original account traceability is maintained, whereas in distribution, the traceability is lost.

Figure 10.16 shows you the process of defining the allocation for the new GL. The first step is to define whether you want to allocate using assessment or via distribution. Then you define the sender and receiver rules that define the amount, percentages, and portions.

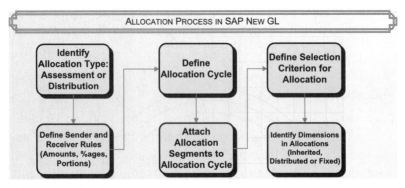

Figure 10.16 Allocation Process

After you have identified the settlement rules, you need to define the allocation cycle and then attach allocation segments to the allocation cycle. You also need to define the selection criterion for the allocation and identify the dimensions in allocations. In the next subsection, you will learn more about financial statements.

10.3.4 Financial Statements

Financial statement versions can be created to customize the balance sheet view per your requirements. You can define the financial statement versions that are then used to prepare and structure the balance sheet or profit and loss statement per your format. This allows you to create one global design of your financial statement. However, you can design multiple financial statements to fulfill local statutory reporting requirements. So if your company is based out of the United States but has operations in India, you can create one global version and one separate version per the Indian requirements. This allows the Indian subsidiary to run both the versions and make sure that they are in sync. The menu path is **IMG • Accounting • Financial Accounting • General Ledger • Periodic Processing • Document • Define Financial Statement versions**, and the Transaction is OB58. In the system, there are reference financial statements available that can be copied and referenced as the starting point. These statement versions can then be run in various financial reports.

On executing OB58, you will see a screen, which displays all the financial statement versions applicable. As an example, let's look at the BAUS (the basic US financial statement version). After you double-click on the **BAUS,** you will see the screen shown in Figure 10.17. Here you can define the maintenance language and chart of accounts. You can also choose to allow the group account numbers and functional areas to be entered in the financial statements. If you select the **Item keys auto.** checkbox, then the system automatically generates an item key as you create your own version.

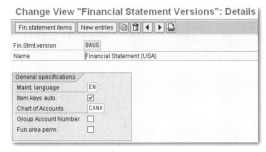

Figure 10.17 Financial Statement Version: BAUS

Figure 10.18 shows you the detailed financial statement version. On each statement, you can create as many groupings as you want. The lowest level assignment is the GL account. The broad groupings are **ASSETS, LIABILITIES**, and **PROFIT & LOSS STATEMENT**. The subgroupings are also detailed. These are **Cash and Cash Equivalents** and then **Petty Cash** under **ASSETS**, for instance. Finally, the GL master record **Cash Desk** is assigned under the **Petty Cash** heading.

> **Note**
>
> The creation of financial statements was also discussed in detail in Chapter 9 (Section 9.3).

In the next subsection, you will learn how to reclassify your GR/IR clearing accounts at month-end.

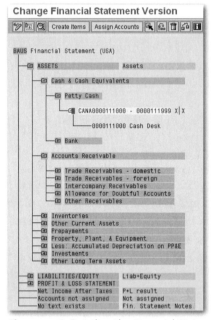

Figure 10.18 Detailing the Financial Statement Version

10.3.5 Reclassify

In this step, reclassification of balances is done for the open items in the GR/IR clearing account. Reclassification of balances allows you to automate the management of your GR/IR account at month-end. This step helps in correctly representing the GR/IR clearing account in the following situations:

▸ Goods are delivered, but the invoice not received (Transaction GNB)

▸ Invoiced but goods not received (Transaction BNG)

In both cases, the system posts an entry to the adjustment account, and an offsetting entry is posted to the target account, which can be configured separately for these two scenarios. The posting is done by reconciliation account on the last day of the month and is reversed on the first day of the month. The menu path is **SAP Menu • Accounting • Financial Accounting • General Ledger • Periodic Processing • Closing • Reclassify • GR/IR Clearing**, and the Transaction F.19.

Figure 10.19 shows you the selection parameters for reclassifying the GR/IR clearing accounts. As you can see, you can reclassify a range of GR/IR

G/L accounts by **Company code** in the **G/L account** selection tab. In the **Parameters tab,** you need to identify a **Clearing Date** and check the **GR/IR Clearing** box.

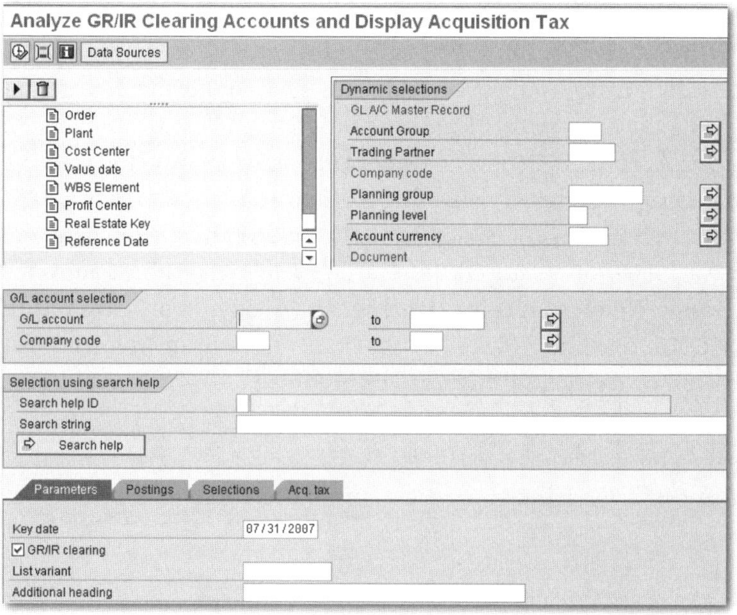

Figure 10.19 Analyze GR/IR Clearing Accounts

If you select the **Postings** tab, you can specify the parameters for posting the GR/IR as shown in Figure 10.20. If you click in **Create Postings**, then the system posts the transaction on execution. You can enter the **Ledger Group, Document date** as **07/31/2007**, **Document type, Posting date** as **07/31/2007**, and **Reversal posting date 08/01/2007**. In addition, you can also maintain the **Posting header text**.

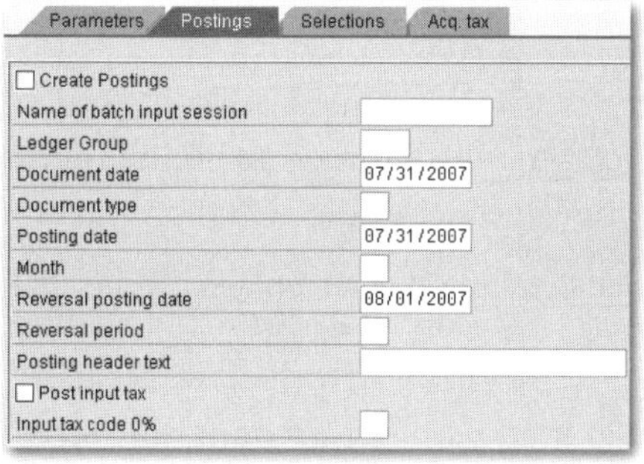

Figure 10.20 Enter Posting Parameters for GR/IR Clearing

565

Now that you understand how you can execute the transaction with selection parameters, let's take a look at configuring the GL adjustment accounts and a detailed scenario to explain the adjustment process from the accounting perspective.

Define Adjustment Accounts for GR/IR Clearing

First you will learn how to configure the adjustment accounts that will get hit when you execute the analyze GR/IR clearing program. Follow the menu path **IMG • Financial Accounting (new) • General Ledger Accounting (new) • Periodic Processing • Reclassify • Define Adjustment account for GR/IR Clearing**, or use Transaction OBYP. Figure 10.21 shows the screen where you can maintain the GL accounts for GR/IR clearing. The transaction **Group** for this is **WRV Goods/invoices receipt clearing**. The two types of **Transaction** keys, **BNG** or **GNB**, depend on whether the goods have been **Invoiced but not yet delivered** or **Delivered but not yet invoiced**.

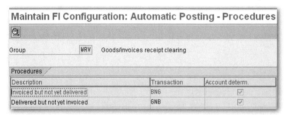

Figure 10.21 Configuring GR/IR Reclassification Automatic Posting

Figure 10.22 shows the screen for maintaining the GL accounts for goods **Delivered but not yet invoiced**. Here you can define the reconciliation account, adjustment account, and target account.

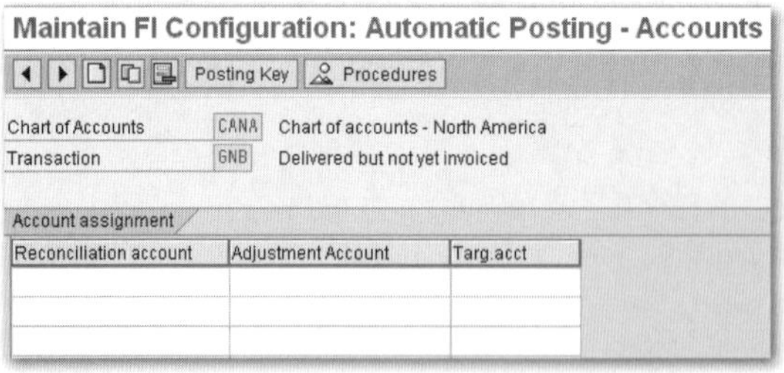

Figure 10.22 Enter the Reconciliation Account and Corresponding Adjustment Account and Target Account

To understand the difference between the adjustment account and target account, look at the following scenario.

A Sample Scenario

If goods were received, but the invoice was not fully received or was partially received, then the following sequence of events will occur. When you receive the goods, the following accounting entry is made:

- **Posting Date: 07/15/2007**
  - *Dr. Inventory 100 USD*
  - *Cr GR/IR Account 100 USD*

If you did not receive the invoice at all, the following accounting entry is made at month-end:

- **Posting Date: 07/31/2007**
  - *Dr. GR/IR Adjustment Account 100 USD*
  - *Cr GR/IR Target Account 100 USD*

Another accounting entry is made on the first of the next month, which nullifies the preceding entry:

- **Posting Date: 08/01/2007**
  - *Dr. GR/IR Target Account 100 USD*
  - *Cr GR/IR Adjustment Account 100 USD*

10.3.6 Check/Count

Check/count refers to the process of validating that the ledgers reconcile with each other. The reconciliation of ledgers is done by comparing the ledgers to ensure that because of some update database termination, the ledgers are not out of sync. These are basically sanity checks to ensure that the subledger ties to the GL. The menu path is **SAP Menu • Accounting • Financial Accounting • General Ledger • Periodic Processing • Closing • Check/Count**. Figure 10.23 shows the transactions for comparing ledgers. This step requires no configuration.

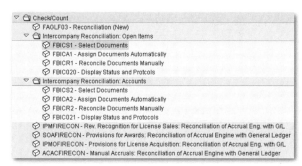

Figure 10.23 Transactions to Reconcile Ledgers

On executing these programs, transaction figures for customer, vendor, and GL accounts within a time period are checked against the balances of the documents posted in that same period. This allows you to check in different parallel currencies as well. These transaction should be definitely checked when you are loading massive amounts of data in one go. So this acts as a check for the sign-off for any data loads, particularly during go-live checks.

10.3.7 Valuate

In this step, you will learn how foreign currency valuation is performed. Valuation of foreign currency is one of the least understood functionalities in SAP ERP Financials. This subsection touches on all the pieces that make it work. Follow the menu path **SAP Menu • Accounting • Financial Accounting • General Ledger • Periodic Processing • Closing • Valuate • Foreign Currency Valuation (New)**, or use Transaction FAGL_FC_VAL.

Figure 10.24 shows the menu path for valuating the foreign currency items. As you can see, the Transactions in the new GL have changed to FAGL_FC_VAL and FAGL_FC_TRANS from F.05. Prior to the new GL, F.05 was used to valuate foreign currency balances and translate the foreign currency balances. Now these have been separated into two transactions. However, the good news is that the configuration settings have not changed at all.

Figure 10.24 Valuate Foreign Currency Balances

Figure 10.25 shows the selection parameters for valuating foreign currency items and the posting details that you can maintain for posting the foreign currency valuation.

General Data Selection

You can perform your valuation by company code and valuation area. You also need to maintain the valuation key date, which helps you identify the open items that have not been cleared.

Postings Tab

In the Postings tab, you can **Create Postings** and specify the **Posting date** and the **Reversal posting date,** and also reset your valuation using the **Reset Valuation** flag.

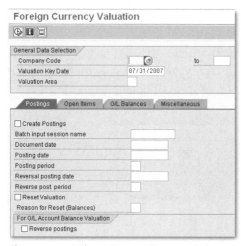

Figure 10.25 Valuate Foreign Currency Balances

If you click on the **Open Items** tab shown in Figure 10.26, you can maintain the selection parameters of the foreign currency open items.

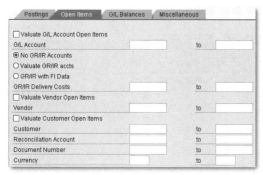

Figure 10.26 Open Items Tab of Valuate Foreign Currency Balances

Figure 10.27 shows the screen for selecting the GL balances along with the **Exchange rate difference key** and the **Currency** of open item differences.

Figure 10.27 GL Balances Tab of Valuate Foreign Currency Balances

Now that you understand the selection parameters for valuating the foreign currency open items, let's discuss how to configure them in the GL.

Configuring Foreign Currency Valuation

The process of configuring foreign currency valuation is shown in Figure 10.28. This section discusses each of these steps in detail.

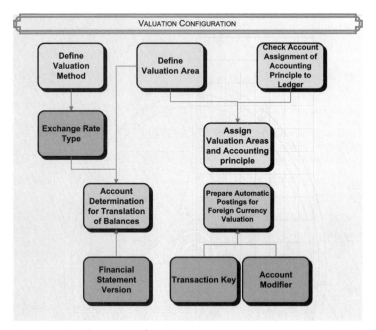

Figure 10.28 Valuation Configuration

Define the Valuation Method

The valuation method allows you to group various parameters that make up the overall valuation procedure. The menu path is **IMG • Accounting • Fi-**

nancial Accounting (New) • General Ledger Accounting (New) • Periodic Processing • Valuate • Define Valuation Method. Figure 10.29 shows the screen for detailing the valuation method. You need to identify and make sure that you maintain the following settings:

▸ **Valuation Procedure**
Choose the appropriate valuation procedure: **Lowest Value Principle** (valuation only happens if there is exchange rate loss), **Strict lowest value principle** (entries are revaluated only if the new valuation has a greater entry than the previous value), **Always valuate**, or **Revalue only**.

▸ **Post per Line Item**
If you check this box, the system posts per open line item.

▸ **Document Type**
This is the document type for posting the clearing entry.

▸ **Group Vendors**, **Group Customers**
If you check this, vendors and customers are grouped together and then valuated per the valuation group.

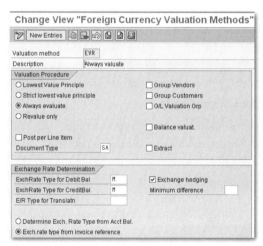

Figure 10.29 Define Valuation Method

▸ **Balance valuat.**
This allows you to balance open items per account, group, or currency per the valuation procedure parameters. This makes more sense if used in conjunction with other valuation parameters.

▸ **Exchange Rate Determination**
Here you can maintain the exchange rate type for credit and debit balances. You can also define whether the exchange rate type needs to be retrieved from account balance or from invoice processes.

Define the Valuation Area

Valuation areas enable you to use different valuation approaches and post to different accounts. After you have defined your valuation method, you can assign it to a valuation area. The menu path is **IMG • Accounting • Financial Accounting (New) • General Ledger Accounting (New) • Periodic Processing • Valuate • Define Valuation Area**.

Figure 10.30 shows how you can maintain the valuation area. **EVR** is the **Valuation method** that has been maintained for the **Valuation** area **US**. Here you have also identified the **Crcy type** (type of currency) as **Company code currency**, which will be used for valuation.

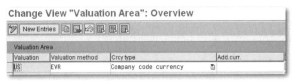

Figure 10.30 Define Valuation Area

You can also assign the valuation area to the valuation method that you defined in the previous step. This allows you to establish the accounting principles for the valuation method. You will learn more about the accounting principles next.

Assign Accounting Principle to the Ledger Group

The accounting principles are legal regulations according to which financial statements are drawn up and rendered. For example, typical accounting principles are US GAAP and International Accounting Standards (IAS). In this step, you can assign the accounting principle to the ledger group. The menu path is **IMG • Accounting • Financial Accounting (New) • General Ledger Accounting (New) • Periodic Processing • Valuate • Check Assignment of Accounting Principle to Ledger Group**. Figure 10.31 shows you the assignment of **Accounting Principle GAAP** to **Target Ledger Gr.. LL**.

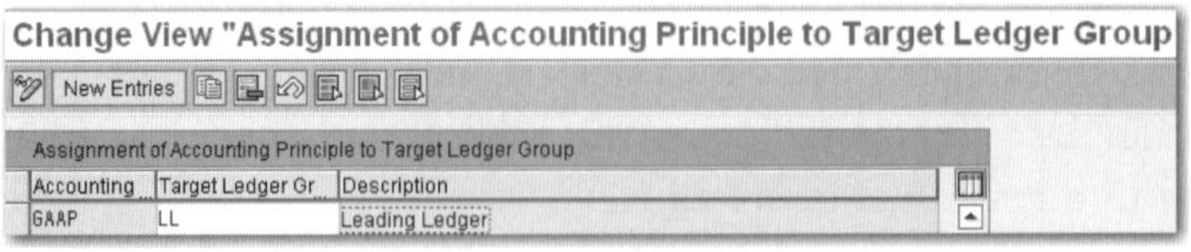

Change View "Assignment of Accounting Principle to Target Ledger Group

New Entries

Assignment of Accounting Principle to Target Ledger Group		
Accounting	Target Ledger Gr	Description
GAAP	LL	Leading Ledger

Figure 10.31 Assignment of Accounting Principle to Ledger Group

Assign Valuation Area to Accounting Principle

This setting allows you to establish the link between the valuation area and the accounting principle. In conjunction with the previous setting, now the valuation area is linked to the ledger group. The menu path **IMG • Accounting • Financial Accounting (New) • General Ledger Accounting (New) • Periodic Processing • Valuate • Assign Valuation Areas and Accounting Principles**. Figure 10.32 shows the screen where you can maintain the assignment of the valuation area to the accounting principle.

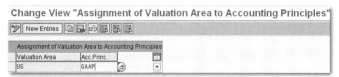

Figure 10.32 Assignment of Valuation Area to Accounting Principle

Account Determination of Translation of Balances

In this activity, you define the account determination for the currency translation. Currency translation is one of the most important financial activities when you have many foreign currency open items that need to be translated at month-end. The menu path is **IMG • Accounting • Financial Accounting (New) • General Ledger Accounting (New) • Periodic Processing • Valuate • Foreign Currency Valuation • Account Determination for Translation of Balances**. Figure 10.33 shows the screen where you can maintain the financial statement items for currency translation.

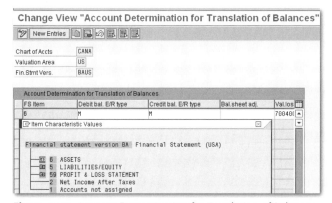

Figure 10.33 Account Determination for Translation of Balances

As shown in Figure 10.33, you can define the credit and debit exchange rate type, financial statement item, and corresponding valuation loss and gain accounts by **Chart of Accts**, **Valuation Area,** and financial statement version (**Fin.Stmt Vers.**). As shown, you can select a group of GL accounts to have the same exchange rate type by selecting **FS Items** from the drop down list as shown in the **Item Characteristic Values** pop up.

Define Automatic Postings for Exchange Rate Differences

In this activity, you define the automatic postings for exchange rate differences. The menu path is **IMG • Accounting • Financial Accounting (New) • General Ledger Accounting (New) • Periodic Processing • Valuate • Foreign Currency Valuation • Prepare automatic postings for Foreign Currency Valuation**.

You can configure the GL accounts by transaction key and account group as shown by the various transaction keys in Figure 10.34. For example, you can define the GL accounts that will be posted for exchange rate differences during **Document Split for Currency Exchange** by choosing the **Transaction Key CEX**. After you select **CEX,** you just need to maintain the appropriate GL accounts.

Maintain FI Configuration: Automatic Posting - Procedures		
🔍		
Group FWA Exchange rate differences		

Procedures		
Description	Transaction	Account determ.
Document Split for Currency Exchange	CEX	☑
Exch. Rate Diff. using Exch. Rate Key	KDB	☑
Exchange Rate Dif.: Open Items/GL Acct	KDF	☑
Payment difference for altern.currency	KDW	☑
Payment diff.for altern.curr.(offset)	KDZ	☑
Internal currencies rounding differences	RDF	☑

Figure 10.34 Prepare Automatic Postings for Foreign Currency Balances

This completes all the configuration settings that need to be maintained for valuation of foreign currency items.

10.3.8 Rollup

In this step, one or several ledgers is rolled up or summarized into a rollup ledger. This concept is heavily used in defining ledgers for consolidation and in defining special purpose ledgers that can be used to analyze different dimensions of summarized information, such as balances by GL account for a particular period. During rollup, all this information is transmitted to the appropriate ledgers. The following transactions are used to perform the rollup functions and define field movements:

- **FAGL21**: Create Rollup
- **FAGL22**: Change Rollup
- **FAGL23**: Display Rollup
- **FAGL24**: Delete Rollup
- **FAGL25**: Execute Rollup
- **GRC1**: Define Field Movement
- **GRC2**: Change Field Movement

The functionality of rollup is summarized in the schematic shown in Figure 10.35. The first step is to define a rollup ledger and assign a company code to a rollup ledger.

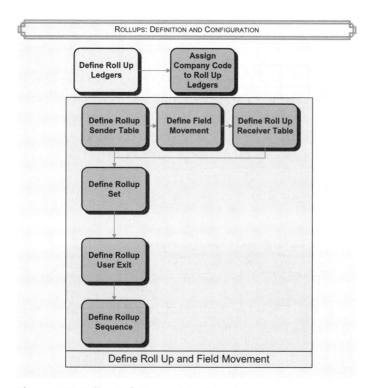

Figure 10.35 Rollup Definition and Configuration

In the rollup process, you need to define the rollup sender table and the receiver table. In the field movement definition, you define how the fields will map from sender table to the receiver table. The rollup set is defined to capture the various dimensions containing the following values: ledger, record type, version, companies, and accounts. You can define rollup user exits to modify the field moving from sender to receiver tables per a particular formula. You can execute a rollup by using Transaction FAGL25.

Note

Standard user exits for rollup are delivered by program RGLVS00 and can be used to modify the data per your requirements.

10.3.9 Carryforward

In this step, balances for GL accounts, customers, and vendors are carried forward to the next fiscal year during the year-end closing process. This ensures that you can display the open balance sheet items in the next fiscal year as well. In case of profit and loss accounts, the account balances are transferred to the retained earnings account specified in the configuration. Balance sheet balances are carried forward to the next year. The menu path is **SAP Menu • Accounting • Financial Accounting • General Ledger Accounting • Periodic Processing • Closing • Carryforward**. The transaction codes for GL balance carryforward are shown in Figure 10.36. Note that the previous carryforward Transaction F.16 has been changed to **FAGLGVTR** to ensure that the balances of all the parallel valuation are carried forward to the new fiscal year.

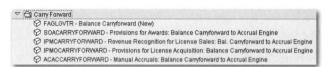

Figure 10.36 Balance Carryforward for the GL

The new Transaction FAGLGVTR is executed by ledger and by company code. In the carryforward to fiscal year, you need to specify the year to which the accounts need to be carried forward.

After you execute the transaction, any transactions made in the previous year are automatically carried forward to the current year. However, it is always better to run the program only after the previous year has been closed. Typically, all these are scheduled as a batch job to run within the first week of the fiscal year closing process.

Figure 10.37 shows the screen for carrying forward GL balances. Here you need to maintain the **Ledger, Company code**, and the new fiscal year (**Carry forward to fiscal year),** along with the **Record type** and **Version** that you need to carry forward. You can also specify that you want to see the new retained earnings balance, after the balance carryforward is run, by checking the **Balances in retain.earng. acct** checkbox.

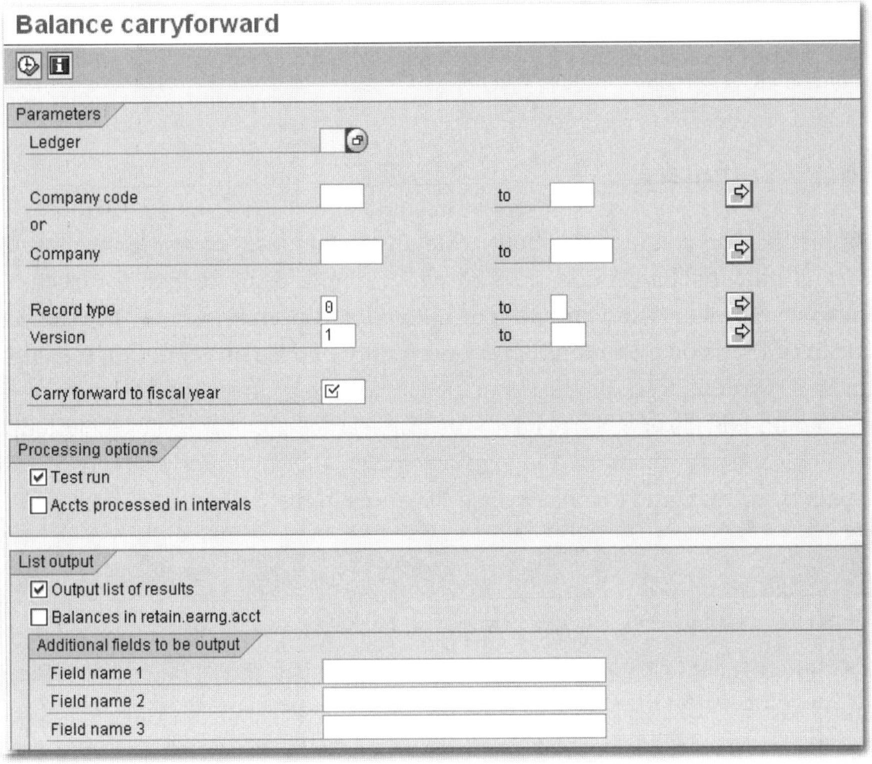

Figure 10.37 GL Balance Carryforward (Transaction FAGLGVTR)

The menu path is **SAP Menu • Financial Accounting • Accounts Payable/ Accounts Receivable • Periodic Processing • Closing • Carryforward ba-lances**, and the Transaction is F.07. Figure 10.38 shows the screen for car-rying forward AP and AR balances.

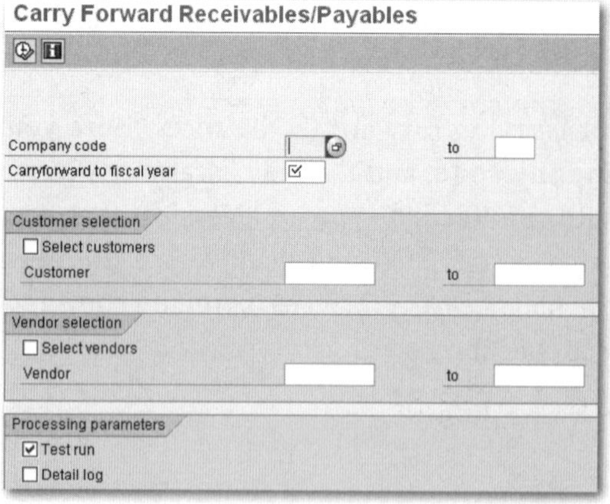

Carry Forward Receivables/Payables

Company code	to
Carryforward to fiscal year	☑

Customer selection
☐ Select customers
Customer ___ to ___

Vendor selection
☐ Select vendors
Vendor ___ to ___

Processing parameters
☑ Test run
☐ Detail log

Figure 10.38 Vendor and Customer Carryforward

10.4 Summary

In this chapter, you learned about achieving faster closes by using the closing cockpit functionality. You learned how to use the closing cockpit to structure and put your month-end processes on auto-pilot to a certain degree. The closing cockpit allows you to communicate your month-end via one common medium and helps you understand the dependencies and task information from an overall month-end closing perspective. You also learned about the key GL periodic activities such as valuation of foreign currencies, allocation, reclassifying GR/IR balances, rollups, and carryforward of balances in the GL.

Key Takeaways

▶ Better planning equals a faster close.

▶ Closing is not just about the GL. Many other modules should be persuaded to perform activities that help the Finance department achieve faster closes.

▶ Identify and communicate the dependencies.

▶ Use the closing cockpit to plan, coordinate, and publish your closing schedule.

This chapter along with Chapter 9 gave you the perspective to understand the GL and the typical month-end closing activities. The key to a faster close is to understand the myriad activities and then plan and organize them in a sequence that makes sense for your organization.

In Chapter 11, you will learn more about the *special purpose ledger*. This will help you appreciate the new GL functionality and will provide you with an additional set of tools to meet your reporting requirements.

The special purpose ledger helps you enhance and add dimensions for summarization, reporting, and analysis. Use this ledger to improve and optimize the reporting capabilities available to you in SAP ERP Financials.

11 Special Purpose Ledger

SAP ERP comes preconfigured with standard ledgers, including the general ledger (GL), profit center ledger, consolidation ledger, and so on. However, prior to the new GL introduction, the only way you could define a ledger of your own was to create a special purpose ledger, which allowed you to define your own tables to meet your business requirements. This chapter describes the special purpose ledger (FI-SL) module of SAP, which is used to define additional dimensions for summarization reporting and analysis.

All the processes in the special purpose ledger allow you to further enhance your reporting without impacting any of your existing systems because FI-SL is just a receiving system that does not impact any other systems. So FI-SL is the safest bet if you want to optimize your reporting, in case there are transient changes in your organization that require new reporting dimensions. When you implement the special purpose ledger, you are trying to improve and optimize the reporting capabilities of SAP ERP Financials without impacting the core functionality.

The processes covered in this chapter are shown in Figure 11.1. First you need to define the basic settings that are followed up by the setting up of the special purpose ledger, which requires a new table group definition. After you have defined the table group, you need to maintain fixed field movements and then define the ledger and the ledger group for your special purpose ledger.

After you have completed the special purpose ledger, you can record business transactions in the special purpose ledger for planning or actual posting. These can be configured to have their own posting periods, number ranges, and versions along with document types, document splitting, and offset account determination. After you are familiar with the routine transactions, you will be introduced to the periodic business transactions such as rollup, currency translation, balance carryforward, and so on.

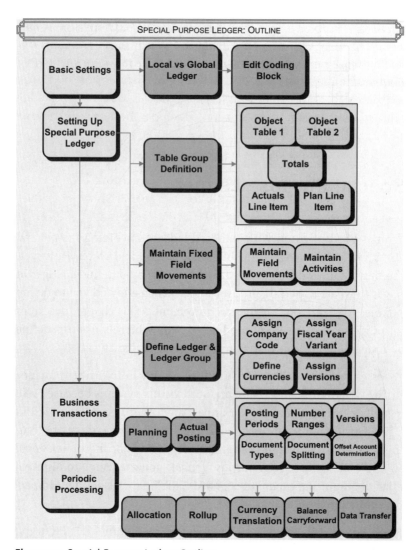

Figure 11.1 Special Purpose Ledger Outline

Most of the special purpose ledger functionality has been packaged by SAP into the new GL, which can now have multiple ledgers built-in to the GL functionality. Therefore, in the new GL, you can create nonleading ledgers that are posted in conjunction with the leading ledger, as you learned in Chapter 9. However, for the special purpose ledger, the main GL (GLT0 table) is posted, and the special purpose ledger is also posted if you assigned a company code to the special purpose ledger.

11.1 Special Purpose Ledger: An Introduction

The information in FI-SL is collected from other SAP applications such as FI, CO, MM, and SD, and from specific postings in FI-SL. The information is then stored in custom tables for reporting purpose. All the data that enters the FI-SL is processed via Integration Manager ,which determines how the data is ultimately posted in FI-SL. The data is posted to FI-SL after the user-defined validation and substitution rules are applied.

You can define special purpose ledgers and generate custom databases by using the FI-SL installation programs. So you can use FI-SL to join tables across applications to get reporting for specific dimensions such as functional year, a different fiscal year variant, and so on. FI-SL can be used to add account assignments and an additional level of detail that was earlier not available in the GLT0 table.

Whenever a document posts in the GL, the corresponding document posts in FI-SL as well. In addition, the data can be processed in planning, allocations, rollup, and carryforward functions. This is very similar to the concept of the leading and the nonleading ledger of the new GL, which you learned about in Chapter 10. The special purpose ledger can be used for the following:

▶ Cost of sales reporting by functional area.

▶ Consolidation purposes.

▶ As an intermediate ledger that can then be rolled up to the ECCS ledger with modifications.

▶ Parallel accounting, although with the advent of the new GL, it is ingrained.

▶ For reporting with a different fiscal year than the company code fiscal year.

▶ For reporting in a different currency than the group currency. For example, if a company is incorporated in Europe but managed from the United States, then the group currency could be Euro but the reporting needs to be in US dollars.

▶ Adding additional fields such as materials, which can then be used for reporting.

Now let's move on to discuss the basic settings for the special purpose ledger.

11.2 Basic Settings

Basic settings identify the main reason you are creating a brand new ledger. You might need additional local reporting, or you might need to add new fields, which in conjunction with other fields, allow you to do reporting on new dimensions that are not possible in standard ledgers. In this section, we will be discussing the basic configuration settings related to linking FI-SL to the local and global ledgers and defining new fields in the coding block.

11.2.1 Preparation for Special General Ledger Implementation

In this step, you establish the link between the special purpose ledger and company code and/or company. Company code establishes the local ledger link, whereas company ties the global link. This allows you to determine whether your special purpose ledger is linked to local company level requirements or it is being used for consolidated reporting. The menu path is **IMG • Accounting • Financial Accounting • Special Purpose Ledger • Basic Settings • Perform Preparation**, and the Transaction is GCVO.

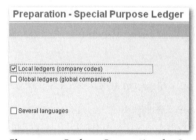

Figure 11.2 Perform Preparation for Special Purpose Ledger

As shown in Figure 11.2, the **Local ledgers (company codes)** have been activated for processing in the special purpose ledger. This allows you to process the company code transactions in FI-SL. If you check **Several languages**, then multiple foreign language texts can be entered in the configuration. This needs to be marked if you have a global implementation and require configuration to be managed from multiple locations.

11.2.2 Edit Coding Block

The coding block identifies the account assignment objects that come preconfigured in SAP ERP, such as cost center, internal order, and so on. In this step, you can define your own fields in account assignment, and these can then be added to the tables in FI-SL. This setting is also provided in the new GL where you can add new fields as well. You learned about the coding block definition in Chapter 9 when you were learning about the new GL. For the editing block you will need to follow the menu path **IMG • Accounting • Financial Accounting • Special Purpose Ledger • Basic Settings • Edit Coding Block**, or use Transaction OXK3. As you can see in Figure 11.3, there are two types of coding blocks: **SAP Standard Account Assignments** and **Customer-Defined Account Assignments**. New fields can be added by clicking on **Add Fields** and then selecting fields from appropriate tables. For more details about the coding block, refer to Chapter 9.

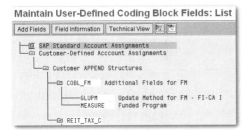

Figure 11.3 Edit Coding Block in Special Purpose Ledger

In the next section, you will learn more about installing the special purpose ledger.

11.3 Installing the Special Purpose Ledger

Now let's learn about the process for installing FI-SL along with the table definition, field movements, and ledger definition. You can install all three together using the express install functionality, or you can configure them in a sequential manner. To get started, you should install all three together in one go and then modify them individually.

11.3.1 Express Installation of FI-SL

The express installation allows you to define the table group, field movement, and the corresponding ledger together in one step. All the technical steps to implement FI-SL are performed in sequence in one go. It is important for you to start off with the express installation to build up the base of your technical implementation; however, you still have to validate and make sure that the settings meet your requirements. Figure 11.4 shows the screen for express installation of FI-SL.

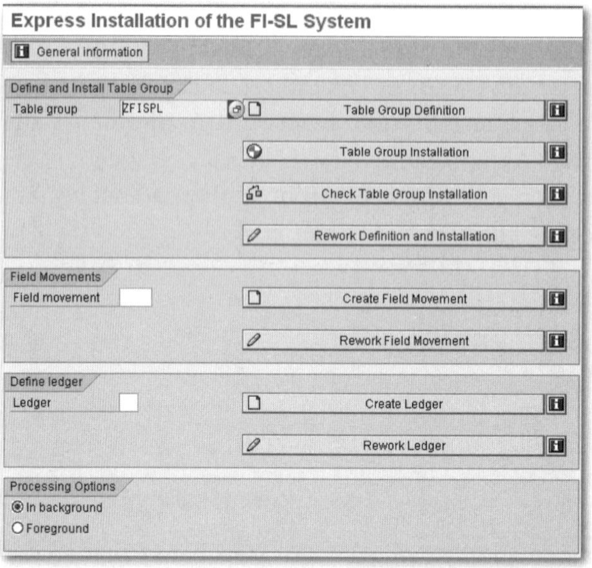

Figure 11.4 Express Installation of the FI-SL System.

Here you define the **Table group ZFISPL**. If you are ready to create your ledger, then click on **Table Group Definition** and subsequently on **Table Group Installation**. After the ledger has been installed, you can check whether everything went fine using **Check Table Group Installation**. The menu path is **IMG • Accounting • Financial Accounting • Special Purpose Ledger • Basic Settings • Tables • Definition • Execute Express Installation**, and the Transaction is GCIQ.

You can choose to perform the installation in the background or in the foreground. Installing in the background is faster and does not produce any errors because the background job runs on the SAP server rather than your machine. However, you will learn about each of these definitions in subsequent subsections.

11.3.2 Define Table group

In this section, you will learn more about the table group definition process, where you define the set of tables together that meet the various reporting needs. Figure 11.5 shows the first screen of the table group definition process. You can create, change, display, check, and delete from the same transaction. After you have defined the table group, the table group can be installed using the **Follow-On Functions**. For defining the table group, follow the menu path **IMG • Accounting • Financial Accounting • Special Purpose Ledger • Basic Settings • Tables • Definition • Define Table Group**, or use Transaction GCIN.

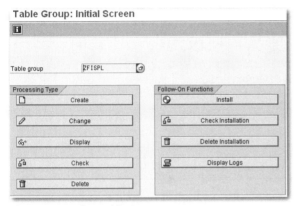

Figure 11.5 Define Table Group

The following tables are automatically defined in this step, based on the Table group **ZFISPL**, as shown in Figure 11.6:

- **Object Table1**: ZFISPLO
- **Object Table 2**: ZFISPLC
- **Totals Table**: ZFISPLT
- **Actual Line Item Table**: ZFISPLA
- **Plan Line Item Table**: ZFISPLP

Field Name	Data elem.	K	Type	Length	Checkt.	Text	Sende
MANDT	MANDT	✓	CLNT	3	T000	Client	
OBJNR	GOBJNR	✓	CHAR	18		Object number for FI-SL tables	
DATIV	DAT_0_VON		DATS	8		Posting date frm which the objc	
DATIB	DAT_0_BIS		DATS	8		Posting date up to which the ob	
DATPV	DAT_1_VON		DATS	8		Posting date frm which the objc	
DATPB	DAT_1_BIS		DATS	8		Posting date up to which the ob	
BUKRS	BUKRS		CHAR	4	T001	Company Code	
ACCT	RACCT		CHAR	10		Account Number	
BUSA	GSBER		CHAR	4	TGSB	Business Area	
CNTR	KOSTL		CHAR	10		Cost Center	
FAREA	FKBER		CHAR	16	TFKB	Functional Area	

Figure 11.6 Table Group Defining Object Table 1

In Figure 11.6, you can see details of the **Object Table 1**. The SAP system automatically assigns the name ZFISPLO (Table Group + O) as Object Table 1. As you can see, Object Table 1 contains the account assignments such as

585

Cost Center, Functional Area, and so on. You can define more account assignments if required. Object Table 2 for the table group ZFISPL is ZFISPLC. For Totals, it is ZFISPLT; for Actuals, it is ZFISPLA, and for Plan Line items, it is ZFISPLP. All these are part of the table group ZFISPL.

Figures 11.7 and 11.8 show the Totals and the Actuals tables, respectively. The Totals Table is very similar to the classic GL table GLT0 or the FAGLFLEXT table for the new GL. It records the summary level data in the special GL.

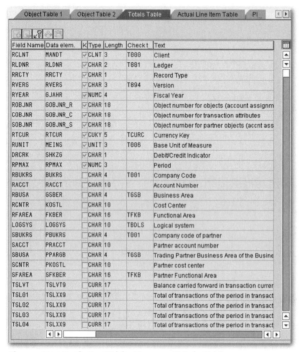

Field Name	Data elem.	K	Type	Length	Check t	Text
RCLNT	MANDT	✓	CLNT	3	T000	Client
RLDNR	RLDNR	✓	CHAR	2	T881	Ledger
RRCTY	RRCTY	✓	CHAR	1		Record Type
RVERS	RVERS	✓	CHAR	3	T894	Version
RYEAR	GJAHR	✓	NUMC	4		Fiscal Year
ROBJNR	GOBJNR_R	✓	CHAR	18		Object number for objects (account assignm
COBJNR	GOBJNR_C	✓	CHAR	18		Object number for transaction attributes
SOBJNR	GOBJNR_S	✓	CHAR	18		Object number for partner objects (accnt ass
RTCUR	RTCUR	✓	CUKY	5	TCURC	Currency Key
RUNIT	MEINS	✓	UNIT	3	T006	Base Unit of Measure
DRCRK	SHKZG	✓	CHAR	1		Debit/Credit Indicator
RPMAX	RPMAX	✓	NUMC	3		Period
RBUKRS	BUKRS		CHAR	4	T001	Company Code
RACCT	RACCT		CHAR	10		Account Number
RBUSA	GSBER		CHAR	4	T6SB	Business Area
RCNTR	KOSTL		CHAR	10		Cost Center
RFAREA	FKBER		CHAR	16	TFKB	Functional Area
LOGSYS	LOGSYS		CHAR	10	TBDLS	Logical system
SBUKRS	PBUKRS		CHAR	4	T001	Company code of partner
SACCT	PRACCT		CHAR	10		Partner account number
SBUSA	PPARGB		CHAR	4	T6SB	Trading Partner Business Area of the Busine
SCNTR	PKOSTL		CHAR	10		Partner cost center
SFAREA	SFKBER		CHAR	16	TFKB	Partner Functional Area
TSLVT	TSLVT9		CURR	17		Balance carried forward in transaction currer
TSL01	TSLXX9		CURR	17		Total of transactions of the period in transact
TSL02	TSLXX9		CURR	17		Total of transactions of the period in transact
TSL03	TSLXX9		CURR	17		Total of transactions of the period in transact
TSL04	TSLXX9		CURR	17		Total of transactions of the period in transact

Figure 11.7 Defining Table Groups: Totals Table

On the other hand, the Actuals table records each line item that was recorded in the system with the currencies identified in the special purpose ledger. This corresponds to the BSEG table in the GL. If you define too many characteristics against which you need to record your actuals, this table will soon have too many entries. So make sure that your Basis person has indexed this appropriately, or it will grow too fast and degrade system performance.

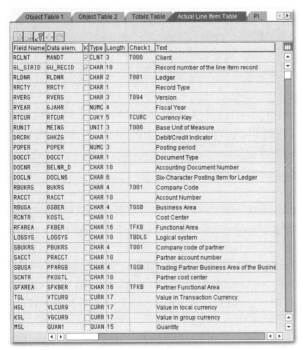

Figure 11.8 Define Table Groups: Actual Line Items Table

Now that you understand the structure of the table definition, you will learn more about the field movements in the next subsection.

11.3.3 Maintain Field Movements

In this section, you will define the field movements from the sender table to the receiver tables and the activities. Field movements help identify the characteristics or fields, such as movement types, material group, customer group, and so on that you want to transfer to the ledger. Activities help categorize the business transactions from other SAP system applications and other external systems. Ledgers are then updated based on the activities. The menu path is **IMG • Accounting • Financial Accounting • Special Purpose Ledger • Basic Settings • Master Data • Maintain Field Movements**, and the transaction codes are GCF1 (Create), GCF2 (Change), GCF3 (Display).

Display Field Movement: Overview

Field	Text	Receiver Table	Sender table
0000	Movements for the G/L Account Transaction Figures	GLT0	ACCHD
0001	Movements Balance C/F for G/L Acct Trnsctn Figures	GLU1	GLU1
0002	Movements FI->GLT3	GLT3	ACCHD
0003	Direct Posting FI->FI-LC	GLT2	ACCHD
0004	Direct Posting to Bus.Area Consolidtn for Rollup	GLT2	ACCHD
0005	Direct Posting + Subst. in Consolidtn of Bus.Areas	GLT2	ACCHD
00PA	G/L Integrated Planning - PA	GLT0	COPABBSEG_GLX
00PL	G/L Integrated Planning	GLT0	COBK
0C03	Field Movement Direct Update to EC-CS	ECMCT	ACCIT_GLX
0F00	Cost of Sales Accounting in FI-SL	GLFUNCT	ACCHD
1001	Bal.Carry Frwrd Cons. Staging Ledger Balance She	GLU1	GLU1
1002	Bal.CarryFrwrd ConsStagingLedger Profit and Loss	GLU1	GLU1

Figure 11.9 Display Field Movement

In Figure 11.9, a sample **Field Movement** is displayed. The field movement type is identified along with the description, the receiver, and the sender table. The menu path is **IMG • Accounting • Financial Accounting • Special Purpose Ledger • Basic Settings • Master Data • Maintain Activities**, and the Transactions are GCV1 (Create), GCV2 (Change), GCV3 (Display). In Figure 11.10, there is a list of activities along with the following details:

- **Trans**
  This represents the business activity for FI-SL direct posting.
- **Transaction Name**
  This is the name of the transaction identified earlier.
- **Table 1**, **Table 2**, and **Table 3**
  These are groups of sender tables used for each activity.
- **AGC**
  This is used to group together the selection conditions for ledger selections.

Display Activity: Overview

Trans	Transaction Name	Table 1	Table 2	Table 3	AGC
COFI	Online Posting from CO	ACCHD	ACCIT_GLX	ACCCR	FI00
GLA0	GL Act. Assessment:Integrative	ACCHD	ACCIT_GLX	ACCCR	FI00
GLD0	GL ActDistribution:Integrative	ACCHD	ACCIT_GLX	ACCCR	FI00
GLU1	Transfer Ext. System -> FI-GLX	GLU1			FX01
GPPA	Cost-Based Profit Planning	COPABBSEG_			
HRP1	HR Payroll	ACCHD	ACCIT_GLX	ACCCR	FI00
JVCB	Joint Venture Cutback	GLU1			JVXX
JVCO	CO Joint Venture	JVAH	JVAP		JVXX
JVE1	JV Equity Adjustment Reverse	GLU1			
JVE2	JV Equity Adjustment Rebook	GLU1			
JVEC	JVA Equity Change	JVAH	JVAP		JVXX
JVFI	FI Joint Venture	JVAH	JVAP		JVXX
JVIU	JV Actual Assessment	COBK	COEP	COIOP	JVXX
JVIV	JV Actual Distribution	COBK	COEP	COIOP	JVXX

Figure 11.10 Display Activity

Now that you understand how you can map the field and define the activity level detail, let's discuss the concept of the ledger and ledger groups in FI-SL.

11.3.4 Define Ledger and Ledger Groups

Ledgers are common grouping of accounting books that must be maintained to support a specific statutory or reporting requirement. Some of the common examples are profit center accounting, GL accounting, and so on. In this section, you will learn how to define the attributes of a special purpose ledger and then assign those attributes to ledger groups. First you will learn about the definition of a ledger's parameters. You can follow **IMG • Accounting • Financial Accounting • Special Purpose Ledger • Basic Settings • Master Data • Ledger • Define Ledger**. You can also use Transactions GCL1 (Create), GCL2 (Change), GCL3 (Display).

Figure 11.11 displays a ledger presupplied in the system. Review the following fields:

▶ **Ledger**
This is the two-digit identifier of the ledger along with the description of the ledger.

▶ **Totals Table**
This is the totals table associated with the ledger. If you create a ledger for the ZFISPL table group, the totals table will be ZFISPLT.

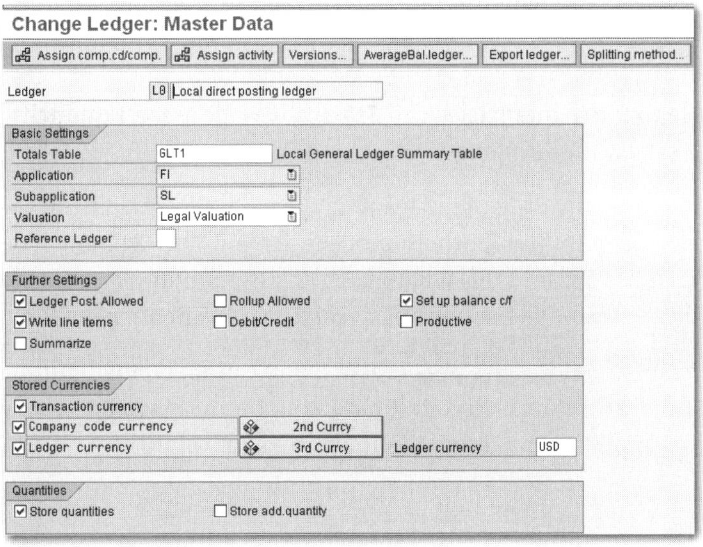

Figure 11.11 Define Ledger

▶ **Application** and **Subapplication**
This refers to FI and SL, respectively.

▶ **Valuation**
The valuation type can be **Legal Valuation, Group Valuation,** or **Profit center valuation.**

▶ **Reference Ledger**
This is the ledger used by FI-SL to update the GL account postings.

▶ **Ledger Post. Allowed, Rollup Allowed, Set up balance c/f, Write line items**
If checked, these options allow postings to be made to the ledger, allow rollup, allow automatic balance carryforward to the next fiscal year, and ensure that you can write line item details, respectively.

▶ **Debit/Credit**
If checked, this option allows you to segregate debit and credit amounts.

▶ **Productive**
If checked, this option ensures that you cannot delete the data from the ledger.

▶ **Summarize**
If you set this indicator, then the FI-SL Line items are summarized according to the coding block summarization.

▶ **Stored Currencies**
The FI-SL ledger can be updated in three currencies: **Transaction currency, Group currency,** and **Ledger currency.**

▶ **Quantities**
You can choose to **Store quantities** and **Store add.** (additional) **quantity,** but it reduces system performance.

You can assign the company code or company to the ledger by clicking on the **Assign comp cd/ comp.** button at the top of the screen. This will take you to the next screen (see Figure 11.12) where you can assign multiple company codes to this ledger or remove the ones that you do not want assigned.

After you have made the necessary assignments, you can then detail out the activities assigned to the company code by clicking on the **Assign activity** button. The next screen that comes up is shown in Figure 11.13.

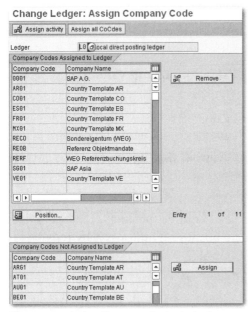

Figure 11.12 Assign Company Codes to Ledgers

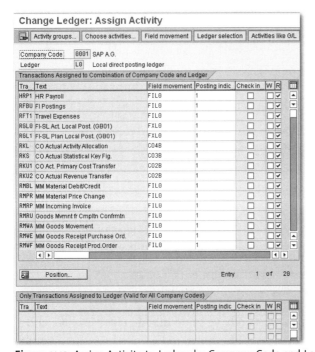

Figure 11.13 Assign Activity to Ledger by Company Code and Ledger

On this screen, you can click on **Field movement** to define the field movements. The fields of Figure 11.13 are detailed here:

▶ **Trans**
Business transaction.

▶ **Text**
Text identifying the business transaction.

▶ **Field movement**
Field movement associated to the business transaction. **FILO** is shown as an example in Figure 11.14.

▶ **Posting indic.**
1: Indicates activity/ledger is updated at direct posting; 2: indicates activity/ledger is updated at subsequent posting; 3: indicates activity/ledger is updated at subsequent and direct posting.

▶ **Check in (Check independent of posting)**
This indicator, if checked, ensures that the ledger is checked even if not posted.

▶ **W (Write Line Items)**
This indicator identifies the combination of ledger and activity for which the line item table is also updated.

▶ **R (Required Posting)**
This ensures that this activity is always posted to the ledger.

Change Ledger: Field Movement

Field movement	FILO	Movements from FI-GLX to local ledgers					
Receiver Table	GLT1	Local General Ledger Summary Table					
Sender table	ACCHD	ACCIT_GLX	ACCCR				
Usage	Direct posting from FI, AM, MM, SD						
Receiver field	Description	Sender table	Sender field	Description		Ex	Edito
KOKRS	Controlling Area	ACCIT_GLX	KOKRS	Controlling Area			
RACCT	Account Number	ACCIT_GLX	HKONT	G/L Account			
RASSC	Trading Partner	ACCIT_GLX	VBUND	Trading Partner			
RBUSA	Business Area	ACCIT_GLX	GSBER	Business Area			
RCNTR	Cost Center	ACCIT_GLX	KOSTL	Cost Center			
RMVCT	Transaction Type	ACCIT_GLX	RMVCT	Transaction Type			
SBUSA	Trading part.BA	ACCIT_GLX	PARGB	Trading part.BA			
UMSKZ	Special G/L ind.	ACCIT_GLX	UMSKZ	Special G/L ind.			

Figure 11.14 Define Field Movement

For a field movement definition, you have to define the receiver table and at most four sender tables. In the example shown in Figure 11.14, three **Sender tables** have been defined. After the tables have been defined, you can map the receiver and sender fields by sender tables. Also **Ex** can be used to define the user exit that can be used to modify or append the data coming from the sender tables at a field level.

Now that you know how to assign the fields within the ledger movement, let's take a look at the versions that can be defined for the local ledger. Click on the back arrow to return to the **Assign Activity** screen. Click on the back arrow until you come back to the initial ledger screen displaying the **Versions** tab. Click on the tab to display the popup shown in Figure 11.15.

Figure 11.15 Define Versions

In Figure 11.15, you can define multiple versions applicable for the ledger and the version record's actual data, plan data, integrated plan data, and rollup data. The translation method and exchange rate type can also be specified by version of the ledger. For each company code ledger combination, you can specify various parameters as shown in Figure 11.16 and detailed here:

▸ **Blocking indicator**
1 indicates that the ledger is released for posting; **0** indicates that the ledger is blocked for posting.

▸ **Fiscal Year Variant**
Here you can define a fiscal year variant that is different from the company code fiscal year variant.

▸ **Write line items**, **Always check**, **Company code currency**, **Ledger currency**
These settings were maintained earlier in the initial ledger screen, but they can be modified by company code here.

▸ **Company code currency** and **Ledger currency**
The currencies are displayed here.

▸ **Validation type**
This is used to control the chart of accounts against which the GL accounts are validated. The options are Blank: operative charts of accounts; 1: corporate chart of accounts; 2L country-specific chart of accounts; 9: separate chart of accounts.

▸ **Carried frwd to FY**

This indicates the fiscal year the accounts will be carried forward to.

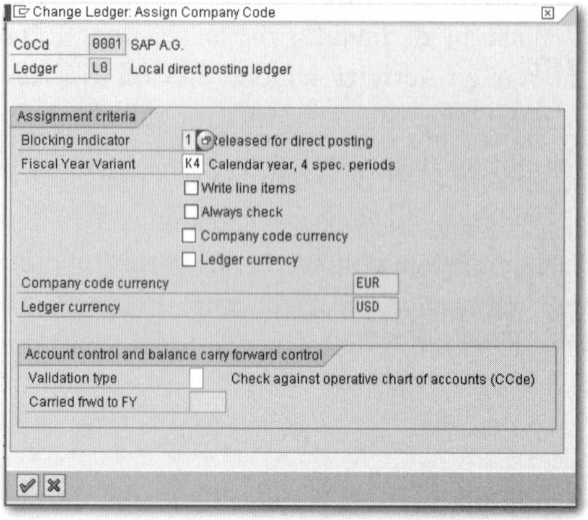

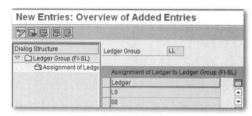

Figure 11.16 Details of the Ledger by Company Code

11.3.5 Ledger Groups

Now that you have completely defined the ledger, you can assign appropriate ledgers to a ledger group. These settings are relevant only if you use parallel accounting. The menu path you will need to follow is **IMG • Accounting • Financial Accounting • Special Purpose Ledger • Basic Settings • Master Data • Ledger • Define Ledger Group**.

Figure 11.17 shows the definition of the **Ledger Group** along with the assignment of ledgers to the ledger group. Initially, you need to create a **Ledger Group LL**, and then you can assign one or multiple ledgers **L0** and **G0** to the ledger group by clicking on **Assignment of Ledger** in the left pane.

Figure 11.17 Define Ledger Group

This completes all the technical settings that you need to make if you want to create a special purpose ledger for your accounting needs. In the next section, you will learn how you can leverage these technical settings to perform some of the common business transactions in FI-SL.

11.4 Business Transactions

Because FI-SL is just a collector of transactions for other SAP modules (MM, FI, and so on), most of the transactions in FI-SL are recorded when the transactions happen in the originating module. However, you can also execute the planning process and record actuals exclusively in the FI-SL. In this section, you will learn about the business transactions that are performed only in FI-SL. First up, you will learn how to execute the planning function in the special purpose ledger.

11.4.1 Planning

In this section, you will learn the planning function in FI-SL that can be used to create budgets, forecasts and other planning reports. The planning process in FI-SL is very similar to the planning process in the new GL, which was discussed in Chapter 9. You can see this configuration in Figure 11.18, and the screen for executing planning in FI-SL is shown in Figure 11.19.

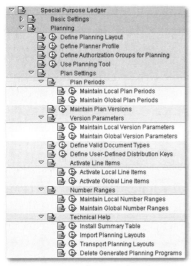

Figure 11.18 Configuring the Planning Process in FI-SL

As you learned earlier in basic settings, the special purpose ledger can be set up at the local level and the global level, so the planning in FI-SL can be done separately in the local ledger and global ledger. You have to define the posting periods and number ranges separately for global and local planning. Also you can run assessment and distribution cycles in FI-SL, which is similar to the new GL functionality. The data can be transferred from CO-OM and CO-PA to start the planning process in FI-SL.

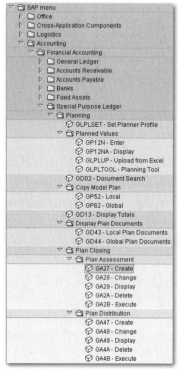

Figure 11.19 Executing the Planning Process in FI-SL

11.4.2 Configuring Actual Postings in FI-SL

You can record the actual postings in FI-SL which can denote various purposes. For example, consolidation entries for elimination if you are using special purpose ledger for consolidation reporting. Posting essentially means recording transactions in the special purpose ledger which can be posted in FI-SL via the following:

▶ Other SAP modules, such as MM, General Ledger Accounting, and so on

▶ Direct entry into FI-SL

▶ External systems

Let's discuss the settings related to the posting period, number ranges for actual postings in FI-SL and document splitting. A diagram showing the configuration process for configuring posting in FI-SL is shown in Figure 11.20. First, you need to set up separate posting periods for local and global ledgers if both are active. Then you need to define actual versions because all the postings in the special purpose ledger need a version.

After you have defined the posting period and version, you need to define the document types for posting in the special purpose ledger, which controls the posting parameters such as number ranges of special purpose ledger documents. Lastly, you can define the settings for document splitting, which are similar to the new GL document splitting discussed in Chapter 9.

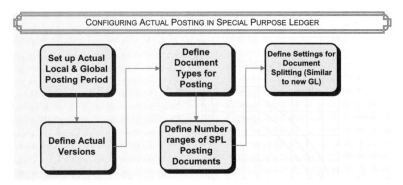

Figure 11.20 Configuring Actual Postings in the Special Purpose Ledger

In the next section you will learn how to define some of the specific settings for configuring FI-SL postings, beginning with defining how you can set up posting periods specific to special purpose ledger.

11.4.3 Define Posting Period

Figure 11.21 displays the local posting period set up. The menu path you will need to follow for this is **IMG • Accounting • Financial Accounting • Special Purpose Ledger • Actual Posting • Posting Periods • Maintain Local Posting Period** or **• Maintain Global Posting Period**. The Transactions are GCP1 (Local), GCP2 (Global).

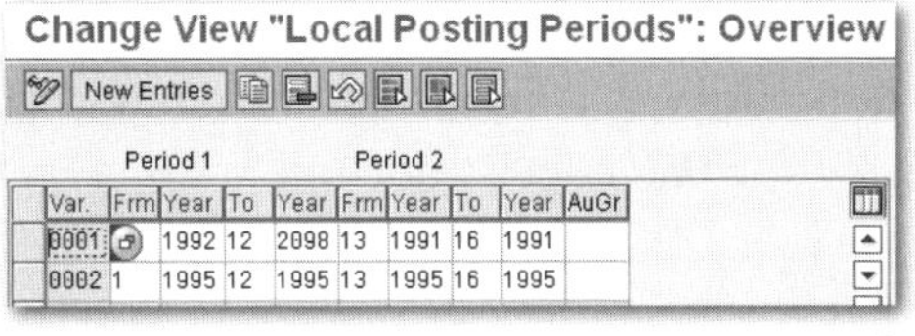

Figure 11.21 Setting Up the Local Posting Period

Let's look at the columns shown in Figure 11.21 in more detail here:

▶ **Var.**
This represents the variant that is assigned to the company code.

▶ **Period 1: Frm + Year**
This represents the from posting period and from year for normal posting periods.

▶ **To +Year**
This represents the to posting period and to year for normal posting periods.

▶ **Period 2: Frm + Year**
This represents the from posting period and from year for special posting periods

▶ **To +Year**
This represents the to posting period and to year for special posting periods.

Now that you have defined the local posting period, let's take a look at document type definitions for the special purpose ledger.

11.4.4 Define Document Type

The maintenance of valid document types for FI-SL postings is shown in Figure 11.22. You can follow **IMG • Accounting • Financial Accounting • Special Purpose Ledger • Actual Posting • Maintain Valid Document Types**, or use GCBX.

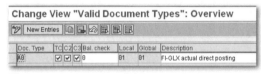

Figure 11.22 Maintain Valid Document Types

The fields shown in Figure 11.22 are explained here:

▶ **Doc. Type**
This shows the document type.

▶ **TC, C2, C3**
These correspond to the transaction currency, the second currency, and the third currency that are populated for the ledger's document type.

► **Bal. check**
This is used to define whether the system will perform a balance check at the time of document entry. The options are **0**: Error if balance is not zero; **1**: Warning if balance is not zero; and **2**: No balance check.

► **Local**
Number range for the document type's local posting.

► **Global**
Number range for the document type's global posting.

► **Description**
This is the description of the document type.

The actual posting transactions in FI-SL are shown in Figure 11.23.

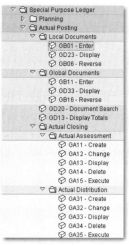

Figure 11.23 Actual Posting Transactions in FI-SL

The configuration settings for document splitting were already covered in the new GL and will not be detailed here.

11.5 Periodic Processing

In this section, you will learn the period-end transactions in FI-SL, which should be part of the closing process at month end. Typically, these processes are the responsibility of the GL person who manages the financial close of your organization. These period-end transactions can be directly executed using the menu path shown in Figure 11.24.

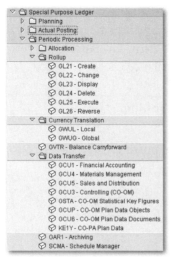

Figure 11.24 Menu Path to Execute FI-SL Period-End Transactions

11.5.1 Allocation

Allocation was covered in Chapter 9 for the new GL, and the functionality is very similar here. Also we have shown the assessment and distribution cycles' menu path in the discussion of planning and actual posting in Section 11.4. This addresses the periodic processing of allocation from sender to receiver objects.

11.5.2 Rollup

Rollup is used to summarize information from one or more ledgers to improve reporting performance. The FI-SL rollup functionality allows you to condense data and substitute data across characteristics. If you want to report by material group instead of by material, you need to execute the rollup function, which allows you to summarize the data at the material group level. In this section, you will learn how FI-SL can be used to rollup the data from multiple ledgers to one ledger for summarization. Rollup is also possible in the new GL functionality and was covered earlier in Chapter 9. The schematic of configuring the rollup is shown in Figure 11.25.

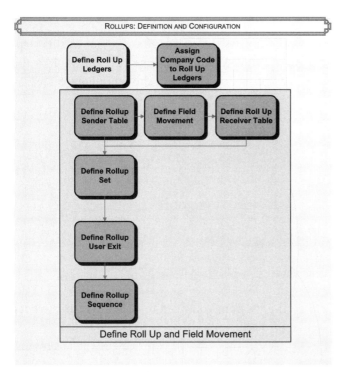

Figure 11.25 Configuring Rollup in FI-SL

11.5.3 Currency Translation

This is used to translate group currency amounts that have already been posted to FI-SL. You can translate the currencies posted in local and global ledgers using currency translation. The screen for currency translation is shown in Figure 11.26.

Figure 11.26 Configuring FI-SL Currency Translation

First let's consider how you can define versions for currency translation in FI-SL.

Define Versions

Currency translation is carried out per the translation version. In this step, you assign the **Translation version 1** and **Exchange rate versn 1** to the ledger's (**L0**) version **1**, using Transaction GCW1 as shown in Figure 11.27.

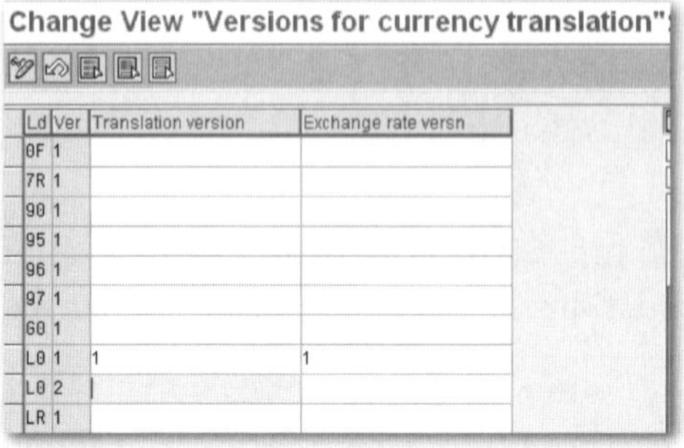
Change View "Versions for currency translation"

Ld	Ver	Translation version	Exchange rate versn
0F	1		
7R	1		
90	1		
95	1		
96	1		
97	1		
60	1		
L0	1	1	1
L0	2		
LR	1		

Figure 11.27 Define Version for Currency Translation in FI-SL

Now that you have defined the version, you need to define which currency translation method is active for FI-SL.

Define Currency Translation Methods

Currency translation methods allow you to group different financial statement items in sets, so that you can apply the correct translation method. For example, the fixed assets must be legally valued at the historical rate, whereas the current assets need to be valuated at the current rate. You can define different currency translation methods to each of these financial statement items. In this step, you can define a currency translation method by copying a preconfigured translation method. The preconfigured currency translation methods available in SAP system are shown in Figure 11.28.

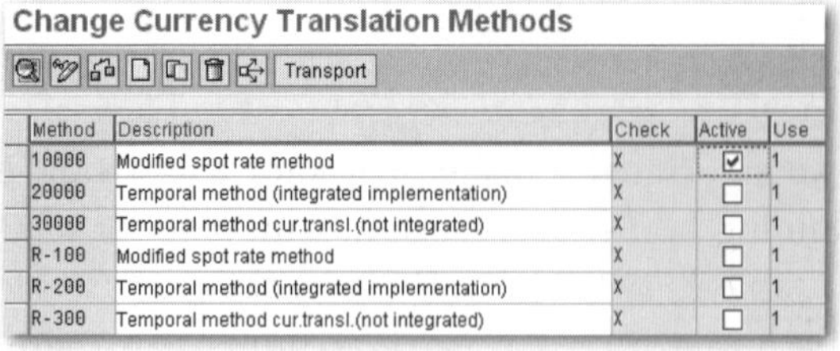
Change Currency Translation Methods

Transport

Method	Description	Check	Active	Use
10000	Modified spot rate method	X	☑	1
20000	Temporal method (integrated implementation)	X	☐	1
30000	Temporal method cur.transl.(not integrated)	X	☐	1
R-100	Modified spot rate method	X	☐	1
R-200	Temporal method (integrated implementation)	X	☐	1
R-300	Temporal method cur.transl.(not integrated)	X	☐	1

Figure 11.28 Define a Currency Translation Method

The fields in Figure 11.28 are explained here:

- **Method**
  This is the identifier for the method.

▶ **Description**

This is the description of the method.

▶ **Check**

This is marked by the system after the error check is complete. **X** indicates no error, blank indicates that the check has not happened, and **E** indicates that the check resulted in errors.

▶ **Active**

This identifies the translation methods that are active.

▶ **Use**

This is the usage indicator that identifies where the currency translation method is being used. **1**: Consolidation; **2**: General Ledger, **3**: Management Consolidation.

Double-clicking on **Method 10000** brings up the screen shown in Figure 11.29.

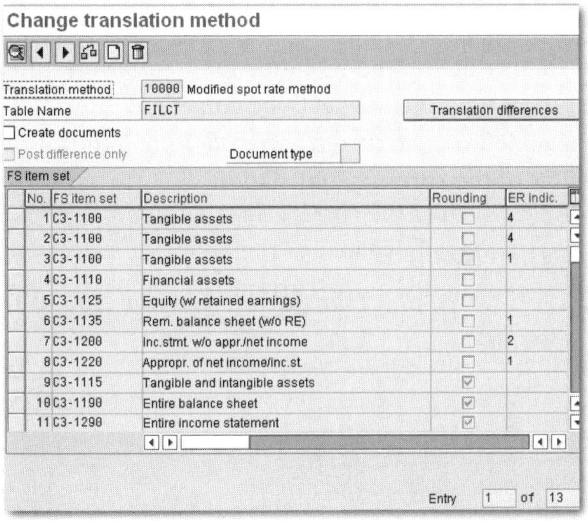

Figure 11.29 Defining a Currency Translation Method: FS Items

In this screen, the **Table Name** associated with the currency translation is maintained. So if you were defining a currency translation method for table ZFISPL, then you would enter table ZFISPLT here. **FS item sets** are used to group together FS items that are used to refer to GL accounts. This helps you translate different GL accounts differently. If you double-click on one of the **FS item sets**, the system takes you to the next screen (see Figure 11.30) where you can enter the parameters for currency translation.

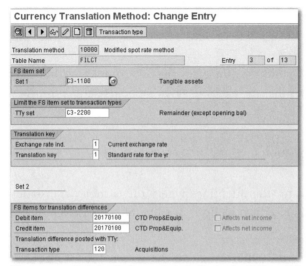

Figure 11.30 Defining Exchange Rate Indicator by FS Item Sets and Identifying FS Items for Translation Differences

The key things you can enter in Figure 11.30 are the **Exchange rate ind** and the **Translation key**. You can also define the FS items for translation differences along with the transaction type that needs to be considered for translation purposes. After you have defined the currency translation method, you need to assign it to the version of the currency translation.

Assign Local Currency Translation Methods

In this step, you can assign local currency **Translation method 10000** to **Version: Cur.transl. 1** as shown in Figure 11.31.

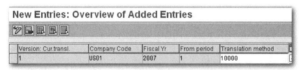

Figure 11.31 Assigning Local Currency Translation Method to Version

Next you will learn about the exchange rate types that can be set up to correct currency translation usage.

Set Up Exchange Rate Types

Exchange rate types need to be set up so that you can indicate which exchange rate (average, historical, current, etc.) will be used to perform the currency translation. In this step, you can define the exchange rate types that are then assigned in an exchange rate indicator as shown in Figure 11.32.

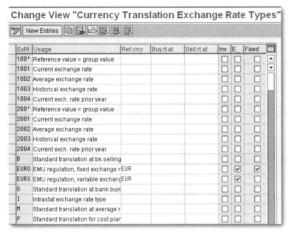

Figure 11.32 Defining Exchange Rate Type

The fields for exchange rate types are described here:

▶ **ExRt**
This is the identifier for the exchange rate type.

▶ **Usage**
This is the description of the exchange rate type.

▶ **Ref crcy**
This identifies the reference currency for the exchange rate type so that the translation always happens with reference to the currency maintained here.

▶ **Buy.rt.at/Sell.rt.at**
These identify the average buying and selling rates that are used as the reference. This helps minimize the data entry required for currency translation.

▶ **Inv**
If checked, this allows calculation with the inverted exchange rate. This setting is only used if the required combination is missing in the table.

▶ **E**
This indicator is used for EMU currencies and requires a reference currency to be maintained.

▶ **Fixed**
This indicates that the exchange rate type uses fixed rates.

Now that you have learned some of the key settings for configuring currency translation, you are ready to execute currency translation in FI-SL.

Executing Currency Translation in FI-SL

You can execute currency translation in FI-SL using Transaction GWUL. The selection parameters for executing currency translation are detailed in Figure 11.33.

FI-SL: Currency Translation

Parameter selection	
Company code	US01
Ledger	L0
Version	0
Actual/plan	0
Year	2007
Period	8
Ref.ex.rate ind.	*
List type	2
☑ Test run	
Distinguish translation differences by:	
☐ Affiliated companies	
☐ Transaction currencies	

Figure 11.33 Local Currency Translation Execution Parameters

The key parameters of executing local currency translation are **Company code, Ledger, Version, Actual/plan, Year, Period**, and **Ref.ex.rate ind.**. All these were discussed earlier as part of the configuration settings for currency translation. **List type** allows you to display the result at various levels:

▶ 1: Highly summarized log

▶ 2: Display FS item sets

▶ 3: Display FS item sets and items

▶ 4: Display the most important control tables and sets

The **Test run** setting allows the program to be executed in test run mode to see the results before the actual run. This completes the discussion on currency translation. In the next subsection, you will learn more about the balance carryforward process in FI-SL.

11.5.4   Balance Carryforward

Balance carryforward is when P&L balances are carried forward to retained earnings account, while balance sheet accounts are carried forward to the next year. In the standard SAP system balance carryforward transfers, the P&L balances to retained earnings account, whereas the balance sheet accounts are carried forward to the next fiscal year.

First, you will learn how to configure the retained earnings account for balance carryforward in FI-SL. The menu path to follow is **IMG • Accounting**

• **Financial Accounting** • **Special Purpose Ledger** • **Periodic Processing** • **Balance Carryforward** • **Retained Earnings Accounts** • **Maintain Local Retained Earnings account** *OR* • **Maintain Global Retained Earnings account**. The Transactions are GCS6 (Local), GCS7 (Global). In Figure 11.34, maintaining the local **Retained earnings account 330000** has been shown for chart of accounts (**ChAc**) **CANA**.

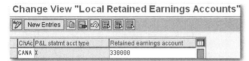

Figure 11.34 Define Local Retained Earnings Account

The global retained earnings account is also defined by the chart of accounts and P&L statement account types, which are maintained in the GL master record. Now that you understand the key configuration settings, let's take a look at the parameters by which you can execute carryforward in FI-SL. You can follow **SAP Menu** • **Accounting** • **Financial Accounting** • **Special Purpose Ledger** • **Periodic Processing** • **Balance Carryforward**, or use Transaction GVTR.

Balance carryforward for FI-SL is executed with the parameters shown in Figure 11.35. You need to enter the Ledger, Company code (local) **or Company** (global), **Record type, Version,** and **Carry forward to fiscal year**. **Record type** options are **0**: Actual; **1**: Planned; **2**: Apportioned Actual; and **3**: Apportioned Plan.

Balance carryforward

Parameters	
Ledger	L0
Company code	US01	to	
or		
Company		to	
Record type	0	to	
Version	1	to	
Carry forward to fiscal year	☑	

Processing options
☑ Test run
☐ Accts processed in intervals

List output
☑ Output list of results
☐ Balances in retain.earng.acct
Additional fields to be output

Field name 1	
Field name 2	
Field name 3	

Figure 11.35 Balance Carryforward for FI-SL

11.5.5 Data Transfer

You can import data from other SAP modules at the time of start-up and correct errors during the course of operation. The data transfer functionality is particularly useful for correcting any errors. For example, if one GL document did not post to FI-SL, you can use data transfer to solve this issue. This is especially useful if you are implementing FI-SL after the standard SAP system functionality has already been implemented. In that scenario, you need to transfer all the relevant data for reporting from the previous months in the fiscal year. The screen for data transfer is shown in Figure 11.36.

The menu path is **SAP Menu • Accounting • Financial Accounting • Special Purpose Ledger • Periodic Processing • Data Transfer • Financial Accounting/Materials Management/Sales and Distribution/Controlling/CO-OM Statistical Key Figures/ CO-OM Plan Data Objects/ CO-OM Plan Data Documents/CO-PA Plan Data**. The Transactions that can be used are GCU1/CU4/GCU5/GCU3/GSTA/GCUP/GCU6/KE1Y.

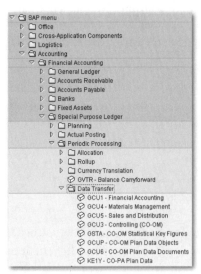

Figure 11.36 Data Transfer to FI-SL

Let's discuss the parameters for executing the data transfer from financial accounting (**GCU1-Financial Accounting** in Figure 11.36), which are shown in Figure 11.37.

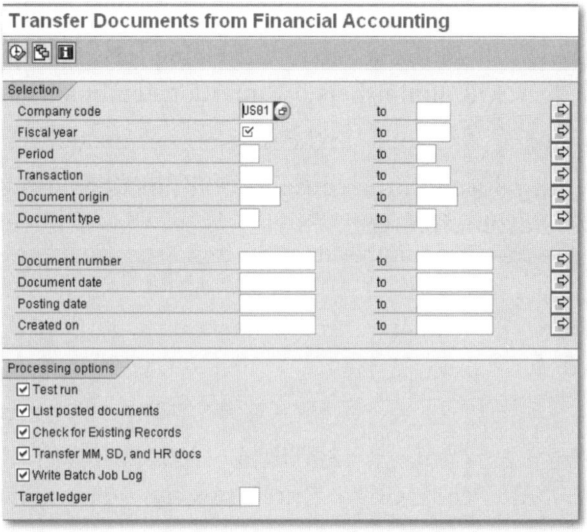

Figure 11.37 Transferring Financial Accounting Documents (GCU1)

As shown in Figure 11.37, you can use a variety of selection methods: **Company code**, **Fiscal year**, **Period**, **Transaction**, **Document origin**, **Document type**, **Document number**, **Document date**, **Posting date**, and **Created on**. You can also use a multitude of processing options: **Test run; List posted documents; Check for Existing Records; Transfer MM, SD, and HR docs**; and **Write Batch Job Log**.

The most important field is the **Target Ledger** to which you want to transfer the documents from FI. This is the FI-SL ledger to which you want the documents to be populated. This allows you to reconcile your ledgers and ensure that their balances match in all the source ledgers of FI-SL.

11.6 Summary

You learned how to install a new special purpose ledger and the key functionality available (planning and actual postings) and the key periodic functions supported by special purpose ledger (allocation, rollup, currency translation, balance carryforward, and data transfer).

The special purpose ledger is an important functionality that can be used to generate another layer of reporting. This module was extensively used prior to the introduction of the new GL to support segment reporting and other required reporting needs. We used FI-SL for getting balance sheets in different fiscal year variants and in different currencies, and we used a host of other applications that were not available in the standard GL. Going forward, the utility of special purpose ledger will diminish as organizations embrace the new GL.

In Chapter 12, you will be introduced to the consolidation functions using Enterprise Controlling-Consolidations (EC-CS).

Consolidation comes to the forefront after all the basic functionality related to SAP ERP Financials has been implemented. This chapter begins with just this premise.

12 SAP Enterprise Consolidation

Most organizations have operations spanning continents that also need decentralization of responsibility. This creates unique challenges for management to come up with an operating legal structure as well as a management-oriented reporting structure. And this complicates the consolidation requirements because you have multiple dimensions against which you want to report, taking into account the global structure of your organization. Overall, this translates into the following requirements for a business consolidation system:

▸ A uniform corporate-wide global strategy

▸ Ability to achieve global synergies and decentralization of responsibilities to react quickly to local market dynamics

▸ Ability to map complex and ever-evolving organizational structures

▸ Ability to unite internal and external reporting under one umbrella for the organization as a whole

Let's first get an idea of what SAP Enterprise Consolidation really is.

12.1 SAP Enterprise Consolidation: An Introduction

SAP Enterprise Consolidation (EC-CS) is the consolidation solution available in SAP ECC Core Enterprise Controlling for consolidating financial data from external and internal accounting and then sharing the reporting with other enterprise controlling modules. Enterprise controlling allows you to combine data from heterogeneous sources in a format that is understood by all. You can also use a Business Information Warehouse (BW) consolidation using SEM-BCS, which was developed as an extension of EC-CS to BW. However, most of the functions available in EC-CS allow you to perform managerial and legal consolidation.

The processes covered in this chapter are shown in Figure 12.1. First you will learn about the master data setup of consolidation, including dimensions, versions, currencies, characteristics, organizational units, financial statement items, definition of sets, and characteristic hierarchies. After you have become familiar with the master data of EC-CS, you will be introduced to the main business transactions in consolidation.

The process of consolidation can be divided in two broad categories: data collection and data processing. Data collection forms the core of the consolidation function. It is very important that you carefully define the business rules for data collection. After you have the data in your format, you need to ensure that you perform consolidation functions such as interunit profit elimination, investments across subsidiaries, and other consolidation processes to finalize your legal and managerial reporting.

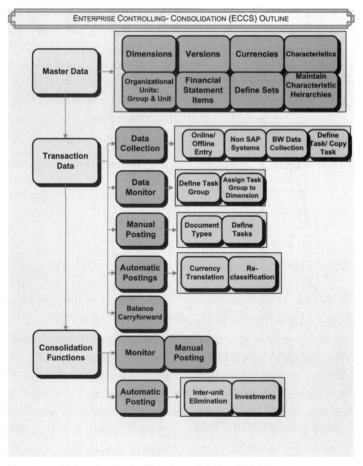

Figure 12.1 Enterprise Controlling-Consolidation (EC-CS)

This chapter describes the consolidation functions available in the SAP EC-CS Solution along with the customizing settings. Typically, the consolidation module is implemented after you have implemented the basic financial functionality related to the GL and the main subledgers such as AP, AR, Asset Accounting, and so on.

Our focus in this chapter will be on identifying tasks that you need to perform for legal consolidation. However, the managerial consolidation also follows the same structure, as you can configure different consolidation types by using different dimensions. All the relevant dimensions collect data appropriately.

First, you will learn about the master data that you need to set up in EC-CS.

12.2   Master Data

As you already learned in Chapter 3, you need to define your enterprise structure to map your organization in SAP ERP Financials. However, in EC-CS, you are allowed to create your corporate structure per your consolidation requirements. So EC-CS provides you with an opportunity to map your organization per legal consolidation and managerial consolidation requirements. You will learn the master data setup in ECCS, which is performed by the corporate department responsible for consolidation. The following key aspects of master data will be explained:

▸ Dimensions

▸ Ledgers and versions in consolidation

▸ Consolidation unit and groups

▸ Financial statement items and sets

▸ Characteristics

But before you go into the definition of these master data components, you need to define the parameters for your session while configuring master data. You define the parameters for the working session in the beginning, and then these global parameters will be applicable for all the configuration settings that you make. The menu Path is **SAP Menu • Accounting • Enterprise Controlling • Consolidation • Global Parameters**, and the Transaction is CXCD. As shown in Figure 12.2, the global parameters pertaining to **Dimension**, consolidation group (**Cons group**), **Version**, **Fiscal Year**, **Period**, consolidation chart of accounts **(Cons chart/acct)**, and **Ledger** can be set in this step.

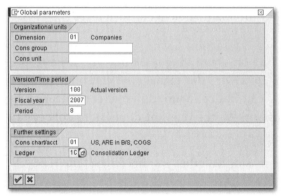

Figure 12.2 Setting Global Parameters

These parameters remain the same throughout the working session unless you change them. After they are set, these parameters are displayed in all the customizing and user settings. Figure 12.3 shows the global parameters displayed in the top half of the **Data Monitor** (Transaction CXCD). You will learn more about the Data Monitor in the next section.

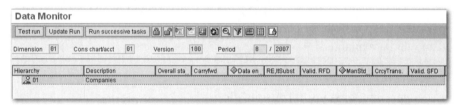

Figure 12.3 Global Parameters in the Data Monitor

Now, let's discuss the significance of dimension. Note that these dimensions appear in all the configuration settings that you will learn in this section.

12.3   Dimension

SAP defines dimension as a specific characteristic of consolidation reporting in SAP Consolidation. You will have the following preconfigured dimensions: company consolidation, business area consolidation, and profit center consolidation. Even though, technically you can map multiple dimensions to a consolidation type, it is recommended that one dimension is mapped to one consolidation type. This ensures that everyone in the business is clear about the functionality behind the specific dimension. In this step, you will learn to look at the attributes of a dimension along with its business significance. The menu path is **IMG • Enterprise Controlling • Consolidation • Master Data • Define Dimensions**, and the Transactions are CX1J (Create)/CX1K(Change)/ CX1L(Display). After executing Transaction CXIK, you come to the screen shown in Figure 12.4.

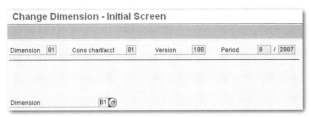

Figure 12.4 Changing a dimension (Transaction CX1K)

After you choose a dimension and press Enter, you will see the screen shown in Figure 12.5. The fields shown in Figure 12.5 are explained here:

▶ **Short text**, **Medium text**
Enter the name of the dimension.

▶ **Length of consolidation unit**, **Length of cons group**
Enter the maximum permitted characters.

▶ **Sets/Hierarchy**
These settings control how the sets get regenerated if there are any changes to the consolidation group hierarchy.

▶ **Apportionment procedure for two-sided eliminations**
Two apportionment procedures are allowed for interunit elimination or during elimination of interunit profit/loss.

▶ **Minimum** or **Product**
For **Minimum**, the difference is multiplied by the smaller of the two differences, whereas for **Product**, the difference is multiplied by the product of the two proportions.

▶ **Treatment of old documents before reposting**
If you have multiple update runs, this setting controls whether the previous documents are deleted or reversed.

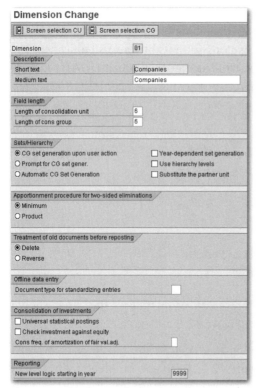

Figure 12.5 Attributes of a Dimension

▶ **Offline data entry: Document type for standardizing entries**
In this setting, you define the document type for offline data entry. The system-provided options are Reclass with and without deferred taxes (11 and 12), and Manual Reclass with and without deferred taxes (15 and 16).

▶ **Consolidation of Investments**
In this setting, you identify the consolidation frequency of the amortization of reported fair value(quarterly versus yearly). Also if you set the **Check investment against equity** indicator, the system checks for any double bookings of investment and equity.

12.4 Consolidation Versions

Consolidated financial statements are prepared against a consolidation version. The version allows you to segregate consolidation areas in EC-CS and consolidate different types of data separately, such as plan, actual, budget, or a separate category of planning. You can also use versions to prepare statements per different accounting principles such as US GAAP, IAS, and so on. In this step, you can define versions for use during consolidation. You can use the menu path **IMG • Enterprise Controlling • Consolidation • Master Data • Define versions** or Transaction CXB1.

Figure 12.6 shows the screen where you can enter a new version. The screen shows how you can change an existing consolidation version. The two versions shown are **100**: **Actual version** and **200**: **Plan version**. Consolidation versions are the ones in which data is posted.

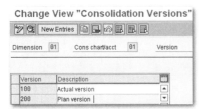

Figure 12.6 Define versions

After you double-click on an existing version (in this case **Actual version**), you reach the screen shown in Figure 12.7. Here you can define the properties of the consolidation version in **Technical settings**:

▶ **Base version**
This version is primarily used for reporting and is same as the consolidation version. You can define a different version than consolidation version if you want to include the totals and journal entries of both the base version and the consolidation version.

▶ **Carry forward version**
Setting this flag allows you to carry forward balances to the new fiscal year.

▶ **Allow overwriting—reported financial data**
This is checked for simulation versions that allow you to copy financial data from other versions.

▶ **Allow overwriting—standardizing/consolidation entries**
This is also checked for simulation versions and allows you to copy consolidation entries from other versions to this version.

▶ **Allow copying to other version—reported financial data**
This allows you to copy financial data from this version to other simulation versions.

▶ **Allow copying to other version—standardizing/cons. entries**
This allows you to copy consolidation entries to other simulation versions.

You can also define **Special versions** for **Data entry**, **Ledger**, **Selected items**, **Structure**, **Tax rate**, **Attributes**, **Translation method**, **Exchange rates**, **Reclassifications**, **Elimination of Interunit profit and loss in inventory**, **C/I method** (consolidation of investment methods), **Investment holdings**, **Investee equity**, **Hidden reserves/FVA**, and **Elim.hidden resvs** (elimination of hidden reserves). You will learn about consolidation tasks in detail in business transactions. The **Special versions** tab allows you to define attributes related to data and how the data entry is managed for each of the specific tasks identified in the preceding list.

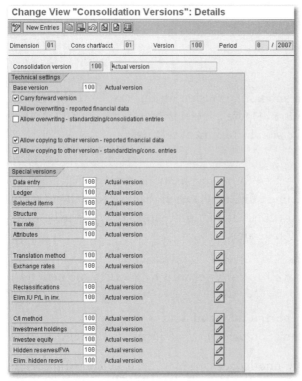

Figure 12.7 Details of a Version

Now that you understand some of the key settings in defining a version, you will learn about defining currencies and defining the ledger.

12.5   Check Currencies and Define Ledger

You can identify the currencies and define ledgers corresponding to currencies. The currencies need to be identified that you will be performing your consolidation with and reporting to your group headquarters.

12.5.1   Check Currencies

Most currencies are predefined and just need to be validated so that the relevant currencies for consolidation are available for use. The menu path you can use is **IMG • Enterprise Controlling • Consolidation • Master Data • Currencies • Check Currencies**. Figure 12.8 show the screen where you can display, change, or create a currency if your consolidation currency is not available.

Currency	ISO code	Alternative key	Long Text
TRY	TRY	949	Turkish Lira
TTD	TTD	780	Trinidad and Tobago Dollar
TWD	TWD	901	New Taiwan Dollar
TZS	TZS	834	Tanzanian Shilling
UAH	UAH	980	Ukraine Hryvnia
UGX	UGX	800	Ugandan Shilling
USD	USD	840	United States Dollar
USDN	USD	840	(Internal) United States Dollar (5 Dec.)
UYU	UYU	858	Uruguayan Peso (new)
UZS	UZS	860	Uzbekistan Som

Figure 12.8 Defining Currency Codes

Currency code is the SAP ERP code for currency while **ISO code** is the international norm for the currency identifier. ISO Code is primarily used for any EDI transactions with outside companies. **Alternative key** is used to define an additional code in addition to the **Currency** code and **ISO code**. Alternative currency is used only in Belgium and Spain.

12.5.2   Define Ledger

Each ledger can have only one ledger currency. So if you need to define multiple consolidation currencies, you also need to define multiple ledgers. The menu path is **IMG • Enterprise Controlling • Consolidation • Master Data • Currencies • Define Ledger,** and the Transactions are CXL1 (Create)/ CXL2(Change)/CXL3(Display)/CXL4(Delete). Figure 12.9 shows the ledger **1C** with the properties of the consolidation ledger such as the **Ledger Name**, **Totals Table ECMCT**, **Valuation**, **Second Currency**, and **Third Currency**.

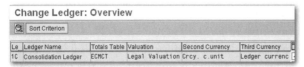

Figure 12.9 Change an existing ledger

After you double-click on the ledger **1C**, you will see the screen shown in Figure 12.10. You can then make the following settings:

▶ **Totals Table**
Typically, **ECMCT** is used for consolidation.

▶ **Application** and **Subapplication**
Defined as **EC** and **CS**.

▶ **Valuation**
The three types of valuation that are possible are **Legal Valuation**, **Group Valuation**, and **Profit Center Valuation**.

▶ **Ledger Post. Allowed**
This allows you to make postings to the ledger.

▶ **Rollup Allowed**
This allows you to roll up the ledger. Note that you can roll up a ledger only to the one that has similar valuation.

▶ **Set up balance c/f**
This indicator ensures that balances are automatically carried forward to the new year.

▶ **Write line items**
This ensures that you can write line items to the ledger.

▶ **Debit/Credit**
If you check this indicator, the system maintains the debit and credit indicator in each posting.

▶ **Productive**
This marks the ledger as productive, and then you cannot delete data posted to the ledger.

▶ **Transaction currency**
This currency is always stored in the ledger.

▶ **Consolidation unit currency**
If this is checked, the system maintains the consolidation unit currency in the ledger as well.

▶ **Ledger currency**
This currency is unique to the ledger and can be maintained in the ledger currency.

▶ **Store quantities**

This ensures that for any logistics transactions, the system also stores the quantities.

▶ **Store add.quantity**

This ensures that any additional quantities are also stored in the ledger.

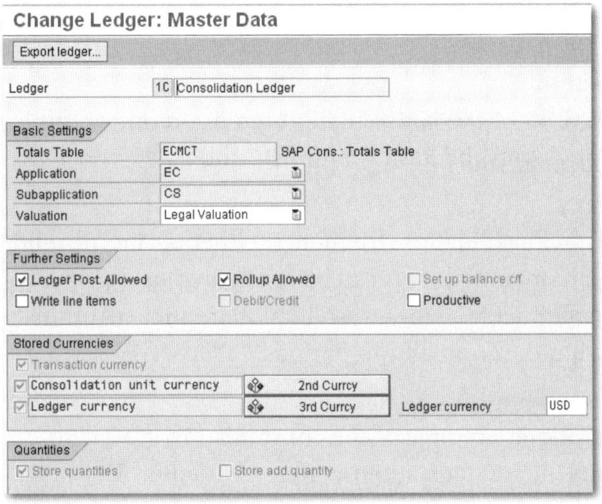

Figure 12.10 Change an Existing Consolidation Ledger

Now that you understand the settings that define a ledger, let's discuss how you can map your organizational structure in EC-CS.

12.6 Define Organization Units and Groups

In this step, you can define organizational units that exist within the corporate structure. This structure enables you to map the corporate group structure into the system. You can map the organization groups into regions, for example, ABC, Inc is divided into Americas, Europe, and Asia. Americas can be further subdivided into North and South Americas, which can then be assigned to companies.

12.6.1 Define Consolidation Group

You need to define the consolidation group to map your organization's consolidation hierarchy by defining consolidation groups and then assigning these to subnodes in the consolidation hierarchy. The menu path is **IMG • Enter-**

prise Controlling • Consolidation • Master Data • Organization units • Consolidation groups • Maintain Consolidation groups individually. The Transactions are CX1P (Create)/CX1Q (Change)/CX1R (Display).

In the initial screen, a **Consolidation group ZABC** is being defined for your organization. You can maintain the details related to **Master data, Correspondence, Methods, Data Transfer**, and **Assignments**. Figure 12.11 shows the **Master Data** tab where you can define the following parameters:

▶ **Short text/Medium text**
This captures the description of the consolidation group. In our example, we are defining the overall consolidation group **ABC Inc**.

▶ **Consolidation frequency**
Here you can define the consolidation frequency either as month end, quarter end, semi-annual, or annual. This can be configured using Transaction CXB2, where you need to define the consolidation frequency (number and name) and then assign the from and to periods.

▶ **Country**
This identifies the headquarter country of the consolidation group. So if a company is listed in the United States, then you need to enter US".

▶ **Ledger**
This identifies the consolidation ledger to which the consolidation group belongs. In this case, we have assigned the ledger **CL**.

▶ **Currency**
You also need to identify the currency of the consolidation group. In this case, we have identified the currency as **USD**.

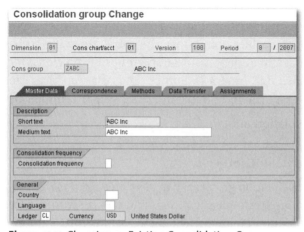

Figure 12.11 Changing an Existing Consolidation Group

In the **Correspondence** tab, you can further define **Name 1** and **Name 2** along with **Address** details. Figure 12.12 shows the screen for maintaining the methods of currency translation and tax rate. The parameters that can be maintained are enumerated as follows:

▶ **Tax rate**
Here you can maintain the tax rate that needs to be applied to the tax base amount to calculate the tax amount.

▶ **Currency**
This gets populated from the ledger to which the consolidation group was assigned in the **Master Data** tab. So in our example **USD** gets populated.

▶ **Entry in group currency**
This indicator identifies the primary currency type (local currency versus group Currency) that you need to enter. If you set this indicator, then you need to enter the group currency. If the local currency is the same as the group currency, then local currency values are also posted; otherwise, the local currency values are not posted. If you do not check this indicator, then you can post in local currency and group currency simultaneously.

▶ **Translation method**
This identifies the currency translation method that will be applicable for the consolidation group. Some of the options are **Straight current-rate method**, **Modified current-rate method**, and **Historical rate method**.

▶ **Period category**
This identifies the relevant periods for which you need to build the validation. You can identify the range from 1 to 16 or each individual period separately.

▶ **Valid. ID for CG**
You can maintain the rules for validating the ID for the consolidation group. You can build validation rules for checking individual statements and charts of accounts for the consolidation group.

▶ **RU CU recordbl**
This indicator allows you to roll up entry and posting of data to the corresponding rollup consolidation unit.

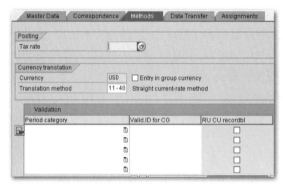

Figure 12.12 Tax Rate and Translation Method

Figure 12.13 shows the screen for maintaining the data transfer rules. The following parameters can be maintained:

- **Financial data type**
  This captures the type of financial data. You can maintain these data types per the chart of accounts to segregate the financial statement items.

- **Year/Prd**
  This is the effective year and period from which the assignment is affected.

- **Period category**
  This identifies the period category for which the assignment is relevant.

- **G.TG. DataMon**
  This identifies the group-dependent task group for use in the Data Monitor. You need to select an appropriate task group in this field, such as 23000, which represents all the tasks in Data Monitor.

- **G.TG. ConsMon**
  This identifies the group-dependent task group that is used in the Consolidation Monitor. 50000 is the task group that can be used to select all the tasks in Consolidation Monitor.

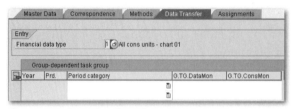

Figure 12.13 Data Transfer Tab

Now that you understand the data transfer schematic, let's take a look at the consolidation group assignments. Figure 12.14 shows the assignments of the consolidation group **ZASIA**, consolidation unit **ZEUR**, and consolidation group **ZZAMER** to the consolidation group **ZABC**.

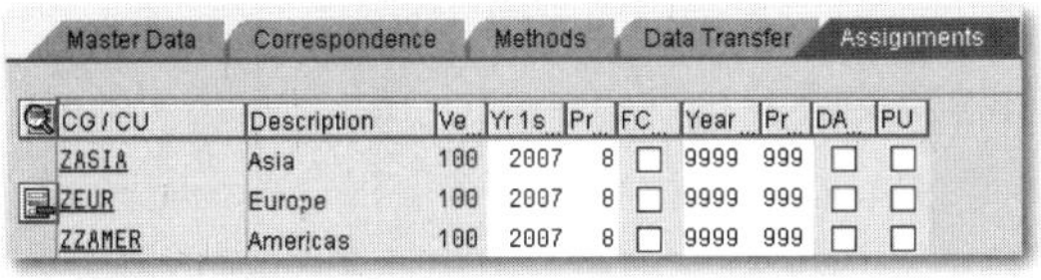

Figure 12.14 Assigning a Consolidation Group

Using similar assignments, you can create a hierarchical structure that allows you to map your organization's consolidation structure. Transaction CX1X allows you to create your consolidation hierarchy quickly. You can even use an Excel upload if you are building your hierarchy for the first time. Now that you know how to set up a consolidation group, you will learn how to define a consolidation unit in the next step.

12.6.2 Define Consolidation Units

The consolidation unit represents the lowest level of consolidation structure that actually receives the data. The consolidation unit can be a company, business area, or a profit center depending on the consolidation type. All these consolidation units actually tie back to the enterprise structure units identified in Chapter 3. The menu path is **IMG • Enterprise Controlling • Consolidation • Master Data • Organization units • Consolidation units • Maintain Consolidation units individually,** and the Transactions are CX1M (Create)/CX1N (Change)/CX1O (Display).

Figure 12.15 shows the screen where you can maintain the master data for consolidation unit ZUSA. You can enter the description and details about the country, language, and local currency. Note that this is very similar to the consolidation group except for the following fields:

▶ **Reason for inclusion**
Here you can specify the reason for inclusion or the reason for exclusion from the consolidation process. Reasons for inclusion can be defined in the system using Transaction CXA9.

▶ **Exempt from inclusion**
This indicator exempts the consolidation group from inclusion in the consolidation process.

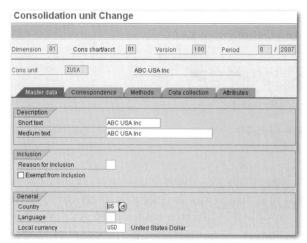

Figure 12.15 Maintain the Consolidation Unit

The **Correspondence** tab is similar to consolidation group where you can maintain the address and correspondence details. The **Methods** tab is similar with the additional ability to maintain the tax rate for investment income. In the **Data collection** tab, you can maintain the data transfer method, which can be online data entry, periodic extract, real-time update from FI, flexible upload, rollup, upload from offline data entry using MS Access, interactive Excel, read from BW copy, or extract from step consolidation. In the **Attributes** tab, you can maintain the K3 Form—Legal Form, Industrial sector, and legal entity.

Tips

▶ You can define additional fields and define new screens for consolidation units and groups by using the enhancement FMC10001. These screens can contain additional fields with special tables.

▶ You can perform mass changes in consolidation group and unit using Transactions CXAS and CXAR, respectively

▶ You can maintain the tax rate by consolidation unit with an **Effective From Fiscal Year** and **Period** using Transaction CXAP.

Now that you understand how to create consolidation units and groups, let's take a look at financial statement items.

12.7 Define Financial Statement Items

Financial statement items perform the function similar to the GL master in GL accounting. However, financial statement items are typically a group of GLs in a business sense and represent primarily the core headings of published balance sheet and P&L statements.

Consolidation uses its own chart of accounts, prescribed by the corporate consolidation department for legal consolidation. You need to define the appropriate chart of accounts and then assign the financial statement items to them to create the hierarchical consolidation structure. You can use the path **IMG • Enterprise Controlling • Consolidation • Master Data • Financial Statement Items • User defined Consolidation Chart of Accounts • Maintain FS Items individually**. You can also use Transactions CX13 (Create)/CX14 (Change)/CX15 (Display).

Figure 12.16 shows the screen where you can define a financial statement item for the balance sheet. The various fields that you need to maintain are as follows:

► **Cons chart of accts**
This is the consolidation chart of accounts. You need to select an appropriate consolidation chart of accounts against which to maintain your FS items.

► **FS item**
This is the consolidation financial item that represents a heading in the balance sheet.

► **FS item type**
This can be a Values item, Totals item, or Text item.

► **Debit/credit sign (+/−)**
"+" indicates debit, whereas "−" indicates credit.

► **Where-applied indicator**
A indicates asset, **B** indicates liability or stockholder's equity, **C** indicates income statement, and **D** indicates that the FS item is statistical.

► **Item category**
This identifies the item category of the FS item.

► **Contra item**
This identifies the corresponding contra item, which is assigned to the FS item. This allows you to post the negative balance in assets to the corresponding liability contra and positive balance in liabilities to the corresponding asset contra, when you are executing the substitution task.

- ▶ **Consolidation item**
  This identifies the item as relevant only for consolidation and is typically used for FS items such as goodwill.

- ▶ **Appropriation item**
  This identifies the FS item as relevant for appropriation of retained earnings.

- ▶ **Breakdown category**
  This identifies the breakdown category that distinguishes by partner type, function area, currency, year of acquisition, and regions.

- ▶ **Breakdown type**
  These columns allow you to define the rules for entering additional parameters for entry in the FS item. The **Breakdown types** can be the following:

  - ▶ **0**
    No breakdown.

  - ▶ **1**
    Optional breakdown with initialized value allowed.

  - ▶ **2**
    Required breakdown; if blank, the default value is used.

  - ▶ **3**
    Required breakdown; entry is forced, default allowed.

  - ▶ **4**
    Required breakdown; entry is forced, default not allowed.

- ▶ **Short text**
  This is the description of the breakdown type.

- ▶ **Fixed value**
  Here you can enter a fixed value for a subitem category such as characteristic.

- ▶ **Set Name**
  This identifies the consolidation FS item set.

Figure 12.16 shows the screen where you can define a financial statement item for a P&L item. Note that the **FS item type** for the travel expense FS item is **1: Value item,** and the **Where-applied indicator** is **C: Income statement**. The **Breakdown category** is defined as **2000: Functional area** with the **Breakdown type 3** where you have to enter a functional area; if nothing is entered, the default value is 2.

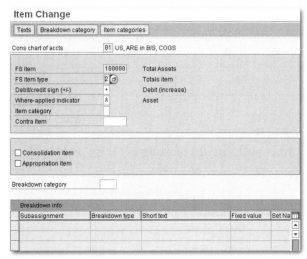

Figure 12.16 Changing a Financial Statement Item

If you click on the **Breakdown category** button shown in Figure 12.17, you will reach the screen shown in Figure 12.18. The fields that can be maintained are as follows:

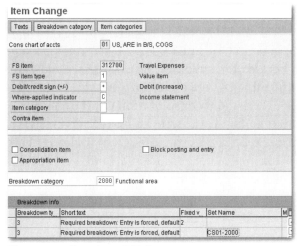

Figure 12.17 Changing a P&L Item

▶ **Char.**
This identifies the characteristics that are relevant for the breakdown category.

▶ **Break. Type/Text.**
This identifies the breakdown type.

▶ **Fixed val.**

This identifies any fixed value defaults that need to be set up for the characteristic.

▶ **Default set**

Here you can identify the default set that can be used for the characteristic.

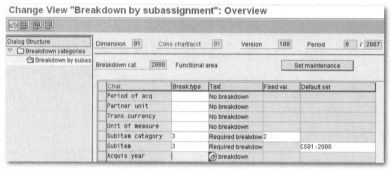

Figure 12.18 Breakdown Category Definition

12.8 Define Sets

Sets are defined to group together similar consolidation units, FS items, subitems, or general objects. You will have to define your own consolidation unit sets depending on the organization structure. However, some presupplied SAP system sets can be used for building your own sets. Follow the path **IMG • Enterprise Controlling • Consolidation • Master Data • Financial Statement Items • User defined Consolidation Chart of Accounts • Maintain FS Items individually,** or use Transactions CXSC (Create) or GS01/CXSB or GS02 (Change)/CXSA (Display) or GS03/CXSD (Delete). Figure 12.19 shows how you can maintain a set for consolidation units. Here the set **NORTH_AMERICAS** is defined as a **Set of cons units**.

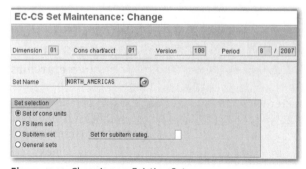

Figure 12.19 Changing an Existing Set

After you press Enter, you can maintain the values of sets as shown in Figure 12.20. Here the consolidation unit **ZUSA** is maintained as part of the **Cons. Unit Set NORTH_AMERICAS**. **Sym. Na.** refers to symbolic names, which are used in report writer as coordinates to address cells in a report.

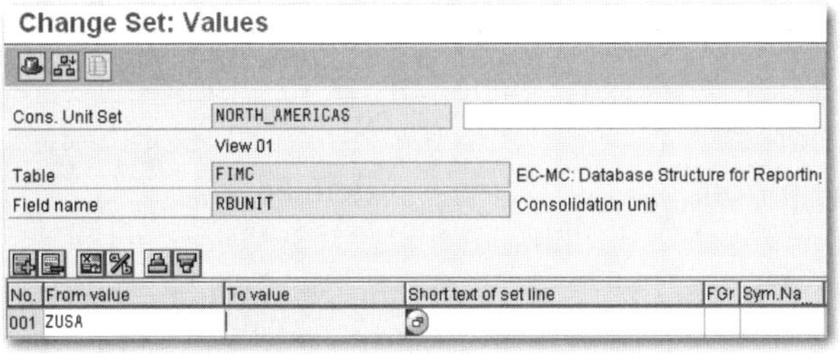

Change Set: Values

Cons. Unit Set	NORTH_AMERICAS			
	View 01			
Table	FIMC		EC-MC: Database Structure for Reporting	
Field name	RBUNIT		Consolidation unit	

No.	From value	To value	Short text of set line	FGr	Sym.Na
001	ZUSA				

Figure 12.20 Maintaining the Values of the Sets

12.9 Define Characteristics

Characteristics are used to define account assignments in EC-CS. Characteristics come predefined in the standard SAP system and include consolidation unit, financial statement item, subitem, and so on. If these predefined characteristics do not meet your requirements, then you can add more characteristics that extend the consolidation database. You should be very careful when you create custom characteristics because it is not possible to delete characteristics if you have posted data in them. The menu path is **IMG • Enterprise Controlling • Consolidation • Add Characteristics**, and the Transaction is CX0A1.

12.10 Define Characteristic Hierarchies

Now you can define hierarchical relationship among custom characteristics defined in the previous step. For example, you can use the characteristic hierarchies to define a hierarchy of products or regions. The relationships defined here can then be used for analysis in drilldown and interactive Excel reports for a more detailed understanding. The menu path is **IMG • Enterprise Controlling • Consolidation • Master Data • Maintain hierarchies of characteristics**, and the Transaction is CXRH.

This completes the typical settings of master data, such as ledger, consolidation groups and units, FS items, characteristics, and characteristic hierarchies. Master data forms the building block of consolidation setup. In the next section, you will learn about the transaction data processing in EC-CS.

12.11 Data Collection

EC-CS is a receiver module of financial and nonfinancial data from multiple applications. So data collection is one of the primary functions of the consolidation module. Consolidation functions are based on the ECMCT table.

Typically, in earlier implementations, we used to define a special purpose ledger to convert the data in a format that made sense for consolidation and then roll up the same to ECMCT. However, with the introduction of the new GL, you can directly roll up from one of the ledgers defined in the new GL. Any entries made only during the consolidation process are recorded in the ECMCA table, which then flows to the totals table. Understanding the EC-CS architecture and data flow will help you in troubleshooting any errors that you might encounter during the consolidation process. The following are the ways you can collect data from the SAP system:

▸ Real-time update from other financial components

▸ Rollup from special purpose ledger or EC-CS component

▸ Periodic extract from the GL

▸ Periodic data entry using Access or Excel

Now you will learn how to enter data online in the system from SAP ERP as well as non-SAP ERP systems. It is very important for you to clearly understand the process of collecting data in EC-CS. There can be a couple of scenarios that you should consider when defining the process of collecting data as follows:

▸ **Decentralized scenario**
Several applications capture the consolidation data and then transmit the data to corporate headquarters to enter the consolidation data. So there are multiple SAP ERP or non-SAP financial applications that need to come together in the consolidation module. This could be the case if your organization is part of a huge conglomerate but needs to publish the consolidation report within the listed companies first. In the decentralized scenario, data is not updated in real-time.

▸ **Centralized scenario**
All the applications are on the same instance and the same client. All the data from subledgers automatically transfers to the GL, which then flows to EC-CS or profit center accounting if it is a profit center consolidation type. All the data gets transmitted to subsequent receivers on an online basis. The centralized approach is much cleaner and highly efficient from the operations perspective.

This can be configured using the settings in **Consolidation • Integration: Preparation for Consolidation**. Depending on your scenario, you need to make appropriate settings in the sender and receiver systems to optimize your data transfer from feeder systems and collection in EC-CS.

12.12 Data Monitor and Consolidation Monitor

Data Monitor allows you to manage the monitoring and collection of financial data. In consolidation, it is very important that you execute your tasks in a particular order. For example, before executing any transactions on data, you need to validate the data. Data Monitor allows you to sequence the tasks and provides you the status of each individual task.

You can also define that a successor task will only begin if the preceding task has been completed without any errors. You can also use the Data Monitor to execute the tasks as well either in test or update mode. Consolidation Monitor helps to control the sequence of the consolidation tasks and to execute the tasks. The tasks of Consolidation Monitor can only be executed after the tasks for Data Monitor are finished. First let's take a look at defining a task group that categorizes similar types of tasks.

12.12.1 Define Task Group

In this step, task groups are defined for the Data Monitor. Task groups can be classified as either global or consolidation dependent task groups. Global task groups are assigned to the dimension and to capture all the tasks in the data collection process. Consolidation group-dependent tasks only show up when a particular consolidation group is entered in the global parameters. Typical tasks that are defined as part of a task group are data carryforward, data validation, validation of reported data, manual standardizing and correcting entries, currency translation, and validation of standardized financial data. Follow the menu path **IMG • Enterprise Controlling • Consolidation • Data • Data monitor • Define task group**, or use Transaction CXE0.

Figure 12.21 shows the details of the **Task Group 23000: Data Monitor-all tasks**. Here you can identify the **Task** that is included in the task groups. For example, **1100 Carryforward** and **7000 Apportionment** have been included as part of the **Task group 23000**. Let's detail the parameters that you can define for each task:

▶ **Block auto**.

If this indicator is set, then the task is automatically blocked after it has been successfully executed without any errors. If this is not set, then you need to manually block any finished task if needed.

▶ **Milestone**

Setting this indicator makes a task a milestone, and automatic processing will stop when Data Monitor reaches this task. Note that **Data entry** and **ManStdEnty** (Manual Standard Entry) will always be marked as milestones. This allows you to initiate other activities manually.

▶ **Position**

This identifies the sequence of tasks that have the same rank. This allows you to execute these tasks in parallel.

▶ **Last Task, DM**

This identifies the last task that, if completed, successfully changes the status of the Data Monitor of the task group to green.

Change View "Assign tasks to task group": Overview

Task	Short text	Block auto.	Milestone	Position	Last task, DM
1100	Carryfwd	☐	☐		○
1110	RE,ItSubst	☐	☐		○
1200	Data entry	☐	☑		○
1300	Valid. RFD	☑	☐		○
1310	CG chgs RD	☐	☐		○
1400	Recl. co.	☐	☐		○
1450	ManStdEnty	☐	☑		○
1500	CrcyTrans.	☐	☐		○
1510	CG chgs SD	☐	☐		○
1600	Valid. SFD	☑	☐		○
7000	Apportion.	☐	☐		○

Figure 12.21 Assign Tasks to Task Group

After you have defined the tasks, you can specify which one is the preceding task for a particular task as shown in Figure 12.22. Here **Balance Carryforward** is defined as a **Preceding task** to **Data Entry**.

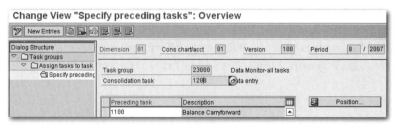

Figure 12.22 Specify the Preceding Task for a Task Group

12.12.2 Assign Task Group to Dimension

You need to assign the task group defined in the previous step to the dimension that is relevant for consolidation. It allows you to customize the task groups per the period, version, and dimension. You can follow the menu path **IMG • Enterprise Controlling • Consolidation • Data • Data monitor • Assign task group to dimension,** or use Transaction CXP1.

Figure 12.23 shows how you can assign the task group **12000** to the **Dimension 01** with an effective fiscal year (**FY effect.**) from **1997** and an effective period (**Period eff**) of **12**. In the same setting, you can also assign a separate task group **40000** to Consolidation Monitor (**Cons mon. task group**).

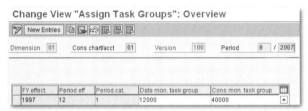

Figure 12.23 Assign Task group to Dimension

Now that you know the key settings that need to be made for defining monitors in EC-CS, let's take a look at currency translation, which is one of the most important functions executed in the consolidation process.

12.13 Currency Translation

Data is collected in EC-CS in local currency. You need to convert the same to your group currency in which you will be reporting your consolidated statements. Currency translation in EC-CS allows you to translate the local currency to group currency. Currency translation, as you know, is based on the translation methods that need to be defined per consolidation unit.

So you will first learn to define translation methods and then learn to define the GL account for the posting of balance sheet translation differences to income statement. Finally, we will reiterate how you can assign a currency translation method to a consolidation unit.

12.13.1 Define Translation Methods

Translation methods are dependent on the FS items. For example, fixed assets are translated using historical exchange rates, whereas current assets are translated using current exchange rates. Income statement items, on the other hand, are based on a period range (month of October) and are translated based on the average rate for the month. The translation method helps zero on the exchange rate that should be used for translating the local currency to group currency. This also controls how the translation differences are posted. The menu path is **IMG • Enterprise Controlling • Consolidation • Data • Automatic Posting • Currency Translation • Translation methods • Define currency translation methods,** and the Transaction is CXD1.

Figure 12.24 shows the standard translation methods that can be copied to build up your own currency translation method. The key parameters for translation method are as follows:

- **Transl. method**.
  This is the translation method identifier.
- **Description**
  Here you can enter the description of your currency translation method.
- **Validation**
  This is a system-determined status signifying whether the translation method has been checked and error free.
- **Active**
  You need to select the translation method that should be activated.

You can also maintain the reference exchange rate indicator against which you will be comparing the translation gains or losses, by double-clicking on the translation method.

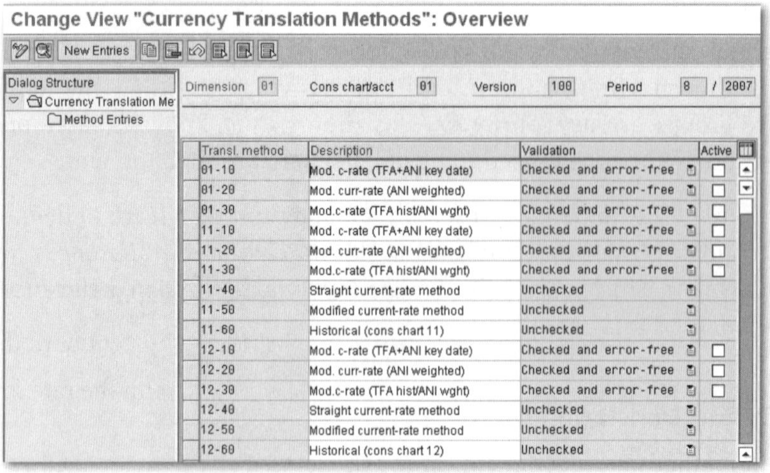

Transl. method	Description	Validation	Active
01-10	Mod. c-rate (TFA+ANI key date)	Checked and error-free	☐
01-20	Mod. curr-rate (ANI weighted)	Checked and error-free	☐
01-30	Mod.c-rate (TFA hist/ANI wght)	Checked and error-free	☐
11-10	Mod. c-rate (TFA+ANI key date)	Checked and error-free	☐
11-20	Mod. curr-rate (ANI weighted)	Checked and error-free	☐
11-30	Mod.c-rate (TFA hist/ANI wght)	Checked and error-free	☐
11-40	Straight current-rate method	Unchecked	
11-50	Modified current-rate method	Unchecked	
11-60	Historical (cons chart 11)	Unchecked	
12-10	Mod. c-rate (TFA+ANI key date)	Checked and error-free	☐
12-20	Mod. curr-rate (ANI weighted)	Checked and error-free	☐
12-30	Mod.c-rate (TFA hist/ANI wght)	Checked and error-free	☐
12-40	Straight current-rate method	Unchecked	
12-50	Modified current-rate method	Unchecked	
12-60	Historical (cons chart 12)	Unchecked	

Figure 12.24 Define Currency Translation Methods

If you select a translation method and then click on **Method Entries**, you will reach the next screen shown in Figure 12.25. Here you can maintain the details of a translation method:

▶ **No.**
This is the sequence number in the translation method.

▶ **R**
This allows you to define rounding entries. To define a rounding entry, you need to enter the relevant item sets that should be checked for rounding.

▶ **Item set 1**
This identifies the FI item sets that are relevant for translation or rounding differences.

▶ **Description**
This details the description of the item set.

▶ **ER ind.**
This identifies the exchange rate indicator that will help in identifying the exchange rates during currency translation.

▶ **Trans.**
This represents the currency translation key that identifies the base currency, method used for translation, and the table from which the system reads the relevant exchange rate. You have the option of defining local or transaction currency as the base currency. The following currency translation keys can be selected:

  ▶ **0**: Translation resulting in consolidated value of zero.

  ▶ **1**: Translation of cumulative local values at current rate.

  ▶ **2**: Historical translation by year of acquisition.

  ▶ **3**: Historical translation using changes in investments table.

  ▶ **4**: Historical translation using changes in investee equity table.

  ▶ **5**: Translation by period at applicable rate for each period.

  ▶ **6**: No retranslation of existing group currency value.

  ▶ **7**: Translation of user-defined exchange rate determination.

  ▶ **9**: Translation of transaction currency values at rate for current period.

  ▶ **A**: Translation of transaction currency values by period with the rate for each period.

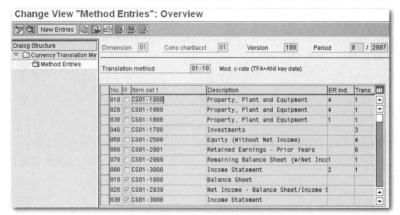

Figure 12.25 Define Translation Method's Item Sets

Double-clicking on the sequence number **10**, will let you see the details of the item set shown in Figure 12.26. Here you can see additional parameters that can be defined:

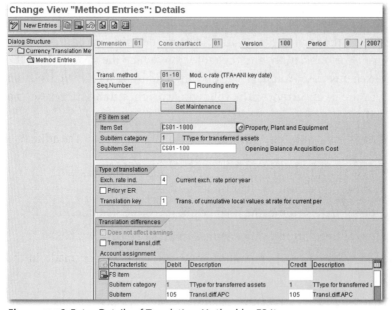

Figure 12.26 Enter Details of Translation Method by FS Item

▶ **Prior yr ER**
  This ensures that the date is determined using the prior year when the transaction actually happened rather than the current year.

▶ **Does not affect earnings**
If you set this indicator, then retained earnings are not affected with translation.

▶ **Temporal transl. diff.**
This stores the temporary translation differences that you find during the currency translation process.

You can also maintain the subitem category and subitems in this screen as shown in **Account assignment**.

12.13.2 Define Posting of Balance Sheet Translation Differences

You can specify that the translation differences in balance sheet accounts are posted to P&L accounts. However, this directly affects the retained earnings, which is a balance sheet account. So some organizations offset this posting by making a journal entry to nullify the impact of balance sheet currency translations. You can use this setting to offset the posting of balance sheet accounts to P&L accounts. The menu path is **IMG • Enterprise Controlling • Consolidation • Data • Automatic Posting • Currency Translation• Translation methods • Define posting of B/S Translation differences in the I/S**, and the Transaction is CXD3.

Figure 12.27 shows the various fields that need to be maintained. They are explained here:

▶ **Bal. sheet item**
This identifies the balance sheet item that will be relevant for the adjusting entry.

▶ **Subitem** and **Subitem category**
This is the subitem and subitem category for the balancing entry for the balance sheet.

▶ **Inc. stmt. Item**
Here you need to enter the offsetting entry that needs to be made in the P&L FS item.

▶ **Subitem** and **Subitem category**
This is the subitem and subitem category for the balancing entry for the P&L entry.

▶ **Statistic. item**
This is the statistical item for the FS balancing adjustment and is used to store the cumulative translation difference for prior periods.

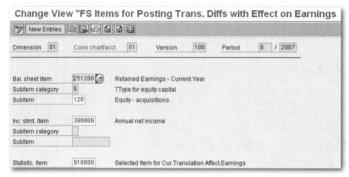

Figure 12.27 Define FS Items for Posting

12.13.3 Assign the Translation Method to the Consolidation Unit

You already learned how you can maintain the translation method in the consolidation unit. You can also maintain this using the following menu path for multiple consolidation units at the same time: **IMG • Enterprise Controlling • Consolidation • Data • Automatic Posting • Currency Translation • Translation methods • Assign translation method to consolidation unit.** The Transaction is CXAO.

12.13.4 Define Exchange Rate Indicators

Exchange rate indicators help in identifying the exchange rates during currency translation. The exchange rate indicator essentially helps you in mapping to the exchange rate type that controls which exchange rates are chosen for currency translation. Figure 12.28 displays the exchange rate indicators that can be defined. Follow the menu path **IMG • Enterprise Controlling • Consolidation • Data • Automatic Posting • Currency Translation• Exchange rates • Define exchange rate indicators,** or use Transaction CXD2.

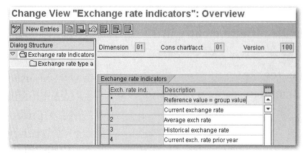

Figure 12.28 Define Exchange Rate Indicators

If you select the exchange rate indicator **1** and then click on the **Exchange rate type a** in the left pane, you will reach the screen shown in Figure 12.29. The most important parameter that you need to maintain here is the **ER type 1001**. This allows you to map to the correct exchange rate maintained in the exchange rate table.

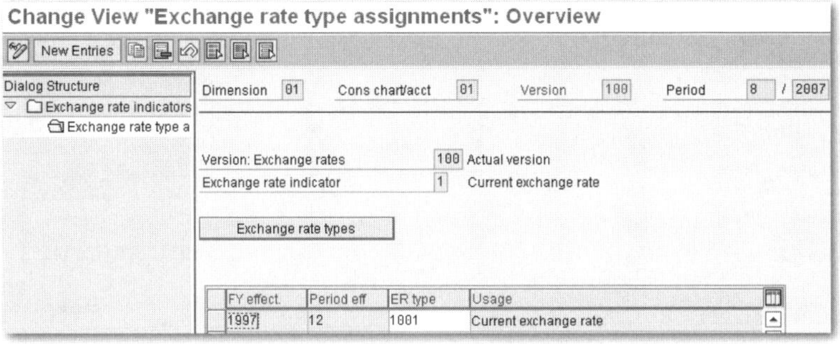

Figure 12.29 Assign Exchange Rate Type to Exchange Rate Indicator

12.13.5 Specify Translation Ratios

Translation ratios can be used to control the number of decimal places used for exchange rate maintenance. These are specified by exchange range type and currency combinations. Figure 12.30 illustrates how you can maintain the translation ratios in **Ratio (from)** and **Ratio (to)**. The menu path is **IMG • Enterprise Controlling • Consolidation • Data • Automatic Posting • Currency Translation• Exchange rates • Specify translation ratios**, and the Transaction is GCRF.

> **Note**
>
> **DEM** and **USD** have a translation ratio of 1:1. This means that you will need to enter the conversion of 1 USD to 1 DEM when you maintain the exchange rates.

12.13.6 Maintain Exchange Rates

Exchange rates need to be maintained in the system so that they can be used for translating local currencies to group currencies. You need to maintain all the currency pairs with group currency. The menu path is **IMG • Enterprise Controlling • Consolidation • Data • Automatic Posting • Currency Translation• Exchange rates • Maintain exchange rates**, and the Transaction is OC41.

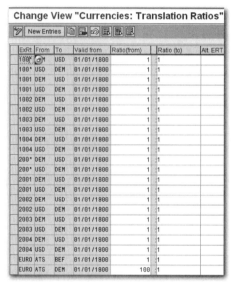

Figure 12.30 Define Exchange Rate Translation Ratios

Figure 12.31 shows how you can maintain the exchange rates by exchange rate type. Both direct and indirect quotes can be maintained. For exchange rate type **1001**, indirect quote of **1.64110 DEM** to **1 USD** has been maintained, whereas the direct quote of **1 USD = 1.64110 DEM** has also been maintained. All exchange rates need to have a valid **From** date. For the current rate, the system will pick up the rate that has the latest data maintained in the **Valid-From** date.

Change View "Currency Exchange Rates": Overview

New Entries									

ExRt	ValidFrom	Indir.quot		Ratio(from)	From		Dir.quot.		Ratio (to)	To
100*	01/01/1997	1.64110	X	1 DEM	=			X	1 USD
100*	01/01/1997		X	1 USD	=	1.64110		X	1 DEM
1001	01/01/1997	1.64110	X	1 DEM	=			X	1 USD
1001	01/01/1997		X	1 USD	=	1.64110		X	1 DEM
1002	01/01/1997	1.64110	X	1 DEM	=			X	1 USD
1002	01/01/1997		X	1 USD	=	1.64110		X	1 DEM
1003	01/01/1997	1.64110	X	1 DEM	=			X	1 USD
1003	01/01/1997		X	1 USD	=	1.64110		X	1 DEM
1004	01/01/1997	1.64110	X	1 DEM	=			X	1 USD
1004	01/01/1997		X	1 USD	=	1.64110		X	1 DEM

Figure 12.31 Maintain Exchange Rates

This completes all the settings needed to make to execute currency translation in EC-CS. Next you will learn about balance carryforward in EC-CS.

12.14   Balance Carryforward

At the end of each fiscal year, financial statement item balances are carried forward to the new fiscal year. During balance carryforward, all the balance sheet items are carried forward. Income statement items are carried forward if they are specified as selected items for carrying forward.

> **Note**
>
> In consolidation and in the special purpose ledger, the balance carryforward period for the each new year is 000. So when you generate reports for balance sheets, make sure that you include 000 as the selection parameters in your report writer reports.

In this section, you will learn how to specify the FS items as relevant for balance carryforward and how to exclude the FS items from the balance carryforward process.

12.14.1   Specify FS Items to Be Carried Forward

You need to maintain these setting for items that are typically not carried forward, such as P&L accounts. However, if you want the financial items to be carried forward to a different financial item in the new year, the same can also be specified here. You will need to follow the menu path **IMG • Enterprise Controlling • Consolidation • Data • Balance carryforward • Specify FS Items to be carried forward** or use Transaction CXS3. Figure 12.32 shows the various balance sheet financial statements that need to be carried forward every year at year end.

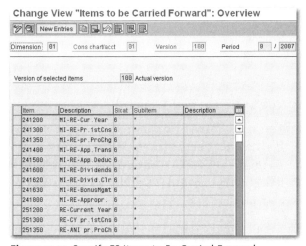

Figure 12.32 Specify FS Items to Be Carried Forward

The parameters shown in the figure are explained here:

- ▶ **Item/Description**
  This identifies the FS item that you want to be carried forward to the new fiscal year.

- ▶ **SIcat**
  This identifies the subitem category.

- ▶ **Subitem**
  If you want the subitems to go to different FS items, then you can maintain these here. Otherwise, ***** is maintained, which covers all the subitems for the FS item.

Figure 12.33 shows the details of the FS items to which the FS item in the old year needs to be carried forward. Here **241100** is maintained as the FS item to which the FS item **241200** gets carried forward.

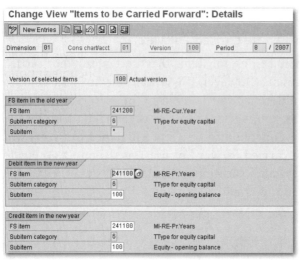

Figure 12.33 Additional Details for FS Items Assignment

12.14.2 Specify FS Items Not to Be Carried Forward

Sometimes you do not want to carry forward balance sheet FS items that are statistical in nature. In this step, FS items that are not relevant for carryforward are defined. The menu path is **IMG • Enterprise Controlling • Consolidation • Data • Balance carryforward • Specify FS Items not to be carried forward**. The Transaction is CXS4.

The configuration settings are similar to the ones previously defined for including the financial items that need to be carried forward. In the next section, you will learn how to configure and optimize your consolidation functions using EC-CS.

12.15 Consolidation Business Transaction Postings

In the previous section, you were introduced to the different functions that need to be executed as part of data collection performed in Data Monitor. Some of the common consolidation functions that happen only in EC-CS are listed here:

- ▶ Standardizing or corrections to reported financial data
- ▶ Reclassifications
- ▶ Interunit eliminations
- ▶ Elimination of interunit P&L
- ▶ Consolidation of investments

However, remember that all the postings that happen only in EC-CS need to be executed from the Consolidation Monitor. Figure 12.34 shows the perspective of posting parameters. First you need to define the **Document types** that are tied to the **Number ranges**. The document types are then assigned to tasks that are assigned to transaction methods. The consolidation transactions can then be posted using the special FS items. These postings are then recorded in ECMCA and ECMCT for consolidation reporting.

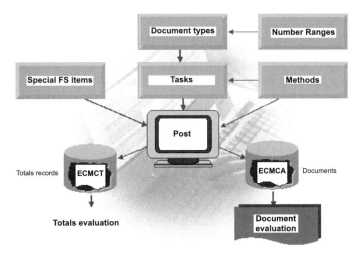

Figure 12.34 Postings Configuration Map (Source: SAP AG)

First of all, let's learn how to define a document type.

12.15.1 Define Document Types

Document types in EC-CS control how the consolidation business transactions will be posted. In this step, document types for manual postings are defined. The menu path is **IMG • Enterprise Controlling • Consolidation • Consolidation functions • Manual Posting • Define Document Type**, and the Transaction is CXEJ. Figure 12.35 shows the **Document type 21** for elimination of inter-unit payables or receivable. The parameters for the document type are detailed as follows:

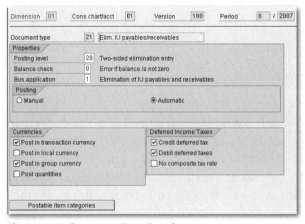

Figure 12.35 Document Type Details

- ▸ **Posting level**
  This allows you to classify the different types of entries. The different posting levels that need to be used appropriately are as follows:
  - ▸ **00**: Reported data.
  - ▸ **Space**: Reported data from real-time update or rollup.
  - ▸ **01**: Adjustment entries to reported data.
  - ▸ **02**: Reported data for consolidation group changes.
  - ▸ **08**: Item substitution and calculation of the retained earnings.
  - ▸ **10**: Standardizing entries.
  - ▸ **12**: Standardizing entries for consolidation group changes.
  - ▸ **20**: Two-sided eliminating entries.
  - ▸ **22**: Two-sided eliminating entries for consolidation group changes.
  - ▸ **23**: Two-sided eliminating entries with special logic.

- ▸ **24**: Two-sided eliminating entries for consolidation group changes with special logic.

- ▸ **30**: Consolidation of investments postings.

▸ **Balance check**
There are three options:

- ▸ **0**: Error if balance is not zero.

- ▸ **1**: Warning if balance is not zero.

- ▸ **2**: No balance check.

▸ **Bus application**
The business applications are classified per the consolidation business transaction as follows:

- ▸ **1**: Elimination of IU payables and receivables.

- ▸ **2**: Elimination of IU revenue and expense.

- ▸ **3**: Consolidation of investment income.

- ▸ **4**: Elimination of IU profit/loss in inventory.

- ▸ **5**: Elimination of IU profit/loss in transferred assets.

- ▸ **6**: Consolidation of investments.

- ▸ **7**: Reclassification.

- ▸ **9**: Other.

▸ **Posting**
The posting can be classified as either **Manual** or **Automatic**. If you choose manual posting, then the document type is excluded from the automatic consolidation transactions.

▸ **Post in transaction currency**
This allows the document type to post in transaction currency.

▸ **Post in local currency**
This allows the document type to post in local currency.

▸ **Post in group currency**
This allows the document type to post in group currency.

▸ **Post quantities**
This allows you to post quantities in the document type.

▸ **Credit deferred tax**
This automatically credits deferred taxes during posting.

▸ **Debit deferred taxes**
|This automatically debits deferred taxes during posting.

▸ **No composite tax rate**
If this flag is set, the system calculates the tax rate by consolidation unit. Otherwise, the system derives a composite tax rate after considering all the consolidation units involved.

After you have defined the parameters for document type, you can assign a number range to the document type as shown in Figure 12.36. Here you have assigned the Number range 05 to the **Document type** as **21** for **Version 100** and **200**. If you check **Auto reversal**, then the document type is automatically reversed in the subsequent period. **CF** represents the consolidation frequency, which can be quarterly, monthly, annually, and so on. **No AutoRe** suppresses any automatic reversals in a new fiscal year.

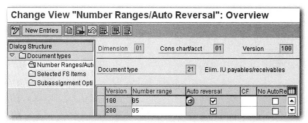

Figure 12.36 Define Number Ranges for Document Type

Figure 12.37 shows how you can maintain the FS items for the following:

▸ **Def. tax, B/S**
In this tab, you can maintain the balance sheet FS item for deferred tax.

▸ **Def. tax, I/S**
In this tab, you can maintain the income statement FS item for deferred tax.

▸ **Clear. Item**
In this tab, you maintain the clearing FS item.

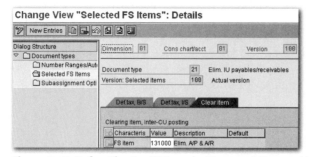

Figure 12.37 Define Clearing FS Items by Document Type and Versions

12.15.2 Assign Tasks to Document Type

Tasks for each activity, such as interunit elimination, reclassification, and so on, are predefined in the system and should not be changed. You should copy a task to modify the task. In this subsection, you will learn how you can assign a task to a document type. Follow **IMG • Enterprise Controlling • Consolidation • Consolidation functions• Manual Posting • Define Tasks,** or use Transaction CXP5. Figure 12.38 shows how you can assign the **Task 1450: Manual standardizing entry** to a **Doc.type** of **15** or **16**. Note that all document types are assigned to a task with an effective from fiscal year and period.

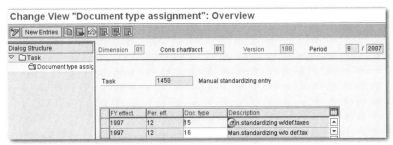

Figure 12.38 Define Tasks and Assign Document Type

12.16   Summary

This chapter introduced you to the consolidation process in SAP ERP by introducing you to master data that needs to be set up for consolidation. These include dimensions, versions, currencies, characteristics, consolidation groups, and units. This was followed by an exposition of the data collection process that is used to import data from SAP ERP Financials and non-SAP applications. You also learned how you can use Consolidation Monitor and Data Monitor to execute various business transactions related to data processing and consolidation business functions.

After this, you learned in detail about the process of configuring currency translation in EC-CS. You also learned about optimizing your balance carry-forward process at fiscal year end. Finally, you were introduced to document types in consolidation and how you can assign number ranges to document types and to tasks defined for various consolidation business transactions.

Now we have concluded the Financial Accounting component of SAP ERP Financials and Part III of this book in which we discussed the GL, the special purpose ledger, and consolidations using EC-CS.

> **Tip**
>
> For more advanced consolidation requirements, Strategic Enterprise Management-Business Consolidations (SEM-BCS) is implemented, which allows you to configure and implement far more diverse dimensions of consolidations per your business requirements.

We are almost at the end of this book, which will conclude in Chapter 13, coming up next.

FINANCE, n. The art or science of managing revenues and resources for the best advantage of the manager. The pronunciation of this word with the i long and the accent on the first syllable is one of America's most precious discoveries and possessions.

—*Ambrose Bierce*

13   Concluding Remarks

The SAP ERP Financials toolkit not only covers the entire breadth of the financial applications but is also extremely deep. It has built-in best practices and processes allowing you to implement all your financial business process quirks and fancies.

The fun with SAP ERP starts when you get into the details. Every day you can learn something new and still hope to find ten new different things that you never knew earlier. This book is not an attempt to cover each and every feature of SAP ERP. Rather an attempt has been made to cover the most important and relevant features of SAP ERP Financials functionality.

The focus of this book is to give you a framework that allows you to launch your optimization initiatives. The implementation should be driven by the functionality that makes sense to implement in a cost-effective fashion to your organization. Many features are available, but you need to determine if you really need that feature in your organization. Good consultants will know whether it makes sense. So there must be a two-way dialog in which you listen to their approaches and alternatives. Be open to suggestions, and make sure that you clearly communicate why you need a certain feature.

Sometimes, you also have to ascertain whether your organization is ready for the kind of sophistication that the feature will give you. Does it make sense to implement integrated planning when you do not have the basic planning structure mapped out? Probably not! But that doesn't mean you can't implement it after establishing your base processes.

Another important consideration is to keep the overall goal of implementing standard functionality whenever possible. There might be situations when you want to customize something that is unique to your organization, but ask the difficult questions amongst yourselves concerning whether you really need that customization or whether it makes more sense to change your business process.

So let us go over what we learned in this book one last time so that you can evlauate whether you got what you wanted.

13.1   What You Learned in This Book

The book helped you to start thinking about financial business processes from a process perspective, which allows you to think of the financial parts as part of a bigger enterprisewide system. This allows you to think about how you can optimize these processes to suit your requirements. For example, you might choose to implement the full-blown product costing with actual costing or material ledger, or you can just choose to get a standard cost estimate using product cost planning. So this book showed you the options and choices that you have with SAP ERP. With all these choices, it's often difficult to know which one is best.

Based on the features and integration effort required, you can choose to implement facets that make sense to your organization. In each chapter you were introduced to the basic building blocks, such as master data and enterprise structure, and then you were exposed to the deep functionality.

Notes
▶ The fun begins when you dive deeper and understand the core reason the functionality exists.
▶ Learning the details will help clients optimize their business processes by choosing the features that make the best sense to them.

An effort has been made to provide you with the features available in the latest SAP ERP 6.0 version so that you understand the baseline functionality available today. You also learned the future direction of SAP ERP in terms of advancements such as the financial shared services extension set and more banking integration.

13.2   Going Forward

Business is continuously evolving, and what makes sense right now will be passé in the future. SAP is always in touch with new business realities and adapts and changes so that you can configure the ever-evolving business processes in SAP ERP.

However, it is especially important that you are not tied down by what the system can or cannot do. More important than any system is creative thinking and the ability to simplify things from the process perspective. Some ingenuity and creative thought processes can allow you to map your existing business processes, and also think about your future organizational map and how the process fits in that scenario. Thinking about the future will clear a lot of cobwebs in your head and will allow you to optimize the process mapping and implement the solution that is best for your organization in the long run.

This book should allow you to undertake several process improvements and optimization efforts in your organization. We hope that this book allowed you to think of your own SAP ERP Financials implementation more deeply and that you will learn how to make the most out of it by optimizing it according to your needs and requirements.

Appendix

A   Glossary and SAP Abbreviations

ABAP   Advanced Business Application Programming, the SAP programming language.

Account determination   System function that determines automatically the accounts in financial accounting to which the postings occur during any posting transaction.

ALV   ABAP List Viewer allows you to sort, filter, subtotal, find, and customize the line layout of the report in a way that makes the most sense to you.

AM/AA   The Asset Management module/Asset Accounting is used to manage your fixed assets.

ALE   Application Link Enabling supports the creation and operation of distributed applications, and application integration is achieved via synchronous and asynchronous communication, not via a central database.

APO   Advanced Planner and Optimizer allows you to run optimization routines on demand planning, supply network planning, and global available to promise (GATP), which allows you to make decisions regarding the supply chain processes.

ATP   Available-to-promise is the quantity of a material or part still available to MRP, which could be used for new sales orders.

BAPI   Business Application Programming Interfaces are SAP supplied data modification routines. You should use many BAPIs

rather than custom ABAP code whenever possible because they are supported by SAP for future releases.

BDC   Batch Data Communication is used to define the processing mode for a batch input session, such as displaying all records, displaying error dialogs, displaying process sessions in the background, and so on.

BW   Business Information Warehouse is used to manage your business intelligence reporting.

CRM   Customer relationship management is used to manage your interactions with your customers.

Company code   The smallest organizational unit for which a complete self-contained set of accounts can be drawn up.

Controlling (CO)   SAP ERP module that controls and monitors internal transactions or reporting processes for nonexternal parties.

Debit and credit (D/C)   This identifies the debit and credit indicator for an account posting.

EDI   Electronic data interchange is the mechanism by which you can communicate with your external partners.

ERP   Enterprise Resource Planning is the philosophy of integrating all your enterprise applications into one, which helps you in supporting your organizationwide efforts at collaboration and integration.

Financial Accounting (FI)   SAP ERP module that organizes and controls the financial accounting processes and transactions of an organization and mostly oriented toward external parties.

Financial Supply Chain Management (FSCM)   SAP ERP module that deals with financial processes such as contract accounts payable and receivable, electronic bill payment and presentment, credit limit management, and working capital management.

GI   Goods issue refers to the issue of goods to a cost object so that they can be used for processing.

GL   General ledger refers to the general ledger master record that is used to structure your balance sheet and income statement.

GR   Goods receipt refers to the receipt of goods with reference to a cost object. Typically, GR refers to the stockable materials and increases the inventory that can then be used in various processes.

GT   Goods transfer allows you to move goods from one location to another location.

GUI   Graphical user interface by which you can access SAP ERP. You can also access SAP via a thin client that does not require any GUI to be installed on the desktop. However, it is recommended that you use the GUI for heavy users.

HR   The human resources SAP ERP module that helps you manage HR function.

IDOC   Intermediate document is the data container for data exchange between SAP systems or between a SAP system and a non-SAP system.

IR   Invoice receipt refers to the recording of invoice in the system with reference to a purchasing document.

IS   Industry specific solutions are SAP supplied solutions to meet the unique needs of an industry-specific problem. For example, IS Oil & Gas for handling petrochemicals industry unique requirements.

LES   Logistics Execution System is the SAP component that allows you to manage your transportation and shipping processes.

LIFO   Last In First Out is an inventory valuation procedure according to which the stocks of a material that were last received are the first to be used or sold.

MM   Materials Management is one of the logistics modules designed to manage and control the material flow of information inside a company such as purchase requisition, bills of material, inventory management, purchasing and supplier information, and others.

KPIs   Key performance indicators are identified at the highest level of aggregation and are of strategic significance for the managers of the process or business unit. However, you can define KPIs for any process area.

MAP   Moving average price is the price indicator that allows you to capture the changes in materials price as these are recorded in the system.

MM SRV Material Management External Services Management allows you to manage the process of requesting an external service, actual execution of the service, and payment of the service in an integrated fashion.

MPS Master production scheduling takes care of those parts or products that greatly influence company profits or that take up critical resources.

MRP Material requirements planning takes into account and plan every future requirement during the creation of order proposals (independent requirements, dependent requirements, and so on).

OLAP Online analytical processing is used to refer to the BW and SEM, which are primarily used for decision making.

OLTP Online transactional processing is the traditional ERP architecture, which is based on recording transactions and avoiding duplicate data entry.

PLM Product lifecycle management refers to a product suite of SAP ERP, which allows you to manage your portfolio of products along with their entire lifecycle from launch to growth and then decline and replacement of the product line

PP The Production Planning module in SAP ERP is used to manage your production order planning and execution.

PS The Project Systems module allows you to manage your projects and integrates with financials to capture costs and revenues.

RFC Remote Function Call allows you to call and process predefined procedures/functions in a remote SAP system.

QM Quality Management is the logistics module, which is used to measure and record quality attributes while processing materials and services.

RFQ Request For Quotation is used in the context of requesting a quotation from the vendor before the purchase order is created for the vendor.

SOA Sarbanes-Oxley Act, which is a U.S. regulatory governance model that increases operational controls and assesses the effectiveness of independent auditors and corporations to guarantee proper financial reporting. This act was introduced in the aftermath of the Enron debacle.

SAP IDES The SAP Training platform that is available as a separate system with pre-configured objects and loaded data, which allows users to train and practice with predefined business content.

SAPScript SAP's word processing system that allows you to design your forms for communicating with your business partners or forms for internal processing. However, this is something that is now increasingly being replaced by Smart Forms and PDF-based forms.

SAPmail Electronic mail system in SAP-office that allows you to transmit messages between SAP and an external messaging system.

SAPoffice The electronic mail system and folder structure in the SAP ERP system that allows you to send documents internally or externally.

SCM   Supply Chain Management refers to all the supply chain components such as PP, APO, capacity planning, consumption-based planning, logistics execution, and purchasing functions. This is the umbrella term for all the logistics functions that allow you to manage your supply chain better.

SD   Sales and Distribution is the logistics module that allows you to manage your sales processes from sales inquiry to billing. Only cash collection is part of financials. The rest of the sales-related processes are part of SD or CRM.

SOP   Sales and Operations Planning is a flexible forecasting and planning tool with which sales, production, and other supply chain targets can be set on the basis of historical, existing, and/or estimated future data.

SRM (SEM component)   Stakeholder Relationship Management is the component in SAP SEM that allows you to manage your relationship with external stakeholders and shareholders

SRM (Purchasing)   Supplier Relationship Management (Purchasing) is the component in procurement that handles the integration with your suppliers allowing you to achieve significant cost savings in terms of invoice reconciliation and provides you with increased visibility to your purchasing process.

WBS   The Work Breakdown Structure element is the lowest level master data element in PS, which breaks down the project work into manageable chunks so that you can assign these and track the costs on WBS elements.

WF   Business Work Flow tool for automatic control and execution of cross-application processes.

B Bibliography

Internet Resources

http://help.sap.com/erp2005_ehp_02/helpdata/en/80/ea89395eb58c4f9d0-c3e837cf0909d/frameset.htm

http://www.sap.com/community/pub/events/2007_04_SAPPHIRE_US/solutions.epx#mySAPERPFinancials

http://www.sap.com/community/pub/showdetail.epx?itemID=8866

Conference Resources

Simplify, Optimize, and Innovate with SAP ERP: 2007_04_sapphire_us_GE1859

Back to School: A Dual Strategy for Innovation, Speed and Success: Hasso Plattner: Creating Roadmaps with SAP Value Engineering, 2007_04_sapphire_us_GE1621.

Benchmarking Study Model: 2006 ASUG SAP Benchmarking Study: SAP Insight, Katherina Mullers-Patel

Customer Success Stories and Best Practices

Top 100 SAP ERP: Customer success stories: http://www.sap.com/solutions/pdf/CS_100_Customer_Successes.pdf

Best Practices Baseline Package: http://help.sap.com/content/bestpractices/baseline/index.htm

Best Practices by SAP ERP Solution: http://help.sap.com/bp/initial/index.htm

C   About the Author

Shivesh Sharma, PMP is a certified project management professional and has worked in multiple end–to–end SAP ERP implementation projects for IBM (ex PwC Consulting), Computer Sciences Corporation and Fujitsu Consulting.

His consulting background combines different ERP team lead positions and project management experiences for multiple Fortune 500 clients while implementing multiple end to end SAP ERP implementations and SAP ERP upgrades. His domain areas for SAP ERP consulting include business process design, change management, project management and hands on configuration experience of SAP ERP Financials (General Ledger, Accounts Receivable, Bank Accounting, Asset Management, Funds Management, Special Purpose Ledger, Cost Center Accounting, Profit Center Accounting, Investment Management, Profitability Analysis and Consolidation using ECCS).

He is currently based out of St Louis, MO and can be reached at *shivesh.sharma@gmail.com.* Shivesh holds an MBA, and in his free time he enjoys traveling, reading, writing, and playing with his son.

Index

**Effectively configure
Controlling-Profitability
Analysis with SAP using the
practical instruction provided**

**.everage CO-PA fundamentals
to improve your company's
profitability**

407 pp., 2008, 79,95 Euro / US$ 79..95
ISBN 978-1-59229-137-3

Controlling-Profitability Analysis (CO-PA) with SAP

www.sap-press.com

Marco Sisfontes-Monge

Controlling-Profitability Analysis (CO-PA) with SAP

Controlling-Profitability Analysis (CO-PA) is a crucial
and important part of SAP. Based on ECC 6.0, this
book explores the required elements for a successful
CO-PA implementation from a process-oriented
perspective. This includes the fundamentals of
profitability management, development of the CO-
PA models and interaction with the FI component of
R/3, configuration of Account-Based and Costing-
Based CO-PA, extraction and retraction, and much
more. This unique reference clarifies CO-PA's integration with other SAP components such as SAP
NetWeaver BI, and also addresses the basic managerial questions required in any implementation.

Gain valuable insight into the workings of SAP NetWeaver BI Integrated Planning

Maximize your return on investment by learning to use this new, valuable tool

318 pp., 2007, 69,95 Euro / US$ 69,95
ISBN 978-1-59229-129-8

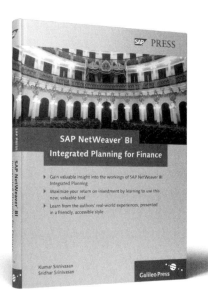

SAP NetWeaver BI
Integrated Planning for Finance

www.sap-press.com

Kumar Srinivasan, Sridhar Srinivasan

SAP NetWeaver BI Integrated Planning for Finance

If you are a functional analyst, consultant, business manager, or a developer this book helps you work on projects to build planning applications in support of business processes.

Readers learn how best to configure, develop, and manage planning applications in a simple and easy-to-follow manner. All the key features and most important aspects are covered in detail, providing you with everything you'll need in order to build a comprehensive planning application. The included examples provide you with a deep understanding of the various features.

esign, customization, application

Ledger definition, document splitting, new profit center ccounting, and parallel valuation in detail

Contains comprehensive information on migration

311 pp., 2007, 69,95 Euro / US$ 69.95
ISBN 978-1-59229-107-6

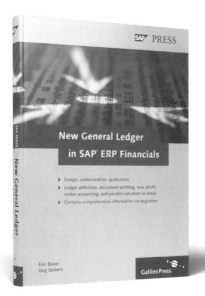

New General Ledger in SAP ERP Financials

www.sap-press.com

Eric Bauer, Jörg Siebert

New General Ledger in SAP ERP Financials

Faster, more efficient, and more transparent: This book enables you to implement and use the New General Ledger in SAP ERP Financials. Readers get an insightful overview of all the most important new functionalities and advantages that the New G/L has to offer. You'll quickly learn about the design and features of ledgers and document splitting, with the help of practical examples. In addition, possible solutions for segment information and parallel valuation are uncovered. A full-length chapter provides key answers on migration. This book shows you how to master your transition to the New G/L and how to get the very most from its vast range of functionalities.

Uncover functionality, processes and complete customization details

Master transaction and position management with hedge management

approx. 700 pp., Feb 2008, 99,95 Euro / US$ 99.95
ISBN 978-1-59229-149-6

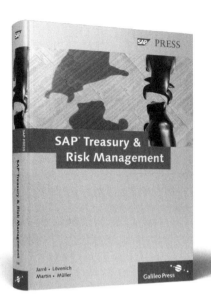

SAP Treasury and Risk Management

www.sap-press.com

Sönke Jarré, Reinhold Lövenich, Andreas Martin, Klaus G. Müller

SAP Treasury and Risk Management

This comprehensive guide introduces you to the functionality and helps you quickly master the usage of SAP Treasury and Risk Management. Learn about the most important customization settings as well as typical use cases and get straightforward solutions to many of the most common problems. With volumes of detailed screenshots, in-depth overviews and practical examples, all components of the tool are covered in detail – from transaction and position management, to risk and performance analyses, to reporting and beyond. Plus, you'll also benefit from expert guidance on interfaces and integration as well as compliance requirements. The book is up-to-date for SAP ERP 6.0.

ain detailed knowledge about
the core functions of Funds
Management

.earn about budget execution,
budget availability control,
year-end closing, key
integration points, and more

approx. 405 pp., May 2008, 69,95 Euro / US$ 69.95
ISBN 978-1-59229-151-9

Streamline Budget Planning and Control with SAP Funds Management

www.sap-press.com

Abhijit Umbarkar

Streamline Budget Planning and Control with SAP Funds Management

SAP Funds Management (FM) helps you monitor and
control funds relevant to the business transactions of your
organization, and with this book you'll find detailed
coverage of the core SAP FM functionality. You'll learn
about the substantial benefits and improvements of FM,
both in the redesigned processes and the related quality of
the services. If you are a project manager, consultant, or a
new FM user, you'll quickly get up to speed on crucial
topics that will help you meet your organizational requirements, including budget execution, budget availability
control, year-end closing, and key integration points. In
addition, financial controllers, budget directors, and finance
managers, will discover how FM can help you streamline
your budget planning and control processes.

Gain unique and practical insights to U.S. tax issues from an SAP perspective

Learn about tax withholding and reporting, record retention, federal income tax integration, tax-related master data, and more

359 pp., 2007, 69,95 Euro / US$ 69.95
ISBN 978-1-59229-155-7

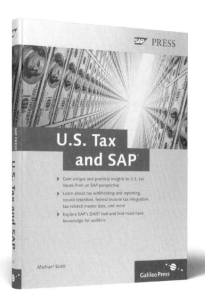

U.S. Tax and SAP

www.sap-press.com

Michael Scott

U.S. Tax and SAP

If you have an SAP implementation and have been frustrated by complex US taxation issues, you've come to the right place for answers. In the post-Sarbanes-Oxley era, this book is the pre-eminent resource that combines US tax knowledge with SAP system knowledge. Based on ECC 6.0, this engaging reference guide written in an engaging conversational style—provides practical information, examples, and tips, to help answer your taxation problems. If you are part of an SAP implementation team, you'll learn about tax requirements and the techniques needed to solve tax-related problems. If you are in the tax group you'll understand what can and cannot be done to solve tax issues, while gaining a detailed understanding of SAP's DART tool. In addition, interested IRS and financial auditors can also learn about the DART tool, and discover the tax solutions and controls offered by SAP.

SOA and the benefits of the enterprise services architecture approach

Architectural concepts, design approach, and standards

Steps to successfully deploy ESA

144 pp., 2006, 49,95 Euro / US$ 49.95
ISBN 1-59229-095-7

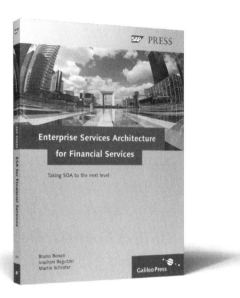

Enterprise Services Architecture for Financial Services

www.sap-press.com

Bruno Bonati, Joachim Regutzki, Martin Schroter

Enterprise Services Architecture for Financial Services

Taking SOA to the next level

Service-oriented architecture (SOA) has become an important topic for financial services organizations, offering new levels of flexibility, adaptability and cost savings. This book cuts through the confusion by clearly describing SAP's approach to SOA—the enterprise services architecture (ESA), shared with leading banks and insurance companies. By illustrating the principles and vision behind ESA, this invaluable guide shows you exactly how it can benefit your financial services firm. In a concise and easy-to-read format, the authors introduce you to ESA and explain exactly how it works. In addition, you'll get a detailed description of the key steps that financial services institutions need to take in order to successfully deploy ESA. This book is written primarily for CIOs, CTOs, IT managers, and consultants.

Understand and implement strategies for maximizing nancials reporting capabilities

Learn and apply best practices for simplifying, streamlining, and automating financial and management reporting

approx. 600 pp., Jan 2008, 79,95 Euro / US$ 79.95
ISBN 978-1-59229-179-3

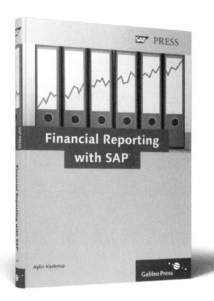

Financial Reporting with SAP

www.sap-press.com

Aylin Korkmaz

Financial Reporting with SAP

This book provides finance and IT teams with best practices for delivering financial reports faster, more accurately, and in compliance with various international accounting standards. Featuring step-by-step coverage of all major FI reporting functions (including Sub-Ledger, Corporate Finance Management, and Governance, Risk & Compliance), this timely book will help you streamline and simplify financial business processes and automate financial and management reporting in SAP ERP Financials. It includes coverage of integrating FI reporting with Business Intelligence, xApp Analytics, and Duet™.

Discover the benefits of why you should migrate to the new SAP General Ledger (GL)

Understand how the new GL functionality affects the migration scope, planning, and staffing

99 pp., 2008, 68,– Euro / US$ 85.00
ISBN 978-1-59229-166-3

Migrate Successfully to the New SAP GL

www.sap-press.com

Paul Theobald

Migrate Successfully to the New SAP GL

SAP PRESS Essentials 34

The new general ledger (GL) is the biggest change to SAP financials since SAP was released. This Essentials guide will show you how to migrate successfully from the SAP classic GL to the new GL in the SAP ERP 2004/2005 releases. You'll learn how to run all aspects of the migration project, including staffing the project team, a proposed project timeline, when and how to engage SAP (SAP provides a migration service), potential problems, and how to avoid them. Tightly focused on technical and accounting issues, this book also provides strategies for ensuring that proper accounting statements and practices are being adhered to. And it teaches you about important new functionality for the new GL such as document splitting, while providing knowledge on the best upgrade strategies. This is the one resource you need for a successful and smooth migration from the Classic GL to the new GL.

Discover what SAP Financials (FI) is all about and whether its right for your organization

Lean how this powerful, time-tested tool can improve your financial processes and save you money

approx. 350 pp., 39,95 Euro / US$ 39.95
ISBN 978-1-59229-184-7, Feb 2008

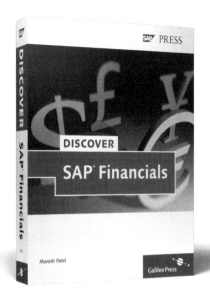

Discover SAP Financials

www.sap-hefte.de

Manish Patel

Discover SAP Financials

Business financials are an essential part of every business, large or small. Whether you just need basic accounting or you perform complex financial audits and reporting, your business needs a software tool that meets your needs. Discover SAP Financials explains how SAP can provide this solution. Using an easy-to-follow style filled with real-world examples, case studies, and practical tips and pointers, the book teaches the fundamental capabilities and uses of the core modules of SAP Financials. As part of the Discover SAP series, the book is written to help new users, decision makers considering SAP, and power users moving to the latest version learn everything they need to determine if SAP Financials is the right solution for your organization. This is the one comprehensive resource you need to get started with SAP Financials.

Interested in reading more?

Please visit our Web site for all
new book releases from SAP PRESS.

www.sap-press.com